AWS®

Certified SysOps Administrator
Study Guide
Third Edition

AWS®
Certified SysOps Administrator Study Guide

Associate (SOA-C02) Exam
Third Edition

Jorge T. Negrón

Christoffer Jones

George Sawyer

To my family, friends, and teammates at AWS, Cloud Academy, and John Wiley, for without your support, encouragement, and remarkable patience nothing worth sharing would have been possible.
— Jorge Tadeo Negrón De Jesús

To my wonderfully supportive friends and family, thank you for unconditionally believing in me.
— Christoffer Jones

First and foremost, I thank God for the opportunities, trials, and triumphs which have brought me to where I am. To my parents, George and Janice Sawyer, and my wife, Mandi Sawyer, thank you for your unwavering support and encouragement.
— George Sawyer

Acknowledgments

I'd like to give special thanks to our editors and leaders Tom Dinse and Kenyon Brown for the trust, inspiration, and patience with the entire process of book writing and publishing with a group of first-time authors. Also, to my friends and co-authors Chris Jones and George Sawyer, who came to my rescue with complete and sincere support when I needed it most: thank you!

My heart goes to my family who endured a significant amount of time without my company for birthdays, holidays, and celebrations while we pursued the best results possible. To Ada De Jesús, Tato, Iván, Mayra, Taileen, Aidia, and Tadeo Negrón, thank you for always being there for me in person and spirit. You are loved!

— Jorge T. Negrón

I'd like to give special thanks to Jorge Negrón, who from the very first day we met, believed that I was something special. I'm eternally grateful for your positive attitude, warm personality, and humble friendship over the years. I knew from the first mention that you wanted to write this book that we would be in this together, and for that, I couldn't be prouder.

I would also like to thank Tom Dinse, our development editor, for spending the time to graciously answer all my questions and for staying truly positive and enthusiastic about the publishing process. You are a credit to the industry, and I could not have been successful without your knowledge and kindness.

A heartfelt thanks to all my wonderful and supportive family and friends. You are such a big part of my life and have always supported my endeavors, no matter how stressing. This includes my close friends Potato, Mark, Dunlop, and my amazingly patient wife, Erin. You each have influenced my life in continually positive ways and for that, I am eternally thankful.

— Christoffer Jones

First, I wish to acknowledge and thank my co-authors, Jorge Negrón and Christoffer Jones, for bringing their exceptional expertise and talents to this project. Of course, authors do only part of the work and I want to express my deep appreciation for the tireless and patient work of the editors and staff at Wiley.

I have been blessed to learn from and work with many great technical trainers in my career. All of these have left an impact on me, and I owe them all a great debt of gratitude. Ultimately, as a teacher, I would be nothing without my students. It has been my students who have taught me and continue to inspire me.

— George J. Sawyer, III

About the Authors

Jorge T. Negrón is part of Cloud Academy's AWS Subject Matter Expert team as well as an official AWS Community Builder based in Atlanta, Georgia. He spends his time building courses, writing blogs, and recording podcasts while helping customers learn and improve their skills in AWS-related technologies.

He was born and raised in Carolina, Puerto Rico, and has traveled the world, enabling customers and partners to gain intimate knowledge of cloud computing skills and development. His passion is in education, training delivery, and contributing to the next generation workforce with cloud computing and machine learning literacy.

In his spare time, you can find him getting tossed around in a Gracie Jiu Jitsu mat or learning the latest magic or mentalism performance from passionate, dedicated, and world-class practitioners.

You can reach Jorge through LinkedIn: `www.linkedin.com/in/jorgetadeonegrondejesus`.

Christoffer Jones is a Principal Delivery Practice Manager for AWS Professional Services based out of Dallas, Texas. Chris has spent the last six years focusing on increasing their AWS skills and sharing their passion of IT operations with customers and students. Chris is also a passionate and dedicated educator who shares knowledge from their prior 18 years of IT operations, networking, and architectural experience.

Chris holds a master's degree from Davenport University in Technology Management and holds the following credentials: AWS Certified DevOps Professional, AWS Certified Solutions Architect Associate, AWS Certified SysOps Administrator Associate, AWS Certified Developer Associate, and AWS Certified Security Specialty.

Chris continues to write about AWS certifications and cloud technologies. You can reach Chris through LinkedIn: `www.linkedin.com/in/christofferjones`.

George Sawyer has been bringing high tech down to Earth for over 20 years as an instructor and learning strategist. George was an early champion of cloud computing and has served as a senior technical trainer with AWS. He is currently writing his dissertation toward a doctorate in education, holds various technical certifications, and is an active AWS Authorized Instructor (AAI).

You can connect with George via LinkedIn at `www.linkedin.com/in/georgesawyer`.

About the Technical Editor

Todd Montgomery has been in the networking industry for over 40 years. Todd holds many AWS, CompTIA, Cisco and Juniper certifications. Todd has spent most of his career in the field working on-site in data centers throughout North America and around the world. He has worked on the advanced networks of equipment manufacturers, systems integrators, and end users in the Data Center and cloud computing environments of private sector, service provider and government sectors. Todd currently works as a data center network automation Engineer in Austin, Texas. He is involved in network implementation and support of emerging data center technologies and AWS public cloud services. Todd lives in Austin, Texas and in his free time enjoys auto racing, travelling, general aviation, and Austin's live music venues. He can be reached at toddmont@tipofthehat.com.

Contents at a Glance

Contents

Introduction

The rate of cloud computing adoption continues to rise, as it has for several years. Technology companies and startups often embrace the cloud early, while heavily regulated industries like healthcare and finance may have a slower adoption process due to security and compliance considerations. This all results in a demand for cloud systems' operators to deploy, monitor, scale, and run the day-to-day operations of a cloud implementation.

This rate of adoption represents an opportunity for systems operators to add to their existing toolset a suite of cloud computing best practices. The best practices put forward by the well-architected framework is intended to allow you to accomplish an implementation that leverages the best and most practical intelligence available. This results in scalable, resilient, highly available, and operationally excellent workloads.

This certification of systems operations for AWS Cloud systems is intended to make sure you understand the variety of critical services that are focused on operations, monitoring, security, and networking. You can dig into the documentation since it's already available online. However, aggregating the reading list from documentation and whitepapers can add up very fast and consume a large amount of time.

We wrote this book so that you don't have to do that aggregation. The idea is to present you with a comprehensive set of services, configurations, and features that are typically in daily use during systems operations. Our hope is that this book saves you time and helps you successfully complete the certifications. We speak from experience; using Wiley cert prep books is how we gained certification our very first time a few years ago. We sincerely hope it does the same for you. Thank you for picking it up.

What Does This Book Cover?

This book covers the topics you need to understand as you prepare to take the AWS Certified SysOps Administrator – Associate exam. The topics that we cover in this book include the following:

- **Chapter 1, "AWS Fundamentals":** The first part of the book starts with the foundational topics that you need to know and understand before you dig into the rest of the book content. These topics include account creation, using the management console, using the command-line interface (CLI), and the Personal Health dashboard. This is basically a review of concepts that should be familiar to you already.

- **Chapter 2, "Account Creation, Security, and Compliance":** The second chapter covers identity and access management, Access Analyzer, AWS Organizations, AWS Directory Service, AWS Control Tower, and AWS License Management. This chapter concentrates on account creation and the different modalities to implement authentication and authorization for users and administrators. Some of the tasks covered in this chapter are:
  - Implementing IAM features (for example, password policies, multifactor authentication [MFA], roles, SAML, federated identity, resource policies, policy conditions)

- Troubleshooting and auditing access issues by using AWS services (for example, CloudTrail, IAM Access Analyzer, IAM policy simulator)

- Validating service control policies (SCPs) and permissions boundaries

- Reviewing AWS Trusted Advisor security checks

- Validating AWS region and service selections based on compliance requirements

- Implementing secure multi-account strategies (for example, AWS Control Tower, AWS Organizations)

- **Chapter 3, "AWS Cost Management":** In the third chapter of this book, the focus shifts to cost analysis and management. The cost and usage report, AWS Cost Explorer, Savings Plan, and Budgets are discussed to give you the tools to manage your costs effectively. Some of the tasks covered in this chapter are:

  - Implementing cost allocation tags

  - Identifying and remediating underutilized or unused resources by using AWS services and tools (for example, Trusted Advisor, AWS Compute Optimizer, AWS Cost Explorer)

  - Configuring AWS Budgets and billing alarms

  - Assessing resource usage patterns to qualify workloads for EC2 Spot Instances

  - Identifying opportunities to use managed services (for example, Amazon RDS, AWS Fargate, Amazon EFS)

  - Recommending compute resources based on performance metrics

  - Monitoring Amazon Elastic Block Store (Amazon EBS) metrics and modifying configuration to increase performance efficiency

  - Implementing S3 performance features (for example, S3 Transfer Acceleration, multipart uploads)

  - Monitoring RDS metrics and modifying the configuration to increase performance efficiency (e.g., Performance Insights, RDS Proxy)

  - Enabling enhanced EC2 capabilities (e.g., Elastic Network Adapter, instance store, placement groups)

- **Chapter 4, "Automated Security Services and Compliance":** The fourth chapter of the book introduces the variety of services that are available. When you activate a service in your account and region, the service operates almost automatically for the protections it provides. Services include Amazon Inspector for EC2s, AWS Security Hub, Amazon Guard Duty, Amazon Detective, Amazon Macie, AWS Shield, AWS WAF, AWS Firewall Manager, AWS Key management services, AWS Secrets Manager, and AWS Certificate Manager. Some of the tasks covered in this chapter are:

  - Enforcing a data classification scheme

  - Creating, managing, and protecting encryption keys

  - Implementing encryption at rest (e.g., AWS Key Management Service [AWS KMS])

- Implementing encryption in transit (e.g., AWS Certificate Manager [ACM], VPN)
- Securely storing secrets by using AWS services (e.g., AWS Secrets Manager, Systems Manager Parameter Store)
- Reviewing reports or findings (e.g., AWS Security Hub, Amazon GuardDuty, AWS Config, Amazon Inspector)

- **Chapter 5, "Compute":** In the fifth chapter we discuss compute services. One of the most common questions here is whether containers are included. As of this writing, Amazon Elastic Container Service and Registry (ECS and ECR) and Amazon Lightsail are "out of scope" for this exam. We cover Amazon Machine Images (AMIs), Amazon EC2, Amazon EC2 Image Builder, Elastic Load Balancers, Auto Scaling, and AWS Lambda. Some of the tasks covered in this chapter are:

  - Configuring Elastic Load Balancing (ELB) and Amazon Route 53 health checks
  - Differentiating between the use of a single availability zone and multi-AZ deployments (e.g., Amazon EC2 Auto Scaling groups, ELB, Amazon FSx, Amazon RDS)
  - Implementing fault-tolerant workloads (e.g., Amazon Elastic File System [Amazon EFS], Elastic IP addresses)

- **Chapter 6, "Storage, Migration, and Transfer":** As its title suggests, in Chapter 6 we cover storage, migration, and transfer services like Amazon S3, Amazon S3 Glacier, Elastic Block Store, Elastic File System, Amazon FSx, AWS Backup, AWS Storage Gateway, AWS Data Sync, and the Snowball AWS transfer family of devices. Some of the tasks covered in this chapter are:

  - Automating snapshots and backups based on use cases (e.g., RDS snapshots, AWS Backup, RTO and RPO, Amazon Data Lifecycle Manager, retention policy)
  - Restoring databases (e.g., point-in-time restore, promote read replica)
  - Implementing versioning and life cycle rules
  - Configuring Amazon S3 Cross-Region Replication (CRR)
  - Performing disaster recovery procedures

- **Chapter 7, "Databases":** It is important to understand all AWS databases in terms of their name and what function they provide, and, more importantly, in which situations to use them. This chapter concentrates on the implementation and operation of Amazon RDS, including Aurora. This should provide a sign that Amazon RDS is a service that needs to be understood well for the exam. It's also important to understand how to use ElastiCache, the engines it supports, and the types of caching process that can be implemented. Some of the tasks covered in this chapter are:

  - Implementing caching
  - Implementing Amazon RDS replicas and Amazon Aurora replicas
  - Differentiating between horizontal scaling and vertical scaling

- **Chapter 8, "Monitoring, Logging, and Remediation":** This is probably the main chapter of the study guide as it contains the material that has the highest percentage of coverage in the exam. In this chapter we discuss Amazon CloudWatch as a service to monitor AWS and third-party tools; Amazon CloudWatch Logs, for the aggregation and processing of log streams; and Amazon CloudWatch Events (also known as Amazon EventBridge), AWS CloudTrail, AWS Config, and AWS Systems Manager as some of the services allowing for scalable deployments and operations. Some of the tasks covered in this chapter are:
    - Identifying, collecting, analyzing, and exporting logs (e.g., Amazon CloudWatch Logs, CloudWatch Logs Insights, AWS CloudTrail logs)
    - Collecting metrics and logs by using the CloudWatch agent
    - Creating CloudWatch alarms
    - Creating metric filters
    - Creating CloudWatch dashboards
    - Configuring notifications (e.g., Amazon Simple Notification Service [Amazon SNS], CloudWatch alarms, AWS Health events)
    - Troubleshooting or taking corrective actions based on notifications and alarms
    - Configuring Amazon EventBridge rules to invoke actions
    - Using AWS Systems Manager Automation runbooks to take action based on AWS Config rules
- **Chapter 9, "Networking":** In Chapter 9 we discuss Amazon VPC and different possible deployments, including traffic mirroring and the AWS transit gateway as a way to interconnect multiple network components. Some of the tasks covered in this chapter are:
    - Configuring a VPC (e.g., subnets, route tables, network ACEs, security groups, NAT gateway, Internet gateway)
    - Configuring private connectivity (e.g., Systems Manager Session Manager, VPC endpoints, VPC peering, VPN)
- **Chapter 10, "Content Delivery":** Chapter 10 could have easily be called "edge services" because the services discussed all use the edge locations of the AWS global infrastructure. We discuss Route 53 and the different routing policies, how to provide private DNS, how to distribute content using Amazon CloudFront, origins, and behaviors. Finally, we discuss AWS Global Accelerator as an alternative to CloudFront to accelerate application response time instead of content distribution. Some of the tasks covered in this chapter are:
    - Configuring notifications (e.g., Amazon Simple Notification Service [Amazon SNS])
    - Implementing loosely coupled architectures
    - Implementing Route 53 routing policies (e.g., failover, weighted, latency based)
- **Chapter 11, "Deployment, Provisioning, and Automation":** Chapter 11 (the last chapter) covers a set of messaging services starting with Amazon SQS, Amazon SNS, and Kinesis

Data Streams. We also discuss deployment automation using Elastic Beanstalk and, more importantly, CloudFormation. Some of the tasks covered in this chapter are:

- Creating, managing, and troubleshooting AWS CloudFormation
- Provisioning resources across multiple AWS regions and accounts (e.g., CloudFormation StackSets, IAM cross-account roles)
- Selecting deployment scenarios and services (e.g., all-at-once, rolling, immutable, and Blue)
- Identifying and remediating deployment issues (e.g., service quotas, subnet sizing, CloudFormation errors, permissions)
- Using AWS services (e.g., Systems Manager, CloudFormation) to automate deployment processes
- Implementing automated patch management
- Scheduling automated tasks by using AWS services (e.g., EventBridge, AWS Config)

Interactive Online Learning Environment and Test Bank

Tools have been developed to aid you in studying for the Amazon Certified SysOps Administrator – Associate exam. These tools are all available for no additional charge here:
`www.wiley.com/go/sybextestprep`
Just register your book to gain access to the electronic resources that are listed here.

- **Practice Exams:** Two 60-question practice exams are available to test your knowledge. These questions are different from the review questions at the end of each chapter.
- **Flashcards:** One-hundred flashcards are available for you to test your knowledge of AWS terms and concepts. If you don't get them correct the first time through, try again! These are designed to reinforce the concepts you have learned throughout the book.
- **Glossary:** Throughout the book, you'll see italicized words that are important key terms. A glossary of these key terms with their definitions is provided. The best part about the glossary is that it's searchable!

> **NOTE** Like all exams, the Certified SysOps Administrator certification from AWS is updated periodically and may eventually be retired or replaced. At some point after [vendor] is no longer offering this exam, the old editions of our books and online tools will be retired. If you have purchased this book after the exam was retired, or are attempting to register in the Sybex online learning environment after the exam was retired, please know that we make no guarantees that this exam's online Sybex tools will be available once the exam is no longer available.

Exam Objectives

The AWS Certified SysOps Administrator – Associate (SOA-C02) exam is intended for system administrators in a cloud operations role. The exam validates a candidate's ability to deploy, manage, and operate workloads on AWS.

As a general rule, before you take this exam, you should have:

- 1–2 years of experience as a system administrator in an operations role
- Experience in monitoring, logging, and troubleshooting
- Knowledge of networking concepts (e.g., DNS, TCP/IP, firewalls)
- Ability to implement architectural requirements (e.g., high availability, performance, capacity)
- Understanding of the AWS Well-Architected Framework
- Hands-on experience with the AWS Management Console and the AWS CLI
- Hands-on experience in implementing security controls and compliance requirements

The exam has the following content domains and weightings:

- Domain 1: Monitoring, Logging, and Remediation (*20% of scored content*)
- Domain 2: Reliability and Business Continuity (*16% of scored content*)
- Domain 3: Deployment, Provisioning, and Automation (*18% of scored content*)
- Domain 4: Security and Compliance (*16% of scored content*)
- Domain 5: Networking and Content Delivery (*18% of scored content*)
- Domain 6: Cost and Performance Optimization (*12% of scored content*)

NOTE
Notice how the Domain 1 for "Monitoring, Logging, and Remediation" has the highest percentage, indicating this is the type of task considered most essential for a systems operator. Also, notice the percentage of the other domains are close to each other. This is one certification where you are required to know the service, the parts of the service, and how to configure the parts to connect to your application or to other AWS services. Experience is essential. Give yourself the chance to do the exercises.

When you register for the exam, you have the choice to either sit for the exam from home or in a Pearson Vue testing center. The details for sitting for the exam from home and searching for a testing center are included in the registration process. As of this writing, the cost for the associate exam is $150 USD. The questions will be in either a multiple-choice or a multiple-answer format. You have 130 minutes to finish 65 questions in the exam.

Objective Map

This table provides you with a listing of each domain on the exam, the weights assigned to each domain, and a listing of the chapters where content in the domains is located. Chapter 1 is included as a refresher and is not specifically tied to exam domains.

Domain	Exam percentage	Chapter number(s)
Domain 1: Monitoring, Logging, and Remediation	20%	
1.1: Implement metrics, alarms, and filters by using AWS monitoring and logging services.		8
1.2: Remediate issues based on monitoring and availability metrics.		8
Domain 2: Reliability and Business Continuity	16%	
2.1 Implement scalability and elasticity.		6, 7
2.2 Implement highly available and resilient environments.		6
2.3: Implement backup and restore strategies.		6, 7
Domain 3: Deployment, Provisioning, and Automation	18%	
3.1: Provision and maintain cloud resources.		5, 11
3.2 Automate manual or repeatable processes.		11
Domain 4: Security and Compliance	16%	
4.1: Implement and manage security and compliance policies.		2, 4
4.2: Implement data and infrastructure protection strategies.		4
Domain 5: Networking and Content Delivery	18%	
5.1 Implement networking features and connectivity.		4, 9
5.2: Configure domains, DNS services, and content delivery.		6, 10
5.3 Troubleshoot network connectivity issues.		4, 9, 10
Domain 6: Cost and Performance Optimization	12%	
6.1 Implement cost optimization strategies.		3, 5, 7
6.2 Implement performance optimization strategies.		5, 6, 7

How to Contact the Publisher

If you believe you have found a mistake in this book, please bring it to our attention. At John Wiley & Sons, we understand how important it is to provide our customers with accurate content, but even with our best efforts, an error may occur. In order to submit your possible errata, please email it to our Customer Service Team at wileysupport@wiley.com with the subject line "Possible Book Errata Submission."

Assessment Test

1. Your senior administrator has asked you to set up notifications for the AWS Budgets configuration in the organization's developer accounts. Which of the following notification options are available for AWS Budgets? (Choose two.)

   A. Posting to the Personal Health Dashboard

   B. Amazon SNS topics

   C. AWS Management Console notifications

   D. Direct integration with ServiceNow

   E. Direct email recipients

2. The two strategies for cache loading include which of the following? (Choose two.)

   A. Arbitrary acquisition

   B. First-in, first-out (FIFO)

   C. Lazy loading

   D. Least effort load

   E. Write-through

3. The compliance officer for the organization has asked you to confirm the maximum length of historical data that AWS Cost Explorer provides. Which of the following options will you provide to the compliance officer?

   A. 24 months

   B. 36 months

   C. 18 months

   D. 12 months

4. Why might you use a geoproximity routing policy rather than a geolocation routing policy?

   A. You want to increase the size of traffic in a certain region over time.

   B. You want to ensure that all U.S. users are directed to U.S.-based hosts.

   C. You want to route users geographically to ensure compliance issues are met based on requestor location.

   D. You are concerned about network latency more than requestor location.

5. In Auto Scaling, what does the desired capacity refers to?

   A. The average capacity that the customer expects to need over the next billing cycle

   B. The capacity that the customer expects to need over the next billing cycle

   C. The initial capacity of the Auto Scaling group that the system will attempt to maintain

   D. The lowest capacity of the Auto Scaling group at which the workload is still able to perform

6. You have an application deployment with endpoints in multiple countries. The application needs to have fast response times, and in the event of a failure, you cannot modify the client code to redirect traffic. Which service can help you implement a solution?

    A. Amazon ElastiCache

    B. Route 53

    C. Amazon CloudFront

    D. AWS Global Accelerator

7. You are securing resources in your VPC. You wish to allow only specific ports and you require stateful connections. Which of the following best fulfills these requirements?

    A. NAT gateway

    B. Network access control lists (NACLs)

    C. Security groups

    D. Web application firewall (WAF)

8. Which of the following saves you from provisioning keys to operate AWS services in a programmatic way?

    A. The AWS Management Console

    B. AWS CloudShell

    C. Session Manager

    D. IAM groups

9. You oversee monitoring of performance for several production data conversion systems running on Amazon EC2 instances. Recently the data engineers reported below normal write and read speeds coming from several application servers. Each application server is a T3.Large using gp2 EBS volumes for the operating system volume and St1 volumes for the data processing volumes. You are concerned that the volumes are throttling. Which Amazon CloudWatch EBS volume metric will confirm EBS volume throttling?

    A. VolumeQueueLength

    B. VolumeWriteOps

    C. VolumeReadBytes

    D. BurstBalance

10. Inline IAM policies are best used when:

    A. Inline policies are not recommended.

    B. Customer-managed policies must be kept secure.

    C. An appropriate AWS-managed policy does not exist.

    D. Resource-based policies must be tightly integrated with identity-based policies.

11. Your organization is undergoing an application modernization effort and focusing on decommissioning and consolidating applications on-premises into a new AWS environment. Several applications require the use of Secure File Transfer Protocol (SFTP) to move files between the

application server and the customer. To reduce cost and assist with consolidation, you want to move all SFTP servers into AWS. Which AWS service provides the most scalable and cost-effective solution?

A. Amazon EFS

B. AWS Transfer Family

C. AWS DataSync

D. Amazon EC2

12. Which AWS services have CLI wizards available? (Choose three.)

A. Amazon EC2

B. AWS Lambda functions

C. Amazon DynamoDB

D. AWS IAM

E. Amazon RDS

F. Amazon S3

13. You have been contacted by the security team because they are receiving too many findings from Macie in Security Hub. The security team has asked if it is possible to change the frequency of findings being sent into Security Hub from Macie. Which of the following frequencies are supported by Macie? (Choose three.)

A. 15 minutes

B. 5 minutes

C. 1 hour

D. 3 hours

E. 6 hours

F. 30 minutes

14. A company wants to analyze the click sequence of their website users. The website is very busy and receives traffic of 10,000 requests per second. Which service provides a near-real-time solution to capturing the data?

A. Kinesis Data Streams

B. Kinesis Data Firehose

C. Kinesis Data Analytics

D. Kinesis Video Stream

15. Which of the following statements about RDS read replicas is true? (Choose two.)

A. A replica can be promoted to replace the primary DB instance.

B. Read replicas are used as read-only copies of the primary DB instance.

C. Read replicas should be created in a different VPC from the primary DB instance.

D. The read replica and primary DB instance replicate synchronously.

16. Your workload spikes every Thursday evening while batch processing runs, and processes are frequently throttled as soon as processing begins. Which of the following scaling methods will most effectively solve this problem?

   A. Predictive scaling

   B. Simple scaling

   C. Step scaling

   D. Target tracking

17. The principal of trust between two unrelated networks is known as:

   A. Distributed computing

   B. Federation

   C. Hybrid computing

   D. Interoperability

18. Which of the following does Elastic Beanstalk store in S3? (Choose two.)

   A. Server log files

   B. Database swap files

   C. Application files

   D. Elastic Beanstalk log files

19. You have been tasked by the CISO to protect all web applications in the production AWS account from SQL injection attacks and cross-site scripting. Which AWS service will you use to accomplish this goal?

   A. Amazon VPC security groups

   B. AWS Web Application Firewall

   C. AWS Network Firewall

   D. AWS Shield

20. You wish to allow administrators to securely connect to hosts in a private subnet in your VPC. Which of the following will best solve this problem?

   A. Bastion host

   B. Client VPN

   C. NAT gateway

   D. Transit gateway

Answers to Assessment Test

1. B, E. When configuring AWS Budgets for notifications, you can select from emailing up to 10 recipients directly from the budget configuration. You can also use Amazon SNS to send SMS messages or take other actions through event triggers with Lambda. See Chapter 3 for more information.

2. C, E. Only options C and E are valid caching strategies. See Chapter 7 for more information.

3. D. AWS Cost Explorer provides current month, prior 12 months, and the ability to forecast the next 12 months of AWS cost and usage using the same dataset as the AWS Cost and Usage reports. See Chapter 3 for more information.

4. A. A geoproximity policy, like a geolocation policy, routes users to the closest geographical region. This means that options B and C are incorrect, as they are common to both types of routing policy. Option D would imply the use of latency-based routing, leaving only option A. This is the purpose of a geoproximity policy: you can apply a bias to adjust traffic to a region. See Chapter 10 for more information.

5. C. There are three limits that are set for an Auto Scaling group: the minimum, desired, and maximum capacities. The minimum is the smallest acceptable group size. The maximum is as large as the group will be allowed to scale. The desired is the initial size of the group. Auto Scaling then attempts to maintain that size. When demand causes the group to scale out, Auto Scaling will then scale in at the end of the event back to the desired capacity. See Chapter 5 for more information.

6. D. The anycast IP addresses provisioned by AWS Global Accelerator will allow you to reach a healthy endpoint without having to switch IP addressing, modify the client code, or be concerned about DNS caching. See Chapter 10 for more information.

7. C. A NAT gateway is used by resources in a private subnet to initiate communication with the Internet. A WAF monitors and protects HTTP(S) requests. NACLs and security groups are very similar, and you will need to know the differences. The security group is stateful and the NACL is stateless. Additionally, the question only asks for traffic to be allowed with no requirement for deny rules. NACLs allow deny rules. Given the choice between a security group and an NACL, the security group is the preferred method if all else is equal. See Chapter 9 for more information.

8. B. AWS CloudShell provides a mechanism for operators to use the AWS CLI without having to provision access keys in a local machine. This adds a new layer of security as it saves time and effort in executing one-line and simple administrative CLI commands. See Chapter 1 for more information.

9. D. In this scenario the data engineers are reporting below normal write and read speeds, which is a great indicator that the volume is throttling. The EBS volumes used in this

deployment are gp2 and st1 volume types, which both use burst bucket balance to maintain performance above the baseline available IOPS for the volume. Checking for depletion of the `BucketBalance` metric for the volume can identify depletion of the burst bucket and result in low performance for the EBS volume. See Chapter 6 for more information.

10. A. While inline policies are available as an option, they are not recommended. Inline policies can be difficult to troubleshoot, and there are almost always better options. See Chapter 2 for more information.

11. B. In this scenario the organization is looking for a scalable and cost-effective solution to migrate SFTP services from on-premises to the AWS Cloud. This automatically eliminates the option of using Amazon EFS and AWS DataSync as they do not offer a method of enabling SFTP. Amazon EC2 is a potential option but would require custom configuration of an SFTP server on Amazon EC2, including the need for configuring scaling using Auto Scaling. This increases the overall cost and complexity of the solution. The most cost-effective and scalable option is to use AWS Transfer Family, which is a managed service that lets you configure an SFTP service that scales to meet customer demand; AWS manages the underlying infrastructure. See Chapter 6 for more information.

12. B, C, D. Wizards will query existing resources and prompt you for data in the process of setting up for the service invoked. As of this writing, wizards are available for `configure`, `dynamodb`, `iam`, and `lambda` functions. For example, the command

    `aws dynamodb wizard new-table`

    will guide you in creating a DynamoDB table. Also, note that the `configure` command does not use a wizard name. It's invoked as `aws configure wizard`. See Chapter 1 for more information.

13. A, C, E. Macie allows customizable frequencies for when findings are published to Security Hub. You can update the publication setting to fit the needs of the security team by adjusting the findings publication from the default of 15 minutes to either every one hour or every six hours. If you modify the publication timings within one region, you will need to modify every other region where Macie is in use as well. See Chapter 4 for more information.

14. A. This is a classic use case for Kinesis Data Streams. See Chapter 11 for more information.

15. A, B. Replication between the primary and read replicas is asynchronous. Creating read replicas in VPCs outside of the primary instance's VPC can create conflicts with the Classless Inter-Domain Routing (CIDR). See Chapter 7 for more information.

16. A. While simple, step, and target tracking scaling will scale out the workload, they only begin scaling after the metric indicates a problem. Predictive scaling anticipates the event based on historical data and scales out ahead of the Thursday evening batch processing so that throttling is avoided. See Chapter 5 for more information.

17. B. Federation is a trust between two parties or systems for the purpose of authenticating users and conveying information needed to authorize their access to resources. Distributed computing is, at its most fundamental, just computing between two or more computers via messaging usually along a network. It does not imply trust. Hybrid computing refers to a

combination of cloud and on-premises resources. Again, no trust is implied. Interoperability is the ability of one computer or application to talk to another. Standards and protocols provide us with interoperability but do not imply trust. See Chapter 2 for more information.

18. A, C. Elastic Beanstalk will store application files and server log files in S3. See Chapter 11 for more information.

19. B. The AWS Web Application Firewall (AWS WAF) is a layer 7 firewall used to protect your web applications from DDoS attacks, SQL injection attacks, and cross-site scripting attacks. You can also allow, block, or count web requests coming into an application based on criteria that you set, such as IP addresses, geolocations, and HTTP headers. See Chapter 4 for more information.

20. A. The NAT gateway and bastion host are often confused. A NAT gateway allows communication out, whereas a bastion host allows communication in. See Chapter 9 for more information.

Chapter

1

AWS Fundamentals

THE AWS CERTIFIED SYSOPS ADMINISTRATOR EXAM OBJECTIVES COVERED IN THIS CHAPTER INCLUDE:

✓ Understand AWS networking resources and security services

✓ Implement security controls to meet compliance requirements

✓ Perform operations by using the AWS Management Console and the AWS CLI

Welcome operators! Thank you for investing in this book and yourself as it will cover the basics of Amazon Web Services (AWS) importance and operation in the event you are not familiar with the fundamentals before getting to start operating workloads using AWS.

As cloud adoption continues to gain traction in the enterprise and startup space, the concept of system operations at scale becomes essential in the implementation of migration and cloud-native initiatives. Amazon Web Services (AWS) Cloud computing brings into play the ideas of rapid and flexible provisioning with a pay-per-use pricing model that is attractive to everyone who can take advantage of it. In general, AWS customers benefit by leveraging agility, cost savings, elasticity, faster innovation by using complex functionality offered by services, and the ability to attain a global scope of accessibility by customers in a matter of minutes if needed.

In this chapter, you'll learn the fundamentals of AWS.

Getting Started 1

To take advantage of cloud computing, organizations must recruit and retain competent systems operators who will be responsible for the migration, deployment, automation, monitoring, maintenance, and troubleshooting of cloud-related workloads. This book will empower you to be successful at the AWS Certified SysOps Administrator – Associate exam and to be able to operate workloads efficiently at scale using AWS. As shown in Figure 1.1, AWS continues to be a leader in the cloud computing space in part due to the remarkable pace of innovation implemented and made available to customers. As of this writing the AWS rate of innovation continues to accelerate with dozens of new services and hundreds of new features added to existing services every year. It's no surprise that AWS hosts millions of active customers and tens of thousands of partners around the globe. According to the Synergy Research Group (a leading technology market analyst) and reported by Statista .com, "Amazon's market share in the worldwide cloud infrastructure market amounted to 32 percent in the second quarter of 2023, still close to matching the combined market share of its two largest competitors" (www.statista.com/chart/18819/worldwide-market-share-of-leading-cloud-infrastructure-service-providers).

As a result of its continuous expansion of services to support virtually any cloud workload, AWS now has more than 200 fully featured services for compute, storage, databases, networking, analytics, machine learning, Internet of Things (IoT), mobile, security, hybrid, virtual and augmented reality (VR and AR), media, and application development, deployment, and management. All you need to do is look at the AWS Management Console to get a sense of the vast and complex ecosystem of services being offered. Let's get started with that process.

FIGURE 1.1   AWS leads cloud market share (Q2 2023).

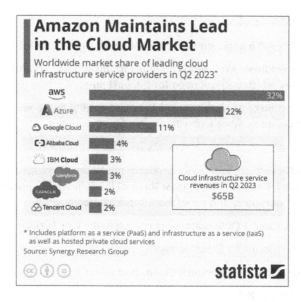

Source: Statista, Inc.

AWS Account Creation

To create an account with AWS, you will need the following information:

- A functional and operable email address
- An idea for what you would want to name your account
- A unique password to assign the account
- A specification for account use as business or personal
- Your full name, address, and phone number
- A credit card to cover expenses incurred
- An idea of what support plan will be needed for your use
- Finally, a web browser and access to your email and phone

The account name, specification of business or personal, and choice of support can be changed later and at any time after you gain access to the console. Exercise 1.1 is optional if you already have an account. You do not need to perform the steps explained, but it will be useful to follow along to note the most recent process of account creation.

EXERCISE 1.1

Creating an AWS Account

1. Using your web browser, navigate to http://aws.amazon.com. If you don't see the Create An AWS Account button at the top right, you may need to use a private browsing session.

2. Click Create An AWS Account.

3. On the Sign Up For AWS page, enter your email address and an AWS account name.

4. Click Verify Email Address. AWS sends an email to the address you provided containing a verification code, which you will need for the next step.

5. Obtain the verification code from your mailbox and enter it in the response page. The code will be a six-digit number and will be valid for 10 minutes.

6. Click Verify.

7. Once your email is verified, enter your choice of password. Passwords need to be at least eight characters and contain at least three of the following: uppercase letters, lowercase letters, numbers, and nonalphanumeric characters.

8. Click the Continue (Step 1 Of 5) button and complete the CAPTCHA check.

9. Click the Continue (Step 1 Of 5) button again.

10. On the next page, enter your personal details and select how you plan to use AWS.

11. Click Continue (Step 2 Of 5).

12. Enter your credit card billing information. (For international users outside the United States, please refer to the following URL for payment methods accepted by AWS: https://aws.amazon.com/premiumsupport/knowledge-center/accepted-payment-methods.)

13. Click Verify And Continue (Step 3 Of 5).

14. Provide your phone number to confirm your identity. You will receive an automated phone call asking you to provide a verification code. Also, you will need to satisfy the CAPTCHA security check before the call happens.

15. Click Call Me Now (Step 4 Of 5). The resulting page will alert you that a call is being made and provide a 4-digit number.

16. Answer the call from AWS, and when prompted, enter the 4-digit number using your phone's keypad.

17. On the next page, select a support plan for your expected use. Your choices are Free – Basic support, Developer support from $29/month, and Business support

from $100/month. Please refer to the following URL to compare AWS support plans and choose the best option for you: `https://aws.amazon.com/premiumsupport/plans`.

18. Click Complete Sign Up.

19. Click Go To The AWS Management Console.

20. Select the Root User option and enter your email.

21. Click Next.

22. Enter your chosen password.

23. Click Sign In.

    Congratulations! You just created a new AWS account. You will be greeted by the AWS Management Console with a brief guide of the main items on the menu bar.

    At the top left of the screen (shown next) and to the right of the AWS logo, you will see the Services menu. The main console for AWS contains a main menu bar, and the Services menu will let you access all AWS services.

Source: Amazon.com, Inc.

24. At the top right you will see your chosen account name as a menu item. Select it to display your account ID and items related to your account, organization, service quotas, billing dashboard, security credentials, settings, and the Sign Out button. See the following image.

EXERCISE 1.1 *(continued)*

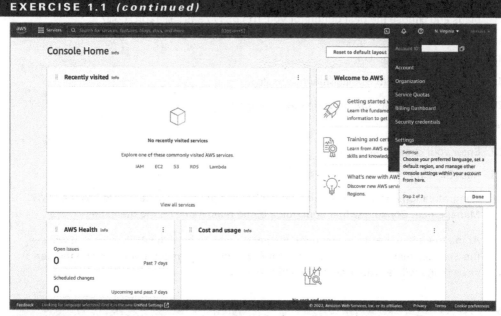

Source: Amazon.com, Inc.

25. Explore the console landing page in detail. You will find interesting items as you scroll up and down the main page.

You have now created an AWS account. Next, let's explore the items on the menu bar.

Console Menu Items

The menu items for the AWS console represent your first steps in operating with AWS. Let's take a quick look at each of these items. The menu bar has 9 items, as shown in Figure 1.2. If you are new to AWS, you want to explore and play with these menu items as much as possible until you become familiar with the functionality provided.

FIGURE 1.2   Menu Items of the AWS Console.

Source: Amazon.com, Inc.

The menu items provide the following functionality:

1. The Console Home Icon   Use this icon to return to the main landing page as you navigate into different AWS services. Sometimes the drill-down sequence for a service configuration can take you a few levels deep. To navigate back to the main landing page, you can select the AWS logo at the top left of your web browser page.

2. The Services Icon   Click this icon to see all the services by category or alphabetically if desired. It also takes you to the Favorites display, where you can mark with a star the services you want for easy access. Marking a service as a favorite will make it appear in the Favorites panel as well as create an icon under the main menu bar of the console.

3. The Search Icon   Clicking this icon allows you to type a service by name or substring and presents you with a list of services and features matching the string used.

> **3a. AWS Resource Explorer**   AWS Resource Explorer is a managed feature that simplifies search and discovery of resources like EC2 instances across regions in your AWS account. You can use Resource Explorer by typing **/resource** in the AWS console search bar. You can also use it with the AWS command-line interface (CLI) and AWS software development kits (SDKs). Resource Explorer may require that you enable and set it up first, and it is available at no additional charge.

4. The CloudShell Icon   CloudShell is an Amazon Linux 2 environment preconfigured to allow you to explore and manage AWS services from a terminal in your browser. You can run scripts and commands as if you had configured the AWS CLI in a local machine.

5. The Notifications Icon   Clicking this icon gives you visibility to open issues, scheduled changes, event log, and any other notification AWS sends to your console for clarity and information.

6. The Support Icon   Clicking this icon gives you access to the AWS Support Center, depending on the support tier you have; the Expert Help landing page for AWS IQ; the AWS re:Post community forums; AWS Documentation; the AWS Training page; the Getting Started Resource Center; and Send Feedback About Your AWS Experience.

7. The Settings Icon   Click this icon to define the settings for your current users. You can choose a language and default region. You can also configure Visual Mode, specify Favorites Bar Icon Size, and choose whether the AWS Management Console remembers your activity by maintaining a list of recently visited services.

8. The Region Icon   Clicking this icon displays your current operating region. Most AWS services have a boundary of operation that is regional even if they contain features for cross-region operations. It is up to the customer to enable inter-region operation in services that have them when needed. Also, there are a few services that are global in scope, and when using them, the Region menu will not allow you to select anything. For example, Identity and Access Management (IAM), Route 53 (for DNS), and CloudFront for content distribution are global services.

9. The Account Icon   Clicking this icon displays your account name and number, and allows you to navigate to your account detailed configuration settings, your AWS Organizations details, the Service Quotas page, your billing dashboard, the Identity Management console (where you can set up your root account security credentials), and the Unified Account Settings page (where you can configure the default region, localization language, and console visual look).

Congratulations! If you didn't have an account, now you understand how to create one. Let's move on to a general discussion of best practices for SysOps.

The AWS Shared Responsibility Model

The shared responsibility model represents the dividing line between what AWS will handle in terms of security and what customers are required to manage to define the strongest security posture possible. AWS manages and controls the components from the host operating system and virtualization layer down to the physical security of the facilities in which the services operate. These include physical datacenter security, separation of the network, isolation of the server hardware, and isolation of storage.

Customers are responsible for building secure applications and protecting data. Customers own workload data and need to always protect it. This includes protecting data as it moves by using SSL or TLS1.2 as well as protecting data at rest by leveraging AES-256 encryption. It is also important for customers to manage the security of applications, especially workloads implemented using the Amazon EC2 service. In this particular use case, the customer takes responsibility for the EC2 instance operating system and application components' security by implementing patching and audits, as would be the case in a physical and local implementation. AWS provides tools and guidance to implement security at scale, and customers can leverage these tools to implement security accordingly. For example, tools like Amazon Inspector will provide visibility of operating systems and application component vulnerabilities. Systems Manager enables customers to automate systems patching according to their requirements and maintenance schedules. There's also a variety of best practices documents, encryption tools, and automated security services, which in general are simple to use and perform a variety of functions across accounts, logs, Amazon S3 buckets, and distributed denial-of-service (DDoS) defense. Finally, customers get a significant number of mechanisms to implement firewall behaviors at the network interface, subnet, and even application layers. Chapter 4, "Automated Security Services and Compliance," focuses on security services and best practices.

This chapter focuses on the initial account setup and best practices, in particular the root account, general guidance about password policies, and provisioning an administrator user using IAM to begin your implementation. You will also want to enable the AWS Security Hub service, which will allow you to get security right the first time.

Security Hub provides you with automatic security checks across your AWS implementation. It consolidates results from other automated security services like AWS Config, Amazon GuardDuty, Amazon Inspector, and Amazon Macie, among others. Security Hub has a built-in set of checks that conform to the Center for Internet Security (CIS) AWS Foundations Benchmarks v1.2.0 and v1.4.0, AWS Foundational Security Best Practices 1.0.0, NIST Special Publication 800-53 Revision 5, and PCI DSS v3.2.1. These will allow you to double-check your fundamental setup right after creating your account. Follow the steps recommended by Security Hub and your account setup will have all the best practices for security and visibility identified by security and operations experts.

Implementing the basic steps outlined in the following sections is a good start but not enough compared to the recommendations provided by AWS Security Hub if you enable the built-in security standards. Try to take advantage of this useful and automated security service.

 You can visit `https://d0.awsstatic.com/whitepapers/compliance/ AWS_CIS_Foundations_Benchmark.pdf` for further details.

General Root Account Best Practices

The AWS root account is a powerful resource. You can do basically anything you want in terms of provisioning and operating AWS services. It also holds your personal and financial information to cover any expenses incurred during implementations. As such, this resource needs to be protected and guarded with the importance it deserves. A breach in security for the root account can result in your account being abused and a bill, which can damage your financial ability to sustain your business. It's not rare to see breached accounts be abused by provisioning bitcoin mining and incurring thousands of dollars in expenses in just a few days. You need to protect accounts by using security best practices for your root and user credentials. Let's get to those best practices, starting with your root account and basic settings.

As you begin to work with AWS, use the following best practices:

Implement MFA for all accounts and users.   The idea of multifactor authentication (MFA) injects an additional piece of information into the authentication process. MFA can be implemented using software or hardware tools and will add protection to your root account and users that goes beyond simple username and password. Use MFA for all accounts and users if possible.

Try to not use the root account after creation and basic setup.   There are tasks that require the root user credentials. For example, you are required to use the root account for changing account settings, registering as a seller in the Amazon EC2 Reserved Instance marketplace, configuring an S3 bucket to enable MFA, activating user access to the billing and cost management console, and closing your account. As a best practice, you should avoid using the root account for service provisioning and day-to-day administration. Instead, create an IAM user with permissions to operate accounts, users, and service provisioning.

Define an account-level password policy.   One of the first items to handle as an operator with the root account is to set up an account-level password policy. This policy
will apply to all users created using IAM. It's important to note that the root account
falls outside the scope of IAM management. Once again, the idea of protecting the root
account cannot be overstated.

Use CloudShell for CLI commands where applicable.   CloudShell provides a mechanism for operators to use the AWS CLI without having to provision access keys in a
local machine. This adds a new layer of security as it saves time and effort in executing
one line and simple administrative CLI commands.

Use Session Manager to connect to Amazon EC2 instances.   Systems Manager Session
Manager provides you with a way to connect to Amazon EC2 instances that does not
require the configuration of SSH or RDP resources to operate a particular instance. This
is a significantly more secure way to manage EC2 instances.

Use IAM roles.   IAM roles are essential to provide cross-account access and enable
AWS services to interact with each other. Learn and understand roles and the mechanics
of role policy creation to maintain a strong security posture.

Know how to get help.   It is essential you understand where and how to go for help
when needed. The AWS Support Center is the primary place for issue resolution if documentation and user forums do not provide clarity on how to resolve an issue. The
AWS console provides a menu for you to gain immediate access to all official sources of
support. Become familiar with each of the options and use them when necessary.

Next we'll discuss how to implement some of these best practices.

Enabling an Account-Level Password Policy

If one is not already configured, your account needs a password policy for users. To accomplish this, complete the steps in Exercise 1.2.

EXERCISE 1.2

Enabling an Account-Level Password Policy

1.   Using your root account and while in the AWS Management Console, open your
     account's Services menu at the top right of the console menu bar.

2.   Click Security Credentials. This will send you directly to the Identity And Access
     Management (IAM) landing page.

3.   You should see a vertical column of items listed to the left of the page. In this list select
     the items listed as Account Settings. The resulting page will display the password
     policy settings for all users.

4. Define a password policy according to your security needs and requirements. At a minimum, passwords should be at least 8 characters and contain at least 3 of the following: uppercase letters, lowercase letters, numbers, and nonalphanumeric characters.

5. Select any other options for the policy. See the following image.

Source: Amazon.com, Inc.

6. Click Save Changes.

Congratulations! You have taken the first step in implementing security best practices for your account. Next let's discuss how to implement multifactor authentication for the root account.

Enabling MFA for the AWS Root Account

If it's not already configured, your root account needs to have MFA enabled. To accomplish this, complete the steps in Exercise 1.3.

Enabling MFA for the AWS Root Account

1. Using your root account and while in the AWS Management Console, open your account's Services menu at the top right of the console menu bar.

2. Select Security Credentials to go directly to the Identity And Access Management (IAM) landing page.

3. You should see My Security Credentials at the center of the page. Under that you will notice a link to change your root password, name, or email address if needed (see the following image). We will not make any changes for this exercise.

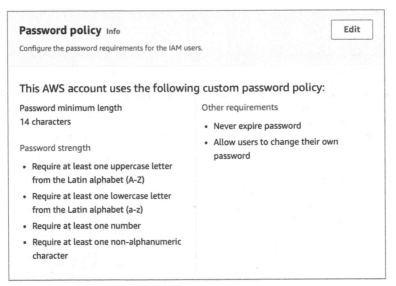

Source: Amazon.com, Inc.

4. Below Password you will see Multi-Factor Authentication (MFA). Click Assign MFA Device, as shown in the following image, and a configuration panel will appear.

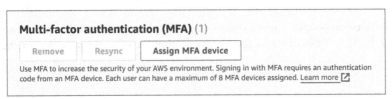

Source: Amazon.com, Inc.

5. Click Assign MFA Device.

    You can use a virtual device, a security key, or other hardware MFA device to configure MFA for the root account. See the following graphic.

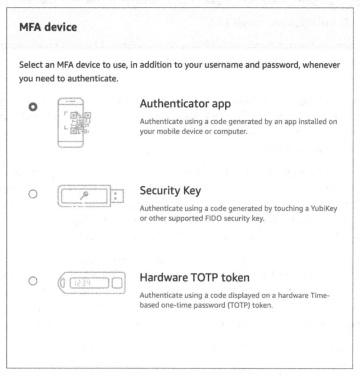

Source: Amazon.com, Inc.

6. Select the option you are prepared to implement. Using a hardware security key is recommended for the best possible MFA protection. Please refer to the following URL to compare MFA support and choose the best option for you; https://aws.amazon.com/iam/features/mfa.

7. Follow the instructions according to the configuration panel for your chosen option. Do not use access keys for your root account. It is best to use access keys with users under the scope of IAM.

    Congratulations! Your root account has MFA enabled.

Provisioning Admin Users with IAM

We've used the IAM service for basic security tasks. IAM represents one of the multiple services available for user provisioning and authentication. It is the first service you need to explore in detail and master its use. Chapter 2, "Account Creation, Security, and Compliance," covers it in detail.

You now need to create a user to begin your operations with AWS. To accomplish this, complete the steps in Exercise 1.4.

Provisioning Admin Users with IAM

1. Using the console Search menu, type **IAM** and press Enter. This will send you directly to the Identity and Access Management (IAM) landing page. It should read in the center IAM Dashboard.

2. You should see to the right of the page a vertical column listing your AWS account details. Make a note of your Account ID. Also note the Sign-in URL For IAM Users In This Account. This is the URL to be used by all IAM users you create. Also note that the URL includes your account number.

3. Click the Create link under Account Alias to provide a name that will be replaced by your account number in the IAM users sign-in URL. This is a good idea to protect your account ID from public exposure. The account alias needs to be a unique name that is not already in use worldwide by DNS or Amazon S3 buckets. The alias must contain 63 characters or fewer. Valid characters are a–z, 0–9, and - (the hyphen).

4. To the left of the page you will see a vertical column listing Dashboard, Access Management, and Access Reports in bold letters. Under Access Management you can see User Groups, Users, Roles, and Policies, among others. These top four items are the fundamental resources for user provisioning. In this exercise we will use User Groups, Users, and Policies. Chapter 2 discusses the IAM service in detail.

5. Select User Groups and then click Create Group at the top right.

6. For User Group Name, type **Administrator**.

7. At the bottom of the page you will see the section Attach Permissions Policies. This section will have hundreds of AWS managed policies representing permissions documents. You can attach up to 10 policies to a user group. All the users in the group will have the permissions that are defined in the selected policies.

8. In the search bar, type **Administrator** and press Enter. You will see all the policies with the string Administrator in their name. Select the AdministratorAccess policy and then click Create Group at the bottom right of the page. This will create the group with the associated permissions to administer everything related to AWS services. The Administrator group will appear listed on the User Groups page.

9. At the left of the page select the items listed as Users and click Add Users at the top right of the page.

10. For Username, type **sysopsadmin** and select both check boxes under Select AWS Access Type. This will allow the sysopsadmin user to use both the AWS Management Console and the AWS CLI when needed.

Please note that you can provision a user to have either access or both. AWS Management Console access will require a password, and programmatic access will create an access key ID and secret access key to be used to configure the AWS CLI or an SDK.

11. Also note that when you select the AWS Management Console access, Console Password and Require Password options appear on the Add User page. Leave these choices as Show By Default. A password will be autogenerated and the user must create a new password at the next sign-in.

12. Click Next: Permissions at the bottom right of the page.

13. On the next page, which is listed as step 2 at the top right of the page, click Add User To Group.

14. Select the check box to the left of your listed Administrator group. This will add the sysopsadmin user to the Administrator group and provision the predefined permissions.

15. Select Next: Tags at the bottom right of the page. Tags are optional but useful as your implementation grows. Also, some services require that resources be tagged to function accordingly.

16. For Key, type **Purpose** and for Value, type **Administrator User**.

17. Click Next: Review at the bottom right of the page.

18. The review page allows you to verify your configuration for the user. Once you do, click Create User at the bottom right of the page.

19. The following page is very important and is labeled as step 5 at the top right. This page indicates that the user has been created and lists the URL to use for AWS Management Console access. The URL will look like this: `https://YOUR_12DIGIT_ACCOUNT_ID.signin.aws.amazon.com/console`.

Please note that your 12-digit account ID will be used as the first item in the URL unless you create an alias for the account as described in step 3. If that is the case, your user sign-in URL will have the following structure: `https://YOUR_ACCOUNT_ALIAS.signin.aws.amazon.com/console`.

20. If you had selected Programmatic Access for a user, the Access Key ID and Secret Access Key will be provided on this page, and you need to make a note of these credentials as they will not be shown to you again. You can always revoke and re-create them, but you will not be provided the clarity and visibility that you are getting on this page. Be sure to click Download .csv so that you get a local copy of the keys. Also, be sure to store them securely.

21. If you chose an auto-assigned password, it will also appear on this page. Please make a note of it.

22. Click Close at the bottom right of the page.

23. From the account's Settings menu at the top right of the page, choose Sign Out.

Congratulations! You have created a user with the name sysopsadmin and assigned it Administrator privileges, a password for console access, and a set of keys for CLI and SDK access. You have also defined an account-level password policy and enabled MFA for the root user. You can use the sign-in URL and credentials downloaded to log into the AWS Management Console and continue exploring some other basic features and services.

The AWS Global Infrastructure

An introduction to AWS Cloud computing always requires a discussion of the AWS global infrastructure. You may already be familiar with the concepts of a region, an availability zone, and edge locations. The AWS global infrastructure components go well beyond these basic three items. For over 10 years, AWS has been evaluated as a leader in the 2021 Gartner Magic Quadrant for Cloud Infrastructure and Platform Services, placing at the top position for its ability to execute and completeness of vision among the top 7 vendors.

You can visit the following URL for details:

`https://aws.amazon.com/resources/analyst-reports/`
`gartner-mq-cips-2021`

As of this writing, AWS operates 33 regions, 105 availability zones, 600+ edge locations, 13 regional edge caches, 36 local zones, 29 wavelength zones, and 115 direct connect locations. There is also a global component called AWS Outposts. The global infrastructure spans 245 countries and territories.

You can visit `https://aws.amazon.com/about-aws/`
`global-infrastructure` for details.

The AWS global infrastructure provides the following items of functionality:

Region   This is a physical location in the world where AWS has clusters of datacenters. Regions are composed of availability zones.

Availability Zone   This is a logical group of datacenters. These groups are isolated and physically separate. Each of them includes independent power, cooling, physical security, and interconnectivity using high bandwidth and low-latency links. All traffic between availability zones (AZs) is encrypted. Also, each availability zone is implemented separately from other availability zones but within 60 miles of each other.

Edge Location   This is the resource used by AWS to deliver reliable and low-latency performance globally. Edge locations are how AWS attains high performance in countries and territories where a region does not exist. The global edge network connects thousands of tier 1, 2, and 3 telecom carriers globally and delivers hundreds of terabits of capacity. Edge locations are connected with regions using the AWS backbone, which is a fully redundant, multiple 100 Gigabit Ethernet (GbE) parallel fiber infrastructure. The AWS edge network consists of over 400 edge locations and 13 regional edge caches in over 90 cities across 48 countries.

Local Zone   This is an extension of a region where you can run low-latency applications using AWS services in proximity to end users. Local zones deliver single-digit millisecond latencies to users for use cases like media, entertainment, and real-time gaming, among others.

Wavelength Zone   This brings AWS services to the edge of a 5G network, reducing the latency to connect to your application from a mobile device. Application traffic can reach application servers running in wavelength zones without leaving the mobile provider's network. They provide single-digit millisecond latencies to mobile devices by reducing the extra network hops that may be needed without such a resource.

Outpost   This is designed to support applications that need to remain in your datacenter due to low-latency requirements or local data processing needs. It brings AWS services, infrastructure, and operating models to your datacenter, co-location space, or physical facility.

Direct Connect Location   This provides a direct connection to AWS using cross-connections from other datacenters operated by the same providers used by AWS. You can access any AWS region from a Direct Connect location using Direct Connect gateways or public virtual interfaces.

As a SysOps administrator, you want to have full visibility of available resources so that you can use the best tool for the right task. The AWS global infrastructure goes beyond the basic items of regions, AZs, and edge locations.

The AWS Command-Line Interface

There are multiple ways in which we can interact and provision resources using AWS. The more common ways include the AWS Management Console, the AWS command-line interface (CLI), and AWS software developer kits (SDKs). The AWS Management Console is a web browser application that allows you to manage your account and AWS services with a visual display of resources and actions. At some point, as SysOps administrators, we will concern ourselves with automation instead of using click streams and sequences. Using shell scripts is one of the primary mechanisms for administrators to perform tasks. Keep in mind that the console, the CLI, and SDKs represent interfaces to the application programming interface (API) for each of the AWS services available.

The AWS CLI provides a set of tools that can be used from a command-line terminal independent of the operating system. You can install and use the CLI in Linux, macOS, and Windows systems. The process of installing and configuring the CLI in your local machine will require a few steps. Fortunately, CloudShell in the AWS Management Console provides an Amazon EC2 instance preconfigured with AWS tools, including the CLI, and provisioned with the same permissions used to log into the console. This allows you to use the CLI without setting up a local set of credentials. CloudShell configures the AWS CLI, Python, and Node.js, among others. It provides 1 GB of free storage per region, and files saved in the home directory are available in later sessions for the same region.

You can use CloudShell to interact with some AWS services to become familiar with the AWS CLI without having to provision a local installation and configuration of the CLI. In general, after the installation of the CLI locally, the steps for a local setup include running the `aws configure` command. The command will ask you for four pieces of information to set up a new CLI account:

- Access key ID
- Secret access key
- Default region name
- Default output format

The Access key and Secret key must exist prior to this configuration and are attached to an IAM user or root user login. The default region is your preferred choice and usually is the region closest to you or your users. The default output for CLI commands is a JSON document. We will discuss the CLI options and output again in more detail later in this chapter. For now, let's explore the CLI using CloudShell.

Exploring the AWS CLI

Using CloudShell, you can explore AWS services, including the CLI. The steps in Exercise 1.5 show you how.

EXERCISE 1.5

Exploring the AWS CLI

1. In the AWS console, log in using the sysopsadmin user you created in Exercise 1.4. If this is the first time you've logged in using the sysopsadmin user credentials, you will be asked to change your password before continuing.

2. Enter the self-assigned password and your new password for the sysopsadmin user. The self-assigned password is part of the credentials file downloaded.

3. Confirm the password change if needed. You will then be asked to log in again to the AWS Management Console using the new password. Be sure to use the console log in link provided in the credentials file.

4. We have already demonstrated how to enable MFA for a user and will leave this task as optional for this exercise. It is a best practice to enable MFA for all users—in particular, users with administrator access, as is the case for the sysopsadmin user created earlier.

5. Click the CloudShell icon in the console menu bar or type **cloudshell** in the search bar and press Enter. CloudShell is a browser-based shell with AWS CLI access from the AWS Management Console.

6. The cloudshell prompt will appear, showing the region of operation at the top left.

7. Using the Actions menu, you can manage the tabs layout as well as download and upload files. You can also restart the AWS CloudShell and delete the CloudShell home directory.

8. Use CloudShell to explore AWS services, including the CLI. We are including a few CLI commands for some of the core AWS services found in Tables 1.1, 1.2 and 1.3. You can experiment and explore as much as you like. Also, please make sure to delete any resources created during your experiments as there may be charges involved with some of the resources provisioned during your experiments.

AWS CLIv2 Features

AWS CLI v2 was released in early 2020 and it includes features and enhancements such as new installers; new configuration options like AWS IAM Identity Center, which is formally known as AWS Single Sign-On (SSO); and interactive features. With v2, you are no longer required to have Python preinstalled to use the AWS CLI. Any issues with compatible Python versions, virtual environments, and conflicting Python packages have been resolved. Installing the AWS CLI has been simplified, and package installers are available for Windows (MSI installer) and macOS (pkg installer). For details about installing, updating, and migrating your CLI, see https://docs.aws.amazon.com/cli/latest/userguide/getting-started-install.html.

TABLE 1.1   CLI command actions and syntax

Common CLI command action	CLI syntax for command
Display the version of the CLI installed	aws --version
Get help for using the CLI	aws help or aws <command> help
Enable the auto-prompt feature of CLIv2	aws <command> --cli-auto-prompt
Configure CLIv2 with creds from a file	aws configure import -csv file:// path/to/creds.csv
Enable a walk-through of configuration	aws configure wizard
Configure CLI creds using AWS IAM Identity Center (AWS SSO)	aws configure sso
The CLI will guide you through values	aws iam --create-user --cli-auto-prompt

AWS CLIv2 includes a new command to import credentials from the CSV files generated by the AWS console when you select programmatic access or provision new keys for a user. Table 1.1 includes some of these you can try to gain familiarity with command-line calls.

AWS CLIv2 New Features (Wizards)

The AWS CLIv2 wizards feature is an improved version of the -cli-auto-prompt command-line option. The wizards guide you through the process of managing AWS resources. You can access this feature by using the command line

```
aws <service-name> wizard <wizard-name>
```

Wizards will query existing resources and prompt you for data in the process of setting up for the service invoked. As of this writing, wizards are available for configure, dynamodb, iam, and lambda functions. For example, the command aws dynamodb wizard new-table will guide you in creating a DynamoDB table. Also, note that the configure command does not use a <wizard-name>. It's invoked as follows: aws configure wizard.

AWS CLIv2 Command Summary for Amazon S3

Table 1.2 is a command summary for Amazon S3.

TABLE 1.2   Amazon S3 command summary

Common S3 CLI commands	CLI syntax for Amazon S3 command
Make a bucket	aws s3 mb s3://my-bucket
List all buckets	aws s3 ls
List the contents of a specific bucket	aws s3 ls s3://my-bucket
Upload a file to a bucket	aws s3 cp file s3://my-bucket/file
Download a file from a bucket	aws s3 cp s3://my-bucket/file file
Copy a file between buckets	aws s3 cp s3://bucket1/file s3://bucket2/file
Synchronize a directory with an S3 bucket	aws s3 sync my-directory s3://my-bucket/

AWS CLI v2 Command Summary for Amazon EC2

Table 1.3 is a command summary for Amazon EC2.

TABLE 1.3   Amazon EC2 command summary

Common EC2 CLI commands	CLI Syntax for EC2 command
Create a VPC	`aws ec2 create-vpc --cidr-block 10.0.0.0/16 --output text --query 'Vpc.VpcId'`
Create Internet gateway	`aws ec2 create-internet-gateway --output text`
Attach Internet gateway to a VPC	`aws ec2 attach-internet-gateway --internet-gateway-id igw --vpc-id vpc`
Create a subnet	`aws ec2 create-subnet --vpc-id vpc --cidr-block 10.0.1.0/24 --availability-zone az --output text`
Create a public route	`aws ec2 create-route --route-table-id rtb --gateway-id igw --destination-cidr-block 0.0.0.0/0`
List all the instances	`aws ec2 describe-instances`
Create an EBS volume	`aws ec2 create-volume`

Amazon VPC and Amazon EBS commands are part of the set included with Amazon EC2 commands.

AWS CLIv2 Outputs

The AWS CLIv2 output default is a JSON document. This is useful when the result is to be processed by other programs. You can also choose a "table" format, which will make the output human readable, and you can choose the output to be a tab-delimited "text" output. For details about CLI output options, visit:

`https://docs.aws.amazon.com/cli/latest/userguide/cli-usage-output.html`

The AWS CLI also provides output filtering options for you to manage the results of a command as needed:

- `--query`: This option can be used to limit the results displayed from a CLI command. The query is expected to be structured according to the JMESPath specification, which defines the syntax for searching a JSON document. Details for the JMESPath specification are available at `https://jmespath.org/specification.html`. For example, using an output of text and a query, you can obtain the specific ID of a resource just created:

```
aws ec2 create-vpc --cidr-block 10.0.0.0/16 --output text --query 'Vpc.VpcId'
vpc-05bad5d48774ec000
```

- `--filter`: This option can also be used to manage the results displayed. However, with the `--filter` option, the output is restricted on the server side whereas `--query` filters the results at the client side.

- `--dry-run`: This is not a filter but a simulation. The `--dry-run` option is used to verify that you have the required permissions to make the request and gives you an error if you are not authorized. The `--dry-run` option does not make the request. It simply verifies that the request is authorized.

AWS SDKs

The AWS CLI can be installed on any computer you choose and can be obtained using an installer by visiting `https://docs.aws.amazon.com/cli/latest/userguide/getting-started-install.html`. Prepackaged installers are available for Linux, Windows, and macOS systems along with detailed instructions for installing, upgrading, and uninstalling the CLI and related tools where applicable.

You will be expected to have an existing username and have an access key ID and secret access key before configuring the AWS CLI. These are required for you to use the CLI or any of the SDKs available. SDKs are available for a variety of languages including C++, Go, Java, JavaScript, Kotlin, Node.js, .NET, PHP, Python, Ruby, Rust, Swift, and many others. Using an SDK, you can develop applications on AWS using your preferred software development language. AWS also makes available tools for integrated development environments (IDEs) and IDE toolkits. For more details, visit `https://aws.amazon.com/developer/tools`.

The AWS Certified SysOps Administrator – Associate exam does not cover setup or utilization of AWS SDKs. It is important to be aware they exist and represent one of the primary ways to interact with AWS services.

AWS Service Quotas

A new AWS account is available with some predefined service usage limits. These limits are intended for your protection. Many of the service limits can be changed by simply making a request to AWS Support. However, it is important to note that some limits are considered hard limits and cannot be changed. Most limits are considered "soft limits" and can be adjusted according to your needs. The Service Quotas page (Figure 1.3) available using your AWS Management Console (`https://us-east-1.console.aws.amazon.com/servicequotas/home`) will provide visibility of the limits for any of the AWS services in your account. You can examine the AWS Default Quota Value, your Applied Quota Value, and if the quota is Adjustable. You will also gain access to the quota request template, which is the document to be used to request up to 10 quota increases for newly created accounts.

You are not expected to memorize service quotas as they are easily referenced using AWS documentation and they tend to change over time. For example, the maximum execution timeout for a Lambda function was originally 5 minutes. Today, the maximum execution timeout is now 15 minutes.

FIGURE 1.3   Service Quotas console panel

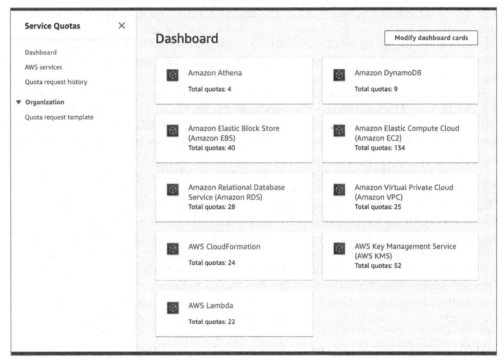

Source: Amazon.com, Inc.

The AWS Health API and Dashboards

AWS pursues a 99.9 percent uptime for most services. In the rare event that a service degradation, scheduled change, or resource-impacting issue takes place, AWS uses the AWS Health API as the main channel to communicate the details and guidance. It powers the AWS Health Dashboards and the AWS Health Aware (AHA) solution.

There are two versions of the AWS Health Client Dashboard. The first version is the public AWS Health Dashboard. It is used to gain visibility to the health of all AWS services. The page displays any reported service event for services across regions. You are not required to have an AWS account to access the AWS Health Dashboard. All you need to do is navigate to https://health.aws.amazon.com/health/status.

If you have an existing AWS account, you can access your AWS Personal Health Dashboard using the AWS Management Console. You can have a personalized view of the performance and availability of the AWS services you're using. You get deeper visibility into resource issues, scheduled changes, and critical notifications. In addition to performance and availability information for AWS services, you can configure your AWS Personal Health Dashboard to use your local time zone settings for published events and receive notifications and detailed remediation guidance when AWS is sustaining a service event that may have an impact on your implementation. You can also receive notifications in advance of AWS scheduled activities, allowing you to prepare for troubleshooting and remediation. Notifications can be delivered to you via email and are also published to the AWS console. Each alert provides the event information, a list of resources affected, and AWS recommendations for the required actions.

If you set up AWS Organizations, AWS Health aggregates all events and displays them in the AWS Personal Health Dashboard. Events from all member accounts are displayed. You can also use Amazon EventBridge to define rules and trigger Lambda functions to perform automated remediation for service events reported or based on the notification of scheduled maintenance.

The AWS Health API is available directly as part of an AWS Business Support or AWS Enterprise Support plan. It allows for chat integration and ingesting events into Slack, Microsoft Teams, and Amazon Chime. It also allows integration with dozens of AWS partners such as DataDog and Splunk, among many others. The result is an automated and immediately actionable incident response to allow you to mitigate any potential customer disruptions. The AWS Health Aware (AHA) solution is provided by AWS and is available in the GitHub AWS Samples repository. AHA implements a serverless infrastructure using CloudFormation that sends alerts from the AWS Health API to your chosen communication channels to actively monitor and respond to AWS Health events. See more details about architecture and implementations by visiting `https://aws.amazon.com/blogs/mt/aws-health-aware-customize-aws-health-alerts-for-organizational-and-personal-aws-accounts`.

Pricing

Pricing for AWS services is structured differently depending on what you are using. For example, Amazon EC2 instances are usually priced per hour of operation and in some cases per second used. Amazon S3 buckets are priced per gigabyte per month. AWS Lambda functions are priced per invocation and resources used.

For new accounts, AWS provides free AWS platform usage up to certain limits for 12 months. You also have short-term free trials to some services, while access to other specific services is always free. The free tier offers are only available to new AWS customers and for 12 months after signing up. After 12 months or if your usage exceeds the predefined tiers, you pay standard, pay-as-you-go service rates. For AWS compute services, the savings plans offer a way to save as compared to on-demand pricing by making a commitment to use a predefined amount of an AWS service for one or three years. You can pay all up-front, partial up-front, or nothing up-front. The discount received will be proportional to the time commitment and how much up-front payment you choose to make.

Also, as your usage increases you can get volume usage discounts. For example, services like Amazon S3 use a tiered pricing model where the more you use the less you pay per GB/ month. For details about service pricing and usage limits included in the AWS free tier, visit `https://aws.amazon.com/free`.

Finally, for any given expected usage you envision using AWS, you can use the AWS Pricing Calculator, which lets you create an estimate without commitments and explore service usage and pricing for your planned architectures. The AWS Pricing Calculator is available at `https://calculator.aws`.

Summary

Cloud computing adoption continues to grow for businesses of all sizes. Essential to cloud migrations and cloud-native implementations is the role of the SysOps administrator. This role is concerned with provisioning, testing, monitoring, and maintaining all of the technology systems used by the enterprise. The idea of visibility by monitoring is crucial to success. Also, the idea of automation as implemented by repeatable and programmatic solutions to provision and deploy applications allows operations to scale in a consistent and reliable way. Finally, security is of the utmost importance as an error in security can possibly result in the loss of resources, data, time, and money. Operating complex computing systems is no easy task, and it takes time, experience, and dedication to embrace the challenges brought on by cloud computing in general. The AWS Certified SysOps Administrator – Associate exam is intended to validate your ability to deploy, manage, and operate AWS workloads. This study guide is intended to help you prepare beyond exam success and into an exciting and rewarding role as an AWS SysOps administrator.

Exam Essentials

Know how to create an AWS account and secure the root user.   The exam validates your ability to implement security controls to meet compliance requirements. Understanding how to operate the IAM service and securing the AWS root account user are essential practices for this exam objective. This includes setting robust password policies, enabling MFA for users, and managing policies.

Understand how to use the AWS Management Console and CLI.   Another important skill validated by the exam is performing operations by using the AWS Management Console and the AWS CLI. Experiment with the AWS CLI and observe the results using the management console. It will provide you with visibility and familiarity with basic commands, options, and parsing results. Keep in mind that the exam may have one or more exam lab components where a scenario made of a set of tasks to perform will be requested. You may be expected to perform the tasks using the AWS Management Console or AWS CLI.

Be familiar with the AWS Personal Health Dashboard.   Identifying, classifying, and remediating incidents is an essential part of your role as a SysOps administrator. Understand how to obtain and respond to AWS service degradation, scheduled changes, or resource-impacting issues by leveraging the AWS Health API and the AWS Personal Health Dashboard.

Understand the AWS global infrastructure and all components.   Implementing high availability and resilient environments will demand that you differentiate between the use of a single availability zone and multi-AZ deployments for a variety of services. Understanding the AWS global infrastructure and all components is critical for such implementation types.

Understand the purpose and function of as many AWS services as possible, starting with those listed in the exam guide.   The easiest type of questions in the certification exam are those that challenge you to remember the name of a service, what the service does, and under what use case you choose the service as compared to a different solution. Navigate to the certification exam guide appendix and make a note of all the services listed as being in scope. For each of those services, try to remember what they do, their anatomy, and how to use them. As of this writing, there are over 65 services and features that might be covered on the exam.

The certification exam guide appendix also shows a list of out-of-scope services and features. While the exam will probably not include complex scenarios that will test deep knowledge of out-of-scope services, it is important that you at least recognize the name and function of all services listed even if you are yet to learn how to operate them.

Hands-On Exercises

To complete these exercises, you will need to use CloudShell in the AWS Management Console. These are one-line fragments for the AWS CLI to create some basic resources. You can execute the command and then examine the console for visual confirmation of the resources created with a service. Use the help command as much as possible to become familiar with the structure and syntax of basic commands. Explore creating different resources for other services. Finally, be sure to delete any resources created during these exercises to clean up after practice and avoid unexpected charges.

Hands-on Exercise 1.1 uses example values for items you need to make a note of and keep track of while performing the steps. Please do not use any of the values provided as examples, as the commands will not work as expected. The goal is to become familiar with the syntax and process of using the CLI. You can always examine the help document for command details.

Hands-On Exercise 1.1: Creating an Amazon VPC with a Public Subnet Using AWS CloudShell

Creating a VPC is a fundamental skill and understanding the different parts and functions is a common item tested during AWS certification exams. In this exercise you will be creating a VPC using the AWS CLI to give you visibility into the syntax and use some of the core AWS services. You are not expected to memorize any commands as they are not tested on exams. However, familiarity with the AWS CLI is the first step toward automating daily tasks as a SysOps. You will need to log into your AWS Management Console and start the CloudShell service from the menu or type **cloudshell** in the service search bar. You will also need your favorite text editor open to take notes on the values provided by your CLI commands.

1. At the AWS CloudShell prompt, type **aws ec2 help** and press Enter.

   Note how for the CLI the EC2 service command includes being able to deploy Amazon EC2 instances, Elastic Block Store (EBS) volumes, and Amazon Virtual Private Cloud (VPC).

2. Use the Enter key to navigate through the help document line-by-line or the space-bar to navigate page-by-page. Type the letter **q** when you want to quit viewing the documentation.

3. At the prompt, type **aws ec2 describe-vpcs** and press Enter. This will display a JSON document describing all the VPCs in the region. At a minimum you will see a description of the default VPC with a CIDR block of 172.31.0.0/16.

4. CLI operations with VPCs usually require that you provide the VpcId of the VPC to be used. You can provision a new VPC using a CIDR of 10.180.0.0/16 using the command:

```
aws ec2 create-vpc --cidr-block 10.180.0.0/16 --output text \
    --query 'Vpc.VpcId'
```

5. Make a note of the VpcId, which should look something like vpc-0fbf21d5550493965.

6. Provision tags for the VPC using the following command:

```
 aws ec2 create-tags --resources vpc-0fbf21d5550493965 \
    --tags Key=vpcname,Value=MyTestVPC
```

7. Provision an Internet gateway—for example:

```
igw-0a500c14869869d02
aws ec2 create-internet-gateway --output text \
        --query 'InternetGateway.InternetGatewayId'
```

8. Attach the Internet gateway to the VPC created earlier by using the command:

```
aws ec2 attach-internet-gateway --internet-gateway-id \
    igw-0a500c14869869d02 --vpc-id vpc-0fbf21d5550493965
```

9. Provision a subnet with a CIDR of 10.180.1.0/24 in the us-east-1a availability zone by using the command:

```
aws ec2 create-subnet --vpc-id vpc-0fbf21d5550493965 \
    --cidr-block 10.180.1.0/24 --availability-zone us-east-1a \
  --output text --query 'Subnet.SubnetId'
```

10. Make a note of the SubnetId—for example, subnet-0747b02d0bb936811.

11. Provision tags for the public subnet by using the command:

```
aws ec2 create-tags --resources subnet-0747b02d0bb936811 \
  --tags Key=subnet,Value=PublicSubnet
```

12. Obtain the route ID associated with your new VPC:

```
aws ec2 describe-route-tables \
  --filters Name=vpc-id,Values=vpc-0fbf21d5550493965 \
  --output text --query 'RouteTables[*].RouteTableId'
```

13. Make a note of the RouteTableId—for example, rtb-008f73396f0e4baa8.

14. Provision a route table entry for public Internet access:

```
aws ec2 create-route --route-table-id rtb-008f73396f0e4baa8 \
  --gateway-id igw-0a500c14869869d02 \
  --destination-cidr-block 0.0.0.0/0
```

15. Associate the route table to the subnet created earlier. This will make it public:

```
aws ec2 associate-route-table \
  --subnet-id subnet-0747b02d0bb936811 \
  --route-table-id rtb-008f73396f0e4baa8
```

Congratulations, you just created a VPC with a public subnet using the AWS CLI.

The preceding exercise is tedious. Usually, using the CLI involves some form of scripting where the corresponding values are stored using variables, the results are validated, and the script is tested before deployment. In our case it is important to become familiar with the syntax and process of using the CLI. You can now examine the results using the AWS Management Console. Please remember to delete all the resources created. You can navigate to the VPC landing page in the AWS Management Console, select Your VPC from the Virtual Private Cloud listing, and select the VPC you created on the main panel. Once it's selected, choose Delete VPC from the Actions menu. You will need to confirm the delete operation and all the resources created before will be deleted.

Review Questions

1. Which of the following injects an additional piece of information into the authentication process?

    A. Defining a secret access ley

    B. Using AWS CloudShell

    C. Implementing MFA

    D. Defining an access key ID

2. Which of the following are required to implement CLI programmatic access? (Choose two.)

    A. Defining a secret access key

    B. Using SSH Keygen

    C. Implementing MFA

    D. Defining an access key ID

3. Which of the following are best practices for AWS account protection? (Choose three.)

    A. Defining an account-level password

    B. Using AWS CloudShell

    C. Implementing MFA for all users

    D. Enabling AWS Security Hub

    E. Using Session Manager for EC2 instances

    F. Using service-linked roles

4. Which of the following is a best practice for cross–AWS account access?

    A. Using AWS Organizations

    B. Using IAM groups

    C. Implementing MFA for all users

    D. Using IAM roles

5. Which of the following saves you from provisioning keys to operate AWS services in a programmatic way?

    A. The AWS Management Console

    B. AWS CloudShell

    C. Session Manager

    D. IAM groups

6. Which of the following saves you from configuring SSH or RDP resources to operate EC2 instances?

   A. The AWS Management Console

   B. AWS CloudShell

   C. Session Manager

   D. IAM groups

7. Which of the following represents the URL to log into the AWS Management Console as an IAM user? (Choose two.)

   A. `https://aws.amazon.com/console/`

   B. `https://accountID.signin.aws.amazon.com/console`

   C. `https://signin.aws.amazon.com/signin`

   D. `https://signin.aws.amazon.com/signin/console`

   E. `https://account_alias.signin.aws.amazon.com/console`

8. Which of the following brings AWS services to the edge of a 5G network?

   A. Edge location

   B. Local zone

   C. Outpost

   D. Wavelength zone

9. Which of the following is an extension of a region where you can run low-latency applications using AWS services?

   A. Edge location

   B. Local zone

   C. Outpost

   D. Wavelength zone

10. Which of the following bring AWS services, infrastructure, and operating models to your datacenter, co-location space, or physical facility?

    A. Direct Connect location

    B. Local zone

    C. Outpost

    D. Wavelength zone

11. Which of the following is the resource used by AWS to deliver reliable and low-latency performance globally?

    A. Region

    B. Local zone

    C. Edge location

    D. Wavelength zone

12. Which of the following represents a logical group of AWS datacenters?

   A. Region

   B. Local zone

   C. Edge location

   D. Availability zone

13. Which of the following CLI commands will guide you through the process of managing AWS resources?

   A. `aws configure wizard`

   B. `aws configure sso`

   C. `aws configure import -csv file://path/to/creds.csv`

   D. `aws configure`

14. Which AWS services have CLI wizards available? (Choose three.)

   A. Amazon EC2

   B. AWS Lambda functions

   C. Amazon DynamoDB

   D. AWS IAM

   E. Amazon RDS

   F. Amazon S3

15. Which of the following CLI commands creates an S3 bucket?

   A. `aws s3 ls s3://my-bucket`

   B. `aws s3 cp file s3://my-bucket/file`

   C. `aws s3 ls`

   D. `aws s3 mb s3://my-bucket`

16. Which of the following CLI commands copies the content of a local directory to an S3 bucket?

   A. `aws s3 cp s3://bucket1/file s3://bucket2/file`

   B. `aws s3 cp file s3://my-bucket/file`

   C. `aws s3 sync my-directory s3://my-bucket/`

   D. `aws s3 mb s3://my-bucket`

17. Which of the following CLI options provide filtering of the output? (Choose two.)

   A. `--query`

   B. `--filter`

   C. `--search`

   D. `--dry-run`

   E. `--cli-auto-prompt`

18. Which of the following support options give you access to the AWS Health API? (Choose two.)

A. Basic

B. Developer

C. Business

D. Enterprise

E. AWS IQ

19. What is the AWS default quota value for EC2-VPC Elastic IPs?

A. 50

B. 5

C. 5,000

D. 500

20. Which of the following URLs are useful for the purpose of pricing a solution using AWS? (Choose three.)

A. `https://calculator.s3.amazonaws.com`

B. `https://aws.amazon.com/free`

C. `https://aws.amazon.com/migration-evaluator`

D. `https://calculator.aws`

E. `https://tco.aws.amazon.com`

Chapter

2

Account Creation, Security, and Compliance

THE AWS CERTIFIED SYSOPS ADMINISTRATOR EXAM OBJECTIVES COVERED IN THIS CHAPTER INCLUDE:

✓ **Domain 4: Security and Compliance**

- ▪ 4.1 Implement and manage security and compliance policies

    - ▪ Implement IAM features (for example, password policies, multi-factor authentication [MFA], roles, SAML, federated identity, resource policies, policy conditions)

    - ▪ Troubleshoot and audit access issues by using AWS services (for example, CloudTrail, IAM Access Analyzer, IAM policy simulator)

    - ▪ Validate service control policies and permissions boundaries

    - ▪ Validate AWS Region and service selections based on compliance requirements

    - ▪ Implement secure multi-account strategies (for example, AWS Control Tower, AWS Organizations)

Account creation, security, and compliance are core responsibilities for sysops administrators. This chapter will have us focused on six services that handle account creation, as well as some aspects of security and compliance. These services are not the only AWS services handling these topics; you will see many more security and compliance services throughout this book.

Chief among the tools in this chapter is AWS Identity and Access Management (IAM), a central collection of features and services for managing access to AWS resources. Included here are controls for such common tasks as user account and permissions policies creation as well as guardrails and audit capabilities at the enterprise level. It will be very important for you to remember where IAM permissions fit in the bigger picture and to have a firm grasp of their scope. The shared responsibility model (discussed in the first section) will be invaluable. The same questions of access and responsibility will apply when you are trying to understand many concepts in the AWS Cloud such as the difference between basic and custom CloudWatch metrics.

Regardless of your job title or which AWS certification you are pursuing, a deep understanding of IAM is essential. AWS IAM is a suite of tools and features centered around authentication and authorization with fine-grained controls.

Authentication vs. Authorization

Don't get these confused—they are foundational to all security. Authentication, in IT security, is being sure the actor is who they say they are. In the broader security sense, we authenticate in three ways: our username/password (what we know), fingerprint or facial recognition (who we are), or a token or smartcard (what we have). Authorization defines what we can do once we are authenticated. IAM is used for both constructs.

Shared Responsibility

AWS is designed to be highly secure by default. Many features and services are included to allow practitioners to protect the confidentiality, integrity, and availability of their infrastructure and data at all levels. As the mantra goes at AWS: Security is job zero.

Understanding security in cloud computing starts with an understanding of the shared responsibility model. This model, illustrated in Figure 2.1, is absolutely essential for understanding how the security of AWS services work and what your role as a customer is. In truth, understanding this model may well be the most important thing that you will learn in your cloud computing journey.

Following the shared responsibility model, the customer and AWS each have a role to play in securing a cloud computing environment and its resources. AWS is responsible for security *of* the cloud and the customer is responsible for security *in* the cloud.

AWS is responsible for the inherited controls, which include the physical and logical infrastructure that the customer's environment runs on. The AWS datacenters are secure by design. The security of a datacenter is complex and begins with site selection. As you may already know, AWS datacenter locations are not publicized but their location is not just security through obscurity. Locations are chosen to minimize and mitigate threats from natural disasters as well. This scheme plays heavily in the design of availability zones by keeping datacenters isolated and autonomous. AWS datacenters have their own fire suppression, power, and security to operate securely and continuously through even unexpected situations, natural or otherwise.

I've been on tours of some very interesting places, including a nuclear reactor, but we don't expect to ever get inside, or even near, an AWS datacenter. Not even as AWS trainers were we allowed to tour an AWS datacenter. Access to the physical and logical infrastructure is strictly limited to those who have reason to be there, and access is closely monitored at many levels. Access to some infrastructure, such as AWS GovCloud in the United States, has additional access controls. Those who do have reason to be in the AWS infrastructure can expect to be closely monitored.

In the event of an incident, AWS has an Incident Management Team which provides 24/7/365 coverage for detection and response. AWS decommissions storage media following the standards of NIST 800-88.

FIGURE 2.1   Roles in the shared Responsibility Model

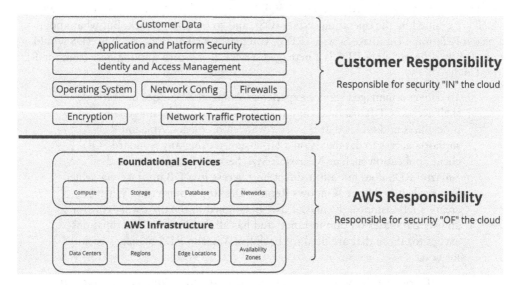

The short and simple way to understand the scope of IAM permissions is to remember that IAM permissions address only what is within the AWS scope of responsibility. Let's take a SQL Server database stack on EC2, as illustrated in Figure 2.2. Before you can run a query on a view, there are several layers that need to be built and each requires permissions from the layer below.

FIGURE 2.2 SQL Server permissions stack

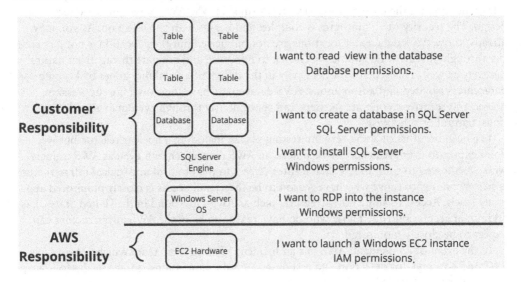

IAM can only grant the permissions necessary to create the instance (`ec2:runinstances`). In order to install SQL Server, Windows permissions are needed, which are granted by the operating system (OS), and so on up the stack. But what about Amazon Relational Database Service (RDS), you may ask? The same stack in RDS would look slightly different since RDS is a managed service. It is worth quoting here from the RDS User Guide:

> To deliver a managed service experience, Amazon RDS does not provide shell access to DB instances, and it restricts access to certain system procedures and tables that require advanced privileges. Amazon RDS supports access to databases on a DB instance using any standard SQL client application such as Microsoft SQL Server Management Studio. Amazon RDS does not allow direct host access to a DB instance via Telnet, Secure Shell (SSH), or Windows Remote Desktop Connection. When you create a DB instance, the master user is assigned to the db_owner role for all user databases on that instance, and has all database-level permissions except for those that are used for backups. Amazon RDS manages backups for you.

> *Microsoft SQL Server on Amazon RDS:* `https://docs.aws.amazon`
> `.com/AmazonRDS/latest/UserGuide/CHAP_SQLServer.html`

What we notice about the RDS stack in Figure 2.3 is that AWS has the responsibility for everything through the database engine (SQL Server). The customer has responsibility for the databases built on the engine. That means that permissions to access and manage the OS and SQL Server engine remain with AWS. However, also note that, as a managed service, AWS limits the customer's direct access to everything below the database. This makes sense when you think about it. If AWS is responsible for maintaining and securing the OS and database engine but then lets the customer get in there and potentially introduce security problems, that just wouldn't work.

FIGURE 2.3   RDS permissions stack

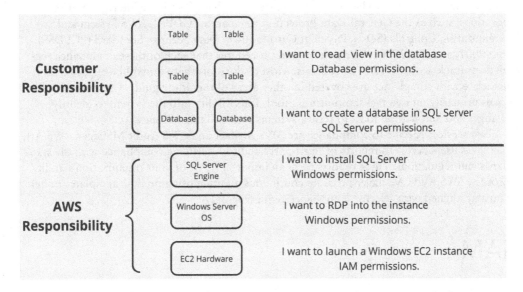

You will continue to see this pattern of a shifting line of responsibility, which moves up as the degree of abstraction increases for the service. By abstraction, we mean that AWS takes on more responsibility and there is less for the customer to manage. Lambda and S3 are more abstracted, whereas EC2 is less abstracted.

Compliance

Compliance is the practice of aligning to standards and frameworks in order to mitigate risk. Most organizations are required by government or customers to meet compliance standards of some kind. These requirements can be highly complex, and violations can be extremely costly. AWS provides the sysops administrator with a variety of tools to help monitor their systems for changes that might indicate trouble or that signal an out-of-compliance state.

Understanding compliance assumes a firm grasp of the shared responsibility model. AWS works with third-party auditors to validate compliance with many certifications, attestations, frameworks, privacy standards, etc. (https://aws.amazon.com/compliance/

programs). However, keep in mind that these certifications are for the elements of cloud computing that are AWS's responsibility as described in the AWS shared responsibility model. We say that the customer "inherits" the certification for the underlying infrastructure from AWS. When a customer builds a workload on that infrastructure or service, the customer is responsible for what they build. Compliance is a two-part process in the cloud. Keep in mind that compliance of a service for a specific compliance program follows three dimensions. Each service is certified by region by compliance program. For that reason you cannot assume that just because a service is Health Insurance Portability and Accountability Act (HIPPA)-compliant in one region that it is also compliant in all regions.

The exam will not expect you to know specifics of the frameworks or standards. However, it would be helpful to be able to recognize some that affect large international corporations, such as the General Data Protection Regulation (GDPR), AWS System and Organization Controls (SOC), Payment Card Industry Data Security Standard (PCI DSS), ISO 9001, and ISO 27001. The policies and procedures that each of these compliance regulations track are referred to as controls. Most of the tools that you will be expected to associate with compliance are covered in other areas of this study guide. Compliance tools focus primarily on two tasks: monitoring tools for visibility into the system to identify changes and automation tools to return systems to their intended state.

Two services specific to compliance are AWS Artifact and AWS Audit Manager. AWS Artifact gives users access to reports of third-party auditors verifying compliance with the standards and regulations. These reports form an important part of your organization's audit process. AWS Audit Manager provides continuous auditing using prebuilt templates to help you stay aligned with selected compliance requirements.

IAM

AWS Identity and Access Management (IAM) is a suite of tools for managing authentication and authorization. In a sense, everything we do in AWS comes back to IAM, so it is imperative that you have a strong working understanding of how permissions work in IAM. This section will survey some of the key features.

IAM Request Context

Every request for access to any AWS resource passes through IAM. That's about 500,000,000 (half a billion) API requests per second. For every request made to IAM there is a context. This context is captured by IAM and taken into account when determining permissions. The context, as illustrated in Figure 2.4, may include data in the request itself or data gathered through the process of making the request.

FIGURE 2.4   IAM request context

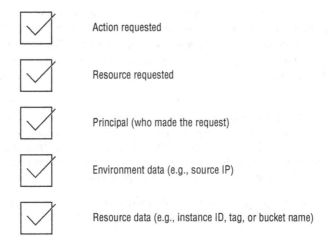

Action requested

Resource requested

Principal (who made the request)

Environment data (e.g., source IP)

Resource data (e.g., instance ID, tag, or bucket name)

The context can include data such as the following:

- What actions are being requested?
- What resource will be accessed (e.g., S3, EC2, DynamoDB)?
- Who (principal) is making the request?
- Where and when (e.g., time of request, source IP, user agent)?
- What specific resource (e.g., tags, instance name, table name)?

The attributes of the context then become vital data for how IAM policies determine access using attribute-based access control.

Attribute-Based Access Control (ABAC)

ABAC is attribute-based access control, which allows you to define permissions based on tags. ABAC is an alternative to the traditional model for granting permissions in IAM, known as role-based access control (RBAC), which is based on the role or function that the user or resource performs. ABAC is much more granular and allows the same user to have different permissions in different contexts. For example, attributes might include time of day, mobile versus desktop, origin IP address, or device security posture.

IAM Policy Types

There are several policy types. Some grant permissions; others do not. You will want to know what each can do and where it is used. In particular, pay attention to identity-based and resource-based policies.

Identity-Based vs. Resource-Based Policies

At a basic level we think of policies as identity-based or resource-based. An identity might be a user logging in with a username and password. A resource might be an S3 bucket. The difference between an identity-based and a resource-based policy is where the policy is attached. In the case of an identity-based policy, the permissions are associated with the user and travel with the user. Identity-based policies can be attached to users, groups, or roles.

When evaluating effective permissions, use the combination of both the resource-based and identity-based policies. The evaluation checks first for a deny. If a deny is found, then access is denied. Then the evaluation looks for allows. Seems complex? It is. That's why IAM Access Analyzer was built and will likely show up on your exam.

With a resource-based policy, the policy resides with the resource rather than with the user and the user comes to the resource for access, as illustrated in Figure 2.5.

FIGURE 2.5   Resource vs. identity policies

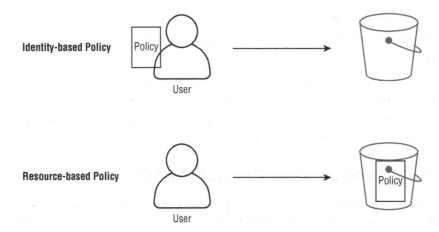

When we talk of IAM policies, there are actually several types. Each one performs a slightly different function. It will be important to recognize in what scenario each might be used in.

- Identity-based policies, which apply to users, groups, and roles.

- Resource-based policies, which apply to resources such an S3 bucket.

- Permissions boundaries, which apply to identity-based policies and define the limits of what the entity can do. Permissions boundaries limit but cannot grant permissions.

- Service control policies, which apply to all identities and resources within an account and limits what they can do but cannot grant permissions, similar to a permissions boundary.

- Access control lists (ACLs), which apply to principals in other accounts. ACLs cannot be used with entities in the same account.

- Session policies, which are used with requests through the command-line interface (CLI) or APIs when assuming a role or with a federated user. Session policies are used to limit, not to grant, permissions.

IAM Policy Evaluation

Resource-based and identity-based policy evaluation is complex, as shown in Figure 2.6. As you just saw, there are many types of policies. Each of these is evaluated and plays into the effective permissions of the user. On the exam you will likely need to be able to parse out what effective permissions a user has based on a combination of policies. In real life, you will certainly need to be able to do this.

    Q: What AWS service do you associate with policy evaluation?

A: IAM Access Analyzer

FIGURE 2.6   Permissions evaluation

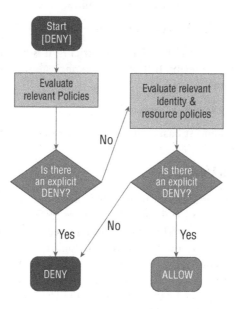

Let's take a look at a policy. (All users are on the same account.)
- The following identity-based policies exist:
  - John Doe can read resource A.
  - Mary Scotts can list and read resources B and C.

- Bob Smith can list, read, and write resources A, B, and C.
- Sally O'Malley has no policy.
- The following resource-based policies exist:
  - Resource A
    - John Doe can list and read.
    - Bob Smith can list and read.
  - Resource B
    - Mary Scotts can list and write.
    - Sally O'Malley can list and read.
  - Resource C
    - Mary Scotts access is denied.
    - Sally O'Malley has full access.

Test yourself:

Q: Can Mary Scotts access Resource C?

A: No, because an explicit deny overrides any allow.

Q: Does Sally O'Malley have access to Resource D?

A: No. "But Resource D wasn't listed, is this a trick?" It is no trick; it is an implicit deny. This is a very important concept. If there is no explicit allow, access is denied even if there is no explicit deny.

Q: Can Sally O'Malley access Resource B?

A: Yes, Sally can read and list based on the resource policy of Resource B.

IAM Policy Conditions

IAM policies have three essential components. These are effect, action, and resource (EAR). Policies can also have optional conditions. There are many conditions and they can be combined to form powerful filters. Common conditions include requiring MFA (`aws:MultiFactorAuthPresent`) or limiting logins to specific CIDR ranges (`aws:SourceIP`). Some keys are global condition keys and others are service-specific. The syntax in a policy looks like this: `"Condition" : { "{condition-operator}" : { "{condition-key}" : "{condition-value}" }}`. The following is an example of a policy statement with two conditions, both of which need to be met:

```
{
  "Version": "2012-10-17",
  "Statement": {
    "Effect": "Allow",
    "Action": "EC2:*",
```

```
    "Resource": "*",
    "Condition": {"IpAddress": {"aws:SourceIp":
["123.4.567.8/24","9.123.456.789.1/18"]
      }
    }
  }
}
```

```
"Condition" : { "StringEquals" : { "aws:username" : "johndoe" }}
```

IAM is also able to make use of variables (e.g., ${aws:username}), wildcards (e.g., "*"), and tags to further expand the capabilities of IAM policies. All of this adds to the granularity of control we have over access using IAM policies.

IAM Password Policies

Passwords are used by users (root and IAM users) to log into the AWS Management Console. It is important to remember the difference between the root and the IAM user. The root user is created when you first create an AWS account. This user authenticates using an email address and password, and the root account cannot be deleted. The root user has complete control over the account, including the ability to control or delete administrators and to terminate the account. There are very few times when the root account is needed for the administration of a system. For that reason, it is best practice to 1) use the root user account only when necessary, 2) never assign security keys to this user account, and 3) apply two-factor authentication.

IAM user accounts, on the other hand, are what you will use most of the time. These types of accounts utilize a username (e.g., "admin") rather than an email address. They are also assigned a password for console access and/or access keys for programmatic access.

AWS provides a default password policy located in IAM ➤ Access Management ➤ Account Settings (see Figure 2.7).

FIGURE 2.7   Change password policy

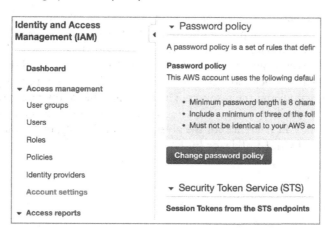

One password policy applies to the entire account, and each account can have only one policy. The default password policy is eight characters in length, a combination of four character types (uppercase, lowercase, numbers, and symbols), and cannot be your account name or email address. In addition to password length and complexity, possible modifications that can be made to the password policy include an expiration, requiring an administrator for resets, and reuse prevention. Be sure you are comfortable modifying the password policy (see Figure 2.8).

FIGURE 2.8   IAM Set Password Policy

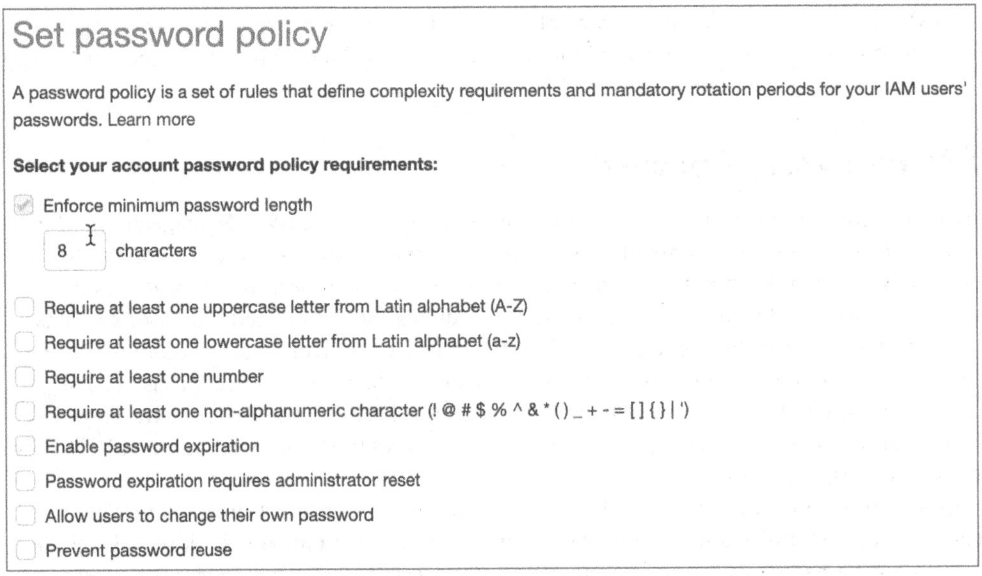

Set password policy

A password policy is a set of rules that define complexity requirements and mandatory rotation periods for your IAM users' passwords. Learn more

Select your account password policy requirements:

☑ Enforce minimum password length

    [8] characters

☐ Require at least one uppercase letter from Latin alphabet (A-Z)

☐ Require at least one lowercase letter from Latin alphabet (a-z)

☐ Require at least one number

☐ Require at least one non-alphanumeric character (! @ # $ % ^ & * ( ) _ + - = [ ] { } | ')

☐ Enable password expiration

☐ Password expiration requires administrator reset

☐ Allow users to change their own password

☐ Prevent password reuse

IAM Policy Example

AWS provides a number of sample policies with both the JSON and detailed explanations of how they work. These examples can be found at https://docs.aws.amazon.com/ IAM/latest/UserGuide/access_policies_examples.html. You will not need to memorize these for your exam, but it would be helpful to review several of them so that you understand what a policy looks like and its main parts. The key parts of every policy are the effect, the action, and the resource. The effect is either allow or deny. The action is the API call for the specified resource(s). The APIs available for a resource can be found in a quick search in the API reference for the given resource. Finally, the resource is any AWS resource such as S3, IAM, Lambda, or EC2.

Here is an example of an IAM policy that grants all S3 actions and all S3-object-lambda actions on a specific bucket. The bucket is uniquely identified by its bucket name and appears as an ARN (Amazon Resource Name): `arn:aws:s3:::bwtgs62jsytehncby`.

```
{
    "Version": "2012-10-17",
    "Statement": [
        {
            "Effect": "Allow",
            "Action": [
                "s3:*",
                "s3-object-lambda:*"
            ],
            "Resource": "arn:aws:s3:::bwtgs62jsytehncby"
        }
    ]
}
```

Note that the ARN does not have all of the elements. Specifically, the region and account ID are omitted. This is normal for an S3 bucket since the bucket name is globally unique within the partition (aws) so no other account ID in any other region can have that name.

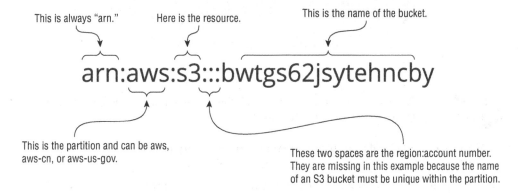

This is always "arn."   Here is the resource.   This is the name of the bucket.

arn:aws:s3:::bwtgs62jsytehncby

This is the partition and can be aws, aws-cn, or aws-us-gov.

These two spaces are the region:account number. They are missing in this example because the name of an S3 bucket must be unique within the partition.

Who can use these permissions on this resource? From this policy, we don't know. The policy itself doesn't specify who can use it. Right now we only know the "what" and the "where." We could attach this policy to a user, group, or role to define the "who."

Policies get very complicated, and there are several other optional elements available such as Sid, Principal, and Condition. Note that Action, Principal, and Resource all have a "Not" variant (NotAction, NotPrincipal, and NotResource). In combination with the Deny effect, these can be very complex and powerful. It is unlikely that you will need to master policies or create any policies from scratch for this exam, but you should have a good sense for how they work. Review a few of the policy examples mentioned earlier.

Permissions Boundaries

Permissions boundaries apply to identity-based principals and define the maximum permissions the identity can be granted. Users and roles can have permission boundaries.

Remember effective permissions. The idea is this: What an entity can do is only the combination of all applicable policies. For identity-based policies (users and roles), it is the permissions shared between both the permissions boundaries and the identity-based policy (see Figure 2.9).

FIGURE 2.9   Policy and boundary effective permissions Venn diagram

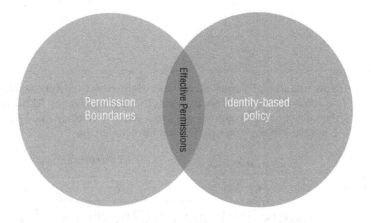

 Permissions Boundaries only limit the scope of permissions, they cannot grant permissions on their own.

AWS provides a helpful example of a permissions boundary policy designed to limit privilege escalation. I suggest you review the policy, available here:

https://docs.aws.amazon.com/IAM/latest/UserGuide/access_policies_boundaries.html

To set a permission boundary, start with creating a permissions boundary policy following the same process as creating a standard IAM policy.

When creating a user:

▪ Add the user to a group.

▪ Copy permissions from an existing user.

▪ Attach existing policies.

You can also set permissions boundaries by selecting a policy from the list of managed policies or creating a new one.

When creating a role:

- Add permissions.
- Add a permissions boundary policy by selecting a policy from the list of managed policies or creating a new one.

Multifactor Authentication

Multifactor authentication (MFA) has become almost an industry norm at this point. However, MFA is not enabled for AWS account users by default.

As shown in Figure 2.10, MFA can use a virtual MFA device (e.g., Google Authenticator), a U2F security key, or a hardware MFA device. SMS is no longer supported.

FIGURE 2.10   Manage MFA Device dialog

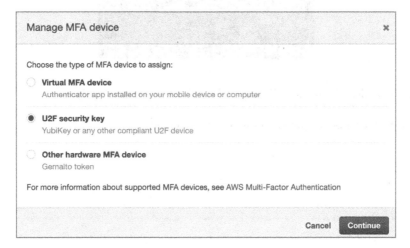

For the exam, you will want to be able to implement and manage MFA for your users. Requiring MFA is managed through permission policies where the MFA condition is set.

From the user perspective, to enable MFA, the user will:

1. Navigate to the IAM console ➢ Users.
2. Select your desired user.
3. Select the Security Credentials tab.
4. For Assigned MFA Device, you will see Not Assigned if the user currently has no MFA devices. Click Manage to assign the device for the user.

5. Click Manage.

    Users can select from three MFA device types, including a virtual MFA device (Authenticator App) such as Google Authenticator, a security key such as YubiKey, or a Gemalto token.

6. Enter the MFA code from the device to sync the device to AWS.

    The user will need to enter the numbers shown in their app or on the Gemalto device or touch the U2F device.

    Some browsers may require authorization to show data about the MFA devices, such as with the Chrome browser (see Figure 2.11).

FIGURE 2.11   MFA browser request to see make and model of security key

Setup is complete. Now the MFA device is enabled (see Figure 2.12).

FIGURE 2.12   Sign-in credentials with MFA enabled

Once the device is enabled, MFA will be required for any console login with that user account.

Removing or Resyncing an MFA Device

Devices can fall out of sync or be lost, causing login issues for users. Resyncing an out-of-sync or deleting a lost device is easy. Follow the same steps described earlier to manage the device. The Manage MFA Device screen will now show Remove and Resync options (Figure 2.13).

FIGURE 2.13 Remove or resync MFA key

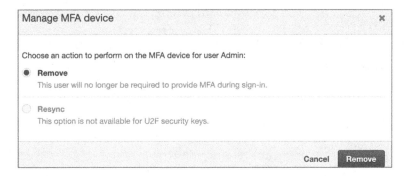

Only one MFA device can be attached to a user at one time. Deleted devices can be reused by the same or other users.

Managing Other Credentials

Several other user credentials can be assigned and managed, including those for CodeCommit (HTTPS and SSH) and Amazon Keyspaces. Make note of what user credentials can be created and how they are created.

Roles

A role consists of two parts: 1) a trust policy, which determines *who* can use the role, and 2) a permissions policy, which describes *what* the entity can do. A role is used to grant fine-grained access and to delegate access. You will want to remember roles as being temporary permissions to do a specific action. IAM allows administrators to grant fine-grained access control through permissions defined in documents called policies. Access control defines who (users or services) can access what (service APIs and resources). Policies are written in JavaScript Object Notation (JSON). While you will not be expected to write a JSON policy from scratch, you should be able to parse a simple policy when you see one. It's a good idea to study example policies to make sure you understand what they will or will not allow.

Creating a role can be done using the APIs, in the console, or via CLI or PowerShell. To create a role in the console, navigate to IAM Roles and click Create Role. Three basic steps include selecting the trusted entity or what you want to give permissions to, such as an AWS service (e.g., EC2 or Lambda); an AWS account; or a web identity provider (Login With Amazon, Facebook, Google, or Cognito). You can also use roles to create a trust policy for users in your account or give permissions through SAML 2.0 federation. For this walkthrough we will assign permissions to EC2 instances. In step 1, shown in Figure 2.14, we select which entity we are creating the role for.

In step 2 (Figure 2.15), we'll select the permissions to assign to the entity, AWS managed permissions policy AWSS3FullAccess.

FIGURE 2.14   Step 1: Select Trusted Entity

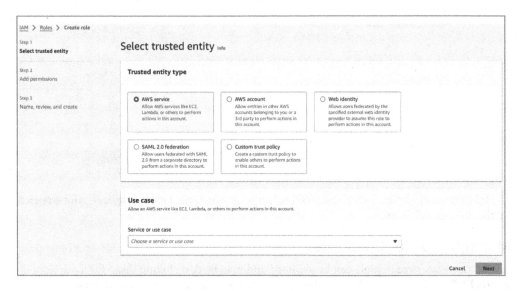

FIGURE 2.15   Step 2: Add Permissions

In step 3 we'll add a role name, description, and tags. We see the trusted entities and policies we selected in steps 1 and 2. In the example, notice that the entities include not only

EC2 but STS, which is now able to AssumeRole. You will notice this for any service you select in step 1 because the service you select needs to use STS (Security Token Service).

Federated Identity

Even small organizations today rely on being able to trust and connect to multiple systems outside their direct control. We see examples of this every day in our personal computing when we sign into websites with our Google or Facebook logins. Identity federation is a mechanism for trusted user authentication between two organizations. AWS provides two different services that can be used for identity federation: AWS Single Sign-on (SSO) and AWS IAM. A third related service, Cognito, will be covered later in this study guide. Identity federation can be used by corporations to allow employees access to AWS resources without requiring them to sign into their corporate network and then again into the AWS console. Mobile apps can use federation so that the app can request temporary credentials using web identity federation. In this model, mobile users can authenticate through a known identity provider (IdP) such as Google or Facebook using SAML 2.0 or OpenID Connect (OIDC). Identity federation is a deep topic with several open standards, each with several protocols. For the SysOps administrator exam, you will not need to be an expert on each. The exam guide states "Implement IAM features (for example . . . SAML, federated identity. . .)." Our focus, then, will be to implement the features associated with federated identity and Single Sign-on.

Open Identity Standards

AWS supports three open identity standards used for identity federation: Security Assertion Markup Language 2.0 (SAML 2.), Open ID Connect (OIDC), and OAuth 2.0. These standards are used by major IdPs such as Facebook, Google, and Amazon.

Identity providers (IdPs) use these standards to provide IAM with authentication and token-based authorization. This simplifies user management so that on-premises users, for example, might be able to gain periodic access to AWS resources without the need of an IAM user account. This both simplifies management (account creation and synchronization) and reduces potential attack vectors (having two standing accounts).

There are three primary standards to be aware of. Each can be used for federation and with an IdP:

- OAuth 2.0 is a protocol used for granting access or delegation but does not confirm identity.
- OIDC is an authentication or identity layer that depends upon, and is used in conjunction with, the OAuth 2.0 protocol.
- SAML 2.0 handles both authentication as well as authorization using tokens containing assertions.

It is useful to understand how the authentication process works with each. Let's start with SAML. SAML uses an IdP to broker the request from the user. The actual identity store could be Active Directory or any Lightweight Directory Access Protocol (LDAP)-based store.

The IdP looks up the user in the store and authenticates them. This is key; the IdP confirms the authentication, not AWS. AWS still does not know who the person is. The IdP sends back a SAML assertion to the user, which includes the role created in the prerequisite steps in the "Roles" section earlier in this chapter.

AWS Single Sign-On (SSO)

AWS Single Sign-on (SSO) uses an identity source, also known as an IdP. The IdP can be one of three possible sources: the AWS SSO identity store, an Active Directory (e.g., AWS Managed Microsoft AD using AWS Directory Services), or an external identity provider such as Azure Active Directory or Okta. Connecting to an external IdP depends on the SAML 2.0 standard. Each AWS organization can have only one identity source, which will serve as your single source of truth. The identity source provides the pool of users who would be trusted. Remember that SSO can be active in only one region in an organization. Consider this in your planning.

AWS SSO supports the System for Cross-domain Identity Management (SCIM) standard, which allows automatic provisioning of users and groups from Okta and Azure AD. AWS SSO also supports ABAC, allowing organizations to define access based on the attributes of a user or group passed through the SAML 2.0 assertion.

Let's look at the process for enabling SSO in an organization. AWS SSO is dependent on AWS Organizations, so that service needs to be set up and all features enabled before SSO can be started. After that, it's as simple as navigating to the AWS SSO console and enabling SSO. Once it's enabled, you will need to select your identity provider. Recall that this can be the AWS SSO identity store, a Microsoft Active Directory (AD), or an external identity provider. You can only have one. Finally, you can connect your accounts and applications and allow them to use SSO.

When you arrive at the new AWS IAM Identity Center dashboard, you will find all the necessary setup steps listed for you (Figure 2.16).

FIGURE 2.16   SSO setup steps

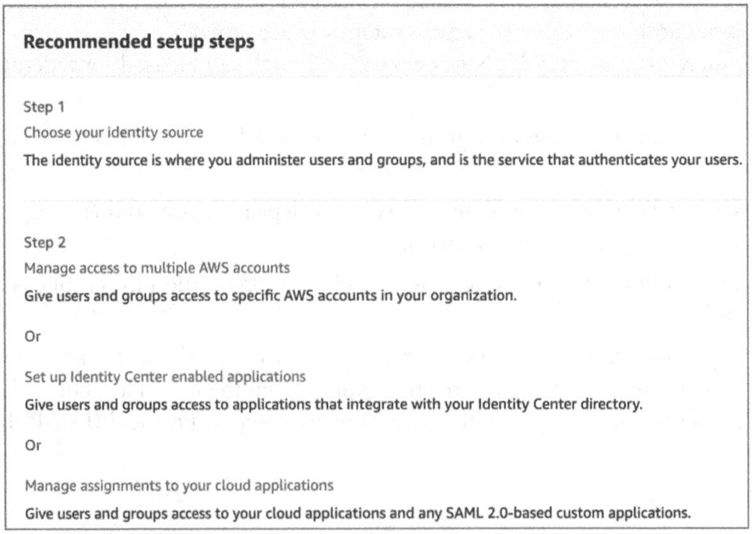

Recommended setup steps

Step 1
Choose your identity source
The identity source is where you administer users and groups, and is the service that authenticates your users.

Step 2
Manage access to multiple AWS accounts
Give users and groups access to specific AWS accounts in your organization.

Or

Set up Identity Center enabled applications
Give users and groups access to applications that integrate with your Identity Center directory.

Or

Manage assignments to your cloud applications
Give users and groups access to your cloud applications and any SAML 2.0-based custom applications.

The first step is setting up the identity store. The option you choose will determine the next steps since setup of each type of store is different.

Using the Identity Central Directory makes use of IAM as the store for all users and groups. Users then access AWS through the AWS access portal configured in a subsequent step.

Selecting Active Directory (AD) will give you the option to connect to an existing directory in the region. The directory must already be set up in AWS and can be either self-managed or an AWS Managed Microsoft AD directory.

Selecting the external identity provider is a bit more involved. The process requires that you manually exchange metadata files between AWS and the IdP so that they can begin the process of establishing the trust relationship (federation).

The second step depends on how you will be granting access. Recall that SSO is integrated with Organizations, so you can provide access to users and groups in any account in your organization. You can also grant access to applications. Applications can be AWS services like SageMaker or IoT SiteWise, many third-party applications such as Salesforce and Office 365, or custom applications using SAML 2.0.

At some point you will want to make a prettier access portal URL. This can be done in the Settings Summary on the dashboard (see Figure 2.17). Keep in mind that you can only set this once. It cannot be changed.

FIGURE 2.17   SSO change access portal URL

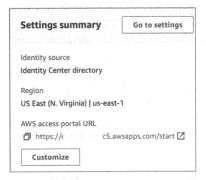

> **Settings summary**   [Go to settings]
>
> Identity source
> **Identity Center directory**
>
> Region
> **US East (N. Virginia) | us-east-1**
>
> AWS access portal URL
> https://(c5.awsapps.com/start
> [Customize]

In July 2022 AWS announced that AWS SSO is now AWS IAM Identity Center. So which should you learn for the exam? As a general rule, new services and changes will not appear on the exam until they have general availability (GA) for six months. That means if you buy this book soon after publication you may have AWS SSO and those who purchase later may have AWS IAM Identity Center.

The good news is that nothing really changed except the name. If you know SSO then you know IAM Identity Center. Just don't let the name change trip you up.

AWS IAM for Federation

AWS IAM can also be used for federation using ABAC and SAML 2.0 or OIDC. Each account within your AWS Organization can have its own SAML 2.0 or OIDC IdP. If your organization already has an identity provider like Azure AD, it is possible to use IAM identity providers rather than creating your users in IAM. AWS IAM uses well-known IdPs, including Amazon, Facebook, and Google, or any other IdP that is compatible with SAML 2.0 or OIDC.

AWS Security Token Service (STS)

A key concept in AWS security is the temporary security credential. Let's say you occasionally cover a systems admin shift every once in a while for your company. To do that occasional job, you need credentials that grant a lot of access to critical systems. Most of the time you never use those permissions, but they are there just in case. That represents a significant opportunity for a bad actor to compromise your account and use those permissions, or there could be any number of other security vulnerabilities due to those unused permissions.

Remember that with STS we are talking about authorization, not authentication. To be granted a credential, the user's identity must have already been authenticated. STS then just passes the credentials.

AWS IAM uses the idea of temporary credentials, which are available to a user or resource just during the time that they need them and just for the specific tasks they need to do. We've already discussed roles, and those are temporary permissions to do a specific task. Now we want to talk about a service that works behind the scenes for roles: the Security Token Service (STS). We will want to associate STS with identity federation, cross-account access roles, EC2 roles, and many other AWS services that can use temporary credentials.

Like IAM, AWS STS is a global service. However, you will notice that STS API calls can be made to specific regional endpoints. This feature exists to reduce latency, but the STS credentials are still global.

Once a token is issued, it cannot be revoked. However, since all permissions are evaluated on every single request, the permissions associated with the token can be revoked, essentially making the token useless almost instantly.

STS APIs

There are a few APIs that you will want to be familiar with. Each of these API calls is used to request temporary credentials from STS in specific settings. The details of what requests and responses look like will be found in the software development kits (SDKs) and is beyond the scope of this exam.

AssumeRole: This API is used by users to gain temporary permissions for an AWS resource. This might include cross-account scenarios where a user needs access to resources in another account. You'll want to remember that this API can make use of MFA. The default expiration of an `AssumeRole` is one hour.

AssumeRoleWithWebIdentity: This API makes use of federated authentication through identity providers such as Facebook, Google, Login With Amazon, or other OpenID Connect (OIDC)-compatible identity providers. We will usually associate this API with Amazon Cognito, though that service is not required to use the `AssumeRoleWithWebIdentity` API call.

AssumeRoleWithSAML: As the name implies, this API uses SAML.

GetFederationToken: For organizations using a custom identity broker rather than OIDC or SAML, this would be the API call to use. A difference to note here is that the expiration is between 15 minutes and 36 hours, with a default of 12 hours.

GetSessionToken: We will want to associate this API call with untrusted environments. MFA can be required on this call, and the expiration for an AWS account root user is limited to a one-hour maximum.

How IAM Does It

Zelkova and Automated Reasoning

It is highly unlikely you would find reference to this on the exam, but it is interesting to know. IAM relies on complex math to drive several of the security tools such as IAM Access Analyzer. For example, your policies can get pretty complex when you start to think of the number of them and how they all interact with one another. Even a team of very smart humans would take a very long time to compute every possible implication of their combined use. To solve for this, automated reasoning translates your policy into mathematic proofs. It becomes possible then to solve for all the possible scenarios for that policy and do this automatically and quickly. This is what allows AWS to check every IAM request that comes in globally in fractions of a second with near-perfect accuracy. The AWS tool behind this is called Zelkova, and it uses a logic problem called satisfiability modulo theories (SMTs). Again, this is highly unlikely to be on your exam but it is always fun to know what's going on behind the curtain.

Running Credential Reports

A helpful report called the credential report can be run from the IAM console, the CLI, or through the API and provides a wealth of data. The report can be run from the console by going to IAM, selecting Credential Report under Access Reports, and then clicking Download Report. The download is a CSV file showing all users. Reports are saved to your local device.

Fields include:

- If MFA is enabled
- Password next rotation
- If access key is active
- The last used data for these fields and more

Of course, the report does not expose any credentials.

IAM Best Practices

Because security is job zero, let's review best practices in IAM:

- Protect your root user account by not using it unless necessary; use an IAM Administrator account instead. Delete the root user access keys unless needed. Enable MFA on the root account.
- Use roles whenever possible rather than granting users permissions directly. Create roles for discrete tasks when possible, and assume the role when the task needs to be done.
- Use least privilege. Start with AWS managed policies, which will cover the most common scenarios. Use Access Analyzer over time to see how permissions are actually being used, and convert your managed policies to custom policies to remove unused or unnecessary permissions.
- Avoid inline policies. Use customer-managed policies instead. Since inline policies exist only in the user/group/role, they are harder to view and manage. Customer-managed policies are all visible in one place in the console.
- Configure password policies. Require strong passwords and password rotation.
- Enable MFA on all user accounts.
- Use roles rather than users for applications on EC2 instances.
- Guard your access keys. Never share your keys; use AWS Secrets Manager or Parameter Store, a capability of AWS Systems Manager. Rotate your keys regularly.
- Leverage attribute-based access control. Add depth to your security by using policy conditions.
- Monitor, monitor, monitor. Learn and make use of CloudTrail, CloudWatch, AWS Config, S3 Server Access Logging, CloudFront Access Logs, and other tools that show user and programmatic activity.

IAM Access Analyzer

IAM Access Analyzer takes a novel approach to intrusion detection and prevention. Rather than identify when someone is actually trying to access your resource, IAM Access Analyzer determines *if* someone can access your resource. IAM Access Analyzer helps administrators identify resources shared outside of their zone of trust, either as an organization or for an account. Using a technique called automated reasoning, Access Analyzer turns IAM policies into mathematical proofs to identify all possible implications of a given policy.

To use IAM Access Analyzer, you will need to create an analyzer. IAM Access Analyzers are region-specific, so you will need to create one for each region within an account that you have resources enabled in. The zone of trust is an important concept here and can be either the current account or the current organization. The zone defines the scope outside of which the analyzer is not concerned. Any resource request coming from within the zone of trust is assumed to be trusted.

Keep in mind that IAM (users, groups, policies, roles) are still global and not region-specific. Don't get confused on this point.

The zone of trust analyzed by IAM Access Analyzer can be your organization or your account. Set to your account, IAM Access Analyzer will identify access from outside your account coming into that region:

IAM Access Analyzer monitors the following resources:

- Amazon S3 buckets

- AWS IAM roles

- AWS Key Management Service (KMS) keys

- AWS Lambda functions and layers

- Amazon Simple Queue Service (SQS) queues

- AWS Secrets Manager secrets

You can also validate policies using policy checks in AWS Access Analyzer. These policy checks evaluate your policy for policy grammar and best practices. You can also generate policies using the AWS Access Analyzer to align your policies to real usage if you so choose.

The IAM Access Analyzer runs periodically. Creating or updating a policy will normally generate findings in about 30 minutes. Some situations, such as the S3 block public access settings, are not updated as frequently and can take six or more hours to update.

Amazon Simple Storage Service (S3)   For Amazon S3, IAM Access Analyzer is looking at the S3 policy, ACL, or access point associated with that bucket to see if it is granted access outside of your organization or account.

AWS IAM Roles   IAM Access Analyzer will look at your role's trust policies. A trust policy defines the principal(s) you trust to assume a role. Principals can be users, roles, accounts, or services.

AWS Key Management Service (KMS)   For KMS, IAM Access Analyzer will assess the key policies and key grants. Keep in mind that permission needs to be granted to allow IAM Access Analyzer in order for it to read the metadata of the key. If you encounter an Access Denied on a KMS key in the findings, check your key permissions. Three additional permissions are required: `kms: Describe Key`, `kms: GetKeyPolicy`, and `kms:List`.

AWS Lambda   IAM Access Analyzer will analyze the policies attached to a Lambda function or layer as well as the permissions associated with an AddPermission operation in EventSourceToken.

Amazon Simple Queue Service (SQS)   Amazon SQS access can be given to external accounts such as partners. This is the type of permissions IAM Access Analyzer will look for.

AWS Secrets Manager   IAM Access Analyzer will scan AWS Secrets Manager policies for any externally accessible secrets stored in AWS Secrets Manager.

The following figures show two findings. Figure 2.18 shows an S3 bucket that can be accessed by an IAM user from another account via a bucket policy. Figure 2.19 shows an IAM role that grants access to an account outside of the zone of trust.

FIGURE 2.18   Access Analyzer scan

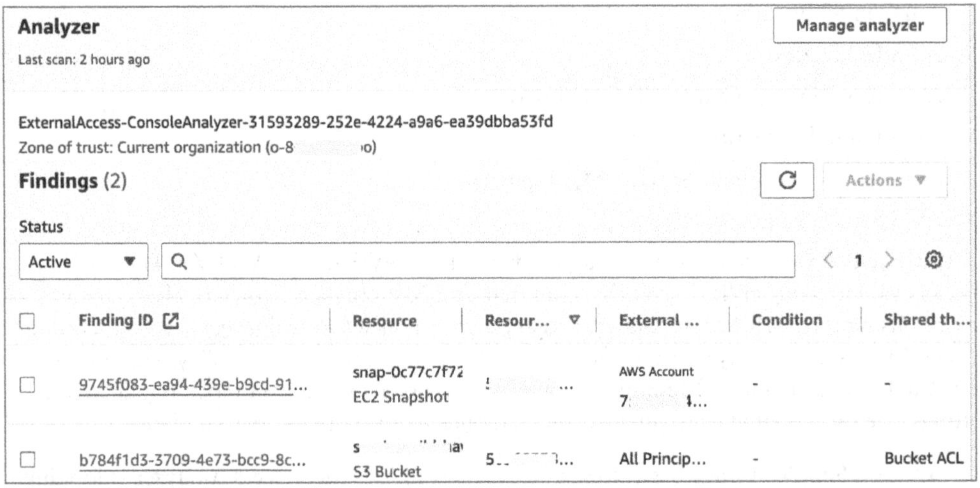

Clicking the second finding (Figure 2.19) reveals details such as the specific offending role, provides the ability to archive the finding if this was intended, and an option to fix the problem. Once you have either archived or fixed the finding, a rescan can be done to be sure the issue is resolved.

Setting Up Access Analyzer

Access Analyzer needs to be set up for each region in each account that you want to analyze. Creating an analyzer is done from within the IAM console. Expanding the Access Reports section reveals Analyzers. In this section, select Create Analyzer to open the window shown in Figure 2.20.

FIGURE 2.19   Access Analyzer finding

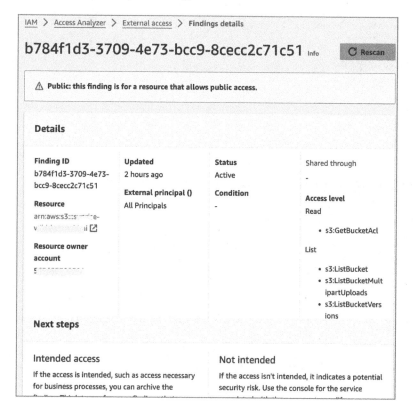

In figure 2.19 we see an example of a finding for an S3 bucket with public access. In the example an external principal has been given four permissions to an S3 bucket. The four permissions are the S3:GetBucketAcl, S3:ListBucket, S3:ListBucketMultiPartUploads, and S3:ListBucketVersions actions. Notice that we can rescan these findings to confirm remediation actions were successful. Next steps listed below give us clear guidance and include the necessary links.

Remember that permissions are for individual API calls. You can look up the API calls in the appropriate Developer API Reference.

IAM Policy Simulator

The IAM policy simulator is used to test identity-based and resource-based policies, including the implications of permissions boundaries and service control policies (SCPs) if the account is a member of an AWS Organization. Testing policies in the IAM policy simulator is safe because no API calls are actually made and no changes to the environment are made. The policy simulator allows the testing of policy conditions with the exception of global condition keys in AWS Organizations SCPs.

FIGURE 2.20   Access Analyzer Create Analyzer

IAM > Access Analyzer > Analyzers > Create analyzer

Create analyzer   Info
The analyzer scans the resources within the zone of trust.

Region

US East (N. Virginia)
You should enable Access Analyzer in each Region where you use AWS resources.

Name

ConsoleAnalyzer-e4cb5d2a-f146-422e-805f-de09c64280b1

Maximum 255 characters

Zone of trust   Info
Policies for all supported resources within your zone of trust are analyzed to identify access allowed from outside the zone of trust.

- ⦿ Current organization (o-
  25   f)

- ◯ Current account
  (63)

Tags   Info
Optionally, add tags to the analyzer. Tags are words or phrases that act as metadata for identifying and organizing your AWS resources. Each tag consists of a key and one optional value.

No tags associated with the resource.

Add tag
You can add up to 50 tags.

ⓘ When you create an analyzer, a trust relationship is created between AWS Organizations and IAM Access Analyzer. Additionally, a service-linked role is created in all accounts in the organization. The service-linked role grants permission to IAM Access Analyzer to interact with AWS resources on your behalf. Learn more ⬈

Cancel   **Create analyzer**

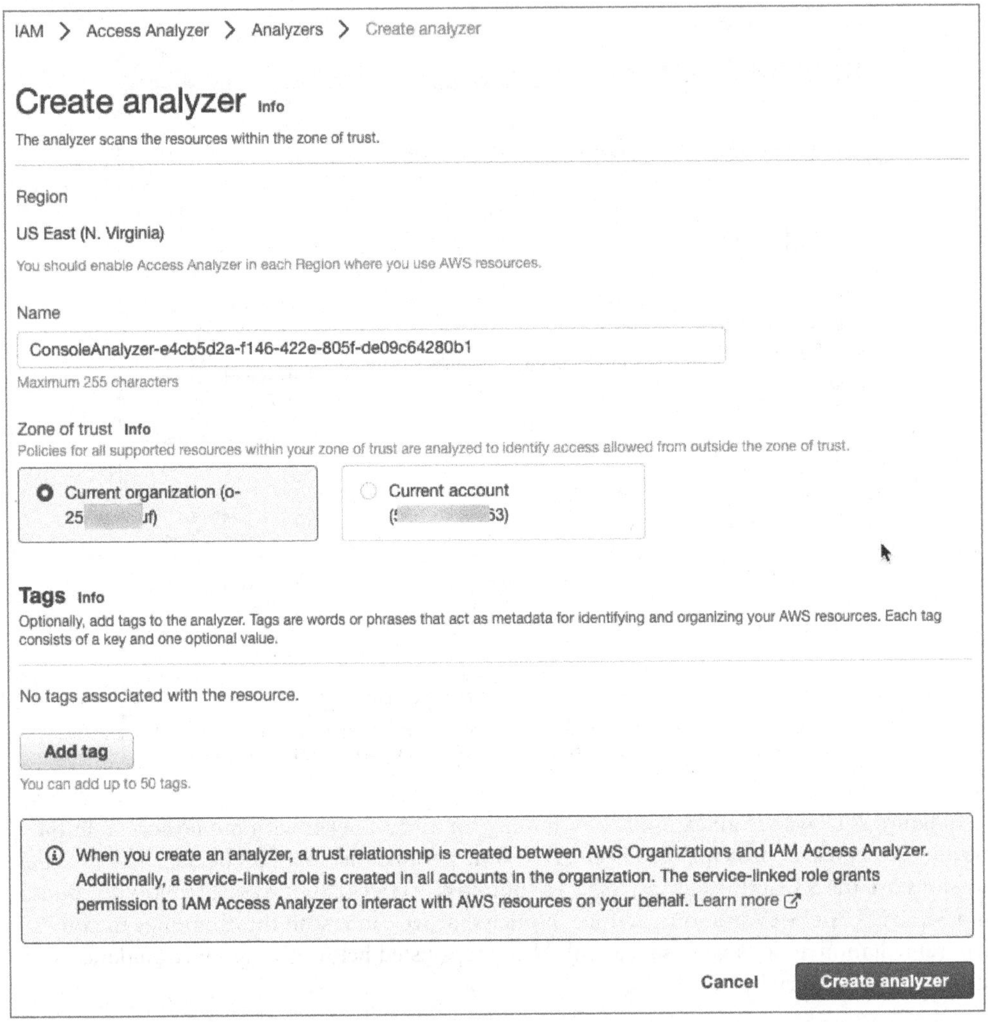

AWS Organizations and Control Tower

It will be helpful to learn AWS Organizations and AWS Control Tower together since Control Tower is dependent on Organizations and we will use many of the same constructs and tools. The aim of both services is to securely manage large sprawling organizations with many accounts and organizational levels or departments without crushing the agility that developers and other users need to be able to spin up services quickly and safely. To do this, AWS builds the organizational framework to which you can apply a variety of controls and automations to facilitate service deployment and account creation without sacrificing security. Figure 2.21 shows the basic AWS Control Tower architecture.

FIGURE 2.21   Basic AWS Control Tower architecture

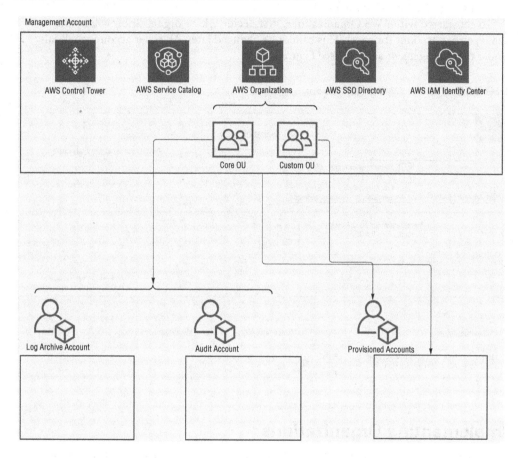

AWS Organizations

Let's start with AWS Organizations. AWS Organizations provides for the central management of accounts with a single bill payer, centralized policies, monitoring, and resource provisioning.

AWS Organizations enables the following:

- Automated account creation and management
- Automated resource provisioning
- Improved security by creating and enforcing structure
- Reduced management overhead
- Simplified auditing for compliance

- Centralized billing
- Simplified AWS service configuration across accounts

There is no cost for AWS Organizations. You only pay for the resources created in the accounts (e.g., EC2 or S3 storage).

To get started with AWS Organizations, first decide which organization will be the management account (or root). This cannot be changed later. All other accounts will fall under the management account (see Figure 2.22).

FIGURE 2.22   AWS Organizations

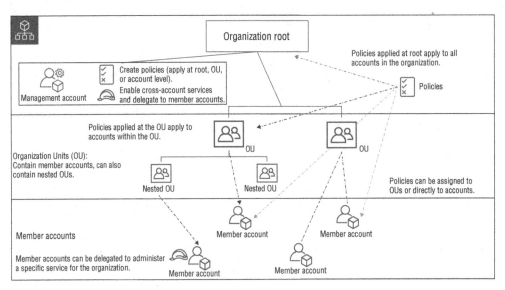

Implementing Organizations

The mechanics of setting up AWS Organizations is very simple. When you create the organization, you will need to be logged in as the administrator of the account, which will become the management account. One thing to note here is that there will be email verifications. Be sure to verify all of the email addresses that you will be using to create the organization and child accounts. A verification email will be sent out, and you will have only 24 hours to confirm. Verification emails can be re-sent, and you can change the email address if needed. Once the management account is established in Organizations, you can either create or invite accounts into the organization.

Now that you have an organization, you will want to organize it with organizational units (OUs). An OU is simply a logical container for accounts, and it can contain other OUs. A useful feature of the OU is that they can have SCPs attached. This allows you to attach an SCP to a group of related accounts very easily. Once an OU is created, accounts and other OUs can be moved into it. To move an account, simply select the account(s) to be moved and choose Move from the Actions menu (see Figure 2.23). Select the Destination OU and click Move AWS Accounts.

FIGURE 2.23   Organizations—Moving an account

Common AWS services can be granted trusted access through AWS Organizations. This allows services such as Amazon GuardDuty or Amazon Macie access to perform their respective tasks on accounts within the organization. This saves considerable time and complexity as accounts are added and removed from a dynamic organization and eliminates the need to manually set policies.

Service control policies can be attached through AWS Organizations. More on SCPs next.

Service Control Policies

A service control policy (SCP) is similar to a permissions boundary in that it defines the limits of permissions that *could* be granted. An SCP does not actually grant permissions itself. SCPs are used within AWS Organizations and are generally not attached to the root but only to accounts or OUs. Remember that SCPs do not apply to users or roles in the management account, only to member accounts in an organization.

To attach an SCP in AWS Organizations, navigate to Policies, select or create a policy, and choose Attach from the Actions menu. You will then have the option of attaching the policy to one or more accounts and/or OUs. Remember that attaching a policy to an OU means that the policy will also apply to all children.

SCPs follow almost the same syntax as identity or resource policies in IAM.

AWS Control Tower

AWS Control Tower solves a common problem in large, multi-account organizations. End users and developers need to create organizations with multiple AWS accounts, and multiple teams may benefit from AWS Control Tower, which provides governance and best-practice capabilities. Control Tower and AWS Organizations tend to go hand-in-hand, with Control Tower adding preventive and detective controls (called guardrails) to AWS Organizations. AWS Control Tower also provides centralized account creation using a feature called Account Factory, which allows end users to self-provision accounts following prescribed templates. A secure audit account is always created as part of AWS Control Tower to store logs.

There is no cost for using AWS Control Tower. However, there are costs associated with increased use of resources related to AWS Control Tower, such as AWS Config, CloudTrail, S3, Amazon CloudWatch, and AWS Service Catalog.

Control Tower has four key features:

- Landing zone
- Guardrails
- Account Factory
- Dashboard

A landing zone is a well-architected, multi-account environment. There can be only one landing zone in an organization. Be careful with naming here; AWS Landing Zone was a solution offered by the AWS Partner Network (APN) of professional services, which stood up a fully customized landing zone. Landing zones became wrapped into AWS Control Tower as a feature. Landing Zone now deploys a blueprint-based landing zone within AWS Control Tower. For the exam, the term *landing zone* will apply to the blueprints deployed by AWS Control Tower. Just be alert when reading any older documentation since the name can be a little confusing.

Guardrails will be discussed in more depth in the next section. For now, you can think of these as high-level rules for the organization.

Account Factory used to be called the Account Vending Machine (AVM). This is a template that allows authorized users in the account to provision accounts on a self-service basis. This is valuable in that it allows organizations speed and agility while maintaining strict compliance and governance.

The dashboard gives the administrators visibility and oversight into the accounts, guardrail enforcement, and any noncompliant services across the organization.

Guardrails

Guardrails (also known as controls) are an important feature of AWS Control Tower. Guardrails allow you to implement preventive and detective controls on a given OU and all OUs below. All guardrails have a behavior and a guidance. Let's dig in a bit here to understand how guardrails work and how to implement them.

But first, one more definition: Are guardrails the same as SCPs? SCPs are used to define permission limits (not to grant permissions) that have effects at the organizational or account level. They can be placed at the organization level to cascade down to all child accounts and OUs. SCPs use IAM policy language to describe the permissions and are a feature of AWS Organizations. SCPs are typically used to set the permission boundaries beyond which no one in the organization can reach rather than setting fine-grained permissions. The management account in AWS Organizations is not subject to SCPs.

All guardrails have a behavior and a guidance (see Figure 2.24). The behavior is either preventive or detective. Preventive guardrails are implemented as service control policies from AWS Organizations. Detective guardrails are implemented using AWS Config rules.

FIGURE 2.24 Guardrails

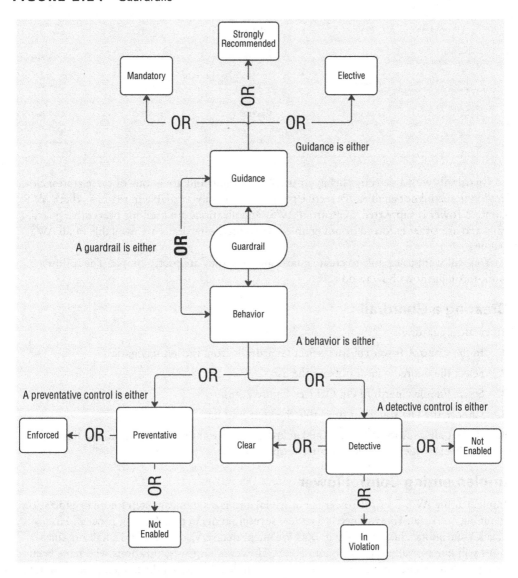

A guardrail's guidance determines the enforcement of the guardrail. Guidance is either mandatory, strongly recommended, or elective (see Figure 2.25).

FIGURE 2.25   Control Tower Guardrail list

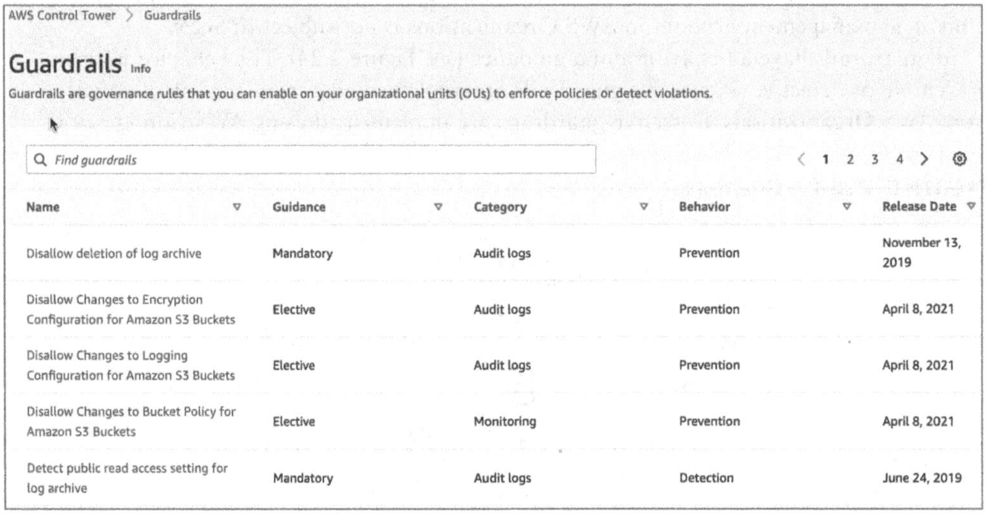

AWS Control Tower > Guardrails

Guardrails Info

Guardrails are governance rules that you can enable on your organizational units (OUs) to enforce policies or detect violations.

Name	Guidance	Category	Behavior	Release Date
Disallow deletion of log archive	Mandatory	Audit logs	Prevention	November 13, 2019
Disallow Changes to Encryption Configuration for Amazon S3 Buckets	Elective	Audit logs	Prevention	April 8, 2021
Disallow Changes to Logging Configuration for Amazon S3 Buckets	Elective	Audit logs	Prevention	April 8, 2021
Disallow Changes to Bucket Policy for Amazon S3 Buckets	Elective	Monitoring	Prevention	April 8, 2021
Detect public read access setting for log archive	Mandatory	Audit logs	Detection	June 24, 2019

Guardrails with a detective behavior use AWS Config and are in one of three states: clear, in violation, and not enabled. Detective guardrails are only available in regions where AWS Control Tower is supported. SCPs from AWS Organizations are used for preventive guardrails and are either enforced or not enabled. Preventive guardrails are available in all AWS regions.

You will want to be able to create guardrails, and they are pretty simple. The following walk-through shows how to do this.

Creating a Guardrail

To create a guardrail:

1. In the Control Tower console, select Guardrails from the left navigation.
2. Select the desired guardrail from the list.
3. Select Enable Guardrail On OU (see Figure 2.26).
4. Choose the OU you want to enable the guardrail on.
5. Repeat all steps for any additional guardrails you want to enable (up to the limit of StackSets, which is 5,000 concurrent operations).

Implementing Control Tower

Implementing AWS Control Tower is not trivial and is a significant step for an organization. Planning is crucial. You will need to review several points in the planning process. First, check your quotas, including the quotas for integrated services. New and small organizations will not typically run into quota issues. However, large organizations who have been using AWS for some time should review quotas in detail to avoid the launch process stalling.

Second, review single sign-on (SSO) and the three available options (AWS SSO User Store, Active Directory, and External Identity Provider). Third, if you have an established AWS account, check AWS Config and CloudTrail for trusted access; this must be disabled. Existing AWS Config recorders, delivery channels, and aggregations need to be modified or removed. Watch out for one-way doors, or things that cannot be changed later. These include the home region and VPC CIDRs. All of this is preliminary work ahead of the actual setup of AWS Control Tower.

FIGURE 2.26 Enable Guardrail On OU

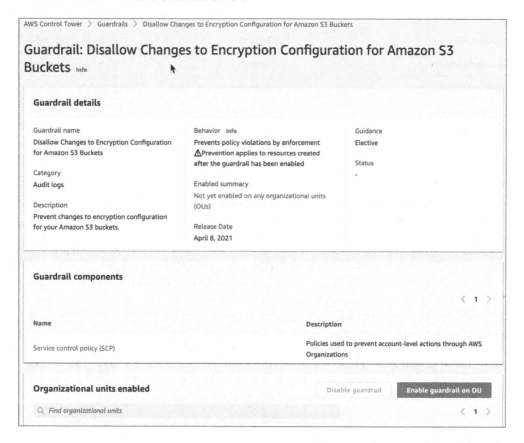

The setup of Control Tower will seem relatively simple, with four basic steps. However, the planning and preparation are nontrivial.

First, select your home region (which can't be changed later) and any additional regions. Regions can be selected as Denied or Not Governed, in which case resources cannot be created later in these regions. If the region Deny setting is enabled, any region that is not explicitly allowed is denied using a preventive guardrail. Otherwise, regions can be selected for Governance, in which case resources can be used from these regions.

Once Control Tower has been set up, regions will appear, as shown in Figure 2.27, in the Landing Zone settings of Control Tower.

FIGURE 2.27   Control Tower Governed regions

Asia Pacific (Singapore)	ap-southeast-1	⊘ Governed
Europe (Frankfurt)	eu-central-1	⊖ Not governed, Denied
Europe (London)	eu-west-2	⊘ Governed
Canada (Central)	ca-central-1	⊘ Governed
Europe (Stockholm)	eu-north-1	⊖ Not governed, Denied
Asia Pacific (Mumbai)	ap-south-1	⊖ Not governed, Denied
Asia Pacific (Tokyo)	ap-northeast-1	⊘ Governed
Asia Pacific (Seoul)	ap-northeast-2	⊖ Not governed, Denied
Europe (Paris)	eu-west-3	⊖ Not governed, Denied
South America (São Paulo)	sa-east-1	⊘ Governed

Next the option is given to rename the foundational OU. By default it is named Security, but you can change it here. An additional OU can be set up at this time as well, or you can opt out of creating it.

At the third step, the audit and audit log accounts are created. A different email account is necessary to create each account. Alternatively, preexisting accounts could be used.

The fourth and final step gives the option to enable (default) CloudTrail at the organization level. This is strongly recommended and is the default. The audit log retention period can be defined here and optional KMS encryption can be enabled. Control Tower does not support multiregion or asymmetric keys.

Control Tower can fail to launch for a variety of reasons. It is recommended that you review the troubleshooting guide as part of your exam preparation at `https://docs.aws .amazon.com/controltower/latest/userguide/troubleshooting.html`. The Control Tower landing zone can be decommissioned in the Landing Zone settings.

AWS Directory Service

AWS Directory Service comes in three flavors. Each has a different use case: AWS Active Directory Service for Microsoft Active Directory, AD Connector, and Simple AD. A fourth directory service, Cognito, is used for mobile and web users but is not covered in this chapter.

When trying to remember the three directory services, try thinking of Simple AD as the oddball. AD Connector and AWS Active Directory Service are both using Microsoft Active Directory and will have similar functionality and prerequisites. For example, both can handle single sign-on (SSO) and multifactor authentication (MFA). However, while Simple AD is Microsoft AD compatible, it is running Samba 4 and lacks advanced features like SSO and MFA.

There are several prerequisites shared by the three directory services. For test taking, it will be helpful to make note of the similarities. This will also help you remember the differences. Any time we have two or more similar services, it is reasonable to expect questions about which would be a best fit for a given customer scenario.

AWS Active Directory Service for Microsoft Active Directory

AWS Active Directory Service for Microsoft Active Directory (also known as AWS Managed Microsoft AD) is a fully managed Microsoft Active Directory (AD) on Windows Server 2012 R2. The Active Directory Service launches inside a virtual private cloud (VPC) as a pair of highly available (two availability zones within the region) domain controllers. More instances can be added manually after the initial build. Directory Services architecture is shown in Figure 2.28.

FIGURE 2.28   Directory Services architecture

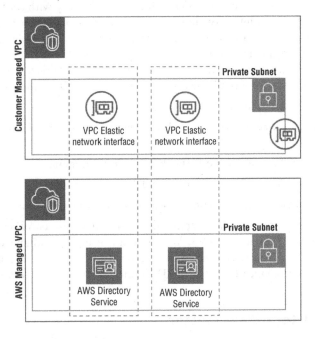

As a managed service, the domain controllers are monitored and automatically replaced in the event of a failure. Daily snapshots are included as well as automatic patching and updates. In other words, as a managed service, administrative tasks are reduced. The AWS Active Directory Service can be managed through the console, the CLI, or through the AWS SDK.

Because AWS Active Directory Service is a managed service, the user has no access to the instances it runs on. This means that you cannot configure memory, CPU, storage, and so forth and you cannot directly access them through SSH or Windows Remote Desktop Connections.

AWS Directory Service for Microsoft Active Directory comes in two editions: standard and enterprise. Standard edition is suited for organizations with up to 5,000 employees and can store 30,000 directory objects (1 GB). The enterprise version will handle up to 500,000 directory objects (17 GB). It would be good to know these two editions.

Pricing

No additional Client Access Licenses (CALs) are required for AWS Managed Microsoft AD since the CALs are included in the service pricing. AWS Directory Service for Microsoft Active Directory is billed at an hourly rate, with additional fees for sharing across accounts and for data transferred across regions.

AD Connector

If you need to connect an on-premises Microsoft Active Directory with AWS services, then AD Connector will be the solution of choice. Active Directory management does not change. When a new user is added to an AWS service such as WorkDocs, AD Connector provides AWS with a list of users and groups to link.

AD Connector creates a trust relationship between an Active Directory (AD) and specific AWS services. AD Connector has a limited set of capabilities. AD Connector can be used to:

- Allow federated sign-in to the AWS Console

- Allow federated user access to Amazon Workspaces, Amazon WorkMail, and Amazon WorkDocs

- Join Windows EC2 instances and S3 buckets to an AD domain

- Integrate with a RADIUS server to enable MFA

- Enforce IAM security policies against resources joined to AD Connector

AD Connector does not store the directory data—it only connects AWS to the authoritative AD store. No data is cached in AWS. AD Connector is highly available deployed across two availability zones. The service is managed and resilient, so updates are automatic and failed instances are automatically replaced. AD Connector does not integrate with RDS SQL Server.

Getting Ready for AD Connector

There are many prerequisites for AD Connector. Detailed prerequisites may not be the best place to spend lots of memorization time for this exam. That said, prerequisites can be a common failure point when setting up a service, so they are something to be familiar with, at least at a high level. Here are some high-level AD Connector prerequisites:

- At least two subnets in different availability zones.
- A VPN or Direct Connect connection to your on-premises network.
- Hardware tenancy for the VPC must be Default rather than Dedicated.
- Check for CIDR range conflicts.
- Check existing VPC endpoints.
- Existing Active Directory domain must be Windows Server 2003 or above.
- Check your service account permissions.
- Check the user permissions for all AD users.
- Note the IP addresses of the primary and secondary domain controllers.
- Open the correct ports on the subnet: TCP/UDP 53, 88, and 389. (It's just a good idea generally to be familiar with the common well-known ports.)
- Kerberos preauthentication is enabled for all user accounts.
- If SSO is going to be used, there are additional requirements.
- If MFA is going to be enabled, there are additional requirements such as an existing RADIUS server.
- Delegate privileges to the service account.
- Know the basic steps for testing the AD Connector and know about the DirectoryServicePortTest test application.

For the complete prerequisites, visit `https://docs.amazonaws.cn/en_us/directoryservice/latest/admin-guide/prereq_connector.html`.

Costs and Sizing

AD Connector pricing is based on the directory size: small or large. The size of the AD Connector is selected when creating the service and cannot be changed.

Simple AD

Unlike AD Connector, Simple AD is a directory store rather than just a connector. Simple AD is a fully managed service built on a Samba 4 Active Directory–compatible server and is best used for cases that have a limited number of users (under 5,000) and where the complexities and features of Microsoft AD are not needed. If Microsoft AD features are required or RDS SQL Server will be used, then Simple AD is not a viable solution. Simple AD is highly available, with two domain controllers placed in separate availability zones within the VPC. Data is encrypted at rest on EBS volumes, and failed domain controller instances are automatically replaced.

AWS License Manager

As shown in Figure 2.29, licenses are of two basic types: AWS-provided licenses and Bring Your Own Licenses (BYOLs). AWS-provided licenses are those that come bundled with EC2 or RDS Amazon Machine Images (AMIs). If your organization already has licenses—for example, from an on-premises datacenter—those can often be brought into AWS and attached to your EC2 or RDS instances. The nuances of licensing are beyond the scope of the exam. You will need to simply understand the basic difference between AWS-provided and BYOL licenses.

FIGURE 2.29   AWS licensing

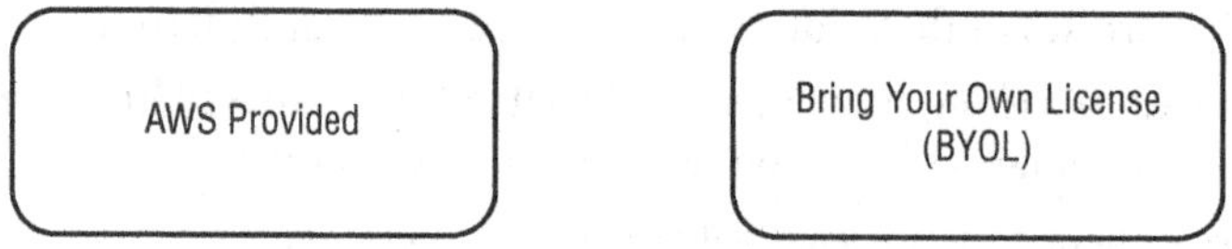

AWS Provided

Bring Your Own License (BYOL)

One of the major challenges of managing an IT system of any size is staying compliant with licensing. Licensing structures vary from vendor to vendor and package to package. You may even have different licensing for on-premises versus cloud for the same package by the same vendor. Violations can be costly and audits can be time-consuming. AWS License Manager is a rules engine that helps track and manage licensing. License Manager safeguards the organization by sending alerts when limits are exceeded and stopping new instances from starting if those instances would exceed the limit. By associating specific AMIs with a license configuration, you can block the launch of AMIs for which you do not have licenses. Figure 2.30 illustrates the actions available, including associating an AMI. Association can be done manually by selecting a specific instance from inventory or by associating the license with an AMI.

FIGURE 2.30   License Manager customer-managed licenses

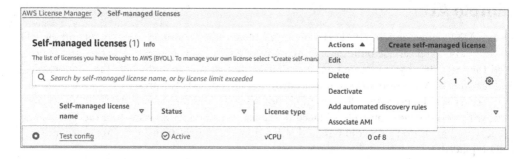

The scope for AWS License Manager can be organizationwide if AWS Organizations is used. Discovery of licensing is automated so that the system knows that if an instance is started, a license is consumed, whereas a terminated instance represents a license that has now become available to use elsewhere. AWS License Manager supports both AWS-provided licenses and BYOLs and allows for switching between the two for a given individual workload. License Manager is a free service—you only pay for the licenses consumed.

Implementing License Manager

The first time you run AWS License Manager, you'll need to grant the necessary IAM permissions (see Figure 2.31).

FIGURE 2.31   License Manager IAM permissions one-time setup

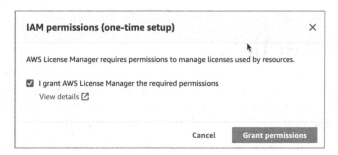

License Configurations

License Configurations are rules reflecting the terms of your software license. These configurations can be applied to AMIs, EC2 Launch Templates, CloudFormation Templates, the Service Catalog, and AWS Marketplace. Each configuration consists of a number of parameters such as name, description, and license count as well as rule parameters like min/max cores, tenancy, and license affinity to host. These parameters combine to describe the license terms.

License Conversion

A common task in License Manager is license conversion. For example, you may have migrated to the cloud bringing your existing licenses (BYOLs). Now those licenses are expiring, and you have decided to use AWS-provided licenses going forward for simplicity. License Manager uses the SSM agent inventory to display instances that can be converted. If instances don't appear in the list, a number of things can be wrong:

- The SSM agent may not be installed or communicating.
- The instance may be running.
- The instance may not have a profile with the AmazonSSMManagedInstanceCore policy.

The current usage operation is said to be the *origin*. The license type you wish to convert to is the *destination*.

Summary

Security is job zero. AWS has an ever-growing tool set for managing accounts and access. This chapter could never begin to dive deep into identity and access management. The most important theory in this chapter is the shared responsibility model. Be thinking about how this applies in everything you do in AWS. The second thing you've learned in this chapter are the services and features, especially IAM. For the exam, you will need to know these and how they are used. Finally, it is important to be able to perform common tasks associated with each of these services and features.

Exam Essentials

Know the shared responsibility model.   The shared responsibility model is fundamental to everything in AWS security. Understand how the line of responsibility shifts as you move from unmanaged services like EC2 to managed services such as RDS or S3.

Recognize that everything is an API.   This fact drives IAM policies but also helps explain the role of services like AWS Organizations and AWS Control Tower and their ability to provide guardrails and service control policies based on API actions.

Remember authentication vs. authorization.   Recall which services serve which function.

Know Directory Services use cases.   There are three directory services and each has a different use case. You will be expected to be able to select the best service for a customer's use case.

Know IAM policies well.   Because everything is an API and policies define authorization based on APIs, you will find policies everywhere. Recognize the different types of policies and where they are used.

Understand the common tasks in IAM.   Be prepared to do common tasks in IAM, such as enabling and managing multifactor authentication, setting the password policy, and running a credential report. This list is not exhaustive, but just a reminder not to forget to review the simple and common tasks of a systems administrator.

Review Questions

1. You have been asked by your manager to gather the AWS reports for an upcoming SOC 3 audit. Which tool would you open to find the report?

    A. AWS Audit Manager

    B. Amazon Reports

    C. AWS License Manager

    D. AWS Artifact

2. You are setting up a directory service for your small but growing company. There are currently about 5,000 objects, but the plan is to double the number of employees over the next three years. You have been directed to use Microsoft Active Directory and the company is cloud native. Which option would be the most cost-effective and lowest management overhead solution for your organization at this time?

    A. AWS Directory Services for Microsoft Active Directory Standard Edition

    B. Microsoft Active Directory on EC2 deployed in two availability zones (AZs)

    C. AWS Directory Services for Microsoft Active Directory Enterprise Edition

    D. AWS Simple AD

3. What are the two types of behavior guardrails on AWS Control Tower?

    A. Preventive and detective

    B. Preventive and audit

    C. Infrastructure and code

    D. Enabled and Disabled

4. A service control policy (SCP) was created in your organization that will allow all users of the Admin role permission to schedule KMS key deletion (`"Action": "kms:*"`). However, when administrators attempt to actually schedule key deletion, they report error messages. Why might this error be occurring?

    A. Users must have the explicit permission `"Action": "kms:ScheduleKeyDeletion"` in order to schedule key deletion.

    B. KMS keys cannot be deleted but only disabled.

    C. Administrators must approve the email sent to their primary email address as a second-factor authentication when attempting to delete KMS keys.

    D. Service control policies do not grant permissions, so allowing an action in an SCP has no effect.

5. Inline IAM policies are best used when:

    A. Inline policies are not recommended.

    B. Customer-managed policies must be kept secure.

    C. An appropriate AWS-managed policy does not exist.

    D. Resource-based policies must be tightly integrated with identity-based policies.

6. What are the three required elements of an identity-based IAM policy? (Choose three.)

   A. Action

   B. Effect

   C. Principal

   D. Resource

7. Which of the following is a way in which AWS License Manager can track Bring Your Own Licenses (BYOLs) consumed by launched instances?

   A. By using a Lambda function to compare the AMI of each instance to an AWS Launch Manager license configuration.

   B. By associating a license configuration with an AMI.

   C. By creating a rule in AWS Config that matches a license configuration in AWS License Manager.

   D. The AWS Systems Manager Agent (SSM) automatically reports license usage to AWS Systems Manager. License Manager integrates with AWS Systems Manager to collect license usage data.

8. Your client with over 50,000 directory objects has an on-premises Active Directory domain running Windows Server 2016. They need to have users access Amazon WorkDocs and Amazon WorkMail using single sign-on. No directory data should be cached in the cloud, but the directory service must be highly available. Which solution best solves the customer's requirements?

   A. Active Directory Connector

   B. Amazon Managed Microsoft AD

   C. AWS Cognito

   D. Simple Active Directory

9. When creating an AWS Organizations member account in your own organization. you notice that you do not have permissions for some actions. The error states that "AWS Account Management trusted access is not enabled. Enable it to view this content." Which of the following will grant the required permissions?

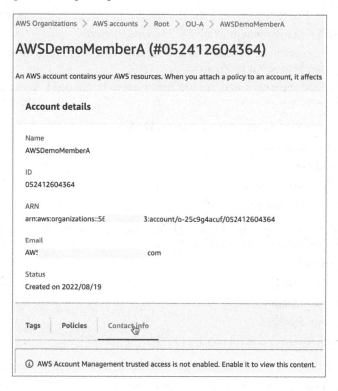

A. In AWS Organizations, navigate to the Policies page and create an SCP that grants administrators of the member account full account management permissions (`ALLOW = admin:*`).

B. Navigate to AWS Organizations Services and enable trusted access on AWS Account Management.

C. Navigate to IAM and add the email address used to create the member account to the Admin role.

D. The account was created using an email address rather than a role. Only root accounts can be created with an email address. The member account must be deleted and re-created using an admin role of the parent organizational unit (OU).

10. Your customer wants to manage licenses across multiple accounts in order to better manage compliance. However, they have not been able to manage license usage in any accounts except the one that License Manager was set up in. What would solve this customer's problem?

    A. AWS License Manager is account-specific and must be set up separately in each account.

    B. Enable AWS Organizations and link AWS License Manager.

    C. From each account to be managed, assign the service-linked roles to the main account where License Manager is configured.

    D. Install the SSM agent on instances in each account to be managed. Assign the SSM agents the service-linked roles in the account where AWS License Manager is configured.

11. By default, Control Tower creates two accounts. These are:

    A. Audit and Log Archive

    B. Security and Log

    C. Management and Sandbox

    D. Security and Management

12. Which two of the following policy types might be attached to an S3 bucket to grant permissions to a specified principal? (Choose two.)

    A. Access control lists (ACLs)

    B. Identity-based policies

    C. Permission boundaries

    D. Resource-based policies

    E. Organizations service control policies (SCPs)

13. Which of the following are characteristics of permission boundaries? (Choose two.)

    A. Permission boundaries apply only to users and roles.

    B. Permission boundaries define permission limits but do not grant permissions.

    C. Permission boundaries grant permissions.

    D. Permission boundary policy statements contain only DENY effects.

14. Which of the following are supported forms of multifactor authentication in AWS IAM? (Choose three.)

    A. Google Authenticator

    B. Hardware MFA device

    C. SMS

    D. U2F security key

15. The Control Tower provides a feature that allows account provisioning following preapproved templates. What is this feature called?

    A. Account Factory

    B. Account Vending Machine

    C. AWS Config

    D. CloudFormation

16. AWS Managed Microsoft AD directories are deployed in what architecture?

   A. In the customer VPC and in the customer's datacenter with a DirectConnect between in an active-active configuration

   B. In two availability zones in a region and connected to the customer VPC

   C. In two availability zones within the customer VPC

   D. In two regions in an active-active configuration and connected to the customer VPC using PrivateLink

17. To add an existing account to AWS Organization, the administrator must do which of the following?

   A. Add the account to AWS Organizations using the account ID, access key, and secret access key.

   B. Invite the account owner to join using the account owner's email address.

   C. Existing accounts cannot be added but can only be created using Account Factory.

   D. Log into the account as root user and accept the invitation.

18. The best explanation of when an `IMPLICIT DENY` occurs is:

   A. A resource-based policy and identity-based policy conflict.

   B. A user attempts to access restricted resources as described in a service control policy (SCP).

   C. IAM attempts to parse a policy but encounters a 500 error.

   D. When no deny statement or allow statement exists.

19. The principal of trust between two unrelated networks is known as:

   A. Distributed computing

   B. Federation

   C. Hybrid computing

   D. Interoperability

20. Which of the following are valid AWS IAM policy types? (Choose three.)

   A. Access control lists

   B. Identity-based policies

   C. Permission boundaries

   D. Service-based policies

   E. System access policies

Chapter

3

AWS Cost Management

THE AWS CERTIFIED SYSOPS ADMINISTRATOR EXAM OBJECTIVES COVERED IN THIS CHAPTER INCLUDE:

✓ **Domain 6: Cost and Performance Optimization**

  ▪ 6.1 Implement cost optimization strategies

AWS cost management is one of the most important skills any cloud operations professional, systems administrator, or cloud engineer can learn. Managing cost has always played an important role in traditional datacenter operations, but the cloud offers even more opportunities and tools to manage cost. The best way to learn how to effectively manage cost is to understand how to monitor, report, and analyze spend within AWS accounts.

This chapter will introduce you to powerful cost management tools used to inspect and optimize spending across AWS services. You will learn about identifying underutilized or unused resources using AWS cost management tools. You'll explore how to configure budgets and billing alarms to build proactive cost optimization strategies.

You will also learn about how—and why—to assess AWS resource usage patterns and implement cost allocation tags to provide improved reporting capabilities. Finally, you will learn how to further improve your cost optimization strategy by identifying opportunities to use managed services, like Amazon RDS, to reduce spend and operational overhead in areas where you should be focusing on developing your product, not worrying about the infrastructure.

AWS Cost and Usage Reports

One of the most daunting tasks a SysOps administrator faces is the collection of cost and usage data. This was true in the days of on-premises datacenters and co-location, and even today with the cloud. However, it does not have to be a daunting exercise of fumbling through logs, reports, and various spreadsheets. In fact, it becomes a very manageable, and some may say enjoyable, experience when you use cloud-native tools like AWS Cost and Usage Reports or AWS Data Exports.

AWS Cost and Usage Reports (AWS CUR) and Data Exports offer a comprehensive dataset of cost and usage data across an AWS account. AWS Data Exports enables creation of billing and cost management data exports using basic SQL, supporting visualization through Amazon QuickSight and have the same information as AWS CUR. These reports allow an administrator to break down costs by the hour, day, month, or even by a product or resource category. More importantly, you can further break down and explore costs using cost allocation tags that you can define yourself. AWS Cost and Usage Reports must be delivered to an Amazon S3 bucket, which occurs up to three times daily. While there is no charge for using the Data Exports or AWS Cost and Usage Reports service, you will incur standard Amazon S3 rates for the reports stored in the Amazon S3 bucket. All AWS Cost and Usage Reports are formatted as comma-separated value (CSV) documents that you can view using spreadsheet software, like Microsoft Excel, or with a custom application using the Amazon S3 API.

 Remember, a tag is any label that you or AWS assigns to an AWS resource. Tags consist of a *key* and a *value*. Tag keys must be unique and have only one value. Cost allocation tags are specifically used to track your AWS costs on a detailed level, such as by department, project, or cost center.

You may be thinking, "Wow! AWS CUR is amazing, but what does it actually do for me as an AWS account owner?" The answer is simple; it provides data, and data is the key to unlocking cost management excellence. AWS Data Exports and AWS Cost and Usage Reports track any AWS usage within your account and then estimates those charges. The reports generated by AWS CUR or AWS Data Exports contain line items for each unique combination of AWS products and can be aggregated by the hour, day, or month. This allows administrators like yourself to dive deep on which AWS products or features are actively being used within an account. This provides an opportunity to evaluate spend on a particular project or architecture and determine potential cost optimization changes to drive down cost.

Importance of AWS Cost Allocation Tags

Cost allocation tags enable organization of resources on the cost allocation report to make it easier for an administrator or organization to categorize or track AWS costs. There are two distinct types of cost allocation tags: AWS-generated tags and user-defined tags. AWS-generated tags are automatically defined, created, and applied, whereas user-defined tags must be manually defined based on the organization's needs and then applied to the AWS Cost Explorer or cost allocation report. You must activate both types of tags separately before they can appear in each report.

Tags can represent business categories to assist in categorizing or organizing cost reports across multiple services. It is important to remember that tags should not include sensitive information, such as personally identifiable information (PII) or data that you would not share publicly, but instead should represent categories that are meaningful to project or business functions. For example, tags can apply across cost centers, project names, or even application names. You can then use these tags to track specific costs for a project through AWS Cost Explorer or the cost allocation reports. The cost allocation report includes all the AWS costs for each billing period and includes both tagged and untagged resources. User-defined tags can take up to 24 hours to appear in the AWS Billing and Cost Management console.

In Exercise 3.1, you learn how to implement user-defined AWS cost allocation tags for use within the Billing and Cost Management console using the AWS Tag Editor. Remember, cost allocation tags appear on the console after you have enabled Cost Explorer, Budgets, or AWS Cost and Usage Reports.

EXERCISE 3.1

Implementing AWS Cost Allocation Tags

1. Sign into the AWS Management Console and navigate to the Management & Governance service section. Choose Resource Groups & Tag Editor, then select Tag Editor in the navigation pane.

2. You need to locate the AWS resource types that you want to tag. In this exercise you will choose Amazon EC2 resources. The Tag Editor by default selects the current region. If you need to find resources outside of your current region, select that region now.

3. In the Resource type drop-down list, choose the AWS::EC2::Instance resource type. Leave the Tags box empty to find all resources of the type selected. Select Search Resources to begin the query.

4. In the Resource Search results area, you will see the results of your query. It is likely that you may see a significant number of resources available if your AWS account is widely used or has been used for production purposes.

5. The Tag Editor will now show any existing tags on the queried resources. If you want to edit any existing tags, you can do so by selecting the box next to the resource or resources you want to edit, and then clicking Manage Tags Of Selected Resources. For example, select all the EC2 instances that are part of a single project.

6. You can edit any existing tags or add a new tag to the collection of resources you have selected. Click Add Tag to add a user-defined tag for your cost center. Under Tag Key, enter **Cost Center** and under Tag value, enter **5858**. When you are done adding any additional tag categories, click Review and apply tag changes. Review the changes and then click Apply Changes To All Selected.

7. Now that the tags have been added to the resources, it is time to activate these tags for use as cost allocation tags. Navigate back to the AWS Management Console GUI and open the AWS Billing Dashboard by using the drop-down menu in the top-right corner of the GUI. In the navigation pane, select Cost Allocation Tags. Select your new Cost Center tag and then click Activate.

8. The Cost Allocation tags are active for use in the AWS Cost Explorer, AWS Billing, and AWS Budget services. Note that it can take up to 24 hours for the tags to appear in the Cost Allocation Tags page, and another 24 hours for the tags to be activated. That's it! Congratulations on applying Cost Allocation tags to your AWS resources.

How Cost and Usage Reports Work

Cost and Usage Reports, up to 10 per account, or AWS Data Exports up to five per account, are placed in an Amazon S3 bucket for review. Each update across any month is cumulative. This means that each time the report is updated, it includes all the cost and usage data for the month to date. Any report data provided throughout the month is just an estimate of your AWS services being used, which means these estimates can change based on how you continue to use the services. Once AWS issues the monthly invoice for all your usage charges, AWS also finalizes the AWS Cost and Usage Report. It is important to remember that the report may change if your AWS account has any pending refunds or credits, or the account support fees change based on your usage for that month. You can tell if your AWS Cost and Usage Report is finalized by looking for the *Bill/InvoiceID* column in your CSV file. If that column is present, the bill has been finalized and will not change.

If at any time you want to analyze or download your AWS Cost and Usage Reports, you can open the Amazon S3 Console and download the CSV file from your Amazon S3 bucket. You can also query the reports using Amazon Athena directly from the Amazon S3 bucket or upload the reports into Amazon Redshift or Amazon QuickSight for further analysis.

How to Create a Cost and Usage Report

Now you know what an AWS CUR does, how different AWS services can integrate with the reports for analytics, and how to check if the data within the Amazon S3 bucket for the CUR is final. In Exercise 3.2 you move on to setting up the AWS Cost and Usage Report with some hands-on practice. We suggest you explore the configuration process for AWS Cost and Usage Reports by following Exercise 3.2.

EXERCISE 3.2

Setting Up a Cost and Usage Report

1. From the AWS Management Console GUI, open the AWS Billing Dashboard by using the drop-down navigation menu at the top right of the screen. Select Cost & Usage Reports from the navigation options on the left, click Create Report, enter a report name, skip adding additional report details, select your preferred option for the Data Refresh settings, and click Next.

2. Configure the S3 bucket by clicking Configure, then either select an existing S3 bucket owned by the same account for which you are configuring the CUR or enter a new bucket name and region to create a new bucket. Click Next.

3. Review the S3 bucket policy and confirm that the policy is correct. Click Save.

4. Enter a Report Path prefix, like the department the AWS account belongs to or the type of account, such as development, production, or staging. Select the Time Granularity, which sets the aggregated time interval for the CUR.

5. Specify if you want to enable Report versioning, which is where you can determine if you want to overwrite the previous reports. Under Enable Report Data Integration, select the integration type you wish to use, if any; click Next; and then click Review And Complete.

6. Now you can explore the Cost and Usage Reports as they start generating in your account. Note that it can take up to 24 hours for AWS to start delivering reports to your S3 bucket. Once the Cost and Usage Reports are delivered to your S3 bucket, you will begin incurring standard Amazon S3 storage charges.

AWS Cost and Usage Reports with AWS Organizations

If you or your organization have multiple AWS accounts, it is likely that AWS Organizations is providing consolidated billing to simplify the billing structure. If this is the case, it is important to know the Amazon S3 bucket that is designated for the AWS Cost and Usage Reports is owned by the account setting up the reports. This means any member or management account within the organization can set up a CUR or AWS Data Exports. If a member account creates a CUR or Data Exports while a member of an AWS Organization, it will only have reporting data for the time it has been a member of that organization. If the account is removed from the organization and joins a new organization, the CUR or AWS Data Exports will only show data from the time it has been a member of the new organization.

What if you don't want your member accounts within your organization to create AWS Cost and Usage Reports or AWS Data Exports? The answer is simple; you can apply a service control policy (SCP) to restrict IAM users within member accounts from setting up a CUR or AWS Data Exports. Keep in mind that SCPs are not retroactive. You may need to manually disable any CUR configuration in a member account that was set up before the application of the SCP.

Accessing AWS Cost and Usage Reports in Amazon S3

Great, you configured AWS Cost and Usage Reports or AWS Data Exports within your AWS account, and you created and configured the Amazon S3 bucket for the reports to be stored, but how do you access and use the reports stored in your S3 bucket? What happens when the chief financial officer (CFO) mandates that you keep all previous AWS Cost and Usage Reports and AWS Data Exports? What if you want to reduce Amazon S3 costs and overwrite the CUR or AWS Data Exports every time it is generated? Let's explore AWS Cost and Usage Reports access and integration a bit further.

AWS Cost and Usage Reports details are accessed from the Cost & Usage Reports page in the Billing and Cost Management console as seen in Figure 3.1, where you'll find a list of your Cost and Usage Reports listed on the page. You can also access the reports by directly accessing the Amazon S3 bucket using the Amazon S3 console. Whichever method you choose is fine—the decision is up to you.

FIGURE 3.1   The AWS Management Console Cost & Usage Reports dashboard

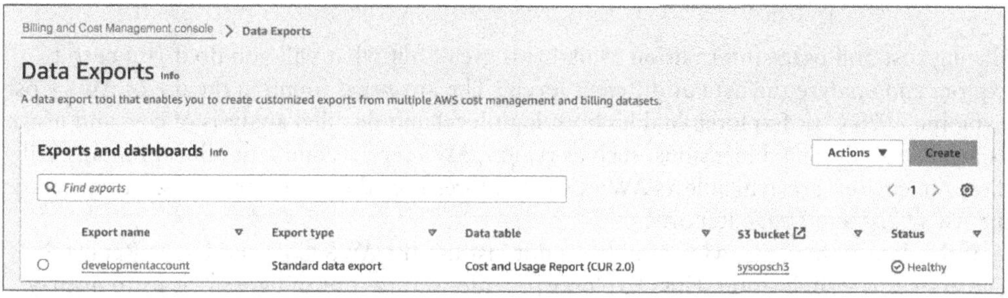

One benefit of the Cost and Usage Reports or AWS Data Exports is ease of use as all reports are stored in a CSV file or a collection of CSV files. As these files can grow quite large, particularly if your organization is a heavy user of a wide variety of AWS services, AWS will split these large reports into multiple files. This multipart CSV file is still stored in the Amazon S3 bucket used by the Cost and Usage Reports, but the naming convention of the AWS CUR files will depend on which parameters you set when you created the reports. AWS will deliver all reports within a specific report date range to the same report prefix.

For example, the naming convention for AWS CUR when a previous version of the report is present will follow this format:

```
<report-prefix>/<report-name>/yyyymmdd-yyyymmdd/<assemblyId>/
<report-name>--<file-number>.csv.<zip|gz>
```

where *assemblyId* is the ID AWS creates when a report is updated, and *file-number* is the indicator used if AWS splits the report into multiple files. The use of .zip or .gz indicates that the reports are compressed. When reports are being overwritten, or you chose to use the Athena specification, the only change to the naming convention is the omission of *assemblyId*. This value is no longer required as new reports are generated.

AWS also creates manifest files, which are used by Amazon Athena, Amazon Redshift, and Amazon QuickSight each time AWS updates the Cost and Usage Reports. The manifest files follow the same naming convention as the AWS CUR and include all the detail columns, a list of report files if multiple files are present due to a split, and the time period covered by the report. The manifest files will also be accompanied by additional files to help set up all the resources you need if you selected Amazon Athena specification, such as an AWS Cloud-Formation template and a SQL file with the code necessary to create the Amazon Athena table manually. If you selected the Amazon Redshift option, the manifest collection also has a SQL file that provides the SQL commands needed to upload your report into Amazon Redshift. Note that if you remove the manifest file, it will break the commands used by Redshift in the provided SQL file. It is best to ensure that the manifest and any supplemental files remain together.

AWS Cost Explorer

Having cost and usage information available is great, but what will you do if you need to explore and analyze the data at different levels? The answer is found in the use of AWS Cost Explorer. AWS Cost Explorer enables both high-level and detailed analysis of cost and usage using several filtering dimensions, such as region, AWS service, and cost allocation tags. All these dimensions are available as AWS Cost Explorer uses the same dataset used to generate the AWS Cost and Usage Reports.

If the data is the same, why would you not just use the AWS Cost and Usage Reports? The answer is visualization! Cost Explorer provides several preconfigured views to display information about your cost and usage trends. For example, you can use Cost Explorer to view a quick visualization of the top five cost-accruing AWS services or an analysis of the overall Amazon EC2 usage within a specific account. Cost Explorer is also extremely helpful in visualization of the Reserved Instance Utilization auditing, planning, and evaluating current reservations. Cost Explorer prepares data for the current month and the last 12 months, and even allows forecasting for the next 12 months. Current month data is available after about 24 hours and is refreshed at least once every 24 hours thereafter. However, you must be patient if you intend to view historical data right away as it will take a few days for Cost Explorer to pull in the remaining usage data for analysis.

You are not stuck in using only the predefined and available reports within Cost Explorer. In fact, you can create up to 50 custom reports to suit the needs of your CFO who consistently asks that you provide a very specific utilization report every month. You can view and build reports using data for up to the last 12 months using the Cost Explorer user interface with no cost. However, if you want to programmatically access your data using the Cost Explorer API, you will incur a charge of $0.01 for each paginated API request.

Enabling and Exploring AWS Cost Explorer Data

To use AWS Cost Explorer data to analyze your Reserved Instance utilization and historical Amazon EC2 usage over the last three months, or to forecast what spend may look like on that super-secret project the CFO asked for, you must first enable AWS Cost Explorer. The process is straightforward and handled using the Billing and Cost Management console. While the process is straightforward, the account status within an organization can affect what cost and usage data is available, and a management account can block access to member accounts within Cost Explorer. Keep in mind that your account is a standalone account, and it joins an AWS Organization; you will no longer have access to cost and usage data prior to joining the organization. Similarly, if the same account leaves the AWS Organization, it will no longer have access to the cost and usage data from the time it was a member in that organization. Don't worry, though; if that standalone account rejoins the same AWS Organization, it will regain access to the historical cost and usage data from the time spent in the organization prior to leaving.

Starting AWS Cost Explorer is easy. Just sign into the AWS Management Console and search for AWS Cost Explorer in the services list. From there, click Cost Explorer and then click Launch Cost Explorer. Once Cost Explorer launches, you will see the Cost dashboard, which shows several predefined reports for you to evaluate.

Controlling Access to Cost Explorer

Just as with any AWS service or feature, it is important to control access to AWS Cost Explorer so that only authorized and required individuals have access to the cost reports. While this information may not be considered sensitive or off-limits in your organization, it is a general best practice to follow the least privilege security model when configuring Cost Explorer. The good news is, we have several methods to control access.

The first method of limiting access is at the management account level. Enabling Cost Explorer at the management account level will allow all accounts in the organization access, and you cannot deny or grant access individually as access is not customizable at individual member account levels. Good news, though; member accounts will only have access to their own cost and usage data—they cannot see any other account's information. Bad news: It is really an all-or-nothing approach using this method to limit access. Either the member accounts will have access to Cost Explorer or they won't, and it will all depend on the management account providing this access.

All-or-nothing access may not work for your organization, and that is perfectly fine. If that is the case, you still can evaluate the use of IAM to manage access to the billing data for individual users. Imagine this: You have a finance department that requires access to the developer member account cost and usage data for analysis each month and has assigned two financial analysts to this task. The management account can enable Cost Explorer and then grant explicit permission to view pages in the Billing and Cost Management console for these two IAM users. With the appropriate permissions, and Activate IAM Access enabled, the IAM users will only be able to view the Cost Explorer data for the AWS account that they belong to.

IAM Access using the Activate IAM Access setting in AWS Cost Explorer is deactivated by default. This setting is only available to the root user of the account. IAM users with administrator access cannot modify this setting.

Setting the appropriate IAM policy to enable IAM users' access to AWS Cost Explorer is required before any reports can be viewed, edited, or removed. As a SysOps administrator, you may be asked to create an IAM policy that allows access to AWS Cost Explorer. In the following policy, you can see an example that enables a user to view, create, update, and delete reports within Cost Explorer:

```
{
   "Version": "2012-10-17",
```

```
    "Statement": [
      {
        "Sid": "ExamplePolicy",
        "Effect": "Allow",
        "Action": [
          "aws-portal:ViewBilling",
          "ce:CreateReport",
          "ce:UpdateReport",
          "ce:DeleteReport"
        ],
        "Resource": "*"
      }
    ]
}
```

Savings Plans

AWS offers several ways to decrease the cost of AWS services, and Savings Plans are no different. Savings Plans is a pricing model used to provide savings of up to 72 percent on AWS compute workloads. Savings Plans require a commitment of using an agreed-on amount of compute power, measured by the hour, over a one- or three-year period. Just like with Reserved Instances (RI), you can pay for the commitment using No Upfront, Partial Upfront, and All Upfront payment options. There are three different types of Savings Plans to be familiar with when considering how to reduce costs within your AWS environment: Compute Savings Plans, EC2 Instance Savings Plans, and SageMaker Savings Plans.

> Remember that Savings Plans commitments cannot be changed after purchase. The EC2 Savings Plans and the Compute Savings Plans apply to underlying Amazon EC2 instances that other services utilize, like Amazon ECS clusters or Amazon EMR, but does not discount the service price itself.

Compute Savings Plans

The Compute Savings Plans target flexibility and pricing, which can offer up to 66 percent off normal On-Demand rates. The biggest benefit to this savings plan is the removal of regional and instance type limitations. For example, the Compute Savings Plans is not region locked and can be used across any region or tenancy, such as Dedicated or Dedicated Host.

The plan also applies across Amazon EC2 instance usage no matter what the instance family, such as *r5* or *c5*, or the size, such as a *r5.xlarge* or *c5.large*. These savings plans are also not exclusive to specific operating systems in use, which means you can run those Microsoft Windows workloads and still gain a reduction in cost. The Compute Savings Plans also apply to any AWS Fargate and Lambda usage within the account. This flexibility of cost reduction is very attractive for organizations that have migrated into AWS and are looking to modernize their application or move into containerized or serverless options. The Compute Savings Plans allow you to make these changes and still receive the cost optimization benefit.

EC2 Instance Savings Plans

If your AWS environment is more heavily utilizing specific instance families in a specific AWS region, the EC2 Instance Savings Plans may offer a better fit with savings up to 72 percent off On-Demand pricing. The EC2 Instance Savings Plans still require a usage commitment over one to three years, but they also require a commitment to a specific instance family. Just like the Compute Savings Plans, the savings apply no matter the instance size, operating system, or tenancy, if the instances are in the specific region and instance family the commitment was configured. The EC2 Instance Saving Plans allow changes to the instance size or operating system within the specific family, such as changing from *m5.2xlarge* (Linux) into *m5.4xlarge* (Windows) while still receiving the discounted rate.

SageMaker Savings Plans

Organizations with heavy SageMaker utilization will benefit greatly from the SageMaker Savings Plans, which provide up to 64 percent off On-Demand SageMaker rates. This savings plan operates like that of the Compute Savings Plans where region, instance size, or instance type doesn't matter, but with one small addition of a component—for example, SageMaker notebook or training. One additional benefit with the SageMaker Savings Plan is the ability to move workloads between regions or migrate usage between *Inference* or *Training* at any time. The plan automatically applies to your workloads and the discount benefit is realized, no matter how your business needs change the configuration of your SageMaker usage.

Savings Plans vs. Reserved Instances

The concept of Savings Plans and Reserved Instances (RIs) are remarkably similar. Each offer a discounted rate for a commitment of time. Savings Plans are considered more flexible than RIs as you can commit to usage on a per hour basis, rather than committing to a specific instance configuration. This flexibility enables organizations to freely adjust compute needs to fit project or business goals and still maintain the cost-saving benefit. Reserved Instances would require a manual exchanging or modifying of the agreement to achieve a similar result, but only when using convertible RIs.

Another major difference between RIs and Savings Plans is capacity reservations. Savings Plans are pricing models only and do not guarantee or provide capacity. To achieve capacity reservations for On-Demand instances, you will need to allocate On-Demand Capacity Reservations (ODCR) in addition to configuring the Savings Plans. Savings Plans also do not apply to spot instance usage or any usage covered by a Reserved Instance. This means that you cannot stack discounts to achieve an even larger discount.

Savings Plans pricing doesn't change with the amount of hourly commitment. If you promise to commit more hours of usage, the discount price will not change. It's also important to note that EC2 instances running SUSE Linux Enterprise Server (SLES) covered under a Savings Plan is different compared to running Reserved Instance pricing. Always check the AWS pricing documentation when designing your cost optimization plan.

Monitoring Savings Plans

As a SysOps administrator you may be responsible for understanding usage of any Savings Plans within your organization. This is an important process when using Savings Plans as you can identify how they apply to overall usage, but more importantly what usage the Savings Plans cover in your AWS account. Evaluating the usage and coverage of the Savings Plans is a critical step in developing and maintaining a cost optimization strategy. Savings Plans have four different methods for evaluating and monitoring usage: inventory, initialization report, coverage report, and budgets.

Monitoring Using Inventory

The Savings Plans Inventory Monitoring option provides an overview of any Savings Plans currently owned or queued for future purchase in the AWS account. The inventory provides detailed information about the Savings Plan, such as type, instance family, region, month-to-date net savings, states, and dates. These inventory categories allow a SysOps administrator to quickly review Savings Plans details to make cost optimization decisions, like when to extend a Savings Plan that may be expiring or just gaining a quick insight on the hourly committed spend for a particular Savings Plan.

What happens when an administrator notices that a Savings Plan is going to expire when reviewing the Savings Plan inventory? That answer depends on the cost optimization strategy and if the Savings Plans are still needed. If the commitment is no longer viable to renew—for example, the project ended or the AWS account is downsizing—the administrator can simply just let the commitment lapse. However, if a renewal is queued to continue coverage of On-Demand usage, the queued purchase must be deleted before the start date. On the other hand, if the Savings Plans have a planned renewal, a purchase can be queued to start as soon as the active Savings Plans expire. Queuing Savings Plans purchases is recommended as it enables continuous coverage and avoids any potential gaps in savings.

One additional benefit of using the inventory method for monitoring Savings Plans is the ability to download the Savings Plans rates and Savings Plans inventory. Within the AWS Cost Management console, you can download a CSV file with detailed information for each Savings Plan within the AWS accounts you own. You can also download the Savings Plans inventory, which provides a CSV file with the same detailed information that is available on the Inventory page. This is useful when you need to run additional analytics or import the CSV file into another management or documentation system. These are great options when you're providing documentation of commitment rates and configurations for auditing or archival needs.

Monitoring Using Utilization Reports

A Savings Plan utilization report provides a visual representation of how the Savings Plans commitment apply to AWS account On-Demand usage over a specified time period. The utilization report also provides a quick glance at several useful metrics and filters to make useful renewal decisions or modifications to the Savings Plans based on new business needs or project changes. All utilization is calculated across a period called a *lookback period*. The lookback period is basically a start and an end date where the visualization and utilization reports are evaluating. This lookback period is what the high-level metrics use to provide utilization details, spend details, and net savings. The utilization report offers metrics for evaluation in the categories of On-Demand Spend Equivalent, Savings Plans Spend, and Total Net Savings.

The On-Demand Spend Equivalent metric provides a look into the amount that would have been spent if no commitment using a Savings Plan was made. This is useful when answering the "What if?" questions presented by CFOs. This metric is also a great way to evaluate the benefit of Savings Plans for additional or future projects and can be included in the Total Cost of Ownership discussion.

The Savings Plans Spend metric provides the committed spent over the lookback period, such as hourly, daily, or even monthly. This high-level metric is useful when evaluating commitment spend over different periods of time or when documenting specific spent for a project. Combining this metric with the On-Demand Spend Equivalent tells a compelling story of the benefits achieved within a cost optimization strategy.

The final metric is the Total Net Savings, which provides the total amount saved from using the Savings Plans commitments over the lookback period. This metric uses a comparison of savings against the On-Demand cost estimate to show net savings. The lookback period can also be adjusted to hourly, daily, or monthly depending on the filters you can define in the utilization report. If you want to share the utilization report or the Total Net Savings, you can download the report to a CSV file from the AWS Cost Management console under the Savings Plans Utilization Report dashboard.

Monitoring Using Coverage Reports

If you want to determine how much spend was covered by the purchased Savings Plans, the coverage report is the place to look. The coverage report, just like the inventory and utilization reports, can be reviewed for a specific time period. The coverage report includes three high-level metrics: Average Coverage, Additional Potential Savings, and On-Demand Spend Not Covered. Each one of these metrics enables an administrator to plan to a purchase, renewal, or removal of Savings Plans from an account.

The Average Coverage metric shows an aggregated coverage percentage based on the lookback period selected. This is useful when evaluating an addition of Saving Plans or changing coverage commitments at renewal time. The Additional Potential Savings metric, shown as a monthly amount, supports reviewing the amount saved by Saving Plans recommendations. This is useful when evaluating if a Savings Plan would provide cost savings over On-Demand pricing. The last metric available is On-Demand Spend Not Covered, which shows the amount of savings spend that wasn't covered by a Savings Plan or Reserved Instance purchase. This metric is particularly useful when updating cost optimization strategies and determining which eligible spend was not covered by the current Savings Plans. You can see usage and coverage rates on an hourly, daily, or monthly level.

Monitoring Using AWS Budgets

AWS Budgets is an option available for setting Saving Plans utilization, coverage, and cost budgets. When designing a cost optimization strategy, it is more than likely you will be using AWS Budgets for awareness of other AWS usage and costs. To enable a centralized view of spend and configure notifications for Savings Plans costs, the use of AWS Budgets is recommended.

In Exercise 3.3 you create a budget for Savings Plans utilization using AWS Budgets. This same process can be used to configure a budget for Savings Plans coverage.

EXERCISE 3.3

Setting Up AWS Budgets to Monitor Savings Plans

1. From the AWS Cost Management console, select the Budgets option in the navigation pane.

2. Click Create Budget and then select the Budget type for Savings Plans.

3. Select Set Up Your Budget and enter a name for the new budget. The budget name must be unique within the account and should follow an easy-to-understand naming convention.

4. Select the period you want to evaluate for the budget. You can choose Daily, Monthly, Quarterly, or Annually. All time periods use UTC time stamps.

5. Next, select the Savings Plans budget type of Savings Plans Utilization. Set Utilization Threshold at a percentage that you want to be notified. You should configure an early threshold warning such as 90 to identify when the overall Savings Plan utilization drops below 90 percent.

6. Click Configure Alerts and choose the option that best fits your needs. If you wish to use email notifications, select the Email Contacts section and fill out up to 10 email addresses to be contacted when the alarm threshold is breached. You can also select SNS Topic ARN if you want to use SNS for notifications. This is an optional step.

7. Click Confirm Budget and the AWS Budget for Savings Plans utilization is successfully configured! Now you can monitor Savings Plan Usage in AWS Budgets with all other budget information within your AWS account.

AWS Budgets

A good cost optimization plan includes methods for tracking AWS cost and usage, but it also includes how to act based on the available data. This is where AWS Budgets comes in as a primary driver of good cost optimization awareness, mixed with a little prevention and early detection. AWS Budgets is used to enable cost and usage tracking within an AWS account and act on any monitored area. AWS Budgets can aggregate utilization and coverage metrics for Savings Plans and Reserved Instances (RIs), which provides a unified location to evaluate cost-saving mechanisms applied against your AWS accounts.

Six budget types are available within AWS Budgets: Cost budgets, Usage budgets, RI Utilization budgets, RI Coverage budgets, Savings Plans Utilization budgets, and Savings Plans Coverage budgets. Each budget type can set up an optional notification based on thresholds configured within the budget. It is important to remember that AWS Budgets information updates up to three times daily. Each update can occur within 8–12 hours after a previous update. When creating budgets and alarms, be sure to consider update intervals to ensure the notifications send within an appropriate window of time.

SysOps administrators use AWS Budgets to solve real-world cost optimization problems and to ensure organizations are aware of spend. For example, AWS Budgets is frequently used for evaluating monthly costs against a set budget or to forecast spend before accruing charges. AWS Budgets also provide a method for organizations to receive forecast notifications to ensure service limits, like Amazon EC2 instance limits, are under the specified limit to avoid any potential launching issues. This advanced planning activity enables organizations to modify spending habits or adjust projects forecasted to run over by AWS Budgets.

The capability for AWS Budgets to raise budget and billing alarms is a highly desired feature for organizations implementing a cost optimization strategy. This feature is also useful for individuals just starting to explore AWS services and looking to stay within a certain spending limit, or even better, within the AWS free tier limits. Budget alerts use Amazon SNS to send notifications and have a one-to-one ratio of Amazon SNS topics to alerts. An AWS Budget alert can also be sent to up to 10 email addresses in addition to the Amazon SNS topic, which offers expanded options in providing automated actions, or advanced notification options like SMS text messaging or AWS Lambda event triggers. The frequency of notifications depends on the alarm type and event. Actual Budget alerts send out once per budget, per period, and only when the first threshold breaches, whereas forecast-based alarms may send out notifications more than once if the budget exceeds the alarm threshold and then goes below. If the budget forecast looks to exceed the threshold again, another alarm trigger will occur. Therefore, AWS requires five weeks of usage data before it can generate budget forecasts. Budget alarms for forecasted amounts will not alert until there is enough historical usage information on the account.

> As with all AWS services and features, to successfully send budget notifications you must ensure that your budget has the appropriate permissions to send a notification to the Amazon SNS topic. You must also accept the subscription to the Amazon SNS notification topic before AWS Budgets will send successfully.

AWS Budgets Reports

Monitoring the performance of existing budgets over a period, such as weekly or monthly, is a crucial step in maintaining a healthy cost optimization strategy. AWS Budgets allows configuration of emailed reports based on your reporting period that can include up to 50 email addresses. You can create up to 50 reports for each standalone AWS account or AWS Organizations management account. The cost for AWS Budget reports does not increase based on the number of email recipients; it increases based on frequency such as daily, weekly, or monthly.

Organizations will typically use weekly AWS Budget reports when first starting on the cost optimization journey. Weekly reports enable organizations to stay close to the spending habits of development organization, migration projects, or the overall AWS accounts within AWS Organizations. Daily reports can often add white noise when trying to determine trends or potential opportunities to reduce cost across an AWS account. Organizations may use daily reports when compliance of financial or regulatory requirements is needed. However, in practical application most organizations will choose to receive reports on a weekly or monthly basis and retain these records for up to a year.

AWS Budgets Pricing

There is a cost associated with AWS Budgets once your account exceeds the two free action-enabled budgets. Each action-enabled budget, which means your budget is taking an action such as sending a notification to an SNS topic or emailing notifications to your finance team, will incur a $0.10 daily cost after the first two action-enabled budgets. Each AWS management account can have up to 20,000 budgets, providing a wide range of potential notifications and alarms. There is also a maximum of 50 AWS Budget reports within the management account, which allow you to monitor the performance of the budget portfolio through emailed reports. If you plan to use this option, it will incur a cost of $0.01 for each report delivered.

While these costs may seem trivial when compared to other AWS service costs, they still have the potential to increase overall AWS spend. When planning the cost optimization strategy, take into consideration the number of budgets and budget actions required to receive the information necessary to make decisions, provide historical cost information, or satisfy any regulatory needs your organization may have.

In Exercise 3.4 you will configure AWS Budget alarms for your AWS account to alarm based on your costs. The process also applies to the setup of Usage, Savings Plans, or RI utilization and RI coverage budgets alarms.

EXERCISE 3.4

Configuring AWS Budget Alarms

1. Sign into your AWS Management Console and navigate to the AWS Cost Management dashboard.

2. In the navigation pane, select Budgets, and then click Create Budget.

3. Select the Customize (Advanced) type of budget using the Choose Budget Type option. In this exercise you will choose Cost Budget, and then click Next. This is where you can choose between the different Budget alarm types.

4. Configure the parameters for your budget. Select the period to specify how often the budget period resets spend under the Set Budget Amount section. You can select between Daily, Monthly, Quarterly, or Annually. For this exercise, select Daily.

5. Now select Budget Effective Date and select Recurring Budget. This tells AWS Budgets to reset the budget after each budget period. You can also choose Expiring Budget for a budget that does not reset after the budget period.

6. Select your start date or budget period to start tracking against the budgeted amount. If you chose Expiring Budget in the previous step, you must choose a date for the budget to end on.

7. As this budget period is Daily, you will need to enter your budgeted amount. This is the total amount that you wish to spend in each budget period, or in this case, daily. If you configured a monthly budget, you must configure additional parameters under the Fixed Budget section. Entering a fixed budget allows you to create a budget that monitors the same amount every month.

8. You can skip the optional Budget Scoping section. Use these optional filters for your budget to include items such as refunds, credits, or taxes.

9. Configure the budget name under the Detail section. This name must be unique within your AWS account. Click Next after naming your budget.

EXERCISE 3.4 *(continued)*

10. To configure an alert threshold for an alarm, select Add An Alert Threshold. Under the Threshold section enter the amount that will trigger a notification. You can enter an absolute value, like 50 dollars, or you can enter a percentage, like 85 percent of your budget. If entering a percentage, do not include the percent symbol. Enter the amount in the Absolute Value or % Of budgeted Amount section, depending on which option you chose.

11. Now choose which threshold type to produce an alert. You can choose Actual or Forecasted. For this exercise select Actual and move on to configuring Notification preferences.

12. Configure an email notification by entering an email address under the Email Recipient section. This is the email that AWS Budgets will notify when a threshold is exceeded.

13. After configuring the notifications for Email Only, click Next and skip the Attach Actions section. This section is used to act on a Budget alarm, such as shutting down an Amazon EC2 instance when an alarm threshold is met. Click Next to finalize the budget creation.

14. Review the budget settings and ensure that the budget has an email recipient. A budget requires a minimum of one parameter within the section to continue. Click Create Budget when you are satisfied with the configuration.

That's it! You now have a Budget alarm configured for daily reporting.

AWS Budgets Actions

AWS Budget can act on an alarm by running actions on your behalf based on a specific cost or usage budget threshold. These actions are particularly useful when automating cost optimization plans to reduce spend when AWS Budgets detect forecasted or actual overages. Configuration of these actions are within a budget and can run either automatically or after manual approval. Setting an action to manual approval is a best practice when first configuring and testing budget actions. This prevents any potential loss of data or production outages as the administrator must first approve and review the action. AWS Budget actions can include applying an IAM policy or service control policy (SCP). This enables you to target specific Amazon EC2 instances within your account. SCPs can be used to prevent provisioning of new resources during the budget period resulting in no spending from additional resources launching during that period. For example, you can apply an SCP to an AWS account to prevent the ec2:RunInstances operation. This prevents an AWS account from launching any new Amazon EC2 Instances until it is removed.

To allow AWS Budgets to perform actions on your behalf, an IAM service role must be in place. This service role provides the appropriate permissions to perform the actions on your behalf once AWS Budgets assumes the role. You should start with the AWS managed policy first when configuring actions and then customize the policy to fit your needs.

What happens if you have an action applied previously that you want to reverse? For example, say you accidentally approved a manual action to add a read-only policy and now need to reverse it. The good news is that AWS Budgets allows the reversal of a previous action in the Action History table within the budget. The action history allows an administrator to review each status and then undo, or reset, any action within the table. If an administrator chooses to reverse an action, it will enter a reversed status where the action is undone, and AWS Budgets no longer evaluates the action for the remainder of the budget period. If the administrator needs to update the action and then reapply, they can click Reset to have AWS Budgets evaluate the budget again and apply the action, as necessary.

Managing Costs with Managed Services

It should be no surprise that using AWS Managed services can offer cost benefits within an organization. The use of AWS Managed services like Amazon Relational Database Service (RDS), AWS Fargate, and even Amazon Elastic File System (EFS) help alleviate a lot of the technical staffing, architectural, and in most cases licensing burdens. One of the largest benefits of using managed services within AWS comes in the form of administrative burden.

Imagine that you have a large fleet of database servers running in your on-premises datacenter. Your CTO has instructed that everything must be migrated over to the organization's AWS Cloud environment; you must ensure that costs are kept as low as possible, and you must ensure that everything is maintained with the highest level of uptime availability. Your first instinct may be to lift-and-shift the existing database environment over to AWS using migration tools and just run the database servers on Amazon EC2 instances. While this is a plausible solution, this requires a significant time investment in ensuring the Amazon EC2 instances are configured correctly, licensed appropriately, and designed architecturally to support the high availability demands from the CTO. This option can also increase spending within an AWS account as several Amazon EC2 instances are required to keep everything highly available, you must consider the traffic in and out of the Virtual Private Cloud (VPC), and there is a significant administrative overhead to keep everything running. Sure, that solution is plausible, and in all honesty, a lot of organizations continue to operate in this manner. However, the better solution may include utilizing a managed service like Amazon RDS.

Using a managed service like Amazon RDS offers several benefits to the organization, but more importantly it frees up a lot of administrative overhead that occurs in just managing database instances. A cost reduction that is often overlooked is the cost it takes for IT administrators or SysOps administrators to manage an environment. When you can make an administrator more efficient or provide them with a reduction in scope of work due to managed services, this enables an intangible cost savings for the organization. When an administrator isn't focused on just keeping the lights on, they can focus on automation, backups, future cost optimization tasks, and more importantly, security of the AWS account. While this is just an example with Amazon RDS, the same principle applies to other managed services.

Let's take another example using Amazon EFS. As an organization you could have your administrators create a shared storage service using Network File System protocols and Amazon EC2 instances. You could manage the underlying operating system and manage or scale the disk space required in each server. This administration takes time, and possibly even more valuable, it takes a specific skill set to keep this type of environment running and highly available. This could mean hours of labor from an administrator or architect; this could mean additional licensing or storage costs for the fleet of Amazon EC2 instances you need to scale and grow this solution. The possibility of costs incurring at almost every turn is evident in creating your own storage solution like Amazon EFS. Alternatively, you could just use a managed service like Amazon EFS, allow the setup and scaling of the underlying storage solution to be completed by AWS, and allow your administrator to focus on where the Amazon EFS connects to be available for your application. You don't have to worry about how much time and money is being spent by the IT staff troubleshooting the installation or performing routine maintenance tasks. The IT staff can just focus on keeping your application at top health and figuring out new ways to save even more money within the AWS environment.

You may be thinking to yourself that IT administration overhead doesn't really account for much in the organization. You have administrators handling 50–75 servers currently and they are doing a great job, and that may be true. What would happen if these same administrators had more native monitoring, automation tools, and visibility into an environment? A conservative estimate of the number of servers that a single administrator can effectively manage would bump up to 150–200. Now what would happen if the same applications and servers this IT staff supports is using managed services? The number may not go up, or down, but the 100 percent allocation in time supporting these servers is now lessened. The IT administrators now have time to review logs, track down bug reports, and focus on optimization of environments for cost, security, and high availability. All these benefits just because your organization is using managed services.

Amazon EC2 Spot Instances and Cost Optimization

Now that you know how to monitor the AWS environment for cost optimization, what do you do with this knowledge? Well, the first thing is to determine the small easy wins in reducing cost within your organization. Often, this small easy win comes with the evaluation of current applications depending on Amazon EC2 and Auto Scaling. Let's say your organization has a large data analytics and Big Data environment or has a massive fleet of web servers running across the globe. These environments will likely require Amazon EC2 instances and Auto Scaling to maintain availability and to scale out compute available to the applications. In these cases, as with any other application use case requiring Amazon EC2 instances, a consideration of using Amazon EC2 Spot instances is a must.

Amazon EC2 Spot instances allow an organization to take advantage of unused Amazon EC2 capacity in the AWS Cloud. These spot instances often come at a savings of up to 90 percent of the cost when compared to the same Amazon EC2 On-Demand pricing. The catch here is a bit more administration and the Amazon EC2 Spot instances potentially being reclaimed with a two-minute warning when Amazon EC2 Spot service interrupts due to capacity no longer being available, the Spot price maximum is exceeded, or during a high-demand spot instance period. However, this catch is just a minor inconvenience to handle through scripting, stopping or hibernating the Amazon EC2 Spot Instances backed by Amazon EBS volumes, and appropriate capacity planning to reduce the overall cost of a high-performing Amazon EC2 fleet.

Let's say your environment is set up to host a large web application with hundreds of thousands of connections per hour. This is a well-known website, and your AWS environment is using Amazon EC2 instances with Auto Scaling. You have your website scaling out and in as required to support the organization, but you just feel there is more that you can do to make this configuration more efficient. Looking back at your cost optimization plan, you have Reserved Instances and Savings Plans configured to reduce the cost of this web application, but you still want to squeeze every penny out of the performance and configuration. The thought hits you hard! You could be scaling your Amazon EC2 environment to meet the demands of your customers using Amazon EC2 Spot instances. These servers are only needed at times of peak capacity, and they don't need to stick around after the demand is gone. Why should you be spending even Amazon EC2 Savings Plans pricing when you could get up to a 90 percent discount on the Amazon EC2 Spot instances? It is at this moment you begin to realize Amazon EC2 Spot instances can help reduce scaling costs for your application while still maintaining the same performance. You run over to your computer, log into the AWS Management Console, create a new launch template, and then continue to configure the use of Amazon EC2 Spot instances under the advanced details. You saved the day; you took every opportunity to reduce the cost of your web application all while maintaining performance and availability. Your cost optimization task is done, but your cost optimization job is far from over.

Summary

An AWS Cost and Usage Report (AWS CUR) contains any AWS usage within your account and then estimates those charges on an hourly, daily, or monthly breakdown. This data is exportable to an Amazon S3 bucket or viewable as a CSV file in your favorite spreadsheet application.

AWS cost allocation tags play an important role in customizing AWS usage and billing reports. These tags enable an organization to track additional information such as cost center, department, project metadata, or any other beneficial billing data. These tags apply at the AWS service level and are easily managed using the Resource Groups & Tag Editor in the AWS Management Console.

AWS Cost Explorer allows exploration of AWS cost and usage at a high level through built-in reports and at a detailed level using filtering dimensions like AWS Region, Member Account, or AWS Service.

It is important to remember to set AWS Cost Explorer IAM permissions using a policy. There is no default access for IAM users within AWS Cost Explorer.

AWS Budgets provides an easily configurable method for setting spend notifications on current and forecasted spend. AWS Budgets supports up to 20,000 budgets and can be configured to send notifications to 10 email subscribers or be published to an Amazon SNS topic. Each budget is allowed to create up to five alerts.

It's important to remember that AWS Budgets can have actions applied to notifications to automate cost optimization tasks when a Budget alarm is triggered. These actions can include modification to Savings Plans or using a custom Deny IAM policy to restrict use of future AWS services.

AWS Cost Savings Plans cover three different types of plans, including Compute, Sage-Maker, and Amazon EC2. The type of Savings Plans you use depends on the AWS services being used and the commitment to compute hours supported by your organization.

Remember that AWS Cost Savings Plans and Reserved Instances are different. Each are used to reduce costs within an AWS environment, but Reserved Instances are the only option to reserve launch capacity, whereas Savings Plans are considered much more flexible than even convertible Reserved Instance types.

The use of Amazon EC2 Spot Instances can drive down costs of an AWS environment. Using Amazon EC2 Spot instances within an Auto Scaling group can maintain scalability and availability while also maintaining the same level of performance for a fraction of the cost compared to using On-Demand instances.

It's important to remember that not all cost savings are tangible within a cost optimization plan. The use of AWS managed services, like Amazon RDS, AWS Fargate, or Amazon EFS, reduces the cost of licensing and, more importantly, administrative overhead.

Exam Essentials

Understand the importance of implementing AWS cost allocation tags.   AWS cost allocation tags provide extended visibility and reporting across AWS Budgets, Cost and Usage Reports, and Cost Explorer in customizable tags such as cost center, project name, or even departmental identification. This can provide a starting point for cost optimization automation tasks.

Understand how to export AWS Cost and Usage Reports.   Properly storing and reviewing AWS Cost and Usage reports provides valuable insight into prior cost optimization initiatives and AWS cost history. Some organizations will be required to meet compliance or regulatory needs and must store AWS Cost and Usage reports for archival purposes. This process is accomplished by storing AWS Cost and Usage Reports in an Amazon S3 bucket and disabling the overwrite feature.

Understand how to create AWS Budget notifications and actions.   AWS Budget notifications provide advanced warning of potential cost overages. This advanced warning provides an opportunity to automate preventive measures to avoid costly overages.

Understand how to identify and remediate unused resources using AWS Cost Explorer.   AWS Cost Explorer can help identify underused or unused services using custom filters and dimensions. The built-in AWS Cost Explorer reports allow a breakdown of the top five cost-accruing AWS Services and analysis of Reserved Instance utilization.

Understand AWS managed service opportunities to reduce cost.   AWS Managed services provide a simplified administration and configuration of commonly used building blocks like containers, databases, and storage. These managed services can reduce IT administration overhead and reduce overall administrative costs.

Understand when to use Savings Plans.   Savings Plans are a flexible pricing model used to lower prices of services utilized under the Compute, EC2 Instance, and SageMaker Savings Plans. AWS Cost Explorer provides recommendations for which Savings Plans will realize the biggest savings.

Review Questions

1. Which of the following tag types are available for use under cost allocation tags? (Choose two.)

   A. User-defined tags

   B. Organization-defined tags

   C. AWS-generated tags

   D. AWS support–generated tags

   E. Cost center tags

2. How long can it take for user-defined cost allocation tags to appear in the AWS Billing dashboard?

   A. 30 minutes

   B. 60 minutes

   C. 24 hours

   D. 8 hours

3. The chief financial officer of your organization has asked you to provide a final Cost and Usage Report for the AWS spend in your development account. How can you determine if the report is finalized before sending it over?

   A. Check that the Cost and Usage Report dashboard is including finalized data.

   B. Check that the Cost and Usage Report has the prefix of Final-Report within the Amazon S3 bucket.

   C. Check that the Cost and Usage Report is present as all reports are final reports.

   D. Check that the Cost and Usage Report has the column Bill/InvoiceID.

4. What is the purpose of a manifest collection found in the Amazon S3 bucket with your AWS Cost and Usage Reports?

   A. The manifest collection provides mapping information for AWS Cost Explorer to import AWS Cost and Usage Report data.

   B. The manifest collection provides connectivity details for AWS analytic services to work with the AWS Cost and Usage Report data.

   C. The manifest collection indicates the order in which multipart AWS Cost and Usage Reports must be structured and viewed.

   D. The manifest collection indicates the naming convention and prefix data for AWS Cost and Usage Reports stored in an Amazon S3 bucket.

5. The annual security audit has just been released and the security team has asked that you prevent any AWS Cost and Usage Reports from being created outside of the primary AWS Organizations management account. What can you do to ensure member accounts cannot create AWS Cost and Usage Reports?

   A. Apply a service control policy to restrict IAM users within member accounts from configuring AWS Cost and Usage Reports.

   B. Apply an IAM policy within member accounts to prevent configuring AWS Cost and Usage Reports.

    C. Apply a service control policy to restrict all Cost and Usage Report use for management accounts.

    D. Apply a managed IAM policy within member accounts to only allow management accounts access to AWS Cost and Usage Reports.

6. The finance department has asked which options are available to perform analytics on the AWS Cost and Usage Reports provided for each AWS member account. Which of the following options are provided within AWS Cost and Usage Reports? (Choose three.)

    A. Amazon Athena 1

    B. Amazon Redshift

    C. Amazon Artifact

    D. Amazon Comprehend

    E. Amazon QuickSight

    F. Amazon PinPoint

7. The compliance officer for the organization has asked you to confirm the maximum length of historical data that AWS Cost Explorer provides. Which of the following options will you provide to the compliance officer?

    A. 24 months

    B. 36 months

    C. 18 months

    D. 12 months

8. You have been tasked with determining the top five cost-accruing AWS Services within your development AWS accounts over the last six months. Which AWS service will provide the fastest visualization of this data?

    A. AWS Cost Explorer

    B. AWS Cost and Usage Reports

    C. Amazon Athena

    D. Amazon Billing Dashboard

9. You have been tasked with securing the organization's AWS developer accounts from having access to AWS Cost Explorer while retaining access to AWS Cost Explorer access for nondeveloper accounts. Which of the following is the best option to accomplish this goal?

    A. Disable AWS Cost Explorer access at the management account level.

    B. Deny AWS Cost Explorer access using a service control policy for developer AWS accounts.

    C. Activate IAM access and configure IAM policies for each AWS member account requiring access to AWS Cost Explorer.

    D. AWS Cost Explorer is disabled for member accounts by default, so no changes are necessary to accomplish this goal.

10. Your AWS Account is a member of AWS Organizations and has access to AWS Cost Explorer. What of the following options best describes the Cost Explorer data that you can view?

    A. As a member of AWS Organizations, the account has access to view all AWS Cost Explorer data for the organization.

    B. Only AWS Cost Explorer data from the time the AWS account joined the AWS Organization.

    C. Only AWS Cost Explorer data from before the AWS account joined the AWS Organization.

    D. As a member of AWS Organizations, the account has access to view AWS Cost Explorer data for all accounts in the same organizational unit.

11. Which of the following Savings Plans options are available from AWS to reduce AWS Service cost? (Choose three.)

    A. SageMaker Savings Plans 1

    B. Network Savings Plans

    C. Compute Savings Plans

    D. EC2 Instance Savings Plans

    E. Lambda Savings Plans

    F. EMR Savings Plans

12. Your organization is looking to cost-optimize a project that runs in North America and in Australia. The project is very heavily using Amazon EC2 instances with Microsoft workloads. The organization has a requirement that if the project moves to another region the cost optimization plan will still be valid. Which option satisfies the need of the organization?

    A. Compute Savings Plans

    B. EC2 Instance Savings Plans

    C. SageMaker Savings Plans

    D. EC2 Reserved Instances

13. Your organization has heavy utilization requirements for machine learning in an upcoming project. You have been tasked with selecting the best cost optimization option to allow changes between regions, but also between inference or training workload types. Which of the following cost optimization option is the best fit?

    A. SageMaker free tier

    B. Compute Savings Plans 2

    C. SageMaker Savings Plans

    D. SageMaker Reserved Instances

14. The finance department has tasked you with determining how much of the On-Demand spend within an AWS account is not covered by a Compute Savings Plan. Which Savings Plan monitoring report will provide the details you are looking for without requiring customization or detailed exports of Savings Plans data?

   A. Savings Plans utilization reports

   B. Savings Plans inventory reports

   C. AWS Cost and Usage Reports

   D. Savings Plans coverage reports

   E. AWS Billing Dashboard

15. Your senior administrator has asked you to set up notifications for the AWS Budgets configuration in the organization's developer accounts. Which of the following notification options are available for AWS Budgets? (Choose two.)

   A. Posting to the Personal Health Dashboard

   B. Amazon SNS topics

   C. AWS Management Console notifications

   D. Direct integration with ServiceNow

   E. Direct email recipients

16. You are developing a cost optimization policy that automatically disables a development organization member AWS account from launching EC2 instances when the account budget goes above 90 percent of forecasted costs. Which of the following AWS Budgets actions will accomplish this goal?

   A. Configure a service control policy to deny Amazon EC2 instances from launching, which is applied once the budget reaches 90 percent.

   B. Configure an IAM policy to deny the developer admin accounts from launching Amazon EC2 instances.

   C. Configure an action using Amazon SNS to send an SMS message to the developers warning them not to launch Amazon EC2 instances once the budget reaches 90 percent.

   D. Configure an action using the Trusted Advisor APIs to record budget overages and notify the AWS Support concierge to disable Amazon EC2 instance launching.

17. The finance department for your company is asking why they are not receiving the forecast Budget alerts you set up for a new account last week. You configured AWS Budget alarms for forecasted amounts at multiple intervals, but on evaluation there is no forecast data. Which of the following options may be a potential cause for not seeing any forecasting data?

   A. AWS Budgets requires a minimum of two weeks of historical billing data to be able to forecast budget spend.

   B. AWS Budgets requires a connection to the AWS Cost and Usage Reports and the account is too new to produce these reports.

   C. AWS Budgets requires a minimum of five weeks of historical billing data to be able to forecast budget spend.

   D. AWS Budgets requires a connection to Trusted Advisor and the account is too new to generate Trusted Advisor checks on spending.

18. Which of the following options is a cost benefit of using AWS Managed services such as Amazon RDS, AWS Fargate, or Amazon EFS?

    A. Managed services are the responsibility of AWS and only require payment for the use of the service, not the configuration of the applications.

    B. Managed services reduce the IT operational overhead as you can focus on developing applications, not running or designing an infrastructure.

    C. Managed services reduce the need for highly available architectural designs as this is now the responsibility of AWS.

    D. Managed services include all operating system licensing costs that AWS pays and manages, essentially eliminating the need to calculate licensing costs.

19. Your organization has asked for a modification of the cost optimization plan to include more cost-effective scaling solutions for their most popular web application. You have settled on the use of Amazon EC2 Spot instances to help scale during peak hours. Which of the following options do you use to implement this change?

    A. Modify the Auto Scaling configuration to relaunch all Amazon EC2 instances as spot instances.

    B. Create a new Auto Scaling group that utilizes Amazon EC2 Spot instances as the primary launch template.

    C. Create a new launch template to replace On-Demand instances with spot instances and apply the launch template to your existing Auto Scaling group.

    D. Create a new launch template to include the use of Amazon EC2 Spot instances when scaling and apply the launch template to your existing Auto Scaling group.

20. Which of the following options represent a potential drawback of using Amazon EC2 Spot instances for cost optimization?

    A. Amazon EC2 Spot instances can be reclaimed with a two-minute warning at any time.

    B. Amazon EC2 Spot instances need to have bids refreshed daily.

    C. Amazon EC2 Spot instances cannot be used with Auto Scaling.

    D. Amazon EC2 Spot instances are only useful for short-term projects.

Chapter

4

Automated Security Services and Compliance

THE AWS CERTIFIED SYSOPS ADMINISTRATOR EXAM OBJECTIVES COVERED IN THIS CHAPTER INCLUDE:

✓ **Domain 4: Security and Compliance**

- 4.1 Implement and manage security and compliance policies

- 4.2 Implement data and infrastructure protection strategies

✓ **Domain 5: Networking and Content Delivery**

- 5.1 Implement networking features and connectivity

- 5.3 Troubleshoot network connectivity issues

Security is such a crucial component for any application or infrastructure design, whether it is fully in the AWS Cloud, on-premises, or any combination of hybrid deployments you can think of. At Amazon, security is the absolute highest priority, and this reflects in all the security and compliance services available for customers in the AWS Cloud. The best way to learn how to effectively secure an AWS environment and enhance compliance is to understand how the various AWS services monitor, document, protect, and prevent security threats and help satisfy compliance requirements.

This chapter introduces several commonly used AWS security and compliance services used to implement security and compliance best practices in the cloud. You'll learn how to implement data and infrastructure protection strategies. The chapter also discusses security checks and logs found across the suite of AWS security and compliance services to satisfy security policy and compliance needs.

You'll also learn the importance of implementing encryption at rest and in transit when implementing networking features and connectivity. Finally, you'll see how to further improve the security posture of your AWS infrastructure and AWS account by securely storing secrets and implementing data and infrastructure protection strategies, such as data classification and network protection services.

Review Reports, Findings, and Checks

One of the key areas of security and compliance is being able to document, analyze, and respond to security events or compliance needs. AWS provides several services to build security reports and compliance findings, and it provides checks to ensure that an AWS account or application is meeting the security requirements of your organization. Without any clear reporting or analytics data available, protecting against security threats is a nearly impossible job. The issue of compliance is also complicated when you are unable to produce verifications of security controls present within the AWS account or designed architecture. Thankfully, AWS offers the tools necessary for you to report, analyze, and act on any findings reported by the AWS security and compliance services.

AWS Trusted Advisor

AWS Trusted Advisor provides you with a quick glance at the security posture of your organization from the lens of best practices and identifies glaringly alarming security configurations you should avoid. Trusted Advisor offers best practice guidance in real time to help you monitor and maintain AWS resources across six categories: operational excellence, cost optimization, performance, security, fault tolerance, and service limits.

Every AWS customer has access to the core Trusted Advisor checks and recommendations. These checks (cost optimization, performance, resilience, operational excellence, and service limits) help provide awareness of problems and can help identify security, provisioning, and cost concerns within an AWS account. For example, the core checks available to everyone help identify security concerns related to Amazon S3 Bucket permissions, multifactor authentication (MFA) status on the root account, and security groups where specific ports like Secure Shell are unrestricted.

> Remember, any AWS account that has Basic or Developer support plans can use the Trusted Advisor console to view all checks in the Service Limits category, but it is limited to the following security checks: IAM Use, MFA on Root Account, Security Groups – Specific Ports Unrestricted, and Amazon S3 Bucket Permissions.

Trusted Advisor includes several useful core security checks to enable any AWS account owner to review some of the most common configuration security problems like unrestricted security groups and MFA disabled on the account root user. However, the real value of Trusted Advisor comes into play when unlocking all security checks available to Business and Enterprise support plans. It is important to know which Trusted Advisor security checks are available in your support plan, and how they can help you in reporting or automating security best practices. You can find a listing of all Trusted Advisor security checks here: https://docs.aws.amazon.com/awssupport/latest/user/trusted-advisor-check-reference.html.

Amazon EC2 Instances with Microsoft SQL Server End of Support

Running any software that is near or beyond the end of support is a security risk. Software that is no longer supported by the vendor will not receive regular security updates and can pose a security vulnerability concern and risk. In Amazon EC2 instances with Microsoft SQL Server, Trusted Advisor verifies that any EC2 instance running a SQL Server AMI in the last 24 hours is within the currently supported versions. The check alerts if the versions are near or have reached end of support. Microsoft supports SQL Server versions for a total of 10 years, which includes 5 years of mainstream support and 5 years of extended support for continued updates.

Amazon EBS and RDS Public Snapshots

AWS Trusted Advisor has two separate checks for Amazon EBS public snapshots and Amazon RDS public snapshots. The checks verify permission settings and alerts of any snapshots marked as public. Any snapshot marked public will give all AWS accounts and users access to the data within the snapshots, which could lead to data or intellectual property leaks. If you intend to share, ensure that you are only sharing with the specific users or accounts that need access using the private snapshot settings.

Amazon RDS Security Group Access Risk

This Trusted Advisor check helps keep databases running on Amazon RDS instances from potentially overly permissive security groups. The check warns when a security group rule is granting overly permissive access to a database, such as being open to 0.0.0.0/0 (Anywhere) instead of a specific IP address or EC2 instance.

Amazon Route 53 MX Resource Sets and Sender Policy Framework

DNS security for email is extremely important for any organization as it helps prevent spam and phishing attacks. This check verifies that each MX record set has a TXT or SPF resource record created with a valid SPF record. The records must start with v=spf1 and indicate which servers are authorized to send email for your domain.

Amazon S3 Bucket Permissions

Security of Amazon S3 buckets is an absolute must since S3 is one of the highest visibility services used by customers. This Trusted Advisor check verifies that no Amazon S3 buckets in an AWS account are allowing open-access permissions (Public) or allowing access to any unauthenticated AWS user. The check runs against bucket policies and explicit bucket permissions that are unused to override these permissions. This check helps identify potential security vulnerabilities in your bucket when permissions exist to grant delete or upload access to everyone. Due to the importance of this security check, it is one of the core Trusted Advisor security checks available to all AWS accounts.

AWS CloudTrail Logging

AWS CloudTrail logging is a security best practice for every AWS account. This check verifies that CloudTrail is enabled and whether it is in use across multiple regions. CloudTrail provides visibility into the AWS account use by recording information about the AWS API calls made on the account. These logs are essential in troubleshooting specific user actions across a specified period. CloudTrail stores these logs in an S3 bucket and requires write permissions.

AWS Lambda Functions Using Deprecated Runtimes

A security best practice for Lambda functions is to ensure that the function is not running on a deprecated, or almost deprecated, runtime. Trusted Advisor refreshes this check multiple times per day and provides details on Lambda functions that are running on deprecated or soon-to-be-deprecated runtimes.

AWS Well-Architected High-Risk Issues for Security

Completing an AWS Well-Architected Framework review of the workloads running in your environment is a best practice. For any findings listed against the security pillar, Trusted Advisor checks workloads for high-risk issues (HRIs). If an AWS Well-Architected Framework review is not available on the account, Trusted Advisor will not display any HRIs.

CloudFront Custom SSL Certificates in the IAM Certificate Store

This Trusted Advisor check looks at custom SSL certificates for CloudFront alternate domain names and alerts when a certificate is expired, about to expire, using outdated encryption methods (SHA-1 hashing), or has a misconfiguration such as the certificate not containing the origin domain name or the domain name.

CloudFront SSL Certificate on the Origin Server

Like the custom SSL certificate check, Trusted Advisor verifies origin server SSL certificate expiration and encryption use. If the certificate is using SHA-1 hashing or is expired or about to expire, Trusted Advisor does not tell CloudFront to issue a 502. CloudFront issues a 502 only if the certificate expires. The Trusted Advisor alert helps us avoid the 502.

ELB Listener Security

Trusted Advisor will check load balancers for listeners that are not configured using recommended security configurations for encrypted communications. If the listeners are not using HTTPS or SSL, updated security policies, or ciphers and protocols that are secure, Trusted Advisor will create an alert. Unless required by an organizational security policy, it is best practice to use Elastic Load Balancing predefined security policies with ciphers and protocols that adhere to the AWS security best practices.

ELB Security Groups

Misconfigured and overly permissive security groups present a significant security threat to an AWS environment. This check verifies that load balancers are not missing an assigned security group or that have security groups that allow access to ports that are not configured on the load balancer. This check helps identify load balancers that may have had security groups associated with a load balancer deleted.

Exposed Access Keys

Having exposed access keys is a critical concern and occurs with surprising frequency to new AWS customers and developers. This check evaluates common code repositories for AWS access keys that may have been exposed to the public. The check also looks for Amazon EC2 usage that could be a result of a compromised access key. While this check is useful, it does not guarantee that checked keys have not been exposed or that all exposed keys have been identified. It is the customer's responsibility to ensure the safety and security of the AWS access keys and AWS resources.

IAM Access Key Rotation

Rotating access keys regularly helps reduce the chance of a compromise without your knowledge. This check verifies that IAM access keys are rotated in the last 90 days and produces an alert for any IAM keys that have not been rotated. This check uses the access key creation and most recent activation date to determine when the keys were last rotated.

IAM Password Policy

Password policies increase the overall security of the AWS environment by enforcing the creation of strong user passwords. This Trusted Advisor check provides alerts when a password policy is not enabled or if password content requirements have not been enabled. When enabling a password policy, it is immediately enforced for any newly created users, but it does not retroactively apply to users already configured and does not force a password change. You should have existing users change their password if you're changing the password policy or enabling updated content requirements.

IAM Use

This Trusted Advisor check is quite simple—it checks for the use of IAM users, groups, and roles in AWS. This basic check is available to all AWS accounts regardless of which support plan they are enrolled in. The check is intended to dissuade the use of root access by verifying that at least one IAM user is present in the AWS account.

MFA on Root Account

This Trusted Advisor check is available to all AWS accounts regardless of the support plan enrollment status. The check verifies that the root account has MFA enabled and issues an alert if the feature is not enabled. AWS security best practices recommend that all AWS accounts be protected by MFA, which requires a unique activation code from a hardware or virtual MFA device to interact with the AWS Management Console.

Security Groups – Specific Ports Unrestricted

It is amazingly easy to create a security group that is open for any IP address in the world when conducting testing, thinking that you will just delete it when you are done testing. However, in some cases you may never return to delete the security group and may unexpectedly use it again to launch resources in the future. This check is included for all AWS accounts regardless of the support plan enrollment status and checks security groups for rules that allow unrestricted access (0.0.0.0/0) to specific ports like those used for remote management. Trusted Advisor will flag ports in red that are the highest risk, in yellow for ports with less risk, and in green for ports that require unrestricted access, such as HTTP, HTTPS, and SMTP. The check evaluates security groups that you create and the IPv4 address rules.

Security Groups – Unrestricted Access

This AWS Trusted Advisor check is like the specific ports unrestricted check as it is verifying IPv4 inbound address rules only in security groups that you create. This check evaluates security groups for rules that allow unrestricted access to a resource and could potentially increase malicious activity opportunities like denial-of-service attacks or hacking.

AWS Security Hub

Just as the Security Hub service provides AWS account owners with a method of viewing compressive information about an AWS account, Trusted Advisor focuses on several distinct categories of checks, including security, whereas Security Hub focuses on providing a comprehensive view of the state of security within AWS and compliance with security standards and best practices. Security Hub provides a centralized location to review findings from across AWS accounts, AWS services, and supported third-party partners. Security Hub helps you analyze security trends and identifies the highest-priority security issues you should address within your AWS account that are visible using aggregated findings in prebuilt dashboards.

One of the most useful benefits of Security Hub is it lets you quickly identify security findings across several AWS accounts and services, like Trusted Advisor. For example, if your organization has Business, Enterprise On-Ramp, or Enterprise support plans, you can view your Trusted Advisor security checks in the Security Hub and follow the recommendations to address any identified security issues. This feature gives you a single convenient location to view security recommendations from Trusted Advisor and Security Hub, saving you valuable time and effort when conducting routine security checks.

Security Hub has prepackaged security standards such as Payment Card Industry Data Security Standard (PCI DSS), CIS AWS Foundations Benchmark, and AWS Foundational Security Best Practices to help you evaluate the security posture of an AWS account and resources. Its security checks use configuration items recorded by AWS Config. Customers are not charged separately for any AWS Config rules enabled by Security Hub as they are referred to as service-linked rules. Because the service-linked rules are owned by AWS service teams, you cannot edit or delete these rules that Security Hub creates for as long as you subscribe to Security Hub.

AWS Security Hub Pricing

Every AWS account and region will have a 30-day free trial of Security Hub. After the free trial, the pricing for Security Hub is calculated across two dimensions: number of security checks and number of finding ingestion events per account/region/month. The first 100,000 security checks are billed at $0.0010 per account/region/month; $0.0008 per check for the next 400,000 checks; and $0.0005 per check for any checks above 500,000.

Finding ingestion events per account/region/month have a perpetual free tier of 10,000 finding ingestion events, and the pricing after the first 10,000 is $0.00003 per finding ingestion event per account/region/month. Any finding ingestion events created by Security Hubs security checks are not billed to the customer.

You may be thinking, what is a finding ingestion event? Security Hub ingests findings from various AWS services and partner products to use for recommendations. Finding ingestions include new findings and updates to existing findings that are coming into Security Hub and are not associated with Security Hub's security checks. Think of this like how Amazon S3 incurs charges for PUT or COPY requests made to the S3 bucket.

It is important to remember that Security Hub is a regional service and that pricing may vary between each region where Security Hub is deployed. This also means if your AWS account is utilizing multiple regions and you want to have Security Hub actively providing recommendations, you will need to configure and enable Security Hub in each region. Resource recording in AWS Config is required for Security Hub in all accounts and in all the regions where you plan to enable Security Hub standards and controls. AWS Config bills separately for resource recording. Check out https://aws.amazon.com/config/pricing for the latest pricing details.

How AWS Security Hub Works

The first step in using Security Hub is to enable it in the region where you want to consume findings from enabled AWS services like Amazon GuardDuty, Amazon Inspector, and Amazon Macie. You can also just use Security Hub to review the findings generated by running continuous automated security checks based on AWS best practices and industry standards.

 To be fully compliant with Center for Internet Security (CIS) AWS Foundations Benchmark security checks, Security Hub must be enabled in all AWS regions.

After you enable Security Hub, it starts to aggregate, organize, and prioritize findings from any of the AWS services that are enabled, including AWS Partner Network (APN) security solutions in use by the AWS account if integration with Security Hub is available. Security Hub then consolidates findings across providers and correlates the findings to allow for prioritization and taking actions on the findings. These findings can be grouped together into insights in Security Hub. *Insights* are a collection of findings grouped by a filter and help identify common security issues that may require remediation actions. You can create custom insights or use predefined AWS managed insights to determine remediation actions.

Insight results display a set of charts summarizing the number of matching findings across security labels, AWS Account ID, Resource Type, Resource ID, and Product Name. Any custom actions configured and associated with a CloudWatch rule for the `Security Hub Insight Results` event type can be selected, and the action can run based on the rule you have configured for automated remediation.

Security Hub also uses managed insights to return results for enabled product integrations or security standards producing matching findings. Table 4.1 represents, as of this writing, the full list of managed insights available for use in Security Hub. The documentation page at `https://docs.aws.amazon.com/securityhub/latest/userguide/securityhub-managed-insights.html` should always contain the latest information available.

TABLE 4.1   Managed insights in AWS Security Hub and their grouping attribute

Managed insight name	Grouping attribute
AWS resources with the most findings	Resource identifier
S3 buckets with public write or read permissions	Resource identifier
AMIs that are generating the most findings	EC2 instance image ID
EC2 instances involved in known tactics, techniques, and procedures (TTPs)	Resource ID
AWS principals with suspicious access key activity	IAM access key principal name

Managed insight name	Grouping attribute
AWS resources instances that don't meet security standards/best practices	Resource ID
AWS resources associated with potential data exfiltration	Resource ID
AWS resources associated with unauthorized resource consumption	Resource ID
S3 buckets that don't meet security standards/best practices	Resource ID
S3 buckets with sensitive data	Resource ID
Credentials that may have leaked	Resource ID
EC2 instances that have missing security patches for important vulnerabilities	Resource ID
EC2 instances with general unusual behavior	Resource ID
EC2 instances that have ports accessible from the Internet	Resource ID
EC2 instances that don't meet security standards/best practices	Resource ID
EC2 instances that are open to the Internet	Resource ID
EC2 instances associated with adversary reconnaissance	Resource ID
AWS resources associated with malware	Resource ID
AWS Resources associated with cryptocurrency issues	Resource ID
AWS resources with unauthorized access attempts	Resource ID
Threat Intel indicators with the most hits in the last week	No Grouping Available
Top accounts by counts of findings	AWS account ID
Top products by counts of findings	Product Name
Severity by counts of findings	Severity label
Top S3 buckets by counts of findings	Resource ID
Top EC2 instances by counts of findings	Resource ID
Top AMIs by counts of findings	EC2 instance image ID

TABLE 4.1   Managed insights in AWS Security Hub and their grouping attribute *(continued)*

Managed insight name	Grouping attribute
Top IAM users by counts of findings	IAM access key user name
Top resources by counts of failed CIS checks	Resource ID
Top integrations by counts of findings	Product ARN
Resources with the most failed security checks	Resource ID
IAM users with suspicious activity	IAM username

Source: Data taken from `https://docs.aws.amazon.com/securityhub/latest/ userguide/securityhub-managed-insights.html/last accessed on 23 December 2023.`

Security Hub supports the creation of custom insights, and you can use any of the managed insights from Table 4.1 or existing custom insights as a starting point. When creating custom insights, you must have a grouping attribute, and you can add an optional filter to help narrow down the matching findings for the insight.

Security Hub also allows you to track the current status of investigations within a finding. This includes being able to send findings to a custom action for processing or remediation. Each finding has a workflow status, which tracks the progress of the investigation into a finding. Each workflow status is specific to an individual finding, and a workflow status does not impact the generation of a new finding. For example, if a workflow status for a finding is set to SUPPRESSED, that does not prevent any new findings for the same issue.

Security Hub automatically updates and deletes findings. All findings are automatically deleted if they were not updated in the past 90 days. It is important to provide updates and set the workflow status for each finding to match the status of your investigation.

Security Hub workflow status should reflect the state of investigation for each finding. The first workflow state for a finding before review is NEW. Security Hub will also reset the workflow status RecordState to NEW from a NOTIFIED or RESOLVED status if the record state changes from ARCHIVED to ACTIVE or Compliance.Status changes from PASSED to WARNING, FAILED, or NOT_AVAILABLE. Changes falling into any of these cases will indicate that additional investigation or action is required.

The next workflow state is NOTIFIED, and it indicates that the resource owner has been notified about the security issue. This is a useful workflow state to use when you are not the resource owner and you need to schedule intervention from the owner to resolve the security issue. This workflow state follows the same reset parameters as the NEW workflow state and will reset from NOTIFIED to NEW if the conditions are met.

An additional workflow state of SUPPRESSED is available that you can use to indicate that the finding has been reviewed and no action is needed. The workflow state of SUPPRESSED does not change if the RecordState changes to ACTIVE. This state is commonly used to reflect if false positives or findings that are not relevant to your organization are identified.

The last workflow status is RESOLVED. This status is used when the finding was remediated and no longer requires action or attention. The finding will remain in the resolved status unless the RecordState changes from ARCHIVED to ACTIVE or Compliance.Status changes from PASSED to FAIELD, WARNING, or NOT_AVAILABLE. When this occurs, the workflow status is automatically changed to the NEW status. Any findings will automatically move the workflow status to RESOLVED if the Compliance.Status is in a PASSED status.

Automating Remediation

Security Hub can use custom actions to automate remediation tasks using Amazon Event-Bridge. This integration allows you to use AWS services to perform remediation actions in response to system events like application availability or resource changes in near real time. Security Hub automatically sends all new findings and all updates to existing findings to EventBridge as EventBridge events. This allows you to configure simple EventBridge rules for events that you are interested in performing automated actions against. Rules can be created to trigger actions across several AWS services such as invoking AWS Lambda functions, invoking Amazon EC2 run commands, activating an AWS Step Function state machine, or notifying an Amazon SNS topic or Amazon SQS queue. Whatever the event requires, you can find an AWS service to help automate the remediation process and avoid manual human interaction where possible.

When creating rules in EventBridge, you can use a predefined pattern to create the rule that automatically fills in the source and detail type from the Security Hub event. Event-Bridge also provides filter values that you can specify to find additional attributes such as AWSAccountID, Compliance.Status, and RecordState. This means you can create an EventBridge rule using these filters to address any changes to the workflow states automatically.

Disabling Security Hub

Security Hub provides several useful reporting and security automation options within an AWS account and is a great addition for increasing security awareness and compliance documentation. However, in some cases you may need to disable Security Hub within an account. Disabling Security Hub can be accomplished from the Security Hub console or by using the Security Hub API. It is important to note that there are some conditions where you cannot disable Security Hub—for example, if you are trying to disable Security Hub in an AWS account that has been designated as a Security Hub administrator account for an AWS Organization. You may also run into issues disabling Security Hub if the account is a member account of an AWS Organization. Before you can disable Security Hub, you must disassociate the account from the administrator account, which can only be done by the administrator account.

 After Security Hub is disabled, it will retain existing findings and insights for 90 days. If you want to save existing findings, you must export them before disabling Security Hub in that region. After 90 days, the findings, insights, and configuration settings are deleted and cannot be recovered.

Amazon GuardDuty

Threat detection is an important consideration when working in the cloud. Even the best laid security plans need active monitoring and threat detection to protect AWS accounts, workloads, and data stored in the cloud. Amazon GuardDuty analyzes continuous metadata streams generated from your AWS account and any network activity found in AWS Cloud-Trail events, VPC flow logs, and DNS logs. GuardDuty uses machine learning to accurately identify threats within your AWS account, and it operates completely independently from your other AWS resources and workloads. Since GuardDuty is a managed service, we can analyze the events discovered by the tool without worrying about the underlying software, licensing, or infrastructure.

Amazon GuardDuty Pricing

GuardDuty does not have an up-front cost associated with the service but does operate using the same pay-as-you-go model that other AWS services use. You only pay for the events analyzed with no additional software to deploy or threat intelligence subscriptions required. The pricing for GuardDuty is based on the quantity of events analyzed from AWS CloudTrail and the volume of VPC flow log and DNS log data analyzed. There is no additional charge from GuardDuty for enabling events for AWS CloudTrail management events, AWS CloudTrail S3 data events, or VPC flow log and DNS log analysis.

GuardDuty offers a 30-day trial at no cost, where you have full access to the entire feature set and detections available. After the trial, Amazon CloudTrail S3 data event analysis and CloudTrail management event analysis are charged per one million events per month and are prorated, whereas VPC flow log and DNS log analysis are charged per gigabyte per month, with tiered volume discounts available. Check the GuardDuty page at https://aws .amazon.com/guardduty/pricing for the most updated pricing per region.

How GuardDuty Works

Once you enable GuardDuty within an AWS account, it begins monitoring your environment immediately. It's important to remember that GuardDuty is a regional service, and any configurations must be replicated to each region that you wish to have GuardDuty monitor. It is a security best practice to enable GuardDuty in all supported AWS regions to help monitor and generate findings about unusual or unauthorized activity in regions you may not be using. It's also best practice to enable GuardDuty to monitor CloudTrail events for global services like IAM.

When GuardDuty is enabled for the first time in any region, a service-linked role for your AWS account is created called `AWSServiceRoleForAmazonGuardDuty`. This IAM service-linked role includes permissions and trust policies that GuardDuty requires to consume and analyze events collected from CloudTrail, VPC flow logs, and DNS logs. GuardDuty also creates a detector in each region when enabled. This detector has a unique 32 alphanumeric ID that is associated with all GuardDuty findings in each region. When configuring CloudWatch event notifications and optional data sources, the detector ID is required.

GuardDuty can pull from various supported data sources in an AWS account. It uses the following data sources for detection and analysis: AWS CloudTrail event logs, CloudTrail management events, CloudTrail S3 data events, Kubernetes audit logs, VPC flow logs, and DNS logs. All logs and log data are encrypted in transit when they are sent to GuardDuty. After analysis, GuardDuty discards the logs. When GuardDuty uses global CloudTrail events for global services such as IAM and Route 53, the events will appear to come from US East (N. Virginia) and nonglobal services will appear from the region where the events are recorded.

When GuardDuty discovers a potential security issue, it creates a finding and is displayed in the GuardDuty console. You can also optionally see your GuardDuty findings through CloudWatch events by sending the findings to CloudWatch via HTTPS. This allows for further customization and remediation actions for each finding discovered. The GuardDuty console also lets you create suppression rules that allow you to hide findings that you have determined as false positives for your AWS environment. Suppression rules are a great way to limit the noise from false positives while still maintaining a complete history of all activity and only focusing on threats that matter.

> Suppression rules defined in the GuardDuty administrator account will apply to all GuardDuty member accounts. Member accounts are not able to modify suppression rules—only the administrator accounts are able to modify these rules.

GuardDuty can integrate with Security Hub and Amazon Detective to serve as a centralized location for reviewing security findings or to build data visualizations to help quickly navigate security issues. Security Hub can use GuardDuty findings, and once enabled in Security Hub, it will automatically pull in findings data to be ingested by Security Hub for review. Integrating Amazon Detective with GuardDuty allows you to create data visualizations of your resources and IP addresses interacting with the AWS environment. You can quickly pivot from GuardDuty finding details to Detective to further investigate security findings once both services are enabled.

GuardDuty for S3 Protection

GuardDuty can monitor object-level API operations when S3 protection is enabled. S3 protection helps identify potential security risks for data stored in your Amazon S3 buckets.

GuardDuty S3 protection uses CloudTrail management events and S3 data events to monitor threats against Amazon S3 resources and analyzes various kinds of activity for Amazon S3 operations. For example, GuardDuty S3 protection monitors for configuration and list events of S3 buckets such as `DeleteBuckets` and `ListBuckets`. GuardDuty also uses the S3 data events to report operations like `DeleteObject`, `PutObject`, and `GetObjects`.

Any S3 objects that you have made publicly accessible will not be processed by GuardDuty; however, it will alert when a bucket is made publicly accessible. Any events discovered based on S3 data event monitoring generates a security finding in the GuardDuty console. When GuardDuty S3 protection is disabled, GuardDuty will immediately stop consuming S3 data event and management event data and stop monitoring data stored in your S3 buckets. It is important to remember that S3 protection is enabled by default for any new detectors created by GuardDuty. If a detector was created before the addition of S3 protection, the data source must be enabled manually before event monitoring of S3 data or management events is possible.

GuardDuty for EKS Protection

GuardDuty offers Kubernetes protection, which enables the detection of suspicious activities and potential compromises in your Kubernetes clusters with Amazon EKS. Kubernetes protection is an optional enhancement and data source for GuardDuty. Amazon recommends enabling Kubernetes protection in GuardDuty to monitor and generate findings for suspicious activities within your Amazon EKS environment as a security best practice.

GuardDuty with Kubernetes protection enabled will detect threats against the Kubernetes API using the Kubernetes audit logs. The Kubernetes audit logs capture chronological API activity from users, applications, and the control plane. When enabled, Kubernetes protection will allow GuardDuty to ingest these logs from Amazon EKS and develop findings for the EKS resources. You are not required to turn on or store these logs for GuardDuty to analyze the data source and produce findings. However, if you disable Kubernetes protection, GuardDuty will immediately stop consuming Kubernetes audit logs and monitoring the EKS clusters. GuardDuty does not manage Amazon EKS control plane logging or make the Kubernetes audit logs accessible in your AWS account. If you have not enabled Kubernetes audit logs for use in your account, you will not have access to view this data.

Amazon GuardDuty Finding Types

What good is having several data sources evaluated and findings produced if you do not review, analyze, and remediate based on those findings? Well, it would be good if you were a digital data hoarder and looking to fill S3 buckets full of log information for fun. For everyone else, it is extremely important to frequently review GuardDuty findings and process remediations as it allows you to keep a pulse on the security posture of your AWS environment. The first step in learning how to review GuardDuty findings is to understand what types of findings are available.

GuardDuty can provide findings for Amazon EC2 resources, and they will always have a resource type of `Instance`. GuardDuty will assign a resource role, which indicates if the EC2 instance was the target or the instigator of the activity. This is extremely useful information when tracking down potential security issues, but it is still a security best practice to examine the resource in question to determine whether it is behaving as expected rather than relying on the findings report. Think of this as a trust-but-verify situation where you should confirm the findings. You may determine that the findings are expected, and false positives need to have suppression rules added. Amazon EC2 findings within GuardDuty have various topics you can evaluate for findings such as Backdoor, Cryptocurrency, Impact, Recon, Trojan, and Unauthorized Access. When GuardDuty detects anomalies in any of these topic areas, it records the event as a finding for you to review in the GuardDuty console.

GuardDuty also provides finding types related to Amazon S3. These findings are specific to Amazon S3 resources and will have a resource type of S3Bucket when related to the S3 CloudTrail data event data source, or a resource type of AccessKey if related to the Cloud-Trail management event data source. Amazon recommends examining permissions on the bucket or any users involved when a finding is made by GuardDuty using the S3 Bucket type finding. GuardDuty uses the following S3 finding types: Discovery, Exfiltration, Impact, Pen-Test, Policy, Stealth, and Unauthorized Access.

IAM finding types within GuardDuty are specific to IAM entities and access keys and will have a resource type of AccessKey. GuardDuty uses the following IAM finding types: CredentialAccess, DefenseEvasion, Discovery, Exfiltration, Impact, InitialAccess, PenTest, Persistence, Policy, PrivilegeEscalation, Recon, Stealth, and Unauthorized Access. Amazon recommends reviewing GuardDuty IAM findings and examining the entity in question to ensure that permissions follow the best practice of least privilege. These finding types assist in determining whether IAM credentials have been compromised.

The final finding type is related to Kubernetes and is specific to Kubernetes resources that have a resource type of EKSCluster. The Kubernetes finding types have the following topics evaluated by GuardDuty: CredentialAccess, DefenseEvasion, Discovery, Execution, Impact, Persistence, Policy, and PrivilegeEscalation. You should review any findings discovered by GuardDuty to determine if the activity is potentially malicious.

Reviewing GuardDuty Findings

Now that you know what the GuardDuty finding types are, you must learn how to use and understand them. When GuardDuty provides a finding, it represents a potential security issue that was detected within your network or detects unexpected or potentially malicious activity. To view and manage findings within GuardDuty, you use the Amazon GuardDuty console on the Findings page. You can also view findings within GuardDuty by using the GuardDuty CLI or API operations.

GuardDuty findings are assigned different security levels and values that reflect the potential risk the finding could have within your AWS environment. Severity values range from 0.1 to 8.9, with higher values indicating higher security risk within the AWS environment. GuardDuty breaks down the numerical range into High, Medium, and Low severity levels. High severity issues with a value range of 8.9 to 7.0 indicate that a resource in question may have been compromised and requires immediate remediation steps. Medium severity issues with a value range of 6.9 to 4.0 indicate suspicious activity that may deviate from normal observed behavior and investigation at your earliest convenience would be recommended.

Low severity issues will have a value range of 3.9 to 1.0 and indicate attempted suspicious activities that did not compromise the network or result in an intrusion. These findings do not require immediate action but should be evaluated for false positives and could indicate someone is looking for weak security points in your AWS environment. While all findings should be considered important, it is up to you to decide when and how to manage remediation of each finding. GuardDuty provides some suggested remediations at `https://docs.aws`
`.amazon.com/guardduty/index.html` for compromised Amazon EC2 instances, Amazon S3 buckets, AWS Credentials, and Kubernetes security issues.

GuardDuty provides sample finding data for evaluating, learning, and visualizing the various finding types. When generating sample findings, GuardDuty will create a sample for each finding type supported. Using sample data, you can plan remediation tasks and test various configurations against CloudWatch events or GuardDuty console filters. You should evaluate the sample findings within the GuardDuty console when using it for the first time. You can see an example of the sample data generated by GuardDuty in Figure 4.1.

FIGURE 4.1 GuardDuty sample findings

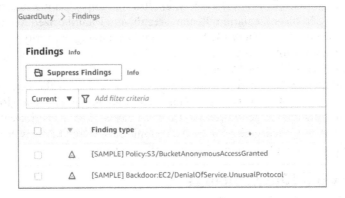

Amazon Inspector

Chances are you will run either Amazon Elastic Compute Cloud (EC2) or container workloads when migrating or running cloud native workloads in your AWS account. This means these compute workloads will need to follow security best practices and be protected from malicious code, actors, or situations. One of these protections comes in the form of vulnerability management and scanning of EC2 instances and container workloads. Sure, you could manually investigate each instance or container and use individual scans to compare findings against known vulnerabilities, but this takes time and is not scalable when working with large numbers of instances or containers. Alternatively, and most preferably, you would use Amazon Inspector to automate the process of scanning for vulnerabilities within EC2 instances and container workloads.

When performing security and vulnerability scans within an AWS account, you should always consider removing as much operational overhead as possible when deploying and configuring the vulnerability management solution. Inspector offers automated discovery and continual scanning to deliver near-real-time vulnerability findings all controlled by a centralized management, configuration, and view of findings within the Inspector console. The console also offers a dashboard that lets you view coverage metrics for accounts, EC2 instances, and Amazon Elastic Container (ECR) repositories scanned by Inspector.

Amazon Inspector Pricing

As with several security services within AWS, there is a free trial for you to evaluate the service and further refine continued running costs after the trial. Inspector offers a 15-day free trial and continually scans EC2 instances and container images pushed to ECR at no cost. To help with cost estimation after the free trial, Inspector also offers a review of estimated spend in the Inspector console.

After the 15-day free trial, if you continue to use Inspector for vulnerability scanning you will be charged monthly based on a combination of two dimensions: the number of Amazon EC2 instances being scanned, and the total number of container images initially scanned when sent to ECR or rescanned during a month. For EC2 instances, you are billed based on the average number of EC2 instances assessed for vulnerabilities in that month. Any instances that are running on an intermittent schedule will impact the cost of Inspector by prorating total time run within a month. ECR container images incur Inspector costs on the initial push to ECR as it scans the container image for software vulnerabilities and the number of times those images are rescanned per month. Just as with other AWS services, you only pay for what you use, and there are no minimum fees or up-front commitments. Always be sure to visit the pricing documentation at https://aws.amazon.com/inspector/pricing for the most updated pricing. Each region may have a different price per instance or per image scan, which you should consider when designing an implementation plan for Inspector.

How Amazon Inspector Works

Amazon Inspector is a regional service and must be configured for each region that has resources you want scanned and monitored for vulnerabilities. Inspector also utilizes Systems Manager (SSM) agents installed and enabled on EC2 instances to provide common vulnerabilities and exposures (CVEs) vulnerability data. The good news is this agent is pre-installed on many EC2 AMI, but it is always a good idea to verify that the SSM agent is installed and enabled when starting to use Inspector. Even if the SSM agent is not installed, Inspector will still scan EC2 instances for network reachability issues.

When you enable Inspector for the first time in any region, it will create the appropriate permissions in a globally service-linked role named AWSServiceRoleForAmazonInspector2. This role is what allows Inspector to collect and analyze VPC configurations and software package information to generate vulnerability findings. It is also a security best practice to configure an IAM user, role, or group to specifically manage Inspector following the least privilege model. Amazon provides a managed policy for use if required under the `AmazonInspector2FullAccess` name. This managed policy is a good starting point should you need to customize access for your specific needs.

You can enable Inspector in a standalone account environment or in a multi-account environment. If you want to enable a multi-account environment, you must be in the same organization as all the accounts you want to manage and have access to the AWS Organizations management account to delegate an Inspector administrator. When enabling Inspector in a standalone account environment, notice that all scan types are enabled by default and that Inspector automatically discovers and begins scanning all eligible resources. This means that EC2 instances with the AWS Systems Manager (SSM) agent installed and enabled will be scanned for vulnerabilities and exposures, as well as network reachability issues immediately after you enable Inspector. Inspector will also convert all container repositories in your private registry that are configured for basic scanning to use enhanced scanning with continual scanning. If you do not want to have continual scanning enabled, you can configure the ECR scanning settings to scan on-push-only (when writing to the ECR repository) or to scan select repositories using inclusion rules.

Inspector uses a purpose-built scanning engine that monitors your resources and open network paths that can lead to vulnerabilities or result in compromised workloads, unauthorized access, or malicious use of resources. Inspector will scan your EC2 instances when first enabled and during specific situations, such as the following:

- When you're launching a new instance
- When you're installing new software on an existing instance
- When new vulnerability and exposure data is added to the CVE item database

Similarly, ECR container images are scanned continuously when Enhanced scanning is enabled and on–push into the repository. Whenever Inspector adds a new CVE to its database, it will rescan eligible container images in ECR repositories configured with continuous scanning.

When Inspector locates a potential vulnerability that impacts one of your resources, it creates a detailed finding report. Each finding is titled according to the detected vulnerability and provides other useful information such as severity rating, information details about the affected resource like Amazon EC2 Instance ID and AMI ID, and additional details on how to remediate the reported vulnerability. Inspector will store all active findings until they are remediated, and any remediated findings are automatically deleted after 30 days. Using the Inspector console, you can assign findings with one of the following statuses: Active, Suppressed, or Closed. An Active finding is any finding that has not yet been remediated or suppressed because of the use of suppression rules. The suppressed status is used for findings that need to be hidden from most views. You can configure suppression rules to exclude findings that may be false positives or known vulnerability testing environments. Any vulnerability that is remediated will be detected automatically by Inspector and change the state of the finding to Closed. Once a finding is in the Closed state, it is removed after 30 days if no other changes are made.

Reviewing and Managing Inspector Findings

The first step in understanding Inspector findings is to learn about the different finding types available from EC2 instances and container images residing in ECR repositories. The first finding type is known as a package vulnerability finding. This finding writes exposed software packages to CVEs. Package vulnerability findings are generated for both EC2 instances and ECR container images scanned by Inspector. It is important to act on package vulnerabilities as attackers can exploit these unpatched vulnerabilities to gain access to your systems and data, or potentially to gain access to other systems and configurations.

The next finding type is networking reachability, which indicated allowed network paths to EC2 instances in your environment. When your EC2 instances have reachable TCP and UDP ports from the VPC edges, like the Internet Gateway or VPC peering connections, these findings are highlighted as they could be overly permissive. These findings are focusing on potentially misconfigured network settings such as security groups, access control lists (ACLs), or even Internet gateways that may allow potentially malicious access. Think along the lines of creating a finding for a database server that has 0.0.0.0/0 open to all IP addresses or that has other remote management ports or non-database-application-specific ports open to 0.0.0.0/0. These networking findings can help identify potential network configuration issues but, more importantly, highlight likely points of entry for malicious attacks. Inspector evaluates configurations for network paths across application load balancers, DirectConnect, elastic load balancers, elastic network interfaces, Internet gateways, network access control lists, route tables, security groups, subnets, VPCs, virtual private gateways, VPC endpoints, VPC gateway endpoints, VPC peering connections, and VPN connections. All these network paths are continually scanned to produce findings that can be viewed in the Inspector console or dashboards.

Now that you know what finding types are available, it is time to learn how to view them and plan for remediation. One of the most useful features of the Inspector console is the Finding Summary section. This section allows you to see all occurrences of a finding and then dig deeper into specific rows to view an overview of the finding, including the AWS account in which the impacted resources reside, the severity, vulnerability type, and when it was last detected. You can also see the affected packages and additional details about the vulnerability by clicking the link to the National Vulnerability Database (NVD) listing. From the summary page, you can also dig deeper into the vulnerabilities and see a brief description of the recommended remediation actions for the finding and the resources affected listed by the Resource ID and type.

Each finding will also be given a severity level by Inspector to help you assess and prioritize your findings. The severity ratings are represented as Untriaged, Informational, Low, Medium, High, or Critical. Each rating is derived from a numerical score, and the score depends on if the finding was discovered in a software package or through network reachability. Software package vulnerability scoring is derived from the NVD Common Vulnerability Scoring System (CVSS). Inspector produces the numerical score on a 1 to 10 scale that reflects the vulnerability's severity. Network reachability scoring is determined by the service, ports, and protocols that are exposed by the type of open path. The severity ratings are defined by and assigned a rating of Low, Medium, High, or Informational.

 Remember that Inspector findings can be viewed in Security Hub when you enable integration with Security Hub. This is a fantastic way to centralize all security and vulnerability information for your AWS accounts.

In the Inspector console, you can view and manage findings using groupings based on specific parameters like finding state, vulnerability, account, EC2 instance, container image, or repository. Using groupings within the console will allow you to filter down to specific types of vulnerabilities or resources to continue investigation. You can also use suppression rules based on filters to exclude findings from the findings view as needed, providing a more highly customized view of findings specific to the needs of your organization.

Now you can view the findings using the Inspector console by applying filters, using the Finding Summary, and using suppression rules. However, what happens when you want to export these findings for notifications or archival purposes? Part of the answer to that question is automatically managed by Inspector as it automatically exports findings to EventBridge, where you can create notifications or take automated remediation actions. For archival purposes, you can optionally send findings to an S3 bucket. Inspector does require that a KMS key be available and accessible by Inspector to encrypt findings sent to the S3 bucket. You will also need to ensure that Inspector has the permissions to upload objects to the bucket before generating the reports.

You have two choices when generating a report from Inspector for the findings. First, you can choose to receive the findings in a CSV or JSON format using the Inspector console, but you can generate only one report at a time. You will need to wait until the report is generated and uploaded to the S3 bucket before you can request another report.

 When exporting Inspector findings to an S3 bucket, you must ensure that the KMS key and S3 bucket is in the same region.

Inspector also offers a dashboard where you can view a snapshot of aggregate statics for your resources in the current region. The dashboard shows metrics about resource coverage and active vulnerabilities, serving as an overview for Inspector health and quick glance reporting. The dashboard displays groups of aggregated finding data for your account resources like EC2 instances with the most critical findings. While viewing the aggregate findings, you can dive deeper into analysis by viewing supporting data for the dashboard items displayed. The Environment Coverage section shows you statistics about the resources that Inspector scans, such as percentage of EC2 instances and ECR images scanned. The Critical Findings section is helpful when determining a count of critical vulnerabilities in your AWS environment and a total count of all findings. This is useful information for quick glance reporting of critical findings to perform deeper analysis on or assign to the security team for further review. The dashboard also provides a section called Risk-Based Remediations, which shows the top five software packages with critical vulnerabilities in your environment and allows you to choose a package name to see additional associated details and impacted resources.

As a SysOps administrator, you'll find that one of the most useful areas of the Inspector dashboard are the sections that help identify accounts with the most critical findings or specific resources like ECR repositories, container images, EC2 instances, or Amazon Machine Images (AMIs) with the most critical findings. These summary findings in the dashboard can help you quickly identify trends in vulnerabilities being continually deployed within an AWS account. For example, the critical AMI findings section shows the top five AMIs in your environment with the most crucial and important findings. You can use this data to develop a remediation plan where each AMI is rebuilt after patching and the found vulnerabilities are remediated.

In Exercise 4.1, you will enable Inspector in a standalone AWS account to begin scanning EC2 instances for vulnerabilities and network reachability. Note that Inspector has a 15-day trial that lets you use it at no cost. Remember to disable Inspector to avoid incurring additional costs beyond the 15-day trial.

EXERCISE 4.1

Enabling Inspector in a Standalone AWS Account

1. From the AWS Management Console, select the US-East-1 (N. Virginia) region.

2. While still in the AWS Management Console, open the Inspector console by searching for Inspector in the list of services or by using the search box.

3. Click Get Started.

4. Click Enable Amazon Inspector. Remember, this is a regional service and we have chosen US-East-1 (N. Virginia) as our region.

5. Once Inspector is enabled, you can manage the enabled scan types from the Account Management page in the Inspector console. For this exercise, we will leave both EC2 Scanning and ECR Scanning enabled.

6. We now have Inspector enabled, and it will automatically discover and scan all eligible resources.

You can leave Inspector enabled in your account for 15 days without incurring cost. If you want to leave it enabled to view reports or findings as you explore EC2 or ECR services, you should set a calendar reminder to disable the service.

Amazon Detective

As a SysOps administrator, you may be asked how to visualize and aggregate some of the findings from GuardDuty, CloudTrail logs, and VPC flow logs to assist in investigation of suspicious activities or to help identify the root cause of security findings. This is where Amazon Detective comes in to provide an automated collection process for the log data from your AWS resources as well as visualizations to help you conduct faster security investigations.

Detective offers prebuilt data aggregations and summaries to help you analyze the extent of possible security issues or findings discovered from GuardDuty findings, VPC flow logs, or CloudTrail logs. Detective uses machine learning, statistical analysis, and graph theory to generate the visualizations. These visualizations help show changes in the type and volume of activity over a selected time period, and then link those changes to GuardDuty findings. Since Detective maintains up to a year of historical event data, it allows organizations to perform more in-depth evaluations over a longer period.

Detective Pricing

Pricing for Detective follows a similar model to other AWS security services where a free trial is available. For Detective there is a free 30-day trial that enables you to use all the Detective features over the 30-day period with no limitations. After the trial is expired, Detective begins the normal monthly pricing model per region. Remember, Detective is a regional service, which means you'll be charged in each region in which it is deployed. Detective is priced based on the volume of data ingested from the various data sources used to produce the visualizations. Data is ingested from CloudTrail, VPC flow logs, and GuardDuty findings. You are charged for each gigabyte ingested into Detective per account, region, and month. Detective does not charge for data stored within the service or for enabling the log sources. As this is a regional service, that means pricing will change for each region in which Detective is enabled. Always check `https://aws.amazon.com/detective/pricing` for updated pricing information for each region in which you plan to deploy Detective.

How Detective Works

Detective extracts time-based events from the data collected in each of the log sources. The extraction of these time-based events, like login attempts, API calls, or network traffic, happens automatically through the Detective service, which also automatically ingests data from GuardDuty. Once the data is collected, Detective uses machine learning and visualization to create a unified interactive view of the resources identified from the logs. This view allows you to see the interactions and behaviors over time as a graph to dive deep into actions such as failed logon attempts or suspicious API calls within CloudTrail. These graphed behaviors allow for rapid investigation of activity that may fall out of normal operations or to identify patterns that may be indicative of security issues or unauthorized access patterns.

Detective can integrate with AWS Organizations to provide the administrator account the analytics and visualizations generated from the member accounts. Each member account must accept a graph and member invitation from the administrator account in the Account Management page of the Detective console. Organization accounts do not control whether their account is a member account. This is the role of the Detective Administrator account, which chooses the organization accounts to enable as member accounts. Member accounts do have the ability to remove their account from the behavior graph after accepting a graph invitation.

Review Reports and Findings of Detective

Detective is a powerful tool for investigating potential security issues and findings. There is an investigation process to follow when working from a GuardDuty finding or an entity. In

Detective, an *entity* is an item extracted from the incoming data. Each entity has a type that helps identify the type of object it represents. For example, an entity could be an IP address, EC2 instance, or AWS user. An entity could also be an AWS resource that you manage or an external IP address that has interacted with your AWS resources.

When investigating a finding or entity, you will progress through phases of investigation known as Triage, Scoping, and Response. The Tirage stage is where the investigation starts because you received a notification about a suspected high-risk or suspected malicious activity, or you were assigned to investigate alerts or findings presented by GuardDuty. This is the phase where you decide if the issue is genuinely a security issue or a false positive. If the issue is a false positive, the process stops here, and you document that it is a false positive. If you decide that the issue is genuine, you continue on to the Scoping phase.

In the Scoping phase, you are determining the extent of the activity and the underlying cause. In this phase, you use the Detective visualizations to identify other entities involved or affected by the activity. The purpose here is to help answer the What, Where, How, and What Else questions. Investigation should help uncover what systems and users were compromised, where the attack originated, how long it has been going on, and whether there are any other related activities. Once you can answer these questions, you move on to the next phase of investigation known as Response. The Response phase is both the simplest phase and the most difficult phase in this process. It is considered simple because it is the last step and you just need to respond to the attack to stop it, minimize the damage, or prevent future attacks like this from happening. It is considered difficult because the work to accomplish the prior goals can take a considerable amount of time, effort, and resources to complete. However, with the AWS security tools available within your accounts, it becomes increasingly easier to mitigate, document, and prevent issues presented in Detective.

Detective has several methods for viewing and locating entities or findings. The first and most likely starting point for any investigation would be the Summary page. The Summary page is where you can go to identify entities that are associated with specific types of unusual activity. For example, say you are assigned to investigate unusual network activity from an external IP address that has repeatedly accessed one of your EC2 instances. From the Summary page, located in the Detective console navigation pane, you can identify entities like EC2 instances that had the largest volume of traffic, or entities involved in an activity that occurred in a new geolocation. Each Summary page panel gives you the opportunity to pivot to the profile for a selected entity. A profile is a single page that provides a collection of data visualizations related to activity for a specific entity. Profiles are used to find supporting information for an investigation and help answer the questions used in the Scoping phase of investigation.

Data Protection Strategies

Amazon takes data protection and privacy very seriously, as you can tell by the numerous AWS services provided to help you protect your data, accounts, and workloads from unauthorized access. These data protection services provide key management for encryption, detection, and protection of sensitive data at scale; mechanisms to rotate, manage, and retrieve secrets used within applications; and methods to provision, manage, and deploy public and private SSL/TLS certificates.

As a SysOps administrator, you will collaborate with various teams within your organization to develop or maintain a data protection strategy when operating in the AWS Cloud. Understanding the services that are frequently used to support data classification, protection, and encryption is critical to developing the appropriate strategy for your organization and customer needs.

AWS Key Management Service

Securing data across AWS services is an essential component of a good data privacy and protection strategy. Using a managed service like AWS Key Management Service (KMS) can enable you to create and control the keys used for cryptographic operations. AWS KMS is a highly available key generation, storage, management, and auditing service for AWS account owners to encrypt or digitally sign data. This service allows you to encrypt and digitally sign data within your own applications or control encryption of data across AWS services through integration.

Central management of encryption operations is necessary when working with any scale of applications or AWS accounts. It just makes sense to keep all encryption keys used for securing and accessing your data in a centralized management environment. This reduces operational complexity and provides improved documentation and improved security controls of who can and cannot create or use encryption keys. AWS KMS is a regional service, which means keys generated in Northern Virginia will not be available in Sydney unless you share the keys into the other regions.

KMS allows you to generate, manage, and use asymmetric keys for digital signing or encryption options where you do not require certificates. This means that KMS should be used between already trusted entities, or you have other mechanisms to prove identity to achieve your encryption and security benefits. This differs from AWS Certificate Manager (ACM), where the purpose is to provide a public key infrastructure (PKI) for the purpose of identifying entities and securing network connections. When you must enable verification of any sender or recipient identity between parties that are untrusted, you would be using ACM and not KMS.

AWS Key Management Service Pricing

Pricing for AWS KMS follows the same model as other AWS services using the pay-as-you-go model. You only pay for what you use, and there are no minimum fees each month. KMS also does not require setup fees or commitments to use the service, and the service is eligible for use within the AWS Free Usage Tier in all regions. This means that KMS has free tier usage that provides a free number of API requests to the service each month. It is important to note that there are some exclusions to the free tier API requests. Any API requests involving asymmetric KMS keys are not included in the free tier offering. API requests to the GenerateDataKeyPair and GenerateDataKeyPairWithoutPlaintext are also excluded from the free tier. KMS provides 20,000 requests per month covered under free tier usage. Free tier usage is calculated across all regions in which the KMS service is available. If you are using KMS in Northern Virginia and Sydney, the free tier request amount will be consumed by both regions.

The pricing model for KMS is straightforward. Each KMS key, whether it is symmetric or asymmetric, that you create will cost $1.00 per month. This price is also the same for multiregion keys, keys with imported key material, or keys in custom key stores. An additional cost of $1.00 per month will enable automatic key rotation where each newly generated backing key costs the additional $1.00 a month. You are paying to have KMS store and retain the previous versions of the key material to enable decryption of older ciphertexts.

Good news; there are some things that you are not charged for within KMS. Any creation and storage of AWS-managed or AWS-owned keys is not charged to your AWS account because you do not have the ability to manage the life cycle or access permissions of these keys. They are entirely under the management of AWS, and you are allowed to use them when encrypting a resource in an AWS service that integrates with KMS, like S3. KMS also does not charge for customer-managed keys that are on a deletion schedule, but if you cancel the deletion during the waiting period you will incur the charges as if the key was available the entire time. Lastly, when KMS generates data keys or data key pairs, there are no monthly charges beyond the charge for the API call.

One important thing to remember about AWS KMS pricing is that each region has a different pricing scale. When designing a data protection strategy with KMS, be sure to check `https://aws.amazon.com/kms/pricing` to factor in any regional price changes. AWS KMS pricing outside of the free tier bills per 10,000 requests. For example, in Northern Virginia you are billed at $0.03 per 10,000 requests and $0.10 per 10,000 ECC `GenerateDataKeyPair` requests. Requests involving asymmetric requests except for RSA 2048 and RSA `GenerateDataKeyPair` are also billed at a separate rate per 10,000 requests. Depending on the needs of your organization and your data protection strategy, you may need to utilize a variety of key types. Always be sure to check the pricing page when factoring in the cost of using KMS.

How AWS Key Management Service Works

You now understand about pricing and the general need for using AWS KMS within your data protection strategy, but how does KMS work if you want to use it for encryption in your AWS account? The entire process starts by requesting the creation of an AWS KMS key. The key is your starting point. You have control over the life cycle and permissions of the KMS key, which means you can determine who will be able to use or manage the key once it is created. The KMS service has hardware security modules (HSMs) that are managed by AWS and used for generation of the key material when creating a key. Of course, you can always import your own key material and associate it with the KSM key if your security policies or organization require this. Alternatively, if you have chosen to use a custom key store feature in KMS, you can generate the key materials in AWS CloudHSM. Once the key material is generated by KMS, you can submit data directly to the service for signing, encryption, or decryption using this new KMS key.

When creating a key in KMS, you must decide between using a symmetric KMS key or an asymmetric KMS key. Which key you use will entirely depend on what you plan on using the KMS key for. A symmetric key is a single 256-bit secret encryption key, which will never leave KMS unencrypted. Using the symmetric key requires a call to KMS. You will use this type of key when encrypting and decrypting data within AWS, and the accounts or services using this type of key must have access to KMS and the proper permissions to utilize the key. An asymmetric KMS key is a public and private key pair that can be used for either encryption and decryption, or signing and verification; however, it cannot be used for both. This is important when determining how many keys your data protection strategy will require when using asymmetric KMS keys. The asymmetric private key never leaves KMS unencrypted, but you can use the public key within KMS using API operations, or if needed, you can download the public key and use it outside of KMS. If you require encryption outside of AWS by users who cannot call KMS, using an asymmetric key is a good choice.

Another use case for asymmetric keys is performing public key encryption, where you can have external AWS parties or applications use the public key to encrypt data, and when needed, you can use the Decrypt operation in KMS to decrypt the data using the public key. It's important to note that when downloading public keys and sharing them outside of KMS, the keys are no longer under the security controls and protections that KMS offers. If you are going to export public keys, always ensure that you are following security best practices by limiting the authorization and sharing of these public keys to only required entities.

AWS has made a change to the terms for some keys in KMS. All references to customer master key (CMK) are replaced with AWS KMS key and KMS key. When browsing documentation or implementing KMS keys, you may see mentions of CMK as AWS is avoiding breaking changes while rolling out the name change across services.

Why Is Envelope Encryption Important?

KMS has a limit on the size of data that can be encrypted using the KMS key. A KMS key is a logical representation of an encryption key and includes the key material to encrypt or decrypt data, as well as metadata like creation date, key state, and description. The KMS key is used to encrypt or decrypt data, but KMS has a limit of 4 KB of data that the service can directly encrypt or decrypt. To encrypt larger datasets using an AWS KMS key, you will use a practice called *envelope encryption*. Envelope encryption is the process of encrypting plaintext data with a data key, and then encrypting that data key with another key. Figure 4.2 summarizes the process of envelope encryption using KMS.

Using envelope encryption, you can encrypt large datasets across S3, EBS, or any other AWS service that can integrate with KMS. The process is straightforward; an API request is sent to KMS to generate the data key using the KMS key. KMS returns the response with a plaintext data key and an encrypted data key. The encrypted data key is encrypted with the KMS key. The data is encrypted using the plaintext data key, and then the key is removed from memory. The encrypted data and the encrypted data key are then moved into a package together and stored. This packaging is called an envelope, and once it is created, the data is stored encrypted at rest.

FIGURE 4.2 AWS KMS envelope encryption process

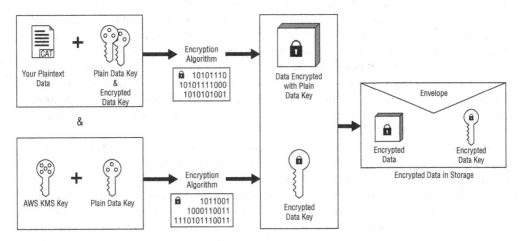

Decryption of an envelope is a similar process, where the encrypted data key is extracted from the envelope, and an API request is sent to KMS using the key that has information about the KMS key that is needed to decrypt the information. KMS will then respond with the plaintext data key used to decrypt the data. When the decryption process is completed, the plaintext data key is removed from memory. That's it! Knowing how envelope encryption works is a key step to using KMS in a data protection strategy.

Required Permissions for Creating KMS Keys

What would a security service be without a permission set to control access and ensure only those permitted to use the service can? That's right—it would not be a particularly good one. As with all services in the AWS Cloud, you must have the proper IAM permissions to access, create, and manage keys in KMS. Let start with a best practice. We all know it is an AWS best practice to use the least privilege model using IAM users when accessing services within the AWS Cloud. KMS is no different and should have an IAM user that has access to create, manage, and delete keys as an administrator. All other users and principals who need to create KMS keys should be managed by an IAM policy.

Be cautious when granting permission to manage tags and aliases within the AWS KMS service. Changing tags or an alias can allow or deny permissions to the KMS key that are set up using attribute-based access control (ABAC).

When creating an IAM policy for a user or principal who requires key creation permissions in KMS, you must confirm that `kms:CreateKey` is included in the IAM policy. If your data protection strategy requires the use of aliases or tags, you will also need to ensure that `kms:CreateAlias` and `kms:TagResource` is included in the policy. You also need to evaluate if the user will be required to create multiregion keys as `iam:CreateServiceLinkedRole` will be required in the policy to enable this feature for the IAM user or principal. One important thing to remember when creating KMS keys is that the key belongs to the AWS account that created the key, not the IAM user. This means the IAM user does not automatically have permission to use or manage the KMS key that was created. To work with the key, the key creator must grant permission through a key policy, IAM policy, or grant function. However, when a principal has the `kms:CreateKey` permission, they can set the initial policy and give themselves permissions for key use and management.

KMS permissions have some nuances that you should remember when working with keys. Statements in a key policy is what determines who has permission to use the KMS key and what actions they can perform with the key. While it is optional for a KMS key to have IAM policies and grants to control key access, every KMS key must have a key policy, which differs from IAM policy as the key policy is regional. It is also important to know that every principal, including the key creator, does not have permissions to a KMS key unless explicitly allowed in a key policy, IAM policy, or grant. If a principal is denied anywhere in a key policy or IAM policy, they will never gain access to the key.

The key policy also has built-in protections to ensure that the keys do not become unmanageable, and this is called the default key policy statement. The default key policy statement allows the account to use IAM policies to allow access to the KMS key, as well as the key policy itself. If the default key policy statement was not present, this would render IAM policies ineffective when granting access to KMS keys. This default key policy also ensures that the root user in the account will never lose access because access cannot be restricted for the root user.

Another critical piece to using KMS keys is understanding how grants are used and how they control cryptographic operations. A grant is simply a policy mechanism that allows AWS principals to use KMS keys when encrypting or decrypting data. You can also use a grant to allow the `DescribeKey` operation and create or manage grants. Wow, that's great, but when would you use a grant over an IAM policy or key policy? The answer is in the longevity of the permission required. Grants are typically used for temporary permissions because you can create a grant, perform the operation, and then remove the Grant All permission without needing to modify a key policy or IAM policy. This adds the power of flexibility and simplified automation when granting access to cryptographic operations. AWS services that integrate with KMS, like EBS, will use grants when encrypting data at rest. The service will create a grant on behalf of the user in the account, perform the operation using the permissions of that account, and then remove the grant once the task is completed. This operation occurs when using KMS keys to encrypt EBS volumes. Remember, each grant allows access to exactly one KMS key. You will need to create different grants when performing actions against a different key in the same account or a different key in another AWS account. As always, be careful when creating grants and when giving permissions to create grants as this can create security implications that may go against your organization's security policies or account governance. Remember, it is important to protect your KMS keys and follow the least privilege model when creating grants, key policies, and IAM permissions.

Rotating AWS KMS Keys

Speaking of protecting KMS keys, best practices discourage the extensive reuse of encryption keys. In short, this means that you should rotate your keys. Key rotation is creating new cryptographic material for your KMS keys, creating a new KMS key, and then making the necessary changes in your applications or aliases to use the newly created keys. This process can be done manually, or you can choose to enable automatic key rotation for a KMS key. When enabling automatic key rotation, KMS manages the new key generation and saves all previous versions of the cryptographic material in perpetuity. KMS saves this key material so that you can decrypt any data that was previously encrypted with any of the rotated key material. This data is saved until you delete the KMS key in AWS KMS. Automatic key rotation is only available for symmetric KMS keys. When setting up a key rotation policy, you will need to manually rotate asymmetric KMS keys and KMS keys in custom key stores.

Wait, do you mean, my keys change and I must update my application every year? No way! That's a lot of work! Well, no, not exactly. Key rotation changes only the KMS key's key material. This is the cryptographic material that was used to generate the key and is used in encryption operations. The KMS key itself remains the same logical resource no matter if you rotate the key manually 100 times, or if AWS handles the automatic key rotation every year. The Key ID stays the same and your applications do not need to change to refer to a new Key ID or alias. Automatic key rotation is a fantastic way to ensure that you are protecting your keys and the data that is encrypted by the AWS KMS keys. However, it is important to note that when a key rotates it doesn't retroactively encrypt data with the new key that was previously encrypted with the old key or mitigate the effect of a compromised key. Therefore, it is especially important to ensure that key policies, grants, and IAM policies are protecting access and use of the keys.

There are some other key rotations that occur within KMS that you should be aware of. AWS-managed keys are automatically rotated every three years (1,095 days) and you cannot manage this key rotation. These are keys in your account that are created, managed, and used on your behalf by AWS services integrated with KMS, like CloudWatch logs, Athena, and Amazon ElastiCache. Similarly, you cannot control the rotation schedule for AWS-owned keys. These keys and the rotation schedule are determined by the AWS service that creates and manages the key.

Implementing Encryption at Rest

AWS KMS keys can be used within your data protection strategy to ensure that data is encrypted at rest, meaning when not moving from point to point, but when it reaches the destination and is in data storage. Various AWS services like EBS, S3, and AWS Systems Manager Parameter Store use KMS to encrypt data at rest. Let's explore some options for EBS and S3 when using KMS for encryption.

S3 offers two KMS-related methods for encrypting data within an S3 bucket. The first option is to use AWS Key Management Service Keys (SSE-KMS) with an AWS-managed service key (aws/s3). This allows AWS to manage the KMS key in its entirety, including rotation and permissions. This is a perfectly good option to use if you do not have any governance requirements to use your own KMS-generated key or if you do not need to rotate your keys more frequently than every three years. If you need to rotate your keys more frequently, or if you want to manage the KMS key creation yourself, you can use the option to use your own AWS KMS key. From here, you can select a preexisting key or create one from the S3 console that fits your needs.

Now any object that is uploaded to S3 will be encrypted at rest using the KMS key of your choice. One thing to keep in mind if you have an active bucket with millions of active objects is that it can generate large volumes of requests to KMS and potentially drive up API costs. This is due to S3 protecting data with your SSE-KMS key that creates an individual KMS data key for every object by making calls against KMS every time a request is made against an encrypted object. To prevent potentially large volumes of overhead API calls to KMS, you can enable the S3 Bucket key for SSE-KMS, and AWS will generate a bucket-level key that is used to create unique data keys for new objects added in a bucket. This cuts down on the calls back to KMS by localizing data key operations to the S3 Bucket key. This reduces the need for S3 to make requests to KMS to complete encryption operations and reduces traffic from S3 to KMS. If you enable S3 Bucket keys on an existing bucket, any existing objects will not use the S3 Bucket key. If you want existing objects to use the new S3 Bucket key, you simply need to run a COPY operation on the objects you wish to use the S3 Bucket keys.

In Exercise 4.2, you will create an AWS KMS symmetric key to use when encrypting data within an S3 bucket. This key can also be used across other KMS-integrated services like DynamoDB and EBS. Always refer to your organization's encryption and security policies for guidance on use of different encryption keys per AWS service.

EXERCISE 4.2

Creating an AWS KMS Key for SSE-KMS Use in S3 and an AWS KMS Key for EBS Encryption Using the AWS CLI

1. From the AWS Management Console, locate the AWS Key Management Service (AWS KMS) and open the AWS KMS Management Console.

2. From the KMS console, click Customer Managed Keys in the left navigation pane.

3. Click Create Key and choose the Symmetric key type. This key will be used for Encrypt and Decrypt data at rest and not digitally signing or verifying operations. For this exercise, we will be creating a Single-Region key in Advanced Options, so you can safely ignore the advanced options. Click Next to continue.

4. Type an alias for the KMS key you are creating. As we are creating a key for S3, you can use an alias such as **s3kmskey** to signify the use of the key in the name.

Remember, in a production environment the KMS key alias can be used for attribute-based access controls and, as such, you should consult with your organization's security or naming convention policy to ensure compliance.

5. You can optionally supply a description of the key. Typically, this can be a single sentence to describe the purpose of the key for future documentation.

6. You can also optionally enter tags to help track AWS costs. This can be useful when viewing the cost allocation report as each tag is represented when attached to an AWS resource. For this exercise, you will skip adding any tags to the AWS KMS key and click Next to continue creating the key.

7. Now you must define the permissions for the key. Under the Key Administrator section ensure that your AWS IAM user is listed. Note: If you are running this exercise from your root AWS account, please proceed to the IAM service, create a new IAM user with Administrator privileges, log out, and then log back in with the IAM user and restart this exercise.

8. Next, ensure that the Allow Key Administrators To Delete This Key option is selected and click Next to continue the key creation process.

9. You must now define who can use the key that you are creating. Ensure that your IAM user is listed under This Account and click Next. If you were allowing other AWS accounts, such as a developer account or shared services account, to use this AWS KMS key, you would add the AWS account number under the Other AWS Accounts section.

10. Now it's time to review the settings used for the KMS key and adjust the key policy if needed. Here you can modify the key policy itself to include conditionals if needed. For this exercise, you will skip modifying the policy directly and accept the default policy configuration. Once you have finished reviewing the policy, click Finish.

11. That's it! You just created your first AWS KMS symmetric key to use for encrypting data at rest! Now you can configure S3 to use this KMS key by enabling encryption on the S3 bucket and choosing the KMS key that you just created.

The next step in this exercise is to create another KMS key for use in encrypting EBS volumes using the AWS CLI. Ensure that you have the AWS CLI installed and configured using your administrator IAM user. You can use the AWS CLI documentation page at https://docs.aws.amazon.com/cli/latest/userguide/getting-started-install.html if you have trouble installing and configuring the CLI.

12. Open the AWS CLI from your local computer. Use the command **aws --version** to verify that you are running version 2.5.2 or higher.

13. Next, we need to create a KMS key for the purpose of encrypting an EBS volume. Type **aws kms create-key help** to view the documentation for creating keys in KMS.

14. Once you have read the documentation, you can create our AWS KMS key. You will create a new key and add tags to help identify the purpose of the key. In the AWS CLI, type `aws kms create-key --tags TagKey="Purpose",TagValue="EBS Encryption" --description " Encrypt EBS volumes"`. This command will generate a new AWS KMS key with the tag key of Purpose and the value of EBS Encryption. The key will also have a description that helps explain the purpose of the key. You should receive output like the following:

```
{
    "KeyMetadata": {
        "AWSAccountId": "123456789012",
        "KeyId": "827cb77a-XXXX-XXXX-XXXX-e9d08db53ff5",
        "Arn": "arn:aws:kms:us-east-1:123456789012:key/827cb77a-XXXX-XXXX-XXXX-
e9d08db53ff5",
        "CreationDate": "2022-04-07T18:53:58.536000-05:00",
        "Enabled": true,
        "Description": "Encrypt EBS volumes",
        "KeyUsage": "ENCRYPT_DECRYPT",
        "KeyState": "Enabled",
        "Origin": "AWS_KMS",
        "KeyManager": "CUSTOMER",
        "CustomerMasterKeySpec": "SYMMETRIC_DEFAULT",
        "KeySpec": "SYMMETRIC_DEFAULT",
        "EncryptionAlgorithms": [
            "SYMMETRIC_DEFAULT"
        ],
        "MultiRegion": false
    }
}
```

15. The key has now been generated. Next we need to create an alias for the key to make management easier. From the AWS CLI, run the command `aws kms create-alias --alias name alias/ebsencryption --target-key-id <KeyId>`. You will be able to find the KeyId from the output of the `create-key` command. Note: Do not include the <> symbols as part of your command.

16. Now that the alias is created, you will need to verify the alias using the AWS CLI. In the CLI, type the command `aws kms list-aliases --key-id <KeyId>` using the KeyId generated by AWS KMS during the `create-key` and `create-alias` commands. You should receive output like the following:

```
{
    "Aliases": [
        {
```

```
            "AliasName": "alias/ebsencryption",
            "AliasArn": "arn:aws:kms:us-east-1:123456789012:alias/
    ebsencryption",
            "TargetKeyId": "827cb77a-XXXX-XXXX-XXXX-e9d08db53ff5",
            "CreationDate": "2022-04-07T18:59:37.468000-05:00",
            "LastUpdatedDate": "2022-04-07T18:59:37.468000-05:00"
        }
    ]
}
```

That's it! You just created a new AWS KMS key to encrypt EBS volumes. When creating an EBS volume, you can select the Encrypt option and use the AWS KMS key you just created.

To clean up after this exercise, you can schedule deletion of the keys you just created. You can do this from the AWS Management Console under the KMS service. To delete the key, select the check box next to the key in the AWS KMS Management Console and click Key Actions, then Schedule Key Deletion. I suggest setting the key deletion waiting period to 7 days.

AWS Certificate Manager

Data protection strategies should also include how to protect data in transit as it moves from service to service or from its source to any other destination. Within AWS it is a best practice to use Secure Sockets Layer/Transport Layer Security (SSL/TLS) certificates when working with internally connected resources. SSL/TLS certificates can be used to establish the identity of websites over the Internet or private networks, as well as to secure network communications. This means you can use the SSL/TLS certificates to encrypt traffic from the source to the destination, also known as *in transit*, to ensure that the data being sent is protected.

This is where AWS Certificate Manager (ACM) enters the data protection strategy as an AWS-integrated service that offers SSL/TSL certificates. ACM helps SysOps administrators by removing the time-consuming manual process of provisioning and renewing SSL/TLS certificates. ACM certificates can be deployed on AWS resources such as elastic load balancers, CloudFront distributions, and API endpoints on API Gateway. The certificates generated by ACM are also capable of being used for private internal resources on AWS to verify identity of resources on a private network like IoT devices, servers, and applications. When issuing private certificates using ACM, you will need to configure ACM Private Certificate Authority (CA), which handles the issuance, validation, and revocation of these private certificates. ACM Private CA eliminates administration overhead and security limitations of self-signed certificates often used to protect private networks. ACM provides the controls and availability to prevent the risk of outages related to certificate expirations often found when using self-signed certificates.

AWS Certificate Manager Pricing

Pricing for AWS Certificate Manager differs when certificates are used with ACM-integrated services like Elastic Load Balancing or CloudFront, or if you are using private certificates with AWS Certificate Manager Private CA. When you use certificates with ACM-integrated services, there is no cost for certificates—you just pay for the resources you create to run your applications. When you use ACM Private CA, it follows the normal pay as you go pricing model, including a monthly fee for the operation of each ACM Private CA in operations. You pay this monthly fee for each ACM Private CA until you delete it. Private certificates created and exported from ACM will have an additional cost.

As of this writing, the ACM Private CA monthly cost is $400 for each ACM Private CA in operation until you delete it, and it is prorated for partial months. When generating a private certificate, you are charged a one-time fee within the account that issues the certificate. Like many AWS services, there are pricing tiers that lower the cost per certificate the more you use. ACM Private CA charges $0.75 for 1–1,000 certificates generated; $0.35 for 1,001–10,000; and $0.001 for 10,001 and above. The more certificates generated within the ACM Private CA, the lower the cost. If you need Online Certificate Status Protocol (OSCP) enabled, you will also pay a monthly fee for OSCP response generation. You only pay for the total number of OSCP queries made for your certificates. If ACM Private CA generated an OSCP response for a certificate, there is a $.06 per certificate per month charge and $0.20 per 100,000 OSCP queries, which is billed on a per-CA basis. Good news, though: AWS Private CA also offers a 30-day free trial for any account new to ACM Private CA—you only pay for the certificates you issue during the trial period. Always be sure to check the latest pricing information at `https://aws.amazon.com/certificate-manager/pricing` when designing the use of ACM for your data protection strategy.

> Remember, AWS Certificate Manager is a regional service. If you need to issue public or private certificates for your applications, Elastic Load Balancing, or API Gateway APIs, you will need to configure ACM in that region. When using ACM for CloudFront you must request or import the certificate in the US East (N. Virginia) region. CloudFront-associated ACM certificates in this region are distributed to all geographic locations configured for a CloudFront distribution.

How AWS Certificate Manager Works

At the most basic level, ACM creates, stores, and renews public and private SSL/TLS X.509 certificates and keys. These certificates and keys protect your websites and applications running on AWS. ACM provides the ability to import third-party certificates into the ACM management system to simplify certificate management for applications that require third-party certificates. ACM is used to secure any mixture of wildcard, singular, or multiple specific domain names used by your applications in AWS. The largest benefit of ACM is the automated renewal of expiring certificates managed by the service.

Requesting certificates with ACM requires that you have a registered fully qualified domain name (FQDN) that can be hosted in Route 53 or any of the commercial registrars available today. You will need to ensure that you can validate that you own the domain name you are configuring with ACM, and this can happen through email validation or using a Certification Authority Authorization (CAA) DNS record. You will need a working email address registered in your domain to process email validation. AWS recommends using DNS validation if you have access to modify the DNS records for the domain. If you choose email validation, remember that you must act every year to process certification renewals; ACM sends renewal notices 45 days before expiration to the domain's WHOIS mailbox email addresses and to five common administrator addresses. When using DNS validation, you must create a CAA record, which ACM uses to validate that it can issue a certificate for you, and these CAA records must remain attached to domain DNS records. ACM will also require you to create one or more CNAME records that contain a unique key-value pair that serves as proof that you control the domain. If ACM can't validate the domain within 72 hours, with either form of validation, the validation will fail, and the certificate status will change to `Validation timed out` in the ACM Management Console.

Requesting Public Certificates

Once the domain has been validated for use within ACM, you can begin requesting and issuing certificates for use in your applications and ACM-integrated services. The first step is to request a public certificate and supply the necessary domain names and type of certificate you need. This creation process is managed through the ACM Management Console, and you will need to determine if a wildcard or bare, or apex, domain name will be used. For example, if you wanted the certificate to support `my.catsdomainname.com`, `store.catsdomainname.com`, and all other subdomains in the leftmost position of the domain name, you will need to use the `*.catsdomainname.com` wildcard. The wildcard name will appear in the Subject field and the Subject Alternative Name extension of the ACM certificate.

Remember that wildcard certificates using the asterisk (*) must be in the leftmost position of the domain name and that it protects only one domain level. Wildcard certificates will only protect the subdomains and not the bare or apex domain. For example, wildcard certifications of `*.example.com` will protect `test.example.com` and `login.example.com` but not `example.com`. To protect both, you will need to add another name to the certificate of `example.com`.

After you configure the names to be listed on the certificate, ACM will ask whether you want to use DNS validation or email validation. Depending on which validation method you select, you will either respond to an email or ACM will validate against the CAA and CNAME records listed for your domain in DNS. This is a protection put in place to ensure that you retain ownership of a domain before issuing certificates. You can also use tagging with ACM to help identify certificates that belong to a specific department, project, or purpose. This is an optional but highly recommended step. Once the certificate is requested, it will enter a pending validation step for up to 72 hours before processing the certificate or failing the validation check. Certificates that can be validated using DNS methods will typically be issued in a few minutes, whereas email validation can take significantly longer.

Importing Certificates into AWS Certificate Manager

An additional feature of ACM is the ability to import certificates obtained outside of AWS for management. Imported certificates from a third party can be used with any ACM-integrated service and will function the same as those provided by ACM itself, with one very important exception: ACM will not provide renewal services for imported certificates. This means you must still manually configure and update the certificates each time they are scheduled to expire before a renewal is completed. To renew imported certificates, you must process the renewal with the third party that issued the certificate and then reimport the certificate into ACM. This maintains the certificate's association and Amazon Resource Name (ARN), resulting in no loss of configuration or association with ACM-integrated services using the certificate.

To import a third-party or self-signed SSL/TLS certificate into ACM, you must have both the certificate and its private key. If importing a third-party certificate signed by a non-AWS certificate authority (CA), you must also include the private key, the certificate, and the public certificate chain. Most third-party certificate providers will allow you to download the certificate chain, the certificate, and the private key as a single package. Importing a certificate also requires that the certificate be valid at the time of import. This means you cannot import an expired certificate or one that has not yet started the validity period as indicated in the certificate's `NotBefore` and `NotAfter` fields.

Importing certificates into ACM also requires you to encode each component in Privacy-Enhanced Mail (PEM) format. This means the certificate, private key, and certificate chain must be in the PEM format before importing. While AWS does not provide any resources or tools for you to convert your certificates into PEM format, the process is straightforward. Remember, you will need to have three separate PEM files for the certificate, private key, and certificate chain. Figure 4.3 shows the format that a PEM-encoded certificate would need when edited in a text editor.

Monitoring and Logging of Certificates

AWS Certificate Manager supports the use of CloudWatch metrics and CloudWatch events to perform notifications and take automated actions against ACM certificates. For example, you can use CloudWatch metrics in the `AWS/CertificateManager` namespace to view, alert, or react to the `DaysToExpiry` metric, which indicates the number of days until a certificate expires. When you use an imported certificate, this CloudWatch metric can help you set up custom alerts for expiration notification or configure automation actions using scripts and CloudWatch events with your third-party certificate provider.

You can also use CloudWatch events to automate actions that happen within ACM. For example, there are several AWS health events that occur with a certificate that CloudWatch events can act on, such as renewal of a public or private certificate, or when needing to act on a renewal for it to occur, such as when you need to complete a renewal by responding to an email when email validation is enabled. CloudWatch events also support ACM expiration events. ACM sends daily expiration events for all certificates that are public, private, or imported starting 45 days prior to expiration. Since ACM automatically manages the renewal of certificates issued by ACM, these expiration notices are more meaningful for automation when using imported certificates as you can automate publishing expiration findings to AWS Security Hub based on the CloudWatch event trigger.

FIGURE 4.3   PEM-encoded certificate

Implementing Encryption in Transit

Now that you know how ACM works, the requirements for requesting and using certificates, and methods you can use to track or monitor expiration, it is time to learn how ACM can be used to encrypt data in transit. ACM by itself isn't enough to encrypt traffic in transit; it is just the source of the certificates used to encrypt the data in transit. This means you will need to use other AWS services that integrate with ACM to encrypt the traffic to and from your application.

Two of the most frequently used AWS services that integrate with ACM to provide encryption in transit are Elastic Load Balancing and CloudFront. In order to serve secure content over SSL/TLS, Elastic Load Balancing (ELB) requires the certificates to be installed on either the load balancer itself or the backend EC2 instance. ACM and ELB are integrated to allow ACM certificates to be deployed on the load balancer and maintained by ACM for renewals. For example, when you create an application load balancer (ALB), you can configure an HTTPS listener and deploy an SSL certificate managed by ACM. The ALB will then use this certificate to terminate the connection and decrypt requests from clients before sending them to the targets. When configuring the listener, just select the source of From ACM and then select the certificate you wish to use for that application.

For CloudFront to secure content over SSL/TLS, it requires that the certificates be installed on the CloudFront distribution or on the backend content source (origin). ACM is integrated with CloudFront to deploy certificates on the distribution. Remember, to use ACM certificates with CloudFront you must request or import the certificates in the US East (N. Virginia) region. When configuring a CloudFront distribution, you must choose to enable HTTPS, and if you are using your own domain name, such as `catsdomainname .com`, you will also need to enable alternate domain names in the distribution. Because ACM is integrated with CloudFront, you can select certificates for your domain, subdomain, or wildcard domains that are hosted in ACM when enabling HTTPS and alternate domain names. When certificates are set to expire, ACM will handle the renewal and update the certificate automatically within CloudFront. In CloudFront you can choose to redirect HTTP requests to HTTPS or to force HTTPS requests only. When you force traffic exclusively over HTTPS, anyone that makes requests using HTTP will receive a 403 Forbidden response when attempting to access an object.

Implementing encryption of data in transit also falls within the shared responsibility model of AWS. All network traffic between AWS datacenters is transparently encrypted at the physical layer, and all traffic within a VPC and between peered VPCs across regions are transparently encrypted at the network layer. AWS also encrypts all data in transit at the AWS service endpoints by using Transport Layer Security (TLS) to create a secure HTTPS connection for API requests. Even though AWS does all this work to help protect their customers, it is still the choice of the customer to encrypt data in transit at the application layer. AWS offers several services like ACM and the ability for AWS services to use TLS to encrypt data in transit, but ultimately if a customer does not want to or understand how to encrypt data in transit, the customer will remain unprotected. It is your job as the SysOps administrator to help educate, architect, and implement data-in-transit encryption strategies.

Amazon Macie

Data protection strategies must include protection for sensitive data stored in AWS. This is where Amazon Macie comes in as a fully managed and regional data security and data privacy service. Macie uses machine learning and pattern matching to discover and protect sensitive data stored in S3 buckets, at scale. Macie can identify several types of sensitive data, including personally identifiable information (PII), which would represent names, addresses, and payment card numbers, and custom data types such as employee ID numbers or unique sensitive data for your organization. Macie is also used to gain visibility in the areas of data security and privacy for any data you have stored in S3.

Think of Macie as a way for you to detect and report on potential issues with the security or the privacy of your data stored in S3—for example, if you have a business unit within your organization uploading CSV files to an S3 bucket, and they contain PII without your knowledge. Macie can scan and analyze objects in the S3 buckets and create detailed findings of all objects with PII found within the bucket. Macie does not stop there; it can also detect and analyze S3 buckets to identify and report on overly permissive or unencrypted buckets for your organization. This is especially useful when validating that security design controls are compliant across your organization's AWS accounts.

Macie Pricing

Pricing for Macie follows a per month, per bucket, and per gigabyte of data processed model. Like many other AWS services, the pricing model differs depending on the region the service is configured to run in. Since Macie is a regional service, you will need to evaluate the pricing guide https://aws.amazon.com/macie/pricing when determining how selecting different regions impact the overall cost of using Macie for data privacy and protection.

Macie uses the number of S3 buckets evaluated for bucket-level security and access controls, as well as the quantity of data processed for sensitive data discovery to determine the total monthly cost. There is a 30-day free trial of S3 bucket-level evaluation of security and access controls to help reduce the initial cost of implementing Macie. During the trial, there are no charges for all buckets evaluated in the first 30 days against the security controls looking for unencrypted buckets and overly permissive bucket policies. After the first 30 days, you are charged by the number of S3 buckets evaluated per month at the rate of $0.10 per S3 bucket. The pricing per bucket is prorated per day when enabling this feature.

Macie also charges based on the quantity of data processed for sensitive data discovery, such as looking for PII or custom data types within an S3 bucket. Macie only charges for the bytes processed during a scan. It is also important to remember that you will incur S3 cost for scanning actions as GET and LIST requests, which are charged the standard S3 fees for these API requests. Macie does use a free tier sensitive data discovery benefit by including 1 GB of processed data at no cost each month. Any data above the 1 GB limit follows a tiered pricing model at $1.00 per GB for the next 50,000 GB each month. For data between 50,000 GB and 450,000 GB, each month the cost is $0.50 per GB, and anything over 500,000 GB per month is charged at $0.25 per GB. Keep in mind that you are charged only for the jobs that are configured to be scanned for sensitive data. If you are only using Macie for security and detective controls, you will not be charged for sensitive data discovery and processing.

Macie offers usage information in its console. It is recommended when enabling the 30-day trial that you view month-to-date spend based on the actual usage of your account. This will provide you with important visibility into the spending as you configure the sensitive data discovery jobs across your S3 buckets. Using this information, you can plan for future spending and growth needed to include or exclude S3 buckets from your data protection strategy. When trying to estimate the spend for sensitive data discovery jobs on a bucket, you can use the Macie inventory view to see detailed information about what S3 has listed as the estimated storage size and object count, and whether compressed objects are included. This is helpful in determining the total numbers of gigabytes that the data discovery job will process.

How Macie Works

Macie is a regional service and needs to be enabled in each region in which you wish to scan S3 buckets for sensitive data and security controls. Enabling Macie is done through the AWS Management Console. Once enabled, Macie will generate an inventory of the S3 buckets for your account in the region where Macie is enabled. Once the inventory is completed, Macie will also start monitoring the buckets for security and access control.

To scan S3 buckets for sensitive data, you must configure and run a data discovery job. Data discovery jobs scan and analyze objects in S3 buckets found during the inventory scan that you select to determine if sensitive data is present. When Macie discovers sensitive data in an S3 bucket, it creates a detailed report called a data finding that you can review in the Macie dashboard. Macie creates a sensitive data discovery result for each object that a discovery job is analyzing. This report is a log that contains details about the analysis of the object, including objects that do not have sensitive data or that may not be supported by the Macie scan.

The Macie dashboard provides sensitive data discovery results for 90 days. If you want to store the results for longer than 90 days, you must enable long-term storage and retention using an S3 bucket. You must configure this archival storage within the first 30 days of enabling Macie by creating an S3 bucket and encrypting the bucket with an AWS KMS key. Once the bucket is created and encryption is enabled, Macie will write your sensitive data discovery results to JSON Lines files (with the file extension .jsonl) and compress the files using gzip before storing the reports in the S3 bucket.

> When you use S3 buckets as long-term storage for Macie sensitive data discovery reports, you must ensure that the KWS KMS key policy is updated to include Macie to use the key for encryption.

You can also use Macie with accounts that belong to an AWS Organization. There are three types of accounts within Macie. An *Administrator account* manages Macie accounts for an AWS Organization. Essentially this account is what centrally manages all Macie accounts that are associated with each other. These associated accounts are called *member accounts*, which are centrally managed as a group within a specific AWS region. You can also use Macie with a *standalone AWS account* that is not part of an AWS Organization. When using Macie with AWS Organizations, you can enable member accounts by integrating Macie with AWS Organizations or by sending and accepting membership invitations individually for each member account.

Monitoring S3 Data with Macie

Macie requires access to S3 buckets to monitor bucket security and privacy and gather details such as metadata about objects. To accomplish this access, Macie uses an IAM service-linked role for your account in the current AWS region. The IAM policy allows

Macie to call other AWS services on your behalf and monitor AWS resources. This role also allows Macie to conduct the inventory of the S3 buckets in the region and evaluate the security and access controls for these buckets.

Macie collects metadata about the S3 buckets in the same region to use this information in assessing the security and privacy of your bucket inventory. The metadata covers information such as the bucket name, creation data, and default encryption settings, as well as account- and bucket-level permissions and settings. Macie also collects metadata about objects within an S3 bucket such as the count and settings for objects in the bucket like storage class, file type, and encryption type.

Once the inventory of all S3 buckets is completed, Macie will use CloudTrail events as a source of information to evaluate bucket security and privacy. When a relevant event occurs on an S3 bucket, like enabling default encryption, Macie will update the inventory data to include these changes. Macie uses account- and bucket-level events within CloudTrail to continually update the bucket inventory. For example, if you add or remove bucket policies, change bucket ACLs, or disable versioning, Macie will update the inventory to reflect these changes. One of the most important actions that Macie tracks within an S3 bucket is the removal or addition of the Public Access Block settings, which should remain enabled to follow AWS security best practice recommendations.

Sensitive Data Discovery with Macie

Discovery of sensitive data within an S3 bucket is a core use for Macie. This process requires the use of sensitive data discovery jobs, which analyze objects within the selected S3 bucket using managed data identifiers, custom data identifiers, or a combination of each. Managed data identifiers are the predefined criteria used to detect specific types of sensitive data like credit card numbers, AWS secret access keys, passport numbers for a particular country or region, and other PII data. These common identifiers help detect many sensitive data types for many countries and regions, including financial data, personal health, and PII data.

Using managed data identifiers is a terrific way to begin checking your S3 buckets for common sensitive data types, including any new type added to the ever-growing list within Macie. However, what happens when you need to check for data types that are considered sensitive to your organization, but not the rest of the world? This is where custom data identifiers can build a more robust sensitive data discovery. Custom data identifiers allow you to define a set of criteria to detect sensitive data that is unique to your needs using a regular expression (regex). You can define which patterns or sequences you want Macie to match based on regular expressions to reflect your organization's sensitive data detection needs. For example, you can configure custom data identifiers to look for patterns or sequences to locate employee IDs, customer account numbers, or any other data classification tags used within the data. This is particularly useful when using Macie to help protect intellectual property for your organization that should not be stored in nondesignated S3 buckets.

Remember, Macie cannot access encrypted objects in an S3 bucket if it does not have access to a key it is allowed to use, or the object was encrypted on the client side before uploading to S3.

Once you have decided which data identifier type you want to use for scanning sensitive data within your buckets, you must define a schedule and scope of the job analysis. You can pick between running a job only once, which is a great way to scan archival S3 buckets or temporary locations, or you can choose to run the job on a recurring basis to support continued sensitive data scanning. For example, if your organization uses S3 as a processing location to store temporary files before moving to longer-term storage, or if S3 buckets are used with AWS Storage Gateway, you may want to schedule a recurring analysis of the buckets that are more frequently changing to ensure that sensitive data is not present. Macie also lets you run any sensitive data analysis job on-demand, which can be useful when you want to scan S3 buckets as part of a security audit or when investigating a security incident report.

Analyzing Macie Findings

Great; Macie is set up to scan every S3 bucket for security and access controls, and you have configured several S3 buckets to be scanned for sensitive data. What happens when Macie detects a potential policy violation, sensitive data discovery, or issues with a security or privacy policy? The answer is to review and analyze the findings generated by Macie and determine if what actions, if any, are needed to remediate the findings.

Reviewing findings with Macie can occur in a few places depending on your specific needs for evaluation. The first area is the Macie console using the Findings pages. This is where you can find the detailed information about individual findings. This page is often used for quick glance analysis and grouping, filtering, and creating suppression rules for improving future analysis. If your organization has a separate analysis application or requires receiving findings in a specific format, you can use the Macie API to query and retrieve the findings data using HTTPS requests. To use the Macie API, you can submit queries using the SDK or CLI of your choice. All results to API queries are returned using a JSON response, which you can then pass to whichever application you require and transform the result into any format needed for analysis. Using the Macie API can be useful when you need to transform findings data into a specific report format or ingest the data in other security or reporting software.

Macie also supports integration with a few other AWS services like EventBridge and Security Hub. EventBridge enables you to act on findings automatically by sending EventBridge data to targets like AWS Lambda or Amazon Simple Notification Service (SNS). Macie automatically publishes new finding events to EventBridge, and it publishes events for subsequent occurrences of existing findings. This integration with EventBridge can help simplify remediation activities by sending notifications to other software and services using SNS, or by processing actions such as replacing S3 bucket policies on an impacted bucket using an AWS Lambda function. If your organization is using Security Hub to analyze the overall security posture, you can review and analyze your Macie findings using Security Hub. The integration between Security Hub and Macie is automatic when both services are enabled within a region. This means Macie will begin publishing new and updated policy findings to Security Hub immediately with no additional configuration or permissions needed within your account. If you need to customize the frequency that Macie publishes findings to Security Hub, you can update the Macie publication settings to fit your needs. By default,

Macie will send all new findings immediately to Security Hub and it will publish updates to findings every 15 minutes as part of the recurring publication cycle. This is a configurable value where you can choose to send publications every hour or every 6 hours. These changes are only applicable to a specific regional Macie configuration. If you require the same publication changes, you will need to update the settings in each region where Macie is enabled. To change the publication settings, visit the Settings page in the Macie Management Console and navigate to the Publication Of Findings section.

Enforcing Data Classification with Macie

Data protection and classification strategies are only as good as the enforcement behind them. Macie helps establish enforcement of data classification by scanning S3 buckets and objects for sensitive data and access control configurations. Data classification strategies for your organization may include simple classification types like public, internal-only, restricted, and sensitive. Having clear definitions for each data classification type will enable better placement and protection of data aligning to the classification type.

For example, data classified as internal-only may reflect customer information like phone numbers or customer account numbers. When an application, or in some cases a human, places data into S3, let's say in the form of a CSV file, the data protection and classification strategy should require the data to be uploaded into an S3 bucket that matches the same classification level of internal-only. This is great when uploading data is automated and the data is classified already, but what happens when a human resources person, developer, or other employee uploads files to an S3 bucket without classification? The answer lies in the use of Macie.

Macie is not only a data protection control; it is an automated identification and classification tool. It is a tool to help implement the correct controls to protect the data stored in S3 buckets. For example, let's assume your organization has several S3 buckets configured for storing data of different classifications. There is a bucket for sensitive information that your organization defines as containing intellectual property and legally privileged information, and another bucket for internal-only data that is used for customer invoices and may contain PII. Data classification is already in place, but there are no protection mechanisms like encryption or limited privileges enforced for data housed in the organization's S3 buckets. Using Macie, you can create a data discovery job to scan all S3 buckets controlled by the organization's AWS accounts in a specific AWS region. You create the job using a managed data identifier to look for PII in the S3 buckets and set up a recurring schedule to ensure that any new data uploaded to the bucket is scanned. This new data discovery job will run against the S3 buckets and report back any findings of objects that may contain PII and other sensitive information for you to review in the Macie console or use automation through the EventBridge integrations to send the findings and notifications to the security team without requiring manual intervention.

After reviewing the findings of all S3 buckets in the account, you may notice that several other buckets not identified as storage locations for internal-only and sensitive data have objects that contain sensitive data. You also notice that several of the S3 buckets do not have encryption enabled, which is required by your data protection strategy. These findings allow you to act and enable encryption on the S3 buckets while moving the sensitive information containing PII into the proper data classification and S3 bucket. Macie isn't enforcing that the data be classified or providing a method for moving data into the classifications itself. However, the Macie findings allow you as a SysOps administrator to locate the potential issue and use other integrated AWS services, like KMS and resource tags, to enforce the data protection and classification strategy.

In Exercise 4.3, we will be enabling Macie and creating a data discovery job to locate sensitive data in an S3 bucket. If you do not have an S3 bucket created in your account, you will need to create one before doing the exercise.

EXERCISE 4.3

Creating a Data Discovery Job to Locate Sensitive Data in S3 Buckets Using Macie

You should only use a *nonproduction* S3 bucket for this exercise and avoid uploading actual sensitive information. Always use fake or sample information when testing configurations where possible.

1. Open the AWS Management Console and log in using an IAM account that has permissions to enable and use Macie.

2. Select the region that your S3 bucket was created in before enabling Macie. Remember, Macie is a regional service and will only be able to access the S3 bucket you created if the service is enabled in the same region.

3. From the AWS Management Console, open the Macie Management Console. You may be presented with an error message box stating that Macie is not enabled. This is normal when Macie has not been enabled within a region.

4. Click Get Started to enable Macie within the region you selected. You will be presented with the Enable Macie screen. This screen also reminds you of the Macie pricing and the 30-day trial. When ready, click Enable Macie to continue.

5. Now that Macie is enabled, it will begin scanning your AWS account for S3 buckets available in the region where Macie was enabled. This process can take between 30 and 60 minutes to complete. Once Macie has finished the inventory, you can continue to create a data discovery job.

6. From the left navigation, select Jobs and then click Create Job.

7. You must now choose an S3 bucket to run this new data discovery job against. Select the option for a specific bucket and under the Select S3 bucket section, select the check box next to the bucket that you want to run this scan against. You would use the other option to specify bucket criteria, such as if you wanted to run this job against S3 buckets that have tags indicating they are HR buckets. Click Next to continue after selecting the bucket you want to use.

8. Review the S3 bucket chosen and take note that the inventory performed by Macie will show the number of classifiable objects and the total size of the objects in the bucket to scan. This screen will also give you an estimate of how much the scan will cost based on the available inventory information. If you are using an existing bucket with objects, be sure to determine that the classifiable size is not above the free tier limit of 1 GB to avoid being charged for this exercise. Click Next to continue.

9. Now you must configure the scope of the data discovery job. Here you can define a schedule and criteria to include or exclude objects the job will analyze. For this exercise, select the One-time Job, which will still enable you to run the job on-demand as many times as you want. Skip modifying any additional settings and click Next.

10. You now will need to define the managed data identifiers that you want to use for this data discovery job. Choose which managed identifiers you want to use by selecting the Include option. For this exercise, only select the ADDRESS sensitive data type, and then click Next to continue.

11. You can now define any custom data identifiers you want to use to help with data classification. For now, don't include custom data identifiers and click Next to continue.

12. Enter a job name and a description, then click Next.

13. You are now presented with a review screen to verify all the options you just selected. Ensure that you have configured the job correctly and the estimated cost. If you are within the free tier limit of 1 GB of data in the bucket, you will see an estimated cost of $0.00. Click Submit to create the job.

The data discovery job is now created, and it will automatically start scanning the selected S3 bucket. Depending on the number of objects and the size of the objects, the scan can take some time to complete. To view an example of findings, you can create a text document and upload it to S3 with a fake address like 1492 Nautical Lane, Columbus, OH, 43223, USA, and run a new scan by creating a new job. Take time to explore Macie and create new jobs and use the Sample Findings. To enable Sample Findings, click Settings and then click Generate Sample Findings in the Sample Findings section. This will place samples of each finding type in the Findings section of the Macie console. Explore what each finding has available for information.

When done with this exercise, be sure to clean up the S3 bucket and disable Macie using the Settings option in the Macie console to avoid any unwanted charges.

AWS Secrets Manager

Security is the highest priority at AWS and this philosophy and best practice carries over to the design of several AWS services. AWS Secrets Manager is one of those high priority security services that exist to enable more secure management of secrets in AWS. Think of a secret, like a password, or a string of characters that you don't want just anyone to see or have access to. These secrets could be database credentials or API keys that your application running on AWS uses to communicate with other components of your architecture. These secrets can be used within the AWS Cloud, on third-party services, or even with on-premises applications. Having a security-minded service like Secrets Manager helps keep security high priority by protecting these credentials and allowing management to implement secrets rotation for added security.

Sure, Secrets Manager is great, but why should you use it? The answer is found in the simplicity of credential management and ensuring that your applications have a single place to rotate secrets. Secrets Manager can natively rotate credentials for RDS, DocumentDB, and Redshift clusters. Credential rotation does not stop there—you can also extend Secrets Manager by using AWS Lambda functions to rotate credentials for Oracle databases hosted on EC2 instance or OAuth refresh tokens used by your application architectures. Accessing the secrets stored in Secrets Manager is as easy as replacing the plaintext secrets with code to retrieve the secrets programmatically using the Secrets Manager API. Just note that Secrets Manager requires an IAM policy permission in order for applications to access specific secrets and the Secrets Manager service. This helps prevent unauthorized applications from using the secrets stored in Secrets Manager.

Keeping secrets safe is also particularly important to AWS. Therefore, Secrets Manager encrypts secrets at rest using KMS keys that you own and store in the KMS service. If you do not have an existing KMS key or do not provide one for use, Secrets Manager will generate a new KMS default key for your account to encrypt the secrets. Secrets Manager also uses the KMS key to decrypt the secret and transmit it using TLS to your local environment and application. This keeps the entire process of storing and retrieving secrets encrypted and protected. This scalable method of storing and managing secrets helps IT administrators and developers in monitoring secrets and rotating them without risk of impacting applications through manual code changes or unsecure transmission of secrets.

AWS Secrets Manager Pricing

Secrets Manager follows the pay-as-you-go pricing model where you only pay for what you use with no minimum or setup fee. Billing occurs on a monthly basis for the number of secrets that you store in Secrets Manager and the API requests made to the service. As with many AWS services, there is a 30-day trial period to use Secrets Manager within your organization. You can use the service fully during the 30-day trial without any restrictions or charges. Once the 30-day trial is over, you will be charged $0.40 per secret per month. If you replicate a secret, you will be billed an additional $0.40 per replica per month. For any secrets stored less than a month, the price is prorated based on the number of hours the secret was stored. Remember that Secrets Manager also charges you for API calls into the service at $0.05 per 10,000 API calls. It is best practice to check the most current pricing information at https://aws.amazon.com/secrets-manager/pricing when determining total cost for your Secrets Manager deployment. If your organization requires more than 100,000 unique secrets, you can reach out to your AWS account team for special pricing and assistance.

How Secrets Manager Works

Not only does Secrets Manager protect credentials used by your applications, it also reduces risk and saves IT administration and developer time when changing credentials. When changing credentials without the use of Secrets Manager, you would need to update the application to use the new credentials, you would need to update any distributed systems that required that credential, and you would also need to ensure the changes were done correctly with no human error introduced. If any of these steps failed, or if an error was found in one of the distributed systems, the entire application could become unavailable. This type of risk is easily avoided with the use of a credential manager like Secrets Manager.

There are four ways to access secrets stored in Secrets Manager:

- The first method is using the Secrets Manager console, which you access through the AWS Management Console and where you would perform administrative tasks to the secrets stored, such as rotating the credentials or retiring the secret.

- The second method is using the AWS CLI or AWS Tools for Windows PowerShell to perform administrative tasks. The CLI is often faster than using the management console and offers flexibility in building and running scripts to automate administrative tasks.

- The third method is using the AWS SDKs to access Secrets Manager and perform tasks using any of the supported SDK languages such as Python, Java, .NET, and Node.js.

- The fourth method is using HTTPS Query API, which provides API-level access to make direct calls to the Secrets Manager HTTPS Query API. AWS recommends using an AWS SDK, when possible, but this feature is supported for any applications that cannot use an available SDK.

Basics of a Secret

Now that you know the various methods for accessing Secrets Manager, it is time to learn about the secrets and how they are stored in the service. When you build a secret in Secrets Manager, the secret will consist of secret information, a secret value, and secret metadata. Secrets can be either binary or a string, and multiple string values can be stored in one secret using JSON text strings with key-value pairs. For example, if you wanted to store connection information for a web application, you could create a JSON file with the hostname, connection port, username, and password to store in Secrets Manager. The JSON output would look like the following:

```
{
  "host"      : "ProdServer-01.databases.example.com",
  "port"      : "8888",
  "username"  : "administrator",
  "password"  : "EXAMPLE-PASSWORD"
}
```

A secret's metadata contains the Amazon Resource Name (ARN), which includes the Region, AccountID, and the secret name (which will include six random characters). The metadata also holds the name of the secret, a brief description, a rotation policy, and any tags associated with the secret. The KMS encryption key ARN is also present within the metadata, which is what Secrets Manager uses to encrypt and decrypt the secret value. Lastly, the secret metadata also has information about how to rotate the secret if rotation is set up.

Secrets also have versioning capabilities, which hold copies of the encrypted secret value. These versions are used when rotating keys or when you change the value of a secret. When a secret has a value of AWSCURRENT, it is the most up-to-date secret that Secrets Manager will use. Secrets Manager uses labels to identify different versions of a secret when performing rotation. When a secret is in the AWSPENDING state, it means that this version will become current once the rotation action is completed. When a secret has a label of AWSPREVIOUS, this means that it is the last known good version of a previous current version of the secret. When using the SDK or CLI, you can specify which version of a secret value to retrieve. If no version is specified within the CLI command or the SDK API call, it will always return the AWSCURRENT value. Secrets Manager also enables custom staging labels that you can attach to a secret. This feature allows up to 20 staging labels to be attached to a secret to help indicate different life-cycle stages such as development, testing, or production when identifying versions.

Secrets Manager Permissions

To access secrets stored in Secrets Manager, you must ensure that the user, group, or role has the appropriate IAM permissions. Using an identity-based policy, you can grant access to multiple secrets for an identity or control who can manage and create new secrets. Identity-based policies allow you to specify which secrets the identity, like an IAM user or group, can access and the actions they can perform on the secret. An alternative method to allow access into Secrets Manager is to use resource-based policies, which allow you to specify who can access the secret and which actions they can perform against the secret. Resource-based policies allow you to grant access to a single secret to multiple users and roles and grant access to users or roles in another AWS account. Resource-based policies are used when operating in a shared security services configuration and the Secrets Manager service is configured in a shared services AWS account controlled by the security team. When configuring the IAM policy, you can use AWS-managed policies as a starting place to grant the appropriate permissions and then set the conditions or access restrictions required for your environment.

Monitoring Secrets Manager Secrets

Monitoring the use of Secrets Manager is a key step to ensure the security of your applications and infrastructure. There are two primary methods: CloudTrail and CloudWatch. Monitoring can help identify when there are issues with a secret and help remediate any discovered issues automatically. CloudTrail captures the API calls and related events made to the Secrets Manager service on behalf of your account and delivers the log files into an S3 bucket. These recorded API calls for Secrets Manager are called *events*. CloudTrail captures API calls from the Secrets Manager console, and it also captures events relating to rotations of secrets, deletions, and version changes. Reviewing the CloudTrail logs for Secrets Manager is a best practice to ensure that only allowed and expected events and management are happening within the service.

CloudWatch is another great service to use for monitoring Secrets Manager. CloudWatch is used to identify and alert when your request rate for APIs reaches a specified threshold. This is an important metric to track as Secrets Manager bills $0.05 per 10,000 API calls, and it can help identify if you have an application that is requesting a secret aggressively, which could indicate a problem with the application or potentially malicious actions. CloudWatch can also be used to monitor estimated Secrets Manager charges to help identify and notify you when Secrets Manager is spending above the desired limit. This can also be helpful when identifying potentially abusive use of secrets creation in the service.

Secrets Manager also integrates with EventBridge for notification of certain events that impact secrets within your account. Using EventBridge can assist in automating notification and remediation actions, such as being notified when any application, SDK, or CLI performs a GET* API call against Secrets Manager. EventBridge will help automate the process of notification by sending generated events to an SNS topic for email or text, or potentially running a Lambda script to capture and parse CloudTrail logs based on the finding to generate a threat report. The possibilities are endless for the automated tasks that can be completed using EventBridge with Secrets Manager.

How to Securely Store Secrets

You now understand how Secrets Manager works and some of the ways you can monitor and secure access to the service. Now you need to learn how to securely store secrets in Secrets Manager for use within your applications. The process starts with learning about the required components of creating a secret for databases and other applications.

A secret can contain a set of credentials for a database or an application like a username and password, or the secret could just be a password or connection string, or even an authorization token. Whatever the secret contains is entirely up to you. However, if you are looking to use secrets with your own applications or with another AWS service like RDS, you may need to specify certain parameters as part of the secret. For example, if you are creating a secret for use within a database service, like RDS, you will need to provide the type of database credentials to store, select an encryption key that Secrets Manager uses to encrypt the secret value, and choose the database that the secret is related to. You also must add a secret name and a description to help with management and administration of the secret. You can optionally add tags to the secret to comply with a tagging strategy or to help identify secrets against a certain project or cost center.

Some of the final options you can select when generating a database secret relate to the creation of resource permissions, replication, and rotation. During the creation of the secret, you can optionally set a resource permission to add a resource policy to your secret, which allows you to grant access to multiple users or roles. You can also optionally replicate your secret to another AWS region by selecting the Replicate Secret option. This is a useful option when you're working with secrets through a centrally managed region or when you're configuring disaster recovery options within another AWS region. If you turn on rotation for the primary secret, Secrets Manager will also update the secret in all replicated AWS regions. Finally, you have the option to configure automatic rotation if your application and secret support rotation. I highly recommend enabling rotation of a secret to increase protection of your secret, but also to increase the security of applications using the secrets. Secret rotation also helps reduce IT administration overhead by eliminating the need to change coded pass-words or secrets in applications manually.

Creating a non-database secret follows a similar process. You still must create the secret with the required information, and in this case, it is a key-value pair or plaintext entry. AWS recommends using JSON format to store secrets when possible, and you can store up to 65,536 bytes in the secret. When storing a secret in a key-value pair, you would have to store something like a key of a username, and the value would be the username for the credential. You could then have another key of the password, and the value would be the password used to access the application. When recalling this secret, it would provide the username and password from the secret to supply the credential to your application. You still need to supply an encryption key for Secrets Manager to encrypt the secret and supply a secret name and description. Optionally you can add tags, resource permissions, and rotation, and con-figure replication options just as you are able to do with the database secrets.

Once a secret is created, you can begin using it within your applications and database. You can also modify the secret within the Secrets Manager console, AWS CLI, or AWS SDK. You have the option to modify the description, resource-based policy, encryption key and tags, as well as the secret itself. However, modifying the secret value directly is not rec-ommended as it can cause the secret and application to be out-of-sync with the latest value. Instead, you should use the Rotation option to modify the secret, which will keep Secrets Manager and the database or application updated when a client requests a secret value.

Retrieving Secrets from Secrets Manager

What good is storing a secret if you would never retrieve it from the service? There are sev-eral ways to retrieve secrets using the AWS Management Console, AWS SDK, or AWS CLI, to name a few. Each programming language supported by the AWS SDK will have differ-ent methods for retrieving the secrets from Secrets Manager, but each will retrieve secrets by calling the GetSecretValue API. To limit the number of API request to Secrets Man-ager, improve speed, and reduce costs, you should use client-side caching within any of the AWS SDKs.

You can also retrieve and use secrets through AWS CloudFormation, which is extremely useful when practicing infrastructure as code within your organization. For example, you can create a secret using Secrets Manager and then retrieve the secret and generated pass-word to use as credentials for a new database being instantiated by CloudFormation. Retrieving secrets from Secrets Manager using CloudFormation requires a dynamic reference for the secret placed in the CloudFormation template. The dynamic reference uses the fol-lowing pattern:

```
{{resolve:secretsmanager:secret-id:SecretString:json-key:version-
stage:version-id}}
```

The *secret-id* is the name or ARN of the secret created and stored in Secrets Man-ager. You will use the ARN of the secret when using a secret stored in a different AWS account. The *json-key* option is the key name of the key-value pair whose value you want to retrieve. This is optional as CloudFormation will retrieve the entire secret text if no *json-key* is provided. The *version-id* option is a unique identifier containing the version of the secret to use. When using the dynamic reference, you will use either *version-id* or *version-stage*, but not at the same time. If you do not specify either, then CloudFormation will default to the AWSCURRENT version of the secret.

That's it! You now can store secure secrets for applications and databases using Secrets Manager. There are several AWS services with integration to AWS Secrets Manager to explore and help protect your credentials. It is always a good idea to check https://docs .aws.amazon.com/secretsmanager when designing an implementation of Secrets Manager within your organization. You can also use the public documentation to view SDK-specific examples of retrieving secrets from Secrets Manager.

In Exercise 4.4, you will store credentials in Secrets Manager using the AWS Management Console and retrieve the stored secret using the AWS CLI.

EXERCISE 4.4

Creating and Storing Credentials in Secrets Manager

1. Open the Secrets Manager console by logging into the AWS Management Console and opening the Secrets Manager service.

2. In the Secrets Manager console, click Store A New Secret.

3. Select the type of secret that you wish to create. For this exercise, select Other Type Of Secret.

4. Next, you will need to determine if you want to use a key-value type of credential or a plaintext one. For this exercise select Key/Value as you will be storing a username and password set. In the first text box, enter the Key as Username, and in the second text box, place the value of DemoSecret.

5. Click Add Row, and in the first text box, enter the Key as Password, and in the second text box, enter password as the value.

6. Next you must select the Encryption key that Secrets Manager will use to encrypt the secret. If you have an existing KMS key that you wish to use, and it has permissions for Secrets Manager, you can use it here. Otherwise, Secrets Manager will create a new AWS-managed KMS key under the aws/secretsmanager name. Once you have selected the key that you want to use, click Next to continue.

7. Now you must enter the name and description of the newly created secret. Enter the name of **DemoSecret** and leave the description blank for this exercise.

8. You can safely ignore the optional configuration items of Tags, Resource Permissions, and Replication for this exercise. In a production AWS deployment of Secrets Manager, you will need to comply with any tagging and governance policies relating to replication and resource permissions. When you are done reviewing the optional components, click Next to continue.

EXERCISE 4.4 *(continued)*

9. On the next screen, you can configure a rotation schedule for the secret. For this exercise you do not need to enable automatic rotation. In a production environment, you would configure a rotation schedule when supported by your application following your organization's security and password policies. When you are finished investigating the rotation schedule, click Next.

10. On the next screen, review the information for the secret and ensure that all configuration items are correct. This screen also provides several code examples for retrieving the newly created secret from Secrets Manager using common AWS SDK–supported languages. When you are finished exploring the sample code items, click Store to create your secret.

That's it! You have created your first Secrets Manager stored secret. Now let's use the AWS CLI to retrieve the secret and verify that everything is working correctly.

11. Open your favorite terminal or command prompt where you have the AWS CLI installed and configured.

12. In the terminal window, type **aws secretsmanager list-secrets** to view a list of all available secrets visible by your configured credentials. You will be presented with a resulting JSON view of the secret created earlier in this exercise and any existing secrets within your configured region. Copy the name of the secret, which should be DemoSecret, and proceed to the next step.

13. To retrieve the secret from Secrets Manager, you must use the command `aws secrets manager get-secret-value` with the `--secret-id` value of `DemoSecret`. So for this exercise, in the terminal type `aws secretsmanager get-secret-value --secret-id DemoSecret` to retrieve the secret value. You will be presented with the JSON result showing the secure string containing the username and password values stored in the secret. Alternatively, you can use the ARN of the secret returned from the `list-secrets` command in step 12 instead of the name. When using secrets from different AWS accounts, you will always use the ARN value instead of the Name value.

You just created a secret using the Secrets Manager console and then retrieved the secret using the AWS CLI. To clean up this exercise, be sure to schedule a deletion of the secret and set the deletion wait time to 7 days. After the wait period is complete, Secrets Manager will remove the secret from your AWS account.

Network Protection Strategies

Network protection involves applying a zero-trust approach for the users of your applications or services within AWS. These users can be located anywhere and need access into your applications, but it is up to you to define a strategy to ensure that these users only have access to the application component or microservice required to service their need. This could mean logical or physical separation of services and applications to ensure that no component or microservice trusts any other explicitly and only allows needed and restricted access to accomplish a task.

AWS has numerous services that can help protect applications connected to the VPC or integrated with AWS services, like DynamoDB or CloudFront. Network protection services like AWS Shield, AWS Web Application Firewall (AWS WAF), and AWS Firewall Manager allow you to provide an elevated level of monitoring and protection against unwanted network traffic or attacks like distributed denial-of-service (DDoS) or SQL injection. When designing a network protection strategy, you must protect both internal and external connections used by your AWS account and applications. The days of just installing a firewall or network access control list to protect a network are long behind us with the advancements in technology and malicious actors.

Network protection strategies will include the use of AWS services across several levels such as host level, application level, and network level. Host-level protection helps minimize network risk by providing fine-grained network segmentation using services and features like VPC Security Groups and AWS Firewall Manager. Application-level protection focuses on web-based attacks that are targeting your applications running in AWS using services like AWS Shield and AWS WAF. Network-level protection provides security policy enforcements for traffic flowing in and out of your virtual networks to protect against malicious activity and utilize services like AWS Shield and network access control lists (NACLs). By combining all three levels of protection in a network protection strategy, you are enabling applications to operate at a much lower risk from malicious attacks.

AWS Shield

Imagine creating the most perfect web application that hundreds of thousands of people enjoy every day. Your application is drawing significant positive attention from the media and sales are good. Life really could not get any better—and then you start receiving alerts from the security team. Your application is starting to become unresponsive from an increase of traffic from unwanted sources. The security team calls you to explain that your application is under a DDoS attack coming from various countries. What do you do? What could you have done to help prevent this from happening in the first place? If you are running this application in a datacenter, you have a couple of options: either block traffic from the offending sources or try to scale beyond the attack. Either of these methods can be cost and time prohibitive and often result in the application being taken down until the attack stops. However, when hosting your application in the AWS Cloud, the answer is, of course, tied to your network protection strategy and the use of native AWS services like AWS Shield to help protect your applications and networks.

AWS Shield is a managed service that provides protection against DDoS attacks for your applications running on AWS. There are two different versions of AWS Shield: One is an optional paid service known as AWS Shield Advanced, and the other is automatically enabled to all AWS customers at no additional cost and is called AWS Shield Standard. AWS

Shield Standard offers protection for all AWS customers against common and frequently used network attacks occurring at the network (layer 3) and transport (layer 4) layers of a network. Shield Standard protects against attacks like SYN/UDP floods and reflection attacks to support high availability of applications run in AWS. AWS also benefits from providing this service free to all AWS customers as it provides an extra layer of security and attack avoidance due to misconfigured applications or servers, which often invite unwanted and malicious attacks by just existing on a network connected to the Internet.

AWS Shield Advanced offers enhanced protection for applications running on AWS services like EC2, Elastic Load Balancing (ELB), and CloudFront. Shield Advanced also covers edge services like AWS Global Accelerator and Route 53 resources against larger and more sophisticated attacks using always-on and flow-based monitoring of network traffic and active application monitoring. These enhanced monitoring options provide near-real-time notifications in the event of a suspected DDoS attack.

AWS Shield is also capable of mitigating incidents by using advanced attack mitigation and routing techniques. Any customers that are Business or Enterprise support subscribers can engage with the Shield Response Team (SRT), which provides 24×7 support to help manage and mitigate application-layer DDoS attacks by assisting your organization with mitigation and defense advice and solutions. Another benefit of Shield Advanced is the DDoS cost protection, which protects against scaling costs associated with mitigation efforts when responding to DDoS attacks. This cost protection helps protect your AWS bill from higher fees due to the usage spikes caused by drastic scaling of AWS resources like EC2 and elastic load balancers during the attack. In the event of an attack, you can request credits to cover these increased scaling costs for any AWS Shield Advanced protected services.

AWS Shield Standard is available in all AWS regions and for all AWS services and edge locations worldwide. This means your disaster recovery solution in Australia is also protected by Shield Standard. Shield Advanced is also available globally for all CloudFront, Route 53, and AWS Global Accelerator locations. However, if you want to enable Shield Advanced directly on ELB or EC2, you'll find that it's only available in certain AWS regions. For an updated list of where Shield Advanced is available, you can check the AWS Regional Services page at `https://aws.amazon.com/about-aws/global-infrastructure/regional-product-services` to verify availability of Shield Advanced in your desired region. It is always a best practice to check service availability when planning an implementation and designing a network protection strategy.

AWS Shield Pricing

Pricing for AWS Shield is split between Shield Standard and Shield Advanced. Shield Standard is built into the AWS services that you are already using for web applications at no additional cost. This means you get the benefit of Shield Standard in every AWS region for every web application you host free of charge. However, Shield Advanced has a monthly fee of $3,000 per month per organization with a one-year subscription commitment. You also must pay for Shield Advanced Data Transfer Out usage fees for any AWS resources enabled with advanced protection, in addition to the standard usage fees for the AWS resources protected. If you are intending to use the Shield Response Team (SRT), you will also have the cost of the Enterprise or Business support subscription in addition to the $3,000 per month, per organization fee for Shield Advanced.

Shield Advanced data transfer out usage fees apply using a tiered pricing model depending on which AWS service Shield Advanced is protecting, such as CloudFront, ELB, AWS Global Accelerator, or AWS Elastic IP for EC2 instances or Network Load Balancer. One important note about pricing with Shield Advanced is there are no additional costs for Route 53 for data transfer out. Pricing for Shield Advanced data transfer out usage fees follow the first 100 TB, then the next 400 TB, then the next 500 TB, and then the next 4 PB. Yes, you read that right, the next 4 petabytes. There are special pricing considerations that require contacting AWS for transfer usage above 5 PB for all services and above 4 PB for ELB and AWS Elastic IP. Always check `https://aws.amazon.com/shield/pricing` for the latest and most current AWS Shield Advanced pricing.

How AWS Shield Works

AWS Shield provides protections against DDoS attacks for your AWS resources at the network, transport, and application layers. You may be thinking, what is a DDoS attack anyway and why does it matter so much? It matters because a DDoS attack can prevent wanted and legitimate traffic and users from accessing your application or website. The DDoS attack can also cause your website or application to crash from being overwhelmed with traffic volume, and potentially increase your AWS costs if auto scaling is being used and Shield Advanced is not in use. During a DDoS attack, multiple computers or connections attempt to flood your website with traffic. These computers or connections are often compromised and the owners are unaware that this type of attack is occurring from their networks.

Shield Standard helps protect the perimeter of your application, which means the first point of entry for external traffic coming into your application. The perimeter of your application can change within AWS depending on which AWS services you are using and the design of your application. For example, if you are hosting a web application using EC2 and serving the traffic directly from the instance, this means that inbound traffic has a first contact point of the AWS region, which places your application perimeter at your VPC. However, if you are using CloudFront, this places your application perimeter at the edge of the AWS network.

While Shield provides DDoS detection and mitigation for your applications running in AWS, it is up to you to design applications and infrastructure to support DDoS resiliency. This means your application should support the ability to continue operating within expected parameters during an attack. For example, your application should be only accessed through a globally distributed network capacity, like CloudFront, and you should provide protection against application-layer DDoS attack vectors by using services like AWS WAF. All AWS customers receive the benefits of Shield Standard to help defend against common network- and transport-layer DDoS attacks. However, when your application uses CloudFront, Route 53 hosted zones, or AWS Global Accelerator, your resources will have comprehensive availability protection against all known network- and transport-layer attacks, not just the common and frequently occurring attacks. These additional benefits can be realized when following DDoS-resilient architecture best practices.

Shield Advanced provides additional capabilities and options to protect your applications running in AWS. Which capabilities and options are available depend on the infrastructure and architecture decisions you made when designing your application. Shield Advanced integrates with AWS WAF and uses AWS WAF ACLs, rules, and rule groups to provide application-layer protections. The Shield Advanced subscription includes the AWS WAF basic fees for web ACLs, rules, and web requests. Shield Advanced also includes automatic application-layer DDoS mitigation by creating, evaluating, and deploying custom AWS WAF rules for protected resources. This automatic mitigation is configurable to allow either counting or blocking of web requests that are part of an attack.

Shield Advanced also helps prevent false positives and provides faster detection and mitigation when a protected resource is unhealthy and using Route 53 health checks. Health-based detection is available for any resource type except for Route 53 hosted zones. Shield Advanced also offers logical grouping of protected resources. These protection groups allow you to define criteria for membership in a group to automatically add new protected resources as they become available. Protection groups can help enhance detection and mitigation efforts of the group, such as placing web applications of similar purpose or configuration in a group and transactional application servers in another. Each group may have unique needs for protection and membership that can be controlled by the protection groups.

Monitoring, management, and visibility is also increased when using Shield Advanced. Shield Advanced provides access to real-time metrics and reports for events and attacks on resources protected by Shield Advanced. These real-time metrics are sent into CloudWatch metrics to support even further reporting capabilities or automation options. You can also automatically apply Shield Advanced protections to new accounts and resources, including deploying AWS WAF rules to web ACLs, all from a centrally managed location. AWS Firewall Manager Shield Advanced protection policies are included for Shield Advanced customers at no additional cost. Using AWS Firewall Manager and Shield Advanced together, you can centralize management and reporting further by integrating with SNS or Security Hubs to report incidents.

An additional option and capability of Shield Advanced is the use of the SRT, a group of engineers with deep experience in protecting AWS, Amazon.com, and subsidiaries from DDoS attacks. You can tap into the experience and skills of the same teams protecting Amazon.com from DDoS attacks to assist with mitigation of attacks that affect your availability of your application. You can also use the SRT to create and manage custom mitigations for your resources. Remember that using the SRT will require a subscription to either Enterprise support or Business support plans. Shield Advanced also has an option to use SRT as a proactive engagement, where the SRT team will contact you directly if an Amazon Route 53 health check you have associated with a protected resource becomes unhealthy during an event detected by Shield Advanced. This option allows you to work faster with the SRT team and limit the impact of an attack when your application availability is affected.

Remember that AWS Shield Advanced will only protect resources that are specified through an AWS Firewall Manager Shield Advanced policy or that you have specified in Shield Advanced. It will not automatically protect your AWS resources.

Using AWS Shield for Network Protection

Using AWS Shield for network protection is best followed by using DDoS-resilient architectures to increase the ability of your application architecture to withstand an attack. This includes designing and configuring architectures to take advantage of the AWS Shield mitigation capabilities using services like ELB, AWS WAF, AWS Global Accelerator, and CloudFront. These services help mitigate and protect against common attacks and provide a best practice approach to application design when protecting web applications and building resiliency for TCP and UDP applications.

Protecting Web Applications

When you're building resiliency for your web application, it doesn't matter which AWS region your application is deployed in as every AWS region receives automatic DDoS protection that AWS provides in the region. These protections are already in place to detect and mitigate DDoS attacks that AWS must deal with when protecting their endpoints used by you, their customer. Even though you have these protections in place, there is still a real chance that a targeted attack against your web application can happen, and you must be sure that the application and application architecture in AWS is prepared to manage the attack.

When protecting a web application in AWS from DDoS attacks, you can choose from four AWS services that can be used in concert to help scale the application and obfuscate the application origin. Using services like CloudFront and Route 53 gives you an additional layer of protection because they provide a fully integrated and inline DDoS mitigation system that mitigates attacks in real time. Figure 4.4 shows an example web application architecture protecting an EC2 instance using Route 53 hosted zones, CloudFront, AWS WAF, and ELB.

FIGURE 4.4 Example web application DDoS-resilient architecture

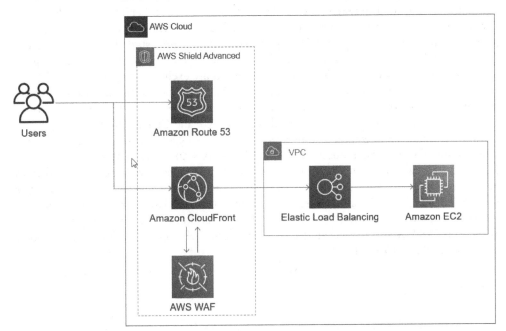

This architecture provides protection against layer 3 and layer 4 DDoS attacks frequently used to affect web applications. The architecture also adds the capability of enabling Shield Advanced for an additional layer of protection. Shield Advanced uses inferred network ACLs (NACLs) to block unwanted traffic and isolate failures closer to the source. These protections are placed further toward the edge of the network to minimize the effect on web application end users. The use of Route 53 also provides protection against common DNS application-layer attacks experienced by web applications.

CloudFront and Route 53 are in place to mitigate and protect against TCP SYN floods using TCP SYN proxy capabilities built into the two services. This TCP SYN proxy challenges any new connection requests to your web application and serves only legitimate users. This combination of protection helps ensure that your web application user will still be able to use your application while mitigating against an attack. To take this a step further, this architecture also uses AWS WAF to provide protection against web application-layer request floods. You can create rate-based rules within AWS WAF that allow you to block source IP addresses if a client is sending more requests than the rule permits. This can help fully mitigate a request attack by blocking the source IPs using the AWS WAF web ACL blocks.

This example architecture is also compatible with extending the support and protection by using Shield Advanced to add proactive engagement with the SRT and automatic application-layer DDoS mitigation for enabled CloudFront distributions. By enabling the optional CloudFront protection with Shield Advanced, your web application gains automated creation, testing, and management of mitigation rules for AWS WAF web ACLs associated with the CloudFront distribution. If you have a web application that is frequently targeted or that has prolonged periods of attacks, it would be worthwhile to investigate using the optional Shield Advanced protections.

Protecting TCP and UDP Applications

Proper network protection does not stop at the web application layer within your AWS account. It is important to take into consideration protection of other TCP- or UDP-based applications running in your environment, like IoT-based applications or voice over IP (VoIP) systems. This also includes web applications that require a static IP address or that are not candidates for using CloudFront—for example, if your customers are requesting a static list of IP addresses to add into their firewall that are exclusive to your web application. Other AWS customers use CloudFront static IP address ranges, and this would not be a viable option for your customer and excludes the use of CloudFront. Figure 4.5 shows an example architecture that offers DDoS resiliency for TCP and UDP applications.

In this example architecture, the purpose is to improve DDoS resiliency for applications that require TCP and UDP requests, and often the use of static IP addresses. The use of Route 53 and AWS Global Accelerator offers static IP addresses to your application that are anycast-routed to the AWS global edge network. These services route end-user traffic to your application, and AWS Global Accelerator can help reduce user latency by up to 60 percent. By combining the use of Route 53 and AWS Global Accelerator with an application load balancer and AWS WAF rules, you can detect and mitigate web application-layer request floods as well as TCP and UDP attacks.

FIGURE 4.5   Example TCP and UDP DDoS-resilient architecture

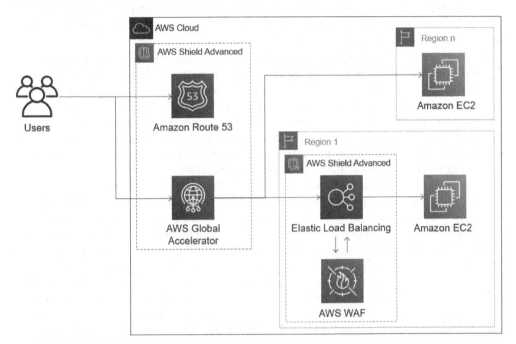

The benefits of this architectural design are like that of the web application resiliency architecture where you obtain protection against layer 3 and layer 4 DDoS attacks, DNS application-layer attacks, and request flooding using AWS WAF rate-based rules. This architecture also supports the addition of Shield Advanced to enable access to proactive engagement with the SRT. The key difference between this architecture is the requirement of the application to use static IP addresses or exclusively TCP or UDP protocols and not only HTTP or HTTPS used for web applications. Choosing to use Shield Advanced with either of these architecture designs will be a decision based on the use case and the level of mitigation and protection your organization requires.

Monitoring and Visibility into DDoS Events

Having AWS Shield and Shield Advanced protecting your environment helps bring peace of mind knowing that DDoS attacks will be lessened. With AWS Shield Advanced you have a team of experts in the SRT to assist. However, it is still a clever idea to monitor and have visibility into the DDoS events taking place against your AWS environment. Shield and Shield Advanced provide various levels of visibility for event categories. Shield offers a look into a global- and account-level category. At a global level, all AWS customers can see an aggregated view of global threats over the last day, last three days, and the last two weeks using the Global Threat dashboard in the Shield console. At an account level, all customers can access a summary of events for that specific account over the period of an entire year. This information describes DDoS events detected by Shield for resources that are eligible for protection by Shield Advanced. This summary is available in the Getting Started section of the Shield Management Console or through the AWS Shield API operation `DescribeAttackStatistics`.

Shield Advanced subscribers also receive additional information about the events and DDoS attacks against resources protected. The Events page in the Shield Management Console provides detailed information about each event, including event metrics that are published to CloudWatch for all resources that Shield Advanced protects. Shield Advanced also offers the ability to see cross-account events when combined with the usage of AWS Firewall Manager to manage Shield Advanced protections. Using Firewall Manager to manage Shield Advanced protections also offers the ability to send events to Security Hub to centralize even more information about the security of your AWS environment.

All the monitoring in the world will not help you identify if there are issues or potential attacks unless you have a baseline to compare against. Baselining your applications is an often-overlooked requirement when protecting against DDoS attacks or deciding on mitigation efforts. When baselining your application, you need to consider what normal would look like during various times of the year or the business seasonality. At a bare minimum, you will want to baseline by monitoring the number of allowed web requests and the number of blocked web requests using AWS WAF. This helps identify what normal would look like on any given day and inform any rate-based rules or advanced notifications of a DDoS or request flood attack. There are several other metrics to be aware of, such as general network traffic averages and network packet averages for your EC2 instances. These CloudWatch-enabled metrics can help you determine if an EC2 instance is receiving packets that are outside of the normal size expected for general operations, or help you identify an increase in overall network traffic that could be a sign of a SYN flood attack.

Using the baseline created and the monitoring logs found in CloudWatch, or whatever you choose to use, you can then determine the best path forward when mitigating an attack. When an attack occurs, you have two options for responding:

- Mitigate the attack on your own.
- Contact AWS support if you are a Shield Advanced customer.

If you are mitigating the attack yourself, the first step is to evaluate any monitoring you have configured to determine a source, if possible, and then create an AWS WAF rule statement in the web ACL with criteria matching the unusual behavior. However, be careful when applying these rules at first as you can inadvertently block legitimate traffic to your application. As a best practice, it is recommended that you only count matching requests for the new rule statements and not actively block them. Good news, though—you do not need to create these rules from scratch. AWS provides several templates within AWS WAF to help you get started quickly when creating rules to help with mitigation. When sufficient evidence is gathered from the counts, and you are sure that legitimate traffic is not being blocked, you can then move the rule to block. Once the rule has been evaluated, you will move into monitoring the event page to ensure that traffic is being mitigated as expected. Once you are comfortable that the event has been mitigated, you can relax for a moment, and then start the process of reviewing the event and logs with your security team. This review process after an event will help strengthen the network protection strategy and improve proactive protections within your environment.

AWS WAF

Protecting web applications is an essential task regardless of where the application is hosted. Any Internet-facing application is subject to a torrent of connections, both legitimate and potentially malicious. As a SysOps administrator you will often find yourself designing or configuring various levels of protection for applications running in the AWS Cloud. If you look at the AWS shared responsibility model, you'll see that it is the customer's role in protecting applications and assets in the cloud, whereas AWS will protect the cloud itself. This means any application protections like limiting network connections, preventing SQL injection attacks, or even designing for DDoS resiliency at an application layer is the responsibility of the AWS account owner. To help you better protect web applications running in the AWS Cloud, we will explore the use of AWS Web Application Firewall (AWS WAF).

AWS WAF helps protect web applications from attacks by using configurable rules that can allow, block, or count (monitor) web requests coming into your application based on definable conditions. You can define conditions to include in rules based on IP addresses, HTTP headers, HTTP body, URI strings, SQL injection, and even cross-site scripting. AWS WAF is tightly integrated with CloudFront, Application Load Balancer (ALB), API Gateway, and AWS AppSync services. When an underlying service like CloudFront receives a request for your website, it forwards those requests to AWS WAF for inspection. Once AWS WAF inspects the requests by evaluating the rules and conditions you defined, it will respond to the underlying service with either a block or an allow. AWS WAF also supports protecting applications not hosted in the AWS Cloud by using CloudFront as you can define an origin that is hosted anywhere.

AWS WAF can help protect web applications from common attacks like SQL injection and cross-site scripting (XSS), on top of also allowing rules that can block or rate-limit traffic from specific IP addresses, user agents, or request headers. This additional functionally is what makes AWS WAF an excellent resource to help control and mitigate DDoS attacks when combined with Shield and Shield Advanced. AWS WAF also provides visibility and control over common pervasive bot traffic attempting to access your web applications. You can optionally use AWS WAF Bot Control to monitor, block, or rate-limit pervasive bots, like scrapers, crawlers, and scanners that may be impacting the performance of your web application. You can also choose which common bots, like status monitors or search engines, that you wish to allow access to your applications. AWS WAF provides several Bot Control–managed rule groups to choose from, or you can create your own custom WAF rules to protect your applications. You can use custom rules and managed rules at the same time to protect your application by allowing more customization and protection. When designing an implementation strategy for AWS WAF, be sure to check `https://aws.amazon.com/waf/pricing` for AWS WAF pricing.

AWS WAF Pricing

AWS WAF follows a pricing model that charges based on the number of web access control lists (web ACLs) that are created in your account. You are also charged by the number of rules that you add per web ACL, and the number of web requests that are received by AWS WAF. There are no additional up-front commitments or costs associated with AWS WAF, but charges for this service are in addition to the integrated services using AWS WAF.

AWS WAF pricing is the same across all AWS regions, and monthly fees are prorated hourly. You will be charged for each web ACL that you create at the rate of $5.00 per month, and each rule that you create per web ACL at the rate of $1.00 per month. AWS WAF also charges based on the number of web requests processed by the web ACL at the rate of $0.60 per 1 million requests. It is also important to note that you will be charged for rules inside rule groups that are created by you. If you add a rule group or managed rule group to your web ACL, you will be charged $1.00 per month for each rule group or managed rule group that you add.

There are several optional security features that you can enable on your web ACL. The charges for these additional features are included with the AWS WAF fees. Where applicable, you must pay a subscription fee, request fee, and analysis fee in addition to the standard AWS WAF fees. For example, AWS WAF Bot Control has a subscription fee of $10.00 per month and a request fee of $1.00 per million requests inspected. When using the CAPTCHA security feature, you are charged an analysis fee of $0.40 per thousand challenge attempts analyzed. A challenge attempt is when a user completes a CAPTCHA challenge that is submitted to AWS WAF for analysis. You are charged regardless of the outcome of the analysis, and a single CAPTCHA response can result in multiple attempts. An additional request fee is charged when the original request is retired after the successful attempt. AWS WAF Fraud Control account takeover prevention (ATP) has an additional subscription charge of $10.00 per month and an analysis fee of $1.00 per thousand login attempts analyzed. Login attempts are defined as when a user submits a username and password through your web application login page.

AWS WAF does offer free tier usage for some of the optional security features like Bot Control and Fraud Control ATP. The Bot Control free usage tier includes the first 10 million requests inspected per month, and the ATP free tier includes the first 10,000 attempts analyzed per month. There is one more pricing consideration to take into account when you're working with AWS WAF: managed rule groups from AWS Marketplace. AWS WAF provides the ability for you to subscribe to a managed rule group provided by an AWS Marketplace seller. When you subscribe to these rule groups, you are charged an additional fee based on the price set by the seller, which is in addition to the AWS WAF fees that the service charges for each rule and rule group. When considering the use of managed rule groups from AWS Marketplace sellers, be sure to check and understand the additional fees before subscribing.

How AWS WAF Works

AWS WAF operates in an equivalent way to other application-layer firewalls. AWS WAF uses web ACLs to protect AWS resources, and you define what is blocked in each web ACL rule. These rules are the statements of conditions that AWS WAF uses to inspect the web requests and to decide whether to block, allow, run CAPTCHA, or count the transaction. AWS WAF supports reusable rule groups that enable you to define groupings of rules for a specific purpose, such as an application type, or you can purchase AWS Marketplace managed rule groups if you have a specific need.

Once the web ACL is created and the rules and rule groups are defined, you can associate the web ACL with one or more AWS resources. There are varying resource types that AWS WAF can protect, including CloudFront distributions, an API Gateway REST API, an application load balancer, and an AWS AppSync GraphQL API. When designing an AWS WAF implementation, use the AWS Service Endpoint documentation at `https://docs.aws .amazon.com/general/latest/gr/rande.html` to ensure that AWS WAF is available in the region you selected.

Web Access Control Lists

At the heart of AWS WAF are the web ACLs. Web ACLs provide a finer level of control over HTTP(S) web requests that your protected applications respond to. When configuring a web ACL to allow or block requests to your application, you must select which criteria the web ACL will use to make the allow or block determination. The criteria used can be an origin IP address of the request, a country of origin, a string match or regular expression (regex) that matches part of the request, a size of a particular request, or a detection of malicious SQL code or malicious scripting. When defining the web ACL, you are not limited to using a single criterion for evaluation; you can use any combination of the criteria options to ensure that you are blocking or allowing exactly the traffic that you intend. Another feature of web ACLs is the ability to block or count web requests that exceed a specified number or requests identified by the criteria in any 5-minute period. This means you can use logical operators to further enhance a rule. For example, you could set up an AWS WAF rule that is looking for a specific country of origin, and that request must come in more than 1,000 times per 5-minute interval before it begins counting or blocking the request. This is useful when determining the viability of a web ACL, or if you are protecting against large traffic spikes from known potentially malicious IP addresses or countries.

 When AWS WAF is processing more than one rule in a web ACL, it will evaluate the rules in order that they are listed for the web ACL. Be mindful of the order that you place rules in to ensure proper evaluation based on your needs.

When applying rules to a web ACL, you also configure the actions AWS WAF uses to handle the matching web request. Allowing and blocking, and sometimes CAPTCHA, are considered terminating actions. This means that these actions stop all other processing of the web ACL on the matching web request. Once a match is found and the action is to allow or block the request, this is the final disposition of the web request for the web ACL. In another way, once it allows or blocks a web request based on the web ACL, it has done its job and stops looking to match other rules for that request. As for CAPTCHA being a terminating action, if a CAPTCHA status is returned with an invalid token, it will terminate the evaluation of rules and supply the requester with a CAPTCHA challenge puzzle to solve.

There are also nonterminating actions such as counting and CAPTCHA. Counting is logging the requests that meet the required conditions, and then AWS WAF moves on to evaluate the remaining rules in the priority order defined. This means that a web request could be counted and then also be blocked or allowed by a rule that is further down the priority list. CAPTCHA will be nonterminating when a valid CAPTCHA token is presented with the request because AWS WAF will continue evaluating the rules that follow the web ACL rule set.

AWS WAF also allows overriding of actions of a rule or group of rules to alter terminating rules by adding a count action instead of allowing or blocking the request. You can use this option to assess a rule group before it is implemented with the normal action settings. For example, if you created a new rule or rule group for a web application to block traffic from a specific country, you can override the block action and change it to count. Once this is done you can test the rule, see that traffic is or is not being counted, and then evaluate if the rule is ready for production. This is also a great option to troubleshoot a rule or rule group that has been generating false positives. By adding the count override, you are preventing that rule from falsely blocking traffic, and you can identify whether traffic is legitimately being blocked or further criteria changes are needed.

In Exercise 4.5, you will create an AWS WAF web ACL to protect resources in your AWS account.

EXERCISE 4.5

Creating an AWS WAF Web ACL

1. Open the AWS Management Console and select the AWS WAF & Shield service.

2. From the AWS WAF & Shield console, click Create Web ACL if this is your first time using AWS AWF. If it isn't, you will be able to click the Web ACLs navigation item and then click Create Web ACL to continue.

3. For this exercise you will use a regional resource, and the region will be US East (N. Virginia). Be sure to select the regional resource and region first as it may clear the name and description fields.

4. Now enter the name of **DemoACL** and a description of **Demo ACL to remove later** and ensure that the CloudWatch metric name is autopopulated to DemoACL. Skip associating AWS resources and click Next.

5. Let's add a managed rule by clicking the Add Rules drop-down menu and selecting Add Managed Rule Groups. Expand the AWS managed rule groups and scroll to the Free rule groups. From here, toggle the switch to add the Admin Protection rule group to your web ACL. Continue to explore the other managed rules that are available under the paid and free options, and when finished, click Add Rules to continue.

6. Under the default ACL action, leave the action as Allow. Because you are blocking the traffic that matches the rule group selected, you want all other traffic to be allowed through for further processing. Click Next.

7. You do not need to set a rule priority for this exercise. However, this is the location where you would set the priority order for processing if you selected multiple rule sets for use. Click Next.

8. Leave the CloudWatch metrics and request sampling options at their default values and click Next.

9. Review the configuration options set during this exercise and click Create Web ACL.

10. The new web ACL is now created and available for use within the AWS account. This web ACL can be associated with AWS resources by clicking the rule and selecting the Associated AWS Resources tab and clicking Add AWS Resources. Remember, you can associate each AWS resource with only one web ACL as the relationship between web ACL and AWS resource is one-to-many. You *can* associate a web ACL with one or more CloudFront distributions, but the web ACL cannot be associated with any other resource type.

This completes the exercise for adding an AWS WAF web ACL to protect AWS resources. To avoid any unnecessary charges to your AWS account, be sure to delete the web ACL after you are done reviewing the process.

Using Rule Groups in AWS WAF

Rule groups are a reusable set of rules that can be added to a web ACL. There are three categories of rule groups: managed, custom (rule groups you own), and integrated (rule groups owned and managed by other services like Firewall Manager and Shield Advanced). Rule groups differ from web ACLs as they can be used across multiple web ACLs and can be reused, whereas web ACLs cannot. Rule groups also do not have a default action; this option is defined for each individual rule or web ACL. Rule groups are not associated with an AWS resource directly. If you want to protect AWS resources with a rule group, it must first be added to a web ACL and the web ACL associated with that resource.

Managed rule groups are like collections of ready-to-use and preconfigured rules that AWS and various AWS Marketplace sellers design and maintain. Most of the AWS-managed rules are available for free to AWS WAF customers, whereas the AWS Marketplace managed rule groups are only available through a paid subscription using the AWS Marketplace. Managed rule groups offer a quick start to protecting AWS resources and can also help with compliance needs. For example, if your organization requires PCI or HIPAA compliance, you may find a managed rule group meets the needs for your web application firewall requirements. Managed rule groups also have the added benefits of receiving automatic updates that keep the rules ahead of the constantly changing threat landscape. It is also important to know that when using a managed rule group, you cannot see the rules themselves. This is a designed restriction to protect intellectual property of the rule group provider and prevent malicious users from designing threats to circumvent the published rule groups.

AWS WAF also allows for the use of your own rule groups, where you can create reusable collections of rules that may not be found in the managed rule group offerings. You may also choose to manage your own rule groups for security, compliance, or governance reasons within your organization. Whatever the reason, when you create a rule group it acts just like any web ACL where you can add rules in the same way. The only difference is that when you create a rule group of your own, you must set an immutable maximum capacity for it, whereas you are not required to set this capacity when using managed rules. If you have a rule group that is working well for your organization, and you want to share it with other AWS accounts, you do this by using the AWS WAF API and the `PutPermissionPolicy`.

The last rule group type is the integrated or rule groups provided by other services. For example, if you use Firewall Manager or Shield Advanced to manage protection of your AWS resources that are using AWS WAF, you will see rule group reference statements added to the web ACLs in your account to indicate that these groups are provided by the other services. The names of the rule groups begin with specific strings, such as `ShieldMitigationRuleGroup`, `PREFMManaged`, and `POSTFMManaged`. The `ShieldMitigationRuleGroup` is managed by Shield Advanced and is added when using layer 7 protections and enabling automatic application-layer DDOS mitigation for the associated resources. It's important to manually remove the integrated rule group as it could cause unintended consequences for resources. The `PREFMManaged` and the `POSTFMManaged` rule groups are managed by the AWS Firewall Manager and will have web ACL names beginning with `FMManagedWebACLV2`.

Using Rules in AWS WAF

Rules allow you to define how to inspect HTTP(S) web requests and which actions to take on a request when it matches the inspection criteria. Within AWS WAF, rules are only defined in the context of a rule group or web ACL. You can define rules to inspect for criteria like cross-site scripting, IP addresses or ranges, geographical location, SQL code, length of a specific part of the request, labels, and strings in the request.

Rules must have one top-level statement, which can contain nested statements at any depth depending on the rule and statement type. Some rule types take sets of criteria, such as specifying up to 10,000 IP addresses or IP address ranges in an IP address rule. Statements can also use logical statements such as `AND`, `OR`, and `NOT` that you can use to combine statements in a rule. For example, if you wanted to combine statements so that a rule inspects IP addresses, SQL-like code in the query string, and a specified user-agent header value, you would use the `AND` logical statement so that all conditions must be true before matching the top level.

It is important to remember that AWS WAF rules cannot exist on their own and are not considered AWS resources. This means they do not have Amazon Resource Names (ARNs) and cannot be independently accessed. All rules must be accessed by name in the rule group or within the web ACL where the rule is defined. Rule names must be unique to every rule in the web ACL or rule group, and the name cannot be changed after it is created. If you want to manage or copy rules to other web ACLs, you use the JSON format of the rule group or web ACL containing the rule. You can also use the AWS WAF console Rule Builder to simplify this process.

Rules can also include a `scope-down` statement to further narrow the scope of requests that the rule evaluates. A `scope-down` statement will evaluate the request against the scope-down statement first, and if a match is found it will continue using the rules standard criteria. Any traffic that does not match the scope-down statement will result as not matching, and AWS WAF will perform no further evaluations. scope-down statements can be used with AWS WAF Bot Control–managed rule groups to help exclude static content by negating matched results. The result of using scope-down statements is removal of unwanted or unnecessary web requests and traffic from reaching your web application.

Using Optional Managed Protections

AWS WAF has several managed protection features where you can include additional, specialized protections in your web ACLs and applications such as AWS WAF Bot Control, AWS WAF Fraud Control ATP, AWS WAF client application integration, and AWS WAF CAPTCHA.

AWS WAF BOT CONTROL

AWS WAF Bot Control is used to help manage bot activity coming into your site by categorizing and identifying common bots, verifying desirable bots, and detecting high-confidence signatures of bots. AWS-managed rule groups and AWS WAF features are combined to allow Bot Control to be customized in how you want to manage bot-related traffic coming into a web application. At the basic level, Bot Control is a managed rule group that provides visibility and control over common and pervasive bot traffic coming into an application. Bot Control can also be used to monitor, block, or rate-limit bots like crawlers and scanners, while allowing common bots like status monitors and search engines to be used without issue.

Bot Control has six basic components for implementation: managed rule group, Bot Control dashboard, logging and metrics, scope-down rules, labels and label matching rules, and custom requests and responses. The managed rule group is called AWSManagedRulesBotControlRuleSet, and this must be included in your web ACL using a managed rule group reference statement. The rule group also adds labels to a web request that it detects as bot traffic. Note that you are charged an additional fee when you use this rule group. The next component is called the Bot Control dashboard, and this is where you can monitor traffic and understand how much of it comes from diverse types of bots. The Bot Control dashboard is a great starting place to review traffic and customize bot traffic. Any changes that you make to bot traffic can be verified in this dashboard.

Logging and metrics are an additional component of Bot Control and help you to understand how the Bot Control–managed rule group evaluates and manages traffic by configuring and enabling logs and CloudWatch metrics for the web ACL. Any labels added by Bot Control are added into the log of the web requests. Using logging and metrics with Bot Control can help provide data to use other Bot Control components like scope-down statements or label-matching rules. scope-down statements allow you to limit the scope of the web requests that the Bot Control–managed rule group evaluates. Traffic that does not match the scope-down statement results as not matching the rule group and is not evaluated by the Bot Control–managed rule group. scope-down statements are a wonderful way to limit the number of web requests that Bot Control is evaluating and reduce the cost of using Bot Control.

Labels and label matching rules are an additional component that Bot Control adds to your web requests. Labels allow you to customize how web requests are managed and identified by the Bot Control–managed rule group. Using label match statements, you can inspect the labels that are on the web requests against a string that you specify. Note that labels do not persist outside of the web ACL evaluation. A label match statement can only see labels from rules that are evaluated earlier in the web ACL. In addition to labels, you can add custom headers to allowed requests. You can also send custom responses for requests that are blocked by using label matching and custom request and response features.

ACCOUNT TAKEOVER PREVENTION

Another optional managed protection within AWS WAF is the AWS WAF Fraud Control ATP, which helps prevent account takeover by gaining unauthorized access to a person's account. ATP provides visibility and control over anomalous login attempts that may be from stolen credentials. This visibility and control can help prevent account takeovers that may lead to fraudulent activities. ATP validates login requests for any username and passwords that match against its stolen credential database. Amazon updates this database regularly to include any new leaked or stolen credentials found on the dark web.

When you configure ATP in AWS WAF, it uses the `AWSManagedRulesATPRuleSet` to detect, label, and manage distinct types of account takeover activities. The rule group inspects HTTP POST web requests sent to the login endpoint of your application. You must supply the details of your applications login page when configuring the managed rule set. This allows the rule group to limit the scope of requests it inspects and avoid any false positives that may occur when using too broad of an evaluation. ATP is also capable of detection against automated attacks that may come from a bot. This is enabled by using the JavaScript and mobile application integration SDKs. Once integrated into your application, the SDK serves as a silent challenge to the user's browser or device to determine if the traffic is legitimate. Just like the Bot Control protection you can use custom requests and responses, labels and label-matching rules, and logging and metrics to further narrow the scope of protection.

AWS WAF CLIENT APPLICATION INTEGRATION

When using AWS-managed rule groups that enable advanced managed integration, you need to integrate the AWS WAF SDK into your application. These advanced managed integration rule groups require an SDK integration, or for you to provide security capabilities that are enhanced by the integration. Currently the AWS-managed rule group for ATP can use this client integration to provide protection against automated login attacks. The integration SDK manages token authorization for your specified client applications and ensures that the protected resources are only accessed after the client has received a valid token. AWS WAF offers a JavaScript SDK that is generally available and offers custom SDKs for Android and iOS mobile applications. If you want access to the custom mobile SDKs, you must contact an AWS sales representative.

AWS WAF CAPTCHA

To assist in weeding out unwanted requests and limiting the ability for non-human logins, you can implement the AWS WAF CAPTCHA component. CAPTCHA stands for Completely Automated Public Turing test to tell Computers and Humans Apart. These challenges are designed to be easy and quick for humans to complete and hard for computers to complete successfully or to randomly complete. This helps ensure that humans are sending requests and prevents activity like web scraping, credential stuffing, and spam.

AWS WAF can be configured to have rules run a CAPTCHA check against web requests that match rule inspection criteria that you defined. A CAPTCHA can be sent as needed to require the client sending a request to solve a CAPTCHA challenge. When the user provides a correct answer, they are allowed through; if the user fails the challenge by providing an incorrect answer, the challenge informs the user and loads a new puzzle. Any successful CAPTCHA response will allow the original web request to be submitted and will include a new CAPTCHA token from the puzzle completion. This makes the use of CAPTCHA favorable for web applications that need to verify user logins or that want to reduce the amount of automated bot traffic to the application overall.

Using AWS WAF for Network Protection

Now that you are aware of the various components and optional protections that AWS WAF provides, it is time to see how AWS WAF provides network protection for an AWS environment. You have already seen the integration potential with CloudFront, ALB, and API Gateway, which often supply most of the applications that need protection behind AWS WAF. When designing a network protection strategy, consider placing AWS WAF as the edge protector for your applications and be mindful of the types of web requests and traffic that you want for your application. This preplanning exercise will drastically reduce the overall cost of AWS WAF implementations and help identify any additional protection services that can achieve goals for CAPTCHA or limiting bot traffic. You can see a sample web architecture using AWS WAF with CloudFront and without in Figure 4.6.

In the architecture shown in Figure 4.6, AWS WAF protects applications at the very edge of the network, where it can prevent the most traffic from reaching an application. When you use CloudFront for caching or protecting the origin, AWS WAF can use CloudFront as an integrated service with additional features and logging available to enhance network protection. AWS WAF can also be used directly with ELB if the architecture does not use CloudFront. This flexibility ensures that any web application has the potential to use AWS WAF for network protection.

You may be thinking "If I'm using AWS WAF, I don't need to use anything else, right?" Wrong. AWS WAF is only one component of protection that is available for applications running in AWS. Just as you would not lock your front door but leave the windows open, or you wouldn't just have the windows up in your car with the doors wide open, you wouldn't want to leave gaps or openings for potential misuse, fraud, or attacks. AWS WAF helps round out the network protection strategy by controlling traffic at the edge and limiting web requests to only what you specify for the application.

However, you will still need to implement other network protections such as Shield and Shield Advanced, Firewall Manager, and even basic protections like security groups and CloudFront to protect the server origin. Network protection is not just about adding one service and stopping for the day. It is about building a strategy around a complement of services, features, and design principles to ensure that your web applications are secure and stable.

FIGURE 4.6   Sample AWS WAF architecture with and without CloudFront

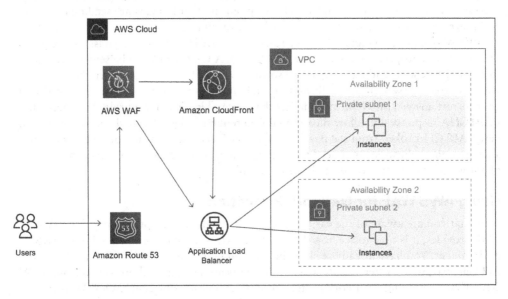

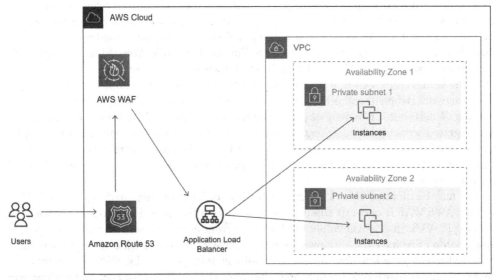

AWS Firewall Manager

Firewall Manager is a security management service used for centralized management and configuration of firewall rules across AWS accounts and applications in an AWS Organization. This means that you have control over enforcement and compliance of a common set of security rules that are applied to new applications and resources as they are added into the AWS Organization. Firewall Manager allows the creation of security policies and firewall rules, and the enforcement of each in a consistent and hierarchical manner across your AWS infrastructure.

The entire purpose of Firewall Manager is to simplify administration and maintenance tasks for AWS WAF, Shield Advanced, VPC security groups, AWS Network Firewall, and Route 53 Resolver DNS Firewall across multiple accounts. When you initially configure Firewall Manager the service will automatically apply those protections across the accounts and resources within the AWS Organization, even when new accounts and resources are added.

Firewall Manager has several benefits when used in an AWS Organization. It helps protect resources across all accounts and particular resources like CloudFront. It automatically adds protection to resources that are added to the member accounts subscribed to an AWS Organizations organization, including allowing subscriptions to Shield Advanced. Firewall Manager also has the extremely useful benefit of allowing security group rules to be applied to all member accounts or specific subsets of accounts in an AWS Organization. This benefit drastically reduces the number of noncompliant applications by automatically applying rules to new in-scope accounts that join the organization. Firewall Manager also allows for the use of custom rules or purchased managed rules from the AWS Marketplace in one location. Always be sure to check `https://aws.amazon.com/firewall-manager/pricing` when designing an implementation plan for Firewall Manager to see the latest pricing information.

AWS Firewall Manager Pricing

Pricing for Firewall Manager follows a per-region monthly fee for use of the Firewall Manager protection policy. This monthly per-region fee applies to five out of the six protection policy types, whereas the Shield Advanced subscription includes the use of Firewall Manager at no additional cost. AWS WAF, VPC security groups, AWS Network Firewall, Route 53 Resolver DNS Firewall, and Palo Alto Networks Cloud Next-Generation Firewalls (NGFWs) all have charges for the AWS Network Firewall protection policies applied monthly, per region.

It is also important to know that pricing for Firewall Manager does not include the AWS Config rules or the individual service fees for protection services such as AWS WAF. When designing your AWS Firewall Manager implementation, consider the fees for the protection services themselves and AWS Config. The pricing for Firewall Manager itself is $100 per policy per public region across all protection services except for Shield Advanced (it is included in the Shield Advanced subscription). AWS WAF protection policy has an additional charge of $100.00 per policy per region for Global (CloudFront locations).

How Firewall Manager Works

When would you use Firewall Manager? The real benefit of Firewall Manager comes into play when you want to protect an entire organization rather than a small number of specific AWS accounts and resources. Additionally, if you frequently add new resources to an AWS account that needs protection, Firewall Manager is a good solution to allow automatic application of protections for these additions. Firewall Manager is also useful when you need to centrally monitor DDoS attacks across an organization. But how does Firewall Manager work?

Firewall Manager is a centralized management tool, which means you only use one Firewall Manager administrator account for management of all Firewall Manager security policies within an AWS Organization. There are a few prerequisites that need to be addressed before you can begin using Firewall Manager. First, the account that you want to be the administrator of must be a member of the organization in the AWS Organizations service where you want to use the Firewall Manager policies. Next, you need to set the Firewall Manager administrator account, which will automatically be set as an AWS Organizations Delegated Administrator for Firewall Manager. These delegated administrator permissions will allow Firewall Manager to access information about your organizational units (OUs) for scoping of any Firewall Manager policies. Firewall Manager requires AWS Config to be enabled within each of the AWS Organization's member accounts, including the administrator account. This means you must ensure that AWS Config is enabled for each AWS region where you have resources located that you want to protect.

If you do not want to enable AWS Config for all resources, you can enable AWS Config for specific resource types according to the type of Firewall Manager policies that you use. Table 4.2 shows the AWS Config resource types that are required when using each Firewall Manager policy type. You can use this table to identify which AWS Config resources you need to enable in a specific region when you do not wish to enable AWS Config for all resource types.

TABLE 4.2   AWS Config resource types required per Firewall Manager policy types

Firewall Manager policy	AWS Config resource types
WAF Policy	Application Load Balancer (select ElasticLoadBalancingV2), API Gateway, WAF Web ACL, WAF Regional web ACL, WAFv2 web ACL
	Amazon CloudFront Distribution protection requires enabling the AWS Config CloudFront distribution resource type in the US East (N. Virginia) region.
Shield policy	Shield Protection, Shield Regional Protection, Application Load Balancer, EC2 EIP, WAF web ACL, WAF Regional web ACL, and WAFv2 web ACL
Security group policy	EC2 SecurityGroup, EC2 Instance, EC2 NetworkingInterface
Network Firewall policy	Network Firewall Policy, Network Firewall Rule Group, EC2 VPC, EC2 InternetGateway, EC2 RouteTable, EC2 Subnet
DNS Firewall policy	EC2 VPC

The next prerequisite for using Firewall Manager is dependent on your use of Palo Alto Networks Cloud NGFW. If you plan to use Firewall Manager for the Cloud NGW firewall, you will need to subscribe to the service in the AWS Marketplace and complete the service deployment steps listed in the Palo Alto Networks Cloud NFGW deployment guide. The next prerequisite is required to manage Network Firewall and DNS Firewall policies. To manage these policies, you must enable sharing with AWS Organizations in the AWS Resource Access Manager, which provides access to Firewall Manager to deploy protections across the member accounts for these policy types. The last prerequisite relates to using Firewall Manager in AWS regions that are disabled by default. If your implementation requires using Firewall Manager in a region that is disabled by default, you must enable the region for both the management account of the AWS Organization and the Firewall Manager administrator account. Examples of disabled regions by default are Africa (Cape Town), Asia Pacific (Hong Kong), Asia Pacific (Jakarta), Europe (Milan), and Middle East (Bahrain). Once all the prerequisites are out of the way for the Firewall Manager policy types, you are ready to configure the security policies that your organization requires.

 When setting up Firewall Manager for your organization, keep in mind that it does not support Route 53 or AWS Global Accelerator. You cannot use Firewall Manager policies if you want to protect these resources with Shield Advanced.

Whenever you add policies to Firewall Manager, it will continuously manage and apply the policies to new AWS accounts and resources as you add them. The policy scope dictates which resources are added or ignored. If a resource becomes out of scope, the protections will not be removed automatically unless you select the Automatically Remove Protection From Resources That Leave The Policy Scope check box when configuring policy scope. The cleanup process is optional but recommended to avoid any unnecessary charges. The default behavior for Firewall Manager when a resource goes out of compliance is to remove the associated AWS Config rules but leave the association of the resource being protected. This means the resources attached to that protection will continue to receive the protection benefit, but without management. When the Automatic Removal option is selected, the AWS Config Manager rules are deleted and any protected resource that is out of scope is automatically disassociated and removed from protection.

AWS WAF Policies

When using AWS WAF policies with Firewall Manager, you specify the rule groups that you want to apply across your resources. When the policy is applied to each account in the policy scope, it will have a web ACL created and managed by Firewall Manager. Individual account administrators can add rules and rule groups to these Firewall Manager–managed web ACLs in addition to those defined by the Firewall Manager administrator. Any web ACLs created by Firewall Manager will have a naming convention of `FMManagedWebACLV2-policy name-timestamp`. The time stamp will always be in UTC milliseconds, and the policy name matches the policy name that is created in Firewall Manager.

Three sets of rules are managed by Firewall Manager AWS WAF policies. The purpose of these rule sets is to help with prioritization for the rules and rule groups in the web ACL. The first rule group is defined by the Firewall Manager administrator in the Firewall Manager AWS WAF policy. AWS WAF will evaluate these rule groups first when web requests are received. The second set applies to rules and rule groups that are defined by the AWS account managers in the web ACLs. The last rule group is also defined within the Firewall Manager AWS WAF policy and added by the Firewall Manager administrator. Any rule groups in this set are evaluated last. Within each set the standard priority settings are followed when evaluating rules and rule groups. The first and last rule group sets only allow the addition of rule groups, which can be AWS-managed, from the AWS Marketplace, or custom rule groups that you create. If you want to use your own rule groups, you must create them before creating the Firewall Manager AWS WAF policy.

AWS Shield Advanced Policies

AWS Shield and AWS WAF are tightly integrated services used in remediation of DDoS attacks. When using Firewall Manager Shield Advanced policies with auto-remediation, each in-scope resource that is not already associated with an AWS WAF web ACL will have an empty one created for it. Shield uses these empty web ACLs for monitoring purposes, and if a resource is associated with any web ACL, Firewall Manager will remove the empty web ACL association. This means you can see several empty web ACLs created within AWS WAF when using Shield Advanced.

AWS accounts and resources change frequently, which can cause these resources accounts to go in and out of scope of a Firewall Manager Shield Advanced policy. For example, if a policy scope setting changes or an account is removed from an AWS Organization, this can cause the scope to change for the resource or account. When this occurs, Firewall Manager stops monitoring the account or resource. For an account that is removed from an AWS Organization, the account will continue to be subscribed to Shield Advanced and receive the benefits of this protection. This also means that the account will receive a prorated Shield Advanced subscription fee. However, if the AWS account is still a member of the organization but it goes out of scope of the policy, no additional fees are incurred. For any resource that goes out of scope of the policy, the resource will continue to be protected by Shield Advanced and incur data transfer charges for Shield Advanced.

One more important note about Firewall Manager Shield Advanced policies is that they are incompatible with AWS WAF classic policies when using automatic mitigation and automatic application-layer DDoS mitigation for CloudFront distributions. The easiest way to correct this problem is to re-create and replace the policy with a new policy, which will automatically use the latest version of AWS WAF, or you can have Firewall Manager create an updated version web ACL for the existing policy and make the switch over to the new web ACLs. Just remember that you must use the Global Region when using Shield Advanced policies with CloudFront distributions.

When implementing an AWS Firewall Manager Shield Advanced policy, you can check the version of AWS WAF that is being used by looking at the parameter keys in the policy AWS Config service-linked rule. The latest version will have a parameter key that includes the `policyId` and `webAclArn`. Earlier versions will have a parameter key that includes `webAclId` and `resourceTypes`. You can use the AWS Config console to evaluate the rules and search for AWS Config rule names that match the `policyId` and `webAclArn`, which means the policy is using the latest version of AWS WAF. If the rules have the `webAclId` and `resourceTypes`, the policy is using AWS WAF Classic and will need to be updated.

Security Group Policies

For AWS Organizations, Firewall Manager security group policies are designed to help manage VPC security groups. Using Firewall Manager, you can centrally control security group policies for your entire organization or even a subset of accounts and resources. Firewall Manager also monitors, audits, and manages any security group policies you create. This means that it will continuously maintain these security group policies and apply updates across the organization. Firewall Manager can apply common security groups to specified accounts and resources as well as audit group rules for noncompliance or the use of security groups to cut down on redundancy and unused groups.

Firewall Manager centrally controls the association of security groups to accounts and resources within your organization. There are common security group policy resource types to be aware of, such as EC2, elastic network interfaces (ENIs), ALBs, and Classic Load Balancer. Firewall Manager applies the policies to these resources and audits, and manages and updates them according to the scope of the policy you define.

Firewall Manager can also work across shared VPCs by setting the security group policy scope settings to include VPCs that are owned by another account and shared with an in-scope account. However, there are a few limitations to consider when applying security group policies that have shared VPCs. For example, you could have duplicates or multipole replicas of a security group in a single shared VPC because Firewall Manager replicates the primary security group once for each in-scope account that the VPC is shared with. If multiple accounts have access to the shared VPC and are in scope, this can lead to multiple replications. Additionally, any shared VPC will not show up in the Firewall Manager security group policy details until at least one resource is created in that VPC that is within scope of the policy. If a shared VPC is removed or the setting is disabled, Firewall Manager will delete the replica security groups that aren't associated with any resources and will leave the remaining replica attached to resources in place. This means you will need to manually clean up the security groups in each shared VPC instance if you wish to fully remove the replicas.

Security group policies within Firewall Manager also require what is known as a primary security group. Primary security groups must be created by the Firewall Manager administrator account, and they can reside in any Amazon VPC instance in the account. Management of the primary security groups is done through either VPC or EC2, and you can assign one or more security groups as primaries for the Firewall Manager security group policies. There is a limit of one security group in a policy, but this is a soft limit and can be changed by requesting a service quota increase by submitting a case to AWS Support.

As for management of the security groups in the VPC, there are policy rule settings that need to be considered when using Firewall Manager. You have a choice to identify and revert any changes made by local users to the replicated security groups, or you can disassociate any other security groups from the AWS resources that are within the scope of the policy. Your choice depends on the governance choices you make when deciding to use Firewall Manager security group policies. If you need to ensure that a security group replica is never changed from your standard set by your organization, you will revert any changes. If you want to ensure that only security groups in scope of the security group policy are used, you will disassociate any other security groups.

Another great benefit of using Firewall Manager security group policies is the ability to *audit security groups*. You can audit the content of audit security group policies to check and manage the rules that are in use within your organization's security groups. Content audits apply to all security groups created by customers within your organization, as well as non-managed security groups like those automatically created by AWS services. The scope of resource types for content audits are EC2 instances, ENI, and VPC security groups.

Note that security groups are considered in scope of the policy if they are explicitly in scope, or the security group is associated with resources that are in scope. You also must choose between the use of managed policy rules or custom policy rules for each content audit policy, but you cannot have both in one policy. A managed policy rule allows the use of application and protocol lists to specify what is allowed and what is denied by the policy. Firewall Manager controls the managed lists, but you can create your own custom application and protocol lists. If you choose to make a custom policy rule, you specify an existing security group as the audit security group for your policy. Think of this existing security group as the template that is being applied for the audit and it defines the rules that are allowed or denied by the policy.

You can also create audit security groups using the Firewall Manager administrator account. Management of the security groups is still completed outside of the Firewall Manager service. Security groups that are in use for content audit policies are used by Firewall Manager as a comparison reference. This reference determines which security groups are in scope of the policy, but Firewall Manager will not associate the security group with any resources in the organization.

When defining the rules in the audit security group, you must either use a managed policy rule or create and use a custom policy rule. The point of these policies is to allow or deny the rules that are defined in the audit security group as a default action. This marks the audited security groups as either compliant when you choose Always Allow, or noncompliant when you choose Always Deny. When using custom policy rules, think of using Allow to say the audited security groups matching the scope are acceptable and when using Deny Any Matches they are not acceptable.

There are some best practices to consider when using security group policies within Firewall Manager. First, you want to be sure that you exclude the Firewall Manager administrator account from the policy scope. When creating an audit security group policy through the console, this is the default option. You also should start with automatic remediation disabled when using audit security group or content policies. This helps eliminate any unwanted remediations before you can fully evaluate and analyze what would happen when automatic remediation is enabled.

Another best practice is to avoid conflicts if you are using outside sources to manage security groups. For example, if you are using a script, or another tool or service other than Firewall Manager, you could run into conflicts where Firewall Manager is attempting to remediate a change placed by the tool, or vice versa. To avoid conflicts, you should always create changes that are mutually exclusive between Firewall Manager and the outside management sources.

Network Firewall Policies

Another Firewall Manager type, *Network Firewall policies*, allow you to manage your VPCs across your AWS Organizations. Network Firewall policies enable you to use centrally controlled firewalls for your entire organization, including the ability to use a select subset of accounts or VPCs. To provide network traffic filtering protection for public subnets in your organization's VPCs, you must use the Network Firewall service. When applying a policy within Firewall Manager, you define what is in scope for the policy across your AWS accounts and VPCs. Firewall Manager then creates a firewall within Network Firewall and deploys the firewall endpoints to the VPC subnets to enable network traffic filtering.

There are a few things that you must do before you can use Network Firewall policies with Firewall Manager. To manage Network Firewall rule groups across the organization accounts, you must have resource sharing enabled. If you want to include the Network Firewall groups in the Network Firewall policy, you must ensure that they already exist in the Firewall Manager administrator account. You can create and manage the Firewall Manager rules and groups as you always do in the Network Firewall console directly. You can specify the stateless rule groups to add, a default stateless group, and the stateful groups within the Network Firewall administrator account to make them available for inclusion in the Firewall Manager policy for Firewall Manager.

Firewall Manager also controls the deployment of firewall endpoints using either a distributed deployment model or a centralized deployment model. With a distributed model, Firewall Manager will create endpoints for each VPC that is within scope of the Network Firewall Manager policy in use. If you want to customize the endpoint location, you must specify which availability zone (AZ) to create the firewall endpoints in, or you can let Firewall Manager automatically create endpoints in the AZs with public subnets. One benefit of specifying the firewall endpoint location is the ability to restrict the set of allowed Classless Inter-Domain Routing (CIDR) blocks per AZ.

Remember, if Firewall Manager is creating firewall endpoints automatically, you must specify whether the service will create a single or multiple firewall endpoints in the specified VPCs.

In a centralized deployment model, Firewall Manager creates one or more firewall endpoint within an inspection VPC. You may be thinking "What's an inspection VPC?" as it is a new term used within the Firewall Manager service when used with Network Firewall policies. An *inspection VPC* is a centralized VPC where Firewall Manager launches the firewall endpoints. You still must specify which AZs to create the firewall endpoints in, and you can't change the inspection VPC after you create your policy. If you want to use a different inspection VPC, you must create a new policy. If there are any changes to the list of AZs, Firewall Manager will attempt a cleanup of any endpoints that were created in the past and that are not currently part of the policy scope. Firewall endpoints will be removed only if there are no route table routes that reference the out-of-scope endpoints. Don't worry; if Firewall Manager cannot remove any of the endpoints, it will mark them as noncompliant and will continue attempting to remove the endpoint until it is safe to delete.

Firewall Manager must also create firewall subnets in the VPC for the firewall endpoints that filter your network traffic. A firewall endpoint must be deployed in a dedicated VPC subnet, and Firewall Manager will create at least one firewall subnet in each VPC that is in scope of the policy. When using a distributed deployment model, Firewall Manager will create firewall subnets only in AZs that have a subnet with an Internet gateway route or a route to the firewall endpoints. If you choose to specify the location of the firewall endpoints, Firewall Manager will create the endpoints in those specific AZs, even if there are other resources already located in the AZ.

You can also provide VPC CIDR blocks to use within Firewall Manager for the firewall subnets, or you can allow Firewall Manager to make the decision based on the available VPC CIDR blocks in scope. If you do not provide CIDR blocks, a query against your VPC is made to determine the available IP addresses in use. When you provide a list of CIDR blocks, Firewall Manager will search for new subnets only in the CIDR blocks provided. When you specify CIDR blocks, you must use /28 CIDR blocks. If you specify a CIDR block that has unavailable or open space in the VPC, Firewall Manager will not create a firewall in the VPC, and it will mark the subnets as noncompliant.

Firewall Manager creates Network Firewall resources using a specific naming convention for any resources in scope of the policy. The naming convention concatenates a fixed string, either `FMManagedNetworkFirewall` or `FMManagedNetworkFirewallPolicy`, depending on the resource type, with the Firewall Manager policy name that you create when you assign the policy. It also concatenates the Firewall Manager policy ID, which is the AWS resource ID for the policy and the VPC ID where Firewall Manager creates the firewall and firewall policy. The resulting name will be a combination of all the attributions, for example: `FMManagedNetworkFirewallMYPOLICYnameMYPOLICYFirewallManagerPolicyIdMY POLICYVPCId`. Once the policy is created, you cannot override the firewall policy settings or rule groups using the VPC account owner permissions.

Firewall Manager currently allows monitoring of VPC route table routes for any traffic destined to an Internet gateway that may be bypassing the Network Firewall, but it doesn't support other target gateways like NAT gateway or NAT instances. Route table management is only available for policies that use distributed deployment models and not centralized deployment models. One important note: When you are using Firewall Manager, it will create VPC route tables for any firewall endpoints it creates, but it will not manage the other VPC route tables. This means an administrator must configure the VPC route tables to direct network traffic to the firewall endpoints that are created by Firewall Manager.

Monitoring of VPC route configurations is a feature of Firewall Manager, and it will issue an alert when traffic bypasses firewall inspection for the VPC in scope of the policy. When a subnet has a firewall endpoint route, Firewall Manager will look for routes that send traffic to the Network Firewall endpoint, traffic from the Network Firewall endpoint to the Internet gateway, inbound routes from the Internet gateway to the Network Firewall endpoint, and routes from the firewall subnet. When a subnet has a Network Firewall route and there is asymmetric routing in the Network Firewall and an Internet gateway route table, Firewall Manager will report the subnet as noncompliant. Firewall Manager will also report on any additional routes in the Network Firewall subnet route tables and your Internet gateway route table that were created for the subnet and mark them noncompliant. Firewall Manager provides suggestions for remediation steps based on the type of violation. These remediation steps will bring the route configuration into compliance, but Firewall Manager does not offer suggestions for all cases. For example, Firewall Manager will not provide suggested remediation actions for non-IPv4 routes, such as IPv6 and prefix list routes.

Firewall Manager Network Firewall policies also have an optional centralized logging that you can enable to get detailed information about the traffic within your organization. This allows you to enable flow logging to capture network traffic flow or alert logging to report traffic that matches a rule within a rule action set for DROP or ALERT actions. You can configure logs generated by the policy's Network Firewall firewalls to an S3 bucket, which will use the reserved Firewall Manager prefix policy-name-policy-id format. When sending logs to your S3 bucket, be sure to include s3:GetBucketPolicy and s3:PutBucketPolicy in the permission sets on the bucket so that Firewall Manager can successfully place logs in the S3 bucket. Also keep in mind that only buckets within the Firewall Manager administrator account can be used for Network Firewall central logging.

DNS Firewall Policies

Another policy type supported by Firewall Manager is *DNS Firewall policies*, which are used to manage associations between Route 53 Resolver DNS firewall rule groups and VPCs across your AWS Organization. DNS Firewall policies offer centralized control of DNS Firewall rule groups in your organization to a select subset of accounts and VPCs, bringing more standardization and control than individual management at each account level. DNS Firewall filters and regulates outbound DNS traffic for VPCs in an AWS account and creates collections of filtering rule groups for association with VPCs that can be reused when needed.

When you're adding DNS Firewall policies to Firewall Manager, an association is created for any account and VPC that is in scope of the policy. This association applies to the Firewall rule group level and priority settings in the policy and with each VPC in scope of the policy. To use DNS Firewall policies, you must ensure that your AWS Organization has resource sharing enabled. Within DNS Firewall, you need to have rule groups defined and created using the Route 53 Resolver DNS Firewall directly using the Firewall Manager administrator account. You will only be able to include rule groups in a DNS Firewall policy if they are created in the Firewall Manager administrator account before you create the policy.

When creating a DNS Firewall policy in Firewall Manager, you must define the lowest-priority associations and the highest-priority associations for your selected VPCs. This is because DNS Firewall filters DNS traffic for VPCs in a specific order. The first rule groups

defined by you in the Firewall Manager DNS Firewall policy with valid values between
1 and 9 are evaluated first. Second, the DNS Firewall rule groups that are associated by
individual account managers directly in the DNS Firewall are evaluated. The final filter is
related to the last rule groups that you define in the Firewall Manager DNS Firewall policy
with valid values between 9001 and 10000. When planning a DNS Firewall policy implementation, pay close attention to the prioritization and filtering order applied to avoid
running filters against policies out of your expected order.

Firewall Manager, with auto-remediation enabled, will create a DNS Firewall association
between the rule groups of the policy and the VPCs within the scope of the policy
when you save the DNS Firewall policy. When Firewall Manager creates these associations,
it will use a naming convention that concatenates the fixed string of FMManaged_ and the
Firewall Manager policy ID. That means an association name would look like
FMManaged_*THISISANEXAMPLE*FirewallPolicyId when viewing the available associations. Once the policy is created, any account overrides to the firewall policy settings or rule
group associations will cause Firewall Manager to mark the policy as noncompliant. Once
a policy is marked as noncompliant, Firewall Manager will attempt to remediate actions to
bring the policy back into compliance. This does not mean that individual account owners
can't create DNS Firewall rule groups. When account owners want to create DNS Firewall
rule groups, they must ensure that associations have a priority setting between the first and
last rule group associations set by Firewall Manager.

Using Firewall Manager for Network

Firewall Manager enhances network protection by enabling central management of a core
set of network services like Network Firewall, AWS WAF, Shield, and Route 53 Resolver
DNS Firewall. Even though centralized management is important, the real benefit of using
Firewall Manager for network protection comes from the findings that Firewall Manager
creates for resources that are out of compliance and for any attacks that it detects. Firewall
Manager integrates with other security services like Security Hub to automatically send findings to Security Hub to further centralize security logging and analysis.

When viewing Firewall Manager findings in Security Hub, you can filter findings based
on Product Name equaling Firewall Manager. If your organization is not using Security
Hub or you wish to disable the integration, you can disable the integration in the Security
Hub console. As you can see, the power of Firewall Manager goes well beyond just the
management component benefit by also enabling auto-remediation and finding reports
against any policy used in Firewall Manager. Understanding the finding types and the auto-
remediation options available will help you create an efficient network protection strategy.

Findings for AWS WAF Policies

Firewall Manager WAF policies apply to AWS WAF rule groups associated with your
resources in AWS Organizations. When you use AWS WAF policies in Firewall Manager, it
will generate findings when a policy goes out of compliance. For example, when a resource is
missing the association with the Firewall Manager–managed web ACLs, a report will be generated back to Firewall Manager. Firewall Manager is capable of remediation automatically

when that option is enabled. When Firewall Manager remediates the compliance issue, it will update the finding and lower the severity from HIGH to INFORMATIONAL. However, if a remediation is completed manually, Firewall Manager will not be able to update the finding. Firewall Manager is also able to remediate when a managed web ACL has misconfigured rule groups in scope of the policy. When the web ACL is missing the rule groups that the policy requires, Firewall Manager can automatically perform a remediation, and when completed, it will move the finding from HIGH to INFORMATIONAL. Just as with the other AWS WAF policy findings, any remediations done outside of Firewall Manager manually will not update the finding automatically.

Findings for Shield Policies

AWS Shield policies used to protect accounts and resources in Shield Advanced also have findings reported back to Firewall Manager. For example, when an AWS resource is lacking Shield Advanced protection when evaluating against the Shield policy, it will generate a finding for noncompliance. Firewall Manager will also report findings when Shield Advanced detects an attack on a protected AWS resource. With both findings, you can enable Firewall Manager to perform remediation automatically. Once the remediation is complete, Firewall Manager will move the finding severity from HIGH to INFORMATIONAL. When remediating findings manually, be sure to set the severity level to INFORMATIONAL in the Firewall Manager console since manually remediated findings are not updated automatically.

Findings for Security Group Policies

Firewall Manager also produces findings for security group content audit policy findings and security group usage audit policy findings. For example, Firewall Manager will produce findings for resources that have misconfigured security groups when evaluated against the Firewall Manager policy. This means when a resource is missing the Firewall Manager managed security group association as defined in the policy, Firewall Manager will produce a finding and then attempt to remediate the issue by creating the associations according to the policy settings. Firewall Manager will also produce findings when a replica security group is out of sync with the defined primary security group. When enabling remediation, Firewall Manager will sync the replica security groups with the primary security group and then update the finding automatically.

Firewall Manager will also generate findings for security groups that are not in compliance with content audit security groups. This finding identifies when an in-scope customer-created security group does not comply with the settings defined by the policy and the audit security group. When remediation is enabled, Firewall Manager will modify the noncompliant security groups to bring them back into compliance according to the security group content audit policy.

When Firewall Manager finds redundant security groups or unused security groups, a finding is generated. When a security group is found to have an identical rule set as another security group within the same VPC, Firewall Manager will attempt to remediate the finding by replacing the redundant security groups with a single security group. A similar action is taken when Firewall Manager identifies an unused security group that is not referenced by any Firewall Manager common security group policy. Once an unused security group is located, Firewall Manager will remediate the issue by removing the unused security group. In both cases, Firewall Manager must have auto-remediation enabled to remediate findings without manual intervention.

Findings for DNS Firewall Policies

Firewall Manager produces findings for DNS Firewall policies when a resource is missing DNS Firewall protection. The finding is generated when a VPC is missing a DNS Firewall group association that is defined in the Firewall Manager DNS Firewall policy. When the finding is generated, it will list the rule group that is specified by the policy to assist in remediation. Firewall Manager does not automatically remediate this finding, which means all remediation efforts will be manual.

Summary

Trusted Advisor provides useful information through the lens of best practices for an AWS account. You can use Trusted Advisor to review best practice guidance across the categories of cost optimization, performance, security, fault tolerance, and account service limits. Every AWS account has access to the core Trusted Advisor checks, but only Business and Enterprise support plans have access to the full suite of checks. Trusted Advisor checks can be reviewed from the AWS console for further investigation and remediation planning.

Security Hub provides account owners with a centralized method of viewing comprehensive information about an AWS account. The largest benefit of Security Hub is the centralized view and dashboards that can be used to view detailed findings from third parties, AWS accounts, and AWS services. Using Security Hub, you can analyze the security trends from various sources and identify the highest-priority security issues to remediate within the target AWS account. Security Hub provides prepackaged security standards for PCI, CIS AWS Foundations Benchmark, and AWS Foundational Security Best Practices. Security Hub also has tight integration with AWS Config for validation of findings, and various AWS services can use Security Hub as a destination to send findings for review through the available dashboard or by creating custom insights. Using EventBridge, you can enable auto-remediation with Security Hub by using custom actions to address security findings.

GuardDuty provides threat detection and active monitoring to protect AWS accounts, workloads, and data stored in the cloud. Using streams of metadata generated by your AWS accounts, GuardDuty will analyze network activity in CloudTrail events, VPC flow logs, and DNS logs for potential threats. GuardDuty uses machine learning to improve accuracy of threat identification and operates independently from the resources running in your AWS account. GuardDuty is considered a managed service provided by AWS, like RDS, where you only need to worry about remediating findings from the tool and not the underlying resources running GuardDuty. GuardDuty also supports integration with Security Hub, where it will send any threat findings for further analysis, enabling a centralized location for viewing security findings.

Inspector enables scalable and automated scanning for vulnerabilities within EC2 and container workloads. Inspector provides automated discovery and continual scanning of resources to deliver near-real-time vulnerability findings to a centralized management location called the Inspector console. The console offers configuration management and dashboard views of coverage metrics for AWS accounts, EC2 instances, and ECR repositories scanned by Inspector. Inspector requires configuration in each region where it is used. AWS Systems Manager (SSM) agents are installed and enabled on EC2 instances to provide CVE vulnerability data. This agent comes preinstalled in many Amazon Machine Images (AMIs), but some manual installation and validation is always advised. Once Inspector locates a vulnerability, it generates detailed findings that can be reviewed in the Inspector dashboard, where you can identify the most critical findings or a specific resource that needs attention.

Detective provides visualization of aggregate findings from GuardDuty, CloudTrail logs, and VPC flow logs to assist in the investigation of suspicious activities and root cause analysis. There are several prebuilt data aggregations and summaries that are useful within Detective that use machine learning, statistical analysis, and graph theory to generate meaningful visualizations. Detective extracts time-based events from the numerous data sources and stores up to one year of data for visualizations. Detective also integrates with AWS Organizations to provide management accounts with the analytics and visualizations generated from the member accounts.

Key Management Services (KMS) is a managed AWS service that provides the ability to create and control keys used for cryptographic operations. AWS KMS is highly available and lets you generate, store, manage, and audit encryption and digital signature keys. KMS also offers centralized management of encryption operations to reduce complexity and improve security controls of who can and cannot access your encryption keys. AWS KMS allows generation of asymmetric keys for digital signing or encryption options where certificates are not required. You can also create symmetric KMS keys for use when encrypting or decrypting data within AWS. KMS does not replicate keys between regions, but you can export and then import the key into another region for use by AWS resources. KMS uses envelope encryption to encrypt data above 4 KB in size. Any access to KMS or the available keys must be granted through IAM policies or KMS grants directly in the key policy. KMS is also quite useful when it comes time to rotate keys since it enables automatic key rotation for keys created and managed by KMS. KMS is used to enable AWS services to encrypt data at rest using the KMS keys, such as within S3.

AWS Certificate Manager (ACM) is used to enable encryption for in-transit operations by generating certificates for use within SSL/TLS. These certificates help ensure that traffic in transit is protected and encrypted. The largest benefit of ACM is the time savings that come from no longer being required to manually process or provision SSL/TLS certificates or run a private certificate authority. ACM certificates can be used with elastic load balancers and CloudFront distributions through tight AWS service integrations with ACM. If private certificates are required, ACM offers a private certificate authority option, which handles the issuance, validation, and revocation of private certificates. ACM offers the ability to create, store, and renew public and private SSL/TLS certifications. You can also import third-party certificates into ACM to simplify certificate management for applications that require third-party certificates. However, ACM is unable to automatically renew or manage the renewal process for any third-party certificates.

Macie provides protection for sensitive data stored in AWS. Macie is also a fully managed AWS service and is configured regionally. This means you must configure Macie in every region where you want to deploy the service. The service operates using machine learning and pattern matching to discover and protect sensitive data stored in S3 buckets and can identify several types of personally identifiable information (PII) such as names, addresses, passport ID numbers, or custom and unique patterns that your organization may require. An organization can use Macie to provide early warnings for potential security issues or breaches of PII for data stored in S3. Macie also supports use across AWS Organizations, where you can configure administrator and member accounts to centrally manage all Macie accounts. You can review findings for Macie in the Macie console dashboards or by querying the Macie API. Additionally, EventBridge is used to automate remediation, and Macie integrates with Security Hub to allow a centralized management of security findings for your AWS accounts.

Secrets Manager is used to protect credentials, such as a password, database connection string, or any string of characters that an application may need and that you don't want the public to know. These secrets are stored securely and managed in Secrets Manager. To retrieve the secrets, you can use the Secrets Manager console or access the Secrets Manager API, including using natively integrated services like RDS, DocumentDB, and Redshift clusters. Secrets Manager handles the rotation of secrets for your account when integrated with other AWS services, but you can store any secret you like in the service without enabling automatic rotation. Key Management Service (KMS) is used to encrypt secrets at rest, and you can use your own KMS key or have one provided and managed by the Secrets Manager service using AWS KMS. To use secrets stored in Secrets Manager, you must set the proper permissions using an identify-based policy applied to IAM users, groups, or roles. You can also use resource-based policies to grant access to multiple users and roles in another AWS account. Secrets Manager is also used when supplying an application secret or database connection string to CloudFormation templates, without needing to share the secret in plaintext with CloudFormation.

Shield and Shield Advanced provide protection for your AWS account and AWS resources against DDoS attacks. Shield is a managed AWS service with a standard and advanced option available. The standard option is available to all AWS customers at no additional cost and provides protection against common and frequently used network attacks occurring at layer 3 and layer 4 of a network for all AWS services and edge locations globally. Shield Advanced offers additional protection and integration with other AWS services, but the real benefit comes in the form of access to AWS security professionals in the Shield Response Team (SRT), which provides 24-hour support to help manage and mitigate application-layer DDoS attacks. Shield Advanced also offers cost protection to help offset the cost of mitigation efforts when auto scaling is used to outperform an attack. Shield Advanced requires a subscription commitment of one year and has a monthly fee of $3,000, which does not include data transfer-out usage fees. Shield Advanced offers integration with AWS WAF and uses AWS WAF ACLs, rules, and groups to provide application-layer protections. The use of AWS WAF is included in the price with AWS Shield Advanced. You can also receive additional information about the security events and DDoS attacks against protected resources in the Shield Management Console or integrate findings with Security Hub to centralize where you view security findings for your organization.

AWS Web Application Firewall (AWS WAF) provides application-layer protections and DDoS resiliency for web applications running in the AWS Cloud. AWS WAF uses configurable rules and rule groups to allow, block, or count web requests coming into the protected web applications. Using configurable conditions for your application, you can choose how the web requests are managed, including which types of requests or locations the requests are allowed to come from. AWS WAF also helps protect web applications from SQL injection and cross-site scripting attacks. Several services are tightly integrated with AWS WAF, such as Shield, CloudFront, application load balancers, API Gateway, and AWS AppSync. AWS AWF also offers additional protection features to control bot traffic, implement CAPTCHA controls, and include account takeover prevention (ATP). AWS WAF also offers client application integration using the AWS WAF SDK to further enhance AWS-managed rule groups for ATP that protects against automated login attacks by managing authorization tokens that require validation before traffic is allowed. Currently AWS WAF offers JavaScript and custom SDKs for Android and iOS mobile applications.

Firewall Manager is a security management service used for centralized management and configuration of firewall rules across AWS accounts and applications in an AWS Organization. You can create, manage, and enforce security policies and firewall rules using Firewall Manager in a hierarchal method across your AWS infrastructure. AWS WAF simplifies administration of tasks for AWS WAF, Shield Advanced, VPC security groups, Network Firewall, and Route 53 Resolver DNS firewalls across multiple accounts. When defining a scope in an AWS Firewall Manager policy, you can define a single resource, account, or collection of resources that are covered by the policy. Firewall Manager is also especially useful in maintaining compliance of VPC security groups across AWS Organization member accounts through the auto-remediation feature, which can be optionally enabled. Several Firewall Manager policies support auto-remediation to return the noncompliant account, resources, or rules into a compliant state. The Firewall Manager console offers detailed information about the findings of noncompliant policies across all AWS accounts within an AWS Organization. This means Firewall Manager requires setup and configuration in a defined AWS administrator account that is often the AWS Organization administrator account. The real benefit of using Firewall Manager is found in the ability to automate remediation steps and ensure VPC security group compliance across a defined standard.

Exam Essentials

Understand how to review Trusted Advisor security checks.   Trusted Advisor offers several security checks and guidance for an AWS account. It offers basic security checks for IAM Use, MFA on Root Account, Security Groups – Specific Ports Unrestricted, and Amazon S3 Bucket Permissions. Understand that Business and Enterprise support unlocks additional security checks, which assist an organization in reporting or automating security best practices.

Understand Security Hub findings and reports.   Security Hub provides a centralized management and reporting location for security findings in an AWS account. Security Hub enables further automation and management of security findings by integrating with other AWS services like GuardDuty, Macie, AWS WAF, and Shield. Automation using EventBridge and Security Hub is important when creating automated remediation actions based on findings from any source.

Understand GuardDuty threat detection findings.   GuardDuty provides analysis of threats for any VPC flow log, DNS log, or CloudTrail network activity. Any threats identified within a GuardDuty-monitored region is available as a finding in the GuardDuty console. GuardDuty provides findings for EC2 resources, S3 resources, and IAM resources, as well as Kubernetes resources within an account. You can review findings for GuardDuty in the GuardDuty console, Security Hub, or the AWS CLI, or by using API operations.

Be able to review findings in Inspector.   Inspector offers findings for vulnerabilities discovered within your web applications hosted in the AWS Cloud. Inspector offers findings for package vulnerability types and network reachability types. You can review findings using the Inspector console and dashboard, or in AWS Security Hub, or by exporting the findings to CSV or JSON format for use with other applications.

Understand how to implement encryption at rest using AWS KMS.   Key Management Service offers the creation and management of symmetric and asymmetric keys to encrypt data stored within AWS at rest. Understand how AWS KMS keys are rotated, managed, and used with envelope encryption to securely store data in AWS services like S3, and how AWS KMS is used to encrypt EBS volumes to protect data at rest.

Know how to implement encryption in transit using AWS Certificate Manager.   The AWS Certificate Manager (ACM) service lets you create and manage certificates to protect data in transit. Understand how ACM integrates with CloudFront, Elastic Load Balancing, and when to use private certificates within an infrastructure.

Know how to enforce a data classification scheme with Macie.   The Macie service offers pattern detection and analysis of data stored in S3 to identify and classify PII. Know how to review Macie findings and create data discovery jobs to enforce data classification in S3 buckets.

Understand how to securely store secrets using Secrets Manager.   The Secrets Manager service tightly integrates with several AWS services. Understand how to create, store, and rotate secrets for use with RDS, DocumentDB, and Redshift clusters. Understand which secrets you can automatically rotate and how to access secrets using CloudFormation.

Be able to configure AWS network protection services using AWS Shield.   Shield offers DDoS protection for AWS resources and edge locations. Know how to enable Shield Advanced and review findings from Shield to mitigate and reduce DDoS attacks.

Understand how to configure AWS network protection services using AWS WAF.   AWS WAF provides protection for web applications running in the AWS Cloud. Understand how to create and apply AWS WAF ACLs, rules, and rule groups. Know when to use AWS-managed rule groups and when to create custom rule groups, and how to review findings and apply remediation using Firewall Manager for out-of-compliance rule groups.

Review Questions

1. Which of the following AWS support plans offer access to all Trusted Advisor security checks within an AWS account? (Choose two.)
   - **A.** Enterprise Support
   - **B.** Developer Support
   - **C.** Basic Support
   - **D.** Business Support
   - **E.** AWS Forums support

2. Which AWS service is required for Security Hub to evaluate security findings and then perform automated remediation actions?
   - **A.** Amazon CloudWatch
   - **B.** AWS Config
   - **C.** Amazon EventBridge
   - **D.** AWS Step Functions

3. The chief information officer has asked you to provide reports and warnings for any S3 buckets that have `DeleteBucket` and `DeleteObject` actions taken on them in the production environment. Which AWS service will you use to accomplish this task?
   - **A.** Amazon Macie
   - **B.** Amazon Detective
   - **C.** Amazon Inspector
   - **D.** Amazon GuardDuty

4. You have been instructed by the security team to locate and evaluate any vulnerabilities in any available EC2 instances that may have reachable TCP and UDP ports from the VPC edges. You have decided to use Inspector for this task. Which of the following finding types will provide the vulnerability information required?
   - **A.** IAM finding type
   - **B.** Network reachability finding type
   - **C.** Package vulnerability finding type
   - **D.** CVE vulnerability finding type

5. You are attempting to encrypt 1,024 KB of data using AWS Key Management Service, and you are receiving errors when sending the data to the service. Which of the following is a potential cause for not being able to encrypt the data directly with AWS KMS?
   - **A.** KMS only allows 4 KB of data to be encrypted or decrypted directly without the use of envelope encryption.
   - **B.** The plaintext data encryption key is using the wrong IAM policy.
   - **C.** Large datasets can only be encrypted when directly accessed from EBS.
   - **D.** The AWS KMS key permissions are not configured to allow encryption of datasets above 4 KB in size.

6. The application security team has asked that you assist in procuring certificates and setting up caching for use in their web applications running in AWS. The infrastructure requires the use of CloudFront, and the applications are spread throughout the US-WEST, AP-SOUTHEAST, and EU-WEST regions. You decide to use AWS Certificate Manager for all web certificates, but when you attempt to locate the certificate for CloudFront you do not see it in the list of available certificates. Which of the following will allow CloudFront to see the certificate for use?

   A. Certificate Manager is a regional service, and you must ensure that is enabled and configured in the US-WEST, AP-SOUTHEAST, and EU-WEST regions.

   B. You cannot use Certificate Manager certificates with CloudFront. You must purchase the certificate from a third party and import IT directly within CloudFront.

   C. CloudFront is a regional service and you will need a different certificate from Certificate manager for each region.

   D. The web certificates must be present in the US-EAST region with AWS Certificate Manager or imported for use by CloudFront before they are selectable when configuring CloudFront.

7. The organization that you work for recently took on a contract to store sensitive proprietary data within S3 buckets for later use by analytical applications. Your CISO is concerned about potential data breaches from developers storing this sensitive data in S3 buckets that are not specified for this project. Which of the following options will provide a report for any sensitive information stored in S3 buckets that should not have this data?

   A. Use GuardDuty to identify the network traffic that is storing the data in the S3 buckets and report back to Security Hub.

   B. Use Inspector to evaluate all S3 buckets for sensitive data vulnerabilities and produce reports on which buckets fall out of compliance.

   C. Use Macie with custom data identifiers to define the criteria to match data stored in S3 buckets and provide reports on which objects and buckets hold noncompliant data.

   D. Use Detective to scan each object uploaded to S3 by developer accounts and produce a report of findings stored in Security Hub.

8. The application development group has reached out stating that they are having issues with Secrets Manager when attempting to retrieve a secret for their database connection. The team is attempting to connect using an EC2 instance that was created via an administrator account. When the application attempts to retrieve the secret, the team is presented with an "Unauthorized" error message. Which of the following actions should you check to resolve the issue?

   A. IAM permissions for the secret. Ensure that the EC2 instance has permissions to access Secrets Manager and the secret.

   B. AWS Secrets Manager API location. Check to ensure that the web application is using the proper HTTPS API endpoint instead of an HTTP endpoint.

   C. Verify that the latest version of the AWS SDK is being used by the application. Ensure that the connection string is formatted in JSON.

   D. Ensure that the web application is retrieving the secret using the AWSCURRENT value and not the AWSPREVIOUS value.

9. You just received an urgent phone call from several panicked application owners stating that their website is down. You also receive several alerts from your monitoring software that the application has become unresponsive. On investigation you realize that your web application is under a TCP SYN flood attack and you do not have any protection in place to stop this attack. Which services can the application utilize to create a TCP SYN proxy to help mitigate this type of attack in the future and receive help from a specialized team if the attack occurs again? (Select three.)

   A. Amazon CloudFront

   B. Amazon Elastic Load Balancer

   C. Amazon Shield Advanced

   D. Amazon Inspector

   E. Amazon Route 53

   F. AWS Security Hub

10. You have been tasked by the CISO to protect all web applications in the production AWS account from SQL injection attacks and cross-site scripting. Which AWS service will you use to accomplish this goal?

    A. Amazon VPC security groups

    B. AWS Web Application Firewall

    C. AWS Network Firewall

    D. AWS Shield

11. The web development team has asked you to deploy a method of limiting scanner and crawler traffic coming into the production web applications. Which AWS WAF feature will accomplish this task?

    A. AWS WAF CAPTCHA

    B. AWS WAF Account Takeover Prevention

    C. AWS WAF Bot Control

    D. AWS WAF client application integration

12. Your organization has recently acquired another web development company and is in process of combining AWS account resources. AWS Organizations was chosen to bring and manage the AWS accounts from the acquisition, but management of the AWS accounts to ensure compliance against security group standards and AWS WAF rule groups is becoming increasingly difficult. Which of the following AWS services will solve this problem?

    A. AWS Firewall Manager

    B. AWS Detective

    C. AWS Web Application Firewall

    D. AWS Security Hub

13. Your organization is using Detective and GuardDuty to visualize and investigate potential security issues and findings. What is the first phase of investigation when you receive a notification about a suspected high-risk activity?

   A. Scoping

   B. Response

   C. Triage

   D. Remediate

14. Your company has been using AWS WAF for all production web applications for a little over a year. During this time, you have created several custom AWS WAF rule groups that you want to share with other SysOps administrators across your global organization. Which of the following methods allows you to share the rule groups with other AWS accounts?

   A. Share the rule group using AWS WAF client application integration and exporting the rule sets to a CSV file.

   B. Share the rule group by entering the AWS account number of the destination account when creating a rule group.

   C. Share the rule group by selecting Share on the WebACL edit screen in the AWS WAF console.

   D. Share the rule group using `PutPermissionPolicy` and the AWS WAF API.

15. Which of the following AWS services is used to view a global level of aggregated threats over the last day and at an account level a list of DDoS events detected over the last year?

   A. AWS Shield

   B. AWS GuardDuty

   C. AWS Detective

   D. AWS Security Hub

16. The security team for your organization has asked for a detailed list of API calls for Secrets Manager used within your organization. The team is looking to validate when a select few secrets were last rotated as part of a recent incident review. What Secrets Manager logs will you pull for the security team?

   A. Provide the security team with access to CloudWatch and filter metrics based on Secrets Manager.

   B. Provide the security team with access to Detective and filter findings based on last rotation.

   C. Provie the security team with access to Security Hub and filter results from Secrets Manager.

   D. Provide the security team with the CloudTrail logs within the region where Secrets Manager is being used.

17. You have been contacted by the security team because they are receiving too many findings from Macie in Security Hub. The security team has asked if it is possible to change the frequency of findings being sent into Security Hub from Macie. Which of the flowing frequencies are supported by Macie? (Choose three.)

    A. 15 minutes

    B. 5 minutes

    C. 1 hour

    D. 3 hours

    E. 6 hours

    F. 30 minutes

18. You are helping the web development team with creating certificates for their new web applications. The team wants to be able to protect all subdomains for their application under a single certificate from AWS Certificate Manager. Which of the following domain name types will need to be used when requesting the certificates with Certificate Manager?

    A. Root domain name

    B. Wildcard domain name

    C. Bare domain name

    D. Apex domain name

19. You have been tasked with generating a new key in AWS Key Management Service for use with a new application hosted on EC2. The key will be used to encrypt and decrypt data within the production AWS account only. Which key type will you select when making the key?

    A. PKI key type

    B. Asymmetric key type

    C. Custom key type

    D. Symmetric key type

20. Your organization has decided to standardize on the use of Inspector for all vulnerability scanning of AWS accounts assigned to production, development, and user acceptance testing. You have received reports that several newly deployed EC2 instances are not being checked for CVE vulnerabilities by Inspector, but they are receiving network reachability findings. Which of the following is a possible cause?

    A. The Systems Manager agent is not running or installed on the EC2 instances.

    B. Inspector will only scan AWS Elastic Beanstalk applications and containers.

    C. A security group is blocking access to the CVE item database.

    D. Inspector is not enabled to scan for CVE vulnerabilities within the same region as the EC2 instances.

Chapter

5

Compute

**THE AWS CERTIFIED SYSOPS
ADMINISTRATOR EXAM OBJECTIVES
COVERED IN THIS CHAPTER INCLUDE:**

✓ **Domain 3: Deployment, Provisioning, and Automation**

- 3.1 Provision and maintain cloud resources

  - Create and manage AMIs (for example, EC2 Image Builder)

  - Identify and remediate deployment issues (for example, service quotas, subnet sizing, CloudFormation errors, permissions)

✓ **Domain 6: Cost and Performance Optimization**

- 6.1 Implement cost optimization strategies

  - Identify and remediate underutilized or unused resources by using AWS services and tools (for example, Trusted Advisor, AWS Compute Optimizer, AWS Cost Explorer)

  - Assess resource usage patterns to qualify workloads for EC2 Spot Instances

- 6.2 Implement performance optimization strategies

  - Recommend compute resources based on performance metrics

  - Monitor Amazon Elastic Block Store (Amazon EBS) metrics and modify configuration to increase performance efficiency

  - Enable enhanced EC2 capabilities (for example, Elastic Network Adapter, instance store, placement groups)

Compute is a foundational service that is used to build large and complex architectures. Whenever you think of cloud computing, it is helpful to think in terms of building blocks. Cloud infrastructure is broken down into discrete elements that can be arranged in any number of ways. You will encounter this with compute. If you have ever built a physical computer, maybe a gaming machine, that knowledge will transfer to our discussion of compute in this chapter.

At the most basic level, compute has four parts: the operating system, the CPU, the memory, and the networking. Launching an EC2 instance will allow you to see and select each of those components in countless combinations. Keep in mind that when you launch virtual machines, there is physical hardware underneath. For example, when you launch a T3 instance there is a physical Intel Xeon (Skylake or Cascade Lake) processor powering it. For this exam, you will not need to know details like the names of physical processors. However, you should be familiar with the various types of instances such as T, C, R, P, and so forth and what they are used for. Compute, however, goes beyond the traditional server and includes AWS Lambda, a managed serverless compute service.

The Hypervisor

The hypervisor is the magic ingredient that makes virtualization. Recall the shared responsibility model and that under everything is physical hardware. In the case of unmanaged services such as EC2, AWS is responsible for the hypervisor and everything below. The hypervisor is that magic layer between the physical devices and what we, as AWS customers, control as virtual machines (VMs) or instances.

You will never see, touch, smell, or hear the hypervisor. It is something of a secret sauce, and for security reasons, AWS shares very little about it. You won't need to know anything on the test specifically about the hypervisor, but in the context of the shared responsibility model, it is helpful to know where it sits in the stack.

Is there an exception to this? Bare-metal instances run directly on the physical hardware without a hypervisor. The hardware itself is still using parts of the nitro system and is protected by the Nitro Security Card but it simply lacks the hypervisor. Bare metal is identified in the instance types with `.metal`.

Amazon Machine Image (AMI)

The Amazon Machine Image (AMI) is a server image used to create EC2 instances with a predefined configuration. AMIs are supplied and maintained by AWS (e.g., Amazon Linux 2023), provided by AWS partners in the AWS Marketplace (free or paid), offered by the community, or created and managed by the customer. An AMI is region-specific but can be copied to other regions.

AMIs can be either EBS-backed or instance store–backed. The setup of each is slightly different. Instance store–backed AMIs can only be created on certain instance types (C3, D2, G2, I2, M3, and R3), and the AMI is stored in S3 as a bundle (image manifest and files). Instance store–backed AMIs incur S3 storage costs. For EBS-backed AMIs, the image is stored as an EBS snapshot, and EBS snapshot charges are incurred. Regarding costs, keep in mind that while an EC2 instance is stopped there is no charge. However, EBS volumes continue to incur cost until deleted.

EBS vs. Instance Store

An EC2 instance has two types of root device used for storage of the AMI. This can be an EBS volume or what is known as an instance store. When you select EBS, the AMI is built from an EBS snapshot. When you select an instance store, the root device is created from a template stored on S3. The best thing to keep in mind here is that the instance store is ephemeral, meaning that when the instance is terminated the data in the instance store is lost. Instance store–backed instances cannot be stopped but only terminated since there is nowhere to store the instance data.

As shown in Table 5.1, there are several significant differences between the two. You should understand the benefits and limitations of each.

TABLE 5.1 Differences between instance stores and EBS

	Instance store	EBS-backed
Storage capacity	10 GiB	64 TiB
Root volume persistence	Ephemeral	Default is delete on termination of instance, but volume can persist
Boot time	Takes longer to boot (<5 minutes)	Quick boot (<1 minutes)
Cost	EC2 instance changes plus S3 cost of storing the AMI	EC2 instance charges plus EBS volume cost plus cost of storing the AMI snapshot
Modifications	Cannot be modified	Can change instance type, kernel, RAM disk, and user data while instance is stopped
Stopping instance	Instance cannot be stopped	Instance can be stopped

EBS Persistence

Understanding the persistence of your EC2 instance and the data on your EBS volume is crucial. What happens to an EBS volume when an EC2 instance is stopped or terminated? The EBS persistence is tied to the instance life cycle (see Figure 5.1). Only EBS-backed instances can be stopped or placed in a hibernate state.

FIGURE 5.1   EC2 instance life cycle

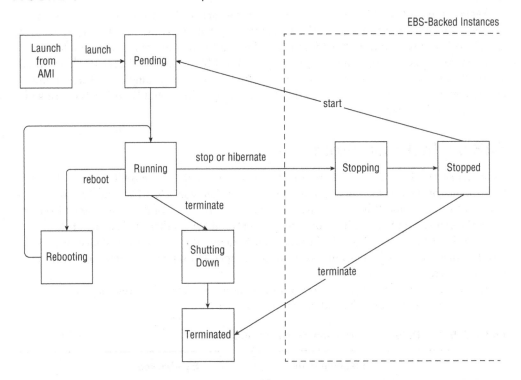

Keep in mind that the AMI is not stored on the instance. The root device image is created from the AMI. The actual AMI is stored as an EBS snapshot. Let's say that you are making changes to an EC2 instance and you want to create an AMI from that particular state of the instance. In that case you will need to create your AMI before terminating. Also remember the DeleteOnTerminate flag, which controls the disposition of the EBS root device after instance termination. This is set to TRUE by default. For non-root EBS volumes, the flag is set to FALSE by default. This is an important difference to remember.

Creating an AMI

Creating a custom AMI is a routine task that you will need to be able to do. You will often make modifications to your base server image to produce a "golden image." Changes may include installing agents, disabling unneeded services, and installing software, among others.

Once every change is made and all tests are passed, you want to produce an image that can be used to clone more identical servers or restore a failed instance. Once you have your instance where you want it to be, simply create an AMI from that instance. The process for creating the AMI differs slightly depending on whether the instance is EBS-backed or instance store–backed.

There are two ways to launch an EC2 instance: from an AMI or from a template. These two methods have a lot in common but there are a few important differences. The AMI is an EBS snapshot of the instance. When creating an instance from an AMI, you still need to go through the whole configuration. A template defines the configuration of the instance, including which AMI to use. The template allows for automation of the instance creation process as well as for versioning.

Keep in mind two things with creating AMIs. First, normally the running instance will power down before creating the AMI. This is to assure that the image is in a stable state. There are some cases where it is not necessary to power down but these are the exception. Second, you are charged for the storage of the AMI as long as the AMI is registered. Deregistering the AMI stops the billing.

EBS-Backed

For an EBS-backed instance that is running, the steps to create an image are as follows:

1. In the EC2 console (shown in Figure 5.2), select Actions ➤ Image And Templates ➤ Create Image.

FIGURE 5.2 Creating AMI

Source: Amazon.com, Inc.

2. The Create Image window will ask you to name the image (see Figure 5.3). Optional settings include the description, tags (tags are an important best practice), and whether you want to include additional volumes. When complete, click Create Image.

Instance Store–Backed

To launch an instance store–backed EC2 instance for practice, browse the community AMIs and use the root device type filter. As always, be careful of costs associated with your practice environment. Creating an instance store–backed AMI follows the same steps as for an EBS-backed except that you must configure the instance. See the user guide at https://docs.aws.amazon.com/AWSEC2/latest/UserGuide/creating-an-ami-instance-store.html.

FIGURE 5.3   Create Image window

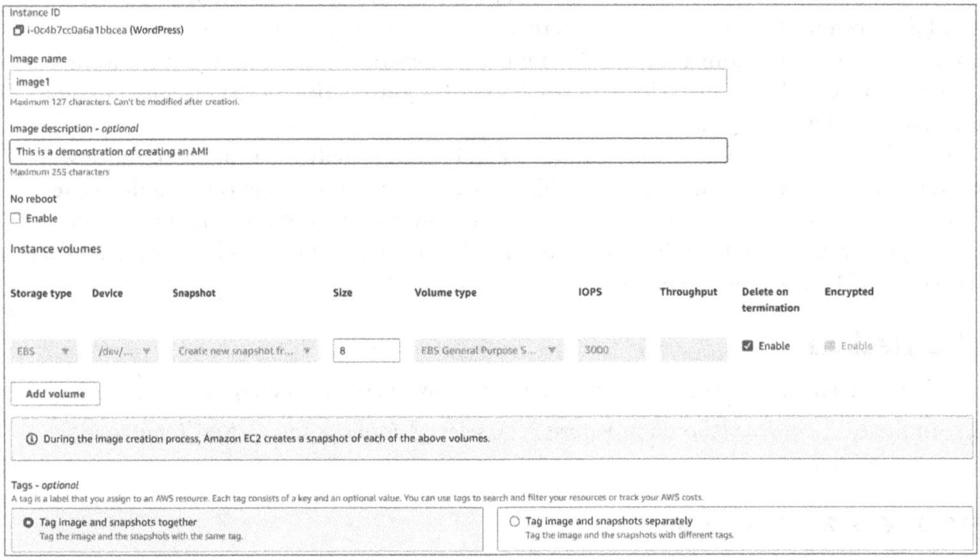

Source: Amazon.com, Inc.

Amazon EC2

Amazon Elastic Compute Cloud (EC2) was one of first services offered by AWS. It is a mature service with a mind-numbing list of options and capabilities. This chapter will give you some guidance. Be sure to review the AWS documentation and, wherever possible, practice.

The EC2 Life Cycle

We mentioned this life cycle earlier, and it is very important. An EC2 instance has a life cycle (see Figure 5.1) that can be affected by a few factors. The most significant is whether the instance root device is an EBS volume or an instance store. Instances can only be in a stopped or hibernate state if they are EBS-backed. Apart from that difference, all instances move from a pending state to a running state and finally to a terminate state. EC2 instances are only billed while in the running state.

Rebooting an instance does not change the hardware; it just restarts the operating system. This is the same behavior as with a physical machine you might be accustomed to. Remember, there is physical hardware under your instance—visualize the shared responsibility model.

EC2 Pricing

Pricing of EC2 is complicated, but it is something you must know well for the exams. Remember that you will not be tested on specific prices since they can vary by region and over time. Two important general points to remember: First, instances only incur charges when in the running state. Second, there are costs separate from the instance itself—for example, EBS storage, data transfer, and elastic IP addresses.

Remember that on the exam you would not be expected to know exact prices. However, you will be expected to understand how to reduce cost for a customer, and that requires an understanding of how the pricing models work in different scenarios. There are four basic pricing models (plus a free tier). EC2 is billed per second of usage with a 60-second minimum so that you only pay for exactly what you use. On-Demand, Spot, and Reserved instances and the Amazon Linux, Windows, and Ubuntu AMIs are eligible.

On-Demand

On-Demand is the baseline model where you are billed per second or hour of usage with no commitment. This model is not the lowest cost but is often used for what we refer to as "short-term, spiky, or unpredictable" workloads. On-Demand would be useful in cases where you might be doing testing or running a short proof-of-concept. For applications that cannot be interrupted, On-Demand would be preferred over Spot instances.

Spot

Spot instances represent the lowest cost for compute with a savings of up to 90 percent over On-Demand pricing. Spot instances are an ideal choice for stateless and fault-tolerant workloads and workloads that can be paused. They are often used for big data, batch processing, and high-performance computing (HPC), where massive scaling of worker nodes is needed.

Capacity Rebalancing is a Spot instance feature that, when enabled, can signal Auto Scaling or Spot Fleet to automatically replace the impacted instance. You can enable Capacity Rebalancing when launching a Spot Fleet either through the console or via the CLI.

Reserved Instances

Reserved instances (RIs) are no longer recommended since savings plans are more flexible. However, test takers should be familiar with RIs since customers will likely still have them. It is worthwhile to review RI pricing models and characteristics. AWS recommends that when reserved instances expire customers move to savings plans.

Saving Plans

Savings plans are a very flexible pricing model that can provide up to 72 percent savings on compute. Whereas reserved instances apply to only EC2 instances, savings plans can be used with EC2, AWS Fargate, and AWS Lambda. In addition, savings plans can apply to any compute regardless of instance type, size, OS, tenancy, or region. Savings plans require a commitment of a number of $/hour of usage over the course of a 1- or 3-year period. Savings plans do not reserve capacity in the way that reserved instances do. However, savings plans can be combined with capacity reservations (see below) to accomplish the same goal.

There are two forms of savings plans: compute savings plans and EC2 instance savings plans. Compute savings plans offer up to 66 percent savings and allow the most flexibility. EC2 instance savings plans are more restrictive but offer higher savings (up to 72 percent). They allow flexibility within an instance family (e.g., moving from an M5.4xlarge to an M5.16xlarge) and between OSs (e.g., Windows to Linux). However, the savings plan is restricted to a specified region.

Capacity Reservations

Capacity reservations can be placed on EC2 instances to reserve capacity in a specified availability zone (AZ) for an indefinite span of time. The capacity reservation works similarly to reserved instances but does not require a 1- or 3-year commitment. Capacity reservations can be combined with savings plans.

EC2 Advanced Features

EC2 has many advanced features. You will want to be familiar with when each of these should be used and how to implement the features. One of the best preparations for AWS exams is to go through the setup screens in the console and be sure that you can explain each setting. This study method isn't perfectly comprehensive, but it helps you to visualize the features and where they are enabled. Remember that most things that can be done in the console can also be done via the CLI or an SDK.

It's important to be aware of the Advanced Details section of the EC2 Launch Instance window for configuration options. Let's walk through some of the Advanced Details section of the EC2 Launch Instance dialog to make sure we know what's there.

Request Spot Instances

Requesting Spot Instances is somewhat straightforward as long as you are familiar with Spot instances (if not, make sure you study Spot). This option says that if Spot is available at the time, launch the instance(s) using Spot, and if not, fall back to On-Demand. Notice that when you select the Spot option several other options become disabled. Your Spot request here can be further customized, and you should be familiar with Spot request configuration.

Domain Join Directory

This option allows you to join the instance(s) to AWS Directory Services. Remember that the instance(s) will need to have a role with sufficient permissions.

IAM Instance Profile

This option lets you specify the role used by the instance(s). The profile serves as a container for the role itself. When you create an EC2 role in the console, the profile is created automatically with the same name. When using the CLI or an SDK to create an EC2 role, the profile must be created separately.

Hostname Type

This option allows the user to choose between the resource name (e.g., i-0123456789abcdef .ec2.internal or i-0123456789abcdef.eu-west-3.compute.internal) or IP name (e.g., ip-10-20-30-40.ec2.internal or ip-10-20–30-40.af-south-1.compute.internal) as the name of the host. The best practice here is to use the resource name where possible since that gives you the most flexibility. The hostname type can be set at the subnet level. If the selected subnet for your instance(s) already has the hostname type set, the instance option will be unavailable.

DNS Hostname

Recall that the hostname is not the IP address. The idea of a DNS hostname is that it abstracts the IP address of the underlying host. What happens if a host IP address changes? If any mapping to the IP address breaks, that's usually bad. Instead, using a DNS name allows the IP address to change without negative impacts. This setting determines if the DNS hostname maps to IPv4, IPv6, or dual stack. Again, the settings at the subnet level can determine what options you have at the instance level.

Instance Auto Recovery

The default for Instance Auto Recovery is enabled. If the instance fails system checks, it is automatically moved to new underlying hardware and rebooted. Metadata such as the instance ID, private IP address, and elastic IP addresses are not changed. However, data in memory (RAM) is lost.

Shutdown Behavior

Recall the EC2 life cycle. Instances can be stopped or terminated. The Shutdown Behavior setting determines what state the instance moves into from an OS-level shutdown command.

Stop-Hibernate Behavior

Hibernate saves the contents of RAM to the root volume. Hibernation can only be enabled before the instance is launched. Hibernate can be used to pre-warm instances that take a long time to fully load. Hibernated instances do not incur charges in the stopped state but they do incur charges during the stopping state while the RAM is being saved. There is cost for the EBS volume.

Termination Protection

Termination protection simply prevents the instance(s) from being terminated through the console, CLI, or SDKs until termination protection is disabled. It serves as a safety mechanism.

Stop Protection

Stop protection is similar to termination protection except it prevents the instance(s) from being stopped.

Detailed CloudWatch Monitoring

Detailed monitoring incurs additional fees. Basic monitoring captures data at 5-minute intervals whereas detailed captures at 1-minute intervals.

Elastic GPU

Elastic GPU is only available on select Windows instance types. It is used to add network-attached graphics acceleration without upscaling to a GPU instance type (P, G, Inf, etc.). Typically you would select Elastic GPU in cases where the workload needs only occasional bursts of GPU acceleration.

Elastic Inference

Elastic inference can be used on EC2 as well as SageMaker and Amazon ECS. It is designed to add deep learning muscles to a non-GPU instance type. Applications typically run inference only in short bursts. This makes the use of a GPU too costly. Instead, elastic inference allows applications to tap into the extra elastic inference capabilities only when you need to save up to 75 percent on inference costs.

Credit Specification

Credit specification applies only to T2, T3, and T3a instance types. Recall that these are burstable instance types, meaning that at normal CPU utilization levels they build up credits that can be used when the instance occasionally needs an increase in CPU above the baseline. Burstable instance types are an excellent way to save cost when workloads run at a predictable utilization but require a periodic CPU spike.

Placement Groups

Placement groups are used to spread or consolidate EC2 instances across the underlying hardware within a single availability zone (AZ). There are three types of placement group:

- *Cluster* placement groups are used to build low-latency, high-throughput workloads such as HPC by placing instances close together within an AZ. Cluster placement is the least fault tolerant of the three models.

- *Spread* placement groups are spread across separate racks, with each instance on its own rack. Spread placement is the most fault-tolerant and is used to reduce the risk of critical failure.
- *Partition* groups are similar to spread placement groups except that instances are grouped together in partitions and the partitions rather than the instances are placed on separate racks. This placement is used to reduce risk of failure for distributed and replicated workloads such as Cassandra and Hadoop Distributed File System (HDFS) where speed of communications must be balanced with protection from failure.

EBS-Optimized Instance

The EBS-Optimized Instance feature is only available on some instance types and provides dedicated throughput between EC2 and EBS attached volumes.

Tenancy

There are three forms of tenancy: shared, dedicated instance, and dedicated host. Shared tenancy is the more common (and least expensive) tenancy. This form will be used for most workloads. However, if your workload requires adherence to certain regulatory compliance or licensing requirements, then a dedicated instance or host may be required. Dedicated hosts and instances are more expensive than shared tenancy for equivalent compute. A dedicated instance gives you an instance running on a host dedicated to your account. No other account can place an instance on that host. However, other instances, both dedicated and shared, can be placed on the host. With a dedicated host, the entire physical host is dedicated to your account. If you stop and start an instance on a dedicated host, the instance returns on the same physical hardware. Dedicated hosts can only run a specified instance type.

Nitro Enclaves

Nitro enclaves are highly secure and fully isolated instances using the Nitro hypervisor. Enclaves can be connected using secure local socket (vsock). The enclave CLI can be installed on an EC2 instance to allow build, run, describe, and terminate commands for enclave.

Amazon EC2 Image Builder

A simple way of thinking of an AMI is that the AMI is the state of a VM boot disk saved at a specific point and made bootable. You can create an AMI from an existing EC2 instance and save that AMI as a custom AMI. Amazon EC2 Image Builder is a tool that makes the creation of images even easier by automating the creation, building, and deployment of the image. Image Builder works for both EC2 AMIs and container images. Microsoft Hyper-V (VHDX), VMWare vSphere (VMDK), and Open Format Virtualization (OFV) virtual machines can also be created when used in conjunction with AWS VM Import/Export (VMIE).

A role will be needed to execute the EC2 Image Builder tasks. The role needs to have `EC2InstanceProfileForImageBuilder` and `AmazonSSMManagedInstanceCore`. Image Builder will briefly create two instances in your account. The first is the build instance, and the second is a test instance if you defined testing in your pipeline. These images may incur nominal fees and are automatically terminated as each step of the pipeline completes.

There are four main configurations for Image Builder. These include the build/test components, the recipes, the infrastructure configuration, and the distribution configuration. Together, these elements will allow the automated creation of AMI and Docker images and distribution in any supported region as a pipeline.

Build/Test Components

Build and test components can be created before you create the pipeline. Build components are similar to user data but much more powerful. With build components you can run updates, install and configure software, or any number of common tasks. Inputs and outputs of actions in a script can be chained together so that the output of one phase can become the input of the next. Components are written in YAML. Test components are similar but specify tests to be run on the image after the build is complete to be sure it is working properly. AWS provides a variety of components, or the user can create their own.

Recipes

Here the base image is defined, either from an existing recipe or one build in this step. Building a recipe includes several elements:

1.   The image type (AMI or Docker).

2.   The name, version, and description. The version number is in the form major .minor.patch.

3.   The base image. This would be the base operating system of a specific version of Linux 2, Windows, Ubuntu, CentOS, etc. For an AMI, a custom AM can be selected, or for Docker images, an existing image from an ECR repository can be chosen. Existing images can also be selected by their ARN.

4.   The instance can be configured with user data in the same way as launching an EC2 instance normally. The SSM agent must be on the image for the user data to run on launch.

5.   The working directory can be defined for build and test workflows.

6.   Build and test components can be added.

7.   Finally, optional tags can be set.

Infrastructure Configuration

Predefined infrastructure configurations can be defined and attached to the Image Builder template. In this section you will define things like the instance type (family and size), VPC, subnet, security groups, key pairs, the role to use for the instance, and so forth.

Distribution Configuration

Depending on whether this will be an AMI or a container image distribution, several settings can be configured. These settings relate to where the image can be distributed including distribution to target regions and accounts.

Pipelines

A pipeline is the combination of the elements discussed above. Building a pipeline involves four main steps, each with some options.

- Step 1 specifies the pipeline details, including name/description, the build schedule (scheduled or manual), and optional tags.
- Step 2 is where the base image is defined, either from an existing recipe or one build in this step.
- Step 3 defines the infrastructure.
- Step 4 defines the distribution.

Compute Optimizer

Optimization is always a trade-off. It is a compromise between performance and cost. As an enterprise scales and as systems grow more complex, the decisions around optimization become exponentially more complex. That's where AWS Compute Optimizer comes in to help analyze utilization and configuration metrics. With Compute Optimizer you get recommendations for EC2 instances, Auto Scaling Groups (ASGs), EBS volumes, and Lambda functions.

There are two versions of AWS Compute Optimizer. The default version looks at Amazon CloudWatch metrics for the past 14 days and provides recommendations on optimization of EC2 instance types, EC2 ASGs, EBS volume configurations, and AWS Lambda function memory sizes. The default optimizer is a free feature. The paid version of Compute Optimizer collects enhanced metrics for the past three months.

Compute Optimizer will deliver up to three recommendations per resource. In addition to recommending resource optimization, Compute Optimizer can identify potential resource performance risks or constraints. The paid Enhanced Infrastructure Metrics feature can be enabled at the organization, account, or resource level. Using Compute Optimizer across an organization requires enabling all features and logging in as the organization's primary account. The Enhanced Infrastructure Metrics feature expands the ingestion and analysis from 14 days to up to three months.

On EC2, the memory utilization metric must be enabled in the CloudWatch agent. EC2 memory relies on passing that data from the operating system to CloudWatch. For EC2 pricing, transient resource pricing such as Spot instances is not considered.

Pricing for AWS Compute Optimizer is based on the collection of Enhanced Infrastructure Metrics. Enabling the enhanced metrics is billed at $0.0003360215 per resource per hour.

Remember that you will not need to know specific prices. Rather, you will want to know that pricing is per resource, per hour.

Elastic Load Balancing

The concept of a load balancer is pretty straight forward: Distribute the incoming load across available resources. AWS load balancers come in three key forms: application load balancers (ALBs), gateway load balancers (GLBs), and network load balancers (NLBs). Each does a specific task well, and you will need to know which one to select for a given use case. Load balancers can be internal (using private IP addresses) or Internet-facing. Load balancers often work in conjunction with AWS auto scaling.

Network load balancers are built for speed and are designed to distribute the load at OSI layer 4 (UDP/TCP). Application load balancers have intelligence built-in to manage OSI layer 7 HTTP/HTTPS traffic. A gateway load balancer is a gateway at layer 3 with balancing at layer 4. A fourth load balancer does exist but is no longer recommended. That legacy load balancer is called the Classic Load Balancer, and you are unlikely to encounter it on the exam. As a rule, if there is an opportunity to migrate the customer from Classic Load Balancer to one of the new models, that would usually be the right answer.

Pricing for all load balancers is based on hours or part of an hour used. There is also cost based on a capacity unit, which is calculated slightly differently for each type of load balancer but is generally the number of connections and bytes processed.

Elastic load balancers work in conjunction with target groups. The target group is a collection of EC2 instances, IP addresses, Lambda functions, or even an application load balancer. Target groups can work with Amazon EC2 Auto Scaling to target dynamically created instances to respond to auto scaling events. Once a target group is created, targets can be registered to them. Target groups are the first step in creating a load balancer.

Classic Load Balancer

The main point to remember with the Classic Load Balancer is that it is no longer being recommended. However, many customers are still using this load balancer, and it is certainly possible you might be involved in a migration to one of the new load balancers. The migration path would be to an ALB or an NLB, depending on the use case. Remember that the GLB has a very specific use case of balancing traffic for third-party virtual appliances.

The migration of Classic Load Balancers is simplified by using the migration wizard. When you select a Classic Load Balancer in the console, the details section will show an option to "Launch ALB migration wizard.", as shown in Figure 5.4. There are also two other migration options, including the load balancer copy utility (found on GitHub) and a manual migration. We will only cover the wizard migration option here.

FIGURE 5.4 ELB Classic Migration tab

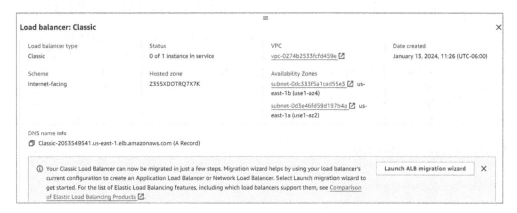

There will be one of two launch buttons available, either ALB or NLB, depending on the configuration (HTTP vs. TCP listener) of the Classic Load Balancer. Clicking Launch Migration Wizard will take you to the review page of the configuration. Clicking Edit here will take you to the beginning of the configuration process for either the ALB or NLB. AWS will then instantiate a new load balancer for you.

Once the new load balancer is running and instances are registered, you will need to begin redirecting traffic. To redirect traffic, create a DNS record with the DNS name of the new load balancer and redirect a percentage of your traffic to test the new load balancer. Typically setting the percentage of traffic is done through a weighting setting, but this may differ among DNS providers. Once all of your traffic is flowing to the new load balancer, be sure to update any policies, scripts, or code to reflect the new load balancer. Finally, delete your old load balancer.

To summarize, the migration follows four main steps:

1. Create the new load balancer using the wizard, the copy utility, or manual migration.

2. Redirect traffic.

3. Update any policies, scripts, or code to reference the new load balancer.

4. Decommission (delete) the old Classic Load Balancer.

Network Load Balancer

Network load balancers (NLBs) operate at layer 4 of the OSI model and are optimized to move packets of data quickly and efficiently at millions of requests per second. The AWS NLB consists of the load balancer in a public subnet, listeners monitoring your specified ports and protocols, target groups, and optional health checks on the targets. Targets for an NLB can be EC2 instance IDs, IP addresses, or an application load balancer. Remember that NLBs are designed to balance loads across two or more AZs and that everything that might be a target for an NLB would reside in a subnet. Never forget that load balancing happens across AZs, not regions. NLBs listen to protocols TCP, TLS, UDP, and TCP_UDP on ports 1–65535.

NLBs integrate with three services: AWS Config, Traffic Monitoring, and AWS PrivateLink (see Figure 5.5). AWS Config can be used to monitor configuration changes. Traffic mirroring is used with a third-party security appliance. Mirroring captures network traffic, copies it, and forwards the copy to an appliance for content inspection, threat monitoring, or troubleshooting. AWS PrivateLink creates an endpoint that can be used by designated AWS accounts, users, and roles.

FIGURE 5.5 NLB integrations

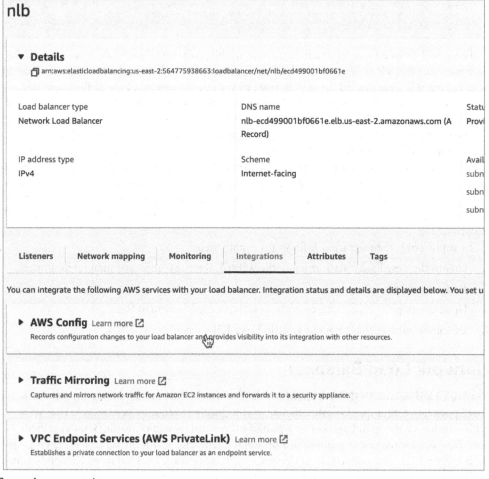

Gateway Load Balancer

The gateway load balancer (GLB) has a very specific use case and is designed for load-balancing third-party virtual appliances using GENEVE (RFC8926). A third-party virtual appliance might be something like a firewall or intrusion detection and prevention system (IDS/IPS). The GENEVE standard operates on port 6081. The GLB operates at layers 3 and 4 of the OSI model, functioning as a gateway at layer 3 and a load balancer at layer 4. GLBs are deployed in the same VPC as the virtual appliance but in different subnets. The virtual appliance is registered with a target group of the GLB.

It is beyond the scope of this chapter to review networking fundamentals. However, understanding routing tables and next hops is essential for all load balancing but especially gateway load balancing. Be sure to review route tables as part of your studies for this exam. Review the examples in the user guide.

At a high level, setting up a GLB requires five steps:

1. In the EC2 console, set up a target group and register targets using the GENEVE protocol on port 6081.

2. In the EC2 console, create a gateway load balancer in the VPC where the appliances live (service provider VPC).

3. In the VPC console under Endpoint Services create an endpoint service.

4. In the VPC console under Endpoints, create a new endpoint in the VPC where the target instances reside (service consumer VPC). Don't forget to accept the endpoint connection request.

5. Finally, configure your route tables.

Application Load Balancer

Shown in Figure 5.6, an application load balancer (ALB) is designed to listen to traffic at layer 7 of the OSI model (HTTP/HTTPS). The ALB will listen on any assigned port for HTTP/HTTPS traffic and forward that to a designated target group.

To create a rule for an ALB listener, first create the ALB. In the load balancer console, select your ALB and select the Listeners tab. For the selected listener, click View/Edit Rules. There will already be a default rule, which forwards traffic matching the protocol/port to the target group. However, additional rules can be created. Up to 100 rules can be created for each ALB. Rules are made up of IF/THEN conditions. For example, if the host headers contain XYZ, then forward to target group A, otherwise forward to target group B.

ALBs have three integrations, as shown in Figure 5.7. AWS Config is used to monitor configuration changes. The Global Accelerator speeds up API workloads by as much as 60 percent by managing routing. ALBs can also be fronted by AWS WAF to provide web traffic filtering to protect your applications from common threats.

FIGURE 5.6 Application load balancer

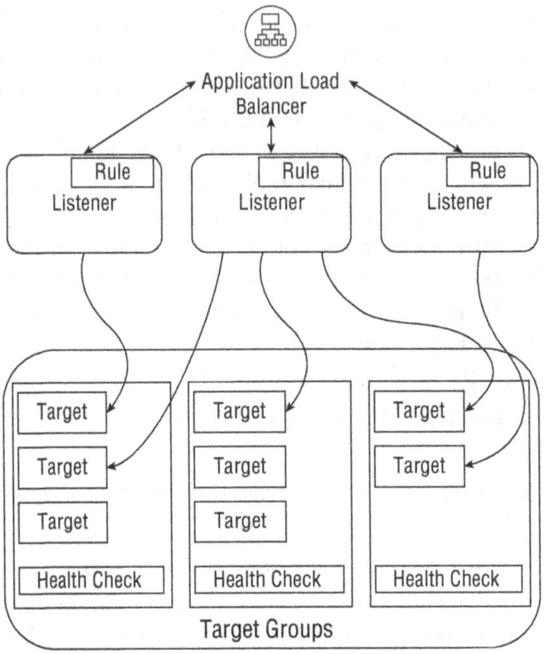

Source: Amazon.com, Inc.

Auto Scaling

Auto Scaling is designed to dynamically add and remove resources and can even predict scaling needs based on patterns. Several AWS resources are scalable, including Amazon Aurora, Amazon EC2, Amazon Elastic Container Service, Amazon DynamoDB, and Spot fleets. Auto Scaling relies on CloudWatch to monitor metrics of the resources. CloudWatch then signals elastic load balancers to add or remove resources. This is what is sometimes referred to as the auto scaling triad, as shown in Figure 5.8.

Auto Scaling is commonly used for rebalancing resources across availability zones. It is also used for capacity rebalancing of Spot instances. Remember that auto scaling works across AZs, not regions. Scaling defines three key metrics: desired capacity, minimum capacity, and maximum capacity, as shown in Figure 5.9. The desired capacity is the initial capacity of the group at the time of launch and the capacity that auto scaling attempts to maintain until scaling policies direct otherwise. The minimum capacity represents the lowest capacity the group should be allowed to scale to and usually represents the minimum needed to maintain availability of the workload. The maximum capacity is the upper limit to which the group can scale and is often determined by cost. A common scenario is to maintain a fixed number of instances, neither growing nor shrinking the group. This might be done in a case where you want to always have one and only one bastion host in a subnet. To accomplish this, you would define one minimum, one desired, and one maximum.

FIGURE 5.7   ALB integrations

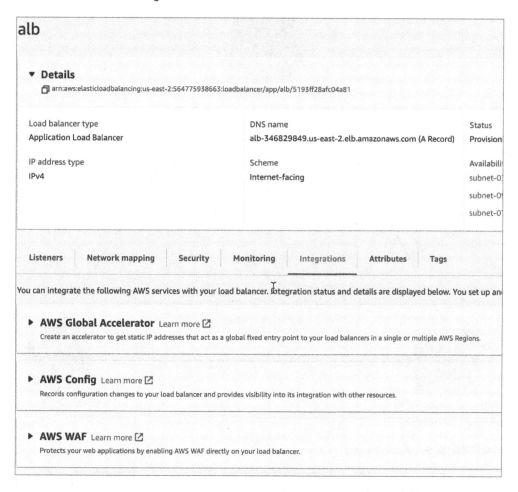

Optimization is always a compromise and can be thought of on a scale from being optimized for availability to being optimized for cost, as shown in Figure 5.10. If you optimize for availability, you will be launching more resources to ensure you have plenty of capacity. If you optimize for cost, you can save money or stay within budget but may have fewer resources than needed to meet demand. The decision is rarely one extreme or the other but some balanced approach on the spectrum.

Scaling Options

The AWS Auto Scaling feature has several options for scaling. Each of them has a particular use case and you should be familiar with them. The first option is to maintain a static number of instances, as in the bastion host example in the previous section. When health checks indicate an unhealthy instance, it is replaced and the instance count remains steady.

FIGURE 5.8   The Auto Scaling triad

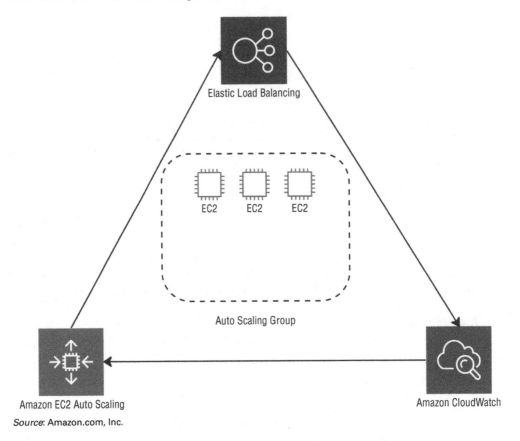

Source: Amazon.com, Inc.

FIGURE 5.9   Auto Scaling

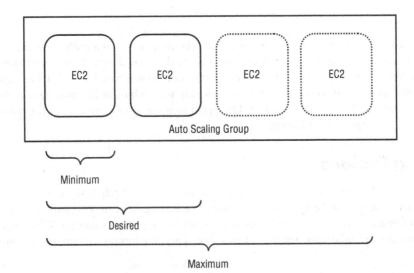

FIGURE 5.10   Auto Scaling availability vs. cost

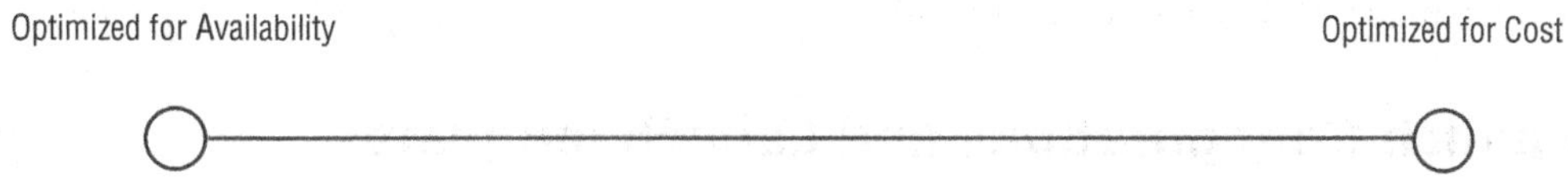

Optimized for Availability   Optimized for Cost

Manual

While most often you will want to automate scaling, keep in mind that scaling can be done manually by modifying the scaling group details.

Dynamic

Dynamic scaling increases or decreases capacity based on some trigger. The triggers are typically a CloudWatch metric such as CPU utilization. Target tracking is a form of dynamic scaling that will maintain a workload at a specified target metric. Let's say you have a workload of 10 instances and you want the average CPU utilization across the workload to stay under 60 percent (the target). Target tracking will add additional instances as needed to keep utilization below 60 percent and remove instances once demand subsides. Another form of dynamic scaling is step scaling. In step scaling, an increment is specified defining the number of instances that will be added, either as a number of instances or a percentage. Target tracking is generally recommended since it scales in proportion to the load on your application. This can help minimize unnecessary cost.

Simple scaling is a third form of dynamic scaling that adjusts capacity based on a single scaling adjustment. Simple scaling requires a cooldown period between each scaling event. The cooldown period is needed to prevent a cycle of instances going up and down (known as flapping) before metrics can recover.

Predictive

Predictive scaling is useful when you have cyclic patterns in utilizations such as high demand during business hours, data analysis, or batch processing. Predictive scaling can have capacity available before demand appears as a CloudWatch alarm. Predictive scaling needs 24 hours of data and will analyze up to 14 days' worth of data. Predictive scaling has two modes: forecast and scale. Forecast mode lets you evaluate the forecast before engaging scaling. Predictive scaling can also be combined with dynamic scaling to provide even more flexibility.

Service Quotas

Service quotas are also known as limits. Since auto scaling launches resources, it is possible to exceed available quotas. It is important to keep quotas in mind and request increases to match the maximum settings in your ASGs.

The high-level steps for auto scaling resources are as follows:

1.   Create a launch template.

2.   Create an ASG.

3. Add elastic load balancers (optional).

4. Configure scaling policies (optional).

Launch Configurations and Launch Templates

In order to create many copies of your instance, auto scaling needs an original template to follow. These used to be called launch configurations, but AWS has been migrating to launch templates. Templates are similar in content to the old configurations but allow for versioning and for more features. Since launch templates are the new preferred method, we will focus on them rather than the old launch configurations. However, you should know the old method and be aware that configurations can be migrated to launch templates.

Creating a launch template follows almost exactly the same steps as launching an EC2 instance. A nice feature of launch templates is the ability to create a new template based on an existing template, which saves time when creating a new version.

Auto Scaling Groups

Auto Scaling Groups are used to logically group EC2 On-Demand or Spot instances for scaling. There are six general steps for creating an ASG. At a high level, these steps are as follows:

1. Define the name of the group and select the launch template.

2. Select the VPC and subnet.

3. Optionally attach the group to a load balancer, enable health checks, enable CloudWatch monitoring of the group, and enable a feature called Default Instance Warmup, which helps CloudWatch obtain more meaningful metrics in step and target tracking scenarios with frequent scaling.

4. Here the desired, minimum, and maximum sizes are set. This is optional but typically specified. Also optional is the scaling policy, which will define a metric for target tracking. Optionally, instance scale in protection can be enabled.

5. Optionally, SNS notifications can be enabled.

6. Finally, optional tags can be added to the group.

Predictive scaling uses machine learning to look at historical CloudWatch trends (up to 14 days) to predict scaling events for the next 48 hours in order to maintain the desired level of utilization. A forecast-only mode is available so that you can evaluate the predictions. Predictive scaling is useful for workloads that follow a repetitive scaling pattern such as regular business hours, weekends, or routine batch processing. To use predictive scaling, you must enable it (see Figure 5.11) on an existing ASG. Predictive scaling needs at least 24 hours of data to make a forecast.

FIGURE 5.11   Predictive scaling policy

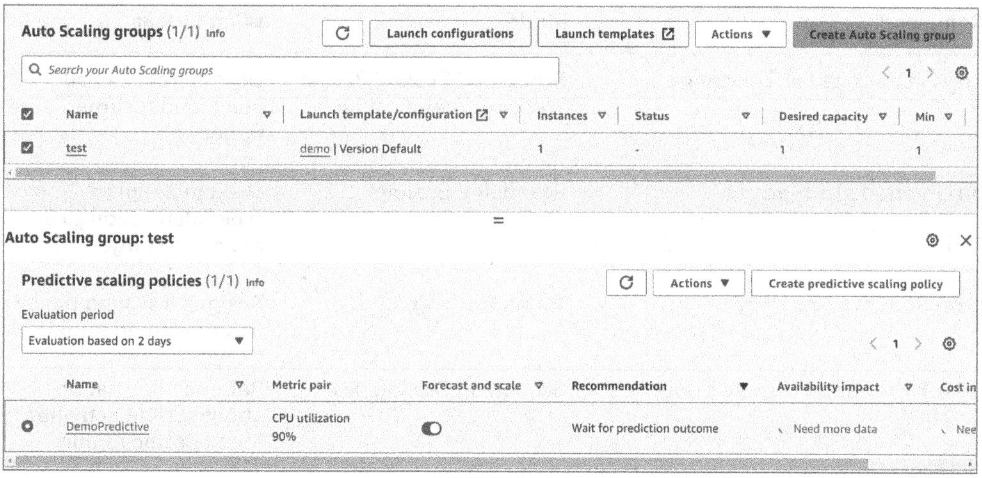

AWS Application Auto Scaling

Not everything that needs to scale is an EC2 instance. That's where the AWS Application Auto Scaling service comes in. Supported scalable resources include the following, among others:

- AppStream 2.0 fleets
- Aurora replicas
- Amazon EMR clusters
- Amazon Neptune clusters
- Spot fleet requests

There are three forms of auto scaling: scheduled, step, and target tracking. Like most actions in AWS, Application Auto Scaling can be done in either the console, the CLI, or via an SDK. Both the console and the CLI are tools of the trade for the systems administrator. While this is not a rule, typically, memorizing the command line is of low priority for the exam taker. However, it is worthwhile to review the commands since they can often show you patterns and insights into what the console is really doing. Commands you may want to be familiar with for Application Auto Scaling include those in Table 5.2. Note the similarities and differences by mode.

TABLE 5.2   Application Auto Scaling commands

Command	Mode	What it does
register-scalable-target	Scheduled Scaling, Target Tracking, Step Scaling	Used to register, suspend, and resume targets
put-scheduled-action	Scheduled Scaling	Used to assign a scheduled action to a registered target
put-Scaling-policy	Target Tracking, Step	Assigns a scaling policy to a registered target
describe-scaling-activities	Scheduled Scaling, Step	Returns information about scaling activities for a specific region
describe-scheduled-activities	Scheduled Scaling	Returns information about scheduled actions for a specified region
describe-scaling-policies	Target Tracking, Step	Returns information about scaling policies in a specified region
delete-scheduled-action	Scheduled Scaling	Deletes a scheduled action
delete-scaling-policy	Target Tracking, Step	Deletes scaling policy

Scheduled Scaling

Scheduled scaling is used when you have predictable patterns of usage—for example, if your usage spikes every Monday morning or if reporting causes a predictable spike at the end of every month. Scheduled scaling allows you to scale out ahead of demand. To establish scheduled scaling, you use a scheduled action, which defines the target to be scaled and when to scale, and sets minimum and maximum capacity. Scheduled actions can temporarily be disabled using a register-scalable-target --suspend state command. Scheduled actions are deleted using the delete-scheduled-action command.

Target Tracking

Target tracking scaling is done based on a CloudWatch metric and a target value for that metric. For example, you might use target tracking to add or remove capacity to maintain a fleet at a given CPU utilization level. Application Auto Scaling automatically creates and deletes the CloudWatch alarms that are used for target tracking. A target tracking policy can have one of three effects:

- It can change capacity up or down by a specified number (`ChangeInCapacity`).
- It can change to a specific value (`ExactCapacity`).
- It can scale up or down as a percentage (`PercentChangeInCapacity`).

Step Scaling

Step scaling is used to increase or decrease capacity by a specified amount. These are known as scaling adjustments. Scaling adjustments are of three types:

- `ChangeInCapacity` changes the capacity by a specific defined value.
- `ExactCapacity` changes to a specific defined value.
- `PercentChangeInCapacity` changes the capacity by a percentage of the existing capacity.

Setting Up Application Auto Scaling

There is no central console for setting up Application Auto Scaling. Instead, auto scaling is enabled in the console of each resource. For example, to auto-scale a DynamoDB table, you enable auto scaling on the Additional Settings tab by editing the read/write capacity (see Figure 5.12).

In RDS Aurora, replicas can be auto scaled. This is done in the Actions menu of the regional cluster, as shown in Figure 5.13 and Figure 5.14.

AWS Lambda

AWS Lambda is a completely managed serverless compute service. Lambda provides a compute resource that runs arbitrary application code in a number of programing languages without the overhead of an operating system. The SysOps exam will not test your ability to write application code. However, there are many administrative tasks related to Lambda. To get some practice with Lambda and to generate metrics, the Innovator Island workshop is a great starter (`https://serverlessland.com/learn/innovator-island`). As always, be aware of associated costs and set a billing alert for yourself.

In planning for Lambda, be aware of quotas. Some are adjustable; others are not. Service quotas can be seen on the Service Quotas dashboard, as shown in Figure 5.15.

FIGURE 5.12   DynamoDB configure RW capacity

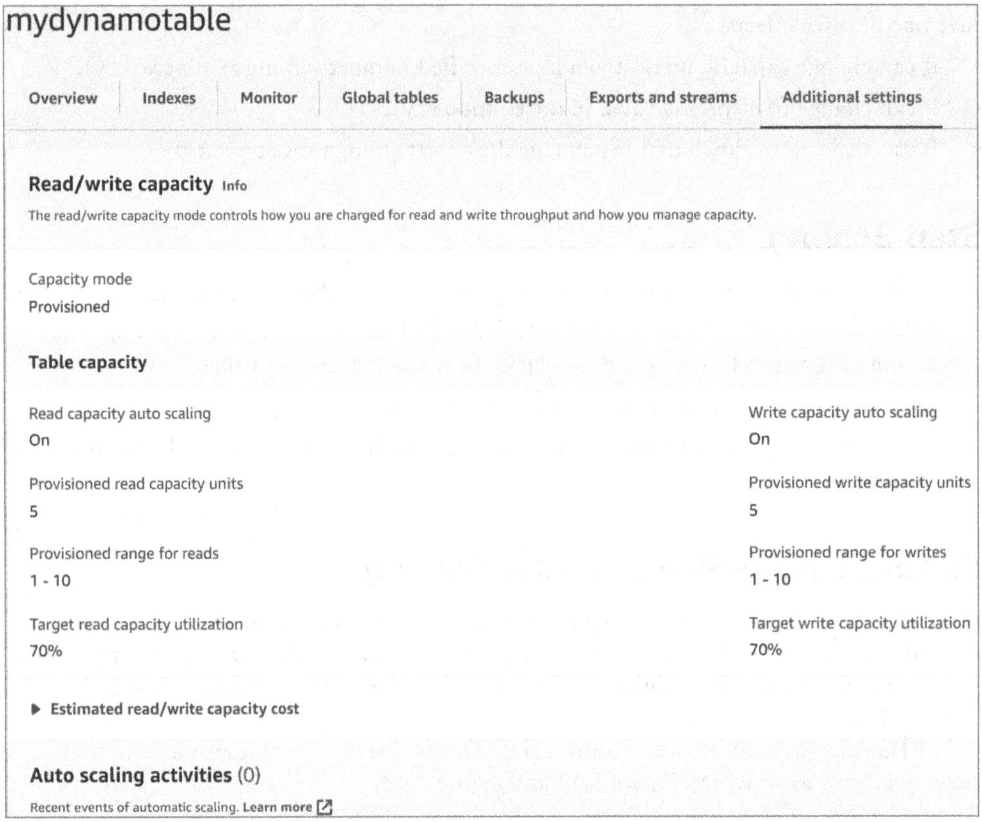

mydynamotable

| Overview | Indexes | Monitor | Global tables | Backups | Exports and streams | Additional settings |

Read/write capacity Info

The read/write capacity mode controls how you are charged for read and write throughput and how you manage capacity.

Capacity mode
Provisioned

Table capacity

Read capacity auto scaling
On

Provisioned read capacity units
5

Provisioned range for reads
1 - 10

Target read capacity utilization
70%

Write capacity auto scaling
On

Provisioned write capacity units
5

Provisioned range for writes
1 - 10

Target write capacity utilization
70%

▸ **Estimated read/write capacity cost**

Auto scaling activities (0)

Recent events of automatic scaling. **Learn more** ▢

Source: Amazon.com, Inc.

Three limits to be aware of are the runtime, memory, and concurrency. Lambda functions have a maximum runtime of 15 minutes and can use a maximum of 10,240 MB of memory. Lambda automatically scales as needed but has a soft concurrency quota of 1,000 instances per minute. Exceeding the limit will throttle requests and return a 429 status code. All Lambda functions in an account within a region share the concurrency limit. If a quota can be adjusted, click the quota in the Service Quotas dashboard, where you can find monitoring and alarms as well as the option to request an increase (see Figure 5.16).

A primary role in systems operations is the monitoring of workloads. Key metrics for Lambda include errors, execution time, and throttling. Errors can be caused by internal application runtime or logic code errors or by problems stemming from the Lambda function's interactions with other services. Execution time is generally looking for the slowest 1–5 percent of responses. Throttling indicates that concurrency limits are being reached and service quotas may need to be increased. Lambda functions are automatically monitored in CloudWatch. Each individual instance of a function creates its own log stream, which shows the RequestID, start/end, duration, billed duration, memory size, max memory used, and init duration, as shown in Figure 5.17.

FIGURE 5.13 RDS Aurora Add Replica Auto Scaling

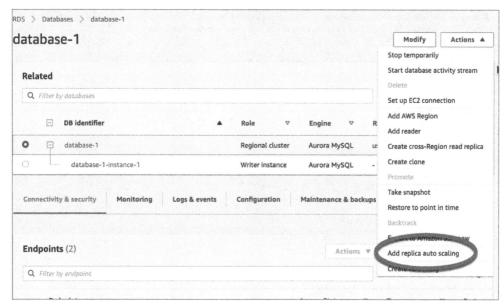

Source: Amazon.com, Inc.

Lambda reports several metrics directly to CloudWatch at a 1-minute interval. These are metrics that would typically be used for alarms. The key Lambda metrics are invocations, duration, errors, throttles, dead letter errors, iterator age, concurrent executions, and unreserved concurrent executions. Application-level metrics can also be captured as custom metrics in CloudWatch. Custom metrics can be either standard or high resolution at 30 or 10 seconds, respectively. An important additional monitoring feature is the optional Lambda Insights. This feature has to be enabled on the function and will add additional metrics, including CPU usage, memory, and networking.

Lambda functions are often loosely coupled with other services and other Lambda functions to create a solution. Having many different parts of the whole can create a challenge for managing and monitoring the various resources. AWS resource groups can help organize these parts by project, team, department, production/development, and so forth. You can create resource groups in the console as well as in CloudFormation stacks and in the AWS Serverless Application Model (SAM) template. Grouped resources are then visible as a group in CloudWatch. Also consider using CloudWatch Log Insights to search across multiple log groups.

FIGURE 5.14   RDS Aurora Add Auto Scaling Policy

RDS > Clusters > Add Auto Scaling policy

Add Auto Scaling policy

Define an Auto Scaling policy to automatically add or remove Aurora Replicas ⧉. We recommend using the Aurora reader endpoint or the MariaDB Connector to establish connections with new Aurora Replicas. Learn more ⧉.

> ⓘ DB instance database-1-instance-1 is not available yet. Try adding the policy again.

Policy details

Policy name
A name for the policy used to identify it in the console, CLI, API, notifications, and events.

    RDS Aurora Replica Auto Scaling

Policy name must be 1 to 256 characters.

IAM role
The following service-linked role is used by Aurora Auto Scaling.

    AWSServiceRoleForApplicationAutoScaling_RDSCluster

Target metric
Only one Aurora Auto Scaling policy is allowed for one metric.

◉ Average CPU utilization of Aurora Replicas View metric ⧉
○ Average connections of Aurora Replicas View metric ⧉

Target value
Specify the desired value for the selected metric. Aurora Replicas will be added or removed to keep the metric close to the specified value.

    50   %

▶ **Additional configuration**

Cluster capacity details
Configure the minimum and maximum number of Aurora Replicas you want Aurora Auto Scaling to maintain.

Minimum capacity
Specify the minimum number of Aurora Replicas to maintain.

    1   Aurora Replicas

Maximum capacity
Specify the maximum number of Aurora Replicas to maintain. Up to 15 Aurora Replicas are supported.

    15   Aurora Replicas

Cancel   **Add policy**

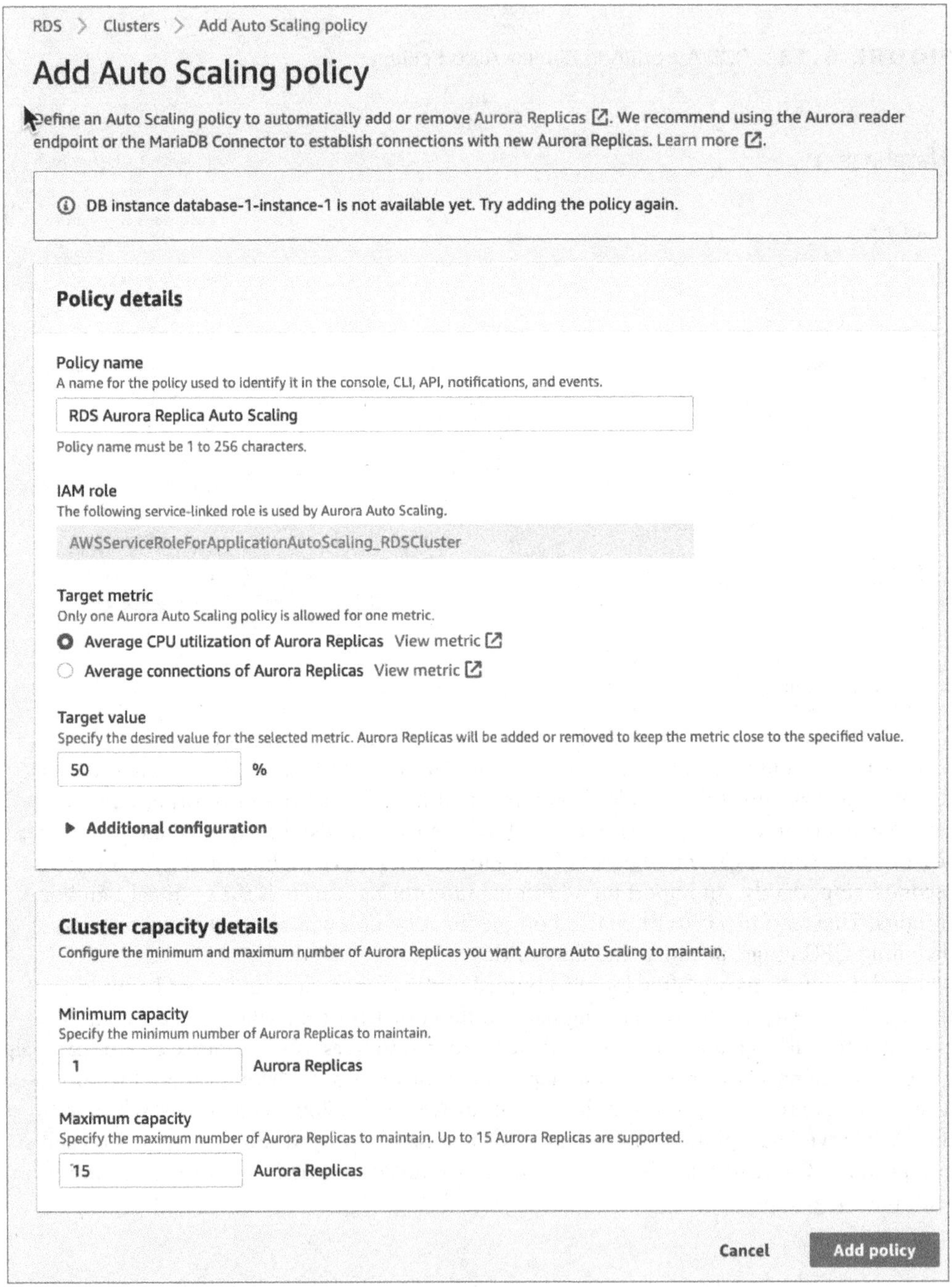

Source: Amazon.com, Inc.

FIGURE 5.15   Lambda Service Quotas page

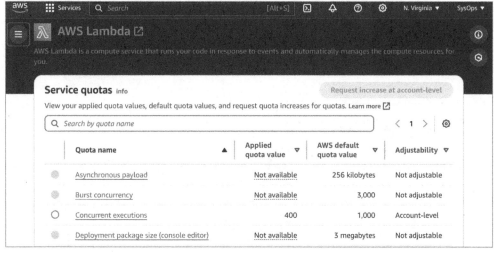

Source: Amazon.com, Inc.

FIGURE 5.16   Lambda Service Quotas Concurrent Executions

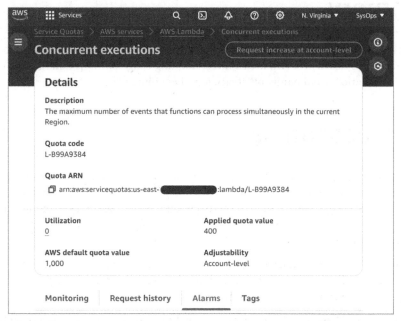

Source: Amazon.com, Inc.

FIGURE 5.17   Lambda CloudWatch log

Source: Amazon.com, Inc.

Summary

Compute is a core function, so there is a lot to remember here. Focus on the exam objectives. This exam focuses heavily on two areas: understanding usage patterns and making optimization recommendations, and hands-on creating and enabling features.

Exam Essentials

Know what to monitor.   Be sure to have basic hands-on knowledge of all the many monitoring and optimization tools such as Cost Explorer, Compute Optimizer, and, of course, CloudWatch. Don't neglect basics like monitoring tab resources such as EC2 and ELB. For each compute type, be sure you know what metrics are important. Know basic versus detailed monitoring.

Know how and when to optimize compute pricing.   Savings plans and Spot instances are very important mechanisms for reducing and managing cost and availability. Know the capabilities and limitations of Compute Optimizer.

Be familiar with EC2 enhanced capabilities.   The best way to learn is to go through the setup screens item by item. Be sure you can give a short explanation of what each feature does and when you would use it. Take a look at the lefthand navigation in the EC2 console. Is there anything there you aren't fluent in? Click each option and explore.

Get hands-on knowledge.   In the console, can you perform every step in the life cycle of an AMI, EBS, EC2, and Image Builder?

Know your auto scaling.   Auto Scaling has a significant number of options. Be sure to review these in more depth and understand which would be appropriate for solving any given scaling problem.

Review Questions

1. Creating which of the following is the first step in setting up EC2 Auto Scaling?

   A. Auto Scaling Group

   B. Launch configuration

   C. Launch template

   D. Target groups

2. What is a key metric for monitoring Lambda performance?

   A. 500 errors

   B. CPU Utilization

   C. Network In

   D. Throttles

3. What are the three placement group types for EC2?

   A. Cluster, partition, and spread

   B. Cluster, shared tenancy, and isolated

   C. Hardware virtualized, para-virtualized, and bare-metal

   D. Tight, loosely coupled, and normalized

4. An EC2 instance only incurs cost when in which state?

   A. Active

   B. Engaged

   C. Online

   D. Running

5. By default, AWS Compute Optimizer looks at how many days of data to make its recommendations?

   A. 7 days

   B. 14 days

   C. 30 days

   D. Three months

6. You have been asked to create a load balancer for a third-party virtual appliance that uses the GENEVE protocol. Which of the following would be the best solution?

   A. Application load balancer

   B. Classic Load Balancer

   C. Gateway load balancer

   D. Network load balancer

7. What is the best choice of load balancer optimized for HTTPS network traffic?

   A. Application load balancer

   B. Classic Load Balancer

   C. Gateway load balancer

   D. Network load balancer

8. You discover that your client has been using several Classic Load Balancers since they created their AWS account in 2019. What would be your best recommendation to the customer?

   A. Convert the Classic Load Balancers to network load balancers using a gateway load balancer to ensure traffic is correctly routed during the transition.

   B. Convert the Classic Load Balancers to network or application load balancers.

   C. Retain the Classic Load Balancers and provision elastic load balancing auto scaling to automatically add more load balancers to meet demand.

   D. Retain the Classic Load Balancers and submit a request to increase the throughput quotas on the Classic Load Balancers.

9. In auto scaling, what does the desired capacity refer to?

   A. The average capacity that the customer expects to need over the next billing cycle

   B. The capacity that the customer expects to need over the next billing cycle

   C. The initial capacity of the Auto Scaling Group that the system will attempt to maintain

   D. The lowest capacity of the Auto Scaling Group at which the workload is still able to perform

10. What is the minimum billing for an EC2 instance?

    A. 1 hour

    B. 1 second

    C. 24 hours

    D. 60 seconds

11. Your customer has asked you to create an isolated EC2 compute environment with cryptographic attestation to process healthcare data. Which feature best meets this requirement?

    A. Amazon Elastic Inference

    B. Instance store volumes

    C. Nitro enclaves

    D. Partitioned placement groups

12. You have been asked to load-balance a workload of TCP traffic. Which of the following is the best solution for your client?

    A. Application load balancer

    B. Classic Load Balancer

    C. Gateway load balancer

    D. Network load balancer

13. What are the three important capacity limits of auto scaling? (Choose three.)

    A. Desired capacity

    B. Maximum size

    C. Minimum size

    D. Optimal capacity

14. You have noticed that during peak demand your Lambda function is being throttled. You suspect you may be exceeding your concurrency quota. Which of the following is the best metric for determining if the concurrency limits need to be increased?

    A. Dead letter errors

    B. Errors

    C. Invocations

    D. ConcurrencyQuota

15. You have a workload composed of several EC2 instances. You wish to keep the average CPU utilization of the workload at or near 60 percent. Which of the following will most efficiently keep your workload as close as possible to the desired utilization?

    A. Manual scaling

    B. Simple scaling

    C. Step scaling

    D. Target tracking

16. AWS Lambda scales automatically to meet demand. By default, Lambda will scale up to the soft concurrency limit. What is the concurrency limit?

    A. 100

    B. 1,000

    C. 10,000

    D. 1,000,000

17. Your workload spikes every Thursday evening while batch processing runs, and processes are frequently throttled as soon as processing begins. Which of the following scaling methods will most effectively solve this problem?

    A. Predictive scaling

    B. Simple scaling

    C. Step scaling

    D. Target tracking

18. EC2 instances have a life cycle. Which of the following are the four principle states of an instance?

    A. Pending, running, shutting down, terminated

    B. Preparing, engaged, shutting down, terminated

    C. Provisioning, provisioned, deprovisioning, decommissioned

    D. Starting, running, terminating, stopped

19. Your client uses a variety of compute resources—EC2, Lambda, and Fargate—with frequent changes in instance sizes and operating systems. Which pricing model would you recommend to them in order to optimize cost?

   A. Dedicated instances

   B. Reserved instances

   C. Savings plan

   D. Spot instances

20. Which of the following is a burstable EC2 instance type?

   A. C

   B. D

   C. M

   D. T

Chapter

6

Storage, Migration, and Transfer

THE AWS CERTIFIED SYSOPS ADMINISTRATOR EXAM OBJECTIVES COVERED IN THIS CHAPTER INCLUDE:

✓ **Domain 2: Reliability and Business Continuity**

  ▪ 2.1 Implement scalability and elasticity

  ▪ 2.2 Implement high availability and resilient environments

  ▪ 2.3 Implement backup and restore strategies

✓ **Domain 5: Networking and Content Delivery**

  ▪ 5.2 Configure domains, DNS services, and content delivery

✓ **Domain 6: Cost and Performance Optimization**

  ▪ 6.2 Implement performance optimization strategies

Storage is a core service area within the AWS service collection as every web application, migration effort, and business continuity plan relies heavily on the safekeeping of data both temporarily and for the longer term. AWS offers a suite of services used for storage and transfer of data into and out of the AWS Cloud. These storage and transfer services are also building blocks available for migrating data from on-premises storage systems when migrating to the AWS Cloud. The best way to know which storage services are right for a project or migration is by evaluating what the storage needs to accomplish, such as archival storage, temporary processing storage, operating system–specific storage needs, or temporary transfer storage while processing or receiving migration data.

This chapter will introduce commonly used AWS storage, migration, and transfer services used to work with data in the AWS Cloud, but also when transferring to and from on-premises applications and infrastructures. You will learn about implementing scalability and elasticity using storage and transfer services. You will also learn about implementing high availability and resilient environments to support migrations and cloud-native workloads. You will explore implementing backup and restore strategies using AWS Data Sync, AWS Backup, migration, and transfer services and the benefits of implementing Amazon S3 performance features. You will learn how to use Amazon S3 as a method for static website hosting. Finally, you will see how to use these storage, migration, and transfer services from the lens of a SysOps administrator supporting migration and transfer efforts within an AWS environment.

Storage vs. Migration

Storage can be a large component of any migration into the AWS Cloud. Data needs a place to live so the various AWS services, custom applications, or workflows can interact with it and produce the desired outcome. Choosing the right storage requires assessing the needs of the business, application, and customer before selecting which AWS storage service is right for the job. The first step in assessing storage needs is to determine if the storage is serving an application-specific purpose, such as root volumes for servers, or shared storage between Amazon EC2 instances. You also must consider if the storage is supporting migration efforts, such as long-term archival storage, inbound data transfer and transformations, or storage connectivity between AWS and an on-premises server.

Requirements gathering is the crucial step in determining which AWS storage option is the best for the situation. This starts with understanding the needs of the application and the business, albeit they do not always have similar or even matching needs. For example, you may have an application designed to operate within block storage, such as Amazon Elastic Block Store for transformation of images or other file types. The application would be perfectly happy running to infinity using block storage connected singly to the application server it lives on. However, the business requires that the storage fit within certain cost parameters and designed to be elastic and sharable if the application becomes popular. This could mean that the block storage the application is using needs more elasticity and availability, which may come from implementing a solution like Amazon Elastic File System or even Amazon FSx. The application requirements are straightforward, but when combining the requirements of the business you will need to consider other architectural or migration options.

Migrations into AWS are no different when evaluating which storage options to use. You must consider the application's architectural, performance, and scalability requirements, but you also need to determine data access and other business requirements that could influence the AWS service selection. When considering just data migration into AWS the decisions align with either long-term storage, like backup, or shorter-term storage options used to transfer data or process using cloud-native solutions. The first requirement to focus on is how data is entering AWS, and what happens to it once it is there.

For example, if an organization needs to migrate backups and long-term storage from an on-premises datacenter, you may consider using Amazon S3 or Amazon S3 Glacier, depending on data access frequency. If the business requires all data to be immediately accessible, you would choose a different service than if the business requires data to be accessible within 4 to 24 hours. Similarly, when migrating applications you must take into consideration the performance, scalability, and long-term collaboration needs of the storage the application will use. Of course, none of this matters if you do not have a method for getting the data into AWS. In the end, as a SysOps administrator, you will need to determine the best storage options to use based on application performance, migration, or transfer needs.

Amazon Simple Storage Service (S3)

When selecting storage options for a migration, web applications, or even log storage within AWS, Amazon S3 is the go-to option when scalability, data availability, security, and performance is a key concern. Amazon S3 is an object storage service, which means you are unable to use it as an operating system root volume and you must use API calls to the Amazon S3 service to upload (PUT), download (GET), or see which files are in the Amazon S3 bucket (LIST). Although the service does not operate like traditional block storage, there are several use cases when using Amazon S3 makes sense.

For example, you would select Amazon S3 when running Big Data analytics or high-performance computing (HPC) workloads on AWS and the solution requires a data lake. Amazon S3 is also useful as a backup destination when the business requires low recovery time objectives (RTOs) and requires aggressive recovery point objectives (RPOs). Amazon S3 offers several replication and tiered storage options to address the backup and restoration of critical data. Additionally, Amazon S3 is an excellent choice for web and mobile applications that are cloud-native and require high scalability. Amazon S3 can scale with the needs of the application and has virtually limitless storage space to grow your application.

Amazon S3 Pricing

Understanding the Amazon S3 pricing model is a crucial skill for any SysOps administrator. Lucky for you, Amazon S3 follows a simple six-component cost structure that provides guidance when evaluating storage costs. When determining the overall cost of Amazon S3, you must consider storage pricing, request and data retrieval pricing, data transfer and transfer acceleration pricing, data management and analytics pricing, replication pricing, and the price to process any data with S3 Object Lambda. These six components of cost will not always apply to every situation. As a SysOps administrator you must evaluate the storage need and determine which component applies to the situation. Always use the Amazon S3 pricing documentation (found at `https://aws.amazon.com/s3/pricing`) when evaluating the use of Amazon S3 in any solution.

When evaluating the use of Amazon S3, keep in mind certain key considerations that can impact the overall price for using the service. Amazon S3 pricing is region-specific—this means that each region can have a different cost per GB. Amazon S3 also has tiered pricing across S3 Intelligent – Tiering, S3 Standard, S3 Standard – Infrequent Access, and S3 One Zone – Infrequent Access. Deciding which S3 storage class to use should not only be a cost consideration, but a decision based on the type of data, amount of data, access requirements, and risk tolerance of the data stored. For example, for any data being migrated into AWS or generated natively that is easy for you to re-create and that requires long-lived storage accessible within milliseconds, using S3 Standard – Infrequent Access may be the best option. Here you are trading lower durability for most cost-effective storage that you access quickly, such as storage for reporting or easily re-created objects.

One last thing to consider when using Amazon S3 as a storage option for migrations or cloud-native applications is the cost of requests and data retrieval and data transfer. Remember, Amazon S3 uses API calls to handle any object manipulation or access in your S3 bucket. This means AWS charges you for request types such as PUT, COPY, POST, LIST, GET, SELECT, Lifecycle Transition, and data retrievals. When considering Amazon S3 for storage, you will need to ensure that you optimize the application accessing and utilizing the Amazon S3 bucket to avoid excessive API calls that could negatively impact the cost of use for Amazon S3 buckets. Data transfer is also a consideration when using Amazon S3 as a migration destination for files or applications. As an Amazon S3 subscriber, you pay for all bandwidth into and out of Amazon S3, except for inbound data transfers in from the Internet, between S3 buckets in the same AWS region, transferred from an S3 bucket to any AWS services within the same AWS region as the bucket, and data transferred out to Amazon CloudFront. When using Amazon S3 for migration storage or backup and recovery, one of the primary drivers of cost is outbound data transfers. As a SysOps administrator, be aware of when using Amazon S3 would invoke data transfer charges.

Backup and Restore Strategies with Amazon S3

Amazon S3 offers several useful features to assist in designing a backup and restoration strategy for an organization. Amazon S3 Replication offers the ability to configure Amazon S3 to automatically replicate S3 objects across different AWS regions using S3 Cross-Region Replication (CRR), or between buckets within the same region using Same-Region Replication (SRR). S3 Replication also supports the use of two-way replication between two or more buckets, which enables further options when designing a redundant backup strategy.

There are several use cases when you may consider using S3 replication within your backup and restoration strategy. The need for data redundancy is one of the leading drivers of using S3 Replication to maintain multiple copies of your data in the same or different AWS regions. Also consider using this use case when you need to enable data sharing across accounts, or the organization has compliance storage requirements. You use S3 Replication when needing to maintain object copies under a different account, such as when you need to change ownership of the objects in the destination bucket to restrict access to object replicas.

Cross-Region Replication (CRR) is a very commonly used feature of Amazon S3 as it enables you to replicate objects and the respective metadata and object tags into other AWS regions. For example, if an organization is using Amazon S3 to store mapping data output in the Northern Virginia (US-EAST-1) region and wants to set up a backup destination in Oregon (US-WEST-2) in the event of a disaster, you can configure CRR to automatically replicate data between buckets in each region. Using CRR, you can also configure replication at the bucket to grab the entire mapping dataset, or you can choose object level using S3 object tags or prefix level if you need to more granularly replicate files into the backup location. Often companies choose to use CRR to support compliance requirements where data storage must span multiple geographically distant locations, even beyond the standard configuration of availability zones.

 NOTE   Amazon S3 Cross-Region Replication (CRR) can satisfy data storage compliance needs. Another common use case is using CRR to improve latency performance for customers when the data is accessed from multiple AWS regions.

Amazon S3 Same-Region Replication (SRR) is another solution when organizations need to back up or store multiple copies of their S3 data within the same AWS regions—for example, if an organization can back up their S3 buckets or objects in the same AWS region but to a different AWS account to satisfy compliance or regulatory requirements. Storing the data in another AWS account also enhances the security of the buckets and objects as it mitigates accidental deletion or loss of data due to credential compromises. You use Amazon S3 SRR typically when aggregating logs, such as security or application logs, into a single bucket. You can aggregate these logs into a specific compliance or security accounts for review or longer-term storage.

Using Amazon S3 CRR or SRR does pose a limit when working with existing buckets and objects. When configuring replication, any new objects placed in the buckets automatically replicate to the destination. However, any existing objects in the bucket after configuring replication would not copy to the replication destination. To address this issue, you can use Amazon S3 Batch Replication to backfill newly created replication buckets with objects from existing buckets.

 NOTE Amazon S3 Batch Replication is a useful tool for migrations. S3 Batch Replication helps preserve metadata and version ID when you're replicating existing S3 objects to other accounts, buckets, or regions.

Another frequently used and helpful feature of Amazon S3 is the ability to create and manage Amazon S3 Lifecycles. This feature allows you to configure a set of rules that allow you to define actions that Amazon S3 applies to a group of objects. There are two different action types to consider: Transition and Expiration actions. Transition actions assist in moving objects between storage classes, such as moving your monthly reports from the Amazon S3 Standard storage class into the Amazon S3 Standard-IA storage class. Expiration actions assist in deletion of objects on your behalf, such as when expiring logs after the compliance period has ended. An expiration action can remove the files after the seven years has elapsed.

Amazon S3 Lifecycle rules can use tags or prefixes to determine which objects or subset of objects in the bucket have the Lifecycle rule applied. You create a Lifecycle rule through the AWS Management Console, AWS CLI, AWS SDKs, or using the Amazon S3 REST API. Organizations use Lifecycle rules as a cost optimization strategy by moving objects between Amazon S3 storage tiers. Using a Lifecycle policy you can configure time durations, object sizes, or other object or bucket conditions to move files between the storage tiers. This enables flexibility for organizations to maintain backup data in Amazon S3, while still having access to the files when needed.

In Exercise 6.1 you will create and enable an Amazon S3 Lifecycle rule to move objects from the Amazon S3 Standard storage class into Amazon S3 Standard-IA after 30 days. To reduce costs of this exercise, create a new Amazon S3 bucket.

EXERCISE 6.1

Configuring Amazon S3 Lifecycle Rules

1. From the Amazon S3 console in the AWS Management Console, create a new Amazon S3 bucket and take note of the name.

2. Open a text editor of your choice and create three documents using the .txt file extension. Fill each document with random words and characters and then save and upload the documents to the newly created Amazon S3 bucket.

3. When the objects upload is complete, edit the tags of two of the objects and include a tag key of **Project** and a value of **Demo**. You will be configuring the Lifecycle policy to use this tag.

4. From the Amazon S3 Management Console, select the bucket you created in step 1. Select the Management tab and click Create Lifecycle Rule.

5. Choose a name for the Lifecycle rule, such as **Demo rule**. The name must be unique within the bucket.

6. Define the scope of the Lifecycle rule to limit the scope by using tags. Click Add Tag and enter the tag key of **Project** and the value of **Demo**.

7. Ignore the filter options for object size, and under Lifecycle Rule Actions, choose the option to transition current versions of the objects between storage classes.

8. Select the storage class transition to Standard-IA and set the days after object creation to 30. Note that S3 Standard-IA and One Zone-IA require a minimum of 30 days after object creation. Intelligent-Tiering and Glacier Instant Retrieval do not have this limitation.

9. Click Create Rule to run an evaluation on the Lifecycle rule to determine if it contains any errors. Creation will proceed when no errors are present, and the rule will show up under the Lifecycle Rules section of the Management tab for the S3 bucket.

That is, it! You set up a Lifecycle rule that moves any S3 objects with the tag of Project and the value of Demo into S3 Standard-IA after 30 days. If you wish to test this Lifecycle rule, you can wait the 30 days and then review the object details. To clean up from this exercise, remove the Lifecycle rule, then delete the objects, and finally remove the bucket from your AWS account.

Using Amazon S3 for Web Hosting

Another common use case for Amazon S3 is hosting static websites. This powerful feature enables organizations to scale short-term, or in some cases long-term, website solutions using the nearly limitless scaling abilities of Amazon S3, and typically for a fraction of the cost when compared to an Amazon EC2 instance or Lambda function. For example, imagine that you are working with a local film festival and the committee wants a location to store and share all the trailers for the upcoming festival. Using Amazon S3 static websites allows Amazon S3 to store the movie trailers as objects, but also allows the creation of a scalable website for viewers to retrieve the files. As the popularity of the festival grows and demand increases, Amazon S3 will scale with the demand, and everyone can continue enjoying the movie trailers. You can further enhance support for increased traffic by implementing Amazon CloudFront to cache frequently accessed files, such as the movie trailer, by using the same Amazon S3 bucket as the origin point. This enables further performance gains by providing connections closer to the end user when they attempt to view the movie trailer.

Using Amazon S3 for web hosting allows for creative solutions to minimize cost, but also utilize the elasticity, durability, and availability of the S3 service to your advantage.

Amazon S3 can host static web content, meaning web content that does not require server-side language and technology to build or display content. Static web content loads faster, is more secure, and is easier to design as it uses HTML. Using Amazon S3 for web hosting opens the possibility of simplifying web presence for disaster recovery by being a location to display a simple web page as part of a failover activity when the primary web server is down. Additionally, you can use S3 web hosting in tandem with web servers running on Amazon EC2 or elsewhere by being an alternate location for specific sales or marketing events that may only be short-lived.

It is highly recommended that any SysOps administrator knows how to configure and access an Amazon S3 static website. AWS has done a fantastic job documenting this process in a tutorial at `https://docs.aws.amazon.com/AmazonS3/latest/userguide/HostingWebsiteOnS3Setup.html` in the Amazon S3 documentation. Before taking the certification exam, be sure to explore the use of Amazon S3 static websites and how to replicate the configuration found in the tutorial.

Amazon S3 Performance Features

Any good migration plan will consider the criticality of data and the importance of the data to the business. This includes which services to store the data on, the availability and durability of the storage options, but also the performance features usable by the organization. Amazon S3 has various performance features that align with the migration use case when moving data from an on-premises datacenter, co-location, or even an office. Amazon S3 offers a performance feature called S3 Transfer Acceleration, which enables fast, easy, and secure transfers of files over long distances between your client and an S3 bucket. S3 Transfer Acceleration helps solve for various data transfer issues, such as having a global customer base that needs to upload into a single S3 bucket, transferring terabytes of data across continents on a regular basis, or if you or your customer cannot utilize all available bandwidth over the Internet when uploading to Amazon S3—for example, when migrating application files during a full app migration.

Amazon S3 also offers the ability to use multipart uploads, which allows you to upload a single object as a set of parts. You can upload the parts in any order either all at once or independently. When all the parts of the object are uploaded, Amazon S3 assembles the parts and creates the object for storage in your S3 bucket. Multipart uploads offer several benefits, ranging from improved throughput due to parallel part uploads, to the ability to pause and resume object uploads. Multipart uploads also serve as a benefit to migration use cases as they can assist in quick recovery from any network issues that may impact restarting a failed upload due to a network error. You would typically use multipart uploads when uploading large objects over a table high-bandwidth network connection and you want to maximize the available bandwidth using multithreaded parallel uploads, and when uploading objects to an Amazon S3 bucket using a spotty or inconsistent network connection. Multipart uploads increase the resiliency against network errors by avoiding upload restarts.

Amazon S3 Transfer Acceleration

You often use Amazon S3 Transfer Acceleration as a method to increase and optimize transfer speeds from across the world into S3 buckets. Amazon S3 Transfer Acceleration uses the Amazon CloudFront edge location network as an upload point to reduce latency and increase transfer speeds. Once the files are uploaded to the edge location closest to you, Amazon S3 Transfer Acceleration transfers the data to Amazon S3 using an optimized internal AWS network path. To use Transfer Acceleration, the destination S3 bucket must be DNS-compliant and not contain any periods, transfer acceleration must be enabled on the bucket, and you must be aware that Transfer Acceleration only supports virtual-hosted style requests, like `examplebucket.s3.us-west-2.amazonaws.com` when using REST API calls. When accessing a bucket with Transfer Acceleration enabled, you must use the endpoint with the following format: `bucketname.s3-accelerate.amazonaws.com` or the dual-stack (IPv6) endpoint of `bucketname.s3-accelerate.dualstack.amazonaws.com`. It is also important to note that unless the bucket owner has delegated permission to set the acceleration state on the S3 bucket, the bucket owner is the only permission that can enable this state.

Enabling Amazon S3 Transfer Acceleration on an S3 bucket from the AWS CLI is straightforward. You use the `aws s3api` command in the following format:

```
aws s3api put-bucket-accelerate-configuration --bucket
  bucketname --accelerate-configuration Status=Enabled
```

You use this command when suspending (disabling) Transfer Acceleration for the bucket by changing `Status=Enabled` to `Status=Suspended`. Remember, only bucket owners or those delegated by the bucket owner can enable or suspend Transfer Acceleration.

To use Transfer Acceleration endpoints with the AWS CLI, you can append the `--endpoint-url https://s3-accelerate.amazonaws.com` parameter to the end of your `aws s3 cp` command. You can also access the Transfer Accelerated endpoint using the Amazon S3 console by viewing the properties for the enabled bucket. Under Transfer Acceleration, Accelerated Endpoint it will display the transfer acceleration endpoint for your bucket. You can then use this endpoint to send accelerated data transfers to and from your bucket. Remember, once you suspend Transfer Acceleration the accelerated endpoints will no longer work. Be mindful when managing this performance feature and hard-coding endpoints for application use.

You can use the Amazon S3 Transfer Accelerator Speed Comparison tool when determining if Amazon S3 Transfer Acceleration is going to improve performance for your application or use case. The Amazon S3 Transfer Acceleration Speed Comparison tool provides both accelerated and non-accelerated speeds across Amazon S3 regions. AWS has great documentation on the use of the comparison tool at `https://docs.aws.amazon.com/AmazonS3/latest/userguide/transfer-acceleration-speed-comparison.html`, which we highly recommended that you evaluate every time Amazon S3 Transfer Acceleration is a consideration.

Amazon S3 Multipart Uploads

Multipart uploads provide several performance benefits when uploading to Amazon S3. The largest benefit is the increased speed, as well as the ability to pause and resume object upload or the ability to recover from network issues. Not all file uploads require the use of multipart uploads. The recommendation is to begin considering the use of multipart uploads when uploading single object sizes above 100 MB. Using multipart uploads with Amazon S3 requires a three-step process: Initiate the upload, upload the object parts, and complete the multipart upload once all part uploads are complete. Amazon S3 will construct the object from the uploaded parts once it receives the complete multipart upload request. When S3 finishes constructing the object from the multipart upload, S3 places the object in the destination bucket just as any other object upload would.

Multipart uploads have various unique identifiers that are either produced or that you select during the process. For example, when uploading an object to S3 using multipart uploads, Amazon S3 will respond with a unique identifier for your multipart upload called the upload ID. You must include this upload ID whenever you upload parts, list the parts, or complete or stop the upload. When uploading a part using multipart uploading, you must include the upload ID and you must specify a part number of your choosing. You can select any part number between 1 and 10,000. Please note that the part number uniquely identifies the part and the position in the object that you are uploading. While AWS does not require you to follow a consecutive sequence when choosing the part numbers, you should be aware that Amazon S3 will overwrite any previously written part when the same part number is in use. Amazon S3 returns an entity tag (ETag) header in the response for each part upload. You must record the part number and the ETag value and include them in the subsequent request to complete the multipart upload.

When you use Amazon S3 multipart uploads, Amazon S3 assigns a unique ID for every upload. After stopping a multipart upload, you cannot upload any part using that unique upload ID again. Ensure that you have completed all parts of your upload before sending the completion response.

For Amazon S3 to consider a multipart upload complete, you must complete the multipart upload by including the unique upload ID and a list of both part numbers and corresponding ETag values. Once Amazon S3 receives these values, it creates an object by concatenating the parts in ascending order based on the part number, as seen in Figure 6.1.

One other consideration when using multipart uploads is cost. After you start a multipart upload, Amazon S3 retains all the parts until the upload is complete, stops, or is canceled. During this time, you incur charges for all storage, bandwidth, and requests (API calls) for the multipart upload and its associated parts. When you stop a multipart upload, Amazon S3 will delete any upload artifacts and any parts. Once the process is complete, AWS no longer bills you for them. As a recommended practice, you should configure a Lifecycle rule using the AbortIncompleteMutipartUpload action to minimize storage costs. You can learn more about configuring this rule at https://docs.aws.amazon.com/AmazonS3/

`latest/userguide/mpu-abort-incomplete-mpu-lifecycle-config.html` in the Amazon S3 documentation.

FIGURE 6.1   Amazon S3 multipart upload process

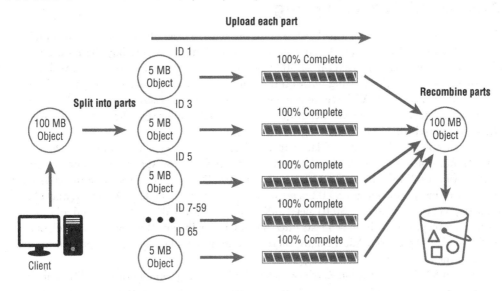

Amazon S3 Glacier

Companies have always required long-term storage of data and information. From the days of office basements filled with filing cabinets and more paper than anyone wanted to see in their entire lifetime, to entire datacenters full of storage racks and systems, this long-term storage has always served the purpose of protection—protection against the loss of data, and in some more extreme cases, protection against liability or compliance and regulatory persecution.

AWS offers several storage services that can store data for an indefinite period, albeit at a widely varying degree of costs. To address long-term storage needs and provide the lowest cost per GB storage option, AWS created the Amazon S3 Glacier storage class. You may be thinking that Amazon S3 Glacier was its own service and just connected to Amazon S3 for data migration efforts, but I am here to tell you that Amazon S3 Glacier is just a storage class within Amazon S3. Granted, this storage class has varying degrees of benefits and levels to consider when planning your longer-term archival needs.

Amazon S3 Glacier has three storage classes: Amazon S3 Glacier Instant Retrieval, Amazon S3 Glacier Flexible Retrieval Storage class (formerly just S3 Glacier), and Amazon

S3 Glacier Deep Archive. Depending on the archival needs of your organization, one of the three storage classes will provide the right mix of cost savings, performance, availability, retrieval time, and security.

Amazon S3 Glacier Pricing

Pricing for Amazon S3 Glacier is dependent on the storage class chosen between Instant Retrieval, Flexible Retrieval, or Deep Archive. As with Amazon S3 pricing, these storage classes also incur charges based on monthly storage, requests based on request type, but with one small difference of including retrieval times in most cases. As always, it is particularly important to check each AWS region pricing at https://aws.amazon.com/s3/pricing when evaluating Amazon S3 Glacier storage classes. Each AWS region has different costs for the varying levels of S3 Glacier storage class options.

For example, the Amazon S3 Glacier Instant Retrieval storage class charges you for the total monthly storage used during that period at the AWS region specific rate. For example, in the US East (Ohio) region, the cost for all storage is $0.004 per GB per month. S3 Glacier Instant Retrieval also charges $0.02 per 1,000 requests for any PUT, COPY, POST, and LIST requests, while also charging $0.01 per 1,000 requests for any GET, SELECT, and all other requests. Lifecycle Transition requests into the S3 Glacier Instant Retrieval storage class costs $0.02 per 1,000 requests. Additionally, there is a data retrieval cost of $0.03 per GB for any data returned to you from this storage class.

Amazon S3 Glacier Flexible Retrieval has a similar pricing model but with different costs for storage, requests, and retrievals. Charges in this storage class are at $0.0036 per GB and PUT, COPY, and POST. AWS bills any LIST requests at $.03 per 1,000 requests. GET, SELECT, and AWS bills all other requests at $0.0004 per 1,000 requests and Lifecycle Transition requests into S3 Glacier Flexible at $0.03 per 1,000 requests. Data retrieval does incur additional costs in this storage class and is dependent on the speed at which you want the data returned to you. Expedited delivery will cost $10.00 per 1,000 requests whereas Standard retrieval will cost $0.05 per 1,000 requests. This storage class additionally charges $0.03 per GB for data retrievals associated with Expedited retrieval request, and $0.01 per GB for Standard retrieval requests.

The final S3 Glacier storage class of Deep Archive also follows pricing models similar to that of Amazon S3 Glacier Flexible Retrieval with differences in storage pricing at $0.00099 per GB per month, $0.05 per 1,000 requests for PUT, COPY, POST, LIST, and Lifecycle Transition requests. All other requests, including GET and SELECT bill at $0.0004 per 1,000 requests. S3 Glacier Deep Archive also charges based on retrieval options with $0.10 per 1,000 data retrieval requests for Standard and $0.025 per 1,000 for bulk. Data retrieval for standard bills at $0.02 per GB and $0.0025 per GB for Bulk retrieval options.

As you can see, the pricing for Amazon S3 Glacier storage classes varies slightly but can drastically change when taking into consideration the speed of retrieval or type of requests made against the service. Understanding the pricing models for these storage classes will assist in determining the most appropriate storage option for any backup and recovery strategy.

Backup and Restore Strategies with Amazon S3 Glacier

Each of the Amazon S3 Glacier storage classes offers a slightly different solution to meet the needs for customers. As a SysOps administrator you should understand the key differences between each storage class to assist your organization in designing the appropriate data archival solution or backup and restore strategy. Choosing the appropriate S3 Glacier storage class will require considerations around cost, availability and durability, retrieval times, object sizes, and storage durations.

Amazon S3 Glacier Instant Retrieval

Amazon S3 Glacier Instant Retrieval offers eleven 9s (99.9999999 percent) of durability and 99.9 percent availability through the redundant storage of data across a minimum of three physically separated AWS availability zones. This positions S3 Glacier Instant Retrieval well against data protection and compliance needs of most organizations when considering long-term storage with rapid retrieval options. The primary usage case for S3 Glacier Instant Retrieval is data that rarely requires access, such as once or twice a quarter, and when accessing the data, you require the data to be available within milliseconds. In this case, S3 Glacier Instant Retrieval is going to be a lower-cost storage option than S3 Standard or S3 Standard-IA, but it will have a slightly higher data access cost, which plays well into the access needed only once or twice per quarter.

Getting data in and out of S3 Glacier Instant Retrieval is just as straightforward as uploading to any Amazon S3 bucket. You can directly PUT into S3 Glacier Instant Retrieval by specifying the GLACIER_IR parameter in the x-amz-storage-class header, or you can set an S3 Lifecycle policy to transition objects from any S3 Standard or Standard-IA bucket into the S3 Glacier Instant Retrieval storage class. When migrating data from an on-premises solution into S3 Glacier Instant Retrieval, the best option is to upload directly using the GLACIER_IR parameter in the header. This removes the reliance on another S3 bucket to serve as a buffer or upload location. One important thing to note: There is a minimum storage duration of 90 days for objects in Amazon S3 Glacier Instant Retrieval storage class. Any objects deleted, overwritten, or transitioned out before 90 days will incur a prorated charge equal to the storage charge for the remaining days.

Amazon S3 Glacier Flexible Retrieval

Another potential candidate for storage classes to support long-term data backups and restoration strategies is Amazon S3 Glacier Flexible Retrieval, formerly known as S3 Glacier. The ideal use case when selecting S3 Glacier Flexible Retrieval storage class is for data that will be accessed once or twice during an entire year and that restores asynchronously. For example, say your organization has an annual audit and wants to review all sales reports stored for the entire year in the S3 Glacier Flexible Retrieval storage class. You retrieve the data only once or twice per quarter because of the audit, but the retrieval can take some time, or rather, the retrieval can be asynchronous and does not require the millisecond retrieval times. This storage class offers up to a 10 percent lower cost than the S3 Glacier

Instant Retrieval storage class for any data that does not require immediate retrieval but also requires the flexibility of retrieving large sets of data, such as backup and disaster recovery, at no cost. S3 Glacier Flexible Retrieval offers the same redundancy and durability as the other S3 Glacier storage classes.

Storing data directly into the S3 Glacier Flexible Retrieval storage class works the same way as other S3 Glacier storage classes. You can directly PUT your data into the storage class using the GLACIER parameter in the x-amz-storage-class header, or you can utilize S3 Lifecycle rules to transition your objects. You can also use the Amazon S3 Management Console, Amazon SDKs, or the Amazon S3 APIs to directly place objects into Amazon S3 Glacier Flexible Retrieval. Retrieval is a bit different compared to the other S3 Glacier storage classes. When restoring objects, the retrieval process is asynchronous. You must first initiate a retrieval request, which creates a temporary copy of the data requested in an S3 Standard storage class. This leaves the archived data intact and untouched in the S3 Glacier Flexible Retrieval storage class. During the request you can specify the duration in days, that the data should remain available in the S3 Standard storage class. Once the duration has passed, Glacier removes the temporary files from the S3 Standard storage class.

When restoring data with S3 Glacier Flexible Retrieval, you can use S3 Event Notification to know when an object is successfully restored and the temporary copy is ready for use within the temporary S3 bucket. Using the same notification process, the bucket owner, or anyone delegated the appropriate permissions, can use AWS Lambda for processing the restored files, with the S3 Event Notification triggering a Lambda function. This opens the door for designing automated systems around the annual restores that may occur within your organization.

Retrieval time for S3 Glacier Flexible Retrieval is dependent on the type of retrieval option selected. You can choose from Expedited, Standard, or Bulk retrieval, and the timing varies within each depending on the size of the objects marked for restoration. Most objects restored using the expedited retrieval option will be available within 1 to 5 minutes. Standard retrieval times will range from 3 to 5 hours, and when processing a bulk retrieval, you can expect 5 to 12 hours before the data is available for use. There is a benefit to using bulk retrievals, as there is no cost associated for the retrieval when using bulk, but it will take additional time to retrieve the files. When designing the backup and restore strategy for the organization, you must consider the retrieval options available and decide which fits the business need based on time of recovery and cost for recovery.

Amazon S3 Glacier Instant Retrieval and Amazon S3 Glacier Flexible Retrieval storage classes have a minimum storage duration applied to objects of 90 days, and Amazon S3 Glacier Deep Archive has a 180-day storage duration applied. Any objects deleted before meeting the minimum storage duration will incur a prorated charge equal to the storage charge for the remaining days. Be mindful of retrieval and storage duration needs when determining which storage class to use for backup and restoration strategies.

Amazon S3 Glacier Deep Archive

Most organizations will have a need for long-term storage of data. Most of the long-term durations are set by compliance or regulatory needs or company-specific requirements depending on the type of data stored. For example, your organization may need to keep annual sales or tax data for 7 years, while another organization like a healthcare provider may need to keep patient records for 10 years or, in some cases, indefinitely. Long-term storage like this can result in considerable cost when handling on-premises, not including the amount of physical space, equipment maintenance, or other costs associated to just keeping the data available. This is where Amazon S3 Glacier Deep Archive becomes so much more valuable. Glacier Deep Archive provides long-term data storage, the type of data access once or twice every few years, at a significantly lower cost than maintaining the storage or magnetic tape libraires on-premises. The use cases are endless for S3 Glacier Deep Archive, and several industries such as financial services, healthcare, and public sectors require this type of storage class to meet regulatory or compliance needs for their business. Not to mention, S3 Glacier Deep Archive can reduce or discontinue the use of on-premises magnetic tape libraries. If you have ever needed to work with magnetic tapes before, you can write AWS a thank-you note—they will appreciate it.

Amazon S3 Glacier Deep Archive is for colder data storage needs. This means the data is much less likely to require access, and when it is, will require larger dataset retrieval or bulk object retrieval. S3 Glacier Deep Archive also has different retrieval options to use such as Standard and Bulk. The Standard retrieval option provides the data within 12 hours and the bulk retrieval option can reduce costs, but data retrieval is complete within 48 hours. As you can see, the retrieval options are much slower than the other S3 Glacier storage classes. When designing your backup and restore strategy, you must take into account these time-frames for retrieval, and whether the cost for Standard outweighs the need for decreasing the retrieval time.

Getting data into Amazon S3 Glacier Deep Archive uses the S3 API and specifying the S3 Glacier Deep Archive as the storage class. You can also use the AWS Management Console, S3 REST API, AWS CLI, or the AWS SDKs to store data into Amazon S3 Glacier Deep Archive. Just like the other S3 Glacier storage classes, you can use S3 Lifecycles to migrate data between an S3 bucket and S3 Glacier Deep Archive. Just be aware that any transitioned data incurs costs at the S3 Glacier Deep Archive upload price. If your organization is looking to transition away from magnetic tapes, you can also use AWS Storage Gateway with the Tape Gateway feature to store the data on the tapes directly into S3 Glacier Deep Archive. This is an excellent feature to begin migration of storage tape archives into AWS for cost reduction, durability, and availability.

Retrieval of data is remarkably like that of the Amazon S3 Glacier Flexible Retrieval storage class. You must first initiate a restore request using the Amazon S3 APIs or Amazon S3 Management Console. Once the request processes, it will create a temporary copy of the data in an S3 Standard storage class, where you can access the data directly using the Amazon S3 GET request. You still need to specify the amount of time, in days, that the data is available. Depending on the request urgency, you can select Standard or Bulk retrieval options. It is important to evaluate the trade-off of time over cost when retrieving objects and selecting the retrieval option. The bulk option will always have a lesser cost at the expense of time.

Amazon Elastic Block Store

By now you have heard of block-level storage volumes used within Amazon EC2, known as Amazon Elastic Block Store (Amazon EBS). You have also likely been using block storage knowingly, or unknowingly for a long time—you know, those little hard drives in your laptop, or smartphone, even the storage in your television. Yep, those are utilizing block storage. The concept is not a new one, but how AWS uses block storage and the service types offered does change how we use, manage, and create block storage in the cloud.

At the root, what you need to know about Amazon EBS is that EBS volumes behave like raw and unformatted block devices (hard drive volumes). You can mount these devices to your Amazon EC2 instances and expose them as persistent volumes, which is until you remove them from the Amazon EC2 instance. They are there for your use, you pay for what you use, and the performance you need, and in the end, you can store files, run operating systems, or anything in between. AWS recommends using Amazon EBS volumes for any data that must be quickly accessible or that requires long-term persistence when connected to Amazon EC2 instances. AWS also positions the Amazon EBS volumes to perform well with database-style applications that rely heavily on read and write operations, or applications that require throughput-intensive actions across long, continuous reads and writes. Overall, Amazon EBS volumes are going to be the most usual form of storage you come across as a SysOps administrator. It is up to you to know how to monitor performance of these volumes and what options are available for backup and restoration of data on the volumes.

Amazon EBS Pricing

Amazon EBS volumes follow the traditional cloud consumption model where you pay for what you use, or rather, what you store. You also have the option to pay for additional performance-related needs, like increasing the amount of input/output operations per second (IOPS), or different volume types to match the workload and volume performance your application requires. As of this writing there are eight different Amazon EBS volume types: General Purpose SSD (gp3), General Purpose SSD (gp2) Provisioned IOPS SSD (io2 Block Express), Provisioned IOPS SSD (io2), Provisioned IOPS SSD (io1), Throughput Optimized HDD (st1), Cold HDD (sc1), and the previous volume type Magnetic (standard). The good news is you will not have to remember the pricing per GB for each volume type. That information is easily available at https://aws.amazon.com/ebs/pricing in the Amazon EBS pricing documentation and searchable when needed. Instead, you will need to know the difference in volumes and what adds additional cost to an Amazon EBS volume and what the advantage or use case is for each volume type. We will not be covering basic

Amazon EBS volume type information in this section, but you should review the EBS volume type section at `https://docs.aws.amazon.com/AWSEC2/latest/UserGuide/ebs-volume-types.html` of the AWS public documentation for Amazon EBS as a refresher before sitting for the exam.

Pricing for Amazon EBS volumes has a per GB per month charge. Newer versions of storage volumes such as gp3 will have a cost savings over the previous generation, gp2. You can also expect an increase in performance or options during each generational change. When using gp3, gp2, st1, and sc1 volumes, you pay for just the storage cost per GB, per month. When using Provisioned IOPS volumes, like io2, io2 block express, and io1, you still pay a per GB per month cost for the storage, but you also pay a fee for Provisioned IOPS per month. Some volumes, like gp3, have additional charges when going beyond the allotted free tier of performance. For example, when provisioning a gp3 volume, you receive 3,000 IOPS free per month; anything over that limit will bill at a reduced fee for Provisioned IPOS over 3,000. The same goes for throughput on gp3 volumes; when exceeding 125 MB/s, you will pay a reduced fee for provisioned throughput MB/s per month over 125.

Amazon EBS also has a unique pricing component to be aware of related to Amazon EBS Snapshots. These snapshots are point-in-time copies of your block data. Amazon EBS Snapshots stored in the Standard Amazon S3 tier are incremental, which means you are only paying for the changed blocks stored per month. This drastically reduces the amount of storage costs per month related to the Amazon EBS volume size. When using the Archive tier, the Amazon EBS snapshot is a full copy of the block data, and AWS bills you for all blocks stored, not just the changed blocks. This means you will see larger snapshot storage costs as it is storing a larger-sized image backup of your volume. In addition to the cost per GB per month to store Amazon EBS volume snapshots, you will also incur a charge per GB of data retrieved when restoring Amazon EBS Snapshots from the Archive tier. When designing a backup and restore strategy for Amazon EBS, consider not only the storage costs, but the costs for snapshot storage and retrieval.

Backup and Restore Strategies with Amazon EBS

Amazon EBS volumes are extremely common in every AWS account. There are several methods for ensuring that EBS volume data is available and backed up as part of a backup and restoration strategy. One of the most useful tools to create, retain, and delete snapshots is the Amazon Data Lifecycle Manager, where you can automate the snapshot process and eliminate manual EBS snapshot administration. The key to a good Amazon EBS volume backup and restoration strategy is to automate as much of the administrative work as possible. Eliminating potential human error is key to developing a solid backup and restore solution that aligns to business needs and scales with the organization.

Amazon Data Lifecycle Manager

Amazon Data Lifecycle Manager allows an organization to automate the creation, retention, and deletion of EBS Snapshots and EBS-backed Amazon Machine Images (AMIs). Data Lifecycle Manager enables cross-account snapshot copy automation and life cycles to reduce storage costs, enforce regular backup schedules, and help create disaster recovery backups and policies across isolated AWS accounts. There is no additional cost to use Amazon Data Lifecycle Manager, but you are responsible for the cost of any stored AMI or EBS volume snapshots created by the tool. The only billing caveat is when using fast snapshot restore as you incur charges for each minute that the fast snapshot restore is enabled. When considering the use of Fast Snapshot Restore, always view the EBS pricing documentation at https://aws.amazon.com/ebs/pricing to evaluate the cost per minute; it can vary per region.

Amazon Data Lifecycle Manager only works with EBS-backed AMIs and volume types. You cannot create, retain, or delete instance store backed AMIs with Amazon Data Lifecycle Manager.

There are a few components to Data Lifecycle Manager you should remember when designing an automated EBS volume snapshot backup or AMI backup process. Snapshots are the primary means to back up the data from the EBS volumes. Successive snapshots are incremental and only contain the volume data changed since the previous snapshots. EBS-backed AMIs include only the EBS volumes attaching to the source instance at the time of creation. Target resource tags and Data Lifecycle Manager tags play a critical role in management and automation process. Target resource tags help identify which resources to back up and are customizable to fit the needs of an organization's backup and restoration strategy. The Data Lifecycle Manager tags apply to all snapshots and AMIs created by a policy to provide distinguishing characteristics from snapshots or AMIs created by other means, such as manual or through other scripts. Data Lifecycle Manager tags will always start with aws:dlm: or just dlm: when applied to resources.

Data Lifecycle Manager uses Lifecyle policies and policy schedules to handle the automation tasks used to back up EBS volumes and EBS-backed AMIs. Lifecycle policies consist of core settings of Policy Type, Resource Type, Target Tags, and Policy Schedules. Data Lifecycle Manager supports snapshot Lifecycle policies, EBS-backed AMI Lifecycle policies, and cross-account copy event policies. Policy schedules enable you to define creation of snapshots or AMIs, and how long to retain them. For example, you can configure policy schedules to retain only the three most recent snapshots or only manage EBS volumes that have a tag key of Production and the value of Webserver.

When using Data Lifecycle Policy Manager, keep in mind that multiple policies can attach to backup volumes or instances. This means you must be mindful when creating policies to ensure that you are capturing the backups at the desired times, and not excessively creating snapshots or potentially increasing the time between snapshots. You must also be aware of which instances and volumes are targets of the snapshot Lifecycle policies as count-based retention schedules will not automatically remove the previously created snapshots. You must manually remove the snapshots when your organization no longer needs to retain copies. Similarly, any age-based retention schedules will continue to remove previous snapshots per the defined schedule up until the last remaining snapshot. This means you must remove the last snapshot manually when your organization no longer requires the snapshot.

In Exercise 6.2 you will enable Amazon Data Lifecycle Manager to create a snapshot Lifecycle policy for backing up EBS volumes with the tag key of Dev and the value of Finance. You will not be using or enabling Fast Snapshot Restore during this process as it will bill for each minute that the fast snapshot restore is enabled. Remember to clean up and remove any undesired policies or snapshots after this exercise.

EXERCISE 6.2

Creating a Snapshot Lifecycle Policy

1. From the Amazon EC2 console select Lifecycle Manager under the Elastic Block Store heading in the left navigation panel.

2. Choose EBS Snapshot Policy from the Create A New Lifecycle Policy Type drop-down menu. Click Next Step to continue.

3. Ensure that you select Volume under the Target Resources section and enter the target resource tag key value of **Dev** and the value of **Finance**. Click Add to save the tag selection.

4. Enter a description for the policy, such as **Development Finance Backup**, and under the IAM Role section ensure that you select Default Role.

5. Under the Policy Status heading, ensure that the policy is enabled and click Next to continue.

6. Next you will need to configure the schedule details for this policy. Provide a schedule name of **Daily**, set the frequency to Daily, and select every 12 hours starting at 06:00 UTC. For this policy you will select an age-based retention type to expire 2 days after creation. You will be ignoring all advanced options for this exercise. When finished, click Review Policy.

7. Review the policy you just created and click Create Policy to complete the process.

That's it! You just completed the creation of an EBS snapshot policy maintained by Amazon Data Lifecycle Manager. To test this policy, you can create an EBS volume with the tag matching the target policy tags. Be sure to remove any volumes and snapshots after testing to avoid undesired costs.

Monitoring and Performance of EBS Volumes

As with all services within AWS, you will need to understand how to monitor the health and performance of EBS volumes. EBS volumes are at the heart of Amazon EC2 instances, and having high-performance and well-monitored EBS volumes is a core component of developing a good backup and restoration strategy for an organization.

There are a few factors that can impact performance of an EBS volume. First, if an EBS volume is performing poorly it is important to ensure that the Amazon EC2 instance type supports the use of EBS optimization. This setting prevents EBS volume traffic from contending with your instances' network traffic and can increase performance. Another factor is understanding the workload that is accessing the EBS volume and ensuring that you select the proper volume type, and in some cases, size and IOPS allotments correctly. This plays a critical role in applications that have read- or write-intensive restrictions, such as database applications. One common performance issue is when initializing volumes from EBS Snapshots as there is a latency penalty applied to the volume. To avoid this latency penalty, you can enable Fast Snapshot Restore on a snapshot, for an additional cost, which creates a fully initialized volume at creation. Alternatively, you can initialize the EBS volume manually by accessing each block prior to putting the volume into production.

You can identify other factors influencing performance by using Amazon CloudWatch when evaluating the EBS volumes. For example, an EBS volume that is performing slowly may have exceeded the read or write IOPS allotted for the volume. Using CloudWatch you can evaluate the metric of `VolumeQueueLength` to determine the number of pending I/O requests for a device. `VolumeQueueLength` is an indicator of a bottleneck on either the guest operating system or the network link to EBS. For transaction-intensive applications that are sensitive to increased I/O latency, it is best to maintain a low queue length and a high number of IOPS available to the volume. However, if you have a throughput-intensive application backed by HDD volumes, they are less sensitive to increased I/O latency and can benefit from maintaining a high queue length when performing large, sequential I/O.

Certain volumes, such as gp2, st1, and sc1, use a burst bucket balance to determine whether the volume has throttling applied at the baseline or has full available IOPS for use. Checking the `BurstBalance` metric in Amazon CloudWatch can identify depletion of the burst bucket and result in low performance of the EBS volume. There are other important metrics to keep track of for EBS volumes using Amazon CloudWatch. `VolumeReadBytes`, `VolumeWriteBytes`, `VolumeReadOps`, and `VolumeWriteOps` all provide valuable information on the performance of an EBS volume. These metrics can help identify if there are I/O size or volume throughput issues between the guest operating system and the EBS volume. Using these metrics, you can define the appropriate I/O size for the volume and application, and the appropriate amount of IOPS in total when using Provisioned IOPS volumes. Remember to get a baseline reading for any application against the EBS metrics as a starting point for setting alerts and determining performance. Without this information it will be exceedingly difficult to know if a volume is performing as expected or having performance issues. AWS has a fantastic explanation of how to design for EBS performance in the AWS re:Invent 2015 video that goes in depth on the best methods for squeezing as much performance as possible out of an Amazon EBS volume (`https://youtu.be/2wKgha8CZ_w`). This video also has wonderful information on how to monitor applications and provides real-world examples.

Amazon Elastic File System

Amazon Elastic File System (Amazon EFS) is a serverless elastic filesystem available to Linux Amazon EC2 instances. Amazon EFS offers automatic scalability up to petabytes of data without the need for provisioning storage or modification to networking for the Amazon EC2 instances accessing the service. Amazon EFS is accessible from Amazon EC2 instances, Amazon ECS containers, Amazon EKS containers, including AWS Fargate, and AWS Lambda functions. Amazon EFS offers scalable and hands-off administration of a filesystem that fits a wide need of workloads and applications such as Big Data and analytics, web serving, and Linux home directories and file storage.

Thousands of individual Amazon EC2 instances can access Amazon EFS filesystems all concurrently with file-locking and strong consistency by mounting the filesystem directly in the guest operating system. Amazon EFS uses the Network File System version 4 (NFS v4) protocol to allow access from Amazon EC2 instances. This enables multiple EC2 instances to connect to the fault-tolerant storage system provided by Amazon EFS. Amazon manages the underlying infrastructure for Amazon EFS, which eliminates the administrative overhead otherwise absorbed by you or your organization.

Amazon EFS also offers two different storage classes when creating the filesystems. You can choose between Amazon EFS Standard or One Zone storage classes. The main difference is the number of availability zones that Amazon EFS stores data across. One Zone storage offers redundant data storage but only within a single availability zone, which results in a lower price point compared to the Standard storage class.

Amazon EFS Pricing

Amazon EFS pricing can vary depending on the region where you implement the solution. It is important to check the Amazon EFS pricing documentation at `https://aws.amazon .com/efs/pricing` when designing an architecture that utilizes Amazon EFS. The pricing structure for Amazon EFS takes into consideration effective storage pricing charged at the price per GB per month for data stored in One Zone or Standard EFS storage classes. Amazon EFS also charges for any applicable storage and data-transfer read or write charges when using Amazon EFS Replication to replicate the filesystem to a region or availability zone of your choice. The charges are applicable to the destination region, including any inter-Region Data Transfer OUT charges. You also will incur charges for same region replication across availability zones as you pay data transferred "out" from the source availability zone.

Using Amazon EFS for Fault Tolerance

Amazon EFS has several uses to increase fault tolerance of applications and architectures within an AWS environment. Any application requiring fault tolerant file storage running in AWS can use Amazon EFS to achieve high availability and storage fault tolerance. This is due to the ability for Amazon EC2 instances, Amazon ECS containers, Amazon EKS containers, including AWS Fargate, and AWS Lambda functions to all access the shared storage using NFSv4.1 and NFSv4.0 protocols, at the same time. AWS designed the service to be highly scalable, highly available, and highly durable with eleven 9s of durability. Amazon EFS also works across multiple availability zones in a single VPC to scale with your highly available applications and offer more availability for the service.

When implementing Amazon EFS for use with compute instances, such as Amazon EC2, each availability zone where compute instances are present and needing access to Amazon

EFS will have a mount target. These mount targets are highly available and complement availability zone failover architectures. This is because the IP addresses and DNS for the mount targets in each availability zone are static and redundant components backed up by multiple resources. For example, in Figure 6.2 you will see a design for a basic application architecture where availability zone failover is present across three availability zones, and there are three separate and redundant Amazon EFS mount targets to support the Amazon EC2 instance failover. When using Amazon EFS One Zone storage class, you are only able to create a single mount target in the same availability zone as the filesystem instead of the multiple targets seen in Figure 6.2, which is using the Amazon EFS Standard storage classes.

FIGURE 6.2 Redundant Amazon EFS architecture

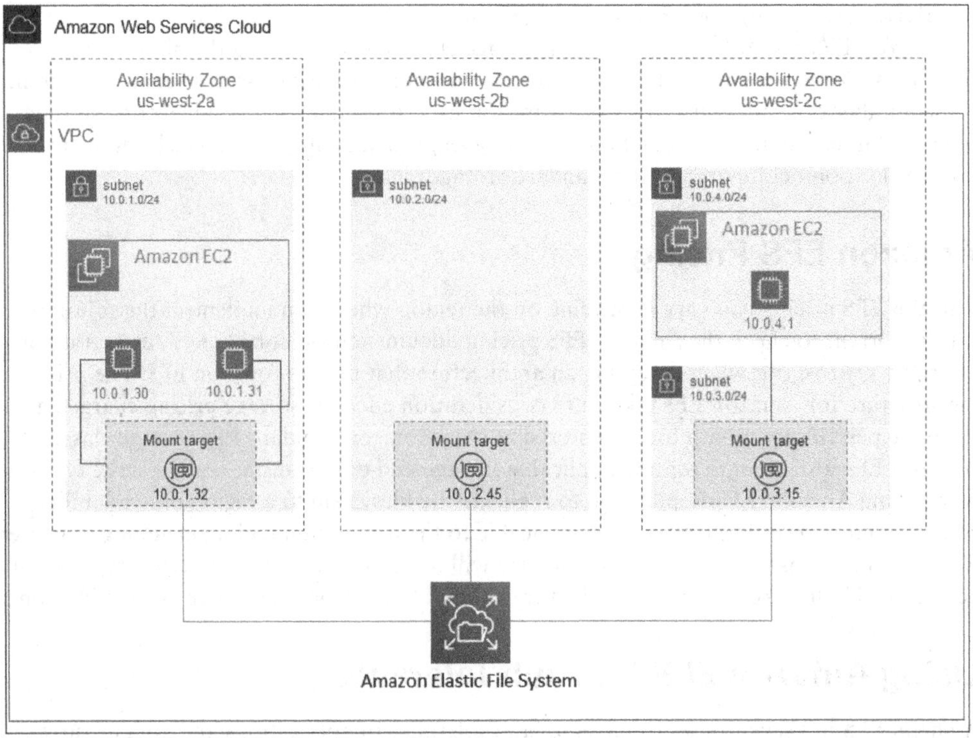

You can also use Amazon EFS locally as a mounted target point on an on-premises server for migration of data into the AWS Cloud–hosted Amazon EFS filesystem. This configuration requires a connection to the AWS environment across an AWS DirectConnect connection or AWS VPN to your Amazon VPC, but there are no additional costs associated with this process. AWS recommends any on-premises server accessing Amazon EFS use a Linux-based operating system with at least the Linux kernel version 4.0 to avoid any potential compatibility conflicts. Using this configuration, you can enhance the fault tolerance of data accessed by multiple systems in the AWS environment while also maintaining a connection to on-premises resources. Any mount target subnet available in the VPC and reachable by the AWS DirectConnect connection between the on-premises server and the VPC is a candidate for using Amazon EFS, if the mount target security group allows inbound traffic on the NFS port (2049) from those on-premises servers.

Amazon EFS offers two additional implementation options to assist in developing fault tolerance for an application. The first is the use of EFS replication, where you can create a replica of the entire Amazon EFS filesystem in the AWS region of your preference. Amazon EFS replication is automatic and transparently replicates the data and metadata located in your Amazon EFS filesystem to the new destination. This can be any supported AWS region that supports Amazon EFS and Amazon EFS replication. This offers a great method to expand fault tolerance to fully redundant web application configurations spanning multiple AWS regions. The Amazon EFS replication process keeps both the source and destination filesystems synchronized. This means you measure the recovery point objective (RPO), and the recovery time objective (RTO) is in minutes, instead of hours, or in some cases days when compared to on-premises options. Using Amazon EFS replication is another solution for creating standby recovery architectures in other AWS regions to support compliance, business continuity goals, or disaster and recovery plans.

 It is important to remember that Amazon EFS filesystems can only be part of one replication configuration at a time. This means you cannot select a destination filesystem as the source for another replication using Amazon EFS replication.

The second implementation option to further advance fault tolerance is the integration with AWS Backup with Amazon EFS. AWS Backup can integrate with your Amazon EFS filesystem to centrally manage and automate data backup across the service. Amazon EFS always prioritizes filesystem traffic over backup operations to ensure that the performance of the filesystem does not decline due to performing backups on the data. In general, AWS backup provides 100 MB/s backup rates for filesystems mostly composed of large files and 500 files/s for filesystems composed of mostly smaller files. AWS Backup will also cap backup duration of an Amazon EFS filesystem to a maximum of seven days.

AWS provides documentation with several opportunities to learn hands-on using walk-throughs for common configurations within Amazon EFS. As a SysOps administrator you should gain hands-on experience with Amazon EFS before taking the certification exam, and the walk-throughs available at https://docs.aws.amazon.com/efs/latest/ug/walkthroughs.html provide a great option for learning how Amazon EFS operates and the common use cases you will come across as a SysOps administrator.

Amazon FSx

Amazon FSx is a fully managed AWS service where AWS handles the hardware provisioning, patching, and backups of the underlying architecture used to deliver the high-performance and scalable filesystem in the AWS Cloud. You can use Amazon FSx with several AWS compute options, including Amazon EC2, Amazon ECS, and Amazon EKS. There are four options to choose from when implementing Amazon FSx: Amazon FSx for NetApp ONTAP, Amazon FSx for OpenZFS, Amazon FSx for Windows File Server, and Amazon FSx for Lustre. The filesystem requirements your organization or application has will help determine which FSx filesystem you should use. The choice is also based on familiarity with given filesystems or by matching the desired feature sets, performance, or data management capabilities of the planned workload. Whichever Amazon FSx filesystem you choose, you can expect a fully managed solution offering up to submillisecond latencies and high throughput.

Amazon FSx is also highly available and replicates data within or across availability zones to protect against failure and increase fault tolerance. Amazon FSx also offers replication across AWS regions and integration with AWS Backup, like the feature sets available from Amazon EFS. One additional benefit of Amazon FSx is the ability to encrypt data at rest and in transit automatically using AWS KMS. Another similarity to Amazon EFS is the ability to run Amazon FSx filesystems with access from on-premises systems for a hybrid-enabled approach to storage.

Great, now you understand the different filesystem types available using Amazon FSx, but how do you select which is right for an application architecture, and when to use it? The answer is completely dependent on the type of workload and knowing which FSx filesystem connects with which type of host. For example, you would use Amazon FSx for NetApp ONTAP when working with a current storage technology running on NetAPP ONTAP or other NAS appliances accessing the filesystem using SMB, NFS, or iSCSI protocols and needing block-level storage options. You would use FSx for OpenZFS when working with a current storage technology running ZFS or other Linux-based file servers accessing the storage using NFS protocols for file-level storage options. You would use Amazon FSx for Windows File Server when the current storage technology is running on Microsoft Windows Server and accessing storage using the SMB protocol for file-level storage options, and you'd use FSx for Lustre when the current storage technology running is Lustre or other parallel filesystems, typically used in high-performance computing configurations.

Amazon FSx Pricing

As you can imagine, pricing for Amazon FSx is determined by which filesystem type is in use. Let's explore the different pricing options for each of the four filesystem types.

Amazon FSx for NetApp ONTAP Pricing

Like several AWS services you pay for the resources that you use and there are no setup charges or minimum fees. Amazon FSx for NetAPP ONTAP pricing takes into consideration the average amount of SSD storage provisioned for your filesystems per month, measured in gigabyte-months. Pricing also varies by the optional additional provisioning of higher-level IOPS, and you pay the average IOPS provisioned above the included rate for the month, measured in IOPS-months. AWS calculates cost depending on the capacity pool storage usage after Amazon FSx automatically transitions data from SSD storage to capacity pool storage based on access patterns. You only pay for the average storage space consumed per month, measured in GB-months. For any data in the capacity pool storage, you also pay requests costs for read and write operations whenever accessing data. Another component of pricing is throughput capacity, where you pay an average throughput capacity provisioned for the filesystem per month, measured in MBps-month. The final component of pricing aligns with backups. You pay only for the average storage space consumed for the incremental backups per month, measured in GB-months. As always, verify pricing using the AWS pricing documentation available at `https://aws.amazon.com/fsx/netapp-ontap/pricing` while planning an Amazon FSx for NetAPP ONTAP architecture.

Amazon FSx for OpenZFS Pricing

The pricing structure for Amazon FSx for OpenZFS only charges for the resources that you use with no setup charges or minimum fees. Pricing does take into consideration the amount of SSD storage provisioned per month, measured in GB-months, and the SSD IOPS provisioned above the allotted rate for the month, measured in IOPS-months. Throughput capacity incurs charges using the average throughput capacity provisioned for the filesystem per month, measured in MB/s-months, and backups incur charges based on the average incremental backup storage consumed per month, measured in GB-months. Pricing for this service can vary per AWS region, and it is best practice to check the AW Public pricing documentation at `https://aws.amazon.com/fsx/openzfs/pricing` when planning to use Amazon FSx for OpenZFS within your AWS architecture.

Amazon FSx for Windows File Server Pricing

Pricing for Amazon FSx for Windows File Server is like the other FSx filesystems as there are no minimum fees and no setup charges; you pay only for what you use. One key difference in this service is how AWS prorates pricing by the hour and billed for the average usage over a month, compared to the pricing quotes, which follow a monthly basis. When using the AWS Public pricing documentation available at `https://aws.amazon.com/fsx/windows/pricing` for Amazon FSx for Windows File Server, be sure to evaluate the costs incurring per hour.

Amazon FSx for Windows File Server charges for storage and throughput capacity that you specify for the filesystem, which is dependent on the deployment type between single-AZ or multi-AZ. The price of storage capacity can depend on the deployment type, such as single-AZ or multi-AZ, and on the storage type, such as SDD or HDD. Backups, taken incrementally, also incur a cost based on the average amount of backup storage per month, measured in GB-months. Another difference in pricing for Amazon FSx for Windows File Server is in the charges for data transfer. Data transferred in and out of the Amazon FSx filesystem across availability zones or VPC peering connections in the same region incur charges at the AWS region rate. Data transfers incurred for replication across availability zones incur charges based on the throughput capacity pricing. Any data transferred out from the Amazon FSx filesystem into another AWS region incurs charges at the inter-region rate for that specific inter-region transfer location.

Amazon FSx for Lustre Pricing

Amazon FSx for Lustre has another unique pricing model you should be aware of when designing an architecture for use within your AWS environment. There are no setup fees or minimum charges, and the pricing follows the typical pay-for-what-you-use model. Cost is associated with the filesystem storage, where you pay based on its storage capacity measured in GB-months, and pricing is dependent on the use of SSD or HDD storage selection. Incremental backups also incur charges for backup data stored, measured in GB-months. A unique cost reduction consideration specific to Amazon FSx for Lustre is the use of data compression to reduce storage consumption for filesystem storage and filesystem backups. When you choose to use data compression, there is different pricing compared to the cost of using uncompressed data. Always verify data compression cost reductions and per AWS region costs using the AWS Public pricing documentation at `https://aws.amazon.com/fsx/lustre/pricing` for Amazon FSx for Lustre. The final cost component to consider is data transfer. Any data transferred in or out from the filesystem across availability zones or VPC peering connections in the same AWS region incurs charges at the rate for data transfers within the same AWS region. When transferring data out to another AWS region, AWS bills at the inter-region rate for that specific inter-region transfer.

Using Amazon FSx for High Availability and Resilient Environments

Data is a critical asset for any organization and requires filesystems that support high availability and resilience to failures. Protecting this asset is only one job of the filesystem; it must also be cost effective and scalable to meet the needs of the business. Amazon FSx provides several options for scalable, highly available, and resilient filesystem use within a familiar and managed environment. Amazon FSx provides scalability and high availability using multiple availability zone architecture support. This also helps build in a margin of resiliency for data stored within any of the Amazon FSx architectures as you can replicate your filesystems across AWS regions and integrate with AWS Backup for additional fault tolerance options.

Amazon FSx offers hybrid-enabled deployment options for each of the filesystem offerings. Using a hybrid-enabled approach—meaning you can migrate and synchronize data from an on-premises datacenter—allows you to expand availability of data both in the AWS Cloud and within your own datacenter. This opens additional avenues of lowering latency for accessing data to those systems and personnel working locally on-premises and need access to the same dataset as the applications in the cloud. Amazon FSx File Gateway or the NetApp ONTAP Global File Cache solution will enable local access of data for on-premises. Depending on which filesystem the business requires, it will depend on which option you deploy as part of the architecture in the organization's AWS account.

Amazon fully manages the availability and durability of Amazon FSx. This means AWS controls the underlying architecture, networking, and software. It also means that only the data and filesystem types are the concerns of the SysOps administrator, thus significantly lowering the administrative overhead seen by many organizations required to manage the entire filesystem architecture and data. Being a managed service within AWS, Amazon FSx also automatically replicates data within or across AWS availability zones to protect from any component failures within the Amazon FSx service. AWS also monitors and maintains the underlying infrastructure components and replaces the failed components or swaps to standby systems in the event of a failure. AWS offers this level of protection in the Amazon FSx service and part of the managed offering.

Of course, there is always room for improvement in resiliency and availability when designing a filesystem for use with any applications. To increase availability, you can choose to replicate data into another AWS region into a secondary configuration of the Amazon FSx filesystem. You can use this information as a passive standby or an active failover configuration. How the data replicates is specific to the Amazon FSx filesystem chosen. There are several walk-through learning tasks to learn common configuration tasks for each Amazon FSx filesystem found in the AWS public documentation available at `https://aws.amazon.com/fsx` for Amazon FSx.

Migration and Transfer

As a SysOps administrator, you will need to migrate data into and out of an AWS environment using a range of different AWS services, depending on the needs of your organization or application. Several AWS services exist to assist in the migration and data transfer process, including some that are meant to operate in a hybrid fashion to assist in migration of on-premises data. It is necessary for a SysOps administrator to understand the benefits and use cases of each data transfer AWS service to recommend the most efficient and cost-effective solution. It is also important to remember that migration and transfer are terribly similar tasks when working with applications. The real difference between a migration and a transfer is the number of times this action occurs. For example, a migration is a one-time task or at least limited to a project duration, with the end goal of completely hosting the application and the data on AWS. A data transfer has no real end date but can potentially link to a migration project. For example, when running in a hybrid on-premises environment an organization may choose to transfer data continuously between the AWS environment and the on-premises systems. This is a persistent task serving a synchronization or data consistency purpose, and not related at all to a migration project. Additionally, data transfers are not just between on-premises and the AWS Cloud. Several AWS services support transfer of data between other AWS locations, regions, and systems—for example, backing up data from an application or Amazon EC2 instances for long-term storage, or synchronizing data between AWS regions for a hot-standby environment.

AWS Backup

AWS Backup allows an organization to centralize and automate data protection across AWS services, including hybrid on-premises workloads. The key value to AWS Backup is the centralized management for backup options across various AWS services like Amazon EC2,

Amazon EBS volumes, Amazon S3, Amazon DynamoDB, Amazon FSx, and AWS Storage Gateway volumes, to name a few. AWS Backup also offers integration with AWS Organizations to centrally manage and deploy data protection policies to govern backup activity across all AWS accounts in the organization.

AWS Backup uses protection policies, also known as backup plans, to define backup frequency and backup retention periods. You assign data protection plans to support AWS resources where AWS Backup then automates the creation of backups and stores the backups in an encrypted vault, designated by the creator of the policy. The AWS Backup console can also manage centralized policies as defined by deployment across an AWS organization, including restoration, monitoring, and backup activities. Another key benefit of AWS Backup is the ability to apply data protection policies to create backups of Storage Gateway volumes and VMware virtual machines on-premises.

AWS Backup Pricing

Pricing for AWS Backup follows the familiar concept of paying for only what you use. Within AWS Backup you will incur charges for backup storage, the amount of backup data transferred between AWS regions, the amount of backup data restored, and the number of backup evaluations. AWS Backup does not require a minimum fee or use, and there are no setup fees or charges. Pricing for backup storage, cross-region data transfer, and restores vary per region and you should always review the current pricing information available at `https://aws.amazon.com/backup/pricing` in the AWS Backup pricing documentation.

AWS Backup has an additional feature called AWS Backup Audit Manager that has separate pricing based on the number of backup evaluations completed. AWS Backup Audit Manager has predefined and customizable controls to ensure compliance of backup usage against the defined policies. AWS Backup Audit Manager relies on AWS Config to record configuration item information, and AWS Config will bill each configuration item separately when used with AWS Backup Audit Manager. When designing the use of AWS Backup Audit Manager, take into consideration the additional cost of the configuration items required by the service.

AWS Backup Use Cases

There are two primary use cases for using AWS Backup. The first is using AWS Backup as a cloud-native backup solution within AWS, and the second is using AWS Backup as a hybrid data protection solution between AWS and on-premises resources. The goal for each use case is to develop a centralized and automated backup plan to meet the data protection needs of an organization.

AWS Backup offers cloud-native backup options through the integration with AWS services such as Amazon S3, Amazon RDS, Amazon DynamoDB, Amazon EFS, Amazon FSx, and Amazon EBS. AWS Backup offers the application of data protection policies to control recovery points, backup frequency, and access of backup data used by AWS services.

Using cloud-native backup solutions increases the ability to automate backup activities and increases the overall resiliency of data stored in AWS.

When creating backup plans for cloud-native AWS services, you have control over the frequency and retention period of the backup plan. This means you can choose to enable continuous backups for supported resources like Amazon S3 to create a point-in-time restore (PITR), or you can configure the plan to only run daily, weekly, or even up to monthly. The backup plan also includes life-cycle information to determine when or if data is to move into cold storage for retention. This can help reduce storage costs for data that you must retain for longer periods of time, such as financial data that you require for long-term archival options.

In Exercise 6.3 you create a backup plan using AWS Backup to create daily backups of Amazon S3 buckets. As this is the first time you are using AWS Backup with Amazon S3, you will need to ensure that you create two in-line IAM policies to ensure AWS Backup has the proper permissions to backup and restore objects. Follow the instructions at `https://docs.aws.amazon.com/aws-backup/latest/devguide/s3-backups.html#one-time-permissions-setup` to complete the IAM setup to enable the role access to the Amazon S3 buckets. When completed, move on to creating the backup plan.

EXERCISE 6.3

Using AWS Backup to Create a Backup Plan for Amazon S3 Buckets

1. Open the AWS Management Console and navigate to the AWS Backup service. Click Create Backup Plan.

2. Under Start Options select the option to build a new plan. Create a backup plan name, such as **S3Backups**.

3. Under the Backup Rule Configuration section, you need to create a rule to handle the backup details. Create a backup rule name, such as **DailyS3Backups**, and leave the backup vault as the default.

4. Under Backup Frequency select Daily and select a backup window. For this exercise we will use the default backup window. You can customize the backup window to fit the needs of your organization.

5. Ensure that Transition To Cold Storage is set to Never and the retention period is set to one month. You are not setting any destination copies or tags for recovery points. Click Create Plan to continue.

6. Now you need to assign resources to the rule so that backups can occur. Under the Resource Assignments section, click Assign Resources.

7. Name the resource assignment, for example, **S3Buckets**, and leave the option set for the default IAM role.

8. Under Assign Resources click the option to include specific resource types and choose S3 from the drop-down list.

9. Select the bucket(s) that you want to back up that have versioning enabled. Once you do, click Assign Resources to complete the creation of the backup plan.

You have just created a backup plan for the selected Amazon S3 buckets that will run daily during the backup period you selected. If you chose to use the default backup window, the next backup will occur at 5:00 a.m. UTC. If you want to force a backup now, you can do so by using the following instructions:

1. On the AWS Backup dashboard, click Create On-Demand Backup.

2. Select the resource type of S3 and the bucket that you want to create the on-demand backup against.

3. Ensure that you select the option to create the backup and then select the default vault. Ensure that the retention period is set to one month. Select the default IAM role. Then click Create On-Demand Backup to continue.

4. You can view the status of the on-demand backup job by clicking Jobs in the left navigation screen.

Congratulations! You just created a backup plan to protect an Amazon S3 bucket daily and a one-time backup of an Amazon S3 bucket. If you selected the same bucket as the daily backup plan, it is creating a full backup of the data. When the daily backup plan runs, it will create incremental backups of the data that has changed. For cleanup of this exercise, you will need to delete the resource assignment from the backup plan, and then delete the backup plan. You will also need to remove the on-demand backup from the backup vault by selecting the default backup vault and deleting the on-demand backup you created.

AWS Backup also offers the ability to centralize data protection management within a hybrid environment using AWS Storage Gateway and providing protection of VMware workloads running in VMware Cloud on AWS. AWS Backup also provides protection for VMware on-premises workloads, including restoration to on-premises datacenters and in VMware Cloud on AWS. Additional on-premises integration comes in the form of AWS Storage Gateway. AWS Backup allows configuration of data protection policies to back up application data stored in AWS Storage Gateway volumes on-premises. With this integration between AWS Backup and AWS Storage Gateway, you can apply the same data protection strategies used for AWS resources that you use for on-premises data stored on AWS Storage Gateway volumes.

AWS Backup when configured with AWS Organizations allows monitoring activities in all AWS accounts in one place. This includes creation and management of backup policies.

Individual use cases for AWS Backup are abundant and relate to automating backups of key AWS services tied to compute resources. You can check the growing list of AWS services that AWS Backup supports in the AWS public documentation available at https://docs .aws.amazon.com/aws-backup/latest/devguide/whatisbackup.html for the most updated services. Here you can find the supported resources and resource types that you can back up and restore using AWS Backup. It is also important to note that not all features of AWS Backup are available for each integrated AWS service. For example, Amazon S3 offers continuous backup and point-in-time restoration (PITR) when using AWS Backup, whereas Amazon EBS volumes do not.

AWS Storage Gateway

Organizations with existing on-premises storage solutions often look for ways to reduce cost, increase availability and durability, and when working in the cloud they are looking for methods to extend their on-premises storage to their cloud applications. This is where AWS Storage Gateway provides the means to accomplish the goal of extending on-premises storage for use within AWS, including extending the AWS Cloud storage benefits into on-premises. AWS Storage Gateway is a hybrid cloud storage service within the storage product category for AWS.

AWS Storage Gateway offers virtually unlimited cloud storage with access using a standard set of protocols such as iSCSI, SMB, and NFS depending on the requirements for existing applications. AWS Storage Gateway also plays a useful role in migrating on-premises storage into the AWS Cloud for hybrid workloads, or when an organization goes all in with an AWS Cloud environment. There are three types of storage interfaces for on-premises applications within AWS Storage Gateway: file, volume, and tape. Amazon S3 File Gateway and Amazon FSx File Gateway enable storage and retrieval of objects or files using application-friendly protocols. Amazon S3 File Gateway stores and retrieves objects using NFS or SMB protocols, which support writing directly through the S3 File Gateway to enable directly accessing these files in Amazon S3. Amazon FSx File Gateway supports access for Windows File Server using the SMB protocol, and any files written are accessible in the Amazon FSx for Windows File Server.

AWS Storage Gateway also supports the use of volume storage interfaces using Volume Gateway. You can use AWS Storage Gateway Volume Gateway when you need to provide block storage using iSCSI connectivity, like the traditional storage area network (SAN) found in on-premises datacenters. Volume Gateway stores data in Amazon S3 and supports point-in-time copies using EBS Snapshots. Volume Gateway also supports integration with AWS Backup to extend backup retention and management of volumes into on-premises. You can restore EBS snapshots to Volume Gateway or to an EBS volume, enabling a much more robust backup and restoration solution.

Many organizations running on-premises backup solutions will be utilizing iSCSI tape libraries for backing up critical data, in some cases entire volumes. AWS Storage Gateway

Tape Gateway offers a method to back up applications with a virtual tape library (VTL) interface consisting of a virtual media changer, virtual tape drives, and virtual tapes. When creating virtual tapes, Tape Gateway uses Amazon S3 for storage where it is possible to enable Lifecycle policies to move data from Amazon S3 into Amazon S3 Glacier or Amazon S3 Glacier Deep Archive. Tape Gateway offers a convenient and efficient method of deprecating often expensive and excessively automation-heavy tape libraries by migrating data into the AWS Cloud.

AWS Storage Gateway Pricing

Pricing for AWS Storage Gateway is dependent on the AWS region and type of storage interface in use. Pricing follows the typical pay-only-for-what-you-use model, and AWS charges based on the type and amount of storage used, the request you make, and the amount of data transferred out of AWS. Always check the AWS Storage Gateway Pricing documentation https://aws.amazon.com/storagegateway/pricing for the most updated pricing information for each of the storage interface options and data transfer costs.

AWS Storage Gateway also has a charge for data transferred into and out of the Storage Gateway service by the gateway, which can vary by region and gateway host. Remember, any storage using Amazon S3 buckets will need to refer to the Amazon S3 Data Transfer pricing for the most updated data transfer pricing. All data transferred into the AWS Storage Gateway service from your gateway appliance has a cost of $0.00 per GB. There are a few more no-cost request types to remember when working with AWS Storage Gateway. For example, EBS snapshot and volume deletes when using Volume Gateway are at no cost, and virtual tape archival when using Tape Gateway is also at no additional cost.

AWS Storage Gateway Use Cases

AWS Storage Gateway has several use cases ranging from extending AWS storage into on-premises resources or extending on-premises data storage into AWS for use by cloud applications. AWS Storage Gateway is also a great option to consider when migrating data or data storage solutions into the cloud due to the use of file, volume, and tape integration types. As a SysOps administrator you will need to assist your organization in determining the best storage options when working in a hybrid environment or migrating data into the cloud. It is important to evaluate the business needs and use cases to determine which AWS Storage Gateway storage interface satisfies the requirements for your project.

One of the more common use cases for AWS Storage Gateway service involves the use of the file storage interface type. The Amazon S3 File Gateway interface type enables on-premises applications to store and retrieve objects stored in Amazon S3 using common file share protocols like NFS and SMB. Any on-premises application would be able to directly interface with objects in S3 using common filesystem interfaces to extend access of the application into the AWS Cloud storage available to applications within your AWS account. The use of Amazon S3 File Gateway also enables migration of data between on-premises and Amazon S3 while maintaining local access to frequently accessed data using a local virtual machine hosting the Amazon S3 File Gateway, as seen in Figure 6.3. This can drastically reduce the latency of accessing files in Amazon S3 by accessing local cached data instead of directly accessing the files in Amazon S3.

FIGURE 6.3   AWS Storage Gateway File Gateway architecture

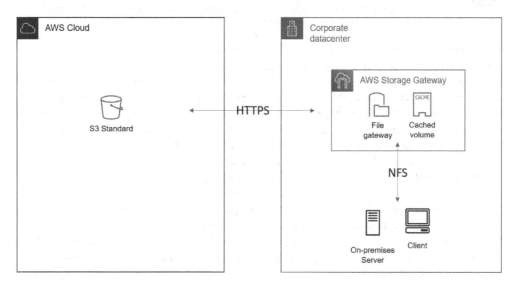

Amazon FSx File Gateway is another option to bring on-premises access to Windows File Shares on Amazon FSx. Amazon FSx creates a local cache from frequently accessed and used data that optimizes data access, increases performance, and decreases transfer traffic. A common use case for Amazon FSx File Gateway is to support on-premises desktop applications that are latency-sensitive and that do not perform well when accessing file shares across the Internet. Amazon FSx File Gateway offers a lower-latency, higher-performance option where these desktop applications are directly accessing the files in AWS from remote locations. This use case has an additional benefit of replacing on-premises storage with fully managed and highly available storage in AWS and avoiding application or network performance drains.

AWS Storage Gateway Volume Gateway is a common service used to back up local applications and for disaster recovery using EBS Snapshots or cached volume clones. Using Volume Gateway enables integration with AWS Backup to provide protection for on-premises application data at the volume level. This means volumes can have point-in-time snapshots automated and managed through AWS Backup. Volume Gateway supports up to 32 volumes for a maximum of one petabyte of data per gateway when using 32 TB maximum per volume in cached mode. Volume Gateway supports stored mode, where each volume can be up to 16 TB for a maximum of 512 TB of data per gateway. One important thing to note is that Volume Gateway compresses data before transferring to AWS and while storing data in AWS. The use of compression helps reduce storage charges and the data transfer costs when using Volume Gateway.

 AWS Storage Gateway Volume Gateway operates as a software-defined appliance deployed on hypervisors such as VMware ESXi, KVM, or Microsoft Hyper-V. For an additional cost, you can purchase a hardware appliance from the supplier, CDW.

For years data storage in on-premises datacenters relied on magnetic tapes for data retention. This process was often time-consuming, requiring consistent testing, maintenance, and other administrative actions to ensure backups were available when needed. Storage of tapes is often difficult and required off-site storage to meet compliance and regulatory requirements. However, restoration of tapes was slow, and standing up recovery environments was time-consuming. Using AWS Storage Gateway Tape Gateway, an organization can migrate existing magnetic tape solutions into the AWS Cloud for disaster recovery or long-term storage. Tape Gateway offers eleven 9s of data durability and data encryption using virtual tape libraries and migrating existing tapes into virtual tapes and storing the data in Amazon S3 Glacier or Amazon S3 Glacier Deep Archive. Tape Gateway offers organizations with up to 1,500 virtual tapes in the virtual tape libraries with a maximum aggregate capacity of one petabyte. You can further extend and scale tape storage using virtual tape libraries by deploying additional Tape Gateways. The real power of using Tape Gateway is the ability to archive tapes for long-term storage for much less cost than traditional on-premises tape storage and archival solutions.

AWS DataSync

When migrating data into the AWS Cloud, you can simplify the process by using the AWS DataSync service. AWS DataSync assists in automating and accelerating copies of substantial amounts of data between on-premises storage systems and AWS Storage services such as Amazon S3, Amazon EFS, FSx for Windows File Server, FSx for Lustre, FSx for OpenZFS, and FSx for NetApp, ONTAP filesystems. AWS DataSync utilizes common filesystem protocols such as NFS, SMB, and HDFS to copy data between on-premises and AWS Cloud storage services.

AWS DataSync allows organizations to move large datasets without using open source tools or paying expensive third-party software licenses with commercial network acceleration and data transfer software. AWS DataSync additionally offers the option to migrate active data to AWS, to archive data on-premises to free up storage capacity, or to replicate data for business continuity. Overall, AWS DataSync is a useful tool to automate data migration when moving data between on-premises storage solutions and the AWS Cloud, and even migrating data from other cloud providers into AWS.

AWS DataSync Pricing

Pricing for AWS DataSync follows the typical pay-for-what-you-use model found within AWS. You pay only for data migrated based on a flat per-gigabyte fee according to your AWS region. AWS DataSync runs on a managed cloud infrastructure, offers data validation and network acceleration technologies, and provides automation capabilities all as part of the flat fee charged. As there are no up-front costs or minimum charges, the pricing for AWS Data-Sync is quite simple. One additional consideration for potential charges when using AWS DataSync comes from the standard request, storage, and data transfer rates when reading or writing to AWS services like Amazon S3. It is always important to check the public pricing documentation at `https://aws.amazon.com/datasync/pricing` for AWS DataSync when designing a migration strategy to evaluate all potential costs.

AWS DataSync Use Cases

AWS DataSync solves the frequent problem many organizations face when moving data between on-premises storage solutions to the AWS Cloud. AWS DataSync provides the connection to existing storage systems using common filesystem protocols like NFS or SMB. AWS DataSync enables migration of data located on-premises, in other cloud providers, or at edge locations to AWS storage services like Amazon S3, Amazon FSx filesystems, or Amazon EFS. You can use AWS DataSync to create an initial dataset copy or allow scheduled incremental transfers of any data that changed to keep on-premises and AWS data the same. As a migration tool, AWS DataSync is extremely useful in ensuring data consistency between on-premises and the AWS Cloud for application cutovers. Once the application is ready for migration and to run fully in AWS, the data will already be up-to-date thanks to AWS DataSync.

You can also use AWS DataSync to provide business continuity data backups or to populate disaster recovery architectures. Using AWS DataSync, you can configure ongoing data transfers from on-premises systems into AWS for disaster recovery or additional processing. Transferring data to disaster recovery configurations often requires significant investment in data transfer software or persistent licensing charges just for continual data copies to be available. AWS DataSync is a lower-cost option to accomplish these data transfers and support broader business continuity and disaster recovery options, including transferring data from other cloud providers to support multicloud architectures.

Another common use case for AWS DataSync is populating data lakes running on AWS. For example, you can use AWS DataSync to transfer entire on-premises datasets into Amazon S3 and then configure incremental copies of the data to ensure synchronization of the data. AWS DataSync offers the ability to schedule these incremental transfers to reduce the impact of data transfer on network bandwidth by moving the transfers to off-business hours. Once the data is in Amazon S3, you can access it with native AWS services to perform machine learning or data analytics against the datasets.

AWS Transfer Family

AWS Transfer Family solves the problem of organizations configuring, running, and maintaining secure and reliable business-to-business (B2B) file transfers. AWS Transfer Family is a fully managed solution for common B2B transfer options to transfer files over Secure Shell File Transfer Protocol (SFTP), File Transfer Protocol over SSL (FTPS), and File Transfer Protocol (FTP) in and out of Amazon S3 or Amazon EFS. As a fully managed service, AWS Transfer Family removes the unnecessary IT administration overhead and allows for seamless migration, automation, and monitoring of file transfer workflows. Using AWS Transfer Family allows for client-side configurations for authentication, access, and firewall configurations to remain the same, resulting in improved customer experiences.

AWS Transfer Family Pricing

When using AWS Transfer Family, you only pay for the access-enabled protocols and the amount of data, in gigabytes, uploaded or downloaded over the chosen protocols. There are no setup fees or underlying resources to manage as part of the AWS Transfer Family configuration. When evaluating AWS Transfer Family for use within your AWS architecture, you should review the pricing documentation at `https://aws.amazon.com/aws-transfer-family/pricing` as service pricing varies per AWS region. Pricing can also vary based on the protocol used in the AWS Region selected and additional charges for reading and writing from Amazon S3 or Amazon EFS may apply. This includes data transfer charges when moving data in and out of Amazon S3 or Amazon EFS services using the standard AWS Data Transfer rates.

AWS Transfer Family Use Cases

Some of the most common use cases for AWS Transfer Family relate to organizations that are deprecating file transfer services within their on-premises networks and datacenters. Administration, security, and maintenance of B2B file transfer can be time-consuming and often results in excessive IT administration overhead for on-premises solutions. AWS Transfer Family allows organizations to lessen the IT administration requirements from these B2B file transfer systems by removing the need for the organization to configure and maintain the hardware, software, security, and networking required to support the business needs. As a fully managed service, AWS Transfer Family allows the focus to be on application integration and maintaining user identities.

Consolidation or migration of B2B file transfer systems is another common use case for AWS Transfer Family. Organizations wishing to migrate from FTP protocols to a more secure option, such as SFTP or FTPS, can use AWS Transfer Family to create a single endpoint hosting multiple protocol access. For example, an organization migrating from FTP to SFTP can create a single AWS Transfer Family endpoint in their AWS VPC and have both FTP and SFTP protocols enabled. The new FTP and SFTP servers will have the same endpoint and DNS updates to point to the FTP server for existing connections. All user authentications map to the AWS Transfer Family service protocol stored directly in the service, or through the integration with Microsoft Active Directory or some other custom identity provider. Once the migration begins, the organization instructs existing users or customers to use the new SFTP option while having an existing FTP server available but running using the AWS Transfer Family service. Once the customer base has been migrated to SFTP, you can remove the service as the customers no longer need access.

 AWS Transfer Family is a resilient and highly available service as it supports up to three AWS availability zones and is backed up by Auto Scaling using a redundant fleet to support transfer requests.

Another useful use case for AWS Transfer Family is the ability to run managed workflows to create, run, and monitor post upload processing of files transferred over SFTP, FTPS, and FTP. For example, once you upload data using any of the supported protocols a workflow can add tags to the data or copy files into other Amazon EFS directories or Amazon S3 buckets. The workflow feature is also extremely powerful in assisting with data classification tasks or scanning for virus or malware activity in uploaded files. You can also identify personal identifiable information (PII) as part of a managed workflow to ensure compliance of data uploading through the AWS Transfer Family service. Managed workflows within AWS Transfer Family solves the problem of requiring multiple software solutions or scripts across multiple systems to accomplish post-upload file processing.

Summary

Amazon S3 provides near limitless object-level storage within the AWS Cloud. Organizations often use Amazon S3 for data migrations, web applications, and log storage. Amazon S3 offers highly durable, available, and scalable storage. Amazon S3 storage operates at the object level and not at the block storage level, which means you cannot use it as a root system volume on an Amazon EC2 instance. Instead, applications access objects stored in Amazon S3 using API calls to the Amazon S3 service. Common use cases for Amazon S3 include data lakes, data analytics, high-performance computing workloads, static website hosting, and backup and disaster recovery storage. Amazon S3 offers replication across buckets and regions to increase architectural resilience and additional backup and disaster recovery use cases. Amazon S3 has several performance features to enhance data transfer such as multi-part uploads and Amazon S3 Transfer Acceleration.

Amazon S3 Glacier offer organizations a solution for long term storage of infrequently accessed data. Amazon S3 Glacier has three storage classes known as Amazon S3 Glacier Instant Retrieval, Amazon S3 Glacier Flexible Retrieval, and Amazon S3 Glacier Deep Archive. Each storage class has different performance, availability, and retrieval times to consider. Amazon S3 Glacier Instant Retrieval is a lower cost storage option compared to

Amazon S3 Standard or Amazon S3 Standard-IA but comes with a slightly higher data access cost. Amazon S3 Glacier Flexible Retrieval, formally known as S3 Glacier, offers additional cost savings for data that you require access to only a few times per year. Amazon S3 Glacier Flexible Retrieval is useful when you do not require immediate retrieval times, or large datasets can take up to five to twelve hours for completion. Most data retrievals with Amazon S3 Glacier Flexible Retrieval storage class occur within three to five minutes. Amazon S3 Glacier Deep Archive offers long term old storage for data that you consider archival and not required for access more than annually. Examples of long-term archival data are Health care records, Tax and Legal filings, and financial documents. Amazon S3 Glacier Deep Archive retrievals can take up to 48 hours using the bulk retrieval option and up to twelve hours for the Standard retrieval option. All data retrievals from Amazon S3 Glacier storage classes use Amazon S3 buckets to create restoration copies for access once the retrieval process is complete.

Amazon EBS provides block level storage for use within Amazon EC2 instances as attached storage volumes. Amazon EBS volumes are the most common type of storage used with Amazon EC2 instances and support connectivity by mapping storage volumes at the Operating System level inside of the Amazon EC2 instance. There are eight different EBS volume types that serve distinct purposes such as General Purpose, Provisioned IOPS, Throughput Optimized HDD, Cold HDD, and magnetic. Each volume type has different performance characteristics to meet the needs of any application. General Purpose and Provisioned IOPS volume types have multiple generations available with varying performance and cost differences to consider. Backups of Amazon EBS volumes use a snapshot process, which results in an EBS Snapshot of the volume. After the initial EBS Snapshot, all subsequent snapshots are incremental and only back up the data that has changed. Amazon EBS offers use of Amazon Data Lifecycle Manager to automate the creation, retention, and deletion of EBS Snapshots and EBS-backed AMIs, including cross-account snapshot copies. Amazon Data Lifecycle Manager assists with retention and cost optimization using Lifecycle policies and policy schedules to handle the automation tasks such as creation and deletion of EBS Snapshots. You can monitor volume performance using Amazon CloudWatch through various volume and IOPS-specific metrics to determine health and overall performance of an EBS volume.

Amazon EFS is a managed serverless elastic filesystem available to Linux Amazon EC2 instances and offers petabyte scalability automatically within the service without modifications to networking or storage systems. Amazon EFS supports connectivity for thousands of instances using the NFS v4 protocol. Amazon EFS offers two different storage classes when creating a filesystem depending on configuration needs. Configurations can consist of Amazon EFS Standard and One Zone storage classes. The main difference between the different storage classes is the number of Availability Zones in which Amazon EFS stores data across. Organizations commonly use Amazon EFS for use cases where the need scalable, fault tolerant, and highly available data shares, such as when working with databases, data analytics, media processing, or web applications. Amazon EFS offers integration with AWS Backup to centrally managed and automated data backups for Amazon EFS data storage.

Amazon FSx is a fully managed service that handles the hardware provisioning, patching, and backups of the underlying architecture to provide a highly available and scalable filesystem in the AWS Cloud. Filesystems available within Amazon FSx include Amazon FSx for NetApp ONTAP, Amazon FSx for OpenZFS, Amazon FSx for Windows File Server, and Amazon FSx for Lustre. Amazon FSx filesystems are highly available and replicate data within or across availability zones to protect against failure and increase fault tolerance. Determining which FSx filesystem to use is dependent on existing filesystems in use, familiarity with the various filesystems, and the performance needs of the applications. Amazon FSx filesystems support hybrid-enabled deployment options to enable synchronization of data between on-premises sources and the AWS FSx filesystem in the Amazon Cloud. Amazon FSx filesystems increase fault tolerance and availability of applications while minimizing the IT administration overhead found when attempting to create and operate these filesystems independently on-premises.

AWS Backup offers a method to centrally organize, manage, and automate data protection across AWS services and hybrid on-premises workloads. AWS Backup integrates with AWS storage services using protection policies to define backup frequency and retention periods for a cloud-native backup solution. Organizations use AWS Backup for automating and managing backup compliance requirements within all AWS accounts using integrations with AWS Organizations, which includes visibility into monitoring metrics and compliance against protection policies.

AWS Storage Gateway offers organizations a way to extend their on-premises storage into the AWS Cloud, extend their AWS Cloud storage for on-premises access, and back up and manage virtual tape libraries. AWS Storage Gateway has three types of storage interfaces for on-premises applications: File Gateway, Volume Gateway, and Tape Gateway. File Gateway supports the use of Amazon S3 and Amazon FSx file gateways to enable storage and retrieval of objects from Amazon S3 or files from the various filesystems available in Amazon FSx. Volume Gateway supports block-level storage using iSCSI connectivity for connectivity within on-premises networks. Tape Gateway allows organizations to utilize iSCSI tape libraries for backing up critical data and migrating existing physical tape medium to the AWS Cloud, reducing physical footprint and lowering long-term storage costs for tape medium.

AWS DataSync offers a solution for migrating data into the AWS Cloud by accelerating the copying of copious amounts of data or datasets between on-premises storage systems and AWS Storage services. AWS DataSync integrates with Amazon S3, Amazon EFS, and Amazon FSx filesystems. AWS DataSync supports automation of data transfers to assist in workload migrations into AWS. Automated data transfers can ensure applications running on-premises and in the cloud are up-to-date to ensure migrations have the latest data. AWS DataSync has common use cases built around migration of data into AWS from on-premises storage systems, such as choosing to migrate all datacenter resources into the AWS Cloud or increasing business continuity by using AWS storage services.

AWS Transfer Family is a fully managed AWS service that solves the problem of configuring, running, scaling, and securing business-to-business file transfer protocols, which often lead to increased IT administration overhead. AWS Transfer Family supports FTP, FTPS, and

SFTP protocols for transferring files into and out of Amazon S3 or Amazon EFS configurations. Using managed workflows, an organization can perform post-upload processing of files to ensure file integrity or compliance, as necessary.

Exam Essentials

Understand how Amazon FSx uses multiple availability zones. AWS FSx as a service is a fully managed AWS service designed to increase fault tolerance and high availability. You can increase fault tolerance and high availability with Amazon FSx storage services by enabling cross-region replication or by extending the storage services using a hybrid architecture approach.

Understand how to use AWS DataSync in migrations. AWS DataSync provides an automated option for keeping migration data updated until the application migration date. Once the application is ready to move fully into AWS, the data has already been synchronously updated and ready for migration completion. You can also use AWS DataSync as a migration tool to transfer large datasets during off-peak business hours to reduce network bandwidth.

Understand how to implement AWS Backup for cloud-native backup management. AWS Backup provides a centralized and automated method for managing backups across supported AWS services. You can create and maintain backups centrally using backup and restoration plans. You can use on-demand backups for resources as needed to augment scheduled frequency backups in backup plans. AWS Backup integration with AWS Organizations allows full management across all AWS accounts in an AWS Organization.

Understand how to implement Amazon Data Lifecycle Manager. Amazon Data Lifecycle Manager provides automated EBS Snapshot and EBS-backed AMI creation and management within an AWS account. Amazon Data Lifecycle Manager creates EBS Snapshots using snapshot Lifecycle policies to automate protection of individual EBS volumes or all EBS volumes attached to an EC2 instance. Amazon Data Lifecycle Manager supports cross-account copy event policies to automate snapshot copies across accounts. Policy schedules handle the frequency of EBS Snapshots, fast snapshot restore settings, and cross-region copy rules.

Understand use cases for enabling Amazon S3 cross-region replication. Amazon S3 cross-region replication increases the fault tolerance of application data stored in Amazon S3 buckets. This feature is also useful in creating backup and disaster recovery options for application data between regions, overall increasing data fault tolerance and in some cases application fault tolerance.

Understand how to implement Amazon S3 Lifecycle rules. You can use Amazon S3 Lifecycle rules to move data between storage classes. Lifecycle rules can assist in reducing storage costs by moving data between Amazon S3 Standard storage class into other longer-term storage classes like Amazon S3 Glacier Flexible Retrieval tier or Amazon S3 Deep Archive tier. You can configure Lifecycle rules to move data based on the needs of your organization and the retention needs using Amazon S3 Deep Archive and Amazon S3 Glacier storage tiers.

Understand use cases for Amazon S3 Glacier storage classes.   You can use Amazon S3 Glacier storage classes for longer-term cold storage of data that does not require frequent access. Financial services, healthcare, and organizations required to maintain data for extended periods of time can benefit from the cost savings of Amazon S3 Glacier storage classes. Depending on the frequency of retrieval, each Amazon S3 Glacier Storage class offers different recovery times and associated costs when retrieving data from the service. When designing a backup and recovery plan, take into consideration the potential duration of recovery that can impact recovery time objectives (RTOs).

Understand how to configure Amazon S3 static web hosting.   Amazon S3 static web hosting enables a cost-effective solution to provide static web content, web redirects, or simple web solutions to expand business capabilities. Organizations often configure Amazon S3 static web hosting to provide splash pages or scalable short-term web file sharing. You can also use S3 static web hosting as a disaster recovery method to supply vital details or serve as a landing page when an organization is experiencing issues.

Understand how to monitor Amazon EBS volume performance.   Each Amazon EBS volume type offers unique performance benefits to applications running on Amazon EC2. Depending on the needs of the application, increasing read or write IOPS can drastically improve performance of an application. Monitoring EBS volume performance using Amazon Cloud-Watch is critical when working with high-performance applications to determine bottlenecks and potential performance risks, or to ensure the proper volume types and features are enabled.

Understand how to implement S3 performance features.   Amazon S3 offers several performance features to enhance upload reliability for network outage sensitive areas using multipart uploads into Amazon S3 buckets and to increase transfer speeds to and from Amazon S3 buckets using Amazon S3 Transfer Acceleration. Multipart uploads offer significant performance benefits when working with large datasets by offering improved throughput, the ability to pause and resume, and quick recovery from any network issues. Amazon S3 Transfer Acceleration shortens the distance between client applications and AWS servers by using the CloudFront Edge locations for Amazon S3 bucket access. Amazon S3 Transfer Acceleration also maximizes bandwidth utilization by minimizing the effect of distance on bandwidth.

Review Questions

1. Which of the following Amazon Simple Storage Service (S3) features allows an organization to scale delivery of temporary HTML pages featuring downloadable podcasts?

   A. Amazon S3 multipart upload

   B. Amazon S3 Transfer Accelerator

   C. Amazon S3 static website hosting

   D. Amazon S3 cross-region replication

2. You work for an organization that requires any content available in an S3 bucket must replicate to two or more additional regions for security and compliance. The solutions architect implemented cross-region replication (CRR) on the source S3 bucket, and all new files uploaded to the bucket are replicating correctly. However, there have been reports that the destination buckets are missing files found in the origin buckets. As the SysOps administrator, you must assist in solving this problem. Which of the following is the best solution for ensuring new and existing files replicate to the destination buckets?

   A. Create a script using the AWS SDK and Amazon S3 REST API to copy the existing files from the origin bucket into the destination bucket before enabling cross-region replication.

   B. Ensure that the IAM permissions and bucket policy configurations allow full bucket replication from the origin bucket.

   C. Turn on the full bucket replication feature in the properties for the origin bucket.

   D. Use Amazon S3 Batch Replication to backfill the existing data of the origin bucket into the new destination buckets.

3. You receive reports from several clients that their uploads into the project Amazon S3 buckets have been slow and unreliable. The clients report the file size to average over 3 GB in size per upload and they have been uploading the files while working on-site in a remote location. Which of the following solutions will best address the upload speed and reliability issue when uploading objects into Amazon S3? (Choose two.)

   A. Enable S3 Transfer Acceleration for the destination bucket and direct the clients to upload files to the `https://s3-accelerate.amazonaws.com` endpoint.

   B. Enable Amazon CloudFront for the project and direct the clients to upload directly to the Amazon CloudFront edge location closest to the remote location.

   C. Instruct the client that the file size is too large and to reduce the file to 1 GB or smaller to avoid reliability and upload performance issues.

   D. Instruct the client to only use the `aws s3 cp` CLI commands with the dual-stack (IPv6) endpoints to ensure the fastest speeds and reliability.

   E. Instruct the client to use multipart uploads for large file uploads into the destination buckets.

4. Your organization has recently decided to not renew the maintenance contract for the data storage array used for long-term storage of financial records. The organization must maintain all financial records for a minimum of 10 years, and the records must be available for audit within 48 hours. Which of the following AWS storage services is the most cost-effective option to replace the long-term storage needs?

   A. Amazon S3

   B. Amazon S3 Glacier Deep Archive

   C. Amazon FSx

   D. Amazon EFS

5. You are designing a storage backup solution that includes the use of Amazon S3 buckets for general file storage and project files. The organization has asked for you to cost-optimize the storage solution and look for ways to cut costs while maintaining durability of the backed-up files. The files only require access once or twice per quarter as part of a standard audit process. Beyond the audit period, the files do not require frequent access. However, when the auditors request the files, they must be immediately available. Which of the following options provides the most cost-effective solution while maintaining the access required for auditors?

   A. Use the Amazon S3 Standard-IA storage class.

   B. Use the Amazon S3 Glacier Flexible Retrieval storage class.

   C. Use the Amazon S3 One Zone-IA storage class.

   D. Use the Amazon S3 Glacier Instant Retrieval storage class.

6. Your organization heavily invests in the use of Amazon EC2 instances to support web applications and critical business applications in the cloud. It has come to your attention that backups for all Amazon EC2 instances are manual and use Amazon EBS Snapshots at a random occurrence whenever the storage administrators think of doing it. As the new SysOps administrator for the organization, you suggest automating the Amazon EBS Snapshot process for these critical systems to enforce a disaster recovery action plan. Which of the following options will accomplish the goal of automating EBS Snapshots and avoiding data loss?

   A. Use AWS Systems Manager to automate the EBS volume snapshots each time the EC2 instance restarts.

   B. Create a script to create a new AMI of each Amazon EC2 instance on a defined schedule.

   C. Use Amazon Data Lifecycle Manager to automate the snapshot process.

   D. Create a script to create EBS Snapshots of each EBS volume present in the AWS account on a defined schedule.

7. You have received reports from several application owners that data reads are slow for an application hosted on an Amazon EC2 instance. You suspect that the EBS volumes are receiving too many read requests for data and performance is suffering. Which of the following CloudWatch metrics can you use to verify read performance for the attached EBS volumes? (Choose two.)

   A. VolumeQueueLength

   B. VolumeWriteBytes

    C. VolumeReadOps

    D. VolumeWriteOps

    E. BurstBalance

8. You oversee monitoring of performance for several production data conversion systems running on Amazon EC2 instances. Recently the data engineers reported below normal write and read speeds coming from several application servers. Each application server is a T3.Large using gp2 EBS volumes for the operating system volume and St1 volumes for the data processing volumes. You are concerned that the volumes are throttling. Which Amazon CloudWatch EBS volume metric will confirm EBS volume throttling?

    A. VolumeQueueLength

    B. VolumeWriteOps

    C. VolumeReadBytes

    D. BurstBalance

9. You recently deployed an Amazon EFS filesystem to handle user home directories for several Linux-based applications hosted across four separate availability zones in your VPC. When attempting to mount the EFS system on each EC2 instance, you find that you are only able to create a mount for EC2 instances in the US-EAST-1a availability zone. What could be the possible issue preventing other EC2 instances from mounting the new EFS storage system?

    A. When configuring the Amazon EFS storage system, only one Amazon EC2 instance is selected as a target.

    B. The Amazon EFS storage system does not have the proper security groups in place.

    C. When configuring the Amazon EFS storage system, the option for One Zone storage class is in use.

    D. The Amazon EFS storage system does not have the proper EC2 instance role policies configured to connect to multiple Amazon EC2 instances.

10. Your organization has successfully implemented and is actively using the new Amazon EFS configuration for six months to share media processing files between production and editing. The production team has recently expanded globally and will be sharing the workload between the Washington, DC and London locations. The London location is worried about latency when connecting to the Washington, DC file share when processing production files and has asked you to evaluate a potential solution. Which of the following options solves the latency issue for the London office?

    A. Configure Amazon EFS replication between the US-EAST and EU-WEST-2 regions.

    B. Configure bastion hosts locally in the EU-WEST-2 region for the London office and have all production staff use this for processing.

    C. Configure an Amazon DirectConnect connection to the local London office to reduce latency when connecting to the Amazon EFS file share.

    D. Configure Amazon EFS mount targets locally in a new VPC located in EU-WEST-2 to locally mount production processing systems to the Amazon EFS mount target.

11. You are assisting the high-performance computing (HPC) department with migration of their data and systems into AWS. The director of the lab has asked for recommendations on a scalable, secure, and fault-tolerant storage solution in AWS to support the parallel filesystems. The department does not have the funds to manage the storage system and is looking for the lowest-cost solution. Which of the following storage solutions would you recommend to the director?

   A. Amazon EBS

   B. Amazon S3

   C. Amazon FSx for Lustre

   D. Amazon FSx for NetApp ONTAP

12. Most of the applications and systems within your organization are now running in the AWS Cloud. The director of IT is concerned that the large investment in the current SAN technologies will go to waste now that most data is moving into AWS. The director has asked for a way to run a hybrid infrastructure where on-premises servers can still connect using the iSCSI protocol, and data is available in both AWS and the on-premises SAN. Which AWS storage solution would you recommend?

   A. Amazon EBS with Windows Files Server cluster

   B. Amazon FSx for NetApp ONTAP with AWS Storage Gateway File Gateway

   C. Amazon FSx for Windows File Server

   D. Amazon EFS with AWS DirectConnect and VPN

13. You receive a task to create a disaster recovery and business continuity plan for your organization's storage hosted on Amazon S3. The IT director requires that any solution must support point-in-time recovery (PITR) for immediate restoration of any data. Which of the following solutions would you recommend?

   A. Amazon S3 Batch Replication

   B. Amazon S3 versioning

   C. Amazon Data Lifecycle Manager

   D. AWS Backup

14. You have chosen AWS Backup as the primary component of the disaster and recovery strategy within your organization. You are using AWS Backup to perform daily backups of four Amazon S3 buckets, but the backup jobs are reporting a failure. On further investigation it appears that the AWS Backup job is failing because it cannot access the Amazon S3 buckets to back up files. What is the cause of this error?

   A. The backup plan is using an IAM role that does not include the necessary in-line IAM policies.

   B. The Amazon S3 buckets are not located in the same AWS region where the backup plan is running.

   C. The AWS Backup plan does not have PITR enabled for the Amazon S3 buckets.

   D. The backup plan within AWS Backup requires an AWS PrivateLink configured to back up Amazon S3 buckets.

15. You receive a task to assist with a major datacenter consolidation project that includes moving several petabytes of archived data into the AWS Cloud. The organization use a tape backup system to maintain weekly and monthly incremental backups of all on-premises servers and storage systems. The CIO is concerned that moving to another backup solution would cause too much training overhead and potential outages as people sort out the new operational processes. Which AWS solution would you recommend to the CIO?

    A. Amazon S3 Glacier Deep Archive

    B. AWS Storage Gateway Volume Gateway

    C. AWS Storage Gateway Tape Gateway

    D. AWS Backup

16. Your organization is in process of migrating hundreds of gigabytes of application data into Amazon S3. You must help to develop a solution that allows on-premises application servers to directly interface with the data now hosted in Amazon S3 using the NFS protocol. Which of the following solutions accomplishes this goal?

    A. Implement AWS Storage Gateway File Gateway.

    B. Implement Amazon EFS.

    C. Implement AWS Storage Gateway File Gateway with Amazon FSx for Windows File Share.

    D. Implement AWS DataSync to synchronize files between Amazon S3 and on-premises.

17. You are the SysOps administrator for an organization that has recently started a new data analytics division. The new director of analytics has asked you to configure a data lake within AWS. The director has also asked to have a local copy of the datasets, which incrementally updates if they want to perform localized analytics from the existing on-premises hardware. Which solution would you recommend to the director?

    A. Implement AWS Backup to incrementally back up and restore data from Amazon S3 onto on-premises storage.

    B. Implement Amazon EFS to share data volumes with on-premises.

    C. Implement Amazon FSx for Windows File Server to enable the SMB protocol and share storage with local servers.

    D. Implement AWS DataSync to copy data between on-premises and Amazon S3.

18. Your organization has tasked you with migrating data from on-premises and a third-party cloud provider into AWS. The CIO is concerned that data between the third-party cloud and AWS will not be in sync, resulting in application downtime while the migration is underway. Which AWS service would you use to accomplish this migration task?

    A. AWS DataSync

    B. AWS Transfer Family

    C. Amazon Storage Gateway

    D. AWS Backup

19. Your organization is undergoing an application modernization effort and focusing on decommissioning and consolidating application on-premises into a new AWS environment. Several applications require the use of Secure Shell File Transfer Protocol (SFTP) to move files between the application server and the customer. To reduce cost and assist with consolidation, you want to move all SFTP servers into AWS. Which AWS service provides the most scalable and cost-effective solution?

A. Amazon EFS

B. AWS Transfer Family

C. AWS DataSync

D. Amazon EC2

20. You work as a SysOps administrator for a data collection and processing organization. Every day a series of FTPS servers receive client information and store local copies for processing by another server. Once a day a data clerk accesses the server to categorize the data into different data classifications, including identifying PII data for processing. During a staff meeting, the manager for the application mentioned that the clerk responsible for completing the data classification is no longer able to complete the work. After some discussion, you offered to develop an automated solution to the problem and migrate the service into AWS. Which of the following solutions meets the needs for this migration without needing additional administrative overhead?

A. Rearchitect the application to use Amazon S3 and apply tags for data classification at upload.

B. Create a new Amazon EC2 FTPS instance and use AWS Lambda functions to process data classification.

C. Implement AWS Transfer Family for FTPS and configure a data classification managed workflow and tagging strategy.

D. Migrate the current FTPS service to an Amazon EC2 instance and use AWS Lambda functions to apply data classification tags to uploaded data.

Chapter 7

Databases

THE AWS CERTIFIED SYSOPS ADMINISTRATOR EXAM OBJECTIVES COVERED IN THIS CHAPTER INCLUDE:

✓ **Domain 2: Reliability and Business Continuity**

- 2.1 Implement scalability and elasticity

  - Implement caching

  - Implement Amazon RDS replicas and Amazon Aurora Replicas

- 2.3 Implement backup and restore strategies

  - Automate snapshots and backups based on use cases (for example, RDS snapshots, AWS Backup, RTO and RPO, Amazon Data Lifecycle Manager, retention policy)

✓ **Domain 6: Cost and Performance Optimization**

- 6.1 Implement cost optimization strategies

  - Identify opportunities to use managed services (for example, Amazon RDS, AWS Fargate, Amazon EFS)

- 6.2 Implement performance optimization strategies

  - Monitor RDS metrics and modify the configuration to increase performance efficiency (for example, Performance Insights, RDS Proxy)

Databases are the heart of most organizations and demand extremely careful maintenance and tight security. AWS offers many types of databases, including purpose-built databases such as Neptune (graph), Timestream (time series), DynamoDB (key-value), Amazon Ledger Database Services (ledger), and Keyspaces (wide column). As important as these database types are, they are not covered in the SysOps exam. The exam will focus on the ElastiCache in-memory databases and Relational Database Service (RDS), including Aurora.

Amazon Relational Database Service

Amazon Relational Database Service (RDS) is a managed database service capable of running common engines, including MySQL, PostgreSQL, MariaDB, Oracle, Amazon Aurora, IBM DB2, and SQL Server (see Figure 7.1). Setting up and maintaining databases is complex, and the exam is not intended to test you as a database administrator. However, it will be helpful for you to know the basics about relational databases. Remember that the database engine, or relational database management system (RDBMS), is what databases are built in, even though both are routinely referred to as "databases." Also remember that RDS is more highly abstracted than running the same RDBMS on EC2. As a managed service, RDS relieves the user of all maintenance of the database engine, operating system, and underlying hardware.

RDS Custom

Normally, RDS gives no direct access to the RDBMS or operating system (OS) that it runs on. RDS Custom, however, is used when customizations are needed to the underlying OS or RDBMS. RDS Custom is still a managed service, but it provides some capabilities similar to running the RDBMS on EC2.

RDS Pricing

RDS instances are provisioned either as on-demand or provisioned instances, just as with EC2. For convenience, pricing is given by the hour but is actually calculated per second, with a minimum of 10 minutes. In addition to RDS compute cost, several other costs are associated with RDS. Storage is charged per gigabyte per month based on provisioned capacity. Provisioned IOPS charges apply to SSD storage only, whereas I/O request charges apply only to magnetic storage and are measured per 1 million per month. Backup storage is billed separately from provisioned RDS storage. Finally, transfer charges apply when moving data to another region or to and from the Internet. Note that when your RDS instance is stopped, you will still be billed for storage.

FIGURE 7.1   Database managed service

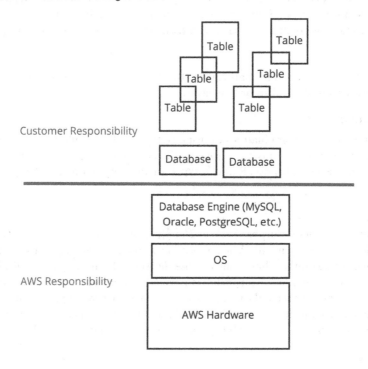

Creating an RDS Instance

When launching an RDS instance, you have many options. We'll take a look at some (but not all) of the key options using the dialog headings to guide us. Don't forget to review each option on your own and know what each does and when to use it. Take advantage of free tier and set up billing alerts. RDS is an expensive service, and an instance accidentally left running can be a costly mistake. Notice that as you select the template and availability and durability settings, the available options below change.

Engine Options

The first of these choices is the database engine, which can be Aurora, PostgreSQL, SQL Server, MariaDB, Oracle, IBM DB2, or MySQL. For each engine you can choose among current or previous versions of the engine. If you select Oracle or SQL Server, then the Amazon RDS Custom option is available.

Availability and Durability

This section gives you the ability to set up multi-availability zone (AZ) instances and multi-AZ clusters in addition to a single stand-alone instance. Depending on your previous selections, you may have the option for a standby instance with a multi-AZ deployment. Remember that a standby is different than a read replica. The standby provides high availability, whereas the read replica off-loads read requests for performance optimization.

Settings

Notice that the master user credentials can be stored in Secrets Manager using a KMS encryption key. This is a useful security measure.

Instance Configuration

There are many available combinations of instance type, vCPU, memory, and networking. Some instance types also have instance store. Available instance types are M, R, T, and X. M type instances are general purpose. R and X types are memory optimized. T type instances are burstable.

Storage

You can select from general-purpose SSD (gp2/gp3), provisioned IOPS SSD (io1), and magnetic disk (not recommended). When allocating storage, remember that you are billed for provisioned storage rather than what you use. Fortunately, auto scaling will allow the expansion of your storage, so starting small is normally a good idea. Databases often need increased input/output per second (IOPS), so io1 volumes are often a good consideration on exam questions asking about improving database IO performance. Keep in mind IOPS comes with a price so io1 volumes will be more expensive than gp2/gp3 volumes.

Connectivity

In this section you can connect the RDS instance to an EC2 instance, assign the VPC and subnet, determine IPv4 or dual stack, assign the security group, and assign a public IP address ("public access"). You can also change the TCP/IP port.

Database Authentication

If you have selected MariaDB, MySQL, or PostgreSQL, there will be an option to use either the database password authentication or IAM authentication. Since the IAM authentication tokens are managed by IAM and the credentials are not stored in the database, IAM authentication is generally more secure and the preferred method.

Monitoring

Performance Insights is enabled by default with the free tier retention of seven days. Performance Insights is very helpful in identifying performance bottlenecks. Enhanced monitoring allows visibility into OS-level metrics, which are not natively visible to CloudWatch. Enhanced monitoring could incur fees if the activity exceeds the free tier of CloudWatch.

Additional Configuration

Additional configuration contains many options worth knowing. Backups are enabled by default and the backup window is configurable. Encryption is also enabled by default using KMS. Logs can be pushed to CloudWatch logs. You can set the maintenance window, and deletion protection is enabled by default.

RDS Backups

Amazon RDS generates daily automatic backups in a configurable backup window (see Figure 7.2). These backups are a snapshot of the entire instance rather than individual database backup. Point-in-time restoration can be done from these backups. When RDS takes the first backup of the instance, it is a full copy. Subsequent backups are incremental (only what has changed). By default, automated backups are deleted when the instance is deleted. The retention period of automated backups can be configured from 0 to 35 days. Setting the retention period to 0 disables automated backups. Backups are stored in S3. There is no additional cost for backup storage during the retention period. If you wish to retain the backup beyond the retention period, the snapshots can be exported to S3 where per-gigabyte-per-month rates apply.

FIGURE 7.2   Database snapshot retention setting

In addition to automated backups, users can take manual snapshots at any time (up to 100 snapshots per region). Manual snapshots persist after the instance is terminated, and costs for storage are incurred unless the backups are deleted. They can be used to restore a database instance but not to a point-in-time in the way that an RDS backup can be restored. Like automated backups, snapshots are stored in S3. Snapshots incur storage costs as soon as they are created. In order to manage costs, snapshot life cycles can be managed using a number of tools such as S3 Lifecycle Management.

AWS Backup

AWS Backup is another service that can create backups of RDS instances with point-in-time recovery at a 5-minute granularity. AWS Backup is fully managed and policy-driven. AWS Backup works across both cloud instances and on-premises resources. RDS backups generated by AWS Backup are manual snapshots, which do not count against your snapshot quota. AWS Backup creates backup plans that are driven by tags.

RDS Replicas

RDS Read Replicas are a particularly important feature for both durability and performance improvement. To understand read replicas, it is important to understand the read and write aspects of a relational database. A key characteristic of a relational database is that they are ACID (atomicity, consistency, isolation, and durability) compliant. The purpose of ACID is to assure that data written to a database is always valid despite any errors that might happen at the hardware or software level. This book isn't the place to dive into ACID or database fundamentals. However, it is important to understand the relationship between the primary RDS instance and the read replicas. As the name suggests, the read replica handles reads and only reads. The read replica serves the purpose of off-loading the read requests to take load off the primary database, which then can focus its resources on write requests. Read replicas improve user experience by providing faster read access and reduces the cost associated with needing to vertically scale a primary to handle both read and write. Remember that databases can only scale vertically, not horizontally.

Read replicas are able to be promoted to become a stand-alone DB instance. This might be done if the original primary were to become impaired, for data definition language (DDL) operations, or other reasons. Since relational databases are designed to have a single primary for write operations, that primary instance becomes a critical single point of failure. Read replicas allow you to place a copy of your data in another availability zone. In the event of the primary becoming unavailable (or for other reasons), the read replica can be promoted to become a stand-alone DB instance and Aurora replicas may serve as the new primary. When a read replica is promoted, it is rebooted and is then available as a stand-alone DB instance. The reboot period should be considered when planning recovery time objectives (RTOs). When data is written to the primary, that data is then automatically replicated to the read replica. However, that replication is not instantaneous. There will always be some lag, and that represents potential data loss that needs to be taken into consideration in your recovery point objective (RPO) planning.

Read Replicas vs. ElastiCache

Both read replicas and ElastiCache will help improve performance, and both can help reduce cost because you won't need to vertically scale the primary instance in response to read demand. However, read replicas and ElastiCache are not exactly the same, so it can sometimes be a difficult decision which to use in a given scenario. In some cases, a combination of both may be the right choice. First, you need to determine what the real problem is. Both solve the problem of heavy read demand on the primary. If that is really the problem, then you would want to know what kind of read requests are coming in. Remember that ElastiCache stores frequently requested data in memory and that there are two different ways to load the cache (lazy loading and write-through). In either strategy, the cache may have misses. If the read requests coming in have a good pattern, then the cache will be able to perform optimally. However, the higher the consistent miss rate, the more read requests will have to travel back to the primary database anyway, and ElastiCache becomes less useful. Since a read replica contains the whole database, there are no misses. For this reason, it is not atypical to see the layering of a read replicate and ElastiCache.

Creating an RDS Read Replica

Read replicas are typically created in a different AZ from the source database using the console, CLI, or the API. The steps are essentially the same as creating the primary database instance. When you create the replica, the primary may pause briefly while a snapshot is taken. The snapshot will be used to create the read replica (see Figure 7.3).

FIGURE 7.3   Create Read Replica

Once a read replica is built, it can be promoted to become a stand-alone (see Figure 7.4). Before promoting a replica, all transactions need to be stopped.

RDS Proxy

An RDS proxy solves the problem of applications that open and close many database connections very quickly. Without a proxy, this fast-paced connecting can exhaust memory and compute resources. The proxy allows pooling of connections and provides resilience, fast scaling, and improved security. The RDS proxy will sit between your application and the database. It is supported on RDS for MySQL and RDS for PostgreSQL, including Aurora and Aurora Serverless (v2 only). An indicator that an RDS proxy would be beneficial includes repeated "too many connections" errors on an RDS instance. On small RDS instance types such as the T family, out-of-memory or high CPU utilization can indicate an opportunity for an RDS proxy. Any pattern of an application opening many short-lived connections (especially common on Lambda) is an indicator to consider an RDS proxy.

FIGURE 7.4   Promote read replica

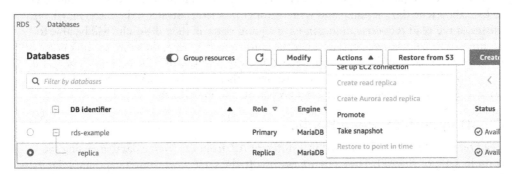

The unit on which pricing for Amazon RDS Proxy is determined is based on the pricing model of the underlying RDS instance. Be sure to familiarize yourself with how RDS provisioned instances and Aurora Serverless are billed. Pricing for Amazon RDS Proxy is per hour with a minimum. Partial hours are billed per second, with a minimum of 10 minutes. The default endpoint is included at no charge, but additional endpoints are provisioned and billed as AWS PrivateLinks. Remember that you will not need to know the exact cost of any given service. What you will want to know is in what situations an RDS proxy will save a customer money or optimize performance and reliability.

Amazon Aurora

Amazon Aurora is a subset of RDS. However, there is much that is different in Aurora. Aurora is a managed distributed storage system that is compatible with MySQL and PostgreSQL engines. However, the architecture of Aurora is vastly different from a traditional relational database and RDS. Storage for Aurora is distributed with six replicas stored across three AZs. In fact, Aurora was built from the ground up to be cloud-native whereas all other RDBMSs were originally designed to work on traditional server hardware in a physical datacenter.

Aurora is backed up continuously by default. These backups are incremental, allowing for point-in-time restoration down to the second. Backtrack is a feature that can be enabled at creation, which allows you to restore a database to a point-in-time.

Pricing

Pricing for Aurora storage is different than RDS. Instances are billed as either a provisioned on-demand instance or a provisioned Reserved instance. The cost of a Reserved instance is, as expected, lower than on-demand. Reserved instances can be at a one- or three-year commitment, with the three-year commitment giving the best pricing. Additionally, either the one- or the three-year reservation can be paid all up-front, partially up-front, or with no money up-front. The best pricing, of course, is for all up-front.

Aurora Serverless is billed based on Aurora capacity units (ACUs) per hour. An ACU is approximately 2 GB of memory with CPU and networking.

Aurora storage is billed per gigabyte per month for actually used data storage rather than provisioned storage. There is also a fee per million for I/O. Aurora Global Database is an additional fee per million replicated I/Os. Backtrack is billed per record change stored, so the cost increases the longer back you wish to be able to restore to.

Amazon Aurora Global Database

Amazon Aurora Global Database is available for both MySQL and PostgreSQL compatibility. The Aurora Global Database creates a single Aurora database, which can span multiple regions with less than one-second latency. This Global Database is automatically kept in sync with an RPO of one second and an RTO of less than one minute. An Aurora Global Database would be used when regional-level disaster recovery and fault tolerance are the primary drivers.

Monitoring RDS Performance

Database performance is complex. Factors from the hardware up the stack to a specific SQL query can have surprisingly large impacts. The exam will focus on monitoring performance metrics and making modifications to improve performance. As usual, CloudWatch will be where we start. Know how to find CloudWatch metrics both in CloudWatch and in the RDS console. Remember that, by default, CloudWatch will display memory, disk space, I/O, network throughput, and database connections. But how will you know when something is going wrong? Metrics, in general, are of limited use if you don't know what the baseline for the workload is. The baseline is the normal performance over a given period of time. CloudWatch alarms are looking for a variance from the baseline. Be sure you know how to create a CloudWatch alarm. CloudWatch metrics receives metrics from each instance every minute.

Recommendations

The RDS console displays several recommendations, which can be found on the lower-left navigation in the console. Trusted Advisor gives recommendations on idle RDS instances, RDS security group access risks, RDS backups, and multi-AZ RDS. Trusted Advisor will also monitor RDS service limits.

RDS Performance Insights

Performance Insights provides additional aggregated metrics at a finer granularity of every second. Insights is turned on by default. The free tier of Performance Insights includes seven days of rolling performance data history with one million API requests per month. Longer historical analysis, up to two years, can be added for an additional fee. The additional retention is billed per vCPU hour per month for provisioned instances and per ACU per month for Aurora Serverless v2. Performance Insights is only available for v2 of Aurora Serverless. The primary metric for Performance Insights is DB Load, which measures average active sessions. This aggregated metric helps give a view of the load placed on the database by running sessions over time.

RDS Enhanced Monitoring

Enhanced Monitoring provides real-time operating system metrics. Enhanced Monitoring is available on all RDS engines except Aurora. By default, Enhanced Monitoring metrics are stored in CloudWatch logs for 30 days. There may be charges for Enhanced Monitoring metrics storage, and costs are based on CloudWatch fees. Enhanced Monitoring can be turned on and off, and granularity can be configured on a per-instance basis. These can be used to manage cost.

Performance Schema

Performance Schema is an additional event monitor available for MariaDB and MySQL databases instances. Events are database engine actions that take server time and have been configured so that they can be collected. Performance Schema data is stored in a database table, which can be queried using SQL. Performance Schema and Performance Insights are separate but connected. Normally both are enabled.

Database Logs

Database logs can be published to CloudWatch logs for storage and real-time analytics. Publishing log data will require a service-linked role.

Events and Notifications

Events are any change in the environment of an RDS instance, parameter group, security group, DB snapshot, or RDS proxy. These events are sent to CloudWatch events and Amazon EventBridge in near-real time. Notifications are handled by Amazon SNS. Events can be used to automate responses to system events.

Amazon ElastiCache

As AWS states in the whitepaper titled "Performance at Scale with Amazon ElastiCache," "An effective caching strategy is perhaps the single biggest factor in creating an app that performs well at scale" (https://docs.aws.amazon.com/whitepapers/latest/scale-performance-elasticache/scale-performance-elasticache.html). Caching is important for both performance and cost optimization. There are two forms of

ElastiCache: Redis and Memcached. Both of these are in-memory caching, meaning that the data is stored in volatile memory rather than being stored on slower disks.

ElastiCache is one of several caching tools that can be used to improve performance and reduce cost. CloudFront is a content delivery network (CDN) that can be used to cache static contact such as images and files. RDS Read Replicas serve as a read-only copy of the database, which reduces load on the database primary and improves read performance. Caching is holding content closer to the user, taking the load off of the source and improving performance for the user. Let's say you need a bolt to fix your tractor. Normally that would mean a drive to town to buy the bolt from a store. However, if you happen to have a few spare bolts in the shed in your backyard, that just saved you a long drive. The shed is your cache of hardware, in this example a bolt. In the case of ElastiCache, we are specifically caching database content rather than bolts.

In any given scenario, you will want to be able to select the appropriate form of Elasti-Cache: Redis or Memcached. Know the differences and capabilities of each at a high level (see Table 7.1). In general, Memcached is a bit simpler to set up and manage but is far less feature-rich than Redis. In addition to just feature selection, you will want to know when to use or not use caching, in general. Caching works well in read-heavy environments when there is some tolerance for slightly stale data. Since caching is stored content, there is always the chance that it may not be the most current version. If your scenario involves something like banking ATM transactions, it's probably best to read from the database. Imagine that your balance is $1,000. You request to withdraw $900. The ATM checks and sees a balance (in cache) of $1,000, so it gives you $900. You immediately (before the cache refreshes) request another $900. The ATM checks and still sees $1,000 in the (now stale) cache and gives you another $900. Where time precision is important, caches are usually not a solution.

TABLE 7.1   Capabilities comparison of Redis vs. Memcached

Feature	Redis	Memcached
Complex data types (lists, hashes, sorted sets, etc.)	YES	NO
Encryption	YES	NO
Compliance Certifications	YES	YES
Pub/Sub	YES	NO
Backups/Restore	YES	NO
Data Partitioning	YES	YES
Sharding	YES	NO
Multithreaded architecture	NO	YES
Snapshots	YES	NO
Replication	YES	NO

Pricing

There are two billing models for ElastiCache: on-demand and reserved. On-demand requires no commitment and you pay only for the resources used per hour. Note that billing is per hour; this is different than EC2 on demand pricing. Reserved nodes are billed hourly and require a one- or three-year commitment. There are three reserved billing models: hourly with no up-front, partial up-front payment with reduced hourly cost, or all up-front with the lowest hourly rate. Additional costs include a per gigabyte charge for backup. There is no charge for data transfer between EC2 and ElastiCache in the same AZ. However, there is a fee for data transfer between AZs. Global Database charges for data transfer out.

Caching Strategies

Not everything could be, or should be, cached, but what *is* cached must be current and not out of date (stale). There are two strategies for populating a cache and keeping it fresh. Each strategy has trade-offs, and you will want to know when to use each. The two strategies are write-through and lazy loading. When an application requests data from the cache and the cache has the data stored, we call that a hit. When the cache does not have the data and the request must continue on to the database to retrieve the data, we call that a miss. The following strategies each attempt to increase hits and reduce misses.

Write-Through Caching

In write-through caching, any data destined for the database is also written to the cache. The advantage here is that data in the cache is always the most current. This model has a write penalty, meaning that it takes more resources to write than to read since each write involves both the database write as well as the cache write. There are disadvantages, however. Since the cache only has what is being written, it will have a lot of missing data, which must then be fetched on request. This can create slow performance when first implemented and scaling out. The second disadvantage is that there may be a great deal of data that is written but never again requested. This leads to unnecessarily large cache sizes. Using a time-to-live (TTL) can help reduce extraneous data in the cache.

Lazy Loading Caching

Lazy loading only populates the database with data that has actually been requested. This has the advantage of keeping cache sizes smaller and more relevant. However, this model will have more misses and higher latency on a miss since the request must first go to the cache, then to the database, then write the data to the cache before serving the request. Data in lazy loading can also become stale since writes and updates to the database are not updated in the cache until a request is made. Again, using a TTL will help. Despite some drawbacks, lazy loading is the most common form of caching.

ElastiCache for Redis

Redis is a very robust in-memory cache for session caching, message queues, and leaderboards (see Figure 7.5). Leaderboards are a good example of a workload that can leverage Redis's sorted sets to handle complex computational sorting of rapidly changing data. Redis is also used for publish/subscribe (pub/sub) scenarios and for message queuing. Redis is highly configurable, and the configuration can be manipulated through the parameter group. It is unlikely that for the exam you will be expected to know the details of setting up a Redis cluster. However, you will want to know the differences between Memcached and Redis from Table 7.1 as well as the common use cases.

FIGURE 7.5   Simple Redis cache architecture

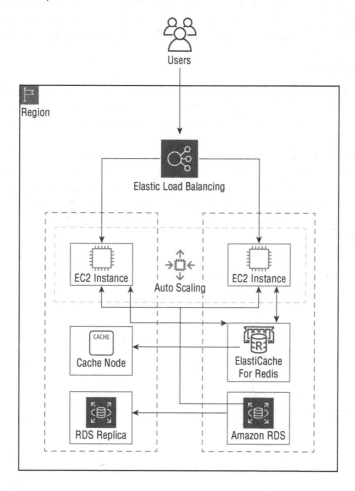

Migrating to Redis on ElastiCache

Customers already using Redis on EC2 or on-premises may choose to migrate to ElastiCache to take advantage of the managed service. Once a Redis ElastiCache cluster is in place, the CLI or an SDK can be used to trigger Online Migration using the `start-migration` command. This will set the primary of your Redis ElastiCache cluster to be a replica of your EC2 or on-premises Redis cluster. Once the data is synchronized, a `complete-migration` command will promote the ElastiCache node to become the primary.

Data Tiering

Data tiering is available on Redis. This feature allows less frequently used data to be moved from memory to solid-state drive (SSD) storage. This reduces cost but slightly increases latency and reduces throughput for data stored on SSD. Movement of data between the tiers is automatic. To gain the data tiering functionality, choose memory-optimized cache nodes with data tiering. These nodes are indicated by "gd"—for example, cache.r6gd.8xlarge.

High Availability

While Redis supports clusters, it still requires a single primary for writing, much like a relational database. For this reason, Redis scales vertically rather than horizontally. Data loss can occur with Redis. However, enabling multi-AZ and using replica nodes can add a level of high availability.

A word here about some terms that can be confusing. Clusters, shards, and nodes are all part of an ElastiCache for Redis implementation. They are also there in Memcached, but with ElastiCache they are less often discussed. Figure 7.6 shows how these elements relate to one another. In the CLI and APIs, shards are called node groups, and clusters are called replication groups. Shards use IP addresses. Be sure that the subnets within the subnet group have sufficient IP addresses allocated.

FIGURE 7.6   Redis cluster shard node

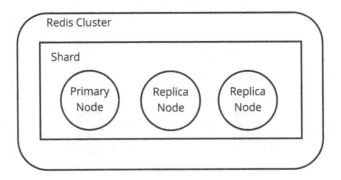

Cluster Modes

Redis provides two cluster modes, and they can be confusing. At a basic level, deciding between the modes concerns three dimensions, as shown in Table 7.2.

TABLE 7.2   Redis cluster modes

	Cluster mode disabled	Cluster mode enabled
Scaling vs. partitioning	Supports scaling.	Supports partitioning.
Node size vs. number of nodes	Only one node, so select largest type needed.	Can have many nodes, so type can be smaller.
Writes vs. reads	If read-heavy, add read replicas to scale.	If write-heavy, use multiple shards, which provide more endpoints.

Replication Across Regions

Global Datastores for Redis are managed and secure read replicas, which provide for low-latency reads and disaster recovery across regions. Each datastore is a collection of one or more clusters in a primary/secondary cluster configuration. Up to two secondary clusters in different regions are supported. Global Datastores are created from the Actions menu of the Redis ElastiCache.

Amazon MemoryDB

MemoryDB for Redis is an in-memory durable database. ElastiCache with Redis and MemoryDB for Redis may seem very similar, but they serve different purposes and differ significantly in durability. MemoryDB would be used for extremely low latency (microsecond read and single-digit millisecond write) with request rates at millions of reads/writes per second and volumes up to 100 TB, and you want durability. This might be in use cases such as session stores, game player stores and leaderboards, real-time analytics and streaming, and financial user tracking or fraud analysis.

Amazon ElastiCache for Memcached

Amazon ElastiCache for Memcached is an in-memory cache well suited to caching relational or NoSQL databases (including DynamoDB) and can be used as a session store.

Designing a Memcached cache can seem challenging. If you are not certain of the capacity needed, AWS recommends starting with a cache.m5.large. Then monitor the metrics memory usage, CPU utilization, and cache hit rate to determine proper sizing.

Actually, creating ElastiCache with Memcached is relatively straightforward. The cache can be created in the cloud or on-premises using Amazon Outposts. The cluster will reside in a subnet group. A subnet group is a collection of subnets that provision IP addresses for your cluster. The subnet group can be created as part of launching your ElastiCache or as a separate configuration step.

Summary

Databases are the most critical and sensitive asset in any business. The AWS Certified SysOps Administrator – Associate exam covers primarily RDS and ElastiCache. RDS supports several database engines, including RDS Aurora, and has several key features. There are a couple of important services that help off-load read requests, including RDS Read Replicas and caching with ElastiCache. Be sure to know when to use which service in response to a scenario. Availability, recoverability, and performance optimization are all important.

Exam Essentials

Know the engines supported by RDS.   This may seem pretty basic, but don't overlook some basic memorization. Amazon Aurora is one of the engines in RDS. Don't be confused that Aurora is compatible with PostgreSQL and MySQL. So, the engines are Oracle, SQL Server, MySQL, MariaDB, PostgreSQL, IBM DB2, and Amazon Aurora.

Be able to compare Memcached and Redis.   Both are supported caching engines in Amazon ElastiCache, but they have different features and capabilities. At a basic level, Memcached is easier to get set up but lacks some of the more advanced features of Redis. You will want to be able to compare and contrast the two engines and recognize when to use each.

Know what can be monitored and where to find the data.   Databases are very resource intensive as well as business critical. Performance monitoring is an essential task, and AWS provides a variety of ways to monitor performance. Of particular importance are Enhanced Metrics and Performance Insights. However, don't forget about common tools like Cloud-Watch, SNS, and EventBridge.

Have a caching strategy.   Given a scenario, be able to select an appropriate caching strategy. Two of the most common strategies are lazy loading and write-through.

Understand pricing.   Remember that for the exam you will not need to know exact prices for any services. Instead, you will need to be able to choose the most cost-effective solution for a given scenario.

Understand performance and cost.   You will almost always be balancing performance and cost. Pay particular attention to which the customer in a scenario is most concerned with.

Understand high availability and disaster recovery.   Be able to differentiate between high availability and disaster recovery. These concerns overlap significantly, but there are differences. There are many options for both, so you will want to be familiar with them and when each should be used.

Review Questions

1. Your customer has asked you to improve the performance of their RDS instance. Their database is consistently under a heavy load due to very large analysis and reporting workloads. Which of the following would be the best solution?

    A. Create a CloudFront distribution.

    B. Implement RDS Read Replicas.

    C. Migrate to Provisioned IOPS SSDs (io1).

    D. Scale up the primary RDS instance.

2. Which of the following database engines are supported by Amazon Relational Database Service (RDS)?

    A. MySQL, DynamoDB, MariaDB, Oracle, PostgreSQL, SQL Server

    B. MySQL, SQLite, Oracle, PostgreSQL, Amazon Aurora

    C. MySQL Oracle, PostgreSQL, SQL Server, MariaDB, Amazon Aurora

    D. MySQL Oracle, PostgreSQL, SQL Server, MariaDB, SQLite

3. ElastiCache supports which two in-memory cache options? (Choose two.)

    A. Apache Ignite

    B. DAX

    C. Ehcache

    D. Memcached

    E. Redis

4. The two strategies for cache loading include which of the following? (Choose two.)

    A. Arbitrary acquisition

    B. First-in, first-out (FIFO)

    C. Lazy loading

    D. Least effort load

    E. Write-through

5. Your customer has asked you to migrate a SQL Server database to AWS. This database will handle heavy read traffic globally but has customizations at the operating system level. Which of the following would be the best solution for your customer?

    A. Amazon EC2 running SQL Server

    B. Amazon Redshift for SQL Server

    C. Amazon Relational Database Service (RDS)

    D. Amazon Relational Database Service (RDS) Custom

6. Which of the following RDS features can best give visibility into load and bottleneck issues on a MariaDB RDS instance?

    A. CloudWatch Performance Alerts

    B. CloudWatch

    C. CloudTrail

    D. Performance Insights

7. To improve the security of an RDS instance connected to EC2 instances, where should the RDS instance be placed?

    A. In a DB subnet group and connected to your EC2 instances using the DB DNS name

    B. In a subnet and connected to your EC2 instance using a bastion host

    C. In the same subnet as the EC2 instances using IPv6 routing inside the subnet

    D. Inside its own DB VPC connected to your EC2 instances using a PrivateLink

8. Automated backups in RDS can be disabled by changing what setting?

    A. Changing the Automated Database Backup setting from Enabled to Disabled

    B. Setting the retention period to 0

    C. Deselecting the Enable Automated Backup setting and typing **confirm** in the dialog

    D. Deselecting the Enable Instance Snapshots setting

9. You have 40 RDS instances in the us-east-1 region, each with 10 unique databases. You attempt to create another RDS instance with 20 additional databases. The creation fails. To correct this issue so that you can add the databases, you must do which of the following?

    A. Create a read replica in a second AZ to free up resources on the primary instance.

    B. Enable Big Tables on the instance.

    C. Request an increase of your RDS instance database quota.

    D. You cannot create more than 10 databases on a SQL Server instance.

10. You are running Amazon ElastiCache for Redis and your engine requires a specific configuration that is not available by default. What would you modify to achieve your goal?

    A. ElastiCache is a managed service and the engine cannot be modified

    B. Parameter Group

    C. `Redis.conf`

    D. Use ElastiCache Custom

11. You have been asked to implement a caching solution for an RDS database. This solution will need to support complex data objects. The solution must be highly available and have persistence. Which solution will you use?

    A. CloudFront Distribution

    B. ElastiCache for Memcached

    C. ElastiCache for Redis

    D. RDS Read Replica

12. RDS Proxy supports most database engines except which one?

    A. Aurora

    B. Aurora Serverless

    C. Oracle

    D. SQL Server

13. Which of the following are indicators that an RDS proxy might be considered? (Choose three.)

    A. Disk full errors

    B. Many short-lived connections

    C. Out-of-memory errors

    D. RDS instances with less than 2 GB of memory

    E. Too many connections errors

14. Which of the following features is best suited to monitoring the operating system of the DB instance in real time?

    A. Amazon EventBridge

    B. CloudWatch logs

    C. Enhanced Monitoring

    D. Performance Insights

15. What is the principal metric found in Performance Insights?

    A. CPU Utilization

    B. DB Activity

    C. DB Load

    D. Memory Utilization

16. Which of the following statements about RDS Read Replicas is true? (Choose two.)

    A. A replica can be promoted to replace the primary DB instance.

    B. Read replicas are used as read-only copies of the primary DB instance.

    C. Read replicas should be created in a different VPC from the primary DB instance.

    D. The read replica and primary DB instance replicate synchronously.

17. You have been asked to recommend a solution that will provide point-in-time recovery for a client's RDS database. Which of the following will most efficiently achieve this goal? (Choose two.)

    A. Add tags to RDS instances and create a backup plan in AWS Backup.

    B. Enable automated RDS backups and set the backup retention period to 0.

    C. Enable automated RDS backups by setting the backup retention period to non-0.

    D. Ship RDS transaction logs to CloudWatch logs.

    E. Use AWS Lambda to automate snapshots every five minutes.

18. When an RDS read replica is promoted, what happens?

    A. A final snapshot is taken of the source DB instance and the source is terminated.

    B. The read replica is immediately available as a stand-alone DB instance.

    C. The read replica is rebooted and is then available as a stand-alone DB instance.

    D. The source DB instance is marked for termination.

19. Your research team has just discovered the cure for cancer, and you have been asked to share the research database with the world. To share this valuable data, what would you do?

    A. Place the database in a public subnet.

    B. Set all security groups on the database to a source of 0.0.0.0/0.

    C. Set the Publicly Accessible property to Yes.

    D. Share the RDS DB snapshot.

20. Your client has a business-critical PostgreSQL database in the us-west-2 region running on Amazon Aurora. The client wants to ensure the database is available even in the event of a regional event. Additionally, the database replication must have low latency and minimal impact on write operations. Which service would best support the client's requirements?

    A. Amazon Aurora Global Database

    B. Amazon Aurora global tables

    C. Amazon RDS Read Replicas

    D. Amazon RDS Proxy

Chapter 8

Monitoring, Logging, and Remediation

THE AWS CERTIFIED SYSOPS ADMINISTRATOR EXAM OBJECTIVES COVERED IN THIS CHAPTER INCLUDE:

✓ **Domain 1.0: Monitoring, Logging and Remediation**

- 1.1 Implement metrics, alarms, and filters by using AWS monitoring and logging services

  - Identify, collect, analyze, and export logs (for example, Amazon CloudWatch Logs, CloudWatch Logs Insights, AWS CloudTrail logs)

  - Collect metrics and logs using the CloudWatch agent

  - Create CloudWatch alarms

  - Create metric filters

  - Create CloudWatch dashboards

  - Configure notifications (for example, Amazon Simple Notification Service/Amazon SNS, Service Quotas, CloudWatch alarms, AWS Health events)

- 1.2 Remediate issues based on monitoring and availability metrics

  - Troubleshoot or take corrective actions based on notifications and alarms

  - Configure Amazon EventBridge rules to trigger actions

  - Use AWS Systems Manager Automation documents to take action based on AWS Config rules

In this chapter, you'll see how *Amazon CloudWatch* works and learn about its three key components: events, targets, and rules. You'll also learn how these relate to the fourth piece of the puzzle: CloudWatch alarms. Put all those together and you've got a robust monitoring solution for your AWS resources.

The chapter starts with an overview of AWS monitoring and quickly moves into specifics of CloudWatch and how it relates to monitoring key AWS resources:

- How AWS defines "monitoring" and how AWS virtualization helps—and at times limits—what can and cannot be monitored

- What structures AWS offers through CloudWatch: events, alarms, and the wiring between these two powerful mechanisms

- How to monitor compute resources like EC2 instances

- How to monitor storage, from S3 to RDS to DynamoDB, and what AWS provides beyond simplistic "How full is my disk?" metrics

- What AWS provides to make reporting, grouping, and interpreting the responses from these monitoring metrics an integrated part of your job (and workspace)

- The ever-present links to key AWS documentation when you forget a particular metric's name or how to create a custom alarm

Amazon CloudWatch is easily one of the most important tools you'll use as a SysOps administrator. Whether you're ensuring things are not going wrong, or responding when they inevitably do, CloudWatch gives you a window into the applications for which you're responsible. From basics like CPU usage and network latency to carefully crafted application-specific metrics, CloudWatch is your friend. In fact, it's your application physician; CloudWatch should be your first stop in seeing whether your application is healthy.

Amazon CloudWatch

The first monitoring tool covered in this chapter is Amazon CloudWatch (see Figure 8.1). If you want to monitor for performance and availability metrics, CloudWatch is the tool you need. You can also monitor for custom application metrics (if the logs agent is installed), and you can create your own log groups and dashboards.

FIGURE 8.1 The Amazon CloudWatch console gives you easy access to alarms, events, and logs within your environment.

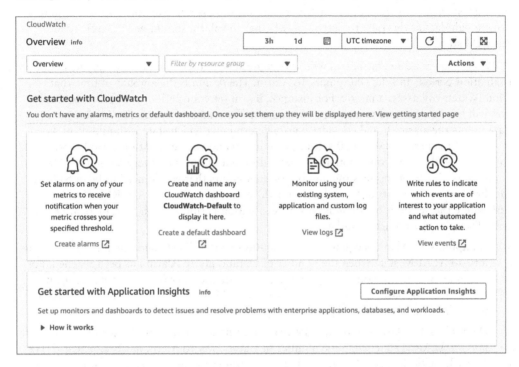

CloudWatch has a lot of different components, all managed from within the same console. We will talk about each of these in more detail in this section, starting with alarms, then moving into logs, events, and finally the dashboard.

CloudWatch Alarms

A CloudWatch alarm is responsible for monitoring a single metric. That may be as simple as an alarm that monitors for a CPU to reach 95 percent or an alarm that takes an average of a 5-minute period to see if the CPU stays at 95 percent and, if so, goes into an alarm state. CloudWatch alarms are a powerful tool in your AWS arsenal; they can be used to drive actions like telling an Auto Scaling group to scale based on that CPU metric I mentioned.

Alarms have three possible states that they can be in at any given point in time:

OK   If your Amazon CloudWatch alarm says it is OK, that means that the metric or the mathematical expression behind the metric is within the defined threshold.

ALARM   If your Amazon CloudWatch alarm says it is in an ALARM state, that means that the metric or the mathematical expression behind the metric is below or above the defined threshold.

INSUFFICIENT_DATA   There are a couple of reasons that your CloudWatch alarm might have INSUFFICIENT_DATA as its state. The most common reasons are that the alarm has only just started/been created, the metric it is monitoring is not available, or there is simply not enough data at this time to determine whether the alarm should be in an OK or an ALARM state.

When you create an alarm, you will have to decide what you want to set for the period, evaluation period, and the Datapoints To Alarm. The *period* is the amount of time that CloudWatch will assess a metric. For instance, if you set your period to 60 seconds, then you will have a new data point every 60 seconds. The *evaluation period* is the number of data points the alarm should consider before determining which state it should be in. For instance, if the period is set to 60 seconds (1 minute) and your evaluation period is set to 5 minutes, then you could potentially get a different alarm state every 5 minutes. The *Datapoints To Alarm* specifies the number of data points that would need to be outside of the threshold, referred to as "breaching," for the alarm to go into an ALARM state. In the case where the period is 60 seconds and the evaluation period is 5 minutes, there are two ways Datapoints To Alarm could go:

- **Datapoints To Alarm is equal to the evaluation period:** The CloudWatch alarm will go into an ALARM state when the number of Datapoints To Alarm has been reached. For example, with the period set to 1 minute, the evaluation period set to 5 minutes, and Datapoints To Alarm set to 5, you will get an ALARM state if the metric is outside of the defined threshold for 5 data points.

- **Datapoints To Alarm is less than the evaluation period:** The CloudWatch alarm will go into an ALARM state when the number of Datapoints To Alarm has been reached. For example, with the period set to 1 minute, the evaluation period set to 5 minutes, and Datapoints To Alarm set to 3, you will get an ALARM state if the metric is outside of the defined threshold for three of the five data points within the evaluation period.

What happens if you are missing data points? For each alarm, you can set how you want CloudWatch to treat missing data points. This allows you to customize your alarms to meet your expectations as far as how missing data points are handled. There are four possible settings: notBreaching, breaching, ignore, and missing. You will get to see these settings when we set up a CloudWatch alarm in an exercise later in the chapter.

CloudWatch Logs

Amazon CloudWatch Logs is a one-stop shop for all things having to do with logging. Not only does it store logs from AWS systems and resources, it can also handle the logs for on-premises systems as long as they have the unified CloudWatch agent installed. If you have chosen to monitor AWS CloudTrail activity through CloudWatch, the activity that is monitored is sent to CloudWatch Logs.

If you need to have a long retention period for your logs, then CloudWatch Logs is also a good fit. By default, logs are kept forever and will never be expired. You should adjust this based on your organization's retention policies. You can choose to keep logs for only a single day or go up to 10 years.

Log Groups and Log Streams

Getting logs in a single destination is a great start; however, to make it more useful, one of the first things most system admins want to do is to put like data with like data. For example, say you have some EC2 instances that handle web traffic. You want the logs grouped together since they are serving a similar purpose. This is where a log group comes into play.

Each web server that sends logs into Amazon CloudWatch Logs is using a log stream. A *log stream* is a collection of the events that have happened on a single source, like an EC2 instance or an AWS service. A *log group* in Amazon CloudWatch is a collection of log streams that will share the same settings in regard to retention and monitoring, as well as IAM settings. In our example, the EC2 instances handling the web traffic would each have a log stream in Amazon CloudWatch, and those log streams would be grouped together into a log group.

Unified CloudWatch Agent

While you can get basic information regarding availability and performance for your EC2 instances, you can get far more detailed information if you have installed the unified *CloudWatch agent*. You can also gather logs from your on-premises servers in the case of a hybrid environment with the CloudWatch agent, and centrally manage and store them from within the CloudWatch console. The agent is supported for multiple Windows and Linux operating systems, including the 64-bit versions of Windows Server 2008, 2012, and 2016 and multiple versions of Amazon Linux, Amazon Linux 2, Ubuntu Server, CentOS, Red Hat Enterprise Linux (RHEL), Debian, and SUSE Linux Enterprise Server (SLES).

By installing the CloudWatch agent on a Windows machine, you can gather in-depth information from the Performance Monitor, which is built into the operating system. When CloudWatch is installed on a Linux system, you can get more in-depth metrics related to CPU, memory, network, processes, and swap memory usage. You can also gather custom logs from applications installed on servers. To install the CloudWatch agent, you need to set up the configuration file. Amazon provides a wizard to make the creation of the configuration file simple.

CloudWatch Events (Amazon EventBridge)

At the beginning of the chapter, we mentioned real-time monitoring. This function is provided by CloudWatch Events, now called Amazon EventBridge. One of the big wins with CloudWatch Events is the ability to use an event as a trigger to kick off something else. For instance, an event related to an HTTP 500 error from a web server might kick off notifications to the administrator or could be used to reboot a backend application server that is having problems. There are quite a few services that can be targeted by CloudWatch Events.

Please note that CloudWatch Events has been renamed Amazon EventBridge and has its own console page.

CloudWatch Dashboard

The CloudWatch dashboard is a fully customizable method to view the data that is most meaningful to you. You can create dashboards with your own custom metrics so that you are presented with the data you need to call attention to. If you create a dashboard and name it CloudWatch-Default, it is displayed in the Overview dashboard, as shown in Figure 8.2. You will create your own dashboard in a later exercise.

FIGURE 8.2   The overview page houses default metrics as well as a CloudWatch-Default dashboard if you choose to make one.

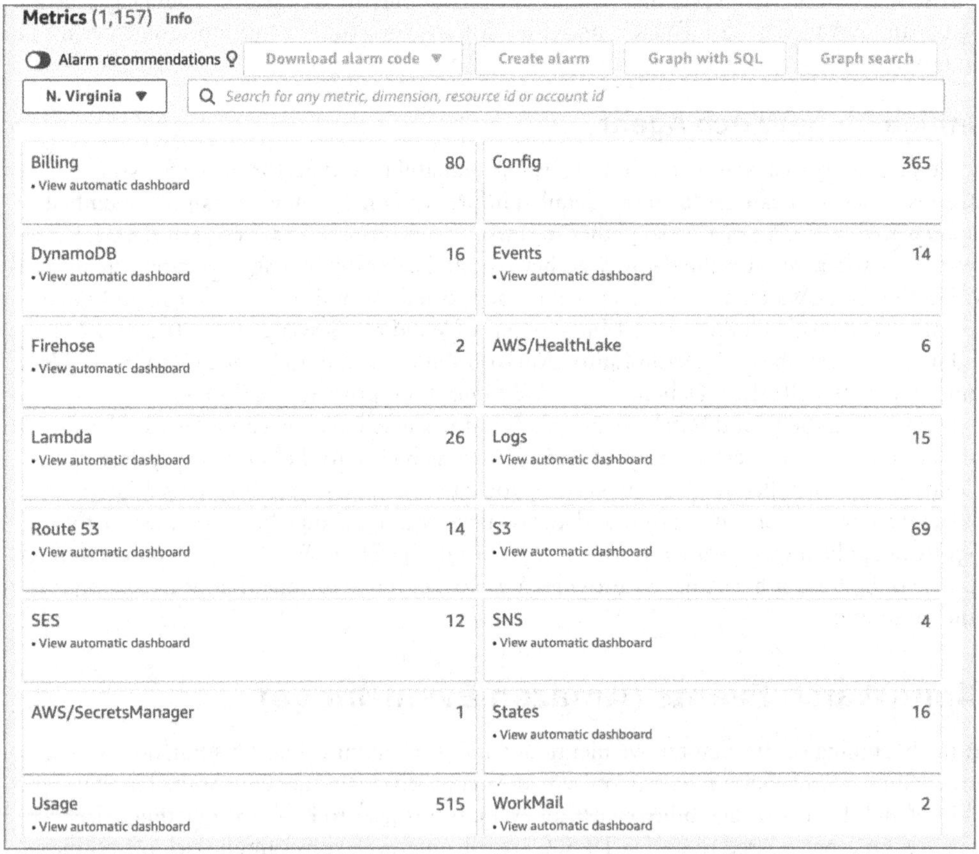

Metrics (1,157) Info			
⬤ Alarm recommendations ♀	Download alarm code ▼	Create alarm	Graph with SQL	Graph search

N. Virginia ▼   🔍 Search for any metric, dimension, resource id or account id

Billing • View automatic dashboard	80	**Config**	365
DynamoDB • View automatic dashboard	16	**Events** • View automatic dashboard	14
Firehose • View automatic dashboard	2	**AWS/HealthLake**	6
Lambda • View automatic dashboard	26	**Logs** • View automatic dashboard	15
Route 53 • View automatic dashboard	14	**S3** • View automatic dashboard	69
SES • View automatic dashboard	12	**SNS** • View automatic dashboard	4
AWS/SecretsManager	1	**States** • View automatic dashboard	16
Usage • View automatic dashboard	515	**WorkMail** • View automatic dashboard	2

Monitoring on AWS

AWS is a cloud platform based on virtualized resources. It comes with some drawbacks. With no accessibility to a datacenter, physical hardware, or racks of storage and networking equipment, there is nothing to "check" to see whether things are behaving. You have a web-based console, a command line, some APIs—but where are the blinking lights? Where are the packet sniffers and patch panels?

In short, they're in CloudWatch. Now, like the rest of AWS, CloudWatch doesn't provide a direct analog for physical devices and on-premises datacenter activities. It does, however, give you a robust system for managing *metrics*. Ultimately, the AWS premise is that as a SysOps admin, you don't care about all those lights and cables as much as you care about metrics: What is the objective number that tells you how something is performing, and what is the acceptable threshold for that number?

Almost every single AWS service and resource provides metrics to CloudWatch, and CloudWatch becomes a sort of repository for all those collected metrics. It gives you tools to wade through the huge amount of collected data and to see those "everything is okay" thresholds for your application.

 Be careful in practical situations when you hear the term CloudWatch. Although AWS and exams use the term specifically as a reference to the service—distinguishing it from other managed services and tools that report to it—it often refers to more in practical usage. You'll often hear CloudWatch as a general term meaning "CloudWatch (the service), the data it collects, the reports within it, and the application of those reports." It can often become a catchall term. This is something you'll need to be aware of.

Monitoring Is Event-Driven

All your monitoring in AWS is event-driven. An *event* (which as you'll later see becomes a CloudWatch event, a more formal idea around this same concept) is simply "something that happens in AWS and is captured." You don't have to do anything with every event, and you certainly won't want to. There are more events than you could ever memorize—and many only make sense to pay attention to in certain contexts.

But when something happens in AWS, it creates an event. For example, when a new EBS volume is created, the `createVolume` event is triggered, and it can either have a result of `available` or `failed`. This event and its result are sent to CloudWatch, the AWS repository.

Monitoring Is Customizable

Now, despite there being an almost innumerable set of events predefined by AWS, there are still times you may need something customized. For instance, perhaps you want to know when the number of queries to a particular queue reaches a certain threshold because there is business logic that should be applied at that stage. You can define these custom metrics easily.

Additionally, once defined, a custom metric behaves just like a predefined one. These custom metrics are added to the event repository alongside standardized metrics and can then be analyzed and interpreted.

You can even build metrics that report on on-premises applications and systems in a hybrid environment, resulting in a complete picture of all your connected systems, rather than just those in the cloud. CloudWatch integrates into your overall system at a very deep layer, providing monitoring that bends to your needs, rather than you bending to it.

One important limitation of CloudWatch bears mentioning: It functions below the AWS Hypervisor, which means that it functions below (and sometimes at) the virtualization layer of AWS. This means that it can report on things like CPU usage and disk I/O, but it cannot see what is happening above that layer.

This means that CloudWatch cannot tell you what tasks or application processes are affecting performance. It can only report on the information it can directly see at the hypervisor layer, or things that are reported to it. That's why it cannot (for example) tell you about disk usage, *unless* you write code that checks disk usage and send that metric to CloudWatch.

This is an important topic, and it sometimes shows up on the exam. You might be asked if CloudWatch can report on memory or disk usage by default; it cannot.

Monitoring Drives Action

The final piece of the AWS monitoring puzzle is what occurs *after* a metric has reported a value or result outside of a predefined "everything is okay" threshold. When this happens, an *alarm* is triggered. An alarm is not necessarily the same as "something is wrong"; instead, think of an alarm as indicating that something needs to happen. That something might be running a piece of code in Lambda, or sending a message to an Auto Scaling group to scale in, or sending out an email via the AWS SNS service.

In short, monitoring in AWS is not just for the purpose of you, the SysOps administrator, actually looking at a dashboard and making a real-time decision. Rather, monitoring is set up in a way that triggers action when you're *not* looking at that dashboard. As you'll see further along in this chapter and then again in later chapters, part of your role is to define these actions. What should happen when CPU usage goes beyond 75 percent? Or when the request queue for your DynamoDB instances really pile up? Monitoring drives these actions.

Basic CloudWatch Terms and Concepts

AWS introduces a number of terms that mean specific things in CloudWatch. You've already seen a few of these, such as alarms and metrics. You'll need to understand these terms to make much sense of CloudWatch or the exam questions about it.

CloudWatch Is Metric- and Event-Based

CloudWatch collects metrics. A metric is anything that can be tracked and is usually discrete: a number or percentage or value. Formally, AWS says a metric is a time-ordered set of data points, which gets at the notion that metrics are reported repeatedly over time. AWS defines a number of metrics, and you can also define custom metrics.

> **WARNING**   Try to keep a metric and an event discrete in your understanding of AWS. An *event* is predefined and is something that happens, like bytes being received by a network interface. A *metric* is a measure of that event, or some facet of that event, like how many bytes are received in a given period of time. Events and metric are related, but not synonymous.

Alarms Indicate Notifiable Change

In addition to metrics, there are alarms. A CloudWatch alarm initiates action. You can set an alarm to respond when a metric is reported with a result value outside of a threshold or result set. For example, an alarm could be set when CPU utilization on your EC2 instances reaches 80 percent. You can also set alarms on lower bounds, such as when that same CPU utilization returns to less than 50 percent.

Events and CloudWatch Events Are Lower Level

CloudWatch also relies heavily on events. An event is something that happens, usually related to a metric changing or reporting into CloudWatch, but at a system level. An event can then trigger further action, just as an alarm can.

Events are typically streamed to CloudWatch; they are reported almost constantly from various low-level AWS resources. Additionally—perhaps just to add a little confusion—CloudWatch Events (CWE) is a specific name for this stream of system events. So CloudWatch Events is the formal mechanism through which events (lowercase "e" this time) get to the CloudWatch system.

CloudWatch Events Has Three Components

Within CloudWatch Events are three key components: events, rules, and targets. An event is the thing that is being reported and is a proxy for that thing happening. A rule is an expression that matches incoming events. If there's a match to an event, the event is routed to a target for processing. A target is another AWS component, typically a piece of code in Lambda or an Auto Scaling group, or perhaps an email that should be sent out.

Choosing Between Alarms and Events

If you've been following along, you may rightfully be a little confused. Metrics make sense, but how is an event related to an alarm? Which is which? And when do you use alarms versus when do you use events? In short, alarms are for monitoring any metric reported on your account, related to your application. These typically deal with request latency on your elastic load balancers (ELBs) or perhaps the throughput of an important query that uses your Amazon Relational Database Service (RDS) instances. Alarms are for your specific application needs. Events describe change in your AWS resources. Think of these as logs, reporting on the general health of your application.

Put another way, an alarm might indicate that a professional football player's fatigue level is increasing and therefore he is running more slowly. It's specific to his function in a performance context. An event might indicate that same player's blood pressure is high when he's walking down the street. It's a *general* indication of health unrelated to his function. Both alarms and events are important, and you'll need to monitor both.

What's in a Namespace?

Another key concept in CloudWatch is that of the namespace. A *namespace* is just a container for a collection of related CloudWatch metrics. Because so many metrics might share a general purpose—CPU utilization on an EC2 instance, an RDS instance, and a DynamoDB instance, for example—AWS provides namespaces to distinguish these from one another. AWS provides a number of predefined namespaces, all beginning with `AWS/[service]`. So `AWS/EC2/CPUUtilization` is CPU utilization for an EC2 instance, while `AWS/DynamoDB/CPUUtilization` is the same metric but for DynamoDB. There is a *long* list of namespaces, and it grows as services are added. You'll also need to work with namespaces yourself. When you create a custom metric, you can place that metric in an AWS namespace or create one of your own. For example, you might create the `Media/photos` namespace to report on usage of photos in your media suite of applications.

To the 10th Dimension

You can also provide up to 10 dimensions for your metrics. A *dimension* is a name/value pair that helps identify a metric. For a metric reported on an EC2 instance, you might have an `InstanceId=1-234567` dimension and an `InstanceType=m1.large` dimension. These pairs provide additional information about the metric that help separate it from other similar metrics, perhaps on different instances or of different classes.

Statistics Aggregate Metrics

Add the term *statistic* to your growing CloudWatch vocabulary. A statistic is just what it sounds like: a value that gives you some sense of a particular metric (or metrics) over time. CloudWatch gives you several helpful default statistics, including minimum, maximum, sum, average, samplecount, and pNN.NN (the value of a specified percentile such as p99.99 or p50).

Statistics are reported over time, so you'll need to specify a time period (more on that later). You can also select a subset of all metrics based on a dimension (or several dimensions). For example, you might want the average for all metrics reported on instances with the dimensions Domain=Rockville and Environment=Prod.

Monitoring Compute

EC2 provides some of the easiest-to-interpret and useful metrics of all of AWS's predefined metrics. Instance metrics are recorded for 15 months to give you easy access to historical data as well.

All instance metrics are provided to CloudWatch in 5-minute increments. You can increase this frequency to 1-minute increments by turning on detailed monitoring.

Activating detailed monitoring is possible through the console. Select your instance and choose Actions ➢ CloudWatch Monitoring ➢ Enable Detailed Monitoring. Please note that detail monitoring will incur a charge to your AWS account.

EC2 Instance Metrics

First, you should realize that there would be pages upon pages of tables if you wanted a list of every single available EC2-related metric. There are metrics for CPU credits, on instances themselves for CPU and disk I/O, status checks, and much, much more.

Fortunately, many of these are things you can simply look up. There are only a large handful of metrics that you will use over and over and that you should be familiar with for the certification exam. For a start, you *should* be comfortable with the usage of instance metrics. Instance metrics include CPUUtilization, DiskReadOps, DiskWriteOps, DiskReadBytes, DiskWriteBytes, NetworkIn, NetworkOut, NetWorkPacketIn, and NetWorkPacketOut.

EC2 EBS Metrics

There are additional compute metrics that are associated with EBS volumes. That may seem a little odd; aren't EBS volumes storage? They certainly are, but many times, metrics for EBS volumes straddle the line between being compute metrics versus storage metrics. EC2 EBS metrics are EBS-related and report on storage volumes, but do that reporting in light of the instance to which the EBS volumes are attached. Predefined instance metrics for EBS include `EBSReadOps`, `EBSWriteops`, `EBSReadBytes`, `EBSWriteBytes`, `EBSIOBalance%`, and `EBSByteBalance%`. These EBS metrics are specifically available for the following instance family types: C, M, R, and T3, among others.

ECS Metrics

With the addition of containers via the Elastic Container Service (ECS), there is a whole new set of metrics that are now relevant to you as the SysOps administrator. These metrics are all available in the `AWS/ECS` namespace, and they give you information about a running cluster rather than a specific container. Several key metrics are shown in this namespace, including `CPUReservation`, `CPUUtilization`, `MemoryReservation`, and `MemoryUtilization`.

Monitoring Storage

When you move from compute into storage, the world of CloudWatch metrics expands even more rapidly. Whereas in compute you essentially have instances and containers, in storage you have S3, DynamoDB, and RDS as central pillars of a storage solution. You could also add to that RedShift and Elastic MapReduce (EMR), and then you start to touch on CloudFront and ElastiCache, which aren't quite storage but are closely associated.

Here, the Internet is your friend; it's always trivial to look up a metric or set of metrics by service. Simply typing **AWS CloudWatch ElastiCache** will get you what you need quickly. However, there are some metrics that you should know off the top of your head, for both your own use and, of course, the AWS exam.

S3 Metrics

There are many S3 metrics—more than makes sense to repeat on the page. The most common are `BucketSizeBytes`, `NumberOfObjects`, `AllRequests`, `GetRequests`, `BytesDownloaded`, `BytesUploaded`, `FirstByteLatency`, and `TotalRequestLatency`. These all exist within the `AWS/S3` namespace.

RDS Metrics

Like S3, there are more metrics for RDS than is reasonable to memorize. A few key ones are `DatabaseConnections`, `DiskQueueDepth`, `FreeStorageSpace`, `ReadIOPS`,

`ReadLatency`, and `ReplicaLag`. They are worth at least recognizing and understanding for your certification exam.

There are some differences when working with RDS compared to other metrics, though. RDS is a managed service, so you can't set the frequency of the metrics or switch between basic and detailed metrics. As a result, RDS sends metrics to CloudWatch every minute, and that's not configurable.

DynamoDB Metrics

You should be sensing a theme with storage metrics: There are a *lot* of them in AWS. This makes sense, though. Most storage in AWS is managed, and you have less direct access. AWS recognizes this and sends you a lot of information so that you can keep up with what's happening in those managed services.

DynamoDB metrics are in the AWS/DynamoDB namespace. Similar to most other managed services, they are reported every minute, and that's not configurable. There's one other wrinkle with these metrics: They are reported to CloudWatch only when they are nonzero. That can skew your averages if you're not careful.

A nonexhaustive list of important DynamoDB metrics includes the following: `ConsumedReadCapacityUnits`, `ConsumedWriteCapacityUnits`, `ProvisionedReadCapacityUnits`, `ProvisionedWriteCapacityUnits`, `ReplicationLatency`, and `SystemErrors`. You should familiarize yourself with these.

The best thing to do in terms of exam preparation is to ensure you understand the terminology used, rather than memorizing specifics of DynamoDB or S3 or RDS metric names. Understand "latency" and "throughput" and "provisioned," and you can generally reason your way through the exam questions.

CloudWatch Alarms

So you've got your metrics, and they're all pouring into CloudWatch. What do you do with all this data? Generally, you want to be alerted and then take action. Of course, one of the key best practices—whether in or out of the cloud—is to automate everything you can. It's much better to build a system that does what you want than to do something manually. Alarms give you the framework to do just that when it comes to monitoring. You create a set of "okay" values, attach an alarm, and then respond to that alarm.

Create an Alarm Threshold

An alarm is intended to go off when a metric is outside of a set of values you consider "okay." You can set a specific value as a high or low value, or a range of acceptable values.

For instance, suppose you want to add instances to an Auto Scaling group when any single instance reports that it is using more than 85 percent of its CPU, and then scale back in when all instances are reporting less than 60 percent CPU utilization.

EC2 instances report a metric for this: CPUUtilization in the AWS/EC2 namespace. You can watch this metric and set an alarm threshold for the metric at 85. You also should specify how many periods the metric must be above that threshold; you might want to scale out only if CPU is above 85 percent for more than four periods.

You'll need to keep up with your monitoring frequency to set good alarms. Basic monitoring reports every 5 minutes, so two successive metrics above a threshold might be enough, perhaps three at most. If you're using detailed monitoring, though, you'll get reports every minute, and then you may want five or six consecutive reports.

It's worth noting that CloudWatch always wants two successive values above/below/in a threshold. It's not intended to trigger an alarm after a single value is reported.

Set Off an Alarm

Once you've set a threshold, CloudWatch takes care of the rest. The new alarm can be in one of three states at any given time: OK, ALARM, and INSUFFICIENT_DATA. These are pretty self-explanatory. When an alarm goes into the ALARM state, you can set off an action. But that's not the only time you can create an action. You could actually set additional actions for when the alarm returns to the OK state (perhaps scaling back in that Auto Scaling group in the example mentioned earlier).

Respond to an Alarm

When the alarm initiates an action, you can do something. That something can be a whole range of things: Send off an email, or provision a new instance, or update an ELB. Basically, anything you can do in AWS, you can do in response to an alarm. Often, you'll invoke code. Part of the beauty of AWS Lambda is that this code can run without a lot of overhead, making the entire CloudWatch alarm framework even more useful.

CloudWatch Events

So far, the focus has been on metrics reported from AWS managed services and your own resources using EC2 instances, EBS volumes, and the like. These metrics will tell you how resources are serving your application, as well as how the things your application is doing in turn affects your overall provisioning and costs. But that's only part of the picture of your AWS environment.

You also need to know how your system is doing, without regard to your application. If certain resources are unhealthy or not performing at capacity, or if the state of a resource is changing, you have to know that. You may also need to make a change in your use of those or related resources.

This is where CloudWatch Events come in. Now, keep clear that *Amazon CloudWatch Events* (capitalized, and sometimes abbreviated as CWE) is distinct from the metrics that are sent to CloudWatch. CloudWatch Events has its own set of constructs, and it operates a little differently than CloudWatch. But it's key to managing your environment, so it can't be discounted.

Events

An event is a change in your AWS environment. Now, as mentioned earlier, an event is part of the overall CloudWatch Events structure. You must be careful to make this distinction; this means that CloudWatch Events has events, which can be pretty confusing.

An event can be generated in one of four different ways:

- An AWS resource changes state. For example, an EC2 instance moves from pending to running, or a database instance moves from running to terminated.

- API calls and console sign-ins occur. These are reported via CloudTrail (which focuses on logging and API calls) but come across as events.

- You generate an event in your code. This is a bit of a melding of two worlds, but your application code can push events to CloudWatch Events for processing.

- A schedule triggers. You can trigger events with cron-style scheduling on a repeated basis.

All of these are simply tools—hooks that allow you to attach behavior when something happens. And that's where rules come into the picture.

Rules

A *rule* is the connective tissue between events and targets. A rule matches incoming events, and if there's a match, sends the event to the specified target. A target can then kick off processing, evaluate the event, send an email, or do anything else you like. (You'll soon see this is similar to an alarm for a metric in CloudWatch.)

A rule can also filter parts of an event or send additional bits of information along with the event. It uses JavaScript Object Notation (JSON) to do this. In fact, JSON is the language used for all of this connectivity, so a rule can simply add or filter the JSON that's passed to a target.

Targets

A *target* processes the JSON data it is sent by a rule, resulting from a match on one or more events. The result is often a stream of JSON to several targets of your choosing.

Typical targets include EC2 instances, Lambda functions (this is a popular one), ECS tasks, step functions, Simple Queue Service (SQS) queues, and Simple Notification Service (SNS) topics. What these targets do with the JSON is really then up to you. You could send off messages via email, scale in or scale out an Auto Scaling group, or provision more instances.

At the point that a target is reached, you can begin to think of further processing as the same as when you've received a CloudWatch alarm, discussed earlier. Although application metrics raising alarms is a different mechanism than events matching rules and being forwarded to targets, once action is taken the system handles things the same way. In fact, there's no reason you couldn't have the same Lambda function triggered by an alarm and function as a target.

Exercises

Once you have metrics—both predefined and custom—and events flowing into CloudWatch, you're going to quickly find that keeping up with them all is a huge hassle. Each metric sits in a different place, and that means you can spend a whole lot of time hopping from screen to screen or running tons of CLI commands. The best way to handle this is to create a dashboard that has your essential metrics all in one place. In this section, you'll do just that.

Exercise 8.1 assumes that you have some resources up and running in your AWS environment. Otherwise, you'll have very little on which to report. If you don't have any resources, you may want to come back to this exercise later in the book. Feel free to start an EC2 instance.

Another idea would be to take this as an opportunity to create some new EC2 instances and S3 buckets to play around with moving data back and forth between buckets. Consider connecting to your instances and updating them. Anything that causes interaction, network I/O, or CPU usage is perfect for this section's metrics. We will use a billing metric as an example.

In Exercise 8.1, you create a custom CloudWatch dashboard.

EXERCISE 8.1

Creating a Custom CloudWatch Dashboard

1. Log into the AWS management console and navigate to the service of CloudWatch.

2. On the landing page, choose the Dashboards link along the left. You should see an empty set of dashboards that relate to custom dashboards. You'll also see the Automatic Dashboards tab, as shown in the following image.

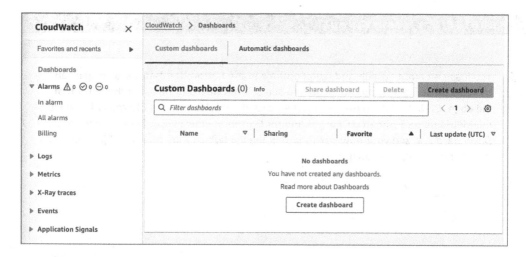

3. Click the Create Dashboard button, and then select a name for your dashboard.

4. Next up, you'll have to select a data source type for the metric to add to the dashboard. You also select the data type as Metrics. Finally, you can select the display widget type from a variety of choices. We leave this setting as CloudWatch for data source type and metrics for the widget configuration data type. You have several options, shown next. For now, click Next.

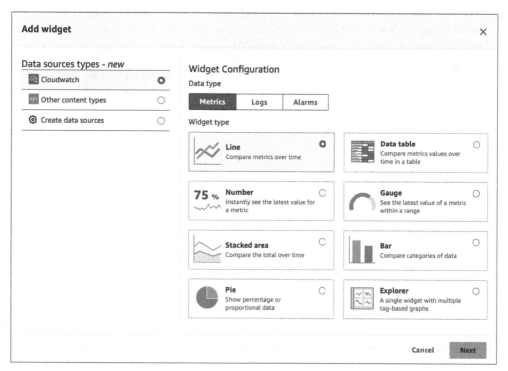

5. You'll see an empty graph and some options at the bottom for metrics, all organized by AWS resource. You should be able to select a metric from the list at the bottom of the page. Click the billing metric and then click the Total Estimated Charge link. Select the Metric name Estimated Charges and for Currency, select USD. Finally, click Create Dashboard and see your new dashboard in the list (which may be a list of just one for you at this point), as shown next.

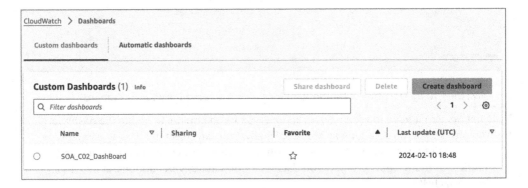

6. If you are using your personal account, you will see your dashboard, and when you select it, you can see a chart of your estimated charges in a line graph. Notice on the top right that you can select a time period like 3H (hours), 1 day, and 1 week. Without a personal account you may not have access to billing metrics. You can add additional widgets to this dashboard by using the Plus (+) sign button to the top right of the screen. You can also change the name of a widget by clicking the pencil icon next to the name.

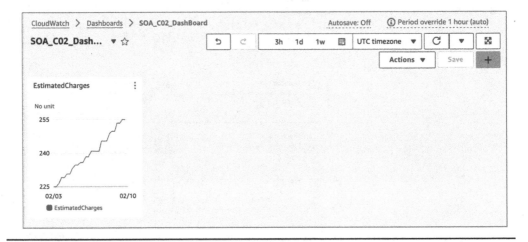

In Exercise 8.2, you add EC2 line metrics to your CloudWatch dashboard.

EXERCISE 8.2

Adding EC2 Line Metrics

1. Click on your create dashboard, name it **EC2_Dashboard**, and then select CloudWatch for the data source type and Metrics for the data type. Click Next.

    You'll see an empty graph and some options at the bottom for metrics, all organized by AWS resource. The following image shows a simple AWS account that has a single EC2 instance and S3 buckets, and not much else.

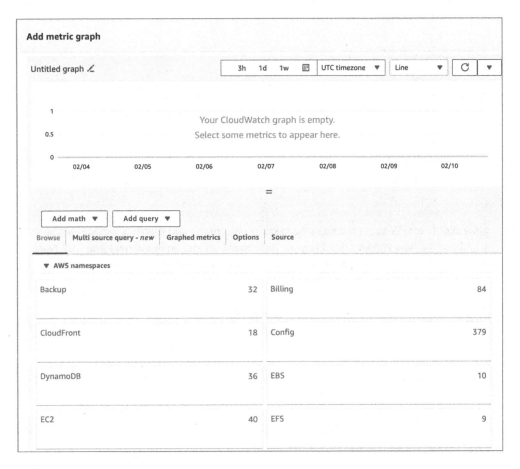

2. Select the EC2 option, and then choose Per-Instance Metrics. You can filter metrics here, as there are a lot to choose from. In this case, assuming you have a few EC2 instances, enter **CPU** in the search box, press Enter/Return, and choose CPUUtilization for all your available instances. This is shown for two instances in the next image.

EXERCISE 8.2 *(continued)*

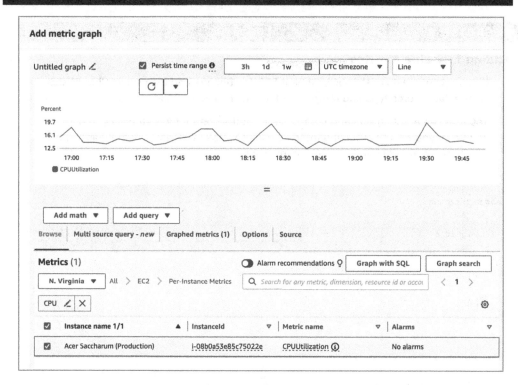

3. Now click Create Widget located at the bottom right of the add metric graph screen, and you'll see the new widget added to your dashboard (as shown in the next graphic). Note that even here, the graph is showing you metrics in real time on your new dashboard.

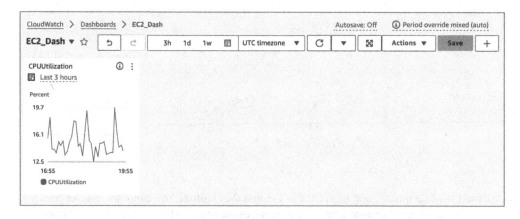

4. Finally, click Save to save the dashboard. This is an important step and often missed! If you don't click Save, you'll lose your updates to the dashboard.

AWS CloudTrail

Have you ever wondered what your users were doing? It's common to monitor for failed logins and, in some cases, successful logins. In a traditional on-premises environment, however, the majority of organizations don't get much more insight than that. Tools are available that can correlate user activity data, but they can be expensive to purchase and difficult to maintain. That's where *AWS CloudTrail* comes in (see Figure 8.3). Not only is it simple to use, but if you use the defaults you are able to view 90 days' worth of account activity free of charge as long as the event is a management event and is a create, modify, or delete operation.

FIGURE 8.3   The free AWS CloudTrail monitoring capture, store, act, and review operations

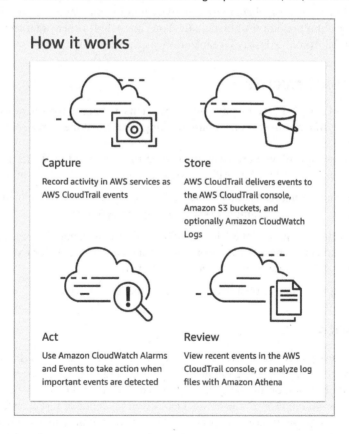

How it works

Capture

Record activity in AWS services as AWS CloudTrail events

Store

AWS CloudTrail delivers events to the AWS CloudTrail console, Amazon S3 buckets, and optionally Amazon CloudWatch Logs

Act

Use Amazon CloudWatch Alarms and Events to take action when important events are detected

Review

View recent events in the AWS CloudTrail console, or analyze log files with Amazon Athena

Do you want to collect more data? You can do so easily by creating a trail. You can create a *trail* that will allow you to gather management and data events from all regions and put that information into an S3 bucket of your choosing. Additionally, if you create a trail you can create custom event metrics and trigger alerts with the integration into CloudWatch. The trail delivers events to both Amazon CloudWatch Logs and EventBridge events.

Management and data events are collected every time there is an API call. One of the most important things to remember is that everything that is done within AWS generates an API call. This includes activity within the AWS Management Console, the AWS CLI, and AWS SDKs, including other AWS services.

Applying a Trail to an Organization

Having an active trail in AWS CloudTrail is the best way to get a full picture of the activity happening in your account. What's even better is that you can manage that one trail and have it applied to all regions where there is activity within your AWS account. A trail created in the console is a multiregion trail by default. You can include other organizations by clicking Enable For All Accounts In My Organization, as shown in Figure 8.4.

Management Events

By default, AWS CloudTrail records management events as long as the operation is create, modify, or delete. *Management events* relate to things that are done to the resources in your AWS account.

When you create a trail, you are given the option to select Read or Write. You can also exclude KMS events and RDS Data API events. Let's look at each of these in more detail.

Read   This setting configures CloudTrail to collect management events related to read actions like `Describe*` (for example, `DescribeSecurityGroups`).

Write   This setting configures AWS CloudTrail to collect management events related to actions that can cause changes to your resources such as `Create*` (for example, `createTags`), `RunInstances`, and `TerminateInstances`.

Figure 8.5 displays the console for CloudTrail Management events.

Data Events

By default, data events are not recorded. *Data events* are related to events that might change data objects in your account. These might include `Get*` and `Put*` in S3, or the invocation of an AWS Lambda function or an operation performed in DynamoDB.

You can choose to monitor all the S3 buckets in your account or just specific buckets. For instance, you may choose to monitor specific buckets that contain sensitive information like personally identifiable information (PII) or personal healthcare information (PHI). Typical API activity for S3 buckets might include `GetObject`, `PutObject`, and `DeleteObject`. As shown in Figure 8.6, you can choose to record read activities, write activities, or both.

FIGURE 8.4   You can apply a trail to all accounts in an entire organization.

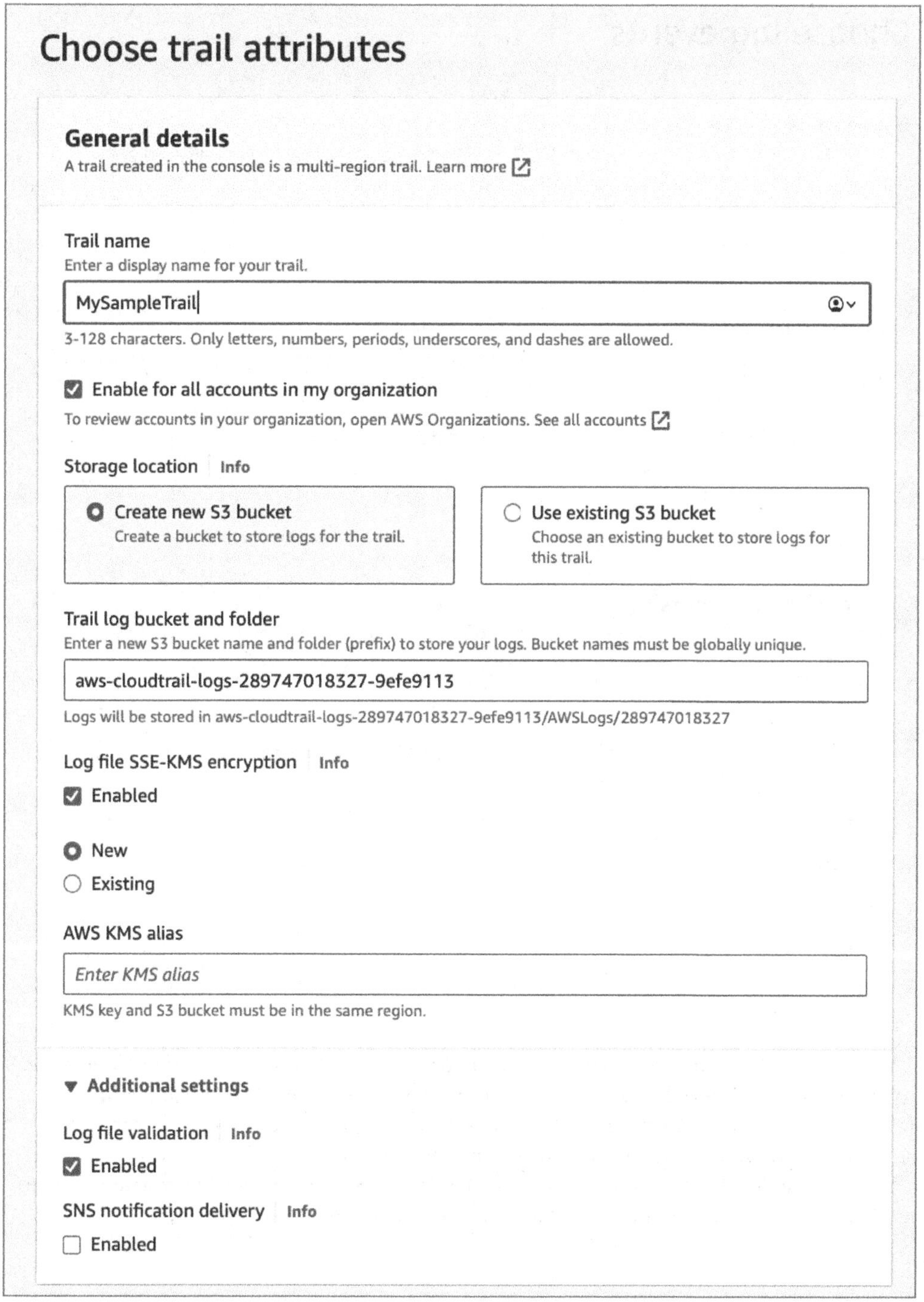

Choose trail attributes

General details
A trail created in the console is a multi-region trail. Learn more 🔗

Trail name
Enter a display name for your trail.

MySampleTrail

3-128 characters. Only letters, numbers, periods, underscores, and dashes are allowed.

☑ Enable for all accounts in my organization

To review accounts in your organization, open AWS Organizations. See all accounts 🔗

Storage location   Info

○ **Create new S3 bucket**
Create a bucket to store logs for the trail.

○ **Use existing S3 bucket**
Choose an existing bucket to store logs for this trail.

Trail log bucket and folder
Enter a new S3 bucket name and folder (prefix) to store your logs. Bucket names must be globally unique.

aws-cloudtrail-logs-289747018327-9efe9113

Logs will be stored in aws-cloudtrail-logs-289747018327-9efe9113/AWSLogs/289747018327

Log file SSE-KMS encryption   Info
☑ Enabled

○ New
○ Existing

AWS KMS alias

Enter KMS alias

KMS key and S3 bucket must be in the same region.

▼ **Additional settings**

Log file validation   Info
☑ Enabled

SNS notification delivery   Info
☐ Enabled

FIGURE 8.5   CloudTrail Management events, read/write

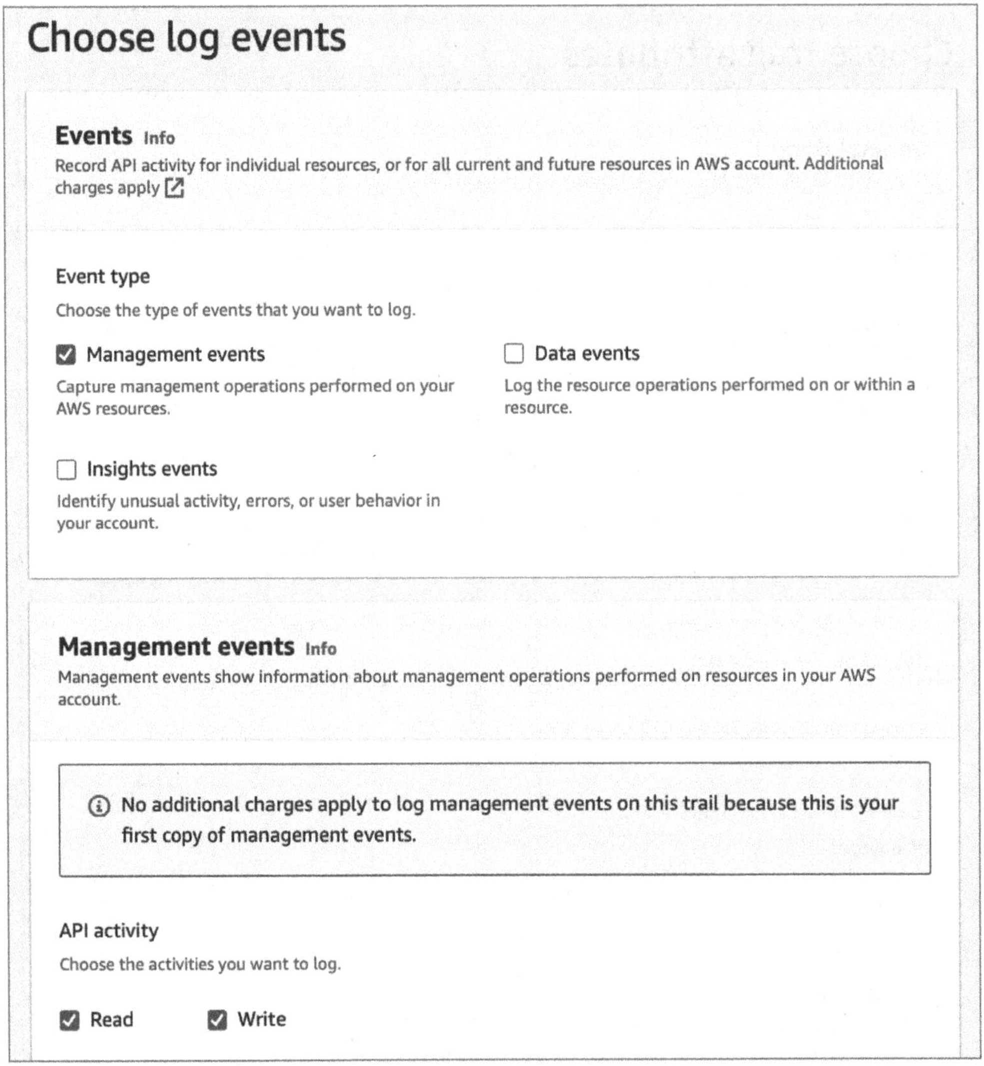

Choose log events

Events Info

Record API activity for individual resources, or for all current and future resources in AWS account. Additional charges apply ↗

Event type

Choose the type of events that you want to log.

☑ **Management events**

Capture management operations performed on your AWS resources.

☐ **Data events**

Log the resource operations performed on or within a resource.

☐ **Insights events**

Identify unusual activity, errors, or user behavior in your account.

Management events Info

Management events show information about management operations performed on resources in your AWS account.

> ⓘ No additional charges apply to log management events on this trail because this is your first copy of management events.

API activity

Choose the activities you want to log.

☑ **Read**   ☑ **Write**

You can also log events from AWS Lambda. You can select specific functions to monitor, or you can choose to monitor all functions. Typical activity for AWS Lambda might include the use of Invoke to kick off a Lambda function. You have the option to monitor your current region or all regions for Lambda events, shown in Figure 8.7.

You can also log events from DynamoDB. You can select read or write for data events to log. You can also select an individual table to monitor, as shown in Figure 8.8.

FIGURE 8.6 You can choose to log read activities, write activities, or both for S3 bucket data events.

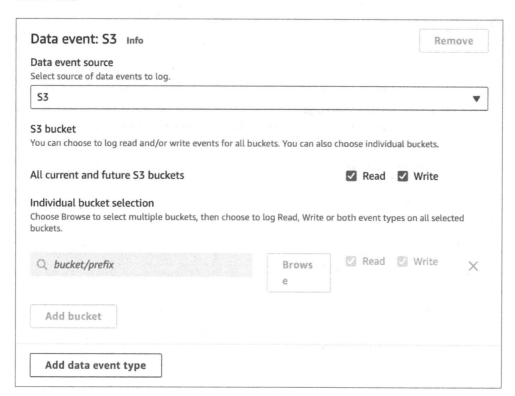

Please note that you have two event selectors: a basic and an advanced event selector. The basic selector targets S3, Lambda, and DynamoDB. The advanced data event selector provides you with fine-grained control over the data events captured by the trail and expands the data event type options. (The advanced selector option is not shown for DynamoDB in Figure 8.8.) For example, SNS and SQS are included in the advanced event selector.

But You Said CloudTrail Was Free . . .

If you are using the default setup for CloudTrail, you will get a history of management events as long as they are related to create, modify, or delete operations. This is completely free. If you create your own trail, the first copy of any management events in each region is free. However, you must pay for the usage of the S3 bucket that they are stored in. You are also charged for additional copies of management events and data events.

FIGURE 8.7   You can choose to log activity for one or more AWS Lambda data events.

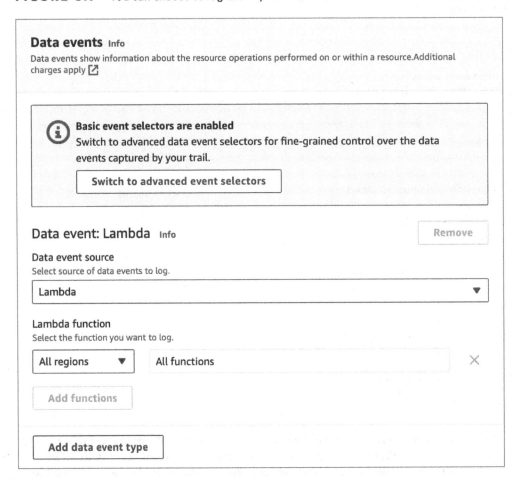

API Logs Are Trails of Data

The cloud strongly favors decoupled and distributed architectures. This means that you don't want your web servers, business logic, and database servers all existing on a single piece of hardware (even if that hardware is purely virtual, as in AWS). It's far more typical—and a better idea for scaling and performance—to separate these components and have them communicate over internal networks. Whether or not you realize it, good application design is all about a set of components that communicate via APIs.

Just as your custom applications can publish APIs, all of AWS's managed services provide APIs. RDS publishes an API. EC2 instances publish metadata through an API, and the Elastic Container Service (ECS) is API-based, just to name a few. That means that even in simpler

FIGURE 8.8   You can choose to log activity for one or more DynamoDB data events.

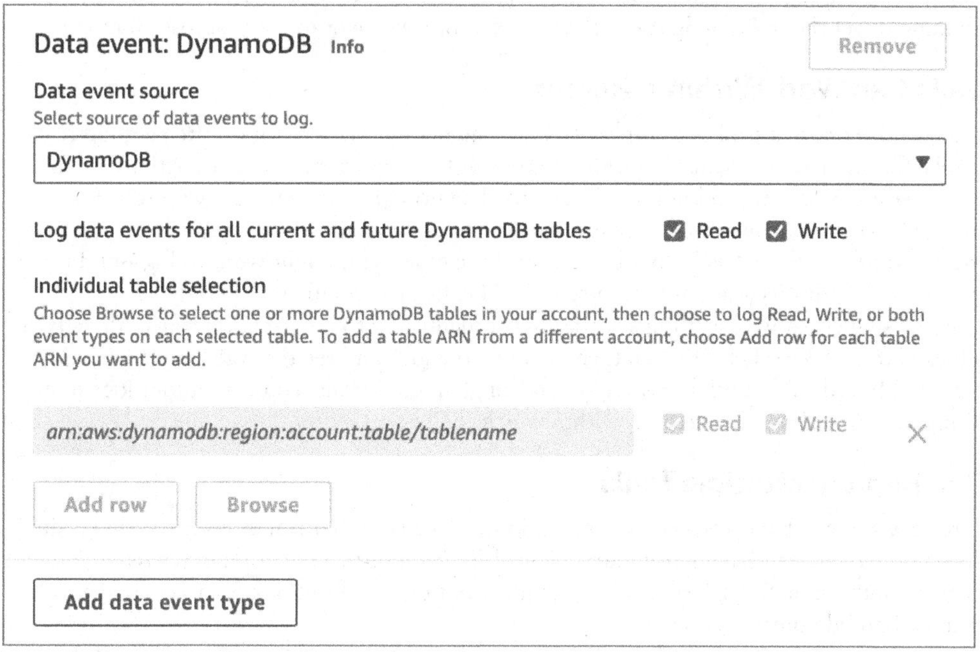

Data event: DynamoDB   Info   Remove

Data event source
Select source of data events to log.

DynamoDB   ▼

Log data events for all current and future DynamoDB tables   ☑ Read ☑ Write

Individual table selection
Choose Browse to select one or more DynamoDB tables in your account, then choose to log Read, Write, or both
event types on each selected table. To add a table ARN from a different account, choose Add row for each table
ARN you want to add.

arn:aws:dynamodb:region:account:table/tablename   ☑ Read ☑ Write   ✕

Add row   Browse

Add data event type

applications, a significant amount of communication is happening between your code and
AWS services.

This communication is what *AWS CloudTrail* is all about. If you can get a handle on this
communication, you'll be able to monitor and react to your application's real-time health
and activity.

What Exactly Is a Trail?

Everything in CloudTrail is based on the concept of trails. A *trail* is just a specific configuration that indicates what events (API calls, inter-resource communication, and so forth) you
want to record and where you want to put the logs of those events. Think of CloudTrail as
having trails and each trail logging a specific event to a specific location. Typically, that location is an S3 bucket.

Trails Can Work Across Regions

There are two types of trails. The first is a trail that applies to all regions. You specify a trail,
and then CloudTrail applies that trail to all regions. The logs still go to an S3 bucket you
choose. Trails apply across all regions by default. All-region trails are ideal because you get a
single configuration that is applied across all your regions consistently. You also get all your

logs from all regions in a single S3 bucket. If you launch resources in a new region, trails that apply to all regions automatically are applied to the new region. You don't have to do anything to get the trail configuration, which is another benefit to trails across all regions.

Trails Can Work Within a Region

You can also create a trail that applies to only one region. There's not as often a good reason to take this approach, because typically if you want to log a certain type of activity in one region, you would want to log it in all regions. The primary use case here would be that you are troubleshooting something very specific—perhaps a certain set of instances are receiving unusual traffic or there has been a breach. In those cases, you might want to log—and log with a lot of verbosity—actions, events, and API calls in a specific region only.

In the single-region case, things work almost identically to cross-region trails. All activity is logged to an S3 bucket. You can then examine the logs and see the trail on your Cloud-Trail dashboard. With both cross-region and single-region trails, you can output logs to any S3 bucket, regardless of the region within which the bucket exists.

One Region, Multiple Trails

In review, you can have a trail across all regions, and a trail that tracks events within a single region. Then, you can have more than one trail for both of these trail types (cross-region and single-region). In fact, that's typical, you might want one trail to track S3 access and another to track Lambda function access.

You also might want multiple trails to report similar things and create variants of the same logs. This is common if you need a trail for developers that logs high-level API usage—for their own performance and improvement tasks—and another more detailed trail tracking the same API usage for security or compliance reasons. AWS allows you to create up to five trails per region, although you can often get this limit raised by contacting AWS support. A trail that works across regions counts as one of the five allowed trails in every region. For example, you could have three cross-region trails and two single-region trails in one region before you hit your limit.

CloudTrail as a Monitoring Tool

Now that you've seen the capturing portion of CloudTrail, it's time to get into actually doing something with the logs it produces. Once you have logs, you can view them, analyze them with a tool like *Amazon Athena*, as well as interpret them and even sound alarms in CloudWatch.

Viewing CloudTrail Logs

CloudTrail places logs in the S3 bucket you specify and does a lot of path-based organization for you. You'll have your bucket name, any prefix you indicated when you set the trail up, and then a folder called AWSLogs. Under this directory, you'll have your AWS account number, then a folder called CloudTrail. From there, logs are organized into more folders: the region, then the year, then the month, and then the date. Within that final folder you'll find actual logs.

For example, a full path to a log might looks like sysops-access/ AWSLogs/860645612347/CloudTrail/us-east-1/2019/01/04. This is a *lot* of navigation, but it makes locating exactly what you want easy (for humans and AWS tools). Individual files have names like 860645612347_CloudTrail_ us-east-1_20181114T1530Z_B8HMwFSVHtT5dEYn.json.gz, which is another mouthful. Logs are GZipped to reduce space; you can unzip them using any standard decompression tool (and most operating systems will handle this automatically as well).

Finally, you can crack open this file and see. . .a lot of information. Here's just a small sample of representative content:

{"Records":[{"eventVersion":"1.05","userIdentity":{"type":"AWSAccount",
"principalId":"","accountId":"ANONYMOUS_PRINCIPAL"},
"eventTime":"2018-11-15T08:06:52Z","eventSource":"s3.amazonaws.com",
"eventName":"HeadObject","awsRegion":"us-east-1",
"sourceIPAddress":"109.86.212.239","userAgent":"[Go-http-client/1.1]",
"requestParameters":{"bucketName":"yellowtagmedia-aws
.com","key":"index.html"},
"responseElements":null,"additionalEventData":{"x-amz-id-2":"q1ANAIW7skRD/
aYAGS927dfjA/27SBRm0fD3WfRHX1YUZgXIaiHmwF6vxpl4RTE096+o+8="},"requestID":
"C56525332834B6C6","eventID":"16a423d1-a9a3-482c-a981-754dd81edc9a",
"readOnly":true,"resources":[{"type":"AWS::S3::Object","ARN":"arn:aws:s3:::
yellowtagmedia-aws.com/index.html"},{"accountId":"860645612347","type":
"AWS::S3::Bucket","ARN":"arn:aws:s3:::yellowtagmedia-aws.com"}],
"eventType":"AwsApiCall","recipientAccountId":"860645612347",
"sharedEventID":"25429b5f-ec72-4b3d-9908-709f31232cb9"}]}

If you're not at all sure what you're looking at, that's okay. There is a lot of useful information here, but for now, just know that every single access of an API generates information like this: the time of the event, information about the event (in this case, access to a static file hosted on an S3 bucket), details about the owner AWS account, and more. All this information is tremendously powerful and useful for monitoring and responding to specific events.

Connect a CloudTrail Trail to SNS

One easy first step in adding some automated monitoring to CloudTrail is to set a trail to notify you via *Amazon SNS* when a trail writes a new log to S3. This is pretty simple, as when you create a trail, you'll have this option available. Just tell CloudTrail to fire off the notification and you're done.

However, keep in mind that with many trails, logs are going to be written to S3 a *lot*—and recall from the previous section how much is captured for every single access. If you're trailing all read access to S3 buckets, for example, and you have buckets that are accessed often, an SNS notification doesn't make sense. You need to be selective about when to send notifications; it can be expensive, and it can create "noise" for administrators and eventually get ignored. Consider a trail that sends out a notification for a security or compliance management event. You would want to be notified only if something abnormal or disallowed occurred.

Exercises

In Exercise 8.3 you set up a trail in AWS CloudTrail.

EXERCISE 8.3

Setting Up a Trail in AWS CloudTrail

In this exercise, we will configure a trail in AWS CloudTrail to monitor for both management and data events.

1. Log into the AWS Management Console and navigate to the CloudTrail page.

2. Click Create Trail.

3. For the trail name, use **SysOpsTrail**.

4. Leave the option "Enable for all accounts in my organization" unchecked.

5. Click Create A New S3 Bucket to create a bucket to store logs for the trail.

6. Make a note of the bucket name. In our example it is
   `aws-cloudtrail-logs-289747018327-4713e77e`.

7. Deselect the Log File SSE-KMS Encryption, Log File Validation, SNS Notification Delivery, and CloudWatch Logs check boxes. Ensure that the Log file SSE-KMS encryption, Log file validation, and SNS notification delivery options are unchecked.

8. Click Next.

9. Under Events, select Management Events and Data Events. Leave Insight Events unchecked.

10. Under Management Events select both the Read and the Write check boxes.

11. Under Data Events, click the basic event selector, and on the S3 tab, select the option All Current And Future S3 Buckets. Ensure that Read and Write are both selected.

12. Click Add Data Event Type and for Data Event Source select Lambda. Then select All Regions and All Functions.

13. Click Next to open the Review And Create page. Verify under Data Events that both S3 and Lambda events configured in the previous steps appear on the page.

14. Click Create Trail. Now you will see your trail in the console under CloudTrail ➤ Trails.

15. Select the trail name to display the trail settings and configuration. You can also delete the trail as well as make it stop logging.

In Exercise 8.4, you set up a CloudWatch alarm.

EXERCISE 8.4

Setting Up a CloudWatch Alarm

This exercise assumes that you have an S3 bucket that can be used. If you do not have an S3 bucket created in your environment, you can easily create one so that you can follow along. We created a bucket called **ahamofomaha**. Keep in mind that bucket names need to be unique globally and not just for the region where the bucket resides.

1. From the AWS Management Console, navigate to the CloudWatch landing page.

2. Under Alarms, select All Alarms and then click Create Alarm.

3. Click Select Metric, select S3, and then click Storage Metrics.

4. Find the bucket you created.

5. You will have two metrics to choose from. Select the NumberOfObjects option.

6. Click Select Metric at the bottom right of the page.

7. On the Specify Metric And Conditions page, do the following:

- Change Statistic to Sum and set Period to 1 Day.

- Under Conditions, set Threshold Type to Static.

- Under Whenever NumberOfObjects Is, choose Greater/Equal and set Than to 2.

- Click Next.

8. Under Configure Action, in the Notification panel choose In Alarm.

9. Under Select An SNS Topic, choose Create New Topic.

10. Add the email address where you want to receive the notification.

11. Click Create Topic. You should see the email listed as an endpoint.

12. Click Next.

EXERCISE 8.4 *(continued)*

13. Name the alarm something that makes sense to you. I called mine **S3ObjectsNumber**. Click Next.

14. On the next screen, if everything looks correct, click Create Alarm.

    Your new alarm should now display INSUFFICIENT_DATA for the state. Assuming you have fewer than two objects in your S3 bucket, it will transition to OK during the next evaluation period. In our case we put 60 objects in the bucket right before, so after displaying INSUFFICIENT_DATA it jumped to Alarm immediately.

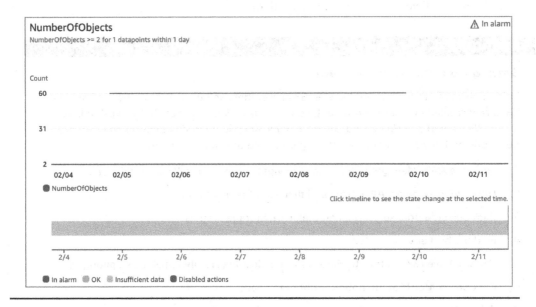

Follow the steps in Exercise 8.5 to set up an Amazon CloudWatch dashboard.

EXERCISE 8.5

Setting Up an Amazon CloudWatch Dashboard

Now that we have our S3 object alarm, let's create a new dashboard and add the alarm to the dashboard.

1. In the CloudWatch console, click Dashboards.

2. Click Create Dashboard.

3. Name the dashboard **My-Awesome-Dashboard**.

4. On the widget configuration, select Metrics and the Line widget type. Click Next.

   Now let's add the alarm that we created.

5. Click Alarms, and then select the check box next to the alarm you created earlier.

6. Choose Add To Dashboard from the Actions menu.

7. Click Save Dashboard.

Now if you go back to your dashboard, you'll see your alarm. This is a simple example, of course, but it gives you a general idea of how to create dashboards and customize their content.

Configure a rule in AWS Config by following the steps in Exercise 8.6.

EXERCISE 8.6

Configuring a Rule in AWS Config

To close this section of the chapter, we will set up AWS Config.

1. In the AWS Management Console, click Services and then choose Config under Management & Governance.

2. Under Settings, ensure that the recorder is on. Also, verify the recording method is set to Record All Resource Types.

3. Verify that the delivery method has an S3 bucket name designated.

4. Select Rules from the left column and click Add Rule on the right.

5. Under AWS Config Rules, select Add AWS Managed Rule, type **cloudtrail** in the search box, and click Cloudtrail-Enabled.

6. Click Next, then click Next again and click Save.

As simple as that, you've created your first rule, and you can evaluate your AWS environment against it. Hundreds of rules are available to you within AWS Config, and we recommend looking through them to find the ones you are most interested in. The following image shows you what a noncompliant resource will look like.

Compliance status

Rules

⚠ 59 Noncompliant rule(s)
⊘ 49 Compliant rule(s)

Resources

⚠ 100+ Noncompliant resource(s)
⊘ 100+ Compliant resource(s)

Noncompliant rules by noncompliant resource count

Name	Compliance
securityhub-s3-bucket-versio...	⚠ 25+ Noncompliant resource(s)
securityhub-s3-bucket-mfa-d...	⚠ 25+ Noncompliant resource(s)
securityhub-s3-bucket-defau...	⚠ 25+ Noncompliant resource(s)
securityhub-s3-default-encry...	⚠ 25+ Noncompliant resource(s)
securityhub-s3-bucket-replic...	⚠ 25+ Noncompliant resource(s)

View all noncompliant rules

AWS Config

AWS Config, like AWS Organizations, doesn't provide functionality that is unique or novel to the cloud. Instead, it addresses a common need of the SysOps administrator: configuration management. Configuration management is a process—and in this case, a tool-based one—for managing the resources and services in place within an environment. In the AWS context, those resources and services are the instances, containers, databases, queues, and other pieces of your applications.

There are some best-of-breed options for configuration management in on-premises enterprise applications, and this chapter addresses those tools and their role in a system. You'll also learn how those tools translate to AWS and how the terms about which they're concerned slightly change meaning in a cloud environment. Finally, you'll see how rules and configuration items are the key components of AWS Config and the AWS approach to configuration management.

This section covers:

- The role of configuration management in an enterprise application
- The differences in on-premises configuration management and cloud configuration management
- The use cases for which AWS Config was created and how each is handled by AWS Config
- Rules and triggers within AWS Config
- Configuration items and their relationship to the resources to which they refer

Managing Configuration Changes

Believe it or not, there was once a time where an "application" was a single server, with software providing web, business logic, and database services. High availability meant having *two* of those servers, networked together. And in *really* large enterprises, there might be a load balancer (or even two!) tying things together.

Of course, that sounds like the dark ages of computing now. It's commonplace to find multiple web servers (each with dedicated hardware, or at least large virtualized machines), application servers, database servers, sharding, and caching on additional virtualized hardware, load balancers, logging, and monitoring. Each component is often redundant, meaning duplicate hardware—physical or virtual—and each component has complex configuration. Rarely is anything run "out of the box" anymore.

The result? A lot of setup and configuration going into a running application. Worse, this configuration needs to be kept in sync; if one web server changes configuration to deal with a new security patch or subnet, all the web servers need the same changes. The same is true of database servers, load balancers, SMS gateways . . . and the list goes on.

For you, the SysOps administrator, this is quite literally a worst-case situation. In addition to all the running machines, you now have a configuration problem. You have to keep all these systems in sync, updated with the latest software (within whatever margin your organization deems acceptable), and running in accordance with your security, network, compliance, and usage policies.

This is the world of configuration management, the process for establishing and maintaining consistency in the systems you manage. You've got to keep these systems performing well and patched, and you have to make sure that web server A looks the same as web servers B and C (except in the case where you explicitly want two servers to be distinct from each other).

Configuration in the Cloud

If you don't have an existing configuration management solution, or you're building in the cloud as your initial platform, you're going to need a configuration management solution. This is where AWS Config comes in; it provides an AWS-native option that doesn't require a lot of previous configuration management experience. AWS Config gives you continuous monitoring and continuous assessment, as well as all the change management and trouble-shooting that comes with these facilities. AWS Config also provides this functionality across accounts and regions. AWS Config is available globally but is enabled on a per-region basis. This allows you to manage costs associated with resource configuration management more granularly.

AWS Config Use Cases

So far, configuration management has been treated as a sort of cluster of functionality: main-taining valid configuration, ensuring compliance, providing a level of security, and more. However, in your role as a SysOps administrator, and in some cases on the exam, you should be able to differentiate between these various pieces of configuration management and understand how each is part of AWS Config's capabilities.

Centralized Configuration Management

First and foremost, AWS Config provides configuration management of all your AWS resources in a single place. This is true across accounts as well.

 Some SysOps administrators will use the management account for an organization in AWS Organizations as the account to which configuration data is aggregated. This approach typically isn't a great idea, though, because this monitoring account will grow. You could easily end up with AWS Config, CloudWatch, CloudTrail, and more. Consider creating an account specifically for your monitoring needs and locking that account down via IAM to yourself and other SysOps administrators.

Audit Trails

AWS Config also provides help with auditing needs. Though it's typical to think of audit-ing in the same breath as AWS CloudTrail, AWS Config is also a help here. Because AWS treats configuration as code and stores historical configuration data, you have the full resource configuration history of your environment. You can even correlate these changes with the logs that AWS CloudTrail provides to show a complete event-driven history of your resources and their configuration changes. Not only do you then know when a resource was changed, but you also have a history of who made the change, from where was the change made, and more.

Configuration as Security

As we've already mentioned, configuration history provides a layer of security that goes beyond the real-time access to your systems. IAM users and roles tend to provide the broadest access to a privileged set of users. Those users are going to be your most experienced operators as well. Unfortunately, that means that if something goes wrong, it's typical that your best engineers are the ones who are most likely to be blamed. However, things go a lot better if you're able to provide an IP address from which a change was made, a time, exactly what the change was, and to how many resources. That sort of clarity in dealing with an unauthorized change can help you isolate a breach—or perhaps an inadvertent change—and remediate quickly.

AWS Config Rules and Responses

Once you understand how AWS Config is used, you must get a handle on how to put rules in place, evaluate those rules, and potentially take remediation action. Fortunately, AWS Config is extremely straightforward, and the rules it provides will cover the majority of your needs.

Rules Are Desired Configurations

A *rule* in AWS Config is simply a desired configuration for a resource. It can describe a specific value, or a set of values, that a property can take. You should think of a rule not as a desired state, but as an allowed state. In other words, a rule being broken meaning something is wrong or incorrect, not just suboptimal.

A configuration item represents a specific configuration. A rule evaluates a resource's configuration at a given point in time. The resource itself provides configuration information through configuration items. A *configuration item (CI)* is an attribute and value (or values) for that attribute, reported against a specific resource. A configuration item includes several key pieces of information, such as the metadata, resource attributes, relationships, and the current configuration of the resource.

Rules Are Evaluated

When you write a rule, AWS Config evaluates the values reported in configuration item attributes against the rule. If the value doesn't match, then the rule is considered broken and the configuration is reported as noncompliant. A notification is then sent, and your AWS Config dashboard will report the noncompliant item.

AWS Provides Prebuilt Rules

AWS supplies you with hundreds of prebuilt rules that can be applied to your resources. For example, Figure 8.9 shows the variety of rules that were available from starting up AWS Config in a very simple account with only a few instances, S3 buckets, static website hosting, and DNS entries. Of course, many of these rules are for "always on" AWS services like CloudWatch and CloudTrail, as well as the various AWS developer tools like CodeDeploy and CodePipeline. Still, this should get you started quickly, and you can avoid having to write custom code just to get basic configuration management in place.

FIGURE 8.9 AWS Config comes with a number of prebuilt rules.

	Name	Remediation ...	Type	Enabled evaluatio...	Detective compliance
○	s3-bucket-versioning-enabled	AWS-Configu...	AWS managed	DETECTIVE	⚠ 25+ Noncomplian...
○	encrypted-volumes	Not set	AWS managed	DETECTIVE	-
○	rds-multi-az-support	Not set	AWS managed	DETECTIVE	-
○	ebs-optimized-instance	Not set	AWS managed	DETECTIVE	-
⊛	securityhub-acm-certificate-expira...	Not set	AWS managed	DETECTIVE	-
⊛	securityhub-access-keys-rotated-9...	Not set	AWS managed	DETECTIVE	⚠ 3 Noncompliant r...
○	ec2-instance-detailed-monitoring-...	Not set	AWS managed	DETECTIVE	-
○	acm-certificate-expiration-check	Not set	AWS managed	DETECTIVE	-
○	db-instance-backup-enabled	Not set	AWS managed	DETECTIVE	-
○	ec2-instances-in-vpc	Not set	AWS managed	DETECTIVE	-
○	restricted-ssh	Not set	AWS managed	DETECTIVE	⚠ 1 Noncompliant r...
○	ec2-imdsv2-check	AWSConfigRe...	AWS managed	DETECTIVE	-
○	iam-user-group-membership-check	Not set	AWS managed	DETECTIVE	⊘ Compliant
○	dynamodb-throughput-limit-check	Not set	AWS managed	DETECTIVE	⊘ Compliant
○	iam-user-no-policies-check	Not set	AWS managed	DETECTIVE	⊘ Compliant
○	iam-password-policy	Not set	AWS managed	DETECTIVE	⚠ 1 Noncompliant r...
○	rds-storage-encrypted	Not set	AWS managed	DETECTIVE	-

Rules

Filter by compliance status
All ▼

〈 1 2 ... 〉 ⚙

You Can Write Your Own Rules

In the event that AWS's rules don't meet your needs, you can write your own. There are three general types of rules. AWS Managed rules are used as is or customized to suit your needs. You can also create a custom Lambda function and add them to AWS Config. You associate each custom rule with a Lambda function containing the logic that evaluates whether your AWS resources comply with the rule. Finally, you can create a custom rule using Cloud Formation Guard. This allows you to create custom rules using a Guard custom policy that evaluates whether your AWS resources comply with the rule.

Trigger Evaluation in Two Ways

You have a rule and AWS Config is reporting via configuration items. What triggers the evaluation? You have two choices. You can turn on proactive evaluation to enable evaluation of resources prior to provisioning. You can also turn on detective evaluation, which enables evaluation of resources that have been provisioned. After selecting the evaluation mode, you define the trigger type. AWS Config can evaluate resources when configuration changes to your specified resources, or you can use the Periodic option, which runs on the frequency that you choose:

Configuration Change Triggers   Set AWS Config to evaluate rules any time a configuration change on a resource is reported.

Periodic Triggers   Set AWS Config to evaluate rules on a specific frequency. You can set this frequency to 1 hour, 3 hours, 6 hours, 12 hours, or 24 hours.

For change triggers specifically, you can choose when evaluations occur. You can select All Changes, which triggers when any resource recorded is created, changed, or deleted. You can also trigger evaluation when any resource that matches the specified type is created, changed, or deleted. Finally, you can trigger evaluation based on tags—when any resource with the specified tag is created, changed, or deleted.

You may want to use a combination of both of these approaches. It's common to have change triggers and then add to that a periodic check for compliance and reporting.

Figure 8.10 shows the console for evaluation mode and trigger type configurations.

FIGURE 8.10   AWS Config Evaluation Mode window

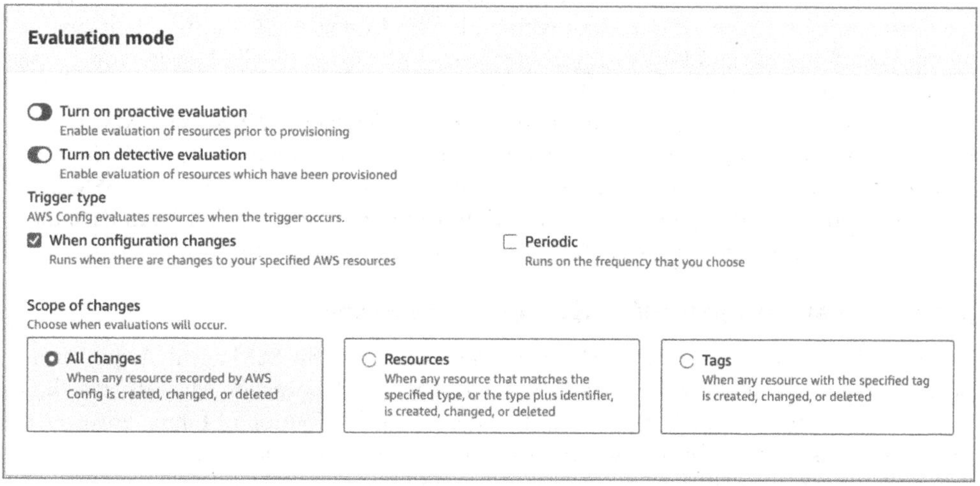

Evaluation mode

◯ Turn on proactive evaluation
   Enable evaluation of resources prior to provisioning
◉ Turn on detective evaluation
   Enable evaluation of resources which have been provisioned

Trigger type
AWS Config evaluates resources when the trigger occurs.

☑ **When configuration changes**
   Runs when there are changes to your specified AWS resources

☐ **Periodic**
   Runs on the frequency that you choose

Scope of changes
Choose when evaluations will occur.

◉ All changes	◯ Resources	◯ Tags
When any resource recorded by AWS Config is created, changed, or deleted	When any resource that matches the specified type, or the type plus identifier, is created, changed, or deleted	When any resource with the specified tag is created, changed, or deleted

AWS Systems Manager

For most SysOps administrators, the challenge in their day-to-day work is not in building servers but in maintaining them. As organizations put more emphasis on keeping their systems secure, it is that much more crucial to keep systems up-to-date on patches and to keep an eye on the overall state of your infrastructure.

AWS Systems Manager gives you the ability to centrally manage, install, update, and configure software for your AWS systems and on-premises systems in addition to some other useful administrative features that will be covered in this chapter.

This section includes:

- How AWS Systems Manager works

- Managing EC2 instances with AWS Systems Manager

- Creating documents in AWS Systems Manager

- Using the Insights Dashboard

- Patching your systems with AWS Systems Manager

- Storing secrets and configurations with AWS Systems Manager

- Connecting to your EC2 instances—no SSH or RDP required

AWS Systems Manager

AWS Systems Manager (SSM) is a free service offered by AWS that provides patching automation, software inventory, and software installation and configuration. It allows you to group systems logically, and it integrates with both AWS Config and CloudWatch. It can monitor both Windows and Linux operating systems by utilizing the *SSM agent*. You can see the AWS Systems Manager console in Figure 8.11.

The SSM agent must be installed on the systems that you want AWS Systems Manager to monitor, install, configure, and update software on. If you choose one of the Windows or Amazon Linux Amazon Machine Images (AMIs) in the Amazon Marketplace, the SSM agent is already installed. Other operating systems in AWS and on-premises will need to have the agent installed before you can use AWS Systems Manager to administer them.

Communication with AWS Systems Manager

To communicate with AWS Systems Manager, you must install the SSM agent. As just mentioned, for the recent Windows and Amazon Linux AMIs in the Amazon Marketplace, the SSM agent is already installed. If you want to use another distribution of Linux, however, or if you want to use a non-AMI image, you will have to install the agent first.

Once the agent is installed on the system, create an Identity and Access Management (IAM) role that will allow the Amazon EC2 instance to communicate with SSM. When you create the role, you need only attach one policy to the role, the AmazonEC2RoleforSSM policy. Once the role has been created with this policy, and the role has been attached to an

EC2 instance, you will be able to manage it with AWS Systems Manager. Remember that you can use AWS Systems Manager for your AWS resources and on-premises systems. The examples in this chapter will focus on using it to manage Amazon EC2 instances.

FIGURE 8.11   The AWS Systems Manager Console is where you will configure the Systems Manager services.

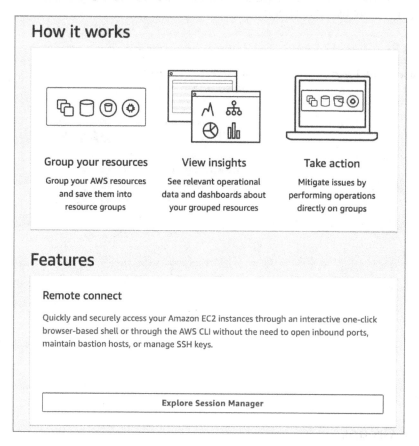

How it works

Group your resources

Group your AWS resources and save them into resource groups

View insights

See relevant operational data and dashboards about your grouped resources

Take action

Mitigate issues by performing operations directly on groups

Features

Remote connect

Quickly and securely access your Amazon EC2 instances through an interactive one-click browser-based shell or through the AWS CLI without the need to open inbound ports, maintain bastion hosts, or manage SSH keys.

Explore Session Manager

AWS Managed Instances

When looking at AWS Systems Manager, a *managed instance* is an Amazon EC2 instance or an on-premises server that is being managed by AWS Systems Manager. This means that it has the SSM agent installed, the role that grants needed access is attached, and it will be visible within the AWS Systems Manager console. Managed instances can be both physical servers or virtual servers and can even be located with another cloud provider.

Once your systems are managed, it is useful to create an inventory of the systems. You can default to selecting all of the managed instances that are in your account, you can select EC2 instances based on tags, or you can manually select systems. The inventory gathers information about current software versions on the managed instances and is a first and very powerful step toward centrally managing your instances. You can configure the inventory by clicking Inventory in the AWS Systems Manager console, shown in Figure 8.12.

FIGURE 8.12 The Inventory screen in AWS Systems Manager provides insights into what types of components are being monitored.

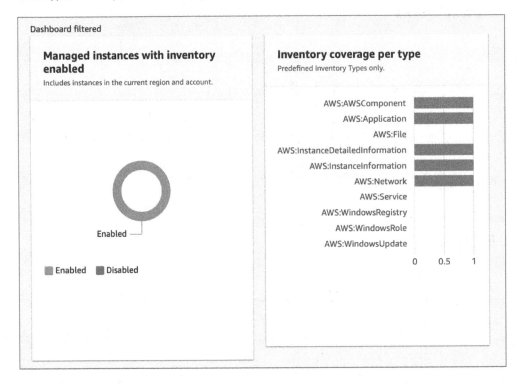

AWS Resource Groups

One of the stellar integrations with AWS Systems Manager is AWS resource groups. By using AWS resource groups, you can logically group your systems, which can simplify management. Systems can be in more than one group, and they can be used for everything from software installation and patching to better monitoring and reporting. For instance, you might create a resource group based on whether a system is Production or Development, or by application, or maybe even by department if you are using tags.

You can execute documents, discussed in the next section, against specific resource groups. Think of a situation where you had to ensure that you patched only the Development systems in your environment and not the Production. You could use an AWS resource group to query for all systems with a tag of Environment:Dev and then execute a document that installs patches against that resource group. AWS resource groups are created on a per-region basis, so if you have resources in more than one region, you will need to create the AWS resource groups in each region.

Taking Action with AWS Systems Manager

AWS Systems Manager uses *documents* to allow you to use configuration as code. Quite a few documents are available from Amazon, and you can also create your own using either JavaScript Object Notation (JSON) or YAML Ain't Markup Language (YAML). Documents can do everything from running commands like installing software from a repository on a Linux box to ensuring a desired configuration state. Documents can be used on both Windows and Linux, though compatibility may depend on what you are asking the document to do. For instance, a script that is being used to install Apache (httpd) with apt on Linux would not work on a Windows system.

There are multiple types of documents that you can use within AWS. Each type has a specific purpose in mind:

Command Document   A document that is meant to be used with the Run command or State Manager (which is part of AWS Systems Manager). Maintenance windows can also take advantage of command documents to apply desired configurations on a schedule that you set.

Policy Document   A document that is meant to be used with State Manager and is used to enforce your policies on the systems that you are targeting within AWS Systems Manager.

Automation Document   A document that is meant to be used for automation and that can also be utilized by State Manager, as well as by maintenance tasks during scheduled maintenance windows.

Session Document   A document that is meant to be used with Session Manager.

Conformance Pack Template Document   A document meant to be used for defining conformance packs used by AWS Config.

Run Command

The Run command uses command documents to execute actions against one or more managed EC2 instances. You can use it to run commands like ls to gather information on a Linux system or dir on a Windows system, or to install software. For instance, I can use a command document to install the Apache web server on my Linux web servers with the Run command.

Patch Manager

The *Patch Manager* is the component of AWS Systems Manager that allows you to patch whole fleets of EC2 instances and on-premises systems automatically. You can patch operating systems as well as the applications that are installed on those systems.

Using maintenance tasks, you can schedule the installation of patches to install only approved patches during a maintenance window. AWS Systems Manager uses *patch baselines*, which list all approved and rejected patches and can contain rules that can automatically approve patches after they have been out for a certain number of days. Why would you want to automatically approve patches? This automates your patching process so that you need to intervene only if there is a patch that is known to cause issues. Think of how much time you could save using SSM Patch Manager to automate patches to be approved and then installed with your AWS and on-premises systems.

For some systems, of course, automatic patching may not be appropriate. For instance, applications that rely on a very specific version of .NET Framework could break if you update the .NET Framework on them, so this is a type of patch that you would not want to automatically approve. Regarding Patch Manager, use your best judgment and your knowledge of the application to determine whether automatic patching is the best option.

Parameter Store

For many organizations, one of the challenges in implementing automation is how to safely store the secrets used for authentication purposes. The *Parameter Store* provides the ability to not only securely store or call secrets (think passwords and certificates), but also store items like database strings and license codes. Did a change occur and now the new secret doesn't work properly? The Parameter Store also includes the ability to use versioning, which allows you to retrieve the old password. All of this can be called by tasks running within AWS Systems Manager. It should be noted that the use of the Parameter Store is free. Parameter Store supports Amazon EC2, Amazon ECS, AWS Lambda, AWS CodeBuild, AWS CodeDeploy, and Amazon CloudFormation.

Session Manager

Remote access to your Amazon EC2 instances can be a security hole if not implemented properly. Windows servers, for instance, need Remote Desktop Protocol (RDP) open if you want to connect to their consoles, and Linux servers need Secure Shell (SSH). One small misconfiguration could open your systems up to the world. This is where Session Manager comes in.

Session Manager allows you to connect remotely to your Amazon EC2 managed instances with no exceptions needed in the security group for that remote access. This feature is currently available for all Amazon EC2 managed instances. The Session Manager Console lists all of your managed instances, similar to what is shown in Figure 8.13. Actions performed with Session Manager can optionally be logged to S3 and/or CloudWatch, and you can also choose to leverage AWS KMS to encrypt session data.

FIGURE 8.13 You can remotely administer your EC2 instances from AWS Session Manager.

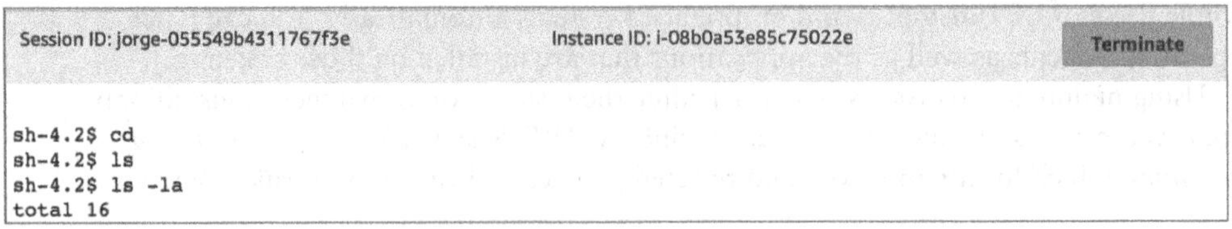

Session ID: jorge-055549b4311767f3e	Instance ID: i-08b0a53e85c75022e	Terminate

```
sh-4.2$ cd
sh-4.2$ ls
sh-4.2$ ls -la
total 16
```

State Manager

State Manager is a compliance tool that allows you to ensure that your instances are running the appropriate versions of software, to define security groups' settings that are permissible, and to join systems to Windows domains or run scripts against Windows and Linux systems.

You create an association that allows State Manager to use documents that define what you want to have happen, set the targets for the documents, and schedule how often you want State Manager to run. If you run the initial inventory job, you will see an association already created in State Manager that uses the `AWS-GatherSoftwareInventory` document.

State Manager will make your security admins very happy, as you can confirm that security applications like antivirus are installed and running the latest versions. It can ensure that systems are joined to a Windows domain and, by extension, receive settings through Group Policy. You can even use State Manager to bootstrap all new instances so that they must download and install all the new security updates right after the OS is installed.

AWS Systems Manager continues to grow in new features and services. It's important to become familiar with its function and operation.

Exercises

These exercises make the assumption that you have the basic networking components set up that will allow systems to communicate with one another. They also assume that you have set up two EC2 instances. Something as simple as launching two instances on the Default VPC's public subnet will work for this example. We are using the Amazon Linux image since it has the SSM agent already installed.

In Exercise 8.7, you create a role for SSM and attach it to your EC2 instances.

EXERCISE 8.7

Creating a Role for SSM and Attaching It to Your EC2 Instances

Before you can manage your EC2 instances, you need to give them permissions to talk to AWS Systems Manager. First, you will need to create a role that the EC2 instance can use.

1. In the AWS Management Console, click Services, then Security, Identity, & Compliance, and then click IAM.

2. Click Roles, then click Create Role.

3. Under Select Type Of Trusted Entity, choose AWS Service.

4. Under Use case, choose EC2. If needed, choose EC2 from the drop-down menu and select the radio button.

5. Click Next: Permissions.

6. In the Filter Policies box, search for **AmazonEC2RoleforSSM**. Click the check box next to it, and then click Next.

7. Click Next:Review.

8. On the Review screen, name your role **EC2toSSM** and then click Create Role.

Now that the role is created, you will need to attach the role to your EC2 instances:

1. In the AWS Management Console, click Services and then click EC2.

2. Choose Instances from the Navigation menu to view your EC2 instances.

3. Click the check box next to one of your EC2 instances, click the Actions button, choose Security, and then click Modify IAM Role.

4. Click the IAM Role drop-down box and select the EC2toSSM role that you created earlier, shown in the next figure.

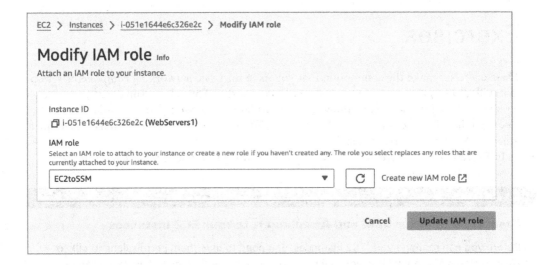

5. Click Update IAM Role.

Repeat the steps for any other EC2 instances you have that you want to manage with AWS Systems Manager.

Tag your EC2 instances by following the steps in Exercise 8.8.

EXERCISE 8.8

Tagging Your EC2 Instances

Tagging your EC2 instances allows you to target them together for use with resource groups, the Run command, the Inventory screen, and so forth. Tags should be used to group like systems.

1. On the EC2 Dashboard, select Instances.

2. Click the check box next to your EC2 instance, click Actions, choose Instance Settings, and then click Manage Tags.

3. Click Add New Tag. For Key, type **Env** and for Value, type **Prod**.

4. Click Save.

Repeat steps 2–4 for all of your EC2 instances that you want to manage with AWS Systems Manager.

Follow the steps in Exercise 8.9 to set up your resource groups based on tags.

EXERCISE 8.9

Setting Up Your Resource Groups Based on Tags

The resource group can be used for patching, among other things. Separating out Prod from Dev systems, for instance, is an excellent use of a resource group.

1. On the AWS Management Console, use the search bar to go to **Resource Groups & Tag Editor**. You will see any saved resource groups.

2. Click Create A Resource Group.

3. For Group Type, select Tag Based.

4. For Grouping Criteria, click the Resource Types drop-down box and select AWS::EC2::Instance.

5. Type **Env** in the Tags field, and type **Prod** in the Value field. Click Add.

6. In the Group Details panel, enter a name for the resource group. I will use **Prod-EC2-Instances**.

7. Click Create Group.

Once the resource group has been created, your screen will show the details of the resource group and you should see your two instances listed under Group Resources, similar to the following image.

EXERCISE 8.9 *(continued)*

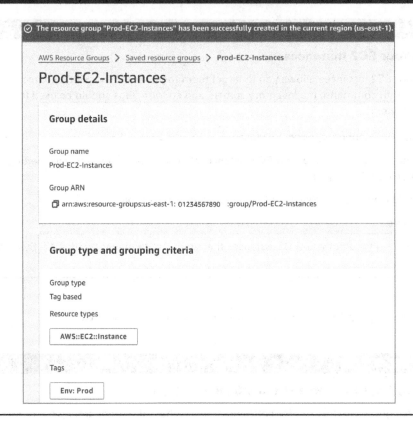

⊘ The resource group "Prod-EC2-Instances" has been successfully created in the current region (us-east-1).

AWS Resource Groups > Saved resource groups > Prod-EC2-Instances

Prod-EC2-Instances

Group details

Group name
Prod-EC2-Instances

Group ARN
arn:aws:resource-groups:us-east-1: 01234567890 :group/Prod-EC2-Instances

Group type and grouping criteria

Group type
Tag based

Resource types

AWS::EC2::Instance

Tags

Env: Prod

In Exercise 8.10, you use the Run command to install Apache on web servers.

EXERCISE 8.10

Using the *Run* Command to Install Apache on Web Servers

Being able to install software without having to log into individual systems is a huge time-saver for most SysOps admins. In this exercise, you'll install Apache on an Amazon Linux EC2 instance.

1. In the AWS Systems Manager Console, navigate to Systems Manager and select Run Command under Node Management.

2. Click Run Command.

3. Select the radio button next to AWS-RunShellScript.

4. Scroll down to Command Parameters, and type the following commands:

```
sudo yum update -y
sudo yum install -y httpd
sudo service httpd start
```

5. Scroll down to Targets, and choose Manually Selecting Instances. Click the check box next to the system you want to do the installation on.

6. Under Output Options, deselect Enable Writing To An S3 Bucket.

7. Click Run.

When installation is successful, the instances you selected will say Success under Overall Status, as in the next image.

Command status

Overall status
⊘ Success

Detailed status
⊘ Success

targets
1

completed
1

error
0

delivery timed out
0

Create a parameter for a license key by following the steps in Exercise 8.11.

EXERCISE 8.11

Creating a Parameter for a License Key

Creating a parameter for a license key allows you to call the parameter when installing software so that the license key can be applied automatically.

1. In the AWS Systems Manager Console, select Parameter Store.

2. Click Create Parameter.

EXERCISE 8.11 *(continued)*

3. For Name, enter **LicenseKey_MyApp**.

4. For Tier, select Standard.

5. Under Type, select String.

6. Enter a string of characters in the Value box; it doesn't matter for this exercise what it is. In a production environment, this would be your actual license key.

7. Click Create Parameter.

Connect to your EC2 instance with Session Manager by following the steps in Exercise 8.12.

EXERCISE 8.12

Connecting to Your EC2 Instance with Session Manager

Connecting to your systems via Session Manager is an excellent way to enable administration without opening up holes in your security groups.

1. In the AWS Systems Manager Console, click Session Manager.

2. Click the Start Session button.

3. Select the radio button next to the instance you want to connect to and click Start Session, shown next.

Your remote session through AWS Session Manager will open to the Linux or Windows console.

Summary

CloudWatch is a far-reaching tool. Although it's simple enough to say, "CloudWatch is the AWS solution for monitoring," there's much more than that to learn and ultimately master. You need a working knowledge of the various functionality that CloudWatch provides, as well as an understanding of the metrics that AWS provides by default. Much of your work with CloudWatch will involve assembling and interpreting these defaults. Finally, all of this comes together in dashboards and reporting. AWS makes dashboards and reporting easy, and you should be familiar with grouping resources through resource groups and then building dashboards for easy review. A metric that takes more than a few seconds to locate and understand probably isn't that valuable a metric.

Like AWS Organizations and AWS Config, AWS CloudTrail isn't particularly complicated. Once you get the basics of how terminology is used and a handle on how trails are processed, it's pretty straightforward. The power in CloudTrail isn't its complexity, though. It's that it—especially along CloudWatch, AWS Organizations, and AWS Config—gives you a more complete picture of your AWS environment and the applications running within that environment.

For the exam, just make sure you understand the basics of trails, that CloudTrail is usually the right tool when it comes to API calls or resource-to-resource communication, and the difference between CloudTrail's log and other system logging. Get those down and you should have no issues.

AWS Config provides a simple, useful framework for ensuring that things don't change unless you *intend* for them to change. If all AWS Config did was provide you with triggers for notification when an instance changes, it would be a helpful service. Add to that rules, periodic triggers, configuration instances, and the ability to monitor managed services like RDS as well as more change-prone ones like EC2, and you've got a pretty powerful tool. While it's true that AWS Config likely will appear on only a few questions on your certification exam, it's still well worth learning to be an effective SysOps administrator.

AWS Systems Manager allows you to perform maintenance tasks such as patching, application updates, and policy enforcements on your AWS and on-premises systems. With the Run command, you can run commands against one or more AWS resources, making configuration a breeze. Using Patch Manager, you can ensure that your systems are patched automatically according to schedules that you define. The Parameter Store makes storing secrets, license keys, and so forth secure and simple, and it integrates seamlessly with a large number of AWS services. Session Manager allows you to remotely administer your systems from their consoles without having to open any ports to the outside world. Finally, State Manager provides a simple method for SysOps administrators to ensure that their systems are compliant with organizational standards related to configuration and software installation.

Exam Essentials

Recognize use cases for which CloudWatch is well suited.   CloudWatch is a monitoring service, and it's going to be your first line of defense in troubleshooting. You'll collect and track metrics and set alarms, from simple metrics such as CPU usage to application-tuned custom ones that you define.

Recite the core components of a CloudWatch event.   An event in CloudWatch has the event itself, a target, and a rule. Events indicate changes in your environment, targets process events, and rules match events and route them to targets. Get these three concepts straight, and you'll be set to handle the more conceptual exam questions.

Recognize names of CloudWatch metrics.   You will be asked about default AWS monitoring—CPU, status, disk, network, but *not* memory—and about the various metric names. Although memorizing all of them is tough, you should review AWS-defined metric names before taking the exam.

Explain how a CloudWatch alarm works.   An alarm is a construct that watches a metric and is triggered at certain thresholds. This alarm can then itself trigger actions, such as an Auto Scaling group scaling out or perhaps a Lambda function running. You should be able to describe this process and recognize its usefulness.

List and explain the three CloudWatch alarm states.   An alarm can be in three states: OK, ALARM, and INSUFFICIENT_DATA. OK means the metric is within the defined threshold; ALARM means the alarm is "going off" because the metric is outside or has crossed the defined threshold. INSUFFICIENT_DATA should be obvious: There's not enough to report yet.

Create custom metrics for anything above the hypervisor.   It's subtle, but important: CloudWatch knows nothing about specific tasks that are affecting performance, because applications all live above the AWS virtualization layer. This is why CloudWatch doesn't provide a memory metric that lives above the hypervisor. You can create custom metrics, but they'll require an agent, and they will be more limited than metrics that can interact below that virtualization layer.

Differentiate between CloudWatch, CloudTrail, and AWS Config.   In a nutshell, CloudWatch is for real-time performance and health monitoring of your environment. CloudTrail monitors API logs and events within your AWS environment. AWS Config monitors the configuration of your environment. All three provide compliance, auditing, and security.

Describe the two types of trails: cross-region and single-region.   A cross-region trail functions in all regions of your account. All logs are then placed in a single S3 bucket. A single-region trail applies to one region only and can place logs in any S3 bucket, regardless of that bucket's region.

Explain how cross-region trails automatically function in new regions.   A cross-region trail will automatically begin capturing activity in any new region that is stood up in an environment without any user intervention. Logs for new activity are placed in the same S3 bucket as logs for existing regions and aggregated in seamlessly.

Describe the best practices for acting on and reviewing CloudTrail logs.   It is not enough to simply turn on CloudTrail and create a few trails. You should set up CloudWatch alarms related to those trails and potentially send events out via SNS. You should also be continually reviewing logs via a CloudWatch (not CloudTrail!) dashboard that has alarms connected to your CloudTrail logs in S3. Further, you may want to consider using a tool like Amazon Athena for deeper analysis of large log file stores.

Explain the use of AWS Config in monitoring, especially as compared to CloudWatch and CloudTrail.   CloudWatch monitors the status of running applications. CloudTrail logs and provides audit trails, especially for API calls. AWS Config is distinct from both of these as it is concerned with the configuration of resources, rather than their runtime state. Anything that affects the setup of a resource and its interaction with other AWS resources is largely under this umbrella.

List the benefits of AWS Config.   AWS Config provides centralized configuration management without requiring third-party tools. It also provides configuration audit trails, a sort of configuration equivalent to the API audit trails provided by CloudTrail. And through both of these AWS Config adds a layer of security and compliance to your application by ensuring changes to your environments are always surfaced and evaluated.

Explain AWS Config rules.   A rule simply states that a certain configuration—or more often, a certain part of a configuration—should be within a set of values. That rule is broken when a change moves configuration outside of allowed thresholds for those values.

Explain how AWS Config rules are evaluated.   There is typically code associated with a rule defining how that rule is evaluated. If you define a custom rule, you'll write your own code to evaluate configuration and report back as to whether the configuration follows or breaks the custom rule. This code is then attached to the rule as a Lambda function.

Describe the two ways rule evaluation can be triggered.   Two triggers cause AWS Config rules to evaluate: change-based triggers and periodic triggers. A change-based trigger causes a rule to evaluate a configuration when there's a change in the environment. A periodic trigger evaluates a configuration at a predefined frequency.

Explain how AWS Systems Manager is able to help with operational tasks.   AWS Systems Manager provides tools that allow you to monitor and maintain your instances, while allowing for the creation of patch baselines and compliance monitoring.

Explain the use of the various components of AWS Systems Manager.   Know what the various components of AWS Systems Manager do. The Run command allows you to execute command documents against AWS resources. Patch Manager allows you to automate the installation of security patches and application updates. The Parameter Store creates a central location to store secrets and other parameters like license keys. Session Manager allows you to remotely administer your systems without opening up ports in your security groups. State Manager helps you monitor the compliance of your systems in regard to versioning and proving that baseline software is installed.

Review Questions

1. You suspect that an application client is nonperformant because it is making more calls than normal to a REST-based API on your application estate. What AWS tool would you use to verify this information and validate any changes you make to correct this issue?

   A. AWS Config

   B. Amazon CloudWatch

   C. AWS CloudTrail

   D. AWS NetReporter

2. You have a number of metrics collecting via CloudWatch on your fleet of EC2 instances. However, you want to gather additional metrics on a number of instances that do not seem to be performing as well as the majority of running instances. How can you gather additional metrics not available through CloudWatch's stock configuration?

   A. Turn on detailed monitoring.

   B. Install the CloudWatch Logs Agent.

   C. Create a new VPC flow log.

   D. Turn on detailed statistics in CloudWatch.

3. Which of the following statements about a CloudTrail trail with regard to regions is true? (Choose two.)

   A. A trail applies to all your AWS regions by default.

   B. A trail collects both management and data events.

   C. A trail can apply only to a single region.

   D. A trail applies to a single region by default.

4. Which of the following is *not* an example of a management event?

   A. An `AttachRolePolicy` IAM operation

   B. An AWS CloudTrail `CreateTrail` API operation

   C. Activity on an S3 bucket via a `PutObject` event

   D. A `CreateSubnet` API operation for an EC2 instance

5. How are management events different from data events? (Choose two.)

   A. Data events are typically much higher volume than management events.

   B. Data events are typically lower volume than management events.

   C. Data events are disabled by default when creating a trail, whereas management events are enabled by default.

   D. Management events include Lambda execution activity, whereas data events do not.

6. Which of the following options for a trail would capture events related to actions such as `RunInstances` or `TerminateInstances`? (Choose two.)

    A. All

    B. Read-Only

    C. Write-Only

    D. None

7. Which of the following is not a valid Amazon CloudWatch alarm state?

    A. OK

    B. INSUFFICIENT_DATA

    C. ALARM

    D. INVALID_DATA

8. You have a CloudWatch alarm with a period of 2 minutes. The evaluation period is set to 10 minutes, and Datapoints To Alarm is set to 3. How many metrics would need to be outside the defined threshold for the alarm to move into an ALARM state? (Choose two.)

    A. Three out-of-threshold metrics out of five within 10 minutes

    B. Three out-of-threshold metrics out of five within 2 minutes

    C. Two out-of-threshold metrics out of five within 5 minutes

    D. Three out-of-threshold metrics out of eight within 16 minutes

9. Which of the following settings are allowed for dealing with missing data points within Amazon CloudWatch? (Choose two.)

    A. `notBreaching`

    B. `invalid`

    C. `missing`

    D. `notValid`

10. Which of the following does AWS Config *not* provide?

    A. Remediation for out-of-compliance events

    B. Definition of states that resources should be in

    C. Notifications when a resource changes its state

    D. Definition of compliance baselines for your system

11. Which of the following would you use to ensure that your S3 buckets never allow public access? (Choose two.)

    A. AWS Config

    B. Amazon CloudWatch

    C. AWS Lambda

    D. AWS CloudTrail

12. Which of the following is not part of an AWS Config configuration item (CI)?

A. An AWS CloudTrail event ID

B. A mapping of relationships between the resource and other AWS resources

C. The set of IAM policies related to the resource

D. The version of the configuration item

13. You have a number of instances based on AMIs with AWS Systems Manager agent installed, but none are able to communicate to the SSM service. What is likely the source of this issue?

A. You need to create an IAM group and assign that group to each instance you want communicating with AWS Systems Manager.

B. You need to create an IAM role and have each instance assume that role to communicate with the AWS Systems Manager service.

C. You need to add the AWSSystemsManager policy to each instance running an SSM agent.

D. You need to use a Linux-based AMI on each instance to ensure it can communicate with the SSM service.

14. Which of the following are supported notation formats for documents in AWS Systems Manager? (Choose two.)

A. YAML

B. JSON

C. CSV

D. Text

15. You are responsible for a fleet of EC2 instances and have heard that a recently released patch has known issues with Rails, which your instances are all running. How would you prevent the patch from being deployed to the instances, given that they are all running the SSM agent?

A. Remove the patch from the automation pipeline.

B. Remove the patch from the patch baseline.

C. Add the patch as an exclusion to the patch baseline.

D. Add the path as an exclusion to the automation pipeline.

16. You have a command document written in JSON for your instances running a Windows AMI and communicating with the AWS Systems Manager Service. You now have inherited several Linux-based instances and want to use the same command document. What do you need to do to use this document with the Linux instances?

A. Convert the document from JSON to YAML and reload it.

B. Copy the document and assign the copy to the Linux-based instances.

C. You cannot use a document written for Windows-based instances with Linux-based instances.

D. Nothing; documents will work across platform operating systems.

17. You need to ensure that a compliance script is executed on all of your managed instances every morning at 1 a.m. How would you accomplish this task?

    A. Create a new `Execute` command and use Systems Manager to set it up on your instances.

    B. Create a new `Run` command and use Systems Manager to set it up on your instances.

    C. Create a new compliance policy document and ensure that all instances' agents reference the document.

    D. Create a new action document and ensure that all instances' agents reference the document.

18. You want to centrally collect and refer to applications, AWS components, network configuration information, etc. installed on multiple EC2 instances that you manage. Which of the following should be adopted to meet this requirement?

    A. Install the Systems Manager Agent on your EC2 instance. Log in with Session Manager, and create and execute a script that collects inventory information.

    B. Install the Systems Manager Agent on your EC2 instance. Use Systems Manager Inventory to collect inventory information.

    C. Use AWS Config to collect EC2 inventory information.

    D. SSH into your EC2 instance. Create and run a script that collects inventory information.

19. You are using an EC2 instance to host a web application. You have configured a CloudWatch alarm for this EC2 instance's CPU utilization metric, which uses SNS to send notifications when it is under heavy load. When you check the alarm status, it says INSUFFICIENT_DATA. Which of the following are common causes of this message? (Choose two.)

    A. The same metric is used in other alarms.

    B. Detailed monitoring has not been enabled for the metric.

    C. The CloudWatch alarm has just started.

    D. S3 bucket for logs does not exist.

    E. The metric is unavailable.

20. A user wants to connect to a Windows instance using Remote Desktop, but the Ops team wants to encourage using Systems Manager features. Which statement is true?

    A. Native RDP is supported and you can enable it in the session properties so that the user can view the desktop instead of the PowerShell prompt.

    B. Map a local port to the RDP port on the instance and start a session. The user can then use remote desktop through port forwarding.

    C. RDP is not supported by SSM. You must open port 3389 in the instance security group.

    D. RDP is not supported by SSM. Use Apache Guacamole over port 80 instead.

Chapter

9

Networking

THE AWS CERTIFIED SYSOPS ADMINISTRATOR EXAM OBJECTIVES COVERED IN THIS CHAPTER INCLUDE:

✓ **Domain 5: Networking and Content Delivery**

- 5.1 Implement networking features and connectivity

  - Configure a VPC (for example, subnets, route tables, network ACLs, security groups, NAT gateway, Internet gateway)

  - Configure private connectivity (for example, Systems Manager Session Manager, VPC endpoints, VPC peering, VPN)

- 5.3 Troubleshoot network connectivity issues

  - Interpret VPC configurations (for example, subnets, route tables, network ACLs, security groups)

  - Collect and interpret logs (for example, VPC Flow Logs, ELB access logs, AWS WAF web ACL logs, CloudFront logs)

  - Troubleshoot hybrid and private connectivity issues

Nothing happens in cloud computing without networking. This chapter will only be able to scratch the surface of the topic. Because networking is so broad, it will be important to focus your studies on the exam objectives and services in scope. This book will not attempt to explain networking theory.

The heart of networking in AWS is the virtual private cloud (VPC). The VPC has many components, including gateways, subnets, CIDR blocks, and security groups. All of these must work together in harmony to allow network traffic to pass through to its destination. This chapter will look at the structure of the VPC and ways to connect with the resources in a VPC.

Networking

The virtual private cloud (VPC) is the logical networking structure for routing packets and connecting all compute resources, both in the cloud and on-premises. The VPC is where all your compute resources will reside, including EC2 instances, RDS instances, and Lambda functions.

One very helpful way to think of a VPC is as an onion (see Figure 9.1). Packets move from the Internet gateway down into the elastic network interface (ENI) of an instance.

Refer to the numbers in Figure 9.1:

Step 1 We visualize network traffic entering the VPC at a gateway. The most common of these would be the Internet gateway, of course. However, virtual private gateways, VPC endpoints (gateway and interface), and DirectConnect also sit on the edge of the VPC. Remember that the Internet gateway provides no firewall or security. It is only an entryway.

Step 2 Next, traffic must discover where the destination resource is located. "Where do we go?" We need a directory, called a router or route table. By default, this is handled by the main route table in the VPC. There may be any number of route tables, but one must always be designated as the main route table. The tables contain the valid addresses of all findable resources. Route tables do not filter traffic but only define valid IP address ranges (CIDR) of resources.

FIGURE 9.1   VPC layers

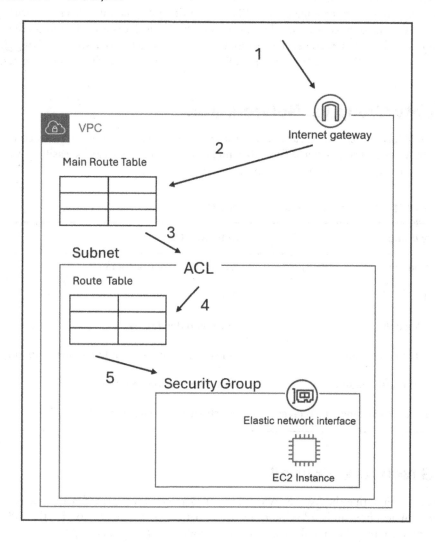

Step 3   The route table directs the packet to a subnet. All resources in a VPC must live in a subnet. At the edge of the subnet is the network access control list (ACL). ACLs are used to filter incoming and outgoing traffic using rules. By default, an ACL has no rules and is open for all inbound and outbound traffic. Packets can be filtered at the boundary, but there is no filtering once a packet is inside the subnet. That means that traffic between resources inside the subnet is not filtered. The ACL is stateless, meaning that both the incoming packet and the outgoing response (or vice versa) are evaluated if any rules are present. This is different from the security group, which is stateful.

Step 4   Packets originating from instances inside a subnet also need to find their path out. For this, each subnet is associated with a route table, which defines the local IP space and the path packets can take when leaving the subnet.

Step 5 Inside the subnet, a packet encounters the security group. This is the last line of defense and sits on the edge of each ENI. A security group is stateful. The security group is depicted in architectures as a box around multiple instances and spanning subnets and availability zones (AZs). This simplifies the drawings but is a little deceiving. Just remember that the security group actually sits on the edge of each ENI on each resource.

Security Group vs. Network ACL

You should have noted that security groups and network ACLs are both ways of controlling packet movement through rules. They are similar enough that they can be easily confused. Be sure you know the differences shown in Table 9.1.

TABLE 9.1 Security groups compared to ACLs

Security group	Network ACL
Associated with instances (ENI)	Associated with the subnet
Stateful	Stateless
Allow rules only	Allow and deny rules
All rules applied equally	Rules applied in order until a match is found
Preferred firewall method	Secondary firewall method
Functions at the instance (ENI) level	Functions at the subnet level

AWS Network Firewall

It is also worth noting the AWS Network Firewall service, which provides a managed, stateful, and stateless firewall in addition to intrusion detection and prevention for the VPC. The Network Firewall can make use of regional endpoints (e.g., `https://network-firewall.<region>.amazonaws.com`) to reduce latency. The firewall has its own subnet, which you assign, and is a target that you define in your route tables. An endpoint is installed for each AZ you wish to protect. You define rule groups and firewall policies to control traffic through the firewall. Suricata is a widely used intrusion detection and prevention system (IDPS) and intrusion prevention system (IPS). AWS Firewall stateful rules are Suricata compatible. The cost of AWS Network Firewall is charged per hour per endpoint plus data per gigabyte.

NAT Gateway

Network address translation (NAT) is used to map private IP addresses to a public IP address. This is the technology used in your home where your mobile phone, laptop, TV, and Alexa devices all have private IP addresses that normally could not communicate with hosts on the Internet, as illustrated in Figure 9.2. With NAT, all these private devices can share one public Internet connection.

FIGURE 9.2   Home NAT

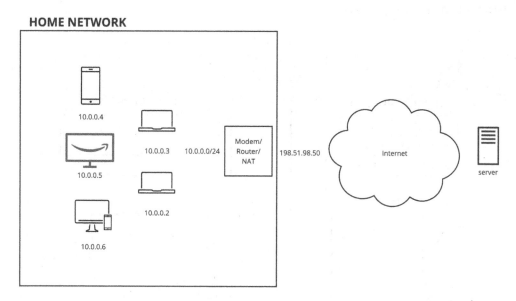

NAT works the same way at the enterprise level. In Figure 9.3, hosts inside the VPC have nonroutable private IP addresses (e.g., 10.0.0.0/16). Normally, traffic from these private addresses cannot be routed on the public Internet. Hosts on the public side are unable to initiate communication directly with the hosts on the private side of the NAT device. However, NAT maps these private IP addresses to a single public IP address. There are many scenarios in which hosts in a private subnet might need to communicate securely with the Internet. One example would be to receive software updates.

In the route table example below, the subnet local CIDR is 10.0.0.0/24, which represents 256 private IP addresses. To allow these hosts to securely communicate with hosts on the Internet while remaining effectively invisible, a route to the NAT gateway is added. Hosts in this private subnet can now only access the Internet through the NAT gateway. The NAT gateway then returns all responding traffic (see Table 9.2).

TABLE 9.2 Example route table

Destination	Target
0.0.0.0/0	nat-gateway-id
10.0.0.0/24	local

FIGURE 9.3 NAT gateway

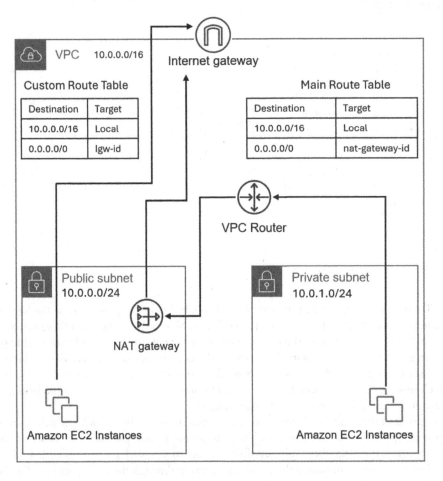

It's worth remembering that IPv6 addresses assigned by AWS are all publicly routable. There are unique local unicast addresses (FC00: :/7) defined in RFC4193 that are not routable on the public network. This is beyond the scope of the exam, but worth noting for real-world application in case your employer implements IPv6.

Pricing for AWS NAT Gateway is billed per hour plus data transfer rates. If you happen to read old study material, there may be references to NAT instances. It is still possible to create a NAT instance on EC2. However, it is no longer recommended and there would be no reason now to select a NAT instance over a NAT gateway.

Troubleshooting

There are many layers within the VPC, and this can make troubleshooting network connectivity issues challenging. It's essential that troubleshooting be done systematically. The three most common connectivity problems are security groups, network access control lists (NACLs), and route table configurations. Be sure to know these three services and how to configure them. Standard Linux diagnostic tools such as ping, mtr, and trace route can be used to diagnose routing and connectivity issues in the cloud but they are not covered on the exam.

The VPC Reachability Analyzer can be a simple and quick way to diagnose connectivity. To dig deep, make use of VPC flow logs.

Lots can go wrong. Be prepared to recognize common networking errors and know how to correct them. Here are some common things to check for:

- Is port 22 enabled on the security group for SSH access?

- Does the instance have a public IP address?

- Are you using the correct key pair?

- Has a conflicting rule been set on the ACL?

- Has a conflicting outbound rule be set on the ACL or security group?

- Is there an Internet gateway attached to the VPC?

- Is there a route to the Internet gateway (0.0.0.0)?

- Are route tables attached to each subnet?

- Is the NAT gateway in a public subnet?

VPC IP Address Manager

IP (Internet Protocol) addresses are essential identifiers for networked resources. IP addresses are either IPv4 (e.g., 53.252.10.76) or IPv6 (e.g., 2001:0da6:85a3:725:0620 :8d2b:8282:5634). While IPv6 is quickly becoming more common, it is less prevalent on the exam. All IPv6 addresses are considered public, meaning that they can be routed on the Internet. IPv4 addresses are separated into public (routable) and private (nonroutable) addresses. Nonroutable simply means that these addresses cannot be routed over the public Internet. They are, however, used in internal networks such as VPCs.

A network such as a VPC or subnet contains a series of private IP addresses. These fall into three ranges of 10.0.0.0–10.255.255.255, 172.16.0.0–172.16.255.255, and 192.168.0.0–192.168.255.255. If that seems like a lot of numbers and a little confusing, you aren't alone. We refer to these ranges as Classless Inter-Domain Routing (CIDR) blocks, and we have a simple notation to make writing the ranges less cluttered. The range 10.0.0.0–10.255.255.255, for example, can be notated as 10.0.0.0/16, which contains 65,536 IP addresses. A /16 address is the largest range that can be used with a VPC. A CIDR of 10.0.0.0/28 is the smallest range used in a VPC and represents just 16 addresses. You will not be expected to calculate CIDRs on the exam. However, you will need to know relative size. For example, /16 is the largest and /28 is the smallest. Remember that CIDR ranges between any two connected networks (VPCs, subnets, on-premises) cannot overlap. This is important and could be a good troubleshooting question to see if you can spot an overlap.

The VPC IP Address Manager (VPC IPAM) allows you to manage IP addresses across your network at any scale. IPAM can manage both AWS private IPV4 CIDRs and AWS public IPv6 addresses as well as your own IPv4 and IPv6 CIDRs. IPAM can be used with AWS Organizations to manage IPs across your entire organization. To use IPAM with Organizations, you must delegate one account as the IPAM management account. You configure this delegation in the settings of the IPAM console. There are three elements to IPAM: the scope, the pools, and the allocations.

The scope serves as a container for all other elements. Each IPAM has two scopes: private and public. Each scope can have pools, which represent a range of IP addresses (CIDR), and pools can be nested. Pools can be allocated for each region and for different environments such as security, production, and development. See Figure 9.4.

FIGURE 9.4   Sample IPAM structure

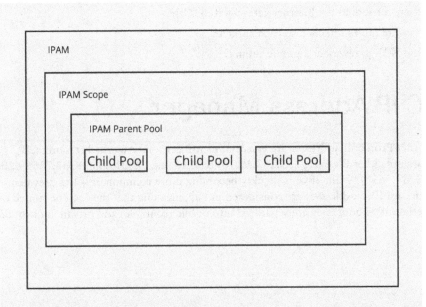

Once created, IPAM provisions two scopes: a public scope and a private scope. IPAM begins discovery of all IPs (CIDR) in the account and will produce a resource list like the one shown in Figure 9.5.

FIGURE 9.5   IPAM discovery

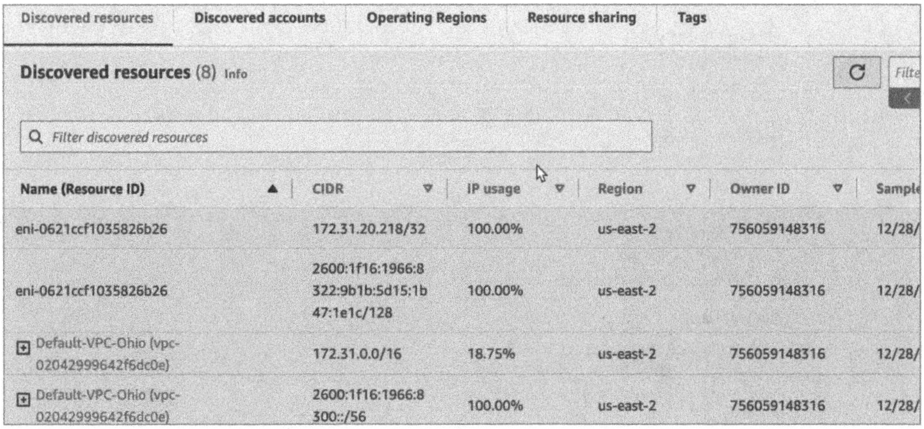

Discovered resources	Discovered accounts	Operating Regions	Resource sharing	Tags

Discovered resources (8) Info

🔍 Filter discovered resources

Name (Resource ID)	▲	CIDR	▽	IP usage	▽	Region	▽	Owner ID	▽	Sample
eni-0621ccf1035826b26		172.31.20.218/32		100.00%		us-east-2		756059148316		12/28/
eni-0621ccf1035826b26		2600:1f16:1966:8 322:9b1b:5d15:1b 47:1e1c/128		100.00%		us-east-2		756059148316		12/28/
⊡ Default-VPC-Ohio (vpc-02042999642f6dc0e)		172.31.0.0/16		18.75%		us-east-2		756059148316		12/28/
⊡ Default-VPC-Ohio (vpc-02042999642f6dc0e)		2600:1f16:1966:8 300::/56		100.00%		us-east-2		756059148316		12/28/

IPs (CIDR) are organized in pools, which can be nested under the scopes. Allocation has two meanings. First, allocation can be done in the pools console where you set aside (allocate) CIDRs to reserve them for future use. Second, you can allocate a CIDR block in IPAM integrated services such as VPC. You can use IPAM pools when creating a VPC, as illustrated in Figure 9.6. Be familiar with both forms of allocation and read your test questions carefully.

Hubs, Spokes, and Bastion Hosts

We are frequently connecting many different networks and services. These can be on-premises networks, AWS services that do not live in a VPC such as S3 or DynamoDB, as well as other VPCs. The routing for all of this could easily become unmanageably complicated. Several services within AWS allow us to centrally manage our cloud or hybrid environment using a hub-and-spoke architecture. The hub and spoke is not a new networking architecture, so it should be familiar to anyone with experience in basic networking.

The service that makes the hub and spoke possible for our VPC is the AWS Transit Gateway, which will be discussed further in this chapter. In addition, you will need to be familiar with several other gateways and endpoints used to connect various services and networks to your VPC.

FIGURE 9.6   Allocating an IPAM CIDR

Create VPC Info

A VPC is an isolated portion of the AWS Cloud populated by AWS objects, such as Amazon EC2 instances.

VPC settings

Resources to create Info
Create only the VPC resource or the VPC and other networking resources.

- ⦿ VPC only
- ◯ VPC and more

Name tag - *optional*
Creates a tag with a key of 'Name' and a value that you specify.

```
ipam-vpc
```

IPv4 CIDR block Info

- ◯ IPv4 CIDR manual input
- ⦿ IPAM-allocated IPv4 CIDR block

IPv4 IPAM pool

```
ipam-pool-0a08109091d7c5233
us-east-1    Private pool for dev in us-east-1                ▼
```

The locale of the IPAM pool must be equal to the current region.

Netmask

```
/26                                              64 IPs ▼
```

IPv6 CIDR block Info

- ⦿ No IPv6 CIDR block
- ◯ IPAM-allocated IPv6 CIDR block
- ◯ Amazon-provided IPv6 CIDR block

Connecting to the Internet

This section covers two ways to connect to the public Internet: an Internet gateway (IGW) and the egress-only Internet gateway (EIGW).

Internet Gateway

An Internet gateway (IGW) is used to connect VPC resources to the public Internet. IGWs are highly available and scalable and handle all traffic, including IPv4 and IPv6, on all ports. There are no settings to configure. An IGW can be attached to or detached from a VPC. In order to route traffic from a subnet, add a route in the route table as shown in Figure 9.7.

Egress-Only Internet Gateway

Like an Internet gateway, the egress-only Internet gateway (EIGW) is a simple passage through the boundary of the VPC with no configuration options. Where the EIGW is different is that only IPv6 traffic passes through. This is useful because all IPv6 addresses are globally unique, which means that, unlike private RFP 1918 addresses, which are not publicly routable, IPv6 addresses are all addressable on the public Internet.

FIGURE 9.7   Adding a route to an Internet gateway

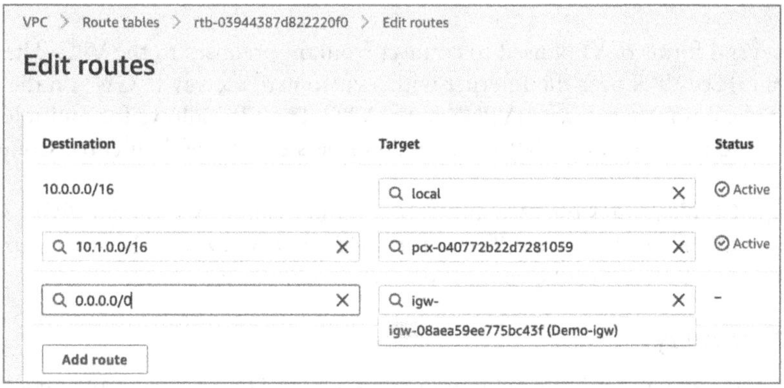

To allow IPv6 resources to communicate with the Internet without allowing resources on the Internet to initiate communications, two mechanisms can be used: a NAT gateway or an EIGW. EIGWs are stateful, meaning that when traffic is sent from the VPC, responding traffic is returned to the initiating resource. Unlike an IGW, the EIGW is not attached to or detached from the VPC.

Connecting to Networks and Services

There are a wide variety of mechanisms for connecting your VPC to an on-premises network, another VPC, or an AWS service. We've already mentioned the Internet gateway as one of the most common gateways. This section will survey a few more with which you should be familiar.

On-Premises to VPC

Connecting your VPC to an on-premises network is a common task, and there are several ways of setting this up.

DirectConnect

DirectConnect is a common enterprise datacenter connection to a VPC. It provides a dedicated connection at speeds from 50 Mbps to 100 Gbps. Implementation of DirectConnect requires working with a DirectConnect delivery partner and takes some time to get up and running. DirectConnect is an expensive option but provides the highest throughput. While DirectConnect is a big networking pipe, it is still a single point of failure and not a highly available service. However, DirectConnect can be architected for high availability. DirectConnect traffic is not encrypted by default.

VPN

There are several forms of VPN used to connect from on-premises to the VPC. The simplest of these is an IPSec VPN over the Internet with a customer gateway (CGW) on the customer side and a virtual private gateway (VPG) on the VPC. The VPG allows for multiple CGW connections and is redundant. A VPN connection is less expensive than DirectConnect but is also slower.

Creating a CGW requires the assignment of a Border Gateway Protocol (BGP) Autonomous System Number (ASN). A VPG can use the default Amazon ASN or a custom ASN. Route propagation must be enabled on the route table.

Transit Gateway

The transit gateway will be discussed in more depth later. This gateway can connect multiple VPCs and acts as a central connection point for all network traffic coming into your AWS environment. Costs for AWS Transit Gateway include a fee per attachment and data processing.

VPC-to-VPC and Services

The VPC is a logically isolated virtual network analogous to an on-premises datacenter. DirectConnect or a VPN can be used to connect on-premises resources to the VPC to form a hybrid network. VPC peering and VPC endpoints can be used to expand your network to additional VPCs and to many other AWS services.

VPC Peering

VPC peering allows you to route IP v4 and IP v6 traffic between two VPCs. VPC peering is very flexible, and we will soon look at architectures thar will allow communication across very large and complex networks.

Peering is nontransitive. In the example shown in Figure 9.8, VPC A and VPC B are both peered to VPC C. However, since there is no explicit peering between A and B, VPCs A and B cannot communicate directly with each other. Just because C trusts A and B, it doesn't mean A and B trust each other; that's nontransitive.

Setting up VPC peering requires several steps, and you will want to know these for the exam. Figure 9.9 gives a rough outline of the steps.

FIGURE 9.8   Nontransitive VPC peering

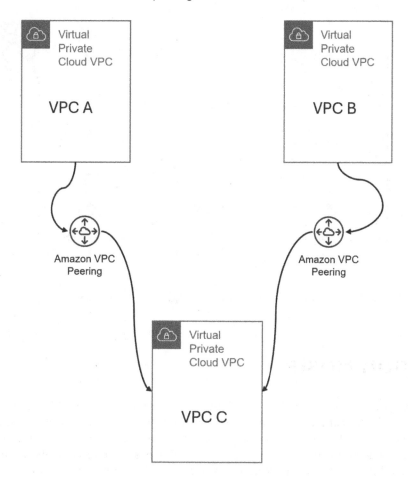

VPC peering does not rely on a VPN or gateway and has no single point of failure. There is no cost for VPC peering, and only data transferred across AZs or regions is subject to fees. As illustrated Figure 9.10, one VPC is designated as the requester, and one is the accepter. When you click Create Peering Connection, the owner of the acceptor VPC will see the new request in their peering connections, and they simply have to accept using the Actions menu. Even if you own both VPCs, the request must still be accepted (see Figure 9.11).

After creating the peering connection, you will need to adjust the main route tables for both VPCs (see Figure 9.12). This is an area where proper planning at the beginning is essential. Since you are letting two different networks using private CIDR blocks communicate, you have a risk of IP address overlap. This would cause inaccessibility issues. Be sure that the VPCs you connect do not have any overlapping IP ranges.

FIGURE 9.9   A VPC peering request

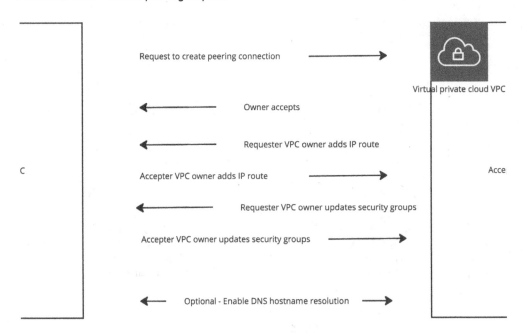

Bastion Hosts

Bastion hosts are often confused with NAT gateways but they serve very different purposes. They are similar in that they serve to hide private instances while still allowing some communication. The NAT gateway allows communication out. The bastion host, on the other hand, allows communication in. Specifically, the bastion host is designed to allow only ports 22 (SSH) or 3389 (RDP) communication. If you consult the dictionary, "bastion" refers to a part of a fort or fortification; think of the Bastille in Paris, France. A bastion host is often also referred to as a jump box or jump server. Using a bastion host supports the security principles of security-in-depth and minimal attack surface.

With a bastion host, the user never connects directly to the server they want to manage. Instead, they connect, via port 22, to the bastion host. The bastion host, then, initiates a port 22 connection to the target instance. A common architecture is to place the bastion host in its own VPC, referred to as a perimeter network, while the target instances reside in private subnets in a different VPC. The bastion host would typically have its own security group as well.

FIGURE 9.10   Create Peering Connection

Create peering connection

A VPC peering connection is a networking connection between two VPCs that enables you to route traffic between them privately. Info

Peering connection settings

Name - *optional*
Create a tag with a key of 'Name' and a value that you specify.

```
VPC-Peering-One
```

Select a local VPC to peer with
VPC ID (Requester)

```
vpc-0                    :b (Demo-vpc)                    ▼
```

VPC CIDRs for vpc-0047f6da395f277cb (Demo-vpc)

CIDR	Status	Status reason
10.0.0.0/16	⊘ Associated	-

Select another VPC to peer with
Account
- ● My account
- ○ Another account

Region
- ● This Region (us-east-2)
- ○ Another Region

VPC ID (Accepter)

```
vpc-03              :a (Trusted-VPC-One)                  ▼
```

VPC CIDRs for vpc-03   :a (Trusted-VPC-One)

CIDR	Status	Status reason
10.1.0.0/16	⊘ Associated	-

FIGURE 9.11   Accept Request

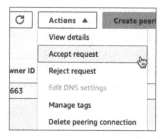

FIGURE 9.12   Editing the peering connection route tables

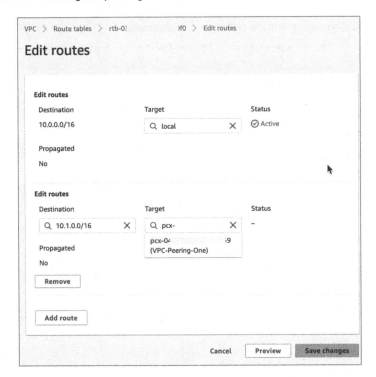

Remember that each bastion host is just an EC2 instance and not a managed service so you would need to take extra steps to assure availability and fault tolerance. For example, to allow your EC2 instance to autorecover after a failure, you can use the EC2 autorecovery feature. An older technique to achieve the same thing was to use an auto scaling group with a minimum of 1 and a desired capacity of 1. However, the autorecovery feature is now preferred. It is also common to have a bastion host in each availability zone for high availability.

There is an excellent reference deployment available at `https://aws.amazon.com/solutions/implementations/linux-bastion`. Be sure to note the costs associated with this deployment before trying it in your own account. However, you can study the architecture and steps. Studying reference deployments (also known as QuickStarts or reference architectures) is extremely helpful when studying for an exam!

Bastion hosts are just EC2 instances, so billing is the same as any EC2 instance. Remember to be careful to right-size your bastion host and use cost control mechanisms such as savings plans.

EC2 Systems Manager

While a bastion host is a standard and essential security feature, it does have weaknesses. A bastion host is still an EC2 instance, so it needs to be patched and incurs costs. A bastion host also requires RSA keys, which must be managed. An alternative to a bastion host is to use AWS Systems Manager (SSM). AWS Systems Manager uses an open source host agent. Using SSM eliminates the need for the bastion host. Users authenticate through AWS IAM and all activity is logged.

Monitoring VPC Traffic

Many monitoring tools are available in AWS such as CloudWatch and CloudTrail. Just a few of these will be covered in this section and those focus on monitoring network traffic. Three key tools are available: Traffic Mirroring, Reachability Analyzer, and a variety of logs. When using logging, always consider the amount of data that could be generated and the cost of processing and storing this data. It would be rare to log everything all the time. Typically, only a subset of the traffic is logged for monitoring and analysis.

Traffic Mirroring

Traffic within a VPC enters a resource through an elastic network interface (ENI). ENIs are useful because they can be detached from one instance and connected to another instance. IP addresses are bound to the ENI, allowing instances to be easily swapped without disrupting network connectivity. Multiple ENIs can be attached to an instance to increase bandwidth on some instances.

Traffic Mirroring allows you to copy inbound and outbound network traffic at an ENI to a security monitoring device. Traffic Mirroring is billed per hour per ENI. There are a few terms to know. A traffic mirror source is an ENI, network load balancer (NLB), or gateway load balancer (GLB). The traffic mirroring destination is where the mirrored traffic is sent, such as a security appliance. Filters are rules used to determine what traffic will be mirrored. A session combines the source, the target, and filters.

Traffic Mirroring uses UDP port 4789 (VXLAN). Mirroring uses filters to determine what traffic to capture. By default, no filters are enabled so no traffic will be captured. A variety of rules can be applied, including inbound versus outbound, accepted versus rejected, protocol (layer 4), source/destination port range, or source/destination CIDR block. Like an ACL, the rules of traffic mirroring are numbered and evaluated in order.

Reachability Analyzer

Reachability Analyzer is a very useful tool for diagnosing IPv4 network connectivity issues between source and destinations in a VPC. Paths across accounts can be analyzed if Enable Trust Access is selected. Reachability Analyzer can be used to identify issues with security group, route table, and network access control list (NACL) configurations.

Reachability Analyzer returns explanation codes, of which there are many. You will not need to memorize all the codes for the exam. Reachability Analyzer can be found in the VPC console. Simply set the source (e.g., an instance), the destination (an Internet gateway), and the protocol. Source and destination must be in the same region and in the same VPC or be connected through VPC peering.

Logs

Logs are your best friend when it comes to troubleshooting. The exam will expect you to be familiar with several types of logs in AWS, including CloudWatch and CloudTrail logs, VPC flow logs, ELB access logs, WAF web ACL logs, CloudFront logs, and CloudWatch logs insights. CloudWatch and CloudTrail are covered elsewhere in this book.

VPC Flow Logs

VPC flow logs are one of the principal tools for monitoring the network traffic through a VPC. They can capture information about traffic on network interfaces in the VPC, including those attached to EC2, ELB, RDS, ElastiCache, transit gateways, and so forth.

A VPC flow log can be created from a variety of consoles, including Network Interfaces in the EC2 console as well as Your VPCs And Subnets in the VPC console (see Figure 9.13).

To create a VPC flow log, determine what network traffic you want to monitor (rejected, accepted, or all), an aggregation interval (1 or 10 minutes), a destination (CloudWatch logs, S3, Kinesis Firehose), and the IAM role.

A lot of data is included in a VPC flow log (see Figure 9.14).

FIGURE 9.13 Create Flow Log

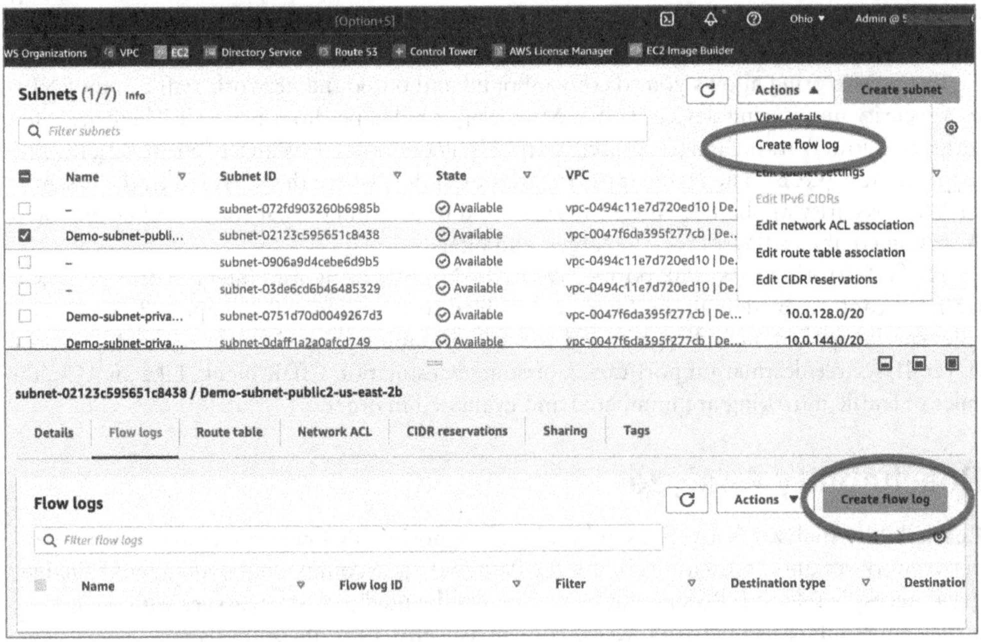

FIGURE 9.14 VPC flow log example

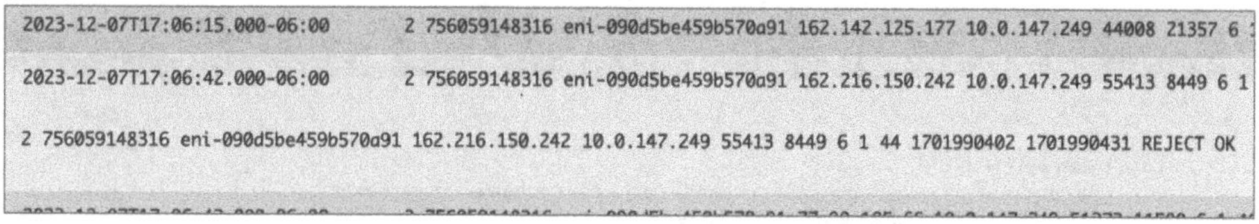

```
2023-12-07T17:06:15.000-06:00        2 756059148316 eni-090d5be459b570a91 162.142.125.177 10.0.147.249 44008 21357 6 :

2023-12-07T17:06:42.000-06:00        2 756059148316 eni-090d5be459b570a91 162.216.150.242 10.0.147.249 55413 8449 6 1

2 756059148316 eni-090d5be459b570a91 162.216.150.242 10.0.147.249 55413 8449 6 1 44 1701990402 1701990431 REJECT OK
```

Figure 9.14 shows an example of a VPC flow log. For the exam you won't have to know what each element means, but you should be able to get a sense for what is happening in the entry.

Our entry contains the following:

2 = Version

756059148316 = The account number

eni-090d5be459b570a91 = The interface, in this case an ENI

162.216.150.242 = Source IP address

10.0.147.249 = Destination IP address

55413 = Source port

8449 = Destination port

6 = IANA protocol number

1 = Number of packets

44 = Packet size in bytes

1701990402 – Start time stamp

1701990431 = End time stamp

REJECT = Action is either ACCEPT or REJECT

OK = Log status is OK, NODATA, or SKIPDATA

Several other fields can appear in the flow logs, but you only need to be able to parse out a few of these. Focus on recognizing the source and destination IP addresses and ports and the action.

Elastic Load Balancer Logs

When enabled (disabled by default), Elastic Load Balancers (ELB) can publish logs for each node every five minutes. The logs contain time of request, client IP, latency, request path, and server response. There is S3 storage cost for ELB logs. To enable ELB logging, first select an S3 bucket to store the logs. The bucket must have sufficient permissions through a bucket policy to receive the logs from the ELB. In the attributes of the selected ELB, enable access logs and specify the appropriate S3 bucket (see Figure 9.15).

FIGURE 9.15   Enabling ELB flow logs

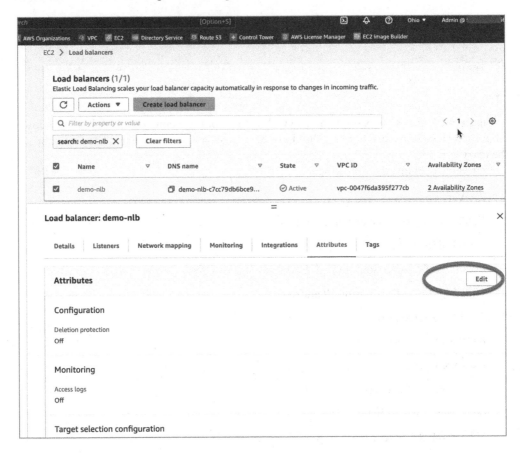

Web ACL Traffic Logs

The AWS WAF (Web Application Firewall) web ACL traffic logs are another method for collecting data about network traffic. The service allows the logs to be sent to a CloudWatch log group, Kinesis Fire Hose, or S3 and is billed for storage in the destination service. The web ACL traffic logs will show information about the time stamp as well as details of the request and which WAF rules were matched.

AWS Client VPN

An AWS Client VPN is a secure, managed TLS VPN service. You would create a client VPN to give users secure access to an AWS resource through the VPC. Users can connect using any OpenVPN-based client. Keep in mind that AWS Client VPN (Figure 9.16) connects client workstations to resources in the VPC. It is not used to connect the VPC to an on-premises network. Client VPN can use three types of authentications: Active Directory authentication, mutual authentication, and SAML-based single sign-on. Pricing for Client VPN is per hour per client as well as data out.

FIGURE 9.16   Client VPN

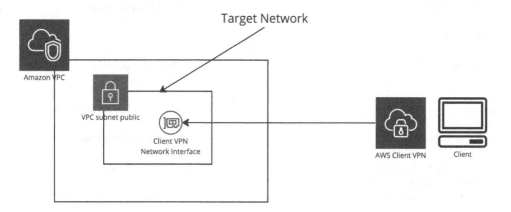

Creating the VPN involves just a few steps:

1. Create a server certificate and load it into AWS Certificate Manager (ACM).
2. Create a client VPN endpoint.
3. Associate a target network.
4. Create an authorization rule in the VPN endpoint.
5. Add routes to VPC-connected gateways and endpoints.
6. Update security groups.
7. Download the client VPC endpoint configuration file.
8. Add the client VPC endpoint configuration file to the VPN client desktop on the user's machine.

VPC Endpoints

Endpoints allow you to connect VPCs to AWS services such as AWS Marketplace. Resources in an on-premises datacenter can use VPC endpoints through DirectConnect. There are three forms of VPC endpoints: gateway endpoints, gateway load balancer endpoints, and interface endpoints.

Gateway endpoints and interface endpoints are used to access AWS services such as DynamoDB or S3 and many other AWS services. While similar, the gateway endpoint and the interface endpoint have several key differences, as shown in Table 9.3.

TABLE 9.3   Gateway endpoints compared to interface endpoints

Gateway endpoint	Interface endpoint
UDP (GENEVE Port 6081)	TCP
Access from VPC only	Access from VPC or on-premises
Not cost	Per-hour billing plus data
In region access	Cross-region access
Uses a route table entry (target = gateway_endpoint_id)	Uses DNS name

A gateway load balancer endpoint is used to direct traffic from the service consumer's VPC to the load balancer in a service provider's VPC (see Figure 9.17 and Figure 9.18). Typically, the target is a virtual appliance such as a web application firewall or an intrusion prevention system. Gateway load balancer endpoints are billed per hour plus data charges. There are three parts to using a gateway load balancer endpoint: the gateway load balancer, the gateway load balancer endpoint service, and the gateway load balancer endpoint. The gateway load balancer (described in Chapter 5, "Compute") is a specialized load balancer for traffic on port 6091 (GENEVE). To create a gateway load balancer endpoint, select Other Endpoint Services when creating an endpoint. You will need to know the service name. Once the endpoint is created, update the route tables to use the endpoint as the target.

AWS Transit Gateway

The AWS Transit Gateway (TGW) is a hub that serves as a single connection point within a region for on-premises networks and other VPCs via VPC peering. The TGW can even be used to connect VPCs of different accounts. See Figure 9.19. Typically, only one TGW would be created in an environment. However, there are scenarios where multiple TGWs might be used to minimize the risk of misconfigured route tables. A specific form of peering, transit gateway peering, is used to connect multiple TGWs. Transit gateway peering can be used to span regions and accounts. When attempting to peer, the owner (accepter) must accept the connection request. Connection requests appear in the VPC console under Transit Gateway Attachments. There is a setting when creating a TGW that allows automatic acceptance of cross-account attachments.

FIGURE 9.17   Connecting to a service without an endpoint

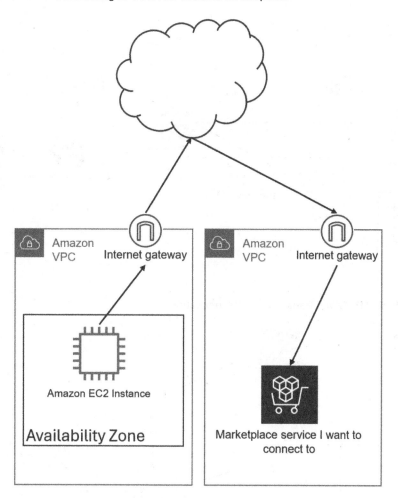

In order to create a transit gateway, you will need to provide an ASN (Autonomous System Number) for the AWS side of the gateway. An ASN is used to identify a network in BGP (Border Gateway Protocol). A variety of options are available, including the ability to enable DNS, automatically associate attachments to the gateway with the route table, and support for multicast.

FIGURE 9.18   Connecting to a Marketplace service with an endpoint

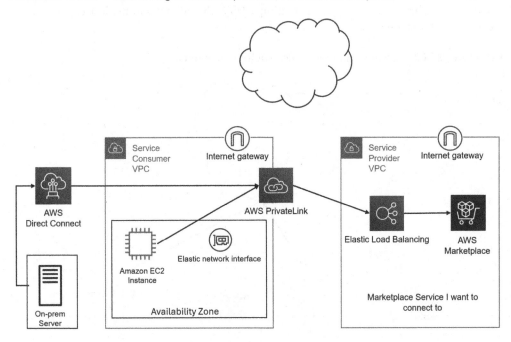

FIGURE 9.19   AWS Transit Gateway connections

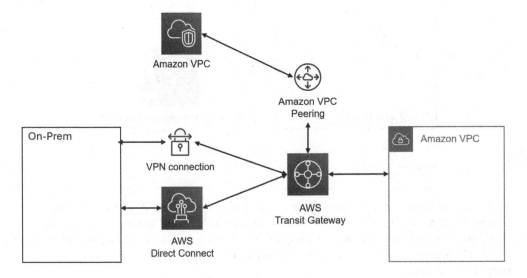

Cloud WAN

A wide area network (WAN) is a common networking construct describing the connection of separate networks over a large geographic area (even globally). AWS Cloud WAN is a managed wide area network connecting on-premises and cloud environments. It helps in aggregating the many different network providers and connections across branch offices and datacenters as well as the cloud into a single dashboard and managed policies.

The global network is the high-level container for your Cloud WAN. Under the global network are core networks, which are at the region level. Each core network has a core network policy that governs configuration of network connections. In the core network are attachments such as SD-WAN, VPCs, and VPN connections. Core networks are connected by the core network edge. A segment is an isolated routing domain.

Billing for Cloud WAN has several dimensions determining the price. The core network edge (CNE) is the managed connection point. Core network edge attachments include VPN, SD-WAN, and VPCs. Peering connections and data processing are also accounted for in Cloud WAN billing.

Summary

Networking is complex with many layers between the source and a destination. For the exam, you will need to have a working knowledge of the VPC and all its parts. Pay particular attention to the flow of packets from the source to the destination. Always ask yourself, where will this packet go next? How does the packet know? What can get in the way?

Exam Essentials

Calculate CIDR.   The exam will not expect you to do math in your head, so you will not need to calculate arbitrary CIDR ranges. However, you will want to be able to recognize large versus small ranges. For example, 10.0.0.0/16 is the largest available range with 65,536 IP addresses. 10.0.0.0/28 is the smallest with 16 IP addresses. Five IP addresses are always reserved for AWS use. That means that the available IP addresses in a /28 CIDR would be 11.

Practice building a VPC.   AWS has published a handy reference deployment (formerly a QuickStart) at https://aws.amazon.com/solutions/implementations/vpc. Study the structure and addresses. Can you set this up manually?

Understand public vs. private IP addresses.   All VPC resources will receive a private IP address. There are three private IP ranges: 10.0.0.0/8, 172.16.0.0/12, 192.168.0.0/16. Public

IP addresses can, optionally, be assigned to most resources. Know how to create elastic IP addresses and attach them to an EC2 instance.

Know your gateways and connectivity. VPCs are designed to be an isolated network environment in the same way that your on-premises datacenter is an isolated network. A variety of gateways and endpoints are available. Be familiar with when to use each. Ask: How would I connect to S3? How would I connect to my on-premises network? How would I connect to another VPC?

Understand how to monitor your network. Many monitoring tools are available in AWS, including CloudWatch, CloudTrail, and X-Ray. For monitoring network traffic in the VPC, Traffic Mirroring will be your best solution. Know how to enable it and what it can monitor.

Understand network architecture. Studying architectural diagrams can be very helpful: for example, see `https://aws.amazon.com/architecture/` `reference-architecture-diagrams`. Make note of the paths and route tables. Note which services are used in a given scenario.

Review Questions

1. The three common types of endpoints are:

   A. Gateway endpoints, gateway load balancer endpoints, and interface endpoints

   B. Gateway load balancer endpoints, elastic endpoints, and static endpoints

   C. VPC endpoints, elastic endpoints, and PrivateLink

   D. VPC endpoints, interface endpoints, and elastic endpoints

2. Which of the following is the best option for creating a hub-and-spoke network to connect on-premises resources and multiple VPCs?

   A. AWS DirectConnect

   B. AWS Gateway Endpoint

   C. AWS Transit Gateway

   D. AWS VPC Peering

3. Which of the following is the best use of a gateway endpoint?

   A. Connect a VPC to S3 without traversing the Internet.

   B. Connect an on-premises network to a VPC.

   C. Connects resources and services using PrivateLink.

   D. Connect two VPCs.

4. You wish to use deny rules to restrict traffic to your resources. Which of the following will allow you to implement deny rules?

   A. Internet gateway

   B. Network access control lists (NACL)

   C. Route table rules

   D. Security groups

5. You are experiencing connectivity errors with IPv4 traffic within your VPC. Which of the following will most efficiently help diagnose the issue?

   A. CloudWatch

   B. Reachability Analyzer

   C. Traffic Mirroring

   D. VPC flow log

6. Your customer wants you to connect their on-premises network to their VPC. The customer is a budget-conscious startup with a small volume of network traffic. They expect to grow at a slow but steady pace over the next year. Which solution will best achieve their goal?

   A. AWS Transit Gateway

   B. DirectConnect

   C. VPC peering

   D. VPN

7. To direct network traffic from an EC2 instance to the public cloud, the destination field of the route table should be which of the following?

    A. 0.0.0.0/0

    B. 0.0.0.0/32

    C. Internet gateway

    D. Local

8. Which of the following represents the largest CIDR block that can be used in a VPC subnet?

    A. 10.0.0.0/32

    B. 172.16.0.0/16

    C. 172.16.0.0/0

    D. 192.168.0.0/28

9. Which of the following is *not* a valid private IP address?

    A. 10.0.0.5

    B. 75.10.150.5

    C. 172.16.0.5

    D. 172.28.10.10

10. You want to route traffic to the Internet from resources in an Ipv6 subnet without allowing external resources to initiate contact. Which of the following best solves this problem?

    A. DirectConnect

    B. Egress-only Internet gateway

    C. Internet gateway

    D. Transit gateway

11. You wish to capture a subset of your VPC traffic in order to diagnose an issue. Which of the following will allow you to capture only the traffic you want and route it to a specified monitoring appliance?

    A. AWS CloudWatch

    B. AWS Systems Manager Distributor

    C. Traffic Mirroring

    D. VPC flow logs

12. You wish to allow administrators to securely connect to hosts in a private subnet in your VPC. Which of the following will best solve this problem?

    A. Bastion host

    B. Client VPN

    C. NAT gateway

    D. Transit gateway

13. Instances in a private subnet must be able to securely initiate software updates with services on the Internet. Which of the following will accomplish this goal?

    A. Bastion host

    B. DirectConnect

    C. NAT instance

    D. NAT gateway

14. Your employer has tasked you with implementing a cost-effective firewall to protect your whole VPC. The solution must be able to process a high volume of traffic with both stateful and stateless rules. Your environment spans two regions (us-east-2 and ap-southeast-1) with three availability zones in each region. Which of the following will you choose?

    A. AWS Network Firewall

    B. Network access control lists (ACLs)

    C. Security groups

    D. Web application firewall (WAF)

15. Your team needs to securely SSH into your fleet. The solution must be highly available and cost-effective, and have auditable logs of the SSH activity. Which of the following will you choose?

    A. Bastion host

    B. NAT gateway

    C. Systems Manager

    D. Transit gateway

16. What is the number of IP addresses reserved by AWS in every subnet?

    A. 3

    B. 5

    C. 7

    D. 10

17. Your employer has a global network with many network providers. You have been tasked with connecting these networks and managing policies centrally. Which of the following will best accomplish this?

    A. AWS Control Tower

    B. AWS Transit Gateway

    C. Cloud WAN

    D. Route 53

18. You have been asked to establish a mechanism for managing IP address blocks (CIDR) across your large, global enterprise. This system must centrally manage both private and public IP spaces. Which of the following AWS services best meets these requirements?

A. AWS Control Tower

B. CloudFormation

C. IP Address Manager

D. Route 53

19. You are securing resources in your VPC. You wish to allow only specific ports and you require stateful connections. Which of the following best fulfills these requirements?

A. NAT gateway

B. Network access control lists (NACLs)

C. Security groups

D. Web application firewall (WAF)

20. The security group provides a firewall at what layer in the VPC?

A. Availability zone

B. Internet gateway

C. Network interface

D. Subnet

Chapter

10

Content Delivery

THE AWS CERTIFIED SYSOPS ADMINISTRATOR EXAM OBJECTIVES COVERED IN THIS CHAPTER INCLUDE:

✓ **Domain 5.0: Networking and Content Delivery**

- 5.2 Configure domains, DNS services, and content delivery

  - Configure Route 53 hosted zones and records

  - Implement Route 53 routing policies (for example, geolocation, geo-proximity)

  - Configure DNS (for example, Route 53 Resolver)

  - Configure Amazon CloudFront and S3 origin access identity (OAI)

  - Configure S3 static website hosting

- 5.3 Troubleshoot network connectivity issues

  - Identify and remediate CloudFront caching issues

As you work more with networks, and the IP addresses that systems use to communicate with one another, it is easy to see that tracking IP addresses and the systems they map to can quickly become a nightmare. IP addresses aren't easily memorable for most people, and even a small organization can quickly outgrow static IP addresses and Excel spreadsheets tracking their names, as well as custom host files.

The Domain Name System (DNS) is a service that has been around for many years. The simplest way to think of it is like your Contacts list on your mobile devices. You remember the names of your friends and family, but you may not remember their phone numbers. When you want to call someone, you click their name, and the phone knows based on the name you selected which phone number needs to be called. DNS does something very similar in that it allows you to use easy-to-remember names like www.wiley.com rather than having to find out or remember the IP address for the site that you want to reach.

This chapter is focused on the AWS implementation of DNS, which is called Route 53, and what you will need to know about Route 53 to use it effectively. In addition, we'll discuss Amazon CloudFront, its use of edge locations for content distribution as well as the fundamental implementation details. Finally, we'll discuss AWS Global Accelerator as a service that also uses AWS edge locations for accelerating the performance and reducing the response latency of your applications.

This chapter will help you understand the following:

- The Domain Name System (DNS) and Amazon Route 53
- The difference between private and public DNS in Route 53
- Routing policies in Route 53 and how they work
- Using health checks in Route 53
- Implementing an Amazon CloudFront distribution
- How to improve cache hit ratios for a distribution
- How to configure a distribution for origin access identity (OAI) and Origin Shield
- How to invalidate cache objects
- AWS Global Accelerator and how it helps your applications

Domain Name System

The *Domain Name System* (DNS) provides a method to translate between human-readable (and easily remembered) addresses and the IP addresses that systems use to communicate over an IP-based network. You may be wondering how DNS is able to convert between friendly names and IP addresses. Let's get into that briefly.

When you look up a site, say like www.wiley.com, your system will reach out to its local DNS server with a DNS query to see if the local DNS server knows the IP address for this site. If your local DNS server has the answer, then it will respond with the IP address. If it doesn't have it, it sends a query to a *top-level domain* (TLD) DNS server for .com. The TLD DNS server will respond with the address of the authoritative DNS server for wiley.com. Your DNS server then sends the query to the DNS server for wiley.com, which responds with the IP address for www.wiley.com. In general, that's how most DNS queries operate.

DNS operates over the network using both Transmission Control Protocol (TCP) and User Datagram Protocol (UDP) over port 53. UDP has historically been used for DNS queries, but large network packets like what you get with IPv6 and/or DNS Security (DNS-SEC) signed records go over TCP. It is also used for zone transfers, the process of propagating name-to–IP address records between servers. Using a bit of humor, Amazon named its DNS service Route 53. It's a DNS server that goes beyond the basic behavior of name-to–IP address translation and implements features unique to the service that allow you to implement health checks on specific points of interest and dictate which result is distributed upon a query based on routing policies. As a summary, Route 53 performs DNS management, including domain name registration, availability monitoring by using health checks, and traffic management using routing policies, among other features. Let's get started with the basics.

DNS Records

Amazon Route 53 supports many of the DNS record types that you might expect, and perhaps a few more. In case you aren't familiar with how each of these types of records is used, let's examine each of them.

A   The A record is used to map a hostname to an IP address. An A record is an IPv4 address.

AAAA   The AAAA record is also used to map a hostname to an IP address. An AAAA record is used for IPv6 addresses.

PTR   A pointer (PTR) record is used to do reverse DNS lookups. The traditional lookup gives you an IP address for a hostname; the PTR does the opposite and gives you the hostname associated with an IP address.

CNAME   A canonical name (CNAME) is used to create a "nickname" to a true and actual name. This is commonly used in web hosting to map a name like www.stuff .com to the actual name of the server that hosts the website. When people type www .stuff.com DNS resolves the address to the web hosting server using the CNAME record. The actual name of the server can be (newproduct.stuff.com) but publicly it can also be reached using its "nickname" of www.stuff.com, which is convenient to say the least. Please note that DNS does not allow the creation of a CNAME record to the top node (apex record) of a DNS name. You cannot create a CNAME for `stuff` `.com` by itself.

SOA   The start of authority (SOA) record is used to define the authoritative DNS servers for an individual DNS zone. This is one of the most important records in a DNS hosted zone. When you register a domain using Route 53 and create a hosted zone, the service automatically creates a SOA record and an NS record for the hosted zone as they are essential to the proper functioning of DNS.

NS   Name Server (NS) records are used to identify the DNS servers for a given hosted zone. These are the actual hosts that will be responding to queries to resolve name-to–IP addresses for your domain. This will typically be expressed as the fully qualified domain name (FQDN) of the server. Route 53 supports wildcard entries for all record types, except NS records. This means all value hosts to route traffic for a related NS record need to have the form `HOST.DOMAIN.TLD.` (i.e., `ns-dns.somedns-38.com.`).

TXT   The text (TXT) record is used to provide information in a text format to systems outside of your domain. It has many purposes, one of which is to present the information for identity validation for Sender Policy Framework (SPF), rather than using SPF records.

MX   Mail exchange (MX) records are used to identify email servers for a given domain. They can also be used to set the priority of the email servers if there are multiple hosts behaving as email servers. For instance, you may have a primary email server with a priority of 10 and a secondary with a priority of 20. The priority number, which is part of the record, defines the order of how the servers are to be used. The lower the number, the more important and higher the priority.

CAA   A CAA record is used to identify valid certificate authorities for your domain. This can prevent unauthorized certificate authorities from being used to issue certificates for your domain.

NAPTR   You will typically find Name Authority Pointer (NAPTR) records linked with service records (SRV). They are used to "chain" multiple records together to create rewrite rules, which can create things like uniform resource identifiers (URIs) or domain labels. You also see NAPTR records in the context of Dynamic Delegation Discovery System (DDDS) applications.

SPF   The Sender Policy Framework (SPF) is used to identify the sender of email messages and validate that the identity presented is true. Due to interoperability issues with SPFv1, AWS recommends that you use TXT records to present the necessary information rather than SPF records. The use of SPF records is not recommended by AWS.

SRV   The service (SRV) record is used to identify hostnames and port numbers for servers that provide services with a DNS zone.

Amazon Route 53 also supports *alias* records. An alias record in AWS is used to route traffic to AWS resources such as an Amazon S3 website endpoint, elastic load balancers, CloudFront distributions, Elastic

Beanstalk environments, VPC endpoints, API gateway endpoints, and global accelerator endpoints, among others. You can also use an alias record to route traffic from one record in a hosted zone to another record. The alias type of record is unique to Route 53, and proper use of it is essential. Alias records in Route 53 are often confused with CNAME records as they are specific to Route 53. CNAME records are more general, and they do incur a charge when used, while Route 53 does not charge for alias queries to AWS resources.

Amazon Route 53

Route 53 behaves in the way you would expect if you have worked with DNS before. However, Route 53 also has features that turn it into a very useful tool for DNS management, including domain name registration or transfer, availability monitoring by using health checks, and traffic management using routing policies, as shown in Figure 10.1.

FIGURE 10.1 The main console for Route 53 makes it simple to choose what you want to do among a variety of options.

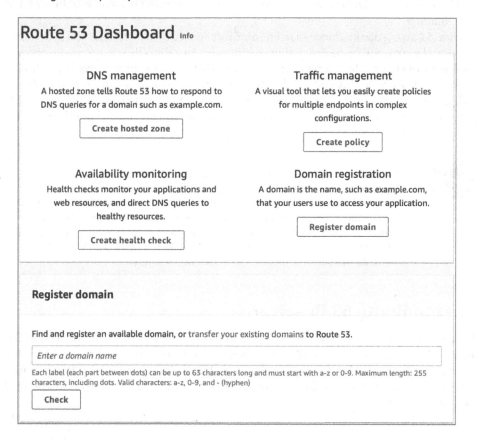

Route 53 includes the ability to register a domain name from a long list of generic and geographic top-level domains (TLDs). There are some restrictions, and some TLDs cannot be registered or transferred to Route 53. However, you can use Route 53 as the DNS service for any domain even if it's not included in the list of Route 53 supported TLDs. The index of supported TLDs is extensive and not worth repeating here.

> You can visit the following URL for a comprehensive list of supported top-level domains: https://docs.aws.amazon.com/Route53/latest/ DeveloperGuide/registrar-tld-list.html.

Route 53 Public and Private DNS Hosted Zones

Independently of how a domain is obtained to use with Route 53, the next step will be to create what is called a hosted zone using the service. Creating a hosted zone is simple; you just need to specify the domain name, an optional description, and most importantly, how you expect to route traffic for the hosted zone. You can select one of two possible types of hosted zones: public or private.

A public hosted zone indicates that traffic related to the zone will be routed on the Internet. This is how most DNS systems operate in that all traffic and resolution is done on the public Internet.

Route 53 gives you the choice to define a private hosted zone, which indicates that traffic related to the zone will be routed within one or more Amazon VPCs. A private hosted zone is isolated from the public Internet and only responds to queries for resources on VPCs that you associate to it. Private hosted zones are useful for you to access resources in your VPCs using custom domain names instead of using private IP addresses or AWS-provided DNS names. When you create a private hosted zone, you will be asked about the VPCs to associate with the hosted zone.

> If you choose to use a Route 53 private hosted zone for custom DNS names in one or more VPCs, you must set both the enableDnsHostnames and enableDnsSupport attributes to true for all VPCs associated with the private hosted zone. To do this, navigate to the VPC landing page in your AWS console. Select the VPC you want, and from the Actions menu at the top right, select Edit VPC Settings. Then enable the settings mentioned above accordingly.

Amazon Route 53 Resolver

The Amazon Route 53 Resolver is available by default in all VPCs. A VPC connects to the Route 53 Resolver at the VPC+2 IP address in an availability zone. The Route 53 Resolver functionality handles all DNS queries, including public domain names, records in private hosted zones, and AWS-assigned names for resources. (i.e., ec2-192-0-3-77.compute-1 .amazonaws.com).

The Route 53 Resolver can also handle DNS queries between your datacenter network and your Amazon VPCs. This will require that you create Resolver endpoints and conditional forwarding rules for the DNS traffic to flow inbound and outbound if needed. The inbound endpoint allows your network to forward DNS queries to the Route 53 Resolver. The outbound endpoint allows the Resolver to forward queries to your datacenter network DNS server if needed.

Route 53 Resolver DNS Firewall

The Route 53 Resolver DNS Firewall is a managed firewall service for DNS queries that originate in your VPCs. You basically create rule groups and then add rules to those rule groups to define how to inspect and filter Resolver DNS traffic coming from your VPCs. Rules define domain names to look for and the action to take when a DNS query matches one of the domains. You can allow a query to move on, you can allow it to move on with an alert, or you can block it and respond with a predefined value. Rule groups need to be associated to VPCs to begin filtering traffic that requires protection. Filtering rules are applied to outgoing VPC traffic.

Route 53 Health Checks

Route 53 health checks monitor availability and performance of endpoints by using a network of health checkers located in regions around the world. Health checkers are in U.S. East (N. Virginia), U.S. West (N. California), U.S. West (Oregon), EU (Ireland), Asia Pacific (Singapore), Asia Pacific (Sydney), Asia Pacific (Tokyo), and South America (São Paulo).

You can use a domain name or an IP address and port combination to define HTTP(S) and TCP health checks. Health checks provide CloudWatch metrics to give you visibility and enable you to set alarms and get automated notifications when needed. Also, you can associate health checks with any Route 53 DNS record to define routing for requests based on the health of your endpoints. The process of automatic failover routing in Route 53 starts with a health check. However, it is important to note that you can apply a health check to any endpoint and any Route 53 record you choose. Health checks are not limited to failover routing policies. You can configure notifications to be sent so that you are aware when an endpoint becomes unhealthy. Also, please note that an endpoint without a health check is always considered healthy.

There are three types of health checks. Each one works differently, so let's look at each one.

Monitor an Endpoint   You can create a health check that will monitor the health of an endpoint defined by IP address or by domain name and at a predefined request interval. You can choose intervals of 30 seconds (Standard) or 10 seconds (Fast). Route 53 sends automated requests to your endpoint to check that it is reachable, available, and functional. You can also configure a health check to make a URL request like requesting a web page. Please note that a faster interval is not necessarily better than the standard 30-second interval. It is common for about 15 health checkers to verify a specified endpoint. Using the standard interval of 30 seconds means the endpoint will receive a health check request every two to three seconds. If you choose the fast interval of 10 seconds, the endpoint will get a request more than once per second, which has the potential of causing saturation on the endpoint.

Monitor Other Health Checks (Calculated Health Checks)   You can create a health check that monitors whether other Route 53 health checks are healthy or unhealthy. If you are operating a web server farm, you can create a health check for each web server instance and then create a health check to monitor all the other health checks and notify you when the number of available servers drops below a set limit. In general, a calculated health check can report healthy under three possibilities:

- At least X of Y selected health checks are healthy.
- All health checks are healthy.
- One or more health checks are healthy.

Monitor CloudWatch Alarms   You can create a health check that can use CloudWatch metrics to determine whether an endpoint is healthy or unhealthy. If you create an alarm, you can also create a health check to monitor the same data that CloudWatch monitors for the alarm. The health check will show healthy if the CloudWatch alarm is in an OK state. When the alarm is in the ALARM state, the health check status is unhealthy. When the alarm is in the INSUFFICIENT state, you can choose to define the health check status as healthy or unhealthy, or use the last known status.

Route 53 health checks for CloudWatch alarms support standard resolution metrics and the statistics of Average, Minimum, Maximum, Sum, and SampleCount only. High-resolution metrics and extended statistics are not supported.

The Structure of a Route 53 Record

Creating a record in Route 53 will require that you provide details about the record. In general, you need to configure the items in the following list, as shown in Figure 10.2.

Record Name   This field holds the name of the record plus the name of the hosted zone. The hosted zone will be predefined and shown as a static value. You only need to specify the name for the record. An example for a value would be www for the name, and stuff.com would be the hosted zone.

Record Type   Select the type of DNS record that you want to create. These were discussed earlier in this chapter.

Alias   This is a radio button where you indicate if the value to use to route traffic is an alias. The setting is OFF by default. If you enable it, then the Value field entry changes to Route Traffic To.

Value/Route Traffic To   This field holds the value that you want the record to have. For example, if you are creating an A record, you would enter an IPv4 address. However, if the Alias radio button is enabled, the Value field entry becomes Route Traffic To and you need to indicate the AWS endpoint, like an S3 website endpoint, and a region, like US-EAST-1, to route traffic to.

TTL (Time to Live in Seconds)   TTL represents how long the value is cached by DNS systems in seconds. AWS recommends starting with a lower value like 300 seconds (5 minutes) until you are sure that everything is working properly. DNS won't be queried again until the TTL has expired.

Routing Policy   In this field you choose how Route 53 routes traffic to your resources. This is a unique feature of Route 53 that allows you to dictate how and what values to use in response to a DNS query. Depending on the routing policy chosen, you may need to provide additional information for the routing to perform as expected. It's important you understand how each of these routing policies operate. Let's examine each of them in the next section.

Record ID   A record ID is a unique value used to identify differences in Route 53 records and is used across routing policies. For example, you can use a date/time stamp or a sequential number for a record ID to identify the primary and secondary records in a weighted failover policy.

FIGURE 10.2   The main console for Amazon Route 53 to create a record in a hosted zone

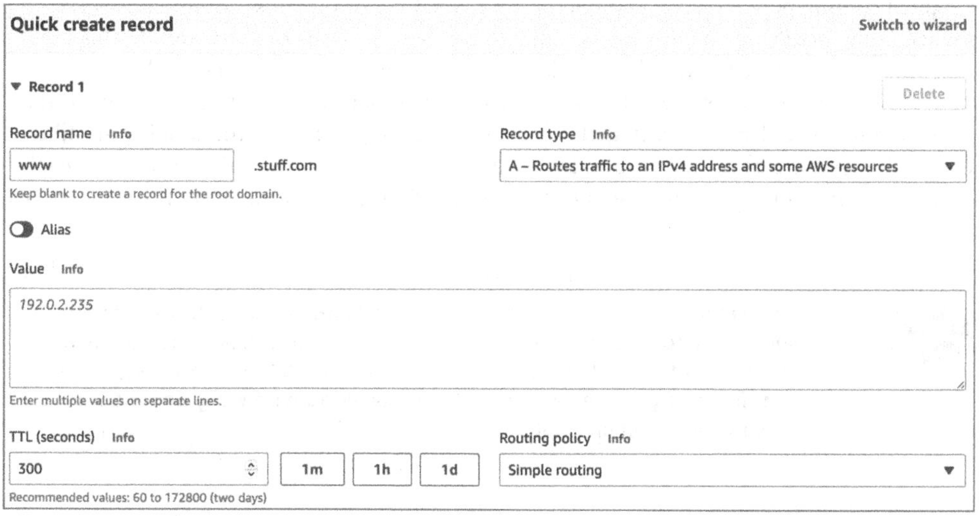

Quick create record	Switch to wizard

▼ Record 1   Delete

Record name   Info

`www`   .stuff.com

Keep blank to create a record for the root domain.

◯ Alias

Value   Info

`192.0.2.235`

Enter multiple values on separate lines.

TTL (seconds)   Info

`300`   ⇕   1m   1h   1d

Recommended values: 60 to 172800 (two days)

Record type   Info

A – Routes traffic to an IPv4 address and some AWS resources   ▼

Routing policy   Info

Simple routing   ▼

Routing Policies

For each record you create in a Route 53 hosted zone, you choose a routing policy. The routing policy is what determines how to return the results of a DNS query, and each type of policy has a different behavior and use case. These routing policies can do some very interesting things, including performance and availability improvements. This section explores each of the types of routing policies and how they are used.

Simple Routing Policy

If you just want Route 53 to route traffic without any special considerations like priorities or geolocation, then a *simple routing policy* is the best fit. Simple routing policies do allow you to apply more than one IP address to a record, but the results are returned in a random order. When you create a record using a simple routing policy, configure it as follows:

- **Record Name:** This field holds the name to be used.
- **Record Type:** Select the type of DNS record that you want to create. These were covered earlier in this chapter.
- **Alias:** No.
- **Value/Route Traffic To:** This field holds the value that you want for the record.
- **TTL (Seconds):** Recommended values are 60 to 172,800 (two days).
- **Routing Policy:** Simple.

Weighted Routing Policy

Weighted routing policies have a couple of use cases. One of the most common use cases is when doing *blue/green deployments* (done to test new versions of software). In this use case, you can configure the weights to allow 10 percent of the traffic to go to the hosts running the new version of the software and route the other 90 percent of the traffic to the hosts running the old software. In general, Route 53 creates a sum of the weights for all the records that you are using and responds to queries based on the ratio of a resource's weight to the total sum. Starting with a number from 1 to 100 is a good idea to get the proportions clearly.

To disable routing to a resource, set the Weight value to 0. Also, if you set Weight to 0 for all records being used, then traffic is routed to each resource with equal probability. Finally, the effect of setting Weight to 0 is different if you are using health checks along with weighted records. Make sure to test carefully.

When you create a record for a weighted routing policy, configure it as follows:

- **Record Name:** This field holds the name to be used.
- **Record Type:** Select the type of DNS record that you want to create.
- **Alias:** No.
- **Value/Route Traffic To:** This holds the value that you want for the record.
- **TTL (Seconds):** Recommended values are 60 to 172,800 (two days).
- **Routing Policy:** Weighted.
- **Weight:** You can enter a number between 0 and 255 in this field. If you specify 0, Route 53 stops using this record in DNS queries.
- **Health Check ID:** Select the health check to be used for the record.
- **Record ID:** You can use a date/time stamp or a sequential number.

Geolocation Routing Policy

If you choose a geolocation routing policy, you can decide where users will be directed based on their location. Users in the United States, for instance, may be routed to the U.S. East region, whereas users in Europe may get routed to a European Union (EU) West region. When you create a record for a geolocation routing policy, configure it as follows:

- **Record Name:** This field holds the name to be used.
- **Record Type:** Select the type of DNS record that you want to create.
- **Alias:** No.
- **Value/Route Traffic To:** This holds the value that you want for the record.
- **TTL (Seconds):** Recommended values are 60 to 172,800 (two days).
- **Routing Policy:** Geolocation.
- **Location:** This field contains the names of the countries that you want DNS to respond to. It is also best practice to include an entry that uses default for the location. This will apply to countries not explicitly called out in this field.
- **Health Check ID:** Select the health check to be used for the record.
- **Record ID:** You can use a date/time stamp or a sequential number.

Latency Routing Policy

Latency routing policies direct your end users or customers to the region that can provide the lowest latency. The most important thing to remember about this is that the region with the best latency may not be the region that is closest to the end user or customer. When you create a record for a latency routing policy, configure it as follows:

- **Record Name:** This field holds the name to be used.
- **Record Type:** Select the type of DNS record that you want to create.

- **Alias:** No.
- **Value/Route traffic to:** This holds the value that you want for the record.
- **TTL (Seconds):** Recommended values are 60 to 172,800 (two days).
- **Routing Policy:** Latency.
- **Region:** The region where the endpoint that will respond exists.
- **Health Check ID:** Select the health check to be used for the record.
- **Record ID:** You can use a date/time stamp or a sequential number.

Failover Routing Policy

You can use a failover routing policy to direct traffic to a primary instance while it's healthy but divert traffic to a secondary instance if the primary becomes unhealthy. When you create a record for a failover routing policy, configure it as follows:

- **Record Name:** This field holds the name to be used.
- **Record Type:** Select the type of DNS record that you want to create.
- **Alias:** No.
- **Value/Route Traffic To:** This holds the value that you want for the record.
- **TTL (Seconds):** Recommended values are 60 to 172,800 (two days).
- **Routing Policy:** Failover.
- **Failover Record Type:** You will need to create at least two records, one for primary and one for secondary.
- **Health Check ID:** Select the health check to be used for the primary record.
- **Record ID:** You can use a date/time stamp or a sequential number.

Multivalue Answer Routing Policy

A multivalued answer routing policy returns multiple values (IP addresses) in response to a query. By using a multivalue answer routing policy, you can be assured that the IP addresses being returned are from healthy hosts, since this routing policy can do health checks if you set it to do so.

 If there are eight or fewer healthy hosts, the query will respond with all the healthy records.

When you create a record for a multivalued answer routing policy, configure it as follows:

- **Record Name:** This field holds the name to be used.
- **Record Type:** Select the type of DNS record that you want to create.
- **Alias:** You can't use an alias record with multivalue routing policies.
- **TTL (Seconds):** Recommended values are 60 to 172,800 (two days).

- **Value/Route Traffic To:** This holds the value that you want for the record.
- **Routing Policy:** Multivalued answer.
- **Health Check ID:** Select the health check to be used for the record.
- **Record ID:** You can use a date/time stamp or a sequential number.

IP-Based Routing Policy

IP-based routing policies enable you to route traffic to resources in your domain based on the client subnet IP. This is similar to geolocation, and it uses your knowledge of the network and your client's IPs to tell Route 53 to use a form of user-IP to endpoint mapping. This is useful if you want to optimize network transit costs to route end users from a particular ISP to specific endpoints. You can also override geolocation routing based on the knowledge of your client's physical locations and have the IP addresses where traffic originates.

 You cannot use IP-based routing policy for records in private hosted zones.

When you create a record for IP-based routing, you are required to group sets of CIDR blocks with CIDR locations into reusable entities called CIDR collections. A CIDR collection has a name and at least one CIDR location specified by name and one or more CIDRs. You can list IP addresses from /0 to /24 for IPv4 and /0 to /48 for IPv6. You need to create CIDR collections separately from Route 53 records that will use IP-based routing. The Route 53 console has an IP-Based Routing section with a subheader called CIDR Collections. To create a record to use with IP-based routing, configure it as follows:

- **Record Name:** This field holds the name to be used.
- **Record Type:** Select the type of DNS record that you want to create.
- **Alias:** No.
- **Value/Route Traffic To:** This holds the value that you want for the record.
- **TTL (Seconds):** Recommended values are 60 to 172,800 (two days).
- **Routing Policy:** IP-based.
- **IP-based:** This field contains the name of the CIDR location within your CIDR collection. You can also select the Default location (*).
- **Health Check ID:** Select the health check to be used for the record.
- **Record ID:** You can use a date/time stamp or a sequential number.

Geoproximity Routing Policy

On the surface, the geoproximity routing policy is similar to geolocation in that it allows you to determine where your users will be directed based on their location. The difference is with a geoproximity routing policy you have fine-grained control of how you configure routing based on the distance between your customers and your resources. This is done by setting a bias. The bias metric allows you to route traffic to specific resources. You can route traffic based on the location of your resources and, if needed, shift traffic from resources in one location to resources in a different location. All you need to do is change the bias value.

 The geoproximity routing policy is only available when you're using a traffic policy created using traffic flow.

Route 53 Traffic Flow

The Route 53 traffic flow feature is a visual editor where you can create complex routing configurations by combining one or more of the routing policies we just discussed. The visual editor saves your configuration as a traffic policy, and there's built-in versioning to help you with management and applying changes. Traffic flow is all about simplifying the process of creating and managing records in large and complex configurations. You can use any of the record types and any of the routing policies we discussed. You can also use health checks as needed. Traffic policies incur no charge no matter how many you create. All versions of a traffic policy exist until you delete them. There's a limit of 1,000 versions per traffic policy.

A traffic policy has the potential to represent multiple records in the scale of dozens or hundreds. Traffic flow enables you to create all the records in a traffic policy automatically by creating a traffic policy record. You define the hosted zone and the name of the record at the root of the tree like `stuff.com` or `www.stuff.com` and Route 53 creates all the records automatically. This becomes a repeatable and reusable resource, which will save you a significant amount of time for large and complex domains. When a query is received for the root record, Route 53 uses the configuration in the traffic policy to generate the response.

Route 53 Application Recovery Controller (ARC)

One of the most complex use cases of Route 53 and health checks is done by the Route 53 Application Recovery Controller (ARC). As the name suggests, this is an application recovery tool intended to leverage health checks and routing policies to allow you to implement an application recovery plan in the event of an availability zone or a regional failure. Route 53 ARC delivers three capabilities, which together allow you to automate complex verification and movement of traffic to resources in the event of a failure. They are readiness checks, routing controls, and zonal shifts. Readiness checks monitor resources, capacity, and network routing policies. If a change takes place that may negatively impact failing over to a replica and recover, the readiness check will notify you about the situation so that it can be mitigated. Consider a readiness check as an advanced form of a health check where not only resources but also routing policies are being monitored to provide you with the fastest and most reliable way to recover from a failure. You can configure rules to manage the recovery process. A readiness check is monitoring readiness for recovery of multiregion or multi-AZ application failure.

The routing controls and zonal shift features are used to shift end-user traffic and restore availability. They apply to active-active or active-standby applications implemented as multi-AZ or multiregion. Route 53 ARC is all about maintaining high availability for large critical applications and simplifying recovery for multi-AZ and multiregion implementations. This is probably the most advanced and complex feature related to Amazon Route 53.

Route 53 Guided Exercise

Now that we have discussed the details of Route 53, let's get some hands-on experience with an exercise on how to use it via the AWS Console.

To do the activities in Exercise 10.1, you need a hosted zone. It will be a good idea (although not necessary) to register a domain name to make sure the steps work as expected and that you get the best understanding. Let's create that first.

EXERCISE 10.1

Registering a Domain and Creating a Hosted Zone

1. Log into the AWS Management Console, click Services, and under Networking & Content Delivery, select Amazon Route 53.

2. On the Route 53 dashboard, you can use the Register Domain panel to find and register an available domain for your personal use. You can register a domain for as little as $9/ year. Domain prices will vary depending on the suffix.

3. Once you have registered a domain, on the Route 53 dashboard select Hosted Zones in the vertical panels to the left of the page. If you don't see the panels, click the icon on the top with three horizontal lines.

4. Click Create Hosted Zone to enter the hosted zone configuration.

5. Type an unused domain name; we are using **sysops.ninja**, which was registered for this exercise and is safe for you to use for this example.

This creates a hosted zone with name servers (NS) and start of authority (SOA) records.

For Exercise 10.2 to work, you need to have two EC2 instances up and running with a web server and a sample page set up properly. You will need to create a security group with a single inbound rule for HTTP from anywhere (0.0.0.0/0). You will also create a role using IAM for the web servers called **EC2SSMRole** and assign it the AWS Managed policy with name **AmazonEC2RoleforSSM** so that you can use AWS Systems Manager Session Manager to connect and operate the servers. These tasks have been covered in Chapter 2, "Account

Creation, Security, and Compliance," and Chapter 8, "Monitoring, Logging, and Remediation." You may need to review how to create a security group and how to create a role for an EC2 instance. We will omit the step-by-step for the sake of brevity.

EXERCISE 10.2

Creating Web Server Hosts and a Health Check

We'll call the web servers **WEB1** and **WEB2**. If you don't have any, you will need to create them to continue. I created two t2.micro instances running Amazon Linux 2023 AMI. I used the default VPC and different subnets for each. For the web server installation, you can use the following script. Put it in the User Data field so it happens while the servers are being provisioned. You will use the index.html page later (change the last line to **WEB2** for the second server). Note that you must allow the software to install before continuing. Also, assign the EC2 Systems Manager Role to the instance in case you need to connect to it using Systems Manager Session Manager.

```
#!/bin/bash
yum update -y
yum install -y httpd.x86_64
systemctl start httpd.service
systemctl enable httpd.service
usermod -a -G apache ec2-user
chown -R ec2-user:apache /var/www
chmod 2775 /var/www
find /var/www -type d -exec chmod 2775 {} \;
find /var/www -type f -exec chmod 0664 {} \;
echo Route 53 Failover Test with WEB1 > /var/www/html/index.html
```

1. Click Services, and under Compute select EC2.

2. Select each of the two instances and take note of their public IP addresses. You will need them for this exercise. Be sure to paste each public IP address into a web browser window and verify that you get the page with the messages "Route 53 Failover Test with WEB1" and "Route 53 Failover Test with WEB2."

3. Click Services, and then under Networking & Content Delivery, select Amazon Route 53.

4. On the Route 53 dashboard, click Health Checks and then Create Health Check.

5. For Name, enter a name that makes sense to you, such as **Web1-HC**.

6. Leave What To Monitor set to Endpoint.

7. Under Monitor An Endpoint, select IP Address, and then enter the IP address of your first instance. Under Path, type **index.html**.

8. Click Advanced Configuration to expand the options. Choose Fast (10 Seconds) for the request interval and 2 for the failure threshold. Leave the rest at the defaults.

9. Click Next.

10. On the Get Notified When A Health Check Fails screen, click Yes for Create Alarm.

11. For Send Notification To, click New SNS Topic. For the topic name, use **Web1-HealthCheck**.

12. Enter your email address under Recipient Email Addresses.

    You will get an email to your address asking you to confirm the subscription.

13. Click Create Health Check.

Click Refresh until the instance is listed as Healthy under the Status column before continuing to the next exercise.

In Exercise 10.3, you'll create the records for the web servers as well as a failover routing policy.

EXERCISE 10.3

Creating the A Records for Failover

1. Click Hosted Zones and then click the domain name you created in Exercise 10.2. Please note how an NS and SOA records already exist.

2. Click Create Record.

3. For Record Name, type **www** and for Record type, select A – Routes Traffic To An IPv4 Address.

4. For Value, type the IP address of the first web instance.

5. For Routing Policy, choose Failover and for Failover Record Type, select Primary.

6. For Health Check, choose the name of the health check you created in Exercise 10.2. For Record ID, use the number **1**.

7. Click Create Records. This will provision the primary in this failover scenario.

8. To create the secondary/failover record, click Create Record.

9. For Name, type **www**.

10. For Value, type the IP address of the second web instance.

11. For Routing Policy, choose Failover and select Secondary.

For Record ID, use the number **2**.

12. Leave the Health Check field empty.

13. Click Create Records.

You have now created a failover set. Based on our test solution, if you went to www
.sysops.ninja, you could be directed to the WEB1 server. If the WEB1 server goes
down (say you stopped it), then the health check for WEB1 will indicate unhealthy and www
.sysops.ninja would direct you to the WEB2 server. The only way to test this is to own
the domain name in question; you can register a domain using Amazon Route 53 for a reasonable cost. The domain used in these exercises was purchased for demonstration. If you
use it, the exercise will not work as indicated above.

In Exercise 10.3, we provisioned two servers using the default VPC and
the feature of auto-assigned public IP addresses. As such, when you stop
the first server and the health check fails, then the secondary IP record
gets used. You get to see the failover to the second web server. However, please keep in mind that when you restore the first web server,
most likely the health check will continue to display as unhealthy. This is
because when you use the subnet auto-assigned IP address feature, if
you stop and then start a server, the IP address will be different. To wit-
ness the health check, return to a healthy state when you start the server
again, and you will need to provision and attach elastic IP addresses to
your web servers. This makes the IP addresses remain the same independently of the server state.

Also, keep in mind that a server without a health check is considered always
healthy.

Amazon CloudFront

When a business adopts AWS Cloud computing and discusses the benefits, it is very common
to read that you can "go global in minutes." Amazon CloudFront is the service that permits
you to do just that. You can have a website anywhere you desire, like an Amazon S3 bucket,
a fleet of EC2 instances with an application load balancer as a customer-facing resource, or
even a site in your own datacenter and CloudFront will make that website available globally
using high-speed data transfers and the AWS global infrastructure of edge locations in a matter
of minutes. CloudFront is a content delivery network (CDN) service that provides security,
low latencies, and high transfer speeds for your chosen dataset. The data to be distributed can

be anything from commonly used static media file sets such as images, videos, or music to dynamic websites, Amazon APIs, and anything else you need to reach your customers globally using secure, low-latency data transfers and using IPv4/IPv6 addressing. CloudFront is a global service and can be used for both distributing content from a point of origin as well as uploading objects when used in connection to Amazon S3 transfer acceleration.

Edge Locations

As discussed in Chapter 1, "AWS Fundamentals," edge locations are the global infrastructure resource used by AWS to deliver reliable and low-latency performance worldwide. Edge locations is how AWS attains high performance in countries and territories where a region does not exist. Also, edge locations exist even in places where an AWS region is present. Edge locations are usually located in highly populated cities around the world. The global edge network connects thousands of Tiers 1, 2, and 3 telecom carriers worldwide and delivers hundreds of terabits of capacity. Edge locations are connected with regions using the AWS backbone, which is a fully redundant, multiple 100 Gigabit Ethernet (GbE) parallel fiber infrastructure. The AWS edge network consists of over 400 edge locations and 13 regional edge caches in over 90 cities across 49 countries.

A regional cache is a midpoint cache between the customer-facing edge locations and the place where datasets originally live and need to be distributed. Regional caches are usually larger in size than edge locations. The idea is for your data to be distributed to remain as close to the customer as possible when compared to where they are originally located. This last item is called an *origin* in CloudFront vocabulary. An origin is where data to be distributed is placed originally.

Edge locations are protected automatically by the AWS Shield standard from distributed denial-of-service (DDoS) attacks and free of charge. You can also leverage a full integration with AWS WAF (Web Application Firewall) to define managed rules for enhanced protection in addition to using SSL/TLS certificate support. In a nutshell, edge locations shorten the distance your data needs to travel to reach your customers.

The CloudFront Cache Process

The CloudFront cache process includes resources worth defining before we discuss the caching mechanism in detail. CloudFront operates based on distributions, the source of the data being cached, such as an S3 bucket, customer datacenter server, or other web servers. A distribution only requires an *origin domain* to be created. Basically, if you have an existing S3 bucket that is publicly available with an image and/or an HTML page, you can create a CloudFront distribution, assign the S3 URL as the origin domain, and then select Create Distribution at the bottom right of the CloudFront configuration page. CloudFront will create a domain name to distribute the content in your S3 bucket. The domain will have a random hostname followed by `cloudfront.net`—for example, `afdm5abcdf77g .cloudfront.net`.

The CloudFront cache process begins by making available the CloudFront domain name as listed above or a reasonable substitute like a CNAME record for your domain name using Route 53. When a request is made, CloudFront detects the closest edge location and performs an *origin fetch* request of the data, which will then be cached on the edge location and distributed to the requesting user. Data is retained on the edge location for 24 hours by default, and any other request for the same dataset will be delivered from the cached dataset in the edge location. A request from a different location will cause the same process to be applied with regard to the edge location closest to the requesting user.

You can modify the default retention time by configuring a Time to Live (TTL) for your objects and distributions. The minimum TTL value you can use is zero (0). This specifies the minimum amount of time, in seconds, for objects to be kept in the cache before performing another origin fetch request. A TTL of 0 indicates that you are using dynamic data and that none of the objects associated with the TTL will be cached. CloudFront will forward all requests for those objects to the origin server.

The metrics gathered when distributing data in the cache versus performing an origin fetch is called the *cache hit ratio*. Ideally you would want to minimize the load on the origin server. Increasing the TTL can result in an improved cache hit ratio simply because the resources are retained longer in the cache. This is practical for static assets.

Another option to improve the cache hit ratio is to enable the Origin Shield option in the CloudFront distribution settings. CloudFront Origin Shield adds another layer to the CloudFront caching infrastructure in addition to the edge locations and regional caches to directly influence the cache hit ratio. Enabling Origin Shield in a CloudFront distribution origin configuration provides a better cache hit ratio, reduced load on the origin server, and better network performance. Origin Shield is a property of the origin configuration in a distribution. When you enable Origin Shield, you should choose the region that has the lowest latency to your origin. Using Origin Shield incurs additional charges for your CloudFront distribution.

Restricting Access to S3 (OAI vs. OAC)

CloudFront provides two ways to control access to an origin implemented using S3. The traditional way is to implement an origin access identity (OAI). This is a virtual user identity used to provide your CloudFront distribution with permissions to fetch objects from an S3 origin bucket. OAI prevents users from accessing your source S3 bucket directly if the S3 access URL is known, as would be the case when you upgrade access to an S3 bucket to use CloudFront. OAI is useful to make sure your S3 data stays protected and only available using your CloudFront distribution URL. However, OAI does not work well with server-side encryption using AWS KMS (SSE-KMS).

As an alternative, AWS introduced origin access control (OAC) as a feature to secure S3 origins by allowing access to designated distributions only. OAC uses IAM principals to authenticate with S3 origins. It is implemented with augmented security like short-term credentials, credential rotation, and resource-based policies. OAC supports downloading and uploading S3 objects using SSE-KMS. It provides comprehensive HTTP methods to support and access Amazon S3 in all AWS regions, including existing regions and all future regions.

OAI will only be supported in existing AWS regions and regions launched before December 2022. Origin access control settings is the recommended best practice to restrict S3 bucket access to only CloudFront.

For details, you can refer to https://aws.amazon.com/ blogs/networking-and-content-delivery/ amazon-cloudfront-introduces-origin-access-control-oac.

CloudFront Functions

You can write code to control how CloudFront processes HTTP requests and responses, to perform authentication and authorization, as well as to generate HTTP responses at the edge. The code you attach to a CloudFront distribution is called an edge function, and you have two ways to write and manage edge functions.

The first are CloudFront Functions. This is a native feature of CloudFront that lets you build, test, and deploy your code within CloudFront. It is intended for lightweight functions in JavaScript with a runtime environment that offers submillisecond start times and scales immediately to handle millions of requests per second.

You can also use Lambda@Edge. This is an extension of AWS Lambda used to execute full application logic closer to your viewers. Lambda@Edge supports Node.js or Python code. When you associate the function with a CloudFront distribution, Lambda@Edge automatically replicates the code worldwide. Lambda@Edge supports network access, file-system access, and access to the request body, which is not possible with native CloudFront functions.

CloudFront Guided Exercise

Now that we have discussed the details of CloudFront, let's get some hands-on experience with an exercise demonstrating how to use it via the AWS console.

Before you define a CloudFront distribution, you must have a source origin to use. Exercise 10.4 shows you how to create an Amazon S3 bucket and upload a few files to have them behave as a simple website.

EXERCISE 10.4

Creating an Amazon S3 Bucket

1. Using you AWS Management Console, open the Amazon S3 landing page.

2. Using the S3 console, click Create Bucket.

3. For the bucket name, follow these rules:

   a. The name must be unique.

   b. The name cannot use uppercase characters.

   c. The name must start with a lowercase letter.

   d. The name must be between 3 and 63 characters long.

   For example, you can use the name **mys3site***NUMBER* and replace *NUMBER* with any sequence of numbers or letters. If an error is displayed, try a different number or sequence until it's created.

4. Choose the region where you want your bucket to be created (i.e. US-EAST-1).

5. Usually you'd want to enable security measures like logging and encryption for your bucket, as well as enable bucket versioning. For this exercise, ignore those settings.

6. Leave the default values of Object Ownership and Block All Public Access enabled.

7. Click Create Bucket. You should see the message "Successfully created bucket "mys3site*XXXX*.""

8. Click View Details in the message or select your bucket name from the list of buckets.

9. Find one or two images you'd like to use for the simple website. Make sure they are different images. (This will become useful later.)

10. Using your choice of text editor, create a file called **index.html**. You can use the following as a model:

```
<!DOCTYPE HTML>
<html>
<head>
<title>CloudFront Exercise S3 Website</title>
</head>
<body>
<h1> CloudFront S3 Website</h1>
<h2>Your Image Title</h2>
<p> <img src="YOUR_IMAGE.jpg" alt="my s3 image" />
</body>
</html>
```

11. Replace the text and the image name according to your choices.

12. Back in your AWS Management Console, on the S3 dashboard click Upload and then click Add Files to select your image file and the index.html file. Finally, click Upload again to close the selection dialog box and then click Upload again at the bottom right of the page. Both files should appear listed under your bucket name in Files And Folders.

Congratulations! You just created a simple website and will host it on S3 and distribute it using CloudFront.

The bucket remains private and its content unavailable if you try to use any of the Object URLs Amazon S3 assigns to your image and index.html file. That is expected since you are blocking public access to the bucket and its content.

If you try to use one of the Object URLs on a browser, you will get an AccessDenied message in your browser window. You accepted the default value for Block All Public Access because CloudFront will serve the content from S3 and you want to limit access to the bucket to be exclusive to CloudFront.

In Exercise 10.5, you create a CloudFront distribution for the s3website site you have on a bucket.

EXERCISE 10.5

Creating an Amazon CloudFront Distribution for the s3website Site

1. Using your AWS Management Console, open the Amazon CloudFront page.

2. In the CloudFront console, Click Create A CloudFront Distribution.

3. For Origin Domain, select the bucket you created in Exercise 10.4. It will appear on the list as:

   mys3site*NUMBER*.s3.us-east-1.amazonaws.com

   The name shown will depend on your chosen **NUMBER** and region. The name of the bucket will automatically appear in the Name field for the origin.

4. Under Origin Access select Legacy Access Identities so that CloudFront will use origin access identity (OAI) to access the S3 bucket.

5. For Origin Access Identity, click Create New OAI and then click Create in the Create A New OAI dialog box.

6. For Bucket Policy select Yes, Update The Bucket Policy.

7. For Enable Origin Shield, leave the default No. You can examine the values of Additional Settings but leave things at their defaults.

For Default Cache Behavior, note that the path pattern is Default(*). The path pattern determines which requests apply to this cache behavior, based on the request's URI path.

8. For all other settings, leave the default values and find the Default Root Object field near the bottom of the page.

9. Set the Default Root Object field to **index.html** since that is the name of the file you created in Exercise 10.4.

10. Leave all remaining values at their defaults and click Create Distribution at the bottom right of the page. CloudFront will deploy your distribution and provide you with a name in the form of: `afdm5abcdf77g.cloudfront.net`. The Last Modified column will show Deploying. It can take a few minutes for the deployment to complete. You will know it's ready when the Last Modified section displays a date and time.

11. Once your distribution is ready, you can copy and paste the Distribution Domain Name to see your site hosted in Amazon S3.

    Notice that a CloudFront distribution consists of General Settings, Origins (one or more), Behaviors, Error Pages, Geographic Restrictions, Invalidations, and Tags.

12. Check the Origins section to see your S3 bucket listed as an origin. Also note the Origin Groups section. These settings are used to create a failover pair of origins.

    The Behaviors page defines a path pattern. The path pattern determines which requests apply to this cache behavior, based on the request's URI path. Path patterns support wildcard matching; (*) matches 0 or more characters; and (?) matches exactly 1 character. Behaviors provide the actual cache behavior for a URI used with CloudFront.

13. Verify that you can see your site. Copy and paste the Distribution Domain Name, **https://d12f94dsvjp9iq.cloudfront.net**, into a browser window.

If you have successfully completed Exercise 10.4, you have an S3 website distributed using CloudFront. If you update the contents of the S3 bucket being used, what would you expect to see as a result?

In Exercise 10.6 you update your cached site dataset and see what happens. CloudFront copied your bucket's files to the closest edge location to you. These copies will remain in the edge location for up to 24 hours by default. Making a change in the S3 bucket will not exactly result in the change getting reflected in the cached data at the edge location. One way to update an object in a CloudFront distribution is to perform an invalidation.

EXERCISE 10.6

Updating Your Cached Site Dataset

1. Using your AWS Management Console, open the Amazon S3 page.

2. In the S3 console, select your site's image filename and click Delete.

3. Type **permanently delete** in the confirmation text box and click Delete Objects.

   You will see the confirmation Successfully Deleted Objects. You are now left only with the `index.html` page in your S3 bucket.

4. Copy and paste the CloudFront distribution domain name into a new browser window.

5. Observe how the website continues to display as if nothing happened with the data in the bucket. This is because the entire site is cached in an edge location for the next 24 hours.

6. To "force" an update to the cached data of your CloudFront distribution, you need to "invalidate" your deleted object. To do so, in your AWS Management Console, first navigate to the CloudFront landing page.

7. Select your distribution's name and then select the Invalidations tab.

8. Click Create Invalidation.

9. In the Object Paths, Add Object Paths field, enter the name of your image file starting with a forward slash (/).

10. Click Create Invalidation. You will see a message showing the invalidation status as In Progress. The invalidation is finalized when the status displays Completed. This may take a few minutes.

11. Once the invalidation is complete, copy and paste the CloudFront distribution domain name into a new browser window.

    Observe how this time the image is no longer part of the CloudFront cached dataset. You have successfully reflected the existing content of your S3 bucket to match your CloudFront distribution cached dataset.

Please note that manually invalidating objects is an expensive operation and should be used only when strictly necessary. If you find yourself performing invalidations frequently, you may want to review the TTL configurations and cache behavior for your distribution.

If you have successfully completed the previous exercises in this section, the time has come to delete all created resources and clean up, which you'll do in Exercise 10.7.

EXERCISE 10.7

Deleting All Created Resources and Cleaning Up

1. Using your AWS Management Console, open the Amazon CloudFront page.

2. Select the check box to the left of your distribution and click Disable, and then click Disable at the bottom of the page.

3. A CloudFront distribution needs to be disabled before deletion. Wait until the entry in the Last Modified column of the distribution changes from Deploying to a date.

4. Select the check box to the left of your CloudFront distribution and click Delete. Then, click Delete at the bottom of the page. This will delete your CloudFront distribution.

5. Again, using your AWS Management Console, navigate to Amazon S3 and delete the `index.html` file and the bucket created earlier. This will complete the cleanup part of these exercises.

AWS Global Accelerator

There is a common denominator between Route 53, CloudFront, and AWS Global Accelerator and that is that they all use AWS edge locations to deliver results. We have discussed how CloudFront uses an origin as the source for data, and when a request comes in, it determines the closest edge location to the customer, then it performs an origin fetch, and it caches the data at the edge location to improve the data delivery performance.

AWS Global Accelerator operates in a similar way to CloudFront, and it works in both directions because it is intended for your applications. Global Accelerator uses the entire AWS high-speed network to bring your application's traffic requests and response items closer to customers and improve latency, agility, security, and availability.

Global Accelerator directs your user requests for application service based on geographic location, application health, and routing policies that you configure. The service also provisions static anycast IP addresses to your application so that client software will not require updates as changes take place.

You can associate your accelerator with applications in front of elastic load balancers (application and network) or elastic IP addresses. Global Accelerator will then provision two anycast IP addresses to operate as the front interface for your applications using the AWS edge network. An anycast IP address allows multiple servers to share the same IP address, and it allows for multiple physical destination servers to be identified by a single IP. It's basically a shared IP address by multiple devices, and this is how Global Accelerator distributes access to your application to customers. Anycast IP addresses simplify allowing listing in firewalls because you only have a few anycast IP addresses to list, instead of potentially needing to list each instance or web server. It can improve application performance by up to 60 percent, and provide fast failover for multi-AZ and multiregion implementations. It also removes DNS cache dependencies so that rerouting if needed happens as fast and pre-dictably as possible. You can test the performance benefits from your location with a speed comparison tool at `https://speedtest.globalaccelerator.aws`.

Pricing

For Amazon Route 53, you pay per hosted zone per month. Additional charges are incurred for queries, traffic flow, health checks, and Route 53 Resolver elastic network interfaces (ENIs). Health check pricing is different for AWS endpoints compared to any other end-point. Alias records are free when the records map to elastic load balancers, Cloud Front distributions, AWS Elastic Beanstalk environments, and S3 buckets configured as a website. Records added to your hosted zones are free. Latency, geolocation, and geoproximity routing incur a charge.

CloudFront bills for data transfers out from edge locations. The free tier includes 1 TB of data transfer out per month, 10 million HTTP(S) requests per month, 2 million CloudFront function invocations per month, and free SSL certificates.

AWS Global Accelerator charges for each accelerator and the amount of traffic that flows through. You are charged by the hour at a fixed rate for each accelerator and for your data transfers. This Data Transfer-Premium plan applies to all traffic that flows through an accelerator in any direction. The DT-Premium charge for an accelerator is separate from any EC2 data transfer-out fees that you incur.

Summary

AWS content delivery services deliver data to customers with improved security and improved latency globally. Networking and content delivery services like Route 53, Cloud-Front, and Global Accelerator are implemented using AWS global edge locations connected by dedicated 100 Gbps redundant fiber to deliver data with single-digit millisecond latency.

Domain Name Service (DNS) allows you to map hostnames to IP addresses and IP addresses to hostnames. You can query the DNS server with a fully qualified hostname (such as `www.wiley.com`) and you get an IP address or the DNS name of an AWS resource as a result. Route 53 is the DNS service within AWS. It provides more than simple name reso-lution. The Route 53 Resolver is the service that performs recursive lookups in response to queries.

Amazon Traffic Flow allows you to associate policies to your traffic, which can improve performance and latency for your customers and/or users.

AWS Private DNS creates a private hosted zone in Route 53 that can act like the internal DNS you are accustomed to using. Endpoints must be within a VPC to take advantage of AWS Private DNS.

Routing policies are assigned to records when they are created. These policies tell Amazon Route 53 how it should respond to queries that are made against that record. There are eight routing policy types: simple, weighted, failover, latency, geolocation, geoproximity, multi-value answer, and IP-based.

Health checks can be created to check endpoints, other health checks, or CloudWatch alarms. Unhealthy health checks can be used to initiate a failover event to ensure that only healthy endpoints are servicing users or customers.

CloudFront represents a content distribution network and caching system that uses edge location to reduce the latency of content delivery. You can configure multiple data sources and implement the execution of code at the edge using CloudFront Functions. You can also implement protection of the origin using OAI or OAC. Also, you get distribution control and cache management, including the ability to implement invalidations.

AWS Global Accelerator allows you to leverage the AWS internal high-speed network to deliver your applications by using anycast IP addresses and allowing the implementation of multiregion and multi-AZ endpoints that are accessible globally. You get full control of routing behavior independent of DNS caching and a significant improvement in latency, security, and high availability.

Exam Essentials

Understand how DNS works.   Domain Name Service (DNS) is used to resolve names to IP addresses, and vice versa. In a forward lookup, a name is resolved to an IP address, and in a reverse lookup, an IP address is resolved to a hostname. Your client will query the local DNS server for a record. If your local DNS knows the address, it will respond with it; if it doesn't, it will reach out to the top-level domain (TLD) DNS servers and work its way down the chain until it locates the authoritative DNS server and gets the response for the query.

Know the various DNS record types.   Know the main DNS record types and when you would want to use them. Know how to use A records, PTR records, CNAME records, alias records, MX records, and TXT. Alias records are important to Route 53 and the exam.

Understand what routing policies do.   You should know how to use the routing policies and set them up, including traffic flows.

Know how health checks work.   Remember the different types of health checks and how they work in relation to failovers.

Remember how CloudFront works.   Know how to implement a distribution, how to invalidate a cached object, and what OAI and OAC do.

Know the purpose of AWS Global Accelerator and when to use it.   Know what an accelerator and anycast IP addresses are.

Review Questions

1. Which of the following services can be used to perform DNS routing and health checks?

   A. Amazon EC2 with DNS and BIND installed

   B. Amazon Route 53

   C. Amazon CloudFront

   D. Amazon ElastiCache

2. Which of the following is *not* a record type supported by Route 53?

   A. NAPTR

   B. NS

   C. SPF

   D. TXT

3. You are setting up a new website for a client and have their website loaded into an S3 bucket. They want to ensure that the site responds to the company name—ourgreatcompany .com—both with and without the www part of the address. What types of record do you need to create?

   A. CNAME

   B. Alias

   C. MX

   D. SRV

4. You are setting up DNS for an application running on an EC2 host in your network. The application exposes its API through an IPv6 address. What type of record set will you need to create for access to this API?

   A. AAAA

   B. A

   C. Alias

   D. MX

5. You have a Lambda-based serverless application. You have several Lambda@Edge functions triggered by a CloudFront distribution and need to set up DNS. What type of record will you need to use?

   A. CNAME

   B. A

   C. Alias

   D. AAAA

6. You have an application running in a VPC with an existing DNS record. You have a backup of the application running as a warm standby in another VPC in a different region. If traffic stops flowing to the primary application, you want traffic to be routed to the backup. What type of routing policy should you use?

    A.   Simple routing

    B.   Failover routing

    C.   Latency routing

    D.   Multivalue answer

7. You have an application deployment with endpoints in multiple countries. The application needs to have fast response times and in the event of a failure you cannot modify the client code to redirect traffic. Which service can help you implement a solution?

    A.   Amazon ElastiCache

    B.   Route 53

    C.   Amazon CloudFront

    D.   AWS Global Accelerator

8. You have an application running with copies in three different regions: US-EAST-1, US-WEST-1, and AP-EAST-1. You want to ensure your application's users always receive a response from the copy of the application with the lowest network traffic response time. Which DNS routing policy should you use?

    A.   Simple routing

    B.   Failover routing

    C.   Latency routing

    D.   Multivalue answer

9. You are working for a startup that wants to test a production-ready version of their shopping cart and perform a trickle test with a small set of actual production traffic. Which DNS routing policy can help you implement this test?

    A.   Simple routing

    B.   Failover routing

    C.   Latency routing

    D.   Weighted routing policy

10. You are responsible for a marketing website running in AWS. You have a requirement from the marketing team to provide an alternate version of the site intended for A/B testing with the current site. However, they only want a small portion of traffic sent to the new version of the site as they evaluate the changes they've made. Which DNS routing policy should you use?

    A.   Multivalue answer

    B.   Failover routing

    C.   Weighted routing

    D.   Geolocation routing

11. A startup has deployed their website to Japan, Australia, and the United States. They want to make sure users get the results from the closest endpoint. Which DNS routing policy can help implement the solution?

A. Failover routing

B. Weighted routing

C. Geolocation routing

D. IP-based routing

12. A startup has deployed a CloudFront distribution with the site hosted in Amazon S3. They want to prevent users from accessing the S3 bucket directly. How can this protection be accomplished?

A. Set the TTL value for the cache to 0.

B. Enable Origin Access Identity (OAI) for the distribution.

C. Enable Origin Shield for the distribution.

D. Define a custom behavior for the largest objects.

13. Which of the following settings need to be configured in a VPC to use private DNS via the Route 53 Resolver? (Choose two.)

A. An Internet gateway needs to exist.

B. The `enableDnsHostnames` attribute needs to be set to `true`.

C. The NACLs for the VPC must include port 53.

D. The `enableDnsSupport` attribute must be set to `true`.

E. The `autoassignIP` attribute must be set to `true`.

14. Which of the following must you configure to control how traffic is routed from around the world to your applications using Amazon Route 53 Traffic Flow? (Choose two.)

A. Traffic record

B. Traffic policy

C. Policy record

D. Policy route

15. A startup will launch their new online game title in the US-EAST-1 region. However, players can be anywhere in the world. Which services will allow the startup to optimize the performance of their online game to a global audience? (Choose two.)

A. AWS Global Accelerator

B. AWS Direct Connect

C. AWS Local Zone

D. Amazon CloudFront

E. AWS Edge Locations

16. Which of the following is a *not* a type of health check offered by Amazon Route 53?

   A. Endpoint

   B. Other health checks

   C. CloudTrail

   D. CloudWatch

17. What happens in Amazon Route 53 if an unhealthy response comes back from a health check? (Choose two.)

   A. Responses are no longer sent to the failing host.

   B. When the host comes back online, responses are automatically sent back to the host.

   C. All responses to the failing host are retried until a response is received.

   D. A CloudWatch alarm is automatically triggered and sent out via notification.

18. A startup has deployed a CloudFront distribution to a global audience and wants to maximize the number of requests that are served from the CloudFront distribution cache. What can be done to improve the cache hit ratio?

   A. Set the TTL value for the cache to 0.

   B. Enable Origin Access Identity (OAI) for the distribution.

   C. Enable Origin Shield for the distribution.

   D. Define a custom behavior for the largest objects.

19. Why might you use a geoproximity routing policy rather than a geolocation routing policy?

   A. You want to increase the size of traffic in a certain region over time.

   B. You want to ensure that all U.S. users are directed to U.S.-based hosts.

   C. You want to route users geographically to ensure compliance issues are met based on requestor location.

   D. You are concerned about network latency more than requestor location.

20. You are seeing intermittent issues with a website you maintain that uses Amazon Route 53, a fleet of EC2 instances, and a redundant MySQL database. Even though the hosts are not always responding, traffic is being sent to those hosts. What could cause traffic to go to these hosts? (Choose two.)

   A. You need to use a failover routing policy to take advantage of health checks on hosts.

   B. You need to turn on health checks in Amazon Route 53.

   C. The hosts are failing a health check but not enough times in a row to be taken out of service by Amazon Route 53.

   D. The hosts should be put behind an application load balancer (ALB).

Chapter

11

Deployment, Provisioning, and Automation

THE AWS CERTIFIED SYSOPS ADMINISTRATOR EXAM OBJECTIVES COVERED IN THIS CHAPTER INCLUDE:

✓ **Domain 3.0: Deployment, Provisioning, and Automation**

- 3.1 Provision and maintain cloud resources

    - Create and manage AMIs (for example, EC2 Image Builder)

    - Provision resources across multiple AWS Regions and accounts (for example, AWS Resource Access Manager [AWS RAM], CloudFormation StackSets, IAM cross-account roles)

    - Select deployment scenarios and services (for example, blue/green, rolling, canary)

    - Identify and remediate deployment issues (for example, service quotas, subnet sizing, CloudFormation errors, permissions)

- 3.2 Automate manual or repeatable processes

    - Use AWS services (for example, Systems Manager, Cloud-Formation) to automate deployment processes

    - Implement automated patch management

    - Schedule automated tasks by using AWS services (for example, EventBridge, AWS Config)

Deployment, provisioning, and automation are foundational components in AWS Systems Operations, and they're crucial for several reasons:

Scalability   Modern applications, especially in the cloud, need to handle varying loads. Automated deployment and provisioning allow infrastructure to scale out (add more resources) or scale in (reduce resources) based on demand.

Speed and Agility   With automation, operations can deploy and provision resources faster than manual processes. This speed enables rapid iterations for developers and accelerates the time-to-market for products and features.

Consistency   Manual deployments and provisioning can introduce human errors. Automation ensures that every deployment is consistent, reducing the chances of issues related to configuration drift or overlooked settings.

Cost Efficiency   Automation can help in optimizing the resource usage. For instance, by automatically scaling down unused resources during off-peak times, companies can save on costs. AWS offers services like Auto Scaling to automate these scaling decisions.

Repeatability   Whether you're deploying in multiple environments (like development, testing, and production) or setting up similar infrastructures in different regions, automation ensures you can repeat the same process without reinventing the wheel each time.

Infrastructure as Code (IaC)   Tools like AWS CloudFormation or the AWS CDK (Cloud Development Kit) allow operations to define and provision AWS infrastructure using code. This approach lets teams version, review, and collaborate on infrastructure changes as they would with application code.

This chapter will help you understand the following:

- Elastic Beanstalk
- CloudFormation
- SQS
- SNS
- Kinesis Data Streams
- Kinesis Data Firehose
- Kinesis Data Analytics
- Step Functions

Elastic Beanstalk

AWS has emerged as a leading cloud platform, providing a variety of services and solutions to businesses worldwide. One of its most powerful and versatile offerings is the AWS Elastic Beanstalk. This platform-as-a-service (PaaS) solution simplifies the process of deploying and managing applications, enabling developers to focus on writing code without having to worry about the underlying infrastructure. This section provides a comprehensive overview of Elastic Beanstalk, exploring its features, layers, deployment options, and security measures.

AWS has simplified the architecting and administering of web applications with Elastic Beanstalk. This product allows you to focus on your web application rather than focusing on software or hardware infrastructure. Elastic Beanstalk automates those tasks.

What Is Elastic Beanstalk?

Elastic Beanstalk is a managed service that simplifies the administration and deployment of web applications within AWS. It takes advantage of CloudFormation to provision all the resources that you need to successfully run your web application. It handles the intricate details of capacity provisioning, load balancing, autoscaling, and application health monitoring, thereby significantly reducing the developers' workload. Moreover, it uses Elastic Load Balancing and Auto Scaling to automatically adjust the application's scale based on its specific needs.

Elastic Beanstalk is a PaaS solution that supports various languages and development stacks, including Java, .NET, PHP, Node.js, Python, Ruby, Go, and Docker. Furthermore, it allows developers to select the EC2 instance type that best fits their application and can retain full administrative control if needed.

Elastic Beanstalk offers a range of features that differentiate it from other PaaS solutions. Here are some noteworthy ones:

Managed Platform Updates   Elastic Beanstalk's Managed Platform Updates feature automatically applies updates for your operating system and platform, including Java, PHP, Node.js, and others, ensuring your environment is always up-to-date.

Customization and Control   Despite being a managed service, Elastic Beanstalk provides developers with full control over the underlying resources. It allows extensive customization, including defining packages to install, creating Linux users and groups, running shell commands, specifying services to enable, configuring a load balancer, and more.

Automatic Scaling   Elastic Beanstalk automatically scales your application up and down based on its specific needs. It leverages the power of AWS's Elastic Load Balancing and Auto Scaling to maintain the optimal number of instances required to run your application efficiently.

Integrated Monitoring and Reporting   Elastic Beanstalk integrates with CloudWatch and AWS X-Ray, providing performance data and metrics. It also presents application health information via a dashboard, giving developers a comprehensive overview of their application's status.

AWS Elastic Beanstalk CLI   In addition to the AWS Management Console, Elastic Beanstalk offers a command-line interface (CLI) known as the EB CLI. This interactive tool simplifies creating, updating, and monitoring environments from a local repository, serving as an alternative to the Elastic Beanstalk console. The EB CLI can be a part of your everyday development and testing cycle.

You may have used the AWS CLI in the past, and you can still use it with Elastic Beanstalk. However, the length of the commands when using the AWS CLI can become a bit unwieldy, especially for scripting functions. AWS released the EB CLI to resolve that issue.

The *EB CLI* contains commands specific to Elastic Beanstalk and allows you to easily create, modify, and delete your environments, all from the command line. The EB CLI makes it far easier to script application environment builds.

For instance, to check the status of your application environment with the AWS CLI, you type the following:

```
aws elasticbeanstalk describe-environment-health --environment-name
  <environment_name> --attribute-names All
```

With the EB CLI, however, the command is much simpler:

```
eb status <environment_name>
```

Versioning and Life-Cycle Policies in Elastic Beanstalk   Elastic Beanstalk can store at most 1,000 application versions. To phase out old versions, you can use a life-cycle policy. This could be time-based, specifying the maximum age, or count-based, specifying the maximum number to retain. Versions that are in use will not be deleted. There is also an option to not delete the source bundle in Amazon S3 to prevent data loss.

Compliance   Elastic Beanstalk gets checked regularly by auditors outside of AWS for many of the popular compliance frameworks and programs, including HIPAA, PCI-DSS, SOC, and FedRAMP. You can download these compliance reports at any time via AWS Artifact, which is available here: `https://console.aws.amazon.com/artifact`. Please note that you will need an AWS login to access these reports.

Elastic Beanstalk Layers

Elastic Beanstalk is composed of several layers, each with a distinct role. Understanding these layers is crucial for effectively leveraging the service:

Application   In Elastic Beanstalk, an application is a collection of different elements, including environments, environment configurations, and application versions. An application can hold multiple application versions, each representing a specific iteration of deployable code.

Application Version   An application version is a unique reference to a section of deployable code. Typically, an application version points to an S3 bucket containing the code.

Environment   An environment refers to a deployed application version on AWS resources. The resources are configured and provisioned by Elastic Beanstalk, and the environment includes all the resources created by Elastic Beanstalk, not just an EC2 instance with uploaded code.

Environment Tier   The environment tier determines how Elastic Beanstalk provisions resources based on what the application is designed to do. There are two main types of environment tiers:

> **Web Server Tier**   Standard applications that listen for and process HTTP requests, typically over port 80.
>
> **Worker Tier**   Specialized applications that perform background processing tasks and listen for messages on an Amazon SQS queue. If an application performs tasks that take a long time to complete (long-running tasks), you can offload them to a worker environment. This allows you to decouple your application tiers. You can also define periodic tasks in the `cron.yaml` file.

Environment Configuration   An environment configuration is a collection of parameters and settings that dictate how an environment's resources are provisioned by Elastic Beanstalk and how these resources behave.

Deployment in Elastic Beanstalk

Elastic Beanstalk provides several options for how deployments are processed. These include various deployment policies and options that allow you to configure batch size and health check behavior during deployments. The deployment options are as follows:

Single Instance   This deployment option is ideal for development. It involves the deployment of the application on a single instance.

High Availability with Load Balancer   This deployment option is great for production. It ensures high availability of the application by deploying it across multiple instances and managing the traffic using a load balancer.

Deployment Policies in Elastic Beanstalk

Elastic Beanstalk offers five main deployment policies: all-at-once, rolling, rolling with an additional batch, immutable, and blue/green deployment.

All-at-Once   In an all-at-once deployment, the new version is deployed to all instances simultaneously. This policy is the fastest but involves a complete service outage during the deployment, making it unsuitable for mission-critical systems. If the update fails, you need to roll back the changes by redeploying the original version to all your instances. However, it is ideal for quick iterations in a development environment and incurs no additional cost.

Rolling   A rolling deployment updates a few instances at a time (a batch), and then moves onto the next batch once the first batch is healthy. The application is running both versions simultaneously, and each batch of instances is taken out of service while the deployment takes place. Your environment capacity will be reduced by the number of instances in a batch while the deployment takes place. This policy is not ideal for performance-sensitive systems. If the update fails, you need to perform an additional rolling update to roll back the changes. No additional cost is incurred in this policy.

Rolling with Additional Batch   The rolling with additional batch deployment is similar to the rolling policy but launches new instances in a batch to ensure full availability. The application is running both versions simultaneously, and you can set the bucket size. A small additional cost is associated with this policy due to the extra batch of instances. The additional batch is removed at the end of the deployment.

Immutable   An immutable deployment launches new instances in a new Auto Scaling Group (ASG) and deploys the version update to these instances before swapping traffic to these instances once they are healthy. This policy ensures zero downtime and quick rollback in case of failures. However, it involves a high cost as double the number of instances are running during updates and it has the longest deployment time.

Blue/Green Deployment   A blue/green deployment refers to using your production environment (blue) and your staging environment (green) side by side to test your new code with real production traffic. It is a fantastic way to find issues with your code not discovered during testing, and it reduces the impact to your customers if an issue is found.

It's important to understand that blue/green deployments are not a direct feature offered by Elastic Beanstalk. You need to create two environments, and then use Amazon Route 53 to use weighted policies to distribute a certain percentage of the traffic to your blue deployment and the other percentage to your green deployment. This requires two different URLs, which are created automatically by Elastic Beanstalk. Once you validate that everything looks good with the new version, you change the weight in the Route 53 policy to 0 for the old environment or remove it from the routing policy altogether. If something does go wrong with the new deployment, you have the ability to quickly fail back to the working version of your application within seconds by adding it back into the routing policy. Once the application has been validated, you can delete the second (staging) environment to reduce cost; just ensure that the Route 53 policy has been edited to point only to the new production environment first.

AWS recommends cloning your current environment when doing blue/green deployments to create your second environment and then updating that second environment. The benefit to cloning your production environment is that you are getting an exact copy of production to work with. This allows you to perform the most accurate and reliable testing of your new application.

In short, a blue/green deployment is not an intrinsic feature of Elastic Beanstalk. It involves creating a new "staging" environment and deploying updates there. The new environment (green) can be independently validated, and you can roll back if there are issues. Route 53 can be set up using weighted policies to redirect a percentage of traffic to the staging environment. Using Elastic Beanstalk, you can "swap URLs" when done with the environment test, ensuring zero downtime.

Security in Elastic Beanstalk

Elastic Beanstalk provides multiple managed policies depending on your organizational security needs. For example, you can provide read-only access or provide full access. These policies can be attached to IAM groups to allow for easier administration of access:

- `AWSElasticBeanstalkFullAccess` is the managed policy that grants full access. It allows you to configure, add, or delete Elastic Beanstalk applications and all their resources.

- `AWSElasticBeanstalkReadOnlyAccess` is the managed policy that grants read access. Users with this policy may view all the resources within Elastic Beanstalk but may not make any changes.

Security is a critical aspect of any cloud service, and Elastic Beanstalk is no exception. It supports HTTPS, and you can load the SSL certificate onto the load balancer. This can be performed from the console or in code (`.ebextensions/securelistener-alb.config`). The SSL certificate can be provisioned using AWS Certificate Manager (ACM) or CLI. For redirecting HTTP to HTTPS, you can configure the application load balancer with a rule or configure it in the application. Ensure that health checks are not redirected.

Elastic Beanstalk Extensions

You can add Elastic Beanstalk configuration files (`.ebextensions`) to your web application's source code to configure your environment and customize the AWS resources that it contains. Customization includes, for example, defining packages to install, creating Linux users and groups, running shell commands, specifying services to enable, and configuring a load balancer.

Configuration files are YAML- or JSON-formatted documents with a `.config` file extension that you place in a folder named `.ebextensions` and deploy in your application source bundle. All the parameters set in the UI can be configured in the code. You can add resources such as Amazon RDS, ElastiCache, and DynamoDB.

You can deploy Amazon RDS within an Elastic Beanstalk environment. However, if you terminate your Elastic Beanstalk environment, you also lose the database. It is therefore preferable to create the RDS database outside of Elastic Beanstalk, especially for production workloads.

For Exercise 11.1, you need only an AWS account to log in with. The default VPC will work just fine for our purposes.

EXERCISE 11.1

Deploying a Sample Application in Elastic Beanstalk

1. Log into the AWS Management Console.

2. Use the search bar or click Services; then click Elastic Beanstalk under Compute.

3. Click Create Application in the Elastic Beanstalk console.

4. On the Configure Environment page, you need to set some values:

   - For Application Name, use **EBHelloWorld**.

   - Scroll down and notice the Environment Information was automatically filled using the name you just used: EBHelloWorld-env.

   - Scroll down and from the Platform drop-down menu, choose PHP.

   - For Application Code, leave Sample Application selected.

   - In the Presets panel, use the preset Single Instance (Free Tier Eligible).

5. Click Next at the bottom right of the page.

6. On the Configure Service Access page, for Service Role select Create And Use New Service Role.

7. For the EC2 Instance Profile, select an EC2 SSM Compatible Role. You may need to create this role if you have not followed all the exercises. It is important for this role to exist and be selected in this step. Leave all other values on this page at their defaults and click Next.

8. The next settings are related to networking, database, and tags:

   - Leave the VPC setting as Default.

   - Select the Public IP Address Activated option. Click Next.

9. You can examine the options on the next page for configuring instance traffic and scaling. For this exercise, leave the page as is and click Next.

10. The next page is used to configure updates, monitoring, and logging. Examine the configuration options but for this exercise, leave the options at their defaults and click Next.

11. On the Review page, examine the details of the environment. Click Submit at the bottom of the page. This launches your Elastic Beanstalk environment.

12. It will take several minutes for the instance to be deployed. Notice that the bottom of the page displays the CloudFormation events that are being executed. You can refresh this panel to keep track of the environment build as it happens.

13. When the build is finished and you see the dashboard for your application, click the URL in the breadcrumb area. The URL will end with `<region-name>`
    `.elasticbeanstalk.com`.

    When you see the Congratulations screen, you have deployed your first application!

To tear down the application so that you aren't charged for anything further, click the Actions button in the application's dashboard and choose Terminate Environment. You will be asked to type the name of the environment you want to confirm. Enter the name and click Terminate. Once you are on the application dashboard, and it is gray with the word (Terminated), click the Actions button again and choose Delete Application. Type the name of the application and click Delete.

AWS CloudFormation

As the digital transformation wave sweeps across industries, organizations are increasingly seeking efficient ways to manage and automate their infrastructure. One such tool that has gained significant traction among cloud architects is CloudFormation. This service allows IT professionals to automate and manage their AWS infrastructure using code.

This section explores AWS CloudFormation, its principles, key concepts, benefits, and best practices. You'll learn about the following:

- An introduction to infrastructure-as-a-service (IaaS)
- Using stacks and templates in CloudFormation
- Customizing stacks with parameters and outputs

Introduction to CloudFormation

AWS CloudFormation is a robust service offered by AWS that lets you define and manage your cloud infrastructure resources using code. This service supports both YAML and JSON formats, offering you a common language to describe and provision all your cloud environment's infrastructure resources.

The principal elements of CloudFormation are templates and stacks. A template is a JSON or YAML file that specifies the AWS resources you want to provision. CloudFormation interprets a template file and makes the appropriate API calls to create the resources you've defined. On the other hand, a stack represents the AWS resources defined by a template that have been provisioned.

CloudFormation facilitates the creation of a broad spectrum of AWS resources, including EC2 instances, S3 buckets, RDS instances, and many more.

CloudFormation's drift detection capability is a critical tool for maintaining the integrity of your stack resources. When configuration changes are made outside of this AWS service, they can lead to discrepancies between the actual resources and their defined templates. With the aid of drift detection, these discrepancies are identified and you can initiate corrective actions.

By updating the drifted resources to align with their original template definition, consistency is restored. Ultimately, addressing these drifts contributes to smoother stack operations and reduces potential issues that could arise from inconsistent configurations.

CloudFormation can be seen as implementing infrastructure-as-code, presenting a more efficient and reliable alternative to manual infrastructure management. It allows you to create, update, version, and delete infrastructure resources using templates. These operations can be carried out through the AWS Management Console, command-line interface (CLI), or APIs.

CloudFormation provides the power and flexibility to address the challenges of:

- Consistently deploying infrastructure across regions
- Updating servers already deployed in a production environment
- Managing dependencies on systems, technologies, and subsystems
- Reclaiming resources from a deployment that didn't go as planned

CloudFormation Templates

A template in CloudFormation provides a blueprint for building your infrastructure. The template file contains instructions for creating and configuring the necessary AWS resources. Logical IDs are used to reference resources within the template, whereas physical IDs identify resources outside of CloudFormation templates, but only after the resources have been created. In a CloudFormation template, only the Resources component is required. Let's get into the structure of a template.

CloudFormation Designer is a visual tool for creating and modifying CloudFormation templates with a drag-and-drop interface. You can add, modify, or remove resources and the underlying JSON or YAML will be altered accordingly. If you modify a template that's associated with a running stack, you can update the stack to conform to the template. Third-party tools like Terraform can help you in the design of your CloudFormation templates.

AWSTemplateFormatVersion

The AWSTemplateFormatVersion section currently has only one valid value for this component: 2010-09-09. Here's an example of what this would look like in JSON:

```
"AWSTemplateFormatVersion" : "2010-09-09"
```

Description

This section must be located underneath the format version. It consists of a string of text that describes what the template is for or what it does. This field is optional. If you choose to use it, this is what the component looks like in JSON:

```
"Description" : "This is my awesome template."
```

Metadata

You can use the `Metadata` section to add more information about your templates. This is typically used if you want to call out information specific to certain parts of your template, as in:

```
"Metadata" : {
  "Instances" : {"Description" : "This template only uses Linux
instances"},
  "Databases" : {"Description" : "This template only builds MySQL in
Amazon RDS"}
}
```

Parameters Intro

Although a static template might be useful, the real strength in using a template comes with the ability to enter a custom value every time you use the template to create a stack (or update it). A common use case might be where you want to define the instance types that you will allow someone to use in the template. This ensures that no one builds a larger instance type than what you want to allow and gives you the ability to define a default as well. The example I just described follows in JSON. We are allowing a template user to choose `t3.nano`, `t3.micro`, or `t3.small`. If they choose nothing, they will be given the default of `t3.micro`.

```
"Parameters" : {
  "InstanceTypeParameter" : {
    "Type" : "String",
    "Default" : "t3.micro",
    "AllowedValues" : ["t3.nano", "t3.micro", "t3.small"],
    "Description" : "Type t3.nano, t3.micro, or t3.small. Default is
t3.micro."
  }
}
```

Parameters are what takes a static template and makes a more dynamic solution. There are four types of parameters that you can use, and their type dictates the input that they are expecting to see:

- String
- Number
- List
- Comma-delimited list

To harness the full potential of CloudFormation parameters, you must understand their application within your stack. The parameters you define can be used as tools to customize your AWS resources during stack creation or updates.

This is achieved by using the `Ref` intrinsic function, which allows CloudFormation to interpret and utilize the parameter's value for provisioning the stack. Moreover, these parameters can also be referenced from the `Resources` and `Outputs` sections of the same template, making them versatile components in stack configuration. Hence, mastering CloudFormation parameters will enable you to create more dynamic and flexible cloud environments.

It is important to validate your inputs whenever you are using parameters. After all, one typo could cause the entire stack to roll back. Four methods are available in CloudFormation to validate inputs:

- `AllowedValues`
- `AllowedPattern`
- `MaxLength/MinLength`
- `MaxValue/MinValue`

Pseudo Parameters

These are parameters that are created by CloudFormation as opposed to parameters that you create in your templates.

- `AWS::AccountID`—AWS account ID
- `AWS::NotificationARNs`—ARNs for notification topics
- `AWS::NoValue`—Removes attribute
- `AWS::Partition`—Returns partition resource is in
- `AWS::Region`—Region of the current stack
- `AWS::StackId`—ID of current stack
- `AWS::StackName`—Name of current stack
- `AWS::URLSuffix`—Returns domain suffix

To use pseudo parameters, you use the `Ref` function and then the name of the pseudo parameter of the argument. For example:

```
"MyRegion" : { "Value" :{"Ref": "AWS::Region"}}
```

Mappings

Mappings allow you to specify a key-value pair. Although you can't use most functions in a mapping, you can use the `Fn::FindInMap` function to retrieve values. The following is an example of a mapping that selects AMI IDs for each region. This allows the same template to be used across regions while still being able to choose the same AMI (whose ID number will be different between regions).

```
"Mappings" : {
 "RegionMap" : {
       "us-east-1"      : { "AmazonLinux" : "ami-XXXXXXXXXXXXXXXXX"},
       "us-west-1"      : { "AmazonLinux" : "ami-XXXXXXXXXXXXXXXXX"}
  }
}
```

Mappings allow you to map keys to values. For each mapping a key must have a unique name, and keys are allowed to contain multiple values. In this example, we have a mapping called RegionAMI. The key in this case is the region name us-east-1 and the values are AmazonLinux and Ubuntu.

```
"RegionAMI" : {
    "us-east-1" : {
        "AmazonLinux" : "ami-XXXXXXXXXXX",
        "Ubuntu" : "ami-XXXXXXXXXXX"
}}
```

A built-in function, Fn::FindInMap, is then used to point to the mapping that you created earlier. This allows you to specify what you want (AmazonLinux) without having to remember the AMI ID for the specific region that you are in. This is demonstrated here:

```
"ImageID" : {"Fn:FindInMap": ["RegionAMI", "Ref":"AWS::Region",
"AmazonLinux"]}
```

Conditions

A condition is used to determine whether a resource should be created or whether a certain property should be assigned. If you want to use conditions, you must not only define your conditions in a Conditions section, you must also set the inputs that you want the conditions to evaluate in the Parameters section and associate the conditions with the resources that you want to create or update. This happens in the Resources and Outputs sections. A great example of this is using a condition to determine whether you are deploying to production or development. In this example, we create a condition called CreateProdResources and we specify that this condition will be true if the EnvType parameter is set to prod:

```
"Conditions":{
    "CreateProdResources" : {"Fn::Equals" : [{"Ref" : "EnvType"},
"prod"]}
}
```

You can then use this condition in a parameter. In the next example, you can see that we have created a parameter named EnvType, which defaults to Dev. We have said that this parameter can be set to either prod or dev. If prod is entered, then the condition will be true and other actions that specify the condition as a requirement will execute. In this way, you can make your dev instances smaller than your prod instances to reduce cost.

```
        "Parameters" : {
        "EnvType" : {
         "Description" : "Environment type.",
         "Default" : "dev",
         "Type" : "String",
         "AllowedValues" : ["prod", "dev"],
         "ConstraintDescription" : "Pick prod or dev."
    }
}
```

Transform

Transform allows you to choose one or more macros for CloudFormation to use. These macros are run in the order in which they are defined. There are two macros hosted by CloudFormation that you should be familiar with. `AWS::Serverless` specifies which version you should use of the AWS Serverless Application Model. This in turn specifies what syntax you are allowed to use and how CloudFormation will process it. `AWS::Include` uses template snippets that are stored outside of your CloudFormation template.

Resources

The `Resources` section specifies the actual resources that you want to create, modify, or delete. This includes things like EC2 instances, storage, and security groups. Examples of types of resources are as follows:

- `AWS::EC2::Instance`
- `AWS::EC2::SecurityGroup`
- `AWS::IAM::Role`
- `AWS::EC2::VPC`

To actually create a resource, you name it, and then declare the type of resource and any properties that are necessary. In this example, `Resources` describe an EC2 instance that CloudFormation will build. You can see the resource type is `AWS::EC2::Instance` and under `Properties`, the AMI ID is displayed:

```
"Resources" : {
  "MyEC2" : {
    "Type" : "AWS::EC2::Instance",
    "Properties" : {
      "ImageId" : "ami-XXXXXXXXXXXXXXXXX"
    }
  }
}
"MyRDS" : {
    "Type" : "AWS::RDS::DBInstance",
    "Properties" : {
        "AllocatedStorage" : "10",
        ...
    }
},
"WebServer" : {
    "Type" : "AWS::EC2::Instance",
    "DependsOn" : [ "MyRDS" ],
    "Properties" : {....
  }
```

With the AWS CloudFormation service, the process of resource creation tasks has been simplified and streamlined, allowing for more efficient implementation. However, with the continuous introduction of new resource types, there could be modifications in sequencing rules. Hence, the utilization of the `DependsOn` attribute becomes invaluable. This attribute ensures a consistent order in task execution regardless of any system updates or resource type additions. By incorporating the `DependsOn` attribute into your AWS CloudFormation strategy, you can maintain consistency and predictability in your resource deployment processes.

Resources and *CloudFormation::Init*

The `AWS::CloudFormation::Init` resource type is an essential component in setting up your Amazon EC2 instance with the required metadata. This specific metadata serves as a crucial input for the `cfn-init` helper script, which is invoked by your CloudFormation template. When executed, the script actively searches for resource metadata within the `AWS::CloudFormation::Init` metadata key. Understanding this process is vital to successful deployment on AWS, as it ensures that your resources are configured accurately according to the specifications outlined in your CloudFormation template. As a best practice, always verify that your `CloudFormation::Init` metadata is correctly structured and relevant to avoid potential misconfigurations or errors during deployment.

You can choose to use either `CloudFormation::Init` or user data to configure an EC2 instance.

Resources and *WaitConditions*

To utilize a `WaitCondition`, you must first create a `WaitConditionHandle` and then associate it with the desired resource in your AWS CloudFormation stack. Once this is accomplished, you can leverage the unique URL provided by `WaitConditionHandle` to signal back to your stack's status. When your initialization code successfully completes its tasks, it sends a signal to this URL, informing AWS CloudFormation that the corresponding resource is ready for use. This mechanism safeguards against premature stack completion and ensures that all resources are fully functional before the stack status changes to `CREATE_COMPLETE`. Hence, understanding and properly using `WaitConditions` in AWS CloudFormation is crucial for effective cloud resource management and operations.

Outputs

With the `Outputs` section, you can do a couple of things. You can set the CloudFormation template to output the results of a stack build to the CloudFormation console, return a response if called, or use the output as the input into another stack. You can have up to 60 outputs in a single template. If a resource creation provides a URL as a result, it is common to see the result URL listed as an output. Here's an example of how you would declare an output:

```
"Outputs" : {
"Logical ID" : {
```

```
        "Description" : "Info regarding the output value",
        "Value" : "<value>",
        "Export" : {
        "Name" : "<value to be exported>"
        }
        }
    }
```

Built-In Functions

Built-in functions allow you to assign values to properties that you can't access until run-time. AWS CloudFormation has several built-in functions that you can use:

- `Fn::Base64`—Converts the string passed to it to Base64. This is needed for passing user data for building EC2 instances.

- `Fn::Cidr`—Used to create an array (a group) of CIDR blocks inside a larger CIDR block.

- `Fn::FindInMap`—Used in the `Resources` section to reference a value in the `Mappings` section of the template.

- `Fn::GetAtt`—Returns an attribute that is used and/or assigned to a resource.

- `Fn::GetAZs`—Returns a list of availability zones available in the region specified in the template.

- `Fn::ImportValue`—Allows you to import a value from the output of another stack.

- `Fn::Join`—Used to append multiple values together using a delimiter that you choose.

- `Fn::Select`—Used to return a single value from an array; values are chosen by their index number.

- `Fn::Split`—Works the opposite of `Fn::Join`. Used to split multiple values using a delimiter that you specify.

- `Fn::Sub`—Can be used to substitute a variable with a string.

- `Fn::Transform`—Chooses a macro for CloudFormation to use to process the stack.

Here's an example to put it into context. When you create an EC2 instance, you can use user data to customize what is installed on the EC2 instance or how certain settings are configured. You can do this with CloudFormation as well, but one of the challenges is that the input must be in Base64. Now, you could manually convert each line of your script to Base64, but you would need to update that whenever something changed. Or you can use the `Fn::Base64` function to simply convert your script to Base64 at runtime. This approach makes it much easier to edit the user data script when you need to. The example that follows shows you how to use two functions to input the user data into a CloudFormation template.

`Fn::Base64`, as discussed, converts everything in user data into Base64. `Fn::Join` joins together two or more strings—in this case, two or more lines (\n is an escape character and is used as the delimiter in this case to represent a new line). The code then installs a web server, changes directories to the root web directory, and then creates a simple HTML page that will display "I am a happy little web server!" when you navigate to it after the web server build has completed.

```
"UserData" : {"Fn::Base64": {"Fn::Join" : ["\n", [
"#!/bin/bash -ex",
"yum install -y httpd",
"cd /var/www/html",
"echo '<html><body>I am a happy little web server!</body></html>'
> index.html",
"service httpd start"
]]}}
```

CloudFormation Best Practices

One of the key aspects of utilizing AWS CloudFormation effectively is planning your use of the tool. Here are a few guidelines to consider:

Organizing Resources   Aim to organize your AWS resources based on their life cycle and ownership. As your stack grows, managing a single stack might become daunting and time-consuming. Therefore, grouping resources with similar life cycles and ownership can simplify the management process.

Replicating Stacks   Once your stacks and resources are set up, consider reusing your templates to replicate your infrastructure across various environments. This allows you to create environments for development, testing, and production, enabling you to test changes before implementing them into production.

Verifying Quotas   Always verify quotas for all resource types before launching a stack. This way, you won't exceed your AWS account limits, thereby avoiding potential disruptions in resource creation.

Monitoring Service Limits   While AWS CloudFormation offers a repeatable infrastructure deployment process, it's crucial to monitor the service limits of EC2 and other AWS services. AWS Trusted Advisor can be utilized to ensure that you won't exceed certain EC2 instance limits.

Using AWS Organizations   Using AWS Organizations in conjunction with CloudFormation can ensure infrastructure created on separate accounts complies with the same IAM policies and organizational controls.

Creating CloudFormation Templates   When it comes to template creation, there are a few best practices to keep in mind:

Avoiding Credentials Embedding   Avoid including credentials in your templates. Instead, utilize input parameters to pass information when you create or update a stack.

Utilizing AWS-Specific Parameter Types   By using AWS-specific parameter types, CloudFormation can rapidly validate values before the stack creation process.

Implementing Parameter Constraints   With parameter constraints, you can specify permitted input values, allowing CloudFormation to catch any invalid values before creating a stack.

Using `AWS::CloudFormation::Init`   This feature allows you to deploy software applications on Amazon EC2 instances. It enables you to describe the configurations you want, eliminating the need for scripting procedural steps.

Validating Templates   Always validate your templates before using them. Doing so can help you catch syntax errors and some semantic errors before CloudFormation creates any resources.

Managing CloudFormation Stacks

The following best practices can assist in managing your CloudFormation stacks:

Managing Stack Resources   Manage all stack resources via CloudFormation. After launching a stack, use the CloudFormation console, API, or AWS CLI to update resources in your stack. Changes made outside of CloudFormation can lead to discrepancies between your stack's template and the current state of your stack resources, which can cause errors.

Creating Change Sets   Change sets allow you to preview how proposed changes to a stack might impact your running resources before you implement them. CloudFormation doesn't make any changes to your stack until you run the change set.

Implementing Stack Policies   Stack policies protect critical stack resources from unintentional updates that could interrupt or replace resources. Always specify a stack policy when creating a stack with critical resources.

Using AWS CloudTrail for Logging   AWS CloudTrail tracks any CloudFormation API calls in your AWS account. Enable logging and specify an S3 bucket to store the logs. This allows you to audit who made which CloudFormation call in your account when needed.

Managing Templates with Code Reviews and Revision Controls   Stack templates describe the configuration of your AWS resources. Code reviews and revision controls can help track changes between different versions of templates, which aids in tracking changes to stack resources. By maintaining a history, you can revert your stack to a certain version of your template.

Issues with CloudFormation Templates

The first issue is that while templates can be used across regions, AMI IDs, EIP IDs, security groups IDs, and a number of other resources identification are unique to the region in which they are located. If your stack fails to build, make sure that you have the right IDs for the resources in that region that you are trying to create.

When a stack is deleted, the resources that are associated with that stack are deleted. The order of deletion is determined by CloudFormation. You do not have direct control over what gets deleted when.

Utilizing CloudFormation, you can ensure the preservation of your resources. This is achieved by setting the `DeleteOnTermination` attribute for an Amazon EBS volume to `False` and by setting the `DeletionPolicy` attribute to `Retain` for other resources.

Keep in mind that some resources, like S3 buckets, might not be deleted when a stack is removed. Similarly, when removing Amazon RDS using CloudFormation it is important to back up database data as it can result in the deletion of user data. Moreover, CloudFormation offers an additional layer of security with its termination protection feature, which can be optionally enabled on a stack. This feature further reinforces prevention from accidental deletions, safeguarding your valuable data and resources.

In Exercise 11.2, you will create a CloudFormation template and stack.

EXERCISE 11.2

Creating a CloudFormation Stack

1. Log into the AWS Management Console.

2. Use the Search bar or click Services; then, under Management & Governance, select CloudFormation.

3. Select Stacks in the CloudFormation console menu.

4. Click Create Stack and, under Prepare Template, select the Use A Sample Template radio button.

5. On the Create Stack configuration screen, under Select A Sample Template, from the drop-down menu choose WordPress Blog found under the Simple heading.

6. Click Next.

7. On the Specify Stack Details screen, enter a name for your stack; I used **SysOpsStackTest**.

8. In the Parameters panel, enter the passwords you want to use for **DBPassword** and **DBRootPassword**.

9. Enter a username in the DB Username field: For example, you can use **admin**.

10. Leave the instance type as t2.small.

11. Under KeyName, select the key pair you will use to authenticate. You should have created a key pair in a prior exercise.

12. Click Next.

13. On the Configure Stack Options screen, accept the defaults and click Next.

14. On the Review page, click Submit.

Once you click Create Stack, CloudFormation goes to work setting up your stack for you. When the status has changed from CREATE_IN_PROGRESS to CREATE_COMPLETE, you have successfully completed your CloudFormation deployment.

If you examine the Outputs tab, you should see A Website URL for the WordPressWebsite provisioned.

These sample templates are a great way to learn, and you can always view the templates you have created by clicking your stack and selecting the Template tab.

Please make sure to delete everything you provision in this exercise in order to prevent unexpected charges.

Amazon SQS

AWS is a globally recognized leader in cloud computing services. One of the core offerings in the AWS suite is the Amazon Simple Queue Service (SQS). SQS is a fully managed, scalable, and reliable messaging service that aids in the decoupling of microservices, serverless applications, and distributed systems. This section will explore the various aspects of SQS.

Overview of SQS

SQS is a distributed queue system that enables applications to rapidly and reliably queue messages generated by one component to be consumed by another. It acts as a temporary repository for messages awaiting processing, serving as a buffer between the component generating and saving data and the component processing the data. This temporary storage facility, known as a queue, is essential in scenarios where the producer is generating work more rapidly than the consumer can process it, or when the producer or consumer is only intermittently connected to the network. This buffering capability, known as decoupling or loose coupling, enhances the elasticity of your application.

SQS is a pull-based system, contrary to push-based systems like Amazon Simple Notification Service (SNS). Messages in SQS can be up to 256 KB in size and can be retained in the queue for a duration ranging from one minute to 14 days, with the default retention period being four days. One of the key at least once offered by SQS is that every message will be processed at least once.

Types of SQS Queues

SQS provides two types of queues: standard queues and first-in-first-out (FIFO) queues.

Standard Queues   Standard queues are the default queue type in SQS. This type of queue supports nearly unlimited transactions per second, ensuring high throughput. A standard queue at least once that a message is delivered at least once. However, occasionally, more than one copy of a message might be delivered, and the sequence might not be in the order of their sending. Standard queues provide best-effort ordering, which generally ensures that messages are delivered in the same order as they are sent.

FIFO Queues   FIFO queues offer exactly once processing. Messages are sent and received strictly in the order they are sent, remaining available until a consumer processes and deletes them. No duplicate messages are introduced in the queue. FIFO queues also support message groups that enable multiple ordered message groups within a single queue. However, they are limited to 300 transactions per second, but they have all the capabilities of standard queues.

Dead-Letter Queues   Dead-letter queues are used for handling message failure. If a message cannot be processed successfully, it is moved to a dead-letter queue for further inspection. This feature allows you to set aside and isolate messages that cannot be processed correctly, allowing you to determine why their processing did not succeed.

SQS Visibility Timeout   SQS uses a mechanism known as visibility timeout to manage the processing of messages. This is the duration for which a message is invisible in the queue after a reader picks it up. If the job is processed within the visibility timeout, the message is deleted from the queue. If not, the message becomes visible again for processing. The default visibility timeout is 30 seconds, with the maximum being 12 hours.

Message Flow in SQS

Working with SQS involves a standard vocabulary consisting of queues, producers, and consumers. The term *queue* is equivalent to an email inbox, while *producers* are applications that put messages into a queue, and *consumers* are applications that pick up these messages.

The general flow of a message in an SQS queue involves the following steps:

1. An application (producer) generates a message and sends it to a queue.

2. An application (consumer) listens or "polls" the queue for new messages and picks them up for processing.

3. Once a message is picked up by a consumer, the message is locked and a visibility timeout is activated. During this timeout, the message becomes invisible to all other consumers, ensuring that each message is processed at least once.

4. The message remains invisible until the consumer finishes processing the message and issues a `DeleteMessage` call to the queue. If the processing fails and the `DeleteMessage` call is not issued, the visibility timeout for the message expires and the message becomes visible for processing again.

SQS API Calls

There are several key API calls in SQS that you should be familiar with:

- `CreateQueue`—Creates a new standard or FIFO queue
- `DeleteQueue`—Deletes the specified queue, regardless of the queue's contents
- `PurgeQueue`—Deletes the messages in the specified queue
- `SendMessage`—Delivers a message to the specified queue
- `ReceiveMessage`—Retrieves one or more messages from the specified queue
- `DeleteMessage`—Deletes the specified message from the queue
- `ChangeMessageVisibility`—Changes the visibility timeout of a specified message in a queue

Polling in SQS

SQS uses two types of polling methods: short polling and long polling.

Short Polling   Short polling returns immediately, even if the queue is empty. It queries only a subset of the available servers for messages and is the default polling type in SQS.

Long Polling   Long polling is a way to retrieve messages from your SQS queues. Unlike the regular short polling that returns immediately, long polling doesn't return a response until a message arrives in the queue or the long poll times out. This method reduces costs and eliminates false empty responses.

Delay Queue in SQS

In SQS, there's a type of queue known as a *delay queue*. In this queue, the delivery of a message can be delayed for a specific number of seconds. The visibility of a message in a delay queue is managed similarly to a standard queue. Once the delay is over, the message behaves like any other message in the queue, with the visibility timeout becoming active once the message is picked up.

Best Practices for SQS

There are several important details to note about SQS:

- The visibility timeout for a message in a queue is 30 seconds by default, with a minimum of 0 seconds and a maximum of 12 hours. If your application takes more than 30 seconds to process a message, you should increase the visibility timeout accordingly. If processing takes longer than 12 hours, you may need to consider using Step Functions instead of SQS.
- Consumers can listen for messages in a queue in two ways: short polling and long polling. Short polling returns a response even if no messages are found, whereas long polling waits until at least one message is available.

- The minimum message size is 1 byte, and the maximum default size is 256 KiB. However, with the Amazon SQS Extended Client Library for Java, you can process large messages up to 2 GB by leveraging Amazon S3 along with SQS messaging.

- While standard SQS queues try to maintain the order of messages, they don't guarantee it. If you need to ensure message order, you should use a FIFO queue instead.

- If a message is not processed successfully, it can be moved to the dead-letter queue after a maximum number of processing attempts. This prevents an infinite cycle of unsuccessful processing attempts. Messages in the dead-letter queue can be examined to determine the reason for the processing failure.

Amazon SNS

AWS Simple Notification Service (SNS) is a robust, fully managed messaging solution for application-to-application (A2A) and application-to-person (A2P) communication. In this section, we will delve into the key concepts and features of SNS, helping you understand how to effectively utilize it to enhance your application's communication capabilities.

Overview of SNS

Amazon SNS is a versatile messaging service that operates in the cloud. It's designed to facilitate both inter-application and application-to-user communications. Capable of dispatching notifications to a variety of devices, including Apple, Google, Fire OS, and Windows, as well as Android devices in China via Baidu Cloud Push, SNS offers a broad spectrum of dispatch methods.

Notifications can be sent via SMS text message, email, SQS queues, any HTTP endpoint, and even trigger AWS Lambda functions. This service follows a pub-sub model where users or applications subscribe to SNS topics and any published message is sent to all subscribers of that topic.

SNS topics act as access points that enable subscribers to dynamically receive identical copies of the same notification. A single topic can efficiently support multiple endpoint types, providing the flexibility to cater to various application requirements. Messages within SNS are stored redundantly across several availability zones, offering high reliability and instant, push-based delivery.

When subscribing to an SNS topic, you can choose from a wide range of endpoint types:

- HTTP/HTTPS
- Email/Email-JSON
- Amazon Kinesis Data Firehose
- Amazon SQS
- AWS Lambda
- Platform application endpoint (mobile push)
- SMS

SNS Fanout

SNS Fanout is a powerful feature that allows publisher systems to distribute messages to a large number of subscriber endpoints, including Amazon SQS queues, AWS Lambda functions, and HTTP/S endpoints. This mechanism supports application-to-application (A2A) messaging, providing the ability to fan out messages to Kinesis Data Firehose delivery streams, Lambda functions, SQS queues, HTTP/S endpoints, and AWS events.

Pairing SNS with Amazon SQS queues can enhance your application's messaging capabilities. When you publish a message to a topic, SNS sends the message to every subscribed queue. This combination facilitates fully decoupled, no-data-loss messaging with the ability to add receivers later, empowering delayed processing and retries of work.

FIFO Topics

Using an SNS FIFO topic, you can configure a message group by including message group IDs when publishing to an SNS FIFO topic and for each message group ID, all messages are sent and delivered in order of their arrival. You can also avoid duplicate message deliveries for the SNS FIFO topic by enabling content-based message deduplication. This is just a check box in the AWS console for configuring a FIFO topic. This feature makes SNS use a SHA-256 hash to generate a message deduplication ID using the body of the message. Any duplicated message sent within a time period is accepted but not delivered.

If an SQS FIFO queue is subscribed to an SNS FIFO topic, the deduplication ID is passed to the queue and SQS uses it to avoid duplicate messages being sent as well. Using SNS FIFO topics, message ordering and deduplication can be achieved at the messaging layer. Strictly preserved message ordering and exactly once message delivery are advanced featured.

Message Filtering

SNS provides a mechanism to selectively receive only the messages that interest the subscribers, as opposed to receiving all messages published to a topic. This is achieved using a subscription filter policy in JSON format.

Using a FIFO topic, you can configure a message group by including message group IDs when publishing to an SNS FIFO topic, and for each message group ID, all messages are sent and delivered in order of their arrival. You can also avoid duplicate message deliveries for the SNS FIFO topic by enabling content-based message deduplication.

Message Delivery Policies

SNS Delivery Policy can be used to control the retry pattern for message delivery when the system that is subscribed becomes unavailable. The retry policies can be chosen as linear, geometric, exponential backoff, maximum and minimum retry delays, and other parameters during message delivery by the SNS topic. When the delivery policy is applied, SNS stops delivery attempts and discards the message unless a dead-letter queue has been defined for the subscription.

Amazon Kinesis Services

Amazon Kinesis services have emerged as powerful tools for real-time data collection, processing, and analysis, offering up-to-the-minute insights and enabling swift responses to new information.

The term *real time* refers to a computational performance level where data transfers and processing must complete quickly enough for the results to be relevant and actionable. This concept plays a crucial role in various sectors, ranging from stock market operations to Internet of Things (IoT) devices.

In the stock market, for instance, real-time data processing is vital for publishing stock prices promptly, allowing traders to respond accordingly. The IoT space is another area where real-time data processing is crucial. IoT devices continually send data to be ingested and processed, enabling actionable results.

Traditional messaging systems—involving queues, topics, or a combination of both—often struggle to implement data transfers in real time, especially for data volumes larger than 256 KB. This is where Kinesis comes into play. Let's get into it!

Introduction to Kinesis Data Streams

As a real-time data collection messaging service, Amazon Kinesis Data Streams (KDS) maintains a replica of all data received in the order of receipt. By default, this data is stored for 24 hours and can be retained for up to 365 days if configured accordingly. Consumers then process the data, which can be saved into another AWS service.

With the help of Kinesis, large datasets can be processed in real time. It offers the ability to read and replay records to multiple consumer applications. The service is particularly beneficial for applications where the speed of data transfers directly impacts the customer experience, such as streaming applications.

Streams, Shards, and Records

A stream in Kinesis is made up of one or more shards, and each shard stores data records sequentially. Each data record consists of a partition key, a sequence number, and the actual data up to 1 MB. KDS retains a copy of all received data, in the order received, for up to 365 days if configured accordingly.

A record in a shard consists of a partition key (which groups data in a shard), a sequence number (unique per partition-key within a shard and maintaining the order of arrival for records), and the actual data (up to 1 MB).

A shard in Kinesis can handle 1,000 records per second, and the data capacity of a stream is proportional to the number of shards being used. With an adequate number of shards, you can collect gigabytes of data per second from tens of thousands of sources.

A shard's capacity in KDS can be configured as on-demand or provisioned capacity mode. Using on-demand capacity, KDS automatically manages and adjusts the number of shards to provide the throughput needed by your workload. In contrast, with the "provisioned" capacity mode, you specify the number of shards for the data stream. You can increase or decrease the number of shards as needed, and you are billed for the number of shards at an hourly rate.

The role of producers and consumers in Kinesis is also significant. Producers send data to KDS, and consumers process this data using the Kinesis Client Library (KCL). The KCL is different from the Kinesis Data Streams API available in the AWS Software Development Kit (SDK). The KCL ensures that for every shard, there is a record processor running and processing the shard. It simplifies the reading of data from a stream by decoupling your record processing logic from the connection and reading of the data stream.

The KCL uses a DynamoDB table to store control data and creates one table per application that is processing data from a stream. It can run on EC2 instances, Elastic Beanstalk, and even your own datacenter servers.

Furthermore, KDS can automatically encrypt data as a producer delivers it into a stream, using AWS KMS master keys for encryption. This feature is particularly useful for collecting and gathering data in real time, such as application log data, social media data, real-time game dashboards, and leaderboards.

Resharding

A single shard provides a capacity of 1 MB/sec data input and 2 MB/sec data output, and it can support up to 1000 PUT records per second. The total capacity of a Kinesis stream is the sum of all its shards' capacities.

KDS supports resharding, which allows you to adjust the number of shards in your stream to adapt to changes in the rate of data flow through the stream. There are two types of resharding operations: shard split and shard merge.

- In a shard split, you divide a single shard into two shards. This process increases the number of shards in your stream, thereby increasing the data capacity of the stream and its cost (since you pay per shard).

- A shard merge combines two shards into a single shard. This reduces the number of shards in your stream, thereby decreasing the data capacity and cost of the stream.

Introduction to Kinesis Data Firehose

Amazon's Kinesis Data Firehose (KDF) is a potent tool for managing large-scale datasets. As an integral part of the Kinesis streaming data platform, KDF has been designed to simplify the process of loading real-time data to multiple AWS storage services. This section will delve deep into the capabilities of KDF, its operation, and the advantages it provides to users.

Amazon Kinesis Data Firehose, often referred to as Kinesis Firehose, is a formidable player in the realm of data ingestion and delivery. Its prowess lies in its ability to handle voluminous datasets effectively and deliver them to a variety of destinations. These include but are not limited to Amazon S3, DynamoDB, Amazon EMR, OpenSearch, Splunk, DataDog, NewRelic, and Amazon Redshift. The key advantage of using Firehose lies in its management of the intricate complexities of infrastructure, storage, networking, and configuration, which are essential to ingest and store your data to a destination. This fully managed service empowers users to efficiently capture, transform, and load data seamlessly.

Kinesis Firehose

The Kinesis Firehose service is fully managed, alleviating the need for users to maintain hardware, software, or write any applications to manage the process. The service scales automatically, and like many other AWS storage services, it replicates data across three facilities in a region, ensuring data security and reliability.

Firehose buffers the input stream to a predefined size and for a predefined time before loading it to destinations. The buffer size can range from 1 MB to 128 MB for S3, from 1 MB to 100 MB for OpenSearch, and 0.2 MB up to 3 MB for Lambda functions. The buffer interval can vary from 60 to 900 seconds.

If the delivery destination is unavailable, Firehose will store data for up to 24 hours. However, if the source is a Kinesis data stream, the data will be retained according to the data stream configuration, not Firehose.

Kinesis Firehose for Delivery

Kinesis Data Firehose is typically used to deliver Kinesis data stream records to AWS storage services. However, it's not limited to KDS, and any application can produce messages for Firehose to deliver to AWS storage services. The Kinesis Agent, a prefabricated Java application, can be installed and configured to collect and send data to your delivery stream. This agent can be installed on Linux systems for web servers, log servers, and database servers. It is also available on GitHub.

Delivery to Amazon RedShift

When delivering data to Amazon RedShift, Firehose uses Amazon S3 as the first step before loading data to your RedShift cluster.

Scalability, Latency, and Backup

Unlike several other services, Firehose does not use shards and is fully automated in terms of scalability. It can even compress and encrypt data before delivering it to storage destinations, ensuring data security.

For certain destinations like Amazon S3, OpenSearch, and Splunk, users have the option to back up the transformed data to another S3 bucket, ensuring a safety net for your valuable data.

Despite its features, users should be aware that Firehose operates fast but not in real time. You should expect a latency of 60 seconds or more when using Firehose to store to destinations. Also, for Firehose, you pay for the amount of data going through it.

Intro to Kinesis Data Analytics

Amazon Kinesis Data Analytics is a tool designed to simplify the analysis of streaming data in real time. It employs Structured Query Language (SQL) to extract, transform, and load (ETL) data residing in KDS and Firehose, facilitating real-time analytics.

With Data Analytics, you can execute complex analytical queries on your stream data, enabling you to gain actionable insights in real time. The service is fully managed by AWS, eliminating the need for manual intervention and reducing the operational overhead as AWS takes care of the operational aspects. It provides automatic scaling to accommodate increasing data loads, ensuring the seamless performance of your applications.

Kinesis Data Analytics

The working of Data Analytics involves creating an application to read and process streaming data. This data is sourced from KDS or Firehose.

The SQL code required for data processing is written using an interactive editor. This SQL code can be tested with live streaming data to ensure its accuracy and efficiency.

For beginner-level projects, AWS offers the Kinesis Data Analytics Studio. This tool simplifies the process of building streaming applications, providing advanced analytical capabilities and enabling quick application development.

Post-analysis, the data can be stored in various AWS services, such as S3, RedShift, or an Elasticsearch cluster. Data Analytics supports Firehose, AWS Lambda, and KDS as destinations for sending the results.

One of the unique features of Data Analytics is its ability to create streams out of real-time queries. This capability allows you to generate new data streams based on the outcomes of your analytical queries.

Step Functions

AWS Step Functions is a fully managed service that simplifies the coordination of components in distributed applications and microservices using visual workflows. It allows you to break down your applications into individual components, each performing a specific function, enabling easier scalability and faster application changes. Step Functions provides a graphical console to arrange and visualize these components as a series of steps, making it easier to build and run multistep applications.

By breaking an application into service components or steps, Step Functions ensures that the failure of one component does not bring down the entire system. Each component can scale independently, and updates can be made to individual components without redeploying the entire system. Orchestration involves managing execution dependencies, scheduling, and concurrency according to the logical flow of the application. Step Functions simplifies this coordination and handles failures, making it easier to build robust and scalable applications.

Defining State Machines

In Step Functions, workflows are defined as state machines using the Amazon States Language, a JSON-based declarative language. State machines describe the steps, relationships, inputs, and outputs of a workflow. They consist of a series of states, each representing a step in the workflow diagram.

State machines can perform various tasks such as work execution, decision-making, parallel execution, parameter passing, timeout management, and termination of workflows. The Amazon States Language provides a rich set of built-in state types to handle these tasks, allowing you to define complex workflows with ease.

The Step Functions console provides a visual interface for designing and organizing workflows. It allows you to arrange and visualize the components of your application as a series of steps, making it easier to build and run multistep applications. The console displays the real-time status of each step and provides a detailed history of every execution.

With the visual console, you can easily define the flow of your application by connecting states and specifying their inputs and outputs. You can also add error handling and retries to ensure reliable execution. The console provides a user-friendly environment for designing and managing workflows without the need for complex coding.

Triggers, Logs, and Error Handling

Step Functions automatically triggers and tracks each step of your application, ensuring orderly execution and efficient handling of errors. It logs the state of each step, allowing for quick diagnosis and debugging of issues. In case of failures, Step Functions provides built-in error handling capabilities, including try/catch and retry mechanisms.

The service integrates with CloudWatch and CloudTrail, enabling real-time monitoring and troubleshooting of workflow executions. You can set up alerts and notifications to stay informed about the status of your workflows. Step Functions also supports detailed logging, providing a comprehensive execution history for auditing and compliance purposes.

How Step Functions Work

Step Functions is a visual workflow service used to build distributed applications, automate processes, orchestrate microservices, and assist developers in creating data and machine learning pipelines. It's a serverless orchestration service that can integrate with Lambda functions and other AWS services by configuring state machines and tasks within the Step Functions service.

State Machines and Workflow Steps

In Step Functions, you define your application workflows as state machines. State machines describe the sequence of steps, their relationships, and the inputs and outputs of each step. Each step represents a specific function or task in the workflow.

The Amazon States Language allows you to define various types of states, including task states, choice states, parallel states, wait states, and more. Task states represent individual units of work, such as invoking a Lambda function or running an Amazon ECS task. Choice states enable branching logic based on conditions. Parallel states allow for concurrent execution of multiple steps. Wait states introduce delays or timeouts in the workflow.

Visualizing and Monitoring Workflow Execution

The Step Functions console provides a visual representation of your workflows, showing the order of execution of each step. You can start an execution to visualize and verify the steps of your application. The console highlights the real-time status of each step, allowing you to monitor the progress of your workflow.

You can set up alarms and notifications to receive alerts on specific events or execution failures. The detailed execution history and logs help in troubleshooting and auditing your workflows.

Step Functions integrates with over 220 AWS services through service integrations. Service integrations allow you to invoke AWS service APIs directly from your workflows, enabling seamless coordination with other AWS services. You can invoke Lambda functions, run ECS or Fargate tasks, interact with DynamoDB tables, publish messages to SNS topics, send messages to SQS queues, start AWS Glue jobs, and much more.

Additionally, Step Functions allows you to incorporate activity tasks, which are integration points with your own custom code or external applications. Activity tasks run in your preferred location, such as EC2 instances, mobile devices, or on-premises servers. Step Functions coordinates the execution of activity tasks, passing inputs and receiving outputs, providing a flexible and extensible way to integrate with external systems.

Step Functions can coordinate any application that can make an HTTPS connection, regardless of where it is hosted. Whether your components are running on EC2 instances, mobile devices, or on-premises servers, Step Functions can coordinate their execution and pass inputs and outputs between them. This flexibility enables you to build distributed applications that leverage AWS services as well as your own microservices.

High Availability and Fault Tolerance

AWS Step Functions is designed for high availability and fault tolerance, ensuring the reliability and resilience of your workflows. The service operates across multiple availability zones within each region, protecting your applications against individual machine or datacenter failures.

Step Functions automatically maintains service capacity to handle the execution of your workflows, even under increasing demand. It scales the underlying compute resources based on the workload, ensuring consistent performance and resource optimization. The distributed nature of Step Functions provides a highly available and fault-tolerant platform for running your mission-critical applications.

Scalability and Serverless Solution

Step Functions is a serverless service, meaning you can scale the operations and compute resources without managing servers or infrastructure. It automatically scales to handle the execution of your workflows based on the workload, ensuring consistent performance and resource utilization.

The serverless nature of Step Functions allows you to focus on building your applications without worrying about infrastructure management. It eliminates the need for provisioning and managing servers, enabling faster development and deployment cycles. Additionally, the pay-per-use pricing model of Step Functions ensures cost optimization, as you only pay for the transitions between states in your workflows.

Step Functions provides a powerful parallel processing capability to handle large-scale workflows efficiently. You can use the Map state to iterate over objects stored in Amazon S3, such as images, logs, or CSV files. Step Functions can launch and coordinate thousands of parallel workflow executions, enabling you to process large volumes of data or perform computationally intensive tasks.

The Map state supports both inline and distributed modes of parallel processing. In inline mode, Step Functions can support up to 40 parallel branches, whereas distributed mode allows for concurrency of up to 10,000 parallel branches. The distributed mode is optimized for S3, allowing you to iterate over objects more easily and overcome payload and execution history limits.

Summary

Elastic Beanstalk is a powerful tool that simplifies application deployment and management in the AWS Cloud. By understanding its features, layers, deployment options, and security measures, developers can effectively utilize this service to streamline their operations and improve efficiency.

CloudFormation is a potent tool in the AWS suite, allowing for efficient resource management. By following the best practices outlined in this chapter, you can optimize your use of CloudFormation, ensuring a more streamlined and effective process. AWS continues to evolve and improve its offerings, so staying updated with the latest best practices is always beneficial.

Remember, the key to mastering CloudFormation or any AWS service lies in understanding, planning, and implementing the best practices effectively.

Templates define how you want your infrastructure to look, and stacks are instances of a template. You can have multiple stacks created from one template, and you can use parameters, mappings, and pseudo parameters to customize stacks, even when deployed from the same template.

SQS is a powerful tool for managing and processing messages between different components of an application. It offers a reliable, scalable, and secure way to decouple and scale microservices, distributed systems, and serverless applications. By understanding the various aspects of SQS, you can leverage its benefits to enhance your AWS-based applications.

SNS is a powerful messaging and notification service that offers a highly scalable, reliable, and cost-effective solution for managing distributed communications. Whether you need to send notifications to end users or facilitate communication between distributed applications, SNS provides the flexibility and robustness required to handle the task efficiently.

The power of SNS lies in its versatility—from decoupling applications and handling high-throughput messaging, to facilitating A2A and A2P communications. With features like topics, Fanout, and advanced messaging with FIFO SNS topics, SNS is an invaluable tool in your systems operations AWS suite.

Kinesis Data Streams opens a realm of opportunities for real-time processing of streaming big data. It simplifies reading and replaying records to multiple Kinesis applications, making it easier to build multiple applications for various purposes, such as counting, aggregating, and filtering. As technology advances, Kinesis's role in harnessing real-time data's power is set to be increasingly significant.

Kinesis Data Firehose is an innovative and efficient solution for data ingestion and delivery. It's fully managed, scalable, and secure, making it a reliable choice for businesses looking to streamline their data management processes. Despite its minor latency, it ensures the safe and efficient delivery of data to multiple destinations. Its integration within the comprehensive Kinesis services further accentuates its versatility and effectiveness.

Kinesis Data Analytics is a robust tool that has revolutionized how businesses handle and analyze streaming data. Its real-time processing, fully managed nature, and SQL-based querying make it an ideal choice for businesses seeking to leverage their data streams for actionable insights.

Finally, Step Functions simplifies the orchestration of distributed applications, providing reliability, scalability, and flexibility. From visual workflow configuration to error handling, parallel processing, and integration with AWS services, Step Functions offers a powerful platform for building complex and efficient applications.

Exam Essentials

Remember that you are responsible for managing your app.   The great thing about Elastic Beanstalk is that you are responsible for managing your application but that AWS is responsible for maintaining the underlying services since Elastic Beanstalk is a managed service. You still need to ensure that your platform is patched, a task that is made simpler with managed updates.

Remember the deployment modes for applications.   Deployment modes are a popular line of questioning on the exam. Remember the differences and use cases between all-at-once, rolling, rolling with additional batches, and immutable.

Understand what CloudFormation does.   CloudFormation allows you to build your infrastructure from a template, which ensures that resources are built the same way every time. CloudFormation allows you to do infrastructure-as-a-service (IaaS).

Define the relationship between templates and stacks. Templates are the definition of your environment, whereas stacks are instances of the template. This means that the stack contains all the resources defined in the template. Stacks are an all-or-nothing deal; if any one resource fails to be built successfully, then the entire stack will fail and be rolled back.

Remember what the sections in a CloudFormation template are used for. You need to remember what the various sections in the CloudFormation template are used for. You won't be expected to write your own template on the exam, but you may be shown samples and asked questions based on what you are seeing.

Review Questions

You can find the answers in the Appendix.

1. A company is having issues with an application's messaging layer becoming saturated at certain times of day. AWS has been adopted, and the messaging layer will be implemented using AWS. Which service will provide a systems operator with the maximum message rate to preserve messages when an application is unresponsive?

   A. Use SQS FIFO queues and an EC2 fleet with an EC2 Auto Scaling Group.

   B. Use SNS topics and an EC2 fleet with an EC2 Auto Scaling Group.

   C. Use SQS standard queues and an EC2 fleet with an EC2 Auto Scaling Group.

   D. Use SNS FIFO topics and an EC2 fleet with an EC2 Auto Scaling Group.

2. A company wants to analyze the click sequence of their website users. The website is very busy and receives traffic of 10,000 requests per second. Which service provides a near-real-time solution to capturing the data?

   A. Kinesis Data Streams

   B. Kinesis Data Firehose

   C. Kinesis Data Analytics

   D. Kinesis Video Stream

3. A company wants to build a click sequence capture, analysis, and store solution. Which services in what function would provide the highest throughput?

   A. SNS to capture the data, Lambda to process, and RDS to store it

   B. SQS to capture the data and a fleet of EC2 instances in an Auto Scaling Group

   C. Kinesis Data Streams to capture the data, Athena to process the data, Kinesis Data Firehose to store the data in S3

   D. Kinesis Data Streams to capture the data, Kinesis Data Analytics to process the data, and Kinesis Data Firehose to store the data in S3

4. A team of systems operators needs to be immediately notified if an EC2 instance is started or stopped. Which service provides the simplest solution?

   A. Use event notifications and SQS.

   B. Use event notifications and Step Functions.

   C. Use event notifications and SNS.

   D. Use event notifications and Kinesis Data Streams.

5. A company's application is implemented in AWS using microservices and Lambda functions. Which service can be used to coordinate the execution and workflow of multiple Lambda functions?

   A. SQS

   B. SNS

    C. Step Functions

    D. Simple Workflow Service (SWF)

6. Which of the following can be used to launch an Amazon Aurora MySQL cluster? (Choose two.)

    A. AWS Organizations

    B. AWS CloudFormation

    C. The AWS Management Console

    D. Amazon Concierge

7. What does the `AWSTemplateFormatVersion` section of a CloudFormation template indicate?

    A. The date that the template was originally written

    B. The date that the template was last processed

    C. The capabilities of the template based on the version available at the indicated date

    D. The date that the template was last updated

8. What is the only required component in a template?

    A. Parameters

    B. Metadata

    C. Resources

    D. Outputs

9. A SysOps administrator is troubleshooting a large CloudFormation stack. It is taking over 2 hours to roll back the entire stack before another test can be performed. How can the SysOps administrator accelerate the test/repair cycle time?

    A. Build a second CloudFormation template to tear down all resources that can then be run as needed.

    B. Enable the `CleanupResources` option within the template.

    C. Disable Automatic Rollback On Error.

    D. Enable Automatic Rollback On Error.

10. A SysOps administrator has a fleet of EC2 instances and then initiates scripts on each instance. However, the next steps in a CloudFormation stack are failing because they depend on resources that those scripts configure. How can the SysOps admin coordinate the creation of resources?

    A. This is not possible using CloudFormation.

    B. The admin needs a separate CloudFormation stack that can run manually after the scripts on instances complete.

    C. The admin needs a separate CloudFormation stack, and must set the initial stack to call the second stack.

    D. The admin must use the `WaitCondition` resource to block further execution until the scripts on the instances complete.

11. Which of the following is not allowed as a data type for a parameter?

   A. List

   B. Comma-delimited list

   C. Array

   D. Number

12. A SysOps administrator wants to accept custom CIDR blocks as inputs to a CloudFormation stack. What validation can be used to ensure the CIDR block is correctly formatted as an input parameter?

   A. `AllowedValues`

   B. `MinLength`

   C. `ValueMask`

   D. `AllowedPattern`

13. The URL to a web application created by a CloudFormation stack is to be provided. What element of a CloudFormation template can be used to accomplish this?

   A. Parameter

   B. Output

   C. Transform

   D. Resources

14. A CloudFormation stack needs to obtain a URL to use by an API call by the application being created. What CloudFormation template elements can be used to do this?

   A. Parameter

   B. Output

   C. Transform

   D. Resources

15. Which of the following are supported deployment models in Elastic Beanstalk? (Choose two.)

   A. Rolling with additional batches deployment

   B. Rolling with incremental updates deployment

   C. Mutable deployment

   D. Immutable deployment

16. Why might you choose to use a rolling with additional batches deployment? (Choose two.)

   A. You don't want the application to completely stop when updates are made.

   B. You want the cheapest possible deployment model.

   C. Your goal is to always maintain maximum capacity in terms of running instances.

   D. You never want two versions of an application running at one time.

17. A SysOps admin is deploying a critical production application that must always be up and running. Any new instances are required to be healthy before accepting traffic. Which deployment model should the sysops admin use?

A. Rolling with additional batches deployment

B. All-at-once deployment

C. Rolling deployment

D. Immutable deployment

18. Which of the following would be required to set up a blue/green deployment? (Choose two.)

A. Amazon Route 53

B. Elastic Beanstalk

C. Multiple application environments

D. Amazon RDS

19. Which of the following is true about a default Elastic Beanstalk deployment?

A. All instances created are private.

B. A custom private VPC is created.

C. All database instances are private.

D. The created application endpoint is publicly available.

20. Which of the following does Elastic Beanstalk store in S3? (Choose two.)

A. Server log files

B. Database swap files

C. Application files

D. Elastic Beanstalk log files

Appendix

Answers to Review Questions

Chapter 1: AWS Fundamentals

1. C. Implementing multifactor authentication (MFA) injects an additional piece of information into the authentication process. MFA can be implemented using software or hardware tools and will add protection to your root account and users that goes beyond simple username and password. Use MFA for all accounts and users if possible.

2. A, D. Configuring programmatic access for the CLI will require four pieces of information: access key ID, secret access key, default region name, and default output format.

3. A, C, D. Defining an account-level password, enabling MFA for all users, and enabling AWS Security Hub are fundamental to protecting your AWS account. Using CloudShell, Session Manager, and/or service-linked roles provides a form of security and protection but are not as fundamental.

4. D. IAM roles are essential to provide cross-account access as well as enabling AWS services to interact with each other. Learn and understand roles and the mechanics of role policy creation to maintain a strong security posture.

5. B. AWS CloudShell provides a mechanism for operators to use the AWS CLI without having to provision access keys in a local machine. This adds a new layer of security as it saves time and effort in executing one-line and simple administrative CLI commands.

6. C. Systems Manager Session Manager provides you with a way to connect to Amazon EC2 instances that does not require the configuration of SSH or RDP resources to operate a particular instance. This is a significantly more secure way to manage EC2 instances.

7. B, E. For console access, IAM users need to use the URL as follows: `https://accountID.signin.aws.amazon.com/console` or `https://account_alias.signin.aws.amazon.com/console`.

8. D. Wavelength zones bring AWS services to the edge of a 5G network, reducing the latency to connect to your application from a mobile device. Application traffic can reach application servers running in wavelength zones without leaving the mobile provider's network. They provide single-digit millisecond latencies to mobile devices by reducing the extra network hops that may be needed without such a resource.

9. B. A local zone is an extension of a region where you can run low-latency applications using AWS services in proximity to end users. Local zones deliver single-digit millisecond latencies to users for use cases like media, entertainment, and real-time gaming, among others.

10. C. Outpost is designed to support applications that need to remain in your datacenter due to low-latency requirements or local data processing needs. It brings AWS services, infrastructure, and operating models to your datacenter, co-location space, or physical facility.

11. C. Edge locations are the resource used by AWS to deliver reliable and low-latency performance globally. Edge locations are how AWS attains high performance in countries and territories where a region does not exist. The global edge network connects thousands of

Tiers 1, 2, and 3 telecom carriers globally and delivers hundreds of terabits of capacity. Edge locations are connected with regions using the AWS backbone, which is a fully redundant, multiple 100 Gigabit Ethernet (GbE) parallel fiber infrastructure. The AWS edge network consists of over 400 edge locations.

12. D. An availability zone is a logical group of datacenters. These groups are isolated and physically separate. Each of them includes independent power, cooling, physical security, and interconnectivity using high bandwidth and low-latency links. All traffic between availability zones is encrypted. Also, each availability zone is implemented separately from other availability zones but within 60 miles of each other.

13. A. The AWS CLIv2 wizards feature is an improved version of the `-cli-auto-prompt` command-line option. Wizards guide you through the process of managing AWS resources. You can access the wizards feature by using the command line:

```
aws <service-name> wizard <wizard-name>
```

14. B, C, D. Wizards will query existing resources and prompt you for data in the process of setting up for the service invoked. As of this writing, wizards are available for `configure`, `dynamodb`, `iam`, and `lambda` functions. For example, the command:

```
aws dynamodb wizard new-table
```

will guide you in creating a DynamoDB table. Also, note that the `configure` command does not use a wizard name. It's invoked as `aws configure wizard`.

15. D. The CLI command to create an Amazon S3 bucket is:

```
aws s3 mb s3://my-bucket
```

You can type **aws s3 help** for details.

16. C. The CLI command to copy the contents of a directory to an Amazon S3 bucket is:

```
aws s3 sync my-directory s3://my-bucket/
```

You can type **aws s3 help** for details.

17. A, B. The `--query` option can be used to limit the results displayed from a CLI command. The query is expected to be structured according to the JMESPath specification, which defines the syntax for searching a JSON document.

The `--filter` option can also be used to manage the results displayed. However, with the `--filter` option, the output is restricted on the server side whereas `--query` filters the results at the client side.

The `--dry-run` option is used to verify that you have the required permissions to make the request and gives you an error if you are not authorized. The `--dry-run` option does not make the request.

18. C, D. The AWS Health API is available directly as part of an AWS Business Support or AWS Enterprise Support plan. It allows for chat integration and ingesting events into Slack, Microsoft Teams, and Amazon Chime. It also allows integration with dozens of AWS partners such as DataDog and Splunk, among many others.

19. B. The AWS default quota value for EC2-VPC Elastic IPs is 5 and will need an adjustment if you need more IPs. You can use the Service Quotas page on your management console to make a request to support and have the limit increased if needed.

20. B, C, D. For details about service pricing and usage limits included in the AWS free tier, you can visit `https://aws.amazon.com/free`.

The logic for AWS TCO calculator now resides in the Migration Evaluator at `https://aws.amazon.com/migration-evaluator`.

The AWS Pricing Calculator is available at `https://calculator.aws`.

The older, simple monthly calculator and TCO calculator have been deprecated.

Chapter 2: Account Creation, Security, and Compliance

1. D. Remember that compliance in the cloud is two parts: AWS and what the customer builds using AWS services. AWS Artifact is used to retrieve security and compliance reports and some online agreements related to AWS's part of the equation. AWS Artifact is accessed through the management console. AWS Audit Manager could easily be confused as the correct answer. However, AWS Audit Manager is used for continual monitoring of compliance, whereas AWS Artifact is used simply to pull reports of AWS compliance.

2. A. Any time there are several services doing something similar, know the use cases for each. Directory services is an example. AWS Simple AD will not work because the requirements specify using Microsoft AD. Deploying on EC2 in two AZs seems like a plausible solution, but a managed service is typically a better option for the customer based on price and management overhead unless the question gives some detail that makes the managed service not feasible. That leaves Microsoft AD Standard and Enterprise Editions. In this case you do not need to know the details of Microsoft AD capacity planning. Simple AD is not recommended for more than 5,000 users, whereas AWS Directory Service for Microsoft AD is. Remember that objects do not equal users and there will generally be more objects than users. That strongly suggests Standard Edition would suffice and that Enterprise Edition would most likely be more expense for capacity that is not yet needed.

3. A. Control Tower and its guardrails are a critical part of governing an enterprise. Be sure to know AWS Control Tower and AWS Organizations and how they work together. Know the various types of policies and when to use each. The structure of guardrails and their terminology can be confusing. Behavioral controls either detect noncompliance or prevent noncompliance.

4. D. While all of these seem plausible, ultimately SCPs are not the correct place to grant permissions. Be sure to know what each policy type does (and doesn't do).

5. A. While inline policies are available as an option, they are not recommended. Inline policies can be difficult to troubleshoot, and there are almost always better options.

6. A, B, D. Remember EAR (Effect, Action, Resource). A fourth common policy option (but not required) is Conditions.

7. B. Recall that licenses from AWS Marketplace will automatically be tracked. What we are considering here would be Bring Your Own Licenses (BYOLs), which License Manager does not automatically know how to associate with an instance. The easiest solution is to associate the license with the AMI. In this way, any instance launched from that AMI will be associated with that license and tracked.

8. A. The key criterion in the question is that no data can be cached in the cloud. Options B, C, and D all store data in the cloud. AD Connector does not.

9. B. Option A is not correct because SCPs cannot grant permissions. Option C is also incorrect since you want to follow the principle of least privilege and granting administrator rights necessarily would violate that principle. Option D is incorrect because creating an account can be done when logged in as either an IAM user or root user, or by assuming a role. However, remember that using the root user account is not best practice when a role can be used instead.

10. B. The service-linked roles for License Manager cannot be manually assigned—they are automatically assigned when setting up the service. The correct answer is that AWS Organizations is required for AWS License Manager to work across accounts to discover compute resources.

11. A. The two accounts created by Control Tower are Audit and Log Archive.

12. A, D. ACLs and resource-based policies can both be attached to a resource such as S3 and grant permissions to a specified principal in the same or another account. Permission boundaries can only deny, not grant, permissions. An identity-based policy is attached to the user and not to the resource. SCPs, like permission boundaries, define the limits of permissions but do not actually grant permissions themselves.

13. A, B. Remember that permission boundaries set the limit of what permissions can be held. They neither grant nor deny permission on their own.

14. A, B, D. AWS no longer supports SMS as an MFA factor for user accounts in IAM. Note that MFA is still a supported option in Cognito user pools.

15. A. Account Vending Machine was an older term and not used now, though you may still see reference to "vending machine" when speaking of Account Factory. The correct term for the feature is Account Factory.

16. C. AWS Managed Microsoft AD resides in a VPC rather than on-premises. PrivateLink does not support AWS Manage Directory Services. Multiregion replication for AWS Managed Microsoft AD is handled by the service using native Active Directory replication.

17. B. Option A is wrong since accounts themselves would not have keys, and sharing of an account's admin keys would not make sense from a security perspective. Option D would not be practical in many cases where the owner of the inviting account is not also the owner of the invited account. Accounts can be both created and invited in AWS Organizations, so option C is also incorrect.

18. D. You will want to be very comfortable with policy evaluation logic. The use of an implicit deny secures resources for which no permission is explicitly given nor denied. See the documentation on identity and resource-based policy evaluation, especially the section on the difference between explicit and implicit denies (`https://docs.aws.amazon.com/IAM/latest/UserGuide/reference_policies_evaluation-logic.html`).

19. B. Distributed computing is, at its most fundamental, just computing between two of more computers via messaging usually along a network. It does not imply trust. Hybrid computing refers to a combination of cloud and on-premises resources. Again, no trust is implied. Interoperability is the ability of one computer or application to talk to another. Standards and protocols provide us with interoperability but do not imply trust.

20. A, B, C. You will want to be very familiar with the six basic policy types and when each is used. Review the IAM User Guide (`https://docs.aws.amazon.com/IAM/latest/UserGuide/access_policies.html`).

Chapter 3: AWS Cost Management

1. A, C. AWS cost allocation tags support two different types: user-defined and AWS-generated. User-defined tags can incorporate useful information such as cost center, project, or department. AWS-generated tags are automatically defined, created, and applied to services.

2. C. When creating user-defined tags for use in AWS cost allocation tags, it can take up to 24 hours for the new tags to show up in the cost allocation reports.

3. D. AWS Cost and Usage Reports (CURs) only enter the finalized state after all pending refunds, credits, or AWS account support fees are updated for that month. When the bill is finalized, the CUR will have a column named *Bill/InvoiceID* in the CSV file. This indicates the bill has been finalized by AWS and will not change.

4. B. AWS Cost and Usage Report exports into an Amazon S3 bucket to produce a manifest collection that holds files to help set up all the resources you need for Amazon Athena, Amazon Redshift, or Amazon QuickSight to analyze the report data. The manifest collection is only created when the option to use these analytics services is selected when configuring the AWS Cost and Usage Reports.

5. A. The only way to prevent AWS member accounts from creating AWS Cost and Usage Reports is to apply a service control policy (SCP) restricting access to the AWS Cost and Usage Report. Be mindful, however, that SCPs are not retroactive for preexisting accounts.

6. A, B, E. AWS Cost and Usage Reports can be configured to include a manifest collection for use of Amazon Athena, Amazon Redshift, and Amazon QuickSight. These additional analytic services provide a deeper look into cost and usage within AWS membership accounts.

7. D. AWS Cost Explorer provides current month, prior 12 months, and the ability to forecast the next 12 months of AWS cost and usage using the same dataset as the AWS Cost and Usage reports.

8. A. AWS Cost Explorer provides several preconfigured views to display cost and usage information trends within AWS accounts. One of the preconfigured reports is the top five cost-accruing services, and you can modify the time period dimension of the visualization to meet the six-month requirement.

9. C. AWS Cost Explorer has two options to restrict access. The first is at the AWS Organizational level, but this provides an on or off approach for the entire organization. It will not limit to specific accounts. To limit specific member accounts, the IAM Access setting must be turned on in AWS Cost Explorer and an IAM policy allowing access to Cost Explorer must be created and applied.

10. B. When a stand-alone AWS account joins an AWS Organization as a member account, the only Cost Explorer data available is from the time the account joined. Any data prior to joining is unavailable for viewing. Once an AWS account is no longer a member account of the organization, the account can view prior stand-alone data once again.

11. A, C, D. AWS offers three Savings Plan models to decrease cost of AWS services up to 72 percent compared to On-Demand pricing. The Saving Plan models currently available are SageMaker Savings Plans, Compute Savings Plans, and EC2 Instance Savings Plans.

12. A. Compute Savings Plans offer flexibility to apply savings to EC2 instances and compute resources across any region, tenancy, or instance type. As the project changes and moves to a new region, the Compute Savings Plans will still apply. Compute Savings Plans are not specific to an operating system, which makes it the best choice for Microsoft Workloads.

13. C. Having the ability to move between regions and change between inference and training workloads is a feature of SageMaker Savings Plans. SageMaker Savings Plans allow region, instance size, and instance type changes as well as changing between workload types without losing the cost savings benefits.

14. D. Savings Plans coverage reports are the best option as the reports include a high-level predefined metric showing On-Demand spend not covered by Savings Plans. This provides a fast method for viewing coverage gaps without needing to manually export detailed information from inventory or utilization reports.

15. B, E. When configuring AWS Budgets for notifications, you can select from emailing up to 10 recipients directly from the budget configuration. You can also use Amazon SNS to send SMS messages or take other actions through event triggers with Lambda.

16. A. AWS Budget actions can automatically or with manual approval take remediation steps to avoid budget overages based on forecasted results being over 90 percent. The best way to limit launching Amazon EC2 instances is to apply a service control policy (SCP) and apply it to the development organizational unit or specific development AWS account preventing the `ec2:RunInstances` operation as the remediation step.

17. C. AWS Budgets requires a minimum of five weeks of historical billing data to provide forecasted spending data. As this data is not available, AWS Budgets is unable to send alerts for forecasted amounts.

18. B. One of the largest benefits to using AWS Managed services to reduce cost comes in the form of removing IT overhead for administration. Managed services allow IT administrators to focus on application maintenance and support as the need to update operating systems, design highly available databases, or configure scalable systems is no longer required for the AWS Managed services. All these actions are the responsibility of AWS.

19. D. To address this configuration change you must create a new launch template and add in Amazon Spot Instances within the scaling policy as we do not want to replace all EC2 instances, only those needed when scaling to meet peak utilization.

20. A. One of the potential drawbacks of using Amazon EC2 Spot instances is the possibility of AWS interrupting or reclaiming the EC2 Spot instance due to capacity limits, high demand of EC2 Spot instances, or the Spot bid price maximum being exceeded. In the event of a reclaim, AWS provides a two-minute warning, which administrators can use to stop or hibernate the spot instance or run a script to move data to permanent storage.

Chapter 4: Automated Security Services and Compliance

1. A, D. AWS Trusted Advisor offers basic security checks to all AWS accounts but only Enterprise and Business support plans can access all available checks within Trusted Advisor.

2. C. Security Hub allows you to automate remediation actions using EventBridge. Security Hub will automatically send all new findings and updates to existing findings to EventBridge as events. EventBridge events can then be used to perform remedial actions using AWS Lambda or notifications using SNS.

3. D. GuardDuty S3 protection uses CloudTrail management events and S3 data events to monitor against threats on S3 resources. GuardDuty will generate findings for actions on an S3 bucket such as `DeleteBucket` and `DeleteObject` and post these findings in the GuardDuty console.

4. B. There are two finding types used in Inspector: package vulnerability findings and network reachability findings. The network reachability findings look for TCP and UDP ports that are open for resources outside of the VPC edge locations, like the Internet gateway or VPC peering connections. This type of access is considered overly permissive, and Inspector will provide detailed information in a finding about the EC2 instances involved, the ports discovered, and the security groups or access control lists (ACLs) involved.

5. A. The Key Management Service can only encrypt and decrypt up to 4 KB datasets when being directly sent to the service. To encrypt larger datasets, you must use envelope encryption to retrieve a plaintext data key and an encrypted data key that are used to encrypt the file, and then package the file with envelope encryption using the encrypted data key. The encryption process is handled outside of KMS and only uses the AWS KMS API to retrieve the data keys.

6. D. In order to use AWS Certificate Manager certificates in CloudFront, you must either import the certificate in the US-EAST (N. Virginia) region or provision a certificate using Certificate Manager before it can be used. CloudFront-associated Certificate Manager certificates in this region are distributed to all geographic locations configured for CloudFront distribution.

7. C. Macie with custom data identifiers is a great solution to identify any sensitive information stored in objects across nondesignated S3 buckets. Using the custom data identifiers, you can define criteria using regex expressions to match values that hold proprietary data. Once this information is found, you can have Macie generate reports or send alerts using EventBridge.

8. A. Secrets Manager requires proper permissions to be set on users, groups, and roles before a secret can be retrieved. In this scenario, an error stating unauthorized indicates that the EC2 instance or application does not have access to retrieve the secret from Secrets Manager. Check the IAM identity-based permissions for the user or check the resource-based policy to verify that the EC2 instance role has permission to access the secret.

9. A, C, E. The application servers are under a TCP SYN flood attack. To stop this type of attack, you need to challenge any new connection requests to your web application and only serve legitimate users. Route 53 and CloudFront have built-in TCP SYN proxy capabilities to remediate this problem. When using Shield Advanced in conjunction with CloudFront and Route 53, you can use the Shield Response Team (SRT) to assist in mitigation of this type of issue if it were to occur again.

10. B. The AWS Web Application Firewall (AWS WAF) is a layer 7 firewall used to protect your web applications from DDoS attacks, SQL injection attacks, and cross-site scripting attacks. You can also allow, block, or count web requests coming into an application based on criteria that you set, such as IP addresses, geo locations, and HTTP headers.

11. C. AWS WAF offers several optional components to enhance the network and application protection. In this scenario the web application team has asked you to limit bot traffic coming from scanners and crawlers. When using AWS WAF, you can enable the optional Bot Control feature to use managed rule groups to identify common bots, verify desirable bots, and detect high-confidence signatures of bots. You can also monitor, block, or rate-limit bots like crawlers and scanners while allowing beneficial bots like search engines to continue.

12. A. AWS Firewall Manager requires the use of AWS Organizations where you can define an organization Firewall Manager administrator account to apply rule groups and policies to every AWS Organization member. The requirement is to manage compliance against security groups and AWS WAF rule groups, which can be accomplished by using AWS WAF policies and security group policies within Firewall Manager. When setting the criteria for each of the policies, you can define an automated action to remediate any security groups that deviate from the standard policy security groups. You can do the same for AWS WAF rules and rule groups to ensure that every member account has the same rule groups applied and available for applications.

13. C. Detective has three phases of investigation when an alert or notification is received from a potential high-risk or suspected malicious activity. The first phase is Triage, which is when you determine whether a report is a false positive or needs further investigation. The next phase is Scoping, where you determine the extent of the activity and the underlying cause. The final phase is Response, where you remediate the action either by resolving the security threat or by marking the threat as a false positive.

14. D. Within AWS WAF you can share custom rule groups by using the AWS WAF API and the PutPermissionPolicy API call. You can only attach one policy in each PutPermissionPolicy request, and the policy must include an effect, an action, and a principal. You also must ensure that you are sharing the rule group from the account and user that is the owner of the rule group.

15. A. The AWS Shield console provides a global aggregated view of threats over the last day, three days, and the last two weeks. The summary view in the AWS Shield Management Console displays the DDoS events detected by Shield for resources that are eligible for protection by Shield Advanced. Alternatively, you can use the AWS Shield API operation DescribeAttackStatistics to retrieve the account-level details.

16. D. Secrets Manager has two logging methods that can be used to evaluate the behavior of secrets: CloudTrail and CloudWatch. In this case, the security team wants to check the details of when a secret was rotated, and this is stored in CloudTrail within the region where Secrets Manager is used. The security team can access the S3 bucket where the CloudTrail logs are stored to do further analysis using third-party software if needed. CloudTrail will provide event details when a secret is deleted, versioned, or rotated. CloudWatch only provides details on the number of requests against the AWS Secrets Manager API and can be useful in identifying applications that are calling the service too frequently.

17. A, C, E. Macie allows customizable frequencies for when findings are published to Security Hub. You can update the publication setting to fit the needs of the security team by adjusting the findings publication from the default of 15 minutes to either every one hour or every six hours. If you modify the publication timings within one region, you will need to modify every other region where Macie is in use as well.

18. B. When requesting certificates that will need to cover all subdomains of a domain name, you need to use the wildcard domain type. This means that the certificate will show a domain name of *.domainname.com, where the * indicates that all names to the leftmost position of the domain name will be covered under the certificate. The wildcard name will appear in the Subject field and the Subject Alternative Name extension of the AWS Certificate Manager certificate.

19. D. Key Management Service offers two choices when generating keys: symmetric and asymmetric. The symmetric key type is used when encrypting or decrypting data within an AWS account and requires direct calls to the AWS KMS service. This is a great option to use when an EC2 instance is required to process encryption using the AWS KMS key as it will call the AWS KMS API to accomplish encryption and decryption actions.

20. A. Inspector requires the use of the Systems Manager (SSM) agent to scan EC2 instances for vulnerabilities against the CVE item database. Network reachability scanning is available even when the SSM agent is not installed or running, which means that the EC2 instances not reporting CVE data must have issues with the SSM agent installation or it is not running.

Chapter 5: Compute

1. C. Launch templates are now recommended over launch configurations. Target groups are for load balancers. Auto Scaling Groups are set up after the launch configuration is defined.

2. D. The error codes in the 500 range indicate a server problem. However, these are HTTP error codes and typically captured at the application level. CPU Utilization and Network In are very common EC2 metrics but are not applicable to Lambda. Throttles are a critical metric for Lambda and indicate invocations exceeding concurrency. Consider either provisioned concurrency or increasing quotas or both.

3. A. The placement groups for EC2 are cluster, partition, and spread placement. Each of these has a use case that you should be familiar with.

4. D. Be familiar with the life cycle of an EC2 instance. In addition to billing, the life cycle determines persistence of data. Be sure to understand how data persists on EBS-backed instances versus instance store–backed and what the EC2 life cycle looks like using an instance store.

5. B. By default, Compute Optimizer looks at the past 14 days of data to make a recommendation. Enhanced Infrastructure Metrics is a paid feature that looks at up to three months of data.

6. C. The gateway load balancer is specifically designed for use with third-party appliances such as next-generation firewalls (NGFWs) and web application firewalls (WAFs) that use the GENEVE protocol on port 6081.

7. A. The application load balancer is optimized for HTTP and HTTPS traffic.

8. B. Classic Load Balancers are being deprecated, and AWS recommends migration to network or application load balancers. Moving to these newer load balancers brings performance and cost optimizations. Elastic load balancers (ELBs) of all types are managed services and do not need auto scaling. Throughput quotas cannot be adjusted for since they are managed services. A gateway load balancer (GLB) is intended for third-party appliances using the GENEVE protocol. A GLB is not used as a transitional load balancer.

9. C. There are three limits that are set for an Auto Scaling Group: the minimum, desired, and maximum capacities. The minimum is the smallest acceptable group size. The maximum is as large as the group will be allowed to scale. The desired is the initial size of the group. Auto scaling then attempts to maintain that size. When demand causes the group to scale out, Auto Scaling will then scale in at the end of the event back to the desired capacity.

10. D. EC2 is billed in 1-second increments after the first 60 seconds. The minimum you would be billed for is 60 seconds.

11. C. Nitro enclaves leverage the Nitro hypervisor components to provide an isolated and hardened compute environment on EC2. A feature of Nitro enclaves is cryptographic attestation, which allows for identification of the enclave and assures that only authorized code is run in the environment. Instance store refers to the boot device, which is either EBS-backed or an ephemeral instance store. Amazon Elastic Inference provides low-cost GPU acceleration on EC2 and SageMaker instances. A partitioned placement group is one of three placement group options.

12. D. Application load balancers handle the HTTP/HTTPS protocols. A gateway load balancer handles the GENEVE protocol. Classic Load Balancers are no longer recommended. Network load balancers handle the TCP protocol.

13. A, B, C. The three limits are desired, maximum, and minimum.

14. D. Each of these can indicate resource configuration issues. The `ConcurrentExecution` metric indicates the number of concurrent executions. When concurrent executions reach the quota or the reserved concurrency, then further requests will be throttled.

15. D. Step scaling is usually an improvement over simple scaling since step scaling can respond to events as they happen without needing to wait for health check replacements and cooldown periods. Target tracking is normally recommended over step scaling since it can stay closer to the desired target value than step scaling. While manual scaling has its place, it is not the best option for automatically scaling this type of workload.

16. B. The soft concurrency limit of AWS Lambda is 1,000. If more concurrent invocations are required, a request can be made to increase the quota.

17. A. While simple, step, and target tracking scaling will scale out the workload, they only begin scaling after the metric indicates a problem. Predictive scaling anticipates the event based on historical data and scales out ahead of the Thursday evening batch processing so that throttling is avoided.

18. A. The states of an EBS-backed EC2 instance are pending, running (rebooting), shutting down (stopping, stopped), and terminated.

19. C. Dedicated instances are typically more expensive for comparable compute power and would not be recommended for cost optimization. Reserved instances and Spot instances offer significant savings. However, savings plans allow for flexibility across EC2, Lambda, and Fargate as well as many dimensions, such as operating system, instance size and family, and tenancy.

20. D. C instances are compute optimized, D are memory optimized, and M and T are both general-purpose instance families. However, T instance types are the only instance types that are burstable.

Chapter 6: Storage, Migration, and Transfer

1. C. Amazon S3 offers a feature that can host static website files, such as HTML documents, which can scale using the underlying architecture of the S3 service. This means outside web traffic is connecting to the S3 bucket hosting the HTML file through the fault-tolerant and highly available S3 architecture. In this scenario, the customer would create a static website with a download link to the S3 object for the podcasts that are temporarily available. The result is a scalable temporary solution for hosting the podcast and the website, without the need for compute resources.

2. D. Amazon S3 cross-region replication and same-region replication pose a limit when working with existing objects and buckets. Cross-region replication will take care of any new object uploads into the bucket by replicating the changes to the destination bucket(s). However, existing objects will not copy using cross-region replication. To accomplish this task, the best option is to use Amazon S3 Batch Replication to backfill newly created replaced buckets with objects from the existing origin buckets. This is a one-time replication required for each destination bucket to bring parity with the existing source bucket.

3. A, E. When uploading objects into an Amazon S3 bucket, larger files can be sensitive to network disruptions and slower Internet speeds. Enabling S3 Transfer Acceleration for the buckets and directing the clients to use the transfer acceleration endpoints will send uploads to the nearest edge location. This will drastically increase the speed of the uploads and reduce latency. Using multipart uploads for larger files will also increase upload speeds as smaller chunks of the overall file upload. Multipart uploads are also a terrific way to solve for network connectivity issues since you can pause the uploads or restart at the last part in process in the multipart upload. This option allows for the file size to remain the same while increasing performance and reliability for the upload process. When paired with S3 Transfer Acceleration, you can achieve the best customer experience.

4. B. In this scenario your organization is looking to achieve a cost-effective solution for their long-term archival and storage needs. They decided to forgo the maintenance contract of the on-premises storage and need a suitable replacement that still maintains access to the files within 48 hours to meet audit compliance requirements. The fact that the organization must maintain files for 10 years, that the recovery time is 48 hours, and that the solution needs to be the most cost-effective are reasons to evaluate the use of Amazon S3 Glacier Deep Archive. Data retrieval for Amazon S3 Glacier Deep Archive is complete within 48 hours using bulk retrieval options, or if the organization needs data faster, they can pay an expedited fee for using the Standard retrieval option in Amazon S3 Glacier Deep Archive to retrieve the files within 12 hours. Amazon S3 Glacier Deep Archive offers long-term cold storage for several use cases, such as storing financial documents, healthcare records, or other data subject to compliance requirements dictating length of time files need to be available.

5. D. In this scenario the organization wants to reduce storage backup costs but also maintain instance access to any files recovered from the system. The organization also wants to maintain the same durability and benefits of Amazon S3. To meet the needs of the organization, you can use Amazon S3 Glacier Instant Retrieval storage class as it matches the durability and reliability of Amazon S3 Standard while reducing the overall storage costs. Amazon S3 Glacier Instant Retrieval also enables the auditors to receive the requested files in milliseconds, which offers similar retrieval times compared to Amazon S3 Standard. The options for Amazon S3-IA and S3 One Zone-A do not apply as they reduce the durability and availability of the stored files, as well as not being the most cost-effective option when storing files for the long term.

6. C. In this scenario the organization is looking to achieve a cost-effective solution for backing up EBS volumes within their environment. There is a concern over automation and the potential for data loss due to manual actions previously taken. To best address the automation and recovery of EBS Snapshots, use the Amazon Data Lifecycle Manager for this process. The Amazon Data Lifecycle Manager automates the creation, retention, and deletion of EBS Snapshots and EBS-backed AMIs. This allows the creation of a schedule backup process to create a disaster recovery backup process to avoid potential data loss. Using the other options available introduces various lag in the data backup options, resulting in potentially missed data during a restoration, where the Data Lifecycle Manager makes incremental backups to reduce cost and reduce the data lost during restoration.

7. A, C. Identifying EBS performance for read operations starts with the evaluation of Amazon CloudWatch metrics related to the VolumeQueueLength, which is an indicator of a bottleneck on either the guest operating system or the network link to the EBS volume. The next metric to check is VolumeReadOps, which indicates how many read operations per second the EBS volume is receiving. This metric helps identify if there is an I/O size or throughput issue between the guest operating system and the EBS volume. Too high a number of read requests on a standard nonprovisioned IOPS volume can lead to queuing and slow read performance.

8. D. In this scenario the data engineers are reporting below normal write and read speeds, which is a great indicator that the volume is throttling. The EBS volumes used in this deployment are gp2 and st1 volume types, which both use burst bucket balance to maintain performance above the baseline available IOPS for the volume. Checking for depletion of the BucketBalance metric for the volume can identify depletion of the burst bucket and results in low performance for the EBS volume.

9. C. In this scenario only one Amazon EC2 instance can connect to the Amazon EFS storage system in a single availability zone. It is likely that the configuration of the Amazon EFS system is using the One Zone storage class, which limits Amazon EFS to a single mount target in only one availability zone, compared to multiple mount targets when using Amazon EFS Standard. The fact that the instances in US-EAST-1a can connect means the system is working with connectivity. There are no mount targets available for each availability zone in the VPC. Amazon EC2 instance roles or security group configurations will resolve this issue.

10. **A.** In this scenario the teams access the same files across the Washington, DC and London offices for production processing. This means the files must stay in sync and the London office is concerned with latency when connecting to the Washington, DC (US-EAST-1) services. To reduce latency and allow the local London office to work on files in the Amazon EFS share the same way the Washington, DC office does, you can enable Amazon EFS replication. Amazon EFS replication automatically and transparently replicates the data and metadata located in the Amazon EFS filesystem to the new destination. The files are in sync and the London locals can work directly on the files and the Washington, DC locals can see the changes as they are replicated.

11. **C.** In this scenario the director has asked for a managed service as they cannot afford a storage administrator, as well as asking for a filesystem that supports parallel filesystems. The entire department focuses on HPC, which means they are a candidate for using the Amazon FSx for Lustre option to manage their parallel filesystems. The use of Amazon EBS or Amazon S3 would increase complexity and cost, and would be an unmanaged solution. Amazon FSx for NetApp ONTAP is not a consideration as it is not the right Amazon FSx filesystem the parallel filesystem needs.

12. **B.** The key indicator in this scenario is the director wants to maintain the current SAN infrastructure in a hybrid deployment while connecting servers using iSCSI. This immediately eliminates the use of Amazon EBS with Windows File Server and the Amazon FSx for Windows File Server options since the connection protocol is SMB. Amazon EFS with AWS DirectConnect and VPN would utilize the NFS infrastructure and be a costly solution. The Amazon FSx for NetApp ONTAP solution using the Storage Gateway File Gateway will enable local access of data for on-premises. This means the SAN is still in use, and data replicates to the FSx filesystem, with eventual migration directly to the Amazon FSx for NetAPP ONTAP solution full-time when the maintenance contract and lifespan of the current SAN has expired.

13. **D.** Data for the organization is already located in Amazon S3, which means the Amazon Data Lifecycle Manager would not be a solution as it relates to EBS and EBS-backed AMIs. Amazon S3 Batch Replication is not the correct solution as it only replicates entire buckets into another destination, usually across regions. Amazon S3 versioning is a recommended best practice when combined with a life-cycle expiration period, and it is a requirement when using AWS Backup. While this is a good manual solution, restoring to a specific point in time with S3 versioning would cause increased administrative overhead. AWS Backup is the correct solution because it natively supports PITR for Amazon S3 and Amazon RDS backups, while maintaining a centrally managed location to configure and restore the backups when needed.

14. **A.** In this scenario AWS Backup cannot successfully complete a scheduled daily backup and is throwing an error that states it cannot access the buckets. The first area to check is that all IAM permissions are correct for the role assigned to the backup plan. The IAM role must have two in-line IAM policies attached to enable backup and restore operations inside of the S3 buckets. It does not matter where the Amazon S3 buckets are located or that AWS PrivateLink is enabled and in use. Having PITR enabled for the backup plan associated to the Amazon S3 bucket would not matter as the IAM permissions are not appropriately set.

15. C. The key indicator in this scenario is the need to continue using a tape backup or tape-like backup system to avoid retraining individuals on a completely new system. The use of AWS Storage Gateway Tape Gateway allows the creation of virtual tape libraries that function just like the on-premises system. This alleviates the need for retraining and only requires configuration of the virtual tape libraries and the Tape Gateway. The use of Amazon S3 Glacier Deep Archive is a component of a good backup strategy with AWS Storage Gateway Tape Gateway, but it is not the complete solution. AWS Storage Gateway Volume Gateway and AWS Backup do not address the needs of the CIO and would require a new backup process and training for the teams.

16. A. The solution to this problem requires the use of NFS file-sharing protocols and the ability to maintain data in Amazon S3 while on-premises servers still have access to use the data once it is in Amazon S3. Implementing AWS DataSync is not an option as this requires on-premises data stores to still be present during the migration. Amazon EFS is not an option as it would require additional copying of data between Amazon S3 and the EFS filesystem. AWS Storage Gateway File Gateway with Amazon FSx for Windows File Share uses the SMB protocol instead of NFS, which does not meet the requirements of this solution. The remaining option is implementing AWS Storage Gateway File Gateway, which enables NFS file share capabilities while maintaining the data within Amazon S3.

17. D. This scenario is a common use case for AWS DataSync. The director wishes to use the power of AWS to perform analytics using a data lake, but also wants to have a localized copy of the data. You can configure AWS DataSync to transfer entire on-premises datasets into Amazon S3 while synchronizing data between on-premises and the Amazon S3 bucket. AWS Backup does not accomplish the synchronization requirement, and Amazon FSx for Windows File Share does not meet the needs of synchronization and assumes that all servers are Microsoft Windows-based. Amazon EFS is not a correct solution because it does not provide a local copy of the data.

18. A. In this scenario the CIO wants to keep data synchronized between the third-party cloud provider, on-premises, and the new AWS environment during a migration. The CIO is also concerned that downtime may occur due to copy methods. This use case is common within AWS DataSync as it provides the connection to existing storage systems, like third-party cloud providers and on-premises systems, to migrate data to AWS storage services like Amazon S3, Amazon EFS, or Amazon FSx. AWS Transfer Family is not the proper solution as the scenario does not mention a migration of SFTP, FTP, or FTPS systems. Amazon Storage Gateway and AWS Backup do not accomplish the data synchronization required for this migration without additional scripting or customization of implementation.

19. B. In this scenario the organization is looking for a scalable and cost-effective solution to migrate SFTP services from on-premises to the AWS Cloud. This automatically eliminates the option of using Amazon EFS and AWS DataSync as they do not offer a method of enabling SFTP. Amazon EC2 is a potential option but would require custom configuration of an SFTP server on Amazon EC2, including the need for configuring scaling using Auto Scaling. This increases the overall cost and complexity of the solution. The most cost-effective and scalable option is to use AWS Transfer Family, which is a managed service that lets you configure an SFTP service that scales to meet customer demand; AWS manages the underlying infrastructure.

20. C. In this scenario it is important that a solution minimize the amount of administrative overhead, which means reducing complexity and the need for manual interactions. Rearchitecting the application and migrating the current FTPS service both require extensive administrative overhead or manual interaction. Creating a new FTPS service using Amazon EC2 and AWS Lambda would accomplish the task, but it requires additional administration to maintain the Amazon EC2 instance and AWS Lambda components. The most scalable and administrative overhead–neutral solution is to use AWS Transfer family configured for FTPS and utilize managed workflows to classify incoming data and scan for potential PII information. Using the managed workflows, you can configure different actions depending on the data classification and eliminate the need for manual data entry or tagging.

Chapter 7: Databases

1. B. CloudFront is used for static content such as images and documents. Provisioned IOPS is used to provide high throughput for RDS instances but is not sufficient to improve performance under high read loads. Scaling the database instance may improve read performance but is a costly solution. The preferred method for improving read performance is to implement read replicas. ElastiCache is another possible tool to improve read performance.

2. C. DynamoDB is a NoSQL key-value database and not a relational database. SQLite is not supported. Amazon Aurora is a relational database service that supports (drop-in compatible) PostgreSQL and MySQL.

3. D, E. Apache Ignite is an open source in-memory distributed database management system. DAX stands for DynamoDB Accelerator and is an in-memory cache for DynamoDB. Ehcache is an open source cache.

4. C, E. Only options C and E are valid caching strategies.

5. D. Amazon Redshift is a relational database used for data warehousing. Redshift does not run SQL Server. SQL Server can be run on EC2 and is an option when a customer needs to customize the database engine or underlying operating system. However, EC2 is an unmanaged service. RDS, on the other hand, is a managed service, which is normally preferred. As a managed service, RDS gives no access to the database engine or operating system of the underlying instance. RDS Customer is a service that allows customization of the database engine and underlying operating system but is still a managed service. RDS Custom is the best solution given the scenario.

6. D. CloudTrail is used to log API activity in the account and does not capture performance data. CloudWatch captures performance metrics above the hypervisor but is not the best at showing bottlenecks. CloudWatch Performance Alerts is not a service. Performance Insights detailed metrics provide visibility into load on the database and can identify bottlenecks.

7.   A. Placing a database instance in a separate VPC would not be an efficient way to improve security. A bastion host is designed to pass SSH traffic and not handle communications between an EC2 instance and the database layer. Placing the database in the same subnet as the EC2 instances violates the principle of security in layers. Additionally, using IPv6 for routing does not add security. The correct answer is to use a DB subnet group. It is highly recommended that you use the DNS name since this protects the connection when an underlying RDS instance fails and is automatically replaced.

8.   B. Disabling the automated backups in RDS is done by setting the retention period to 0. This isn't particularly intuitive, so it's a good one to try to remember. You would rarely want to disable automated backups on important production data, but it is something you may want to do on test and development databases to save cost. Remember that snapshots and automated backups operate differently.

9.   C. The question is not about your knowledge of a specific database engine. Rather, what is important to notice here is that you are creating an instance. The number of databases per instance is an RDBMS concern. The number of RDS instances in a region is an AWS quota concern. You won't be expected to know quota limits, but you should be able to recognize when quotas might be causing the problem.

10.   B. There is an RDS Custom that allows engine- and OS-level customization of RDS, but ElastiCache does not have an equivalent capability. Redis.conf is not accessible in ElastiCache. Using Parameter Groups in ElastiCache provides the ability to make modifications, which can be applied to one or more ElastiCache clusters.

11.   C. CloudFront is used for static content such as images and files. Read replicas can help offload read requests from the primary database instance, but replicas are not a true caching solution. Memcached does not support complex data objects or high availability, or have persistence. In general, Redis is going to be more feature-rich and robust than Memcached.

12.   C. Amazon RDS Proxy is not supported on RDS for Oracle.

13.   B, C, E. Indicators that an RDS proxy might benefit a workload include errors related to too many connections, out-of-memory errors, or high CPU utilization. The amount of memory that an RDS instance has is not necessarily an indicator since a small instance with low load may handle that load easily without a proxy. Disk full errors can occur due to runaway log activity but are not necessarily an indicator of connection overload.

14.   C. CloudWatch logs are able to collect data from the operating system but are not designed, alone, to present that data in real time. Amazon EventBridge is used to connect applications using event-driven architectures. Performance Insights looks for patterns in aggregate DB metrics over time. Enhanced Monitoring gives real-time visibility into DB instance operating system metrics.

15.   C. DB Activity is not an available metric. CPU and memory utilization can be found in other monitoring tools. DB Load is an aggregated metric capturing average active sessions and giving insight into the load being placed on a database instance over time.

16. A, B. Replication between the primary and read replicas is asynchronous. Creating read replicas in VPCs outside of the primary instance's VPC can create conflicts with the classless inter-domain routing (CIDR).

17. A, C. Setting RDS automated backup retention to 0 disables backups. CloudWatch logs are best used for storage and monitoring of system and application logs. Using AWS Lambda to create snapshots is unnecessary.

18. C. When a read replica is promoted, no action is taken against the original primary DB instance (source). No final snapshot is taken of the source.

19. D. Changing the subnets and security groups are networking actions that would expose the database to bad actors but not give access to other researchers. The Publicly Accessible property enables or disables Internet connectivity to the database but does not grant permissions. RDS snapshots can be shared unencrypted with other accounts.

20. A. DynamoDB global tables are used for cross-region replication of DynamoDB tables. There are no Amazon Aurora global tables. The correct answer is an Amazon Aurora Global Database, which is a single Aurora database spanning multiple regions. RDS Read Replicas are used for cross-region disaster recovery, and a replica can be promoted to become the primary. An RDS proxy is used to pool and share database connections.

Chapter 8: Monitoring, Logging, and Remediation

1. C. AWS CloudTrail provides insight into API calls, and a client interacting with a REST API is exactly that.

2. B. The Amazon CloudWatch Logs Agent, when installed on an instance, provides metrics not available in any other manner, including using the basic CloudWatch capabilities.

3. B, D. CloudTrail trails apply to a single region by default (option D) but can be applied to all regions (meaning options A and C are both false). They also collect both management and data events (option B).

4. C. Management events in CloudTrail relate to security, registering devices, configuring security rules, routing, and setting up logging. In the options, this would include A, B, and D. Option A is a security event, B is setting up a security rule for routing, and D is a routing data rule. Option C, on the other hand, is related to data and is a data event rather than a management event.

5. A, C. Because data events capture the movement, creation, and removal of data, they are typically much higher volume than management events (option A). Data events are also disabled by default (option C), making them different from management events.

6. A, C. The `RunInstances` and `TerminateInstances` events are considered write events. This is easiest to remember because they are not read events, and AWS provides only two options: read and write. Collecting these events, then, would require a trail be set to Write-Only or All (which collects all events).

7. D. CloudWatch alarms have three states: OK, ALARM, and INSUFFICIENT_DATA. INVALID_DATA is not a valid alarm state.

8. A, C. In this scenario, there would need to be three out-of-threshold data points within the evaluation period of 10 minutes to trigger an alarm. This means that both options A and C would trigger an alarm. Note that it is *possible* that the scenario in option D would trigger an alarm, depending on when the out-of-threshold metrics occurred (inside 10 minutes), but it is not clear from the answer, so options A and C are better answers.

9. A, C. There are four possible settings for handling missing data points: `notBreaching` (A), `breaching`, `ignore`, and `missing` (C).

10. A. AWS Config does not provide mediation mechanisms. You can write code to remediate situations that cause notifications via AWS Config, but the remediation capability is not a standard part of Config itself.

11. A, C. AWS Config will notify you if a bucket has been granted public access (provided you have set that baseline up in AWS Config). You would then need to remediate that access, and that would require AWS Lambda (option C).

12. C. Configuration items do not include IAM-related information (option C). They do include event IDs (option A), configuration data about the resource, basic information about the resource such as tags, a map of resource relationships (option B), and metadata about the CI, including the version of the CI itself (option D).

13. B. Any instance running an SSM agent will need to assume an IAM role for connecting to the AWS Systems Manager service (option B). There is no such policy as AWSSystemsManager (option C).

14. A, B. AWS Systems Manager supports documents in JSON and YAML.

15. B. A patch baseline stores the patches that will be automatically deployed to your instances. If you want to avoid a certain patch, simply remove it from the baseline.

16. D. AWS Systems Manager documents can be used cross-platform without any changes (option D).

17. B. The Run command allows you to execute scripts and other commands on instances. In this case, a Run command could execute the compliance script needed.

18. B. When using Systems manager agent on EC2 instances, it enables the collection of meta-data types such as network configuration, AWS components, and other useful information. The agent can be installed across several EC2 instances with the same configuration to collect the inventory information required for your organization.

19. B, E. The most common causes of the INSUFFICIENT_DATA message for CloudWatch alarms are conditions responsible for the alarm not having enough data to evaluate its status.

20. A. It is true that native RDP is supported and can be enabled in the session properties so that the user can view the desktop instead of the PowerShell prompt.

Chapter 9: Networking

1. A. The three types of endpoint are gateway endpoints, gateway load balancer endpoints, and interface endpoints.

2. C. AWS Transit Gateway allows several VPCs and the on-premises network to be connected to a central gateway in a hub-and-spoke architecture. VPC Peering is required with the AWS Transit Gateway in order to connect the resources with multiple VPCs. However, VPC Peering cannot, alone, connect the VPC to an on-premises network. DirectConnect is an important service for connecting the VPC to an on-premises network but cannot connect VPCs to each other. A gateway endpoint is used to connect directly to S3 or DynamoDB without routing through the public Internet.

3. A. There are many gateways and endpoints and you will want to know when to use each. Using a gateway endpoint within a VPC enables traffic to be sent to S3 without traversing the public Internet. The gateway endpoint does not use PrivateLink and does not allow access to S3 from an on-premises network, peered VPCs, or through a transit gateway.

4. B. Security groups and NACLs are very similar and it will be important to remember the differences. One of the key differences is that NACLs offer deny rules whereas security groups only use allow rules. Route tables do not use rules.

5. B. CloudWatch and VPC flow logs can be very helpful in diagnosing errors. Traffic Mirroring creates a copy of inbound and outbound traffic that can be used to route traffic to appliances for threat monitoring and troubleshooting. However, the most efficient tool for diagnosing most connectivity issues is the Reachability Analyzer.

6. D. AWS Transit Gateway and VPC peering are used to connect VPCs. VPNs and DirectConnect are used to connect an on-premises network to a VPC. The customer is budget-conscious and has light network traffic. DirectConnect is designed for high traffic and is significantly more expensive than a VPN. This makes the VPN the best solution for this customer at this time.

7. A. 0.0.0.0/0 is the shorthand for any public destination. The Internet gateway is the target but would not be in the destination field. It would be in the target field and be in the form of igw-id. Local represents the local network CIDR. 0.0.0.0/32 is a single IP address.

8. B. CIDR blocks can range from /28 containing 16 IP addresses to /16 containing 65,536 IP addresses.

9. B. The valid RFC 1918 address ranges are 10.0.0.0–10.255.255.255, 172.16.0.0–172.31.255.255, and 192.168.0.0–192.168.255.255.

10. B. An Egress-only Internet gateway allows outbound communication over IPv6 from instances in your VPC to the Internet, and prevents the Internet from initiating IPv6 connections with your instances. External traffic can initiate communications through an Internet gateway. DirectConnect is used to connect the VPC to an on-premises network. A transit gateway serves as a hub to connect on-premises networks and VPCs.

11. C. Distributor is used to package and publish software to nodes on your network. CloudWatch is used for application and infrastructure monitoring. It can be used to give indications of system health and performance but is not used to capture and route network traffic. VPC flow logs and Traffic Mirroring may seem similar but are fundamentally different. Flow logs collect information about network traffic whereas Traffic Mirroring actually captures the network data and is able to route a copy to another location.

12. A. The NAT gateway and bastion host are often confused. A NAT gateway allows communication out whereas a bastion host allows communication in.

13. D. The NAT gateway and bastion host are often confused. A NAT gateway allows communication out whereas a bastion host allows communication in. A NAT instance is still available but is an old method and is no longer recommended.

14. A. The WAF operates at the endpoint level to protect resources like the application load balancer and CloudFront. A WAF is only stateless. Security groups operate at the instance (ENI) level and are only stateful. Network ACLs operate at the subnet level and are only stateless. Only the AWS Network Firewall has both stateful and stateless capabilities, and it operates at the VPC level.

15. C. Transit gateways and NAT gateways are not used for SSH connectivity. A bastion host is normally used for secure SSH connections, but Systems Manager offers a more cost-effective, highly available, and auditable solution.

16. B. AWS reserves five IP addresses in each subnet's CIDR block. In a 10.0.0.0 network these are the network address (10.0.0.0), the VPC router (10.0.0.1), reserved (10.0.0.2 and 10.0.0.3), and the broadcast address (10.0.0.4).

17. C. AWS Transit Gateway is used to connect various networks together and can span the globe. This gateway, however, lacks the automation, ability to segment, and configuration management found in Cloud WAN. AWS Control Tower and Route 53 are not able to meet the requirements.

18. C. AWS IP Address Manager (IPAM) is designed to centrally manage IP addresses (CIDR) globally. AWS Control Tower is an important service for centrally managing large enterprise environments. However, it is not capable of managing CIDR blocks. CloudFormation is for provisioning and managing AWS and third-party resources through code. Route 53 manages DNS.

19. C. A NAT gateway is used by resources in a private subnet to initiate communication with the Internet. A WAF monitors and protects HTTP(S) requests. NACLs and security groups are very similar and you will need to know the differences. The security group is stateful and the NACL is stateless. Additionally, the question only asks for traffic to be allowed with no requirement for deny rules. NACLs allow deny rules. Given the choice between a security group and a NACL, the security group is the preferred method if all else is equal.

20. C. The security group provides protection at the network interface level.

Chapter 10: Content Delivery

1. B. Route 53 is a DNS web service and can be used to perform domain registration, DNS routing, and health checks.

2. D. Although Route 53 does support text records, the record type is TXT, not TEXT, so option D is incorrect. Route53 does support NAPTR, NS, and SPF records.

3. B. You will need an alias record to map the apex record (`ourgreatcompany.com`) to the S3 bucket. You can then use another alias record to map the subdomain, `www .ourgreatcompany.com`, to the same S3 bucket website.

4. A. You would need an AAAA record set because this is an IPv6 address.

5. C. Whenever you need to associate a domain name with an AWS service such as CloudFront, S3, an ELB, or a VPC endpoint, you use an alias record.

6. B. This is the main use case for a failover routing policy. If traffic cannot reach a primary instance or service, Route 53 will "fail over" routing to a backup or secondary instance. Please remember that a health check needs to be defined for failover routing to work as expected.

7. D. The anycast IP addresses provisioned by AWS Global Accelerator will allow you to reach a healthy endpoint without having to switch IP addressing, modify the client code, or be concerned about DNS caching.

8. C. Latency routing policies return responses to users based on network latency.

9. D. Using weighted routing, you can choose what proportion of traffic will go to one endpoint versus another. For a trickle test, you can use a weight of 95 for the main production systems and a weight of 5 for the new version to be tested.

10. C. This is a good use case for weight routing. You can send (for example) 10 percent of traffic to the new site and the remaining traffic to the existing site using weighted values.

11. C. Geolocation routing will deliver the closest endpoint to users based on the region or country where they are located.

12. B. Enabling Origin Access Identity or Origin Access Control will limit access to the S3 bucket to the CloudFront distribution exclusively.

13. B, D. If you choose to use a Route 53 private hosted zone for custom DNS names in one or more VPCs, you must set both the `enableDnsHostnames` and `enableDnsSupport` attributes to `true` for all VPCs associated with the private hosted zone.

14. B, C. For Amazon Route 53 Traffic Flow to work, you'll need both a traffic policy (option B) and a policy record (option C). The traffic policy contains the rules that define how traffic should flow, and a policy record connects that traffic policy to a DNS name.

15. A, D. AWS Global Accelerator can distribute your application traffic globally with significant performance improvements. CloudFront is a content delivery network that can be used to distribute video, images, and audio globally at high transfer rates.

16. C. You can set up health checks in Amazon Route 53 to check an endpoint, other health checks already set up, or alarms in CloudWatch. You cannot directly monitor via CloudTrail (option C), although you could monitor CloudWatch alarms triggered by CloudTrail events.

17. A, B. Amazon Route 53 will stop sending requests to health check failing hosts and will also re-send requests when that host responds as healthy again (options A and B).

18. C. Enabling Origin Shield for the distribution will improve the cache hit ratio.

19. A. A geoproximity policy, like a geolocation policy, routes users to the closest geographical region. This means that options B and C are incorrect, as they are common to both types of routing policy. Option D would imply the use of latency-based routing, leaving only option A. This is the purpose of a geoproximity policy: You can apply a bias to adjust traffic to a region.

20. B, C. Health checks are not always turned on in Amazon Route 53 (and generally are not by default), so that's the first thing to check (option B). All policies can use health checks, so option A is incorrect, and an ALB is not required to use health checks, making option D incorrect as well. It takes three successive failures of a health check by default to take a host out of commission, so option C is also a possible answer.

Chapter 11: Deployment, Provisioning, and Automation

1. C. Standard queuing offers higher throughput than FIFO queuing. SNS does not preserve messages.

2. A. This is a classic use case for Kinesis Data Streams.

3. D. This is the only option that provides the speed and data retention with the highest throughput.

4. C. SNS can provide notification for an AWS region such as an email message, a text message, or a call to an HTTP endpoint. Most AWS services include event notification features.

5. C. Coordinating the execution of Lambda functions is one of the classic use cases for Step Functions.

6. B, C. CloudFormation and the AWS console are the only two items that can deliver the needed results.

7. C. AWSTemplateFormatVersion indicates the version of the template—and therefore what its capabilities are—by indicating the date associated with that version.

8. C. CloudFormation templates allow for all the provided answers, but they require only a Resources component to be present.

9. C. CloudFormation provides an Automatic Rollback On Error option that will cause all AWS resources created to be deleted if the entire stack doesn't complete successfully. Its default value is enabled. You can disable it to troubleshoot the point where the stack failed and not repeat deployment and rollback of resources that are working.

10. D. The admin can use CloudFormation's WaitCondition to act as a block of action until a signal is received from the application (in this case, when the instance scripts complete).

11. C. Parameters can be lists, comma-delimited lists, numbers, and strings. They cannot be arrays.

12. D. CIDR blocks use specific decimal and hexadecimal number patterns, and therefore the admin should use AllowedPattern to ensure they are properly supplied.

13. B. The URL to a web application created by a stack is an output value. One way to think of this is to see that the value cannot be created until the stack runs.

14. A. This is an input value, as it is something user-supplied and required by the template at runtime. Parameters are the way to import data to a stack.

15. A, D. Elastic Beanstalk supports a number of deployment models, including rolling with additional batches and immutable (options A and D). The other two options are made-up terms.

16. A, C. Both the rolling deployment and the rolling deployment with additional batches deployment models allow you to ensure your application is always running (option A). But you would then use the additional batches option to ensure you maintain maximum capacity throughout the process (option C).

17. D. An immutable deployment is often slower and more expensive than the other models, but it ensures both the health and maximum confidence in a new deployment.

18. A, C. Blue/green deployments require multiple environments (option C) that can run side by side as well as Route 53 (or something similar) for weighted routing policies. Although you can use Elastic Beanstalk, it is not required, and Amazon RDS is unrelated.

19. D. Elastic Beanstalk automatically creates a publicly available endpoint for your application in a default deployment.

20. A, C. Elastic Beanstalk will store application files and server log files in S3.

Index

Online Test Bank

To help you study for your AWS Certified SysOps Administrator certification exam, register to gain one year of FREE access after activation to the online interactive test bank—included with your purchase of this book! All of the chapter review questions and the practice tests in this book are included in the online test bank so you can practice in a timed and graded setting.

Register and Access the Online Test Bank

To register your book and get access to the online test bank, follow these steps:

1. Go to www.wiley.com/go/sybextestprep. You'll see the **"How to Register Your Book for Online Access"** instructions.
2. Click "here to register" and then select your book from the list.
3. Complete the required registration information, including answering the security verification to prove book ownership. You will be emailed a pin code.
4. Follow the directions in the email or go to www.wiley.com/go/sybextestprep.
5. Find your book on that page and click the "Register or Login" link with it. Then enter the pin code you received and click the "Activate PIN" button.
6. On the Create an Account or Login page, enter your username and password, and click Login or, if you don't have an account already, create a new account.
7. At this point, you should be in the test bank site with your new test bank listed at the top of the page. If you do not see it there, please refresh the page or log out and log back in.

SYBEX®

A Wiley Brand